1715

1715

The Great Jacobite Rebellion

DANIEL SZECHI

Yale University Press
New Haven and London

For information about this and other Yale University Press publications, please contact:
U.S. Office: sales.press@yale.edu   www.yalebooks.com
Europe Office: sales@yaleup.co.uk   www.yaleup.co.uk

Set in Minion by J&L Composition, Filey, North Yorkshire

Library of Congress Cataloging-in-Publication Data

Szechi. D. (Daniel)
1715: the great Jacobite Rebellion/Daniel Szechi.
p.cm.
Includes bibliographical references and index.
ISBN 0–300–11100–2 (alk. paper)
1. Jacobite Rebellion, 1715. 2. Scotland—History—18th century. 3. Great Britain—History, Military—18th century. 4. Jacobites. I. Title: Great Jacobite Rebellion. II. Title.
DA814.3.S94 2006
941.07′1—dc22   2005034841

A catalogue record for this book is available from the British Library.

Published with assistance from the Annie Burr Lewis Fund.

For my fierce and loving grandmother, Jessie Fairbank,
who never forgot she was Scottish

SUCH A PARCEL OF ROGUES IN A NATION

Fareweel to a' our Scottish fame,
Fareweel our ancient glory;
Fareweel e'en to the Scottish name,
Sae famed in martial story.
Now Sark rins o'er the Solway sands,
And Tweed rins to the ocean,
To mark where England's province stands:
Such a parcel of rogues in a nation!

What force or guile could not subdue,
Through many warlike ages,
Is wrought now by a coward few,
For hireling traitors' wages.
The English steel we could disdain,
Secure in valour's station,
But English gold has been our bane:
Such a parcel of rogues in a nation!

O would, or I had seen the day
That treason thus could sell us,
My auld grey head had lain in clay,
Wi' Bruce and loyal Wallace!
But pith and power, till my last hour
I'll make this declaration,
We're bought and sold for English gold:
Such a parcel of rogues in a nation!*

*G. S. Macquoid, *Jacobite Songs and Ballads* (1887), pp. 30–31.

Table of Contents

Illustrations

1 Queen Anne by Michael Dahl, 1705.
2 John Campbell, 2nd Duke of Argyll and Greenwich, by William Aikman, *c.* 1720–1725.
3 Henry St John, 1st Viscount Bolingbroke, by Alexis Simon Belle, 1712?.
4 King George 1 by Sir Godfrey Kneller, 1714.
5 King George II when Prince of Wales after Sir Godfrey Kneller, 1716.
6 James Butler, 2nd Duke of Ormond, by or after Michael Dahl, 1714.
7 James Stanhope, 1st Earl Stanhope, attributed to Johan van Diest, *c.* 1718.
8 James Francis Edward Stuart, studio of Alexis Simon Belle, *c.* 1712.
9 Charles Townshend, 2nd Viscount Townshend, after Sir Godfrey Kneller, *c.* 1715–1720.
10 John Erskine, 6th or 22nd Earl of Mar.

Illustrations 1–9 are reproduced by kind permission of the National Portrait Gallery, London. Illustration 10 is reproduced by kind permission of the National Trust for Scotland.

Maps

Notes

Map 1 originates from Paul Kléber Monod, *Jacobitism and the English People, 1688–1788* (1989), p. 189, with additional material from Nicholas Rogers, *Crowds, Culture, and Politics in Georgian Britain* (1998), pp. 28–32, and appears here with the kind permission of Cambridge University Press and Paul Kléber Monod.

Maps 5–7 originate from British Library, MAPSC9616, and are published with the permission of the British Library.

Map 9 originates from British Library, ADD 33954 f30, and is published here with the permission of the British Library. I am grateful to Dr Margaret Sankey for drawing it to my attention.

Preface

This book had its genesis on a quiet summer afternoon in the National Library of Scotland in Edinburgh in 1996. I had the day before finished doing the final bit of research necessary to complete the project I was then working on (a biography of the Jacobite MP George Lockhart of Carnwath), and had a little time left before I was due to leave that wonderful city. For no very good reason I thought I would use it to revisit an interesting memoir I had last looked at over a decade previously: John, Master of Sinclair's, *Memoirs of the Insurrection in Scotland in 1715*. It is a vibrant, anguished text, full of savage sneers, diatribes and guilt. And it was so rich as a historical source that it quickly drew me in. I had, of course, encountered the 1715 Jacobite rebellion many times before. It was the looming nemesis waiting just offstage in my first book, constituted the watershed in the history of the Jacobite cause I published in 1994 and played a pivotal role in the story of Lockhart of Carnwath I was then completing. Yet revisiting it through Sinclair's vivid eyewitness account was somehow different that time. Perhaps I now knew enough to sense the deep problems Sinclair's text mutely hinted at. In any event, I decided to try writing an article on an aspect of the '15 that had interested me for some time: the experience of the exiles of the '15 and its impact on the Jacobite community in Scotland. From there, as is the way of these things, one thing led to another and this book is the final result. One thing it is not, however, is the final word on that great rebellion. The well of sources is so deep and the sweep of the phenomenon is so broad that even this book really only constitutes an introduction to the subject. Young scholars come hither; there is a great deal more work for you to do.

Though historians may write alone, they truly never work alone, and this book owes a huge intellectual debt to many other scholars of the seventeenth/eighteenth-century British Isles whose names will be found listed in the bibliography below. In particular, the excellent work (to say nothing of the friendship, advice and help) of Jeremy Black, David Hayton, Allan Macinnes, Paul Monod, Murray Pittock, Éamonn Ó Ciardha and Chris Whatley made this book possible. Without them it would at best have been in gestation a great deal longer. I also owe a special debt to my former student, Margaret Sankey, for her kindness in allowing me to cite extensively from the proofs of her forthcoming book on the Jacobite prisoners of war of 1715–16. This will without doubt only be the first of many on the eighteenth century we can look forward to from her; she is destined to become one of the leading scholars of the next generation. This book would also have been much tardier in appearing were it not for the fine work of the professional archivists and librarians who guard the banks of source material that are the real core of Scotland's historical heritage. Their names are legion, but I must mention three in particular: David Brown and Tristram Clark at the National Archives of Scotland and Iain Beavan at Aberdeen. The archives they tend are the measure of their achievement: nowhere in the world is any nation getting better value for its money.

I am, too, indebted to Her Majesty the Queen for permission to cite from the microfilm of the Stuart Papers held at Ralph Brown Draughon Library in Auburn; to Sir Robert Clerk of Penicuik for the use of the Clerk of Penicuik MSS, the Earl of Dalhousie for permission to use the Dalhousie Papers, the Earl of Seafield for permission to use the Seafield Muniments and Sir Archibald Grant for permission to use the Grant of Monymusk papers, all of which are held at the National Archives of Scotland. I am grateful, too, to the Duke of Atholl for permission to use the Atholl Papers at Blair Atholl. My thanks are due also to the Keeper of the Records of Scotland for permission to see the Eglinton and Montrose Papers. All Old Brotherhood material from the collection held at the Westminster Diocesan Archives is published here with the kind permission of the Old Brotherhood, for which I am also grateful. The costs of transatlantic research are formidable, and without the financial help I received from the Scouloudi Foundation, the Society of Antiquaries of Scotland and the Auburn University History Department, this book would have taken a great deal longer to research. I am very grateful to them all. I must, too, thank the University of Chicago Press for permission to reuse material from my article, '"Cam Ye O'er Frae France?": Defeat, Exile and the Mind of Scottish Jacobitism, 1716–27', which appeared in *Journal of British Studies*, 37 (1998), 357–390,[1] and Oxford University Press, the Past and Present Society and my co-author, Margaret Sankey, for permission to reuse material from our article, 'Elite Culture and the Decline of Scottish Jacobitism, 1716–1745', which was published in *Past and Present*, 173 (2001), 90–128.

Abbreviations and Conventions

AECP	Affaires Étrangères, Correspondance Politique (Angleterre)
BL	British Library
Blackader	A. Crichton [ed.], *The Life and Diary of Lieutenant Colonel John Blackader of the Cameronian Regiment, and Deputy Governor of Stirling Castle* (1824)
Blairs Letters	Scottish Catholic Archives, Edinburgh, Blairs Letters
Glenbuchat	modern rendering of contemporary placename usually spelled 'Glenbucket' by contemporaries and historians
HMC	Historical Manuscripts Commission
HMC *Stuart*	*Calendar of the Stuart Papers Belonging to His Majesty the King Preserved at Windsor Castle* (8 vols, 1902–20)
NAS	National Archives of Scotland, Register House (formerly the Scottish Record Office)
NLS	National Library of Scotland
PRO	Public Record Office, Kew
SP	State Papers Domestic
Steuart *Newsletters*	A. Francis Steuart (ed.), *News Letters of 1715–16* (1910)
Stuart Papers	Stuart Papers microfilm, Ralph Brown Draughon Library, Auburn University, Alabama

The place of publication of all works cited in the endnotes and bibliography is London unless otherwise stated.

The citations from the State Papers Domestic in the notes below are in two forms. One derives from the standard notation used by the Public Record Office at Kew, e.g. 'SP 54/9/1: instructions for General George Wade, St James, 1 Oct. 1715'. The second derives from the National Archives of Scotland, which holds a complete set of negative photocopies of the State Papers

Domestic relating to Scotland (which are in some instances easier to read than the originals). The standard notation for these is different, e.g. 'RH 2/4/306/75: Lord Justice Clerk Cockburn to Townshend, Edinburgh, 22 Oct. 1715'. The fourth number in the RH sequence (in the indicated example '75') is, however, the same in both sets of notations, as is the date, and scholars wishing to see the documents in question should be able to use either to locate them. The *Descriptive List of Secretaries of State: State Papers Scotland, Series Two (1688–1782)* (3 vols, List and Index Society, 262–264, 1996), is also very helpful in this context. In addition, the original State Papers Domestic documents have over the years accumulated a number of pencilled and stamped-on numbering systems added by successive generations of archivists. This can be confusing, so in all instances I have followed the numeration for any particular document found in the List and Index Society volumes.

The spelling and punctuation of all quotations have been modernised wherever this helps elucidate the meaning of the text. Commonplace contractions and abbreviations have all been silently expanded.

Since the British Isles remained on the Julian calendar until 1751, dates there were eleven calendar days behind those of continental Europe in 1715. The dispatches of the French ambassador in London – which used new-style dating – and correspondence cited below stemming from continental locations have therefore had the old-style, British Isles, date added. Thus a letter written in Paris on 14 May would be cited below as having been written on 3/14 May.

Introduction

On 5 November 1688 Prince William of Orange, Stadholder (military commander-in-chief) of the Netherlands and collateral heir to the thrones of England, Scotland and Ireland held by his father-in-law King James II (of England and Ireland) and VII (of Scotland), landed in Torbay with a Dutch army at his back. William proclaimed to all who would listen that he had come to save Protestantism in the three kingdoms from the danger it lay under from the Catholic James and his new-born son and heir, James Francis Edward Stuart, the future Old Pretender. And an apparently Protestant-inclined providence certainly smiled on the bold Dutchman. Within two months King James had fled to France and within less than two more William was offered, and graciously accepted, the crowns of England and Scotland (thereby becoming William III of England and Ireland and II of Scotland). All that remained was to secure control of the rest of the British Isles and consolidate the new order's hold on the institutions of church and state.

Which was, of course, easier said than done. Not everyone in the archipelago was willing to accept either the overthrow of the main line of the Stuart dynasty or the new order, and for most of the next century there were always two dynasties contesting the crowns of the British Isles. The Protestant Stuart line died out with William's successor, James II and VII's daughter by his first marriage, Queen Anne, in 1714, and the Guelph Electors of Hanover (the nearest Protestant heirs) succeeded her. James II and VII died in exile in 1701, but his son James and his grandson Charles carried on the struggle to restore the Catholic Stuart line for nearly sixty more years. The main line of the Stuart dynasty was only finally extinguished when Charles's brother, Cardinal Henry Benedict Stuart, died in 1807. Until the late 1750s adherents of the main line of the Stuarts, the Jacobites (so called from the Latin form of James's name: *Jacobus*), plotted, intrigued and, periodically, rebelled against the heirs of the Revolution. The subject of this book, the '15 rebellion, is thus the second of three major attempts by the Jacobites to resist or overthrow the 'Glorious' Revolution. The first occurred when the revolution that had begun so promisingly with William III and II's easy capture of England in 1688 was contested by Stuart loyalists in Ireland and Scotland from 1689 to 1691. The third took place when Charles Edward Stuart – Bonny Prince Charlie – famously led the last Jacobite uprising against the government of George II in 1745–46. And both of these wars/rebellions, but especially the '45, have overshadowed the '15. It has become something of an orphan child within our vision of the eighteenth century.

For most contemporaries it was soon characterised as the 'unnatural' rebellion,[1] and in the same vein subsequent generations of historians have found it to be 'the obscure rising', the 'impossible' rebellion, and 'a series of contradictions'.[2] It is easy to see why. The Jacobite rebellion of 1745 in particular is spectacularly full of drama and potential. A prince (Charles Edward) arrives in Scotland out of the blue. The Scottish Jacobites allow themselves to be seduced by his charm and promises and follow him to victory in Scotland and a daring invasion of England. He and his officers fall out, their army is forced to retreat, and, despite further victories, is finally cornered and defeated. The prince flees through the heather and after desperate adventures escapes into embittered exile; his followers are brutally harried by way of reprisal.[3] There is just so much there that it is not surprising that the '15 has attracted a great deal less interest. It is a dowdier bird. There is a prince: James Stuart, the Old Pretender (father of Charles Edward), but he has precious little impact on the rising proper. His followers, though they are far more numerous than their counterparts in 1745, win no glorious victories and conquer no great cities. The rebellion finally disintegrates piecemeal and in retrospect merits little but contempt from the victors. Looking back, the winners wonder why they were ever alarmed or frightened by the vanquished and soon the great majority of the erstwhile rebels are allowed to creep home by one means or another.

Compared to the dogged, bloody war in the Highlands and Ireland in 1689–91 and the excitement and sweep of the '45, the '15 is manifestly a damp squib. Yet, in the opinion of this historian, all of the above makes it a more, rather than less, interesting phenomenon. Implicit within the history of the '15 is a set of intriguing questions. Why did the Jacobites rebel when their prince was not even there to lead them? Why did they do it at the worst possible time from a geopolitical point of view? Why were they able to achieve so little militarily? Why did the rebellion finally disintegrate so pathetically? Why were their enemies so willing to stay their hand in the aftermath? What follows is in many respects a study in historical sociology. This does not mean that I am a sociologist by training (beyond a very basic level), but rather that the questions I am primarily engaged in answering are sociological (in the broadest sense): how and why the Jacobite communities of the British Isles and diaspora generated this rebellion and what innate social and cultural dynamics within those communities trended the rebellion towards its eventual outcome. The reader will nonetheless find plenty of social, political and military history in the pages below; only the underlying thrust of the analysis needs to be focused on these questions, and this author has no aversion to trying to tell a good story. History should be readable and interesting and it is my hope that this book will satisfy many more readers than those interested in such matters.

In a more general European context, the '15 is, furthermore, important because of the way it, like all the Jacobite rebellions, differed so fundamentally from the great majority of the popular revolts that contemporary governments had to face at some time or other in the eighteenth century.[4] Unlike the classic peasant revolts that were the main expression of popular discontent in this period, whose participants sought to block or reform policies and replace or attack unpopular officials while leaving the existing order intact, it aimed from the outset at the overthrow of the existing political order. This does not mean that the '15 was different in every respect. It has long been accepted among historians that early modern European rebellions were never discrete phenomena. Because the actors were human beings with lives, loves and experiences that tied them into the complex, shifting network of human affairs surrounding them, all early modern European rebellions were necessarily deeply embedded in a time and a place. They did not just occur anywhere; they occurred where they did for reasons that were vital to the participants in that specific context.[5] Then, as now, all politics was local and this was emphatically the case with the 1715 and other Jacobite rebellions.

Where the Jacobite revolts departed most strikingly from most of their peers was in the intensity of commitment they demanded from their participants. For any rebellion to break out, a mass of people sufficient to seize power from the customary institutions of government in that particular place at that political moment had to be so angry with their circumstances, or fearful that their situation was about to change for the worse, that they were willing to abandon the ordinary course of their lives and follow their leaders into a frightening, dislocated world suffused with the implicit threat of grief, pain and violent death. Even so, most peasant rebels could at least make believe that it would never come to that. In spirit they were more akin to armed demonstrators than radical insurrectionaries. The Jacobites, by contrast, knew they were embarking on a civil war. And the grief, pain and violent death that would inevitably follow were not just for themselves, but for their neighbours, friends and kinsfolk.

As well as being a political act the '15 was, therefore, also an implicitly arrogant event, undertaken by a section of the community convinced of their own superior righteousness with respect to the everyday mores by which they had hitherto lived their lives. To do what they did, the rebels had to believe that they knew better than their neighbours what must be done to save the community from its current crisis (as was the case with their peers, there was a crisis associated with the rebellion, at least in the minds of the rebels).[6] Such confidence in their own judgement was, moreover, made even more essential by the likelihood of condign punishment in the event of the rebellion's failure. By the early eighteenth century the dreadful consequences of defeat were well known throughout the British Isles and, indeed, the rest of Europe. In England and Wales, Scotland and Ireland the punishment for rebellion was fiendishly cruel: a convicted rebel would be hanged until he passed out, then revived and forced to watch his own disembowelment, before being cut into pieces for public exhibition throughout the kingdom. Though in practice this dreadful ordeal was inflicted only on selected victims deemed specially obnoxious by the authorities, undertaking actions that brought on even the risk of such punishment took real resolution.[7] Thus well before the rebels began openly to defy the state they had further to convince themselves of the likelihood of victory, for without that conviction the horrors that putative rebels well knew would follow their defeat must have acted as a deterrent.

In addition, in order to amount to more than a violent demonstration or riot the public defiance of existing state authority that was at the heart of the Jacobites' rebellion had to be sustained, and the economic and human resources of the rebel community mobilised to support an alternative authority. In order to do this – in effect, to create a temporary alternative state – the rebels had to mobilise the wherewithal, technical, experiential and material, to construct an administrative infrastructure sufficient to sustain them through their struggle with their enemy. The physical resources – the food, weapons and money the rebels would need to keep going – were, too, a *sine qua non*. Without muskets, powder and shot, to say nothing of food in their bellies and somewhere to shelter from the elements, the Jacobites were not going to be able to confront the armed forces of the early modern British state with any prospect of success. They also had to find the moral resources to keep themselves going over the long term. Anger could help bring them to the point of rebellion, but it could not fuel the rebels' perseverance for weeks and months; for that an ideology, in the sense of a system of interconnected, mutually supporting ideas, beliefs and values, was required. And an ideology is fixed in the hearts and minds of its adherents by upbringing, education and experience, usually over a long period of time.

Anger and fear, self-righteousness, confidence, the ability to construct a war effort and the physical resources and ideology to sustain it: these, then, were the necessary conditions for the outbreak of a Jacobite rebellion in the British Isles in 1715. Without them there might have been riots and individual acts of public defiance by Jacobites, but there could have been no rebellion capable of truly threatening the authority of the state and its controllers. Moreover, every one of these components was embedded in community, time and place. Thus to understand what happened in the British Isles during the seven months between September 1715 and April 1716 we need to comprehend the context in which they came together to make a rebellion. This will be the subject of the first two chapters.

Despite its partial affinity with contemporaneous European rebellions in terms of general physical and psychological characteristics, the '15 differed from its peers in that it stemmed from, and was powered by, the ideological and political dynamics intrinsic to a peculiarly alienated community within the British polity. The ideological momentum this Jacobite community developed, inclining it towards rebellion, is, therefore, the subject of Chapter 3, while the way this momentum crystallised into a far-reaching conspiracy will be dealt with in Chapter 4. Rebellions in any era reveal a great deal about the internal social relations of the affected communities, in the sense that as the rebels step forward to try and seize control, possible reactions from their fellow subjects who do not share their views range from fierce resistance to fearful submission, which in turn can tell us a good deal about the internal workings of society in a particular locality. By deriving a general pattern from the way the rebellion broke out in Scotland and northern England, Chapter 5 explores these relationships, preparatory to looking at how, and how successfully, the Jacobites created an alternative army and an alternative state. This naturally leads into a broad consideration of the progress of the rebellion as it grew into a latent civil war. Hostilities in all four theatres of conflict, northern, central and western Scotland; Lowlands and Borders Scotland; and northern England are correspondingly the subject of Chapters 6 and 7. The military conclusion to the rebellion was, though, not the end of the affair. The victorious Whig regime was left holding over 2,000 prisoners of war after the '15 collapsed, and was facing a long-term political problem with respect to the hundreds of élite Scots and some dozens of English former rebels who were either fugitives within the kingdom or had fled overseas to escape its vengeance. How it dealt (and failed to deal) with the aftermath of the rebellion – and how, in particular, Scottish civil society was regenerated in the process – is the subject of Chapters 8 and 9.

There is, too, a further context that needs to be considered here. It is universally recognised that history is an imaginative, dynamic subject. Historians are simply trained, knowledgeable intellectuals who knit what they can find out about a place, an event and a moment into a coherent literary vision that (hopefully) helps the present understand its own development a little better. In doing so they are implicitly answering questions posed by the present. This is an uncomfortable truth for historians who – quite rightly – aspire to scientific detachment and would like to think of themselves as addressing larger issues than the grubby, humdrum neuroses of their own era. It is nonetheless so. Hence it is appropriate in any historical study to reflect on what present and previous generations of historians have made of the same phenomenon.

This is especially the case with respect to the subject of Jacobitism in general and the 1715 rebellion in particular. Jacobitism has not had much respect. Romantic popular history aside, it is implicitly viewed by many historians of the early modern British Isles as an irrelevance.[8] Jonathan Clark has argued that this treatment of Jacobitism essentially stems from the fact that, do what the historians will, it just does not fit within the prevailing orthodoxy.[9] This projects the long eighteenth century (1660–1832) as an era of rapid social change, accelerating economic advancement usually described as 'the industrial revolution' and the acquisition of a global empire. It is Victorian Britain in the making, and thus a dynastically inspired, anti-British (in the sense that it directly connected with Scots and Irish proto-nationalism) movement with strong religious overtones looks decidedly out of place. The Jacobites and Jacobitism have therefore tended to be pushed to the margins of our vision of the long eighteenth century. No historian of the era would argue that the Jacobite rebellions and the Jacobite movement are completely irrelevant to the course of development of the British Isles, but they are generally viewed as far less important than a great many other phenomena; hence they can be briefly treated or otherwise dismissed in the author's literary progress towards more important things.[10] This then diffuses into the general understanding of the era, so that, for example, at the time of writing (October 2004) even so quietly significant a place as the National Library of Scotland's shop bookshelves – replete with interesting new works on Scottish society, politics and culture from the Middle Ages to the present – implicitly drop the subject of Jacobitism by leaving it to the novelists. Robert Louis Stevenson's *The Master of Ballantrae* is a rattling good yarn which was backed up by some research on the author's part, but history it is not. The historians' blind spot with respect to Jacobitism is something this book alone cannot repair. Suffice it to say that the prevailing orthodoxy on the long eighteenth century is going to remain flawed and misleading until it can encompass apparent anachronisms like the Jacobite movement.[11] Indeed, a clear signal that a Kuhnian paradigm shift[12] towards a new orthodoxy is in progress may come when a broad school of historiography ceases to perceive the Jacobite movement in such terms and projects it instead as a natural, unsurprising outgrowth of the institutions and mores of the era.

The story of the '15 has also been dealt with before by some fine historians who have taken a very different approach to that which follows below. The most important recent book focused exclusively on the '15 was published by John Baynes in 1970.[13] Baynes was a former soldier and had a soldier's eye for terrain and the critical details of military affairs. His book correspondingly offered an excellent account of the military side of the campaign, given the sources available to him. Since then, however, three decades of fine work by the National Archives of Scotland have given scholars access to a great deal more unpublished manuscript material. Our understanding of the economy, politics and society of early eighteenth-century Scotland has correspondingly broadened and deepened and new sources have set many of the military events described by Baynes in a new light. The differences between Baynes's interpretation and that advanced below, indeed, stem primarily from this modern vision of the British Isles and those new and rediscovered sources.[14] Before Baynes the redoubtable and industrious brother-and-sister team of Alistair and Henrietta Tayler produced a disappointingly bitty account of the rebellion in 1936, which effectively comes across as a series of semi-digested sketches rather than a coherent treatment.[15] Prior to the Taylers, there were a few incidental works that dealt with particular aspects of the rising,[16] but the only works that dealt with the '15 as a whole were contemporary polemics.[17]

The upshot of all of this is that the subject has been profoundly neglected. Many other books, theses and dissertations have a chapter or two on the rebellion as part of a general consideration of the Jacobite movement and related phenomena,[18] few of them as percipient and stimulating as Bruce Lenman's *The Jacobite Risings in Britain* or as well researched as Jonathan Oates's lengthy consideration of responses to the '15 and the '45 in north-eastern England.[19] Yet even the cursory examinations that came before Baynes acknowledged that the '15 was on a substantially larger scale than the '45, drew considerably more English support, and thus *prima facie* should have been a greater threat to the Whig regime.[20] That it was not is generally ascribed to the military incompetence and political chicanery of John Erskine, Earl of Mar, an interpretation that rests firmly on the basis of charges levelled at the time and by none more bitterly and eloquently than John Sinclair, the Master of Sinclair

('Master' was the honorific title given at that time to the heir apparent to a Scottish Lord of Parliament).[21] There is a great deal of justice in this, but the rebellion was much bigger than Mar, and in many ways he was simply riding a tiger. Another actor who comes in for a good deal of blame is James, the Old Pretender, the exiled son of James II and VII. He was slow to reach Scotland after the rebellion broke out (in fairness, through no fault of his own) and allowed himself to be dominated by Mar when he did arrive. James has consequently been criticised almost as much as his commander in Scotland for the failure of the rebellion.[22] Interestingly, the criticisms even of modern historians (and novelists) tend to go back to his alleged weak-mindedness, an interpretation directly traceable to eighteenth-century Whig polemics which essentially portrayed him as stupid because he was a Catholic.[23] No true Englishman could be a superstitious, priest-ridden Catholic, so he had to be dim. In fact James was a sophisticated, well-educated man, who had some military experience and thoroughly understood the duties of a king.[24] He did not always do a very good job even as a shadow monarch, but there again, neither did his German cousins who actually reigned in the British Isles.[25] He was certainly no dimmer than they were.

Reassessing the '15 offers us the chance to gain a new insight into the Jacobite phenomenon. Though the drama and sweep of the '45 have generated a massive historiography, we should not assume that the essence of the Jacobite cause lay therein.[26] The Jacobite moment in the history of the British Isles was much bigger than one uprising late in the history of the movement. It is, therefore, necessary to broaden our understanding of what Jacobitism was about and what it was capable of, and a reassessment of the '15 will serve that end very well. For it was an event the Jacobites in Scotland and northern England created for themselves, by themselves, in the face of the British state (albeit they were encouraged underhand by the French government). In the process they revealed a great many strengths and weaknesses not just within their own community, but in the new British polity as a whole. Uprisings, rebellions and civil wars always expose the political and social pathology of a people and a state. This book is an attempt to recapture that pathology for the Jacobite community, the state it opposed and the larger polity of which both were a part. It is also to be hoped it will be a further step towards the reintegration of the Jacobites into the discipline's vision of the eighteenth-century British Isles.

CHAPTER 1

'To Mark Where England's Province Stands':
the Economy and Social Structure of the British Isles
in 1715

The 1715 rebellion took the course it did because of its context in the three
kingdoms. And if the historiographic devil is always in the details, this is most
emphatically the case when dealing with such complex phenomena as the
intertwined economic, social and political contexts of a major uprising.
Precisely because of the historiographically charged nature of that context
even my use of the term 'three kingdoms' is one that demands explanation. In
strict legal terms there were only two kingdoms in the British Isles in 1715, as
the kingdoms of Scotland and England had formally ceased to exist when they
merged in the kingdom of Great Britain in 1707. Yet in 1715 Scotland
remained an uneasily semi-autonomous zone within the overall embrace of
the new British state. From an administrative point of view all that had
occurred in 1707 was that certain elements of the Scottish state, notably its tax
collection system, army and political institutions, had been subsumed by the
English polity, which otherwise still functioned very much as it had done
before the Union except that it was now called Great Britain.[1] For the
purposes of the analysis that follows Scotland, England and Ireland will, then,
be taken as having each retained a distinct economy and society in the early
eighteenth century, albeit that burgeoning ties of interest, kinship and culture
were slowly drawing the three together.[2] The net effect was to create a shifting,
episodic commonality that could sometimes overcome the centrifugal force
set up by each kingdom's divergent economic and social circumstances. The
question as to why those developing ties – in particular the economic and
social elements therein – nonetheless failed to prevent the Jacobite rising lies
at the heart of this chapter.

The Economy of the British Isles in 1715

The long since conjoined polity of England and Wales was in 1715 by far and away the wealthiest of the three kingdoms and, indeed, per capita, the wealthiest in the world.[3] This economic preponderance within the British Isles had been the case since before the Roman era and the economic divergence between England and the other two kingdoms had grown even greater over the course of the previous two centuries.[4] Though England and Wales remained a predominantly rural nation, the proportion of the English and Welsh population who earned their living primarily from the land was lower (at around 45 per cent) than anywhere else in the British Isles.[5] In London England and Wales also had at its economic heart the only contemporary mega-city in the archipelago, and one so large – with a population of approximately 575,000 – that it acted as the engine of the Anglo-Welsh economy, drawing goods, generating wealth and bringing on a steady, cyclical population movement, all to service its needs and fuel its continued growth.[6] Yet London was in many ways an aberration. At any one time it subsumed over 10 per cent of the population of England and Wales, but it was a city of migrants, there to complete apprenticeships or to amass some money before returning whence they came, and a great many of London's inhabitants regularly cycled out of it and back to the cities, towns and villages of the Anglo-Welsh hinterland after only a few years in the Great Wen.[7] They carried their skills and experience back to the rural and small town world from which they came and in the process reinvested in the larger English and Welsh economy. This cycle and its fruits had been operating and, as London grew, accelerating, for centuries. As a result, by the early eighteenth century industries and enterprises moving goods and services of all kinds on a national scale could be found in virtually every major Anglo-Welsh city and a great many smaller towns.[8] The massive increase in production we generally designate as the industrial revolution was not yet on the economic horizon, but England and Wales were already well on the way to developing a truly national economy, where craftsmen in Taunton and Bristol reworked goods and materials produced in Yorkshire and Kent to make products that sold in London, Manchester and Bangor.[9]

England and Wales was also, in 1715, still in the throes of a surge of economic development occasioned by the explosion of financial and commercial innovations, or, more accurately, intensifications, known as the commercial revolution. This took off in the late seventeenth century and basically involved a huge expansion of the mercantile and commercial sectors of the economy. There had been a strong export component to the English economy since the Middle Ages, and exports of Anglo-Welsh manufactured products and raw materials, plus re-exports of goods and materials brought in increasing quantities from the Caribbean and North American colonies and overseas trading posts in India and Africa, now became the principal focus of investment and government support. The European market for sugar, tobacco, Indian calicos, tea and other hitherto exotic and expensive products seemed nigh insatiable at this point, and England's commercial sector rapidly expanded to try and meet the demand. In the process new modes of doing business, securing capital and financing trade were developing in tandem with a huge expansion in Britain's mercantile marine. The stock market, insurance companies and banks were becoming regular players in all major commercial enterprises and money was begetting money on a hitherto unimaginable scale. The groundwork for Britain's nineteenth-century global commercial hegemony was being laid.[10]

But what did all this mean for the ordinary English or Welsh man or woman? For the rural labourer or the small tenant farmer it meant that there was an incremental increase in expectations from two directions. Employers and landlords were demanding ever greater productivity and steadily rising rents.[11] The rural workforce had for a long time often had by-employments such as spinning and weaving which they took up during slack periods in the agricultural cycle; these now became of critical importance within their domestic economies.[12] Often they meant the difference between poverty and a mild prosperity. The small tenant farmer was in a pernicious bind: though agricultural prices were depressed throughout the early eighteenth century the general trend was for rents to rise. The only way he could defend his standard of living was to exploit the land and his crops more intensively.[13] In failure to do so lay arrears, possible eviction and poverty; but even small success could offer new levels of comfort and access to goods previously only available to the very wealthy. Sugar, tea, oriental textiles and imported, rather than locally manufactured, consumer durables – the staples of Britain's future consumer society – were beginning to make their appearance in the homes even of the modest tenant farmer. For the small manufacturer or tradesman the changing economic order was both an opportunity and a threat. The man who could increase the output of his workshop or business could find investors for still further expansion and a multiplicity of new outlets for his products.[14] Conversely, he could find his wares undercut by goods produced more cheaply elsewhere in the increasingly national economy. Thus a small master running a textile workshop in Tiverton or Ipswich could find himself squeezed by similar goods produced at a lower price in Norwich or Halifax.[15] Landowners were in some ways best placed to take advantage of the new opportunities for profit. They had access to a continuing stream of income and judicious investment could now produce a steadily rising standard of living and consolidate their families' economic position for the foreseeable future. But alongside the profits came the demands of social station. Landowners were expected to maintain a certain lifestyle and the quality and expense of that lifestyle were rising in tune with the broader prosperity being generated by the commercial revolution. The architectural glories of the eighteenth-century Anglo-Welsh urban renaissance thus came at a price. Elite families were being ruined by extravagance, debt and failed investments all the time in the early eighteenth century.[16]

The upshot of all of this is that England and Wales was generally prospering and the English economy in particular was surging and expansive, yet this did not necessarily generate emotional security in the population. Prosperity, whether enjoyed or observed, must often have seemed very precarious, and there was a corresponding undercurrent of economic anxiety running through English life.[17] A recession, such as the one that hit important sectors of the economy in England and Wales between 1713 and 1717, was more than sufficient stimulation to set concern and apprehension racing.[18] In any such trend towards broad economic expansion there are liable to be losers as well as winners, and in England and Wales in the early eighteenth century the impact of the new-found prosperity was regionally patchy. South-eastern and Midland England benefited a great deal more than the rest of the country.[19] South-western England was tending towards economic stagnation.[20] Wales was only lightly touched by any of the new developments.[21] North-eastern England was just beginning to feel the upsurge in economic expansion.[22] Parts of the English Border region were in the throes of an economic crisis brought on by both the postwar recession and the commercial opening of the Scottish frontier in 1707. Hitherto defended against cheaper Scottish goods by English customs tariffs, northern England was suddenly exposed to the full blast of Scottish low-wage competition in the English national market and lost most of the illicit revenues it had accrued for centuries from illegal cross-border traffic. Those commodities, such as salt, that were protected in Scotland after the Union and could therefore still be profitably smuggled across the border were accordingly even more fiercely defended against government attempts to intercept them, and violent confrontations between bands of smugglers, 'armed in great bodies', running salt, 'in defiance of all opposition', and customs officers became all too regular an occurrence.[23] On the English border hard times were being felt at all levels of society.[24]

On the other side of the old frontier the Scottish political nation had, of course, been drawn, in part, towards political union with England precisely because of the comparative prosperity and higher standard of living Scots observed in early eighteenth-century England.[25] Scotland's economy had struggled to recover from the impact of the Great Civil War, which had been far more devastating in Scotland than south of the border. A fragile recovery only really began in the 1670s and 1680s and it was aborted by the disasters of the 1690s.[26] Between 1689 and 1691 Scotland suffered renewed civil war, the costs of which effectively bankrupted the Scottish state, and the war was not long over when Scotland was struck by the famines of 'King William's ill years' in the mid- to late 1690s, which may in some areas have killed or driven out as much as one-third of the population.[27] The net result was a stagnant, depressed economy and no obvious way to remedy the situation.[28]

In such circumstances, desperate measures came to seem worth trying, and one particularly bold initiative, the Darien venture, was launched in the late 1690s. This projected the seizure of Spanish territory in the isthmus of Darien by the specially created Royal Company of Scotland Trading to Africa and the Indies with a view to establishing a trading entrepôt there. The subtext was that Scots merchants would then smuggle huge quantities of goods in and out of Spanish America, reap vast profits and rescue Scotland's economy from its economic doldrums. Unfortunately for the enthusiastic investors, who sank, according to one estimate, one-quarter of Scotland's liquid capital in the venture, the Darien scheme totally failed. William III and II was furious at such a freebooting expedition launched against his Spanish ally in time of peace and refused any state help at all. In this he was backed up by the English Parliament, which was determined to prevent England's lucrative Iberian and South American trade being undermined by an interloping Scots rival. English investment in the Darien venture was blocked and the Scots could not carry it through on their own resources. The net result was that the colony failed, the money was lost and Scotland was left worse off than when it started.[29]

By the early eighteenth century Scotland was apparently in dire need of substantial economic stimulation. Something in the region of 80 per cent of Scots made a living from the land, and the bulk of Scotland's exports, such as they were, were in the form of livestock and raw materials. The only major manufacture exported was Scots linen, and that trade seemed to be faltering and declining in value.[30] Only one Scottish city was showing some visible improvement in its economic situation: Glasgow, and its wealth was based on an unabashedly illicit trade with the English colonies in North America, bolstered by extensive smuggling of tobacco and other colonial products into

England and re-exports to Europe. There is, however, the tantalising possibility that Glasgow was only the tip of the iceberg and that by the early eighteenth century there was good deal more hidden, illicit prosperity in Scotland's economy than has hitherto been realised.[31] The extent of such economic activity is, though, very difficult to gauge because of the fact that it rarely leaves records. In any event, a substantial minority of the Scots élite saw Scotland's economic salvation only in union with England, which, of course, finally came to pass in highly controversial circumstances – and virtually certainly against the wishes of most of the Scots people – in 1707.[32]

To make matters worse, the economic uplift so certainly promised during the political furore surrounding the passage of the Act of Union was very slow in arriving. Apart from a brief burst of profiteering by Scots merchants who had laid in stockpiles of French wine at the lower Scots rate of duty, which they then sold off on the English market post-Union, the Scots economy as a whole did not show much immediate benefit from the Union. In 1714 even a stalwart supporter of the Union was forced to admit that 'Edinburgh indeed has suffered by the Union, and so has the countryes about it in some measure, that used to furnish the town, for there is not that consumption nor employment for trades people that has been formerly.'[33] Other parts of Scotland suffered equally.[34] Even Glasgow's growth stalled and the rest of the Scottish economy remained stagnant.[35] English investment was slow in arriving and reimbursements of Scotland's share of national, British taxation servicing the English national debt (the so-called Equivalent) were episodic and made little impact on the overall economic situation. The Scots linen industry had lost its previous state protector and its interests were subordinated to more powerful economic interests at Westminster.[36] The cattle trade seems to have expanded, but because of cross-border smuggling prior to the Union which only became overt after 1707 this may be more apparent than real.[37] Scottish coal had trouble competing on the English market.[38] Scarcely surprising then that most Scots felt a profound sense of economic disappointment with the Union.[39] The Reverend Robert Wodrow, though a firm upholder of the Union on political and religious grounds, believed in 1724 that:

The poverty and debts of many are increasing, and I can not see hou it can be otherwise. Ther are no ways to bring in specie into this country. Trade is much failed, and any trade we have is of that kind that takes money from amongst us, and brings in French brandy, Irish meal, tea, etc, which are all consumed; and unles it be a feu coals from the west, and some black cattell from the south, and many of these are not our breed, but Irish, I see no branch of our business that brings in any money. Our tobacco trade, and other branches to the West Indies, are much sinking; and the prodigiouse run of our nobility and gentry there, besides the corruption in principle, and practise, takes away a vast deal of monney every year. Besides, its plain that we are overstocked with people, considering their idlenes, and that makes the consumpt very great; and when there are no incomes, nor incouragement of manufactorys among ourselves, this will infallibly at lenth impoverish us.[40]

And gloom continued to characterise Scots thinking on the economy until the mid-eighteenth century, though there may have been a few small swallows presaging summer, or at least better times, by the 1730s.[41] More dangerously, threatened extensions of higher levels of English taxation to such staples as malt in Scotland produced violent protests in 1713, and the anger generated then was easily reignited in 1715. Thus when John Erskine, the Earl of Mar, arrived in Scotland in August 1715 he quickly bruited it about that:

the Parliament . . . designed to lay unsupportable taxes upon the nation: on lands, corn, cattle, meal, malt, horse[s], sheep . . . even on cocks and hens, and that this was no mean reason for him to take up arms since otherwise in a very short time the nation should sink under such burdens.

Unsurprisingly, 'this took extreamly with the comon people and animated them to take up arms',[42] as may be seen from the 'loud acclamations' of 'No Union! No malt, no salt tax!' with which the rebel soldiers and people of Kelso greeted the proclamation of the Jacobite king James III and VIII.[43]

Moreover, as in the Lowlands, poverty was the principal experience of the economy in the Highlands in the first generation after the Union.[44] Within a Scottish context the Lowland economy was considerably more advanced and better capitalised than its Highland counterpart. Yet the Union's impact on the Highland economy was probably relatively beneficent, as it set the vital cattle trade on track for steady expansion. Mounting élite indebtedness, however, seems to have more than counteracted the impact of the profits from droving black cattle southwards to the English market. Throughout the period from 1660 to 1715 clan élites were raising rentals and yet still accumulating debts.[45] The net effect was to tighten the hold of subsistence agriculture on the Highland economy, which is as much as to say that for the mass of the population poverty begat poverty.[46] The Highland élites, too, found it difficult to break out of their own version of this cycle, as indicated by the mounting levels of debt they continued to take on in order to live an 'appropriate' lifestyle. Indeed, they were only finally able to do so in the vastly changed circumstances of the late eighteenth century.[47]

The result of all of this was that in 1715 Scotland was still poor despite the Union. Eight years with little or no improvement in the economy had broadly disappointed the high hopes of economic salvation that sustained many of the supporters of Union during its bitterly contested passage through the Scots Parliament in 1707.[48] Scotland was also subject to the same postwar economic recession that was affecting England and Wales, and the number of unemployed poor had even begun to concern the government at Westminster by the end of 1714, when the new Commission of Police was instructed to look into the matter because it had 'become grievous to the country'.[49] Given, though, the economic slough in which Scotland was enmired, the recession probably did not make much difference to the lives of most ordinary Scots men and women. The mass of the Scottish people, whether labourer or small farmer, probably registered that times were hard (and the winter of 1714–15 particularly difficult);[50] there again, very likely few could remember when things had ever been any different. As far as the élites were concerned, the Union had lamentably failed to fulfil its promise and there seemed little prospect that it would do so in the foreseeable future. Only on a few islands of prosperity, such as the Ayr coalfields and Glasgow, was there much sense of improvement, in terms of rising standards of living, by 1715.[51] Support for the Union outside those exceptional places could only stem from political/religious commitment, because it had so little economic basis.

In principle the case of Ireland was similar to that of Scotland, largely as a consequence of war-related damage in the seventeenth century, but some important differences had developed by the early eighteenth century. Of the three kingdoms there can be no doubt that it was Ireland that suffered the most economically during the Great Civil War. One stark measure of this is that Ireland's population loss as a result of war and its associated epidemics of disease and bouts of famine may have reached as much as 40 per cent.[52] Such staggering human losses over an eleven-year period are, moreover, an indication of equally appalling infrastructural economic damage, in terms of ruined businesses, destroyed farms and lost capital stock. Ireland emerged from the mid-seventeenth century not so much in an economic slough as in a very deep pit. Nonetheless there was a substantial recovery between the late 1650s and the late 1680s, though returning to anything approaching normality was liable to look very good given where the Irish economy was coming from. From the 1660s, if English producers' demands for protection are anything to go by, Ireland's export trade in cattle, wool and butter began to recover, and certainly the infrastructural damage of the mid-century began to be repaired.[53] This hopeful trend was, however, aborted by the outbreak of renewed civil war in 1689. Though King William's War was nowhere near as devastating as the previous struggle (principally because the fighting lasted only two years), the Irish economy suffered grievously as plundering armies once again marched and countermarched, fought battles and besieged towns from one end of the island to the other.[54] Partisan warfare, initially waged by the Protestant Williamites of Ulster, and subsequently by Catholic Jacobites elsewhere in the country, added to the damage. Nonetheless, Ireland's economy was not reduced to the nadir it experienced in the 1650s, though it was certainly set back.[55]

Economic recovery from the turmoil of the early 1690s was, indeed, apparently relatively quick and strong. By the mid-1690s English producers were once again complaining about Irish competition. In addition, in a grim vindication of the old adage that it is an ill wind that blows nobody any good, Ireland may have drawn a backhanded economic benefit from the Scottish famines of the late 1690s. South-western Scotland, the main source of previous generations of Scots settlers in Ulster, was hard hit by the crop failures of 'King William's ill years', and consequently generated a new wave of migration to Ireland. From an economic point of view this was pretty much an unalloyed good, as the new settlers compensated for the war-related population losses of the early 1690s and, because they mostly came from farming communities and were soon busy working the Irish land (which, fortuitously, had a longer growing season than Scotland), substantively contributed to the recovery of the Irish agricultural sector. Since, as in Scotland, this furnished a basic livelihood for some 80 per cent of the population, its return to a comparatively normal level of output was a positive gain. Correspondingly, secondary, more export-related sectors of the economy, particularly linen manufacture, began to expand again by the late 1690s and were soon competing with equivalent English and Scots products.[56] Moreover, because, ironically, the number of politically powerful English and Welsh landowners who also owned estates in Ireland had increased as a result of confiscations of Irish land and their sale or gift to supporters of the new order, Ireland had acquired a tranche of MPs and peers concerned to advance its economic interests at Westminster.[57] These Anglo-Welsh landowners, simply by seeking to improve the profitability of their Irish estates, acted to defend Irish interests. This did not save the Irish economy from initially suffering when trade was disrupted by the outbreak of the War of the Spanish Succession in 1702, but it did facilitate its subsequent revival after 1704. This was based on supplying the Royal Navy and smuggling Irish products into France and culminated in a positive boom between 1711 and 1714. The good times, however, came to an end around the same time as the Hanoverians came to the throne, and the next two decades at least very likely saw a decline in per capita income for most of the population.[58]

That said, Ireland was probably still doing better per capita than Scotland in the early eighteenth century. Ireland was, indeed, to experience a general economic expansion in all sectors over the next eighty years that would eventually improve the standard of living of the majority of its people, although this economic advance was only just beginning in the 1700s.[59] Inevitably, there were also ups and downs and in 1715 Ireland, too, was under a cloud economically as a result of the diminution in state purchasing brought on by the end of the war. The export trade to Iberia and France, supported by the Irish diaspora in both places, that was to facilitate Ireland's economic uplift was only starting to get in gear.[60] As in Scotland, as far as most of the Irish population were concerned, times were hard, though this was perhaps less keenly felt given where Ireland's economy was coming from. In Ireland's case there can, too, be no doubt that the religious discrimination to which the majority of the population was subject also had a negative impact on the economy, both because it encouraged migration by young adult males (a major economic asset in a preindustrial labour force) and discouraged the reinvestment of trading profits in Ireland by Catholic merchants. The dynamics of Irish society, like their English and Welsh and Scots counterparts, were bound to influence the pattern of economic development.

The Social Structure of the British Isles in 1715

Those who thought and wrote about the structure of English and Welsh society in the early eighteenth century still did so in terms of the hierarchy of orders.[61] This is best envisaged as a number of horizontal tiers with vagrants and beggars at the bottom, labourers next up, then husbandmen (small farmers), followed by yeomen (larger, more independent farmers), small manufacturers and merchants, wealthy manufacturers and merchants, and finally landowners at the top.[62] Social status within this hierarchy was influenced by wealth, but not set by it. Hence a landowner, particularly an aristocratic one, who was poorer than a merchant, or even a well-to-do farmer (there were a few destitute nobility), still enjoyed a higher status than his/her social inferiors even when they were economically better off. Indeed, most contemporary English and Welsh men and women defined their status by who deferred to them and showed them public respect, and who they themselves had to defer to and show public respect for. Since sumptuary laws had long ceased to operate in England and Wales, and clothes and fashions regularly trickled down the social hierarchy, whom you took your hat off to, and conversely, who took their hat off to you, created a public image which every individual jealously guarded.[63] In a broad sense it was, too, an honour-bound society even at the lower levels; hence the importance of public reputation and the seriousness with which gossip, rumours and slander reflecting adversely on a particular individual were taken.[64]

There was very little sense of horizontal affinity within the bands that made up the social hierarchy. A yeoman from Wiltshire or Suffolk, for example, would have little sense of common interest with a yeoman from Pembroke or Cumberland. The one exception to this was at the top end of society. The noble and gentry landowners of England and Wales displayed class consciousness (i.e. a sense of mutual, supporting interests and solidarity in the face of perceived threats to those interests) redolent in many respects of classically Marxist descriptions of such phenomena. It has even been argued that there was only one class in early modern England and Wales: the ruling class.[65] Class solidarity below the landowning élite was rare and, when it did occur, was almost invariably local. What impeded the development of a sense of common interest with neighbours and peers was the paternalist dynamic. Benevolence, charity and concern for those below you in the social hierarchy were expected, even demanded, and in a sense were literally the price of deference. If you wanted to have your social inferiors show you cheerful public respect (the visible mark of your social station) you had to make an appearance of paternalism. Failure to do so would lead to increasing degrees of public and secret defiance, ranging from surly uncooperativeness to attacks on property in the form of arson and vandalism and on to public demonstrations/riots aimed at humiliating those who had not lived up to their social obligations.[66] Edward Thompson, possibly the greatest social historian of eighteenth-century England, in 1971 characterised English and Welsh social relations in this period as a kind of 'collective bargaining arbitrated by riot', and while this analysis may need to be nuanced, its basic insight remains valid.[67] The ruling élite expected to command its social inferiors, but tacitly understood that in order to do so it needed to be perceived to be upholding its side of the social compact.[68] As Thompson put it, there was a 'moral economy' in operation.[69]

Cutting across these horizontal status bands with their vertical paternalism/deference ties were a number of other affinities that could powerfully influence the social outlook and connections of an individual. In some parts of England and Wales exceptional concentrations of de facto industrial workers periodically showed signs of incipient class consciousness. Groups such as textile workers and tin miners in the West Country, sailors in the port of

London and coal miners in Northumberland at various times organised themselves into collective bodies (effectively proto-unions), went on strike and bargained with their employers for better wages and conditions. Such local social movements were illegal and shocking, as far as the social élite was concerned, but were to become more and more frequent as the eighteenth century went on.[70] Likewise bonds created by the distinctively different language and culture in Wales and Cornwall and bonds of neighbourhood and community more generally could create vertical solidarities against perceived 'outsiders' of all kinds.[71] Overarching these there was, too, a sense of Englishness or Welshness, which could become sufficiently powerful and mobilising, depending on news from the political centre, to overcome customary bonds.[72] If, for some reason, local landowners came to be perceived as 'unpatriotic' in such crises it was far from unknown for their social inferiors ostentatiously to defy them and even usurp their social leadership.[73]

Equally unsettling for those at the top of the social hierarchy were the ties created by religious dissent. From 1689 all Protestant churches whose members were willing to swear loyalty to the crown were entitled to worship freely without interference from the authorities, and all over England and Wales hitherto illegal Presbyterian, Congregationalist, Baptist and (eventually) Quaker churches emerged from the religious underground to take advantage of the opportunity. This provoked periodic bouts of hysteria within the established Church about the threat posed to the cause of true religion in the nation by these Dissenting congregations, and the Dissenters' efforts to extend the legal limits of religious toleration and evangelise more broadly were vigorously, and successfully, resisted by the Church of England. Dissent was consequently well contained until the end of the eighteenth century and probably never drew more than 7 per cent of the population, though because Dissent was rapidly becoming a primarily urban phenomenon, local concentrations in English and Welsh towns and cities could far exceed this overall figure.[74] Nonetheless, where any numbers of Dissenters were present their ties with each other tended to trump customary social ties whether vertical (towards social superiors) or horizontal (bonds of neighbourhood and community). They thus became a group apart within the community and one that was often suspect and resented.[75]

And if this was the case with the Protestant Dissenters, it was ten times more so with respect to the tiny Catholic minority in England and Wales. By the early eighteenth century the proportion of Catholics in the Anglo-Welsh population had dwindled to about 2 per cent, primarily located in small communities on the lands of the few remaining Catholic landowners. Their Church and the practice of their religion were absolutely illegal, and rewards

were publicly offered for the discovery of Catholic chapels and property
and the apprehension of Catholic priests. Even so, a certain amount of tacit
toleration was extended by neighbours and kinsfolk (in effect, neighbourhood and kinship ties overcoming patriotic orthodoxies depicting Catholics
as the enemy within). As far as most of the population were concerned,
'their' Catholics were good Catholics, it was just the other, unknown,
Catholics who were the problem. Certain regions, notably north-western
England, also contained larger numbers of Catholics than was the case elsewhere. In parts of Lancashire, for example, the Catholic minority may have
been as much as 25 per cent, hence the county was always a source of
anxiety for its neighbouring counties and the central authorities.[76]
Moreover, since, as with the Dissenters, Catholic religious ties were liable
to trump bonds of deference, neighbourhood and community, they were
not wrong to be apprehensive. In a confessional state such as eighteenth-
century England and Wales religious dissent in any form was at the very
least mute defiance, and always carried the potential for more serious
resistance to authority.

Scottish society had many affinities with its English and Welsh counterpart
in terms of the way it was structured and functioned, but there were some
critical differences that were to prove especially significant in 1715–16.
Scotland's population numbered approximately 1 million, of whom about 30
per cent were primarily Gaelic-speaking inhabitants of the Highlands and
Islands. The remainder of the population were Scots-speakers living in the
southern, central and north-eastern Lowlands. In addition, around half of the
total population lived in the two-thirds of Scotland geographically north of
the River Tay, primarily in the north-eastern Lowlands.[77]

The social structure of the Highlands was unusual in that the clan system
that made it so distinctive was still fully functional in the early eighteenth
century. The basic concepts of the clan and clanship are generally well known,
but for the sake of clarity it is worth briefly elucidating its central features with
an eye to the way the social élite's authority operated on a day-to-day basis.
The chieftain was the apex of clan society, and theoretically enjoyed great
power over his people, but *de facto* he was far from being an absolute
monarch.[78] All chieftains were in a reciprocal relationship with both their
extended families (brothers, uncles, cousins, etc.), who in some degree shared
their dynastic legacy, and a wider circle of clan gentry composed of former
cadet branches of the ruling house and others whose ancestry was more
obscure, legally known as 'tacksmen'.[79] Members of this broad stratum below
the chieftain were known in Highland society as the *fine* and it was they who
were the primary land managers of clan society and the immediate rulers of

most of the ordinary clansmen because they were the ones who leased large tracts of land from the clan chief, and then sublet them to humbler tenants in return for goods or services part of which they then paid back to the chief.[80] Most clans were quite small in terms of numbers (no more than 5–6,000 in total), so the ruling dynasties played a visible, major role in all their clansmen's lives, but the day-to-day exercise of power within the clan for the most part remained firmly in the hands of the *fine*. Their relationship with the clansmen was, however, trammelled by both parties being members of the same cultural entity. Because both *fine* and clansmen were members of the clan and partakers in its myths of common identity their relationship had certain limits. The *fine* generally could not evict clan tenants, nor could ordinary clansmen decamp in search of better terms of employment elsewhere. Consequently, as long as the whole of the clan, and especially the ruling dynasty, accepted their common identity and associated responsibilities, the clans were intrinsically stable and the bonds of loyalty strong.[81]

In the Lowlands the social structure was akin to that prevailing in England and Wales, albeit with a Scottish cast.[82] In particular, there was a fundamental distinction between the heritors (those who owned the land and the considerable legal rights that went with possession of it) and the tenants (those who worked it). There was, of course, a very wide range of gradations in land ownership and tenancy corresponding to the horizontal tiers that characterised English and Welsh society, but there was a basic difference between the two in terms of simple authority. In Scotland, because of the still overwhelmingly rural, traditionally paternalist dynamics of Scottish Lowland society, a tenant was generally under a much greater social (and economic) obligation to respect and defer to the heritor whose land he farmed than was usually the case in England and Wales. Even so, the heritors' authority was not *ipso facto* powerful enough to allow them imperiously to summon their people to war in the fashion of their sixteenth-century ancestors. The common people of Lowland Scotland may have been under a greater necessity of deferring to their social superiors than their English and Welsh counterparts, but this did not make them pawns in their masters' games, and they were quite capable of resisting and obstructing demands from their landlord for obedience if they disapproved of his cause.[83] What made so many Scottish plebeians nonetheless willing to accept commands from the élite that went far beyond the regular mores of deference and submission were the religious divisions that became embedded in Scottish society in the late seventeenth century.

After the Restoration in 1660 the Presbyterian Kirk of the mid-seventeenth century was reconstructed by the state on thoroughly Episcopalian lines. Most of the Scots population accepted this change, but a substantial minority were alienated. This minority, the direct ecclesiological and spiritual heirs of the Covenanters of the Great Civil War era, withdrew from the Kirk to worship in field conventicles and private homes and were episodically prosecuted and harassed by the authorities for their defiance, from the early 1660s to the late 1680s.[84] The conventiclers obdurately resisted these attempts to drive them into the new, Episcopal Kirk for the most part peacefully, but occasionally by assassination and armed rebellion, greatly embittering relations between them and those Scots who had embraced the Episcopal order.[85] In 1689, however, the situation abruptly reversed when the bishops of the Kirk chose to stand by what they felt to be their divinely ordained allegiance to James II and VII, and refused to acknowledge William III and II as their *de jure* monarch. William, for his part, badly needed a loyal Kirk backing up his failing state in Scotland and so reluctantly allied himself with the conventiclers.[86] For most Scots this was the element of the Revolution that most directly touched their lives, as all over Scotland the former Episcopalian incumbents of parish kirks found themselves either actually or potentially liable to eviction by the triumphantly Presbyterian conventiclers who were now back in charge of the Kirk as a whole. Once again a majority of Scots seem to have been more or less willing to conform to the new order, but as was the case in the Restoration era, a substantial minority defiantly resisted.[87] In due course these resisters formed an illegal counter-Kirk on Episcopalian principles and the division between 'Episcopalian' and 'Presbyterian' became entrenched in families and communities across Scotland.[88] Moreover, once the religious lines were drawn they inevitably spilled over into politics. According to Edmund Burt, Episcopalian ministers regularly interweaved 'the people's civil rights with religion . . . teaching them, that it is as unchristian not to believe their notions of government as to disbelieve the gospel'.[89] In the north-eastern heartland of Episcopalianism, by 1715 the Episcopal clergy also regularly denounced members of their congregations who showed any willingness to compromise with the Kirk by law established, and made Episcopalianism synonymous with Jacobitism (somewhat unfairly; there were a few non-Jacobite Episcopalians).[90] Episcopalian meeting-houses thus became, by and large, 'the nurseries of rebellion', that served 'only to keep up the spirit and courage of the faction that favour it'.[91]

Broadly speaking, the southern Lowlands, below the Tay, went overwhelmingly Presbyterian; the Lowlands north of the Tay were more evenly divided, with Episcopalians enjoying parity or even a majority in some areas, such as Aberdeenshire and Angus.[92] The Highlands were just as polarised, but there was an extra complexity there added by the historical traditions associated with particular septs in some clans. Hence it was possible to find Catholic and Presbyterian sub-groups within what were otherwise emphatically Episcopalian entities, and vice versa with respect to the small number of predominantly Presbyterian or Catholic clans.[93] With the advantage of state backing the Presbyterian Kirk was slowly gaining the upper hand by the early eighteenth century, but between 30 and 40 per cent of the population was probably still in the Episcopalian camp in 1715.[94]

The net result of all this with regard to northern, and particularly north-eastern, Lowland society was to create a reciprocally hostile siege mentality. The Presbyterian community in the north felt beleaguered and threatened by the Episcopalian hordes whom it regarded as 'next door to popery or the devil', and it actively sought outside intervention to protect itself and smite its foes.[95] This was intermittently forthcoming, usually when the central authorities felt espe-cially alarmed by reports of Jacobite activity. At such times the northern Presbyterians could count on government agencies to physically attack the fabric of the Episcopalians' religious community by arresting and harassing their clergymen and closing down their chapels.[96] Such collaboration with outsiders by the Presbyterians, of course, antagonised the Episcopalians on two counts. By offending localist sentiment it boosted the regionalist patriotic aspect of the Episcopalians' perception of themselves, and by invoking what was in effect overwhelming force in the shape of government intervention it kept the Episcopalian community in a mirror-image siege-like state of hostility and tension with its Presbyterian neighbours.[97]

So when the rebellion finally came in 1715 it is not in the least surprising to find the Synod of Glasgow and Ayr exhorting its congregations to fulfil their duty to King George, 'as you would escape the curse of Meroz, which stands branded with infamy, for not coming out to help the Lord against the mighty', and the Synod of Lothian and Tweeddale declaring, 'there is no place for neutrality here. *For he that is not with us, is against us.* Exert your zeal for the true religion.'[98] On the other side their Episcopal counterparts taught their congregations that adherence to the Jacobite cause was 'essential to salva-tion'.[99] Local Jacobites also could not resist the temptation to harass Presbyterian ministers in areas that fell under their control in 1715, and Mar had to make a particular effort to restrain them and enforce religious toleration within Jacobite-controlled areas.[100] Even so, Episcopalian ministers ousted Presbyterian incumbents and intruded themselves into kirks in many parishes in Jacobite-held territory, particularly in the north-east.[101]

In such circumstances, too, it is not surprising to find that the power to command their tenants traditionally enjoyed by the heritors of the Lowlands was considerably enhanced in areas with a substantial Episcopalian popula-tion. In the face of religious harassment by Kirk and state, the lower orders naturally cleaved to the traditional protectors of the local community: the heritors whose lands they worked.[102] Thus, in effect, state hostility allowed, even encouraged, the heritors in strongly Episcopalian regions such as the north-east to maintain a latent military potential more associated with land ownership in previous centuries. The consequences are evident in the major Jacobite risings after 1707. In both 1715 and 1745 north-eastern Lowland tenants in their thousands followed local heritors to fight for the Jacobite cause, whereas southern and central Lowland Episcopalian heritors who joined the Jacobite risings did so either alone or with a handful of kinsmen and domestic servants.[103]

In the Highlands religion played a distinctly secondary role in the social bond between the *fine* and the ordinary clansmen. The majority of the non-Presbyterian clans were Episcopalian in religion, but a significant proportion were Catholic.[104] The corollary of this was that, in so far as the central authorities could ever enforce the Presbyterian ascendancy in the Kirk on the remote and inaccessible Highlands, the *fine* acted as protectors of local customs in religion and everyday life in much the same way as the heritors of the Episcopalian areas in the Lowlands.

By contrast with Scotland, where religious polarisation was felt to be a new and highly unwelcome development, in Ireland religious divisions were intrinsic to everyday life. Broadly speaking, the social structure in Ireland resembled that prevailing in England and Wales and Lowland Scotland. The old pastoral, tribal communities of sixteenth- and early seventeenth-century Ireland had virtually disappeared by the late seventeenth century and a landowner–tenant hierarchy had replaced it. In terms of the ranking of occupational and social status this hierarchy – which was a long-standing Irish adaptation of the English and Welsh 'model' that had spread from areas of English medieval colonisation in Ireland, rather than a recent imposition – was very similar indeed to that found in England and Wales. Moreover, again as in England and Wales, the system was powered by reciprocal deference and paternalism on the part of tenants and landowners.[105] What made the Irish case markedly different with respect to the quality of this relationship were the religious divisions that suffused it.

In the early eighteenth century approximately 25 per cent of Ireland was Protestant; 75 per cent of the population was Catholic.[106] To be a Protestant was automatically to be legally privileged in the sense that only Protestants had access to government office and full political representation (though a few Catholics retained the right to vote until the 1720s). Protestants could also count on state support for their churches and rest assured that – barring some form of truly egregious behaviour – their ministers of religion would not be harassed by the authorities or their churches physically attacked by government militia or regular troops. Catholics could not expect any of the above, though in practice persecution tended to be episodic and localised.[107] This should not be taken to suggest that the Catholic community in Ireland was simply a miserable mass of poverty-stricken peasants oppressed by their landlords and abused by the state. On the contrary, in the early eighteenth century as much as 14 per cent of Ireland was still in the possession of Catholic landowners, there were prosperous Catholic yeomen farmers and graziers to be found in many parts of the island and there was a strong Catholic merchant community in the major towns and cities, particularly in the west of the country.[108] The Protestant community was also itself highly polarised and often mutually antagonistic. Of the 25 per cent of the population who were Protestants over half were Presbyterian descendants of primarily Scots settlers in Ulster; the other moiety were adherents of the Church of Ireland, which was an offshoot of the Church of England. Only those who adhered to the Church of Ireland were fully legally privileged. The Presbyterians were socially discriminated against and had only partial access to the sweets of the Protestant hegemony. In addition, only a very small proportion of Ireland's ruling class, the landowners, were Presbyterian. The vast, increasing majority (probably 85 per cent and climbing) were Irish Anglicans. The overwhelming majority of Presbyterians were either more, but some distinctly less, prosperous tenant farmers, or part of a thriving Presbyterian business and manufacturing network. And though all three religious communities lived alongside each other, and were obliged to do business with each other, each intrinsically favoured its own confession.[109] One helpful way of envisaging Irish society, then, may be as three overlapping but separate communities, each with a social hierarchy that in its basic outlines echoes that found in England and Wales.

Nonetheless, in practical terms, the disproportionate share of Ireland's land and wealth held by non-Catholics meant that the majority of Irish Catholics were either tenants of, or workers for, Protestants of one variety or another.[110] Most of the time this probably made little or no difference to their lives. In physical and financial terms Ireland's ruling élite generally treated the lower orders neither better nor worse than their peers elsewhere in the British Isles.[111] In cultural terms, however, the religious divide between landowner/employer and tenant/worker seems to have quietly acted to make a brittle relationship between the two. Any possibility of a Jacobite rising automatically threw the Protestant community as a whole into an antagonistic stance *vis-à-vis* their Catholic neighbours, tenants and servants. Thus when news of Jacobite plotting reached Ireland in the summer of 1715 a senior government official immediately envisaged the Protestants as a beleaguered minority: 'You may be sure that the report of the Pretender's preparations must sufficiently alarm a country in which, besides Nonjurors, Jacobites, etc., there are at least 6 papists to one Protestant.'[112] Protestants and Catholics did have a common identity, as Kerrymen, Corkmen, inhabitants of Athlone and so on, but it was clearly overshadowed by their antagonistic religious identities.[113] This is most clearly, and for our purposes here most relevantly, seen in Catholic Ireland's enduring emotional commitment to the cause of the exiled Stuarts.

This had both practical and psychological aspects. Part of the treaty of Limerick which completed the Williamite conquest of Ireland was a set of provisions allowing those Jacobite troops who wished to do so to leave Ireland and continue the war in French service. Some 21,000 and an unknown numbers of their dependants accordingly departed Ireland between 1690 and 1692.[114] In France they reinforced an existing, extensive Irish mercantile and religious diaspora that already reached into every part of Catholic Europe.[115] Their good service to the crown of France during the rest of the Nine Years War led, furthermore, to the creation of a permanent Irish Brigade in the French army, and later a smaller, more transient Irish Brigade in the Spanish army. This French brigade became over the course of the next fifty or so years the embodiment of Catholic Ireland's hopes of liberation from the Protestant Ascendancy.[116] Every year, alongside the existing little stream of Irishmen migrating to the continent for business reasons, or to take up religious vocations, an additional stream of young Catholic Irishmen took ship for France to enlist in what they saw as the army of Catholic Ireland overseas. Estimates of how many did so are as yet guesswork, but it must have been in the tens of thousands, given that the proportion of first-generation Irish immigrants in the ranks of the Irish Brigade remained high well into the mid-eighteenth century.[117] The exploits of the Irish Brigade in battle against the British army, and the hopes the brigade represented, were also of major and abiding interest to the Catholic community back home, and were celebrated in their stories, songs and poetry.[118] There could be no clearer instance of the Catholic community's alienation from the prevailing order in Ireland.

Conversely, for all that they increasingly saw themselves as Irish, rather than the English or Scots in Ireland, and despite their mutual antagonism, the Presbyterians and Anglicans in Ireland both still perceived the Catholics as a threat to their position in the kingdom and the English connection as vital to their survival.[119] Every Irish Protestant had heard tales of the great massacre of Protestant settlers in Ulster carried out by Irish Catholic rebels in 1641, and many still alive in the early eighteenth century had lived through the Catholic Jacobite triumph of 1685–89, during which the Protestant Ascendancy was briefly overthrown. And out of these experiences there came a united, and rarely questioned, commitment to the English connection. If they ever felt under threat (and Catholic Ireland's fascination with the Irish Brigade ensured that a sense of threat was chronic rather than episodic) there was no doubt that the two halves of the Irish Protestant community would unite in defence of the status quo.

* * *

Every polity contains economic fault lines. The kingdoms of the British Isles in 1715 were no exception. The distribution of wealth between and within each one was grossly unequal and the balance between and within them showed few signs of change. Within each kingdom, too, economic developments were enriching some and impoverishing others. Economic anxiety was, correspondingly, as commonplace an experience as the new luxury goods that were transforming people's lives and aspirations. Yet none of these were new phenomena. Change was built into the early modern economy of the British Isles. The only thing that was different about 1715 was the postwar economic recession affecting all three kingdoms, which may well have promoted social unrest in badly affected areas,[120] and, rather more importantly, Scotland's profound disappointment at the failure of the Union to deliver the prosperity for which it had given up its (theoretical) independence. And, as the French ambassador sardonically noted in April 1715, regardless of who or what was responsible, when the small tradesmen of cities like London found their businesses in trouble they automatically blamed the government.[121]

Socially, the three kingdoms were set in a mould which had, by and large, endured for over a hundred years and would continue for another hundred years more. To be one of the lower orders was to be patronised and genteelly bullied; to be one of the élite was to be sucked up to and surreptitiously defied. Even the religious tensions which characterised social interactions in all three kingdoms were not new. They were, however, more intensely felt in the years leading up to 1715 than they had been for some time previously. The tension was there in England and Wales, was more keenly felt in Scotland and was at its most extreme in Ireland. And therein lay the necessary cause for civil war. In the early modern era only religion could justify killing and maiming one's neighbours, friends and kinsmen by the hundreds and thousands. Moreover, in England and Wales, but even more in Scotland, the tension was between rival Protestant communities. Catholics there would at most feature as auxiliaries in a larger struggle for the Protestant soul of a Protestant polity. In other words, unlike Ireland, the Catholic 'threat' was insufficient in England and Wales and, especially, Scotland to deter Protestant communities who detested each other from taking their struggle to God's Acre.

CHAPTER 2

'Fareweel e'en to the Scottish Name': the Politics and Geopolitics of the British Isles in 1715

If making a living and getting along with your fellows is one half of human existence, politics is the other half. Rebellions are inevitably political events. Hence we must not only look to the economic and social context, but also comprehend the politics of the three kingdoms and the geopolitics of the British Isles and the European great powers in 1715. The inter-state relations of the British Isles had been part of a much greater European whole for a very long time, and this was still emphatically the case in 1715. The attitude of the European great powers to events in the British Isles, and their actual and potential involvement, accordingly played a major role in the eventual outcome of the rebellion.

The Political Structures of the British Isles in 1715

Constitutionally speaking, the kingdom of Great Britain was a monarchy like many others in contemporary Europe, and George I theoretically retained virtually all the powers enjoyed by his medieval predecessors. In principle, he was only required to answer to God for his stewardship. *De facto*, however, centuries of accumulated legal precedents and government custom had long since created an unwritten constitution and a generally accepted practice of government that sharply limited the power and authority of the monarch. In reality George I was only one element (albeit a major one) in a composite political arrangement. The king shared power with the House of Commons and the House of Lords. The Commons, as an elected chamber, presented itself as the representative of the people at large and over the previous century had arrogated to itself the sole right to initiate taxation. Since governments have always been fuelled by money this necessarily made it the single most important element in the triad. The Lords, though, saw themselves as representing the fundamental interests of the nation and as the component of the constitution most committed to political stability. Indeed, the chamber has been described as the constitutional fire brigade of British politics.[1] Because the men who sat in the Lords were also the greatest landowners in England and Wales they had a considerable influence on who was elected to the Commons and between that indirect social authority and the constitutional equality of both houses in Parliament (all legislation had to pass both houses) they remained enormously powerful.[2] The monarch nonetheless retained the right to choose his or her ministers, and while a wise monarch would take into account the political state of play in Parliament, and the balance of interests in Lords and Commons, when making such choices, this right lay at the heart of the monarchy's continued centrality within British politics. Without the monarch's favour no party, and no politician, was liable to succeed in office. The monarchs also had the final word in the making of policy, both foreign and domestic, and thus must be considered major political actors in their own right. The old conceit that by the early eighteenth century the monarchy was merely the figurehead on a ship of state steered as they pleased by Parliamentary politicians has long since been exploded.[3]

Within the kingdom of Great Britain that subsumed Scotland and England and Wales there were two unequal elements. The Parliamentary Union of 1707 was at least accepted, and probably more generally supported, by the English and Welsh political nation (i.e. those with a legal right to the franchise, which in the Scottish, Anglo-Welsh and Irish populations as a whole was a small proportion), but in Scotland it came to pass in direct defiance of the outspoken protests of the majority of the Scottish political nation, and probably the Scottish nation at large.[4] Various special provisions were therefore inserted in the Union treaty during its passage through the Scots Parliament to take the edge off opposition to it on the part of powerful interest groups, such as the Kirk and the lawyers, who might otherwise have added their (considerable) weight to the opposition. The result was that the final, working Union was a hybrid arrangement. Scotland retained its distinctive, Roman law-based legal system and a separate, Presbyterian state church along with partially representative institutions like the Royal Convention of Burghs and the General Assembly of the Kirk, which for all practical purposes gave Scotland a quietly semi-autonomous status within the British polity that was to last until the nineteenth century.[5] In the long term these softened Scotland's complete subordination at Westminster. There, the Union simply grafted 45 Scottish MPs and 16 Lords, these latter elected every general election by the rest of the peerage of Scotland, on to the 513 existing English and Welsh MPs and approximately 160 English and Welsh Lords, plus 26 bishops of the Church of England.[6] As a consequence of this overwhelming Anglo-Welsh superiority Scotland's interests were intrinsically vulnerable even when the Scots' representation was united (which it virtually never was). And in the years immediately after the Union the Westminster Parliament acted with casual indifference to Scotland's economic and other interests.[7] This provoked episodic outrage and public protests in Scotland and profoundly disillusioned key constituencies there. Most saliently, the legal chicanery implicit in the English and Welsh peers' refusal in 1711 to allow James Douglas, Duke of Hamilton, the right to sit in the Lords on the grounds that his newly created British peerage was negated by his existing Scottish peerage infuriated the Scots peers.[8] The passage of the Scottish Toleration Act of 1712, which broke the Kirk's legal (and treaty of Union-endorsed) monopoly on the practice of religion in Scotland and legalised its Episcopalian rival, produced protests in the General Assembly and schism in the Kirk.[9] And the extension of the malt tax at English rates to Scottish malt in 1713 provoked riots and an attempt to end the Union by a body of the Scots representatives in Parliament. The origins of this latter measure well illustrate the nature of the Scots' problem at Westminster, because it arose purely as a result of political manoeuvring by English and Welsh backbenchers to try and force the reduction of their own rates of the malt tax by holding Scotland hostage.[10] Shortly thereafter, however, the Union fulfilled its basic purpose: when Queen Anne died without heirs of her body on 1 August 1714, Scotland, committed by the Union to the succession of Georg Ludwig, the Protestant, Guelph, Elector of Hanover, automatically acquiesced in the change of dynasty.

This question of who would succeed Queen Anne, the last Protestant Stuart in the direct line of descent from James VI and I, had lain at the heart of the English negotiators' determination to hammer out a treaty of Union with their Scottish counterparts in 1706, and as the ageing queen grew visibly frailer it became a steadily more live issue in British politics.[11] That her successor had to be a Protestant was laid down by the legislation that consolidated the Revolution of 1688 in England and Wales; and the Hanoverian Guelph dynasty were the queen's nearest Protestant kin. The problem was that antagonism between the two great political parties into which the Anglo-Welsh political nation was divided, the Whigs and the Tories, steadily grew sharper and more bitter as her reign ran on. Both parties collaborated in dethroning James II and VII in 1689, and subsequently they cooperated (however bad-temperedly) in passing the English Act of Succession, laying down that the Guelphs would succeed Anne, in 1701.[12] But in 1702 the War of the Spanish Succession broke out and in the course of that eleven-year struggle with France, England and Wales became more and more polarised between the two parties.[13]

The Whigs saw themselves as the defenders of Protestantism in the British Isles in all its forms, and beyond that as being staunch opponents of popery and France in Europe.[14] They were an odd amalgam of aristocrats, landed gentry and new business interests with roots in (and some covert sympathy with) the Parliamentarian party of the Great Civil War, as a result of which they were regularly smeared by their Tory opponents as anti-monarchical.[15] It is more accurate, perhaps, to view them as conditionally pro-monarchical. As long as the monarchy was committedly Protestant and cooperated with Parliament, and themselves in particular, in ruling the three kingdoms they were thoroughly monarchist; if not, not. Their view of the Revolution of 1688 was that it was a human act blessed by God and triumphantly vindicated by England's military and commercial successes since then.[16]

The Tories, by contrast, had come by the early eighteenth century to see themselves first and foremost as the defenders of the Church of England and its religious hegemony within the British Isles and England in particular. Though they generally accepted the religious toleration of Protestants that had come in with the revolution settlement, they remained suspicious of Protestant religious dissent and viewed Dissenters as schismatics (at best) or heretics (at worst).[17] As far as their Whig enemies were concerned a Tory would 'rather be a papist than a presbyterian',[18] but in fact most Tories were equally hostile to Catholics, except in so far as they saw them as a lesser threat to the Church of England than the Dissenters.[19] The Tories also saw themselves, with some justice, as the heirs of the Cavaliers of the Great Civil War era, and maintained that they were likewise the party of monarchy. They squared their role in the Revolution with their principles by taking it to have been a unique, divine, providential act designed to save the Church of England, in which human will played a minor role. Nonetheless, they generally endorsed the revolution settlement in terms of the constitution and practice of government. Consequently, while they were ostensibly still the self-proclaimed champions of monarchical power they had *de facto* developed a similarly conditional attitude to the Whigs in terms of their monarchism. The Tories, too, were pro-monarchical power so long as that power was exercised, as they saw it, in support of the Church of England (and, of course, its principal upholders, themselves).[20]

And herein lay the source of their gathering ambivalence towards the incoming Guelph dynasty. In 1710, in a series of adroit political manoeuvres, Robert Harley, subsequently Earl of Oxford and Mortimer, persuaded the queen to dismiss her Whig ministers and bring in a new, moderately Tory ministry with the express purpose of reaching a negotiated peace with France.[21] Oxford was a consummate intriguer and an excellent Parliamentary tactician, and over the next two years he matter-of-factly sold out the interests of Britain's continental allies, and reneged on Britain's treaty commitments, as the price of a favourable separate peace for Britain with France.[22] Already aggrieved by the way Oxford had ousted them from office, the Whigs were alarmed and infuriated by his destruction of the military coalition they had so painstakingly built up against France. When added to measures promoted by Oxford's militantly Tory backbenchers that hit at the Whigs' Dissenting political allies, the Whigs became convinced that Oxford was plotting to overturn the Protestant succession and restore the Catholic James Stuart, the Old Pretender, who was still living in exile in France as a pensioner of Louis XIV. There was even some basis to the Whigs' fears, in that Oxford was secretly in apparent negotiations with James over a potential restoration. In reality, though, these negotiations owed more to Oxford's attempts to save himself from his internal Tory party enemies by enlisting the aid of a crypto-Jacobite faction within the Tories' ranks than to any serious commitment to the Jacobite cause.[23]

Still, the appearance of Jacobite sympathies proved crucial. Until 1712 the Guelphs had been careful to maintain a friendly demeanour towards both the Whigs and the Tories. As the terms of the Peace of Utrecht were revealed, however, they were forced to take a stand on the issue, and their continental interests led to Hanover aligning with Britain's wronged allies, particularly the Holy Roman Emperor, Charles VI. Georg Ludwig did so in a temperate fashion and tried hard to maintain his lines of communication with both parties, but in the increasingly febrile atmosphere at Westminster his actions inevitably antagonised many Tories.[24] The Whigs were not slow to grasp the opportunity to secure the reversionary interest and in 1713 and the first half of 1714 they worked hard to ingratiate themselves with the Guelphs and convince Georg Ludwig that they were the only reliable friends his dynasty would have when he succeeded to the British throne.[25] So acrimonious and hysterical had the political climate become, moreover, by the spring of 1714 that the Whigs – apparently sincerely – came to believe that the mass of the Tory party stood poised to betray the Protestant cause (as the Whigs conceived it) and reverse the Revolution of 1688, and accordingly the Whigs began to arm and prepare for a rebellion or civil war in support of the Guelph dynasty.[26] Many Tories, for their part, construed what they saw as the Electoral family's increasing alignment with the sworn enemies (so they believed) of the Church of England as a direct threat to the future security of the Church, and this distinctly muted their enthusiasm for the incoming dynasty and increased the drift towards Jacobitism of a minority within their ranks.[27]

This was the situation at the time of the queen's death. Despite internal party feuding which had just brought down Lord Treasurer Oxford, the Tories were riding high, solidly ensconced in power at Whitehall, and enjoying a large majority in the Commons and a smaller one in the Lords.[28] They correspondingly felt their fall from power all the more keenly. The new king, George I, did not wholeheartedly accept the Whigs' claim to be the only friends he had, and he conscientiously tried to bring into office Tories who had overtly maintained their commitment to the Hanoverian succession in the last years of Queen Anne. These 'Hanoverian' Tories, however, generally loathed the Whigs as much as any of their fellow Tories and would not come into office without the rest of their party. The majority of them refused George I's overtures and he was forced to turn to the Whigs in the autumn of 1714.[29]

Triumphant and vindicated, the Whigs made the most of their opportunity both to install themselves in power and to revenge themselves on their Tory enemies. Tories of all stripes were swept from office at every level of government, even down to the gardener at Dublin castle. The army was also thoroughly purged, and senior officers appointed under the Tories for the most part forced to sell their commissions. Some Tories were allowed to remain on the Commissions of the Peace, which were the main agency of local government and thus needed to include men with sufficient local, personal authority to influence and direct local communities, but even there they were carefully reduced to a minority, so as to make sure the Commissions could not become focuses of opposition.[30] From early August the Whigs, too, began to threaten impeachments of the Tory former ministers as soon as the first Parliament of the new reign met.[31] Party politics in the early eighteenth-century British Isles definitely still had a civil war edge, and just as the Tories had come in in 1710 determined to 'get off five or six heads',[32] so did the Whigs in 1714. Fighting talk of this kind, along with Whig triumphalism and the purge of Tory officers and office-holders, inevitably provoked a Tory backlash, and by the autumn of 1714 the parties' mutual antagonism had risen to such heights that there were even anti-Whig riots in a scattering of localities in England on the king's coronation day.[33] By then the Tories were also trumpeting their most powerful rallying call, 'the Church in Danger', to which the Whigs retaliated by accusing the Tories of favouring 'popery and wooden shoes', and as the general election campaigning gathered steam a significant number of local communities in England and Wales became progressively polarised.[34]

Though only about 20 per cent of the male population of England and Wales had a vote at any given election in the early eighteenth century, a significantly greater percentage would have voted, or could look forward to voting, at some point in their lives. It has been estimated that not until 1884 would the electorate be larger and more diverse in England and Wales than it was in the early eighteenth century.[35] The net effect of this was much greater popular involvement in politics, at least in terms of personal alignment and episodic displays of party support, than would be the case later in the century. Hence when the parties' mutual hostility was stoked to new heights, as it was during the run-up to the 1715 general election, civil disorder of some kind was virtually certain to follow. There were some serious election riots in January and February in various parts of England and Wales, though they were perhaps not as bad as they might have been because the social élite who led the Tory party still entertained hopes of securing a majority in the Commons which would force George I to deal with them, and so they were more inclined to restrain than to incite their plebeian supporters.[36]

Direct government support, funding and patronage for Whig candidates, including a speech by the king when dissolving the last Parliament of Queen Anne which encouraged the voters to 'have a particular regard to such as shewed a firmness to the Protestant Succession, when it was in danger' (i.e. the Whigs),[37] however, led to an overwhelming Whig victory at the polls.[38] And as soon as the new Parliament met the leaders of the Whig party promptly set in motion impeachment proceedings against former Lord Treasurer Oxford, former Secretary of State Henry St John, Viscount Bolingbroke (the key negotiator of the Peace of Utrecht on the British side), and the former commander-in-chief of the army, James Butler, the Duke of Ormond, along with a couple of lesser lights of the former ministry with whom they had scores to settle.[39]

These proceedings alarmed and angered the remaining (unindicted) leaders of the Tory party, such as Sir William Wyndham and George Granville, Lord Lansdowne, and whether because they actually incited their ordinary supporters to show their disapproval, or because they no longer chose to restrain them, in the spring and summer England and Wales were swept by waves of Tory riots, primarily directed at the Whigs' Dissenter allies (who were an easy target because they tended to be locally visible and vulnerable).[40] The government was at first taken aback by the intensity of this wave of popular hostility to its actions, but soon recovered and confronted the rioters with military force, draconian legislation (the infamous Riot Act was passed at this point) and swingeing punishments.[41] In London the ministry even went to the length of forming gangs of toughs of their own, led by no less a party luminary than the future Whig premier minister, Thomas Pelham-Holles, Duke of Newcastle, to contest the streets with their Tory rivals.[42] Civil disorder, apprehension and uncertainty were thus the keynotes of the political atmosphere in England and Wales by the summer of 1715.

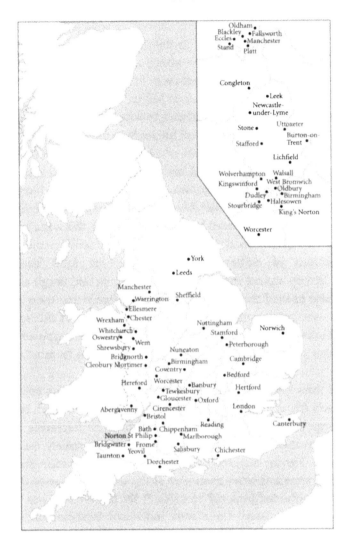

Map 1: English and Welsh towns that experienced one or more Tory/Jacobite riots, 1714–15.

Scottish politics in the autumn and winter of 1714–15 was, on the surface, much calmer and more subdued than its English and Welsh counterpart. In part, this stemmed from the élitist nature of politics in Scotland. By contrast with England and Wales, which generally had large county, and some large city, electorates, the county franchise in Scotland was limited to those owning land valued at 40 shillings rental 'of old extent' or a freehold of £400 Scots.[43] This effectively limited the vote to substantial heritors; the common people only participated in so far as they were allowed, or willing, to applaud their betters' choice of a representative.[44] In the burghs a syndicate system was established at the time of the Union which arranged Scotland's chartered towns and cities entitled to representation in the Scottish Parliament in groups which would collectively return an MP to Westminster. Each burgh in a group would send forward one delegate to vote at a joint meeting of the group, and each group had a strictly set hierarchy, with the vital casting vote at each election devolving in turn from one burgh to the next in sequence.[45] Given the complexity of these post-Union political arrangements, and the long-standing alliances and antagonisms between particular burghs and beyond them with their heritor neighbours (many burghs were quite small and consequently easily influenced by local landowners), this was a recipe for some intense and heated local politics, though not usually at the popular level.[46] Coalitions of noblemen, heritors and the local bourgeoisie campaigned fiercely against each other in both county and burgh elections. This could have opened the way to civil disorder except that these political antagonisms were publicly muted by the social conventions of élite society in Scotland.[47] Kinsmen, neighbours and gentlemen were not supposed to deal with each other acrimoniously, so their disputes tended to be more publicly decorous.[48]

To assume from this greater apparent seemliness that Scottish politics was not as intensely felt as English and Welsh politics would, however, be totally wrong. In large part because of the religious divisions fracturing Scottish society, but even more because of the Union, Scottish society was deeply divided in 1715. For the majority of the Scottish political nation the Union remained a live issue and bitter memories of the way it had passed the Scots Parliament still poisoned personal relations.[49] Yet the division was compli-cated by the religious issue. There were individual Presbyterians, such as Robert Hepburn of Keith, who were so anti-Union that they were willing to ally themselves with anyone who would help overturn it.[50] There were also extreme Presbyterians who rejected all uncovenanted government, whether presided over by a Catholic Stuart or an Anglican (formerly Lutheran) Guelph.[51] Neither of these groups represented, however, more than a tiny minority. The great majority of Presbyterians in Scotland (and thus in all like-lihood the majority of the population) were undoubtedly unhappy with the way the Union had worked out, but were irredeemably suspicious of the motives behind opposition to it when that opposition was voiced by Episcopalians.[52] To further complicate matters, there were personal and factional rivalries within Scotland's élite that set groups that might otherwise have been natural allies at odds with each other.

In the years immediately before the Union Scottish politics was contested by four main groupings: the Cavaliers, the Squadrone, the Court party and the proprietary, or magnate, factions. The Cavaliers (whose name deliberately aligned them with Stuart loyalism during the Great Civil War) were Episcopalian in religion and tended towards 'Country', or anti-government (in the sense of opposing the extension of the government's powers), politics. The great majority were also Jacobite in sympathy and overwhelmingly anti-Union.[53] The Squadrone, by contrast, were Presbyterian to the core, and though their sobriquet – which derived from the designation, *Squadrone volante* (flying squadron), normally applied to a unit of hard-riding, crack cavalrymen – was consonant with their origins as the Whig wing of the defunct Country party, they were steadily developing into a party much like the English Whigs in that their main focus was on securing power rather than a specific ideological agenda. Though individual adherents of the Squadrone were disturbed by the Union at the time of its passage, the group as a whole supported it strongly before and after 1707, though they were not above exploiting its unpopularity in 1713 to curry favour with the at that point highly disgruntled electorate.[54] They can fairly be regarded as unequivocally committed to the Union, though some of them did privately advocate revisions in its terms.[55] The Court party was a loose amalgam of Episcopalians and Presbyterians held together by government patronage (or the hope of it), political clientage and personal friendships with the ministers of the crown in Scotland. Some were basically civil servants who were bound and determined to see the government's business done regardless of its political complexion, others were content to be guided or directed in their political views by powerful ministers, still others were ambitious politicians trying to work their passage into office.[56] As far as this grouping was concerned support for the government's measures was a given, though a few did signal their disapproval of the Union by absenting themselves or even voting against it.[57] The proprietary, or magnate, parties were the personal followings of great noblemen, who could pretty much be relied upon to support their leader's position regardless of the issue. The leaders, in turn, were primarily interested in securing office for themselves and their followers, though they did have certain basic political inclinations. At the time of the Union there were three significant proprietary parties: Hamilton's, Atholl's and Argyll's. Hamilton most often aligned himself with the Cavaliers, as did John Murray, Duke of Atholl, whereas John Campbell, Duke of Argyll, was quite clearly Whiggishly inclined, but personally hostile to the Squadrone. Correspondingly, Hamilton havered on the Union issue, which he may have seen as a golden opportunity to advance himself by obliging the government to buy him off, and tried to assume the leadership of the Cavaliers while making sure his opposition to it was ineffective. Atholl was more resolutely anti-Union, despite his public Presbyterianism, in the hope of drawing the Cavaliers to himself instead of Hamilton. Argyll was staunchly pro-Union.[58]

After 1707 practical politics ensured that these native alignments shifted in response to the Anglocentric dynamics of politics at Westminster. In order to get legislation passed there and best protect the interests of their constituents the Scots MPs and peers had to find allies in the British Parliament. The Cavaliers duly attached themselves to the Tories and soon faded into a Scottish version of the Tory party, though with a much stronger Jacobite tendency.[59] The Squadrone became more and more aligned with the English and Welsh Whigs.[60] The Court party, initially led by the Duke of Queensberry, and after his death in 1711 by Mar, was badly hurt by the growing strength of party affiliation amongst the Scots representatives in Parliament, especially after 1710, and went into terminal decline.[61] The magnate parties were likewise badly disrupted. Hamilton's significance was much reduced by the transition to a larger political arena, and his proprietary party did not survive his murder in 1712. Atholl's following was even worse hit: he was unable to secure office for himself or his followers, and his party withered away to a single (often recalcitrant) kinsman.[62] Only Argyll was able to retain his former political clout. Ably backed by his brother, Archibald Campbell, Earl of Islay, he bargained his way into political office, provided for his following and contested the leadership of the Presbyterian and Whig interest in Scotland with the Squadrone. The outcome of these developments was that by the time of Queen Anne's death there was a Scots version of the Tory party contesting the day with Squadrone and/or Argathelian (i.e. Argyll-connected) Whigs in almost every constituency in Scotland.[63]

Politics in England and Wales, moreover, now had immediate repercussions in Scotland. Thus when the English and Welsh Whigs came into office in the autumn of 1714 their Scots allies soon followed. In practical terms this meant that several of the leaders of the old Scottish Court party were out of power for the first time since 1704. Mar subsequently claimed that he had always been a secret Jacobite, and he certainly tentatively established contact with the exiled Stuarts in 1710, but this had no apparent impact on his conduct in office while serving the Oxford ministry and its Whig predecessor in Scotland's administration and even as the rebellion broke out his own brother found it hard to believe he had turned Jacobite.[64] It therefore seems reasonable to assume that he was only precipitated into truly Jacobite politics by his dismissal from office in September 1714. This was not, it should be added, the universal response of the leaders of the Court party to their loss of power. The Earls of Findlater (formerly Seafield), Northesk and Aberdeen stayed well clear of Jacobite plotting, perhaps in the hope of ingratiating themselves with the new monarch at some later date. Mar, however, was facing financial ruin without his ministerial salary (or at least the credit he could get on the expectation of its eventually being paid – Oxford cynically manipulated the non-payment of salaries to keep his followers in line between 1710 and 1714 and Mar's salary was far in arrears), and needed to get back into office quickly to save himself serious embarrassment.[65] One obvious way to do this was to make himself a political nuisance who would be best bought off by the new regime, and though his thinking at this time is obscure, it is indicative that (despite his support for the original passage of the Union and efforts to subvert the Parliamentary attempt to overturn it in 1713) Mar now chose to put himself at the head of a new popular campaign for the dissolution of the Union that took off in the autumn of 1714.[66]

To get such a campaign under way Mar clearly had to mobilise the Scots peerage, who were still very much the natural leaders of the Scots political nation. Mar's obvious allies were the Scots Tories, and as soon as it became clear he was not going to be retained in office he set about trying to enlist their support, assuring Atholl that, 'If we who were formerly in measurs stick togither we will signifie something upon the occation of the elections, let the other side have what designs against us they please'.[67] Equally predictably, most of the Tories responded positively, though some privately expressed doubts about his motivation, and once they were on board Mar duly sought to broaden the campaign's appeal so as to bring in the more marginal elements on the Whig side: those beyond the charmed circle within the Squadrone and Argathelian parties and thus unlikely to be put forward as court-favoured candidates in the Representative Peer elections.[68] Mar personally drafted an appeal, warning, 'It is not Whig or Tory, friend or stranger. The very being of our state of peerage depends upon the next approaching elections',[69] and a team of his allies, including Alexander Montgomery, Earl of Eglinton, Thomas Hay, Earl of Kinnoull, James Livingstone, Earl of Linlithgow, John Fleming, Earl of Wigton, and John Elphinstone, Lord Balmerino, personally approached likely recruits such as William Ross, Lord Ross, and William Boyd, Earl of Kilmarnock.[70]

The drum Mar and his allies particularly beat to stir up the nobility was their claim that the Whigs at Westminster intended to end the system of Representative Peers' elections and instead create a number of hereditary British peers who would permanently represent the Scots peerage at Westminster.[71] Any such proposal was liable to be deeply unpopular with the

Scottish nobility, who, though they resented the implicit derogation of their status the peers' election entailed, virtually all cherished some hope of one day being summoned to the fount of honour and patronage in London.[72] Mar and his associates also implied that it was going to be the Squadrone and the Argathelians who would benefit by this hereditisation scheme. The initial response was certainly encouraging, Eglinton, for example, reporting of Kilmarnock that 'He is as much and violent against the hereditarie perage as I am.'[73] Yet even at this stage it was clear that if the campaign was too closely identified with Mar and the Tories potential Whig recruits would shy away from involvement, as Eglinton admitted in the same letter:

> I spake to him only at a distance about the address, which he apeared to be much taken with. I told him I would waitt upon [him] at his oun hous the begining of the nixt week, and bring in writting my thoughts of the skeem of ane address, for should I [have] puled it out at our first metting I was affrayd he would a suspected a project.[74]

The Squadrone and the Argathelians were also aware of what Mar was up to by this time and sought to neutralise the key issue with respect to the Scots peerage by joining with Mar in London in November in a joint petition to George I asking for redress of the Brandon decision (the exclusion of Hamilton from the Lords in 1711).[75] Argyll and the Squadrone had completely backed away from any notion of a dissolution of the Union, so that found no mention in the petition to the king, and back in Scotland, despite their mutual suspicions and rivalry, the two Whig factions now united in trying to stop the anti-Union movement. James Graham, Duke of Montrose, now third Secretary of State (i.e. *de facto* the Secretary of State responsible for Scotland), reinforced their efforts in early January 1715 with the official assurance that 'the King looks upon all this matter no otherwise than as a measure calculated by his enemies to disturb the quiet of his government . . . and does expect that his good subjects will lay themselves out to prevent honest people's being catchd by the snares that are laid for them'.[76]

By the time Montrose blasted the anti-Union campaigners with this public statement of royal disapproval, however, the more politically marginal elements on the Whig side were clearly wavering. Whig stalwarts like the Lord Justice Clerk, Adam Cockburn of Ormiston, John Leslie, Earl of Rothes, and Principal John Stirling of Glasgow University had to work hard to dissuade groups like the Presbyterian Nonjurors[77] and the leaders of the more depressed trades in cities like Edinburgh and Glasgow from joining in the anti-Union campaign.[78] Nonetheless they gradually gained the upper hand,

and by mid-December Lord Justice Clerk Cockburn was able to report with respect to the Presbyterian Nonjuring clergy in Edinburgh that 'thow they were against the Union and would be satisfyed to see it dissolved, yet they are not of opinion this is the fitt time, for they would see King George better fixt and have a tryall of this new Parliament first'.[79] Securing the likes of the alienated freemen of Edinburgh took longer, but even that was achieved by the time of the general election.[80] The final blow to the anti-Union campaign came on 21 January 1715 when the Faculty of Advocates formally considered a proposal to send up a loyal address to George I with a clause asking him to dissolve the Union. The Faculty was one of those elements of the pre-1707 Scottish polity preserved by the Union (as part of the separate Scottish legal system) and was a widely respected institution. Its opinion was likely to be influential and both sides regarded the outcome as of the first importance. The address was brought forward by two of Mar's clients, James Murray of Stormont (the future Jacobite Earl of Dunbar) and John Carnegie of Boysack, who had apparently taken 'great pains' to secure a majority in advance of the meeting. They approached it with confidence and 'braged that certainly they would carry their address'. Instead, after 'a warm and long debate for near to three hours', the Whig Lord Advocate, Sir David Dalrymple of Hailes, secured the defeat of the proposal by 58 votes to 42.[81] Emboldened by this victory, the Whigs proceeded to break up further meetings to discuss anti-Union addresses by the threat of prosecution for sedition.[82]

Mar's problem was that Scotland was already too politically polarised by the autumn of 1714 for such a putatively national movement to take off. Presbyterian/Whig suspicions of anything of this kind associated with Episcopalians/Tories simply ran too deep.[83] Though solid Kirkmen like John Flint could still fervently express the hope 'that God who hath so surprisingly brought King George to the throne will put it in his Royall heart and those of Revolution Principles to dissolve this Union', their response to the draft petitions being diligently put about by Mar and his allies was ultimately bound to be negative. Flint, explaining his opposition to Robert Wodrow, simply stated: 'Consider the promoters'.[84] Andrew Fletcher of Saltoun accordingly dismissed the whole project as 'redicoulus', and urged his Tory friends to put their efforts instead into securing the largest possible representation in the Commons. In doing so Fletcher showed he was out of touch with the political realities of post-Union Scotland, where a determined, coordinated effort to win the elections by a government-aligned, well-funded and well-patronised political party was always liable to be overwhelmingly successful. More ominously, he clearly did understand the likely Scots Tory reaction to failure both in the petitioning movement and at the polls when he warned against 'fomenting an humor of violence in the ordinary people and therby bringings things to blows'.[85] By that stage it was, perhaps, not yet too late to avert civil strife in Scotland, but the highly charged political atmosphere created by the double failure of the Tories' hopes certainly made such strife more likely. Significantly, when Alexander Macdonald of Glengarry sought to explain his decision to lead out his clan for King James he pointed particularly to 'King George having refused to accept of our address'.[86]

Ironically, if there was one of the three kingdoms that could in any way be described as politically quiescent in 1715 it was the one most fundamentally alienated from the existing structure of power in the British Isles: Ireland.[87] It was not that the Catholic majority of the population accepted the existing order – their keen interest in the affairs of Ireland overseas and the Stuart court in exile strongly suggests they remained intrinsically opposed to it – but, rather, that they were usually unconcerned with what was going on in Irish politics.[88] At source, this stemmed from the simple fact that legal barriers designed to prevent Catholics voting were already formidable and they were excluded from any legal involvement in the administration of Ireland.[89] Episodically, whenever Protestant zealots in the Dublin Parliament sought to bring in still more penal laws, the surviving Catholic landowners would discreetly lobby there and in London to avert the threat.[90] Otherwise Ireland's Catholics were, in the main, both legally and emotionally observers of, rather than participants in, the Irish political scene.

The Irish Protestants' politics was, however, periodically (the Irish Parliament met just once every two years) quite lively in the years before 1715. By then the Protestant community as a whole was fast recovering its self-confidence, of which there can be no more telling indication than its polarisation into Whig and Tory parties during the reign of Queen Anne. Given that many of the major Irish Protestant landowners and officers of the crown also owned lands in England and Wales and regularly shuttled between the two kingdoms, this development almost certainly stemmed from the 'rage of party' running through Anglo-Welsh politics at the same time. And the Irish Whigs and Tories reflected, too, the opposed ideological positions espoused by their English and Welsh counterparts.[91] There was, though, one crucial difference: the Irish Tories overwhelmingly supported the Hanoverian succession. A few amongst them, such as Sir Constantine Phipps, the Lord Chancellor, and others associated with the increasingly Jacobite-leaning James Butler, Duke of Ormond, were beginning to think more positively about the possibility of a Stuart restoration by 1714, but they were an anomaly.[92] When the Protestant succession, and with it, as far as most Irish Protestants were concerned, the associated Protestant Ascendancy in Ireland, was felt to be in danger their interests and the recent history of Ireland practically dictated that the Irish Protestants, Whig and Tory, Church of Ireland and Dissenter, would unite in support of the Protestant cause, regardless of their grievances against each other.[93] Thus when the crisis materialised in 1715 Edward Budgell was able proudly to report to the Irish Chief Secretary of State, Joseph Addison, 'I must acquaint you that the Presbyterians in the north of Ireland are all generously resolved to come into the array notwithstanding the civil disabilities they labour under, and will serve the king though they must afterwards ly at the mercy of the government for doing so.'[94] This in turn meant the Irish Tory party was bound to be badly hit by any suggestion that Toryism elsewhere in the British Isles was inclining towards the exiled Stuarts. And, indeed, the Irish Tory party was effectively killed by the Protestant community's united response to the Jacobite rebellion.[95] Thus the more inflamed politics became in mainland Britain and the closer the political nation there came to civil war, the more united the Irish Protestants were; hence Ireland's apparent political quiescence in 1715.

Ireland overseas, however, was another matter. The Irish diaspora had long been involved in supporting the Stuart cause financially and politically, and the succession crisis in the British Isles was bound to attract their interest.[96] Strategically, the most significant element in the Irish emigrant community comprised Irish soldiers in the service of the various continental powers. Of these, the élite Irish regiments in French service were the most important.[97] They were, however, facing a crisis of their own in 1714–15. Louis XIV's government was in desperate financial straits by the end of the War of the Spanish Succession and with the peace came a wave of cuts in state expenditure.[98] As part of these cuts several Irish regiments were facing disbandment or transfer to Spain. This was most unwelcome news both to the regiments in question and to the Stuart court in exile.[99] As far as the officers and men of the affected regiments were concerned they had enlisted in the service of the king of France for many reasons, including adventure, escape from discrimination in Ireland, excellent career opportunities and relatively good rates of pay. Foremost among their reasons, though, at least in the sense that it was an overarching justification of their service in the armies of the enemies of the rulers of the British Isles, was that they believed that in France lay their best hope of serving the Jacobite cause and restoring the exiled dynasty.[100] By doing so, these expatriate Irish soldiers obviously expected to overturn the existing order in Ireland. Disbandment threatened them with poverty; transfer to Spanish service would put them further from their goal of returning to Ireland as part of a liberating army, as well as placing them in less congenial circumstances (the Irish exiles were generally hospitably received in France).[101]

During the winter of 1714–15 well-connected Irish officers and other Jacobite exiles were correspondingly focused on dissuading Louis XIV from reducing or transferring their regiments. As, indeed, was the Stuart court. It, too, wanted to keep a strong Irish contingent in the French army for future service in the vanguard of any Franco-Jacobite invasion of the British Isles. Energetically backed by James and his mother, the dowager Queen Mary of Modena, James Fitzjames, the Duke of Berwick, a bastard son of James II and VII and the most eminent of the Jacobite officers in French service, therefore diligently lobbied the old king to save as many of the Irish regiments as he could.[102] And though he only enjoyed partial success in this endeavour, Berwick and his brother's efforts effectively refreshed the Irish regiments' Stuart connection at exactly the time when reports of civil disorder in England and Wales first began to arrive in France.[103] Quite apart from the ideological commitment many of the officers and men of the Irish Brigade felt towards the exiled Stuarts they now had the prospect of material advantage to incline them towards active support of any uprising in the British Isles. With France clearly exhausted militarily there were unlikely to be any wars involving France for some time to come and thus a much reduced chance of promotion and preferment, and the pending disbandment and transfers meant uncertain career prospects for many officers and men. It was, therefore, natural for the army of Catholic Ireland overseas to respond positively to what looked like a golden opportunity. Correspondingly, the Irish diaspora as a whole solidly backed efforts organised from France to support the rebellion in Scotland, and if less aid arrived there than the leaders of the rebellion had hoped for at the outset, it was not for want of will on the part of the Irish expatriates.[104]

European Geopolitics in 1715

Europe was virtually never completely at peace at any point during the early modern era. European states were inherently bellicose, in that their major purpose was to wage war, and European dynasties aggressively pursued their own interests whenever they felt opportunity beckoned. For all the superficial politeness associated with the era's 'lace wars' image, international relations were vicious; tantamount, indeed, to a contest for survival of the fittest.[105] The price of failure was clear to all involved: between 1500 and 1714 the number of European great powers shrank from about sixteen to about nine. In such circumstances securing any possible advantage over another great power, however meanly gained or theoretically ideologically distasteful that advantage might be, was simply standard practice, and nowhere was this *realpolitik* more clearly exposed than in the attitude of Europe's dynasties towards rebels and rebellion.

Publicly, every European dynasty abhorred and rejected any notion that subjects ever had the right to be so insubordinate and irreligious as to resist their divinely sanctioned rulers. Actually, rebellion was far too useful a tool of statecraft for any dynasty to ignore. It was a plain fact, of which all concerned were well aware, that rebellion and civil war had knocked France out of the great power game in the late sixteenth century, that Spain's decline had been precipitated by the Dutch revolt, that Poland had been (ultimately fatally) weakened by the Cossack uprising led by Bogdan Chmielnicki and that Russia had nearly ceased to exist as an independent entity during the 'Time of Troubles' of the early seventeenth century. As I have noted elsewhere, successfully sparking a major rebellion in an enemy great power's territory was potentially the thermonuclear device of contemporary statecraft.[106]

This meant that the Jacobites were of considerable interest to all of Britain's European rivals. Moreover, because the Jacobite underground in Britain was attached to a legitimate dynasty, albeit one in exile, the Jacobites were specially attractive to strongly monarchical and/or Catholic powers. After all, what could be more generally supportive of the divine right of kings, or better demonstrate one's commitment to the true faith, than aiding a fellow dynast/co-religionist in the recovery of his rightful throne? Breaking the supposed rules of inter-monarchical relations by supporting rebels against an enemy dynasty could be argued to be legitimate in such a case.[107] More importantly, perhaps, the Jacobite movement episodically appeared to have strong support in parts of Britain, and even a cursory examination of the phenomenon by diplomats resident there would reveal a widespread, potentially insurrectionary network with strong regional bases and alleged friends well embedded in the very structure of power.[108] A major Jacobite uprising would thus, at the very least, seriously divert resources from any British war effort, and there was always the possibility that such a dynastic rebellion might cascade into a full-blown civil war which would remove Britain from the great power game for some considerable time.

Britain's rivals were, therefore, bound to explore the possibility of using the Jacobites whenever they came into conflict with the British state or the incumbent dynasty. That said, their interest in the Jacobites was not going to produce the support the Jacobites most needed: a foreign invasion that would provide them with ample supplies of money, modern weapons and a corps of professional, regular troops with which to oppose the British army, except in time of war.[109] This was unfortunate for the Jacobites because Britain was at peace in 1715. The War of the Spanish Succession ended for Britain at the Peace of Utrecht in 1713. The Great Northern War was still raging around the Baltic littoral, but Britain was not formally involved in this conflict, for all that George I was assiduously working on getting a British naval squadron dispatched to the Baltic in the hope that this would precipitate a war between Britain and Sweden which he could exploit to the advantage of Hanover.[110]

The consequence of all of this was that the international situation was distinctly unpromising from the Jacobite point of view in 1715. Britain was not at war and there was little prospect that it would be in the immediate future. France remained generally sympathetic to the Jacobite cause, but the Jacobites living there well knew that France could not afford to contemplate open hostilities. France was militarily exhausted by the War of the Spanish Succession and Louis XIV was ailing and tired, and had come to the realisation, as he told his great-grandson and heir as he lay on his deathbed, that he had 'loved war too much'.[111] Spain had been the great loser, in terms of territory, at the Peace of Utrecht, where it was forced to cede its possessions in Italy and the southern Netherlands, and it was consequently set on overturning the peace settlement. To this end a full-scale rearmament programme was under way, energetically directed by Cardinal Giulio Alberoni, Philip V's premier minister. Spanish Bourbon revanchism, though, was focused on the Mediterranean and at this stage, despite their undoubted sympathy for their Stuart co-religionists, the Spanish Bourbons were unwilling to pick a fight with Britain.[112] Charles XII of Sweden, 'the valiant Swede' of Jacobite song,[113] was a formidable warlord and much desired as an ally by Protestant Jacobites in Britain for religious reasons (a Swedish-backed Stuart restoration offered the enticing prospect of locking James into a rock-solid Protestant church settlement in the three kingdoms).[114] So much so, indeed, that the Swedish ambassador to London, Count Karl Gyllenborg, was secretly approached in 1715 by a delegation of prominent Tories who offered to loan substantial sums to support the Swedish war effort on the understanding that Charles XII would invade Britain as soon as he could spare the necessary resources.[115] This overture was ultimately to develop into a fully fledged Jacobite plot, exposed in 1717, but Sweden was clearly too embattled in 1715 for it to yield results in the immediate future.[116] Sweden was already at war with Denmark, Russia, Poland-Saxony and Prussia, and understandably loath to add Britain to the list.[117] The Holy Roman Emperor, Charles VI, was an embittered former ally of Britain who had been sold out at Utrecht, but in 1715 he was on cordial terms diplomatically with the Guelph dynasty as Electors of Hanover, and was set on renewing the drive against the Ottoman empire in the Balkans that had been brought to a close by successive wars with France beginning in the 1680s.[118] So the Jacobites could expect no help from the Habsburgs. As for the Netherlands, it was a declining power by the end of the War of the Spanish Succession and in any event, as one of the premier Protestant powers in Europe, and the one responsible for overthrowing the main line of the Stuarts in 1688, was not about to support the restoration of the Catholic Stuarts to the British throne. Denmark, Russia and Prussia were too deeply involved in the Great Northern War to be concerned with anything else.[119] In sum, for all that they were potentially the most useful tool of their kind in the European great game, if the Jacobites were going to rise in 1715 they were going to have to do it alone, or with, at best, surreptitious support from France and Spain.

* * *

Antagonism between Whig and Tory was the engine of politics in the British Isles in 1715. Each regarded the other as inimical to the best interests of the three nations and did its best utterly to vanquish the foe. Party politics, moreover, still had a potentially warlike quality to it. How could it be otherwise when religion lay at the core of party identity? Not only were one's party political enemies corrupt, malicious and extravagant, their religious iniquity threatened Truth itself. Thus the rage of party was bound to raise political passions to heights we would more normally associate with civil war. The intensity of the conflict certainly increased during the reign of Queen Anne, so that by the time of the Hanoverian succession it had become peculiarly angry and bitter. Yet there was no civil war in the British Isles during the reign of Queen Anne, despite massive popular upheavals like the Sacheverell riots of 1710, because, by and large, the political élite kept their struggle within minimally civil bounds.[120] Although a Whig or a Tory was occasionally murdered because of his political views it was a very infrequent event.[121] Hence while the increasing heat of contemporary political passions was a necessary component in the confluence of phenomena inclining the British Isles towards civil war in 1715, it was by no means sufficient to cause that civil war of its own accord.

An inclination towards rebellion and war on the part of the Jacobites should, in any event, have been positively counteracted by the configuration of contemporary great power relations in Europe. The situation could not have been worse from the point of view of would-be Jacobite rebels. None of the great powers was in a position where it might be moved to support them and in all likelihood would not be able to do so for some time. Rebellion in such circumstances was nothing less than foolhardy. But the Jacobites were not fools. They understood international affairs as well as their Whig foes. So if they rebelled they must have seen something in their circumstances that does not jump to the modern eye, and it is to that we must now turn.

CHAPTER 3

'What Force or Guile Could not Subdue':
the Jacobites in 1715

On 6 September 1715 at Kirkmichael in Braemar John Erskine, eleventh Earl of Mar, proclaimed James Francis Edward Stuart as King of Scotland, England and Ireland. The ceremony was solemnly witnessed by some 200 of Mar's tenants, newly mustered as a military unit, and twenty or so gentry on horseback led by the Earl of Linlithgow, who now styled themselves the Jacobite 'royal squadron'. It was apparently a breezy day, because as James VIII and III's newly made royal standard was unfurled an ornamental globe at the top fell off, 'which many looked upon as a bad omen and did call to mind the story of King Charles the 1st whose staff head fell off when he stood before the judges'.[1] By that point, however, those present and those preparing to rise in other parts of Scotland considered themselves irrevocably committed. As one former Jacobite remembered in 1717, 'jacta est alea . . . they had gone such a length as made it impossible upon them to look back'.[2] The 'unnatural' Jacobite rebellion of 1715 had formally begun.

But why there, and why then? Opposition to the Union with England was undoubtedly *a*, if not *the*, major motivation for most of the Scots who volunteered to fight for the Jacobite cause (as opposed to those who were forced out by their landlords and superiors) in 1715.[3] But the Union was over eight years old, and the Jacobites could have risen against it at various times since April 1707 and quite possibly garnered more support than they did in 1715.[4] The Hanoverian dynasty was facing unprecedented popular opposition on the streets of England. But the tide of popular discontent was clearly ebbing by August in the face of draconian measures by the authorities and the deployment of regular troops on the streets of disaffected towns and cities.[5] The Scottish Jacobites were rising against a government which had very few troops in the country with which to oppose them; certainly less than a thousand. But Scotland's small garrison was primarily composed of veterans of the War of the Spanish Succession and reinforcements were already mustering in England.

Mar was a desperate, ruined politician and the Tory party throughout the British Isles seemed to be facing its nemesis.[6] But by 1715 the days when a disgraced politician would, in the words of the great Hugh O'Neill, 'go quietly home and rebel' were long gone. An implicit but major question thus hangs over the Jacobites' decision to take up arms in September 1715.

As we have already seen, moreover, the question is compounded by the Jacobites' poor geo-strategic situation in autumn 1715. There was little prospect of overt, substantive military support from any of the great powers. So it is scarcely surprising to find that many Whigs doubted that there would be an uprising even when confronted with clear evidence of Jacobite preparations for war. 'Sure these people, whatever their principals, are not quite mad, which however must be the call if they pretend to stirr . . . ', expostulated Montrose, the *de facto* Secretary of State for Scotland, in March 1715.[7] And the death of Louis XIV, 'so seasonably', on 21 August/1 September seemed to Hew Dalrymple, Lord President of the Court of Session, clear evidence 'that heaven favors us and that it is tyme for them to lay assyd their interpriz'.[8] Yet despite their unpromising circumstances and the odds against them the Jacobites did rebel, and in large numbers in Scotland. So who were the rebels and how did they persuade themselves this was their time?

The Jacobite Shadow-State and the Jacobite Communities of the British Isles

Each of the three kingdoms had its own Jacobite underground. These were linked to each other through the personal and social connections of individual Jacobites and beyond the British Isles to the Jacobite diaspora in continental Europe. The focus of the entire movement was always the exiled king, who was resident in France at Saint-Germain-en-Laye until 1713 and Bar-le-Duc in Lorraine from 1713 to 1715. For practical purposes, however, there were actually two centres of Jacobite 'government' between 1713 and 1715. Though James received regular updates on Jacobite business by correspondence and occasional visitors to Bar, and was certainly regarded as the final authority within the movement, his mother, James II and VII's widow, Queen Mary of Modena, continued to preside over the exiled court's business at Saint-Germain until 1716, and it was there that Jacobites of the three nations intersected – and sometimes clashed – most publicly.[9]

Theoretically, state business at the Jacobite court was the province of the official, Jacobite, Secretary of State, but his actual authority depended on his relationship with James and Queen Mary. From 1693 to 1713 the principal, and eventually sole, Jacobite Secretary of State was Charles Middleton, Earl of

Middleton. He was originally foisted on James II and VII by a combination of Protestant Jacobite factional power within the movement and French pressure outside it, for primarily religious reasons (Middleton was a Protestant, though not a very devout one).[10] Nonetheless he rapidly gained his master's confidence and by 1695 was the leading Secretary of State (at that point there were two) and James II and VII's main man of business. When the king died in 1701 Middleton was so moved by the way the old man bore his last travail that he underwent a sincere conversion to Catholicism and tried to retire from office, and whether out of religious sympathy or genuine recognition of his administrative ability, James, now nominally James III and VIII, and Queen Mary decided to keep him on as Secretary of State.[11] This broke the religious compact of 1693 and from 1702 to 1713 James came under mounting pressure from the Protestant Jacobites in the British Isles to dismiss Middleton and replace him with a man with the appropriate religious credentials. James bitterly defended his minister, but was eventually obliged to part with him at the end of 1713.[12] Middleton was honourably retired to become James's Master of Horse and was replaced by the Protestant Jacobite knight Sir Thomas Higgons, a quiet and unassuming man who had been resident at Saint-Germain since the 1690s and a gentleman usher of the Privy Chamber since 1701. Higgons was, however, merely a figurehead. His written French was poor, he had no real experience of administration at the exiled court and James had little regard for his advice.[13] De facto, serious court business, such as Jacobite plotting and relations with France and other powers, was taken over by Berwick between 1713 and the summer of 1715, with Middleton also making a reappearance as a confidential adviser in autumn 1714.[14] Berwick finally fell from James's good graces in autumn 1715 when he refused to accompany his brother to Britain, and James replaced him with the newly exiled Bolingbroke, who (as at least a nominal Protestant) was also able to replace the figurehead Higgons (though Higgons was not formally deprived of his office until 1716).[15] Bolingbroke was to remain Jacobite Secretary of State, however, only until the end of the rebellion, being summarily dismissed as soon as James returned from Scotland in March 1716.[16] Mar succeeded him as sole Secretary of State and held the office until 1719. Throughout this ministerial back-and-forthing Queen Mary continued to exert a considerable influence on policy-making and play a major role in the public relations of the Jacobite court, and there were also several lesser figures, such as David Nairne, James's private secretary (from 1713), and the Queen's Almoner, Father Lewis Innes, who were also episodically important in shaping Jacobite policy.[17]

Notwithstanding the fact that the exiled Stuarts did quite a good job, given their resources, in presenting themselves as a bona fide dynasty with a real royal court, the Jacobite court's claim to significance ultimately rested on its power to mobilise its supporters in the British Isles.[18] And the Stuarts had a constituency in each of the three nations. The lineaments of that support were, however, profoundly different in each kingdom and thus we need to examine them separately to get a true sense of the dynamics of the Jacobite movement as a whole.

Because of the plain fact that England and Wales was the richest, most populous and most powerful of the three kingdoms, English and Welsh Jacobites tended to dominate the politics of the Jacobite movement. This was something of a paradox, in that in many respects Jacobite support in England and Wales was weaker than anywhere else in the British Isles: there was a tiny, core Jacobite community and a larger, shifting group that was intermittently more or less sympathetic to the Jacobite cause. The core community, in turn, contained two elements: the Nonjurors and the Catholics. We have already looked at the Catholics in the context of English and Welsh society as a whole, but the Nonjurors require further explanation. The term 'Nonjuror' refers to the fact that the first members of this definitively Protestant group refused to take the oaths of allegiance (legally speaking: 'jure') to William III and II and his successors in 1689. The Nonjurors of 1715 were the spiritual, and often lineal, descendants of these uncompromising Anglicans. Their rejection of the Revolution stemmed from the fact that the leaders of the political nation in 1689 had all sworn an oath of allegiance to James II and VII. Such oaths, the Nonjurors believed, were divinely sanctioned, binding and unbreakable as long as the king lived, and after his death obliged them to pledge allegiance to his legitimate heirs regardless of their religion. They were initially a dispro-portionately clerical community, but over the course of the generation following the Revolution they gradually assumed a more natural social profile, including every tier of society. At the same time they also formally went into schism with the Church of England by founding a self-perpetuating line of Nonjuring bishops initially consecrated by survivors of James II and VII's episcopate who had been removed from office. In so far as they had bases they tended to be in the larger cities, where the anonymity vouchsafed by a shifting population meant they could practise their religion as long as they were reasonably discreet, and on the country estates of landowners who were also Nonjurors. The Nonjurors were probably never as much as 1 per cent of the English and Welsh population and were thus of even less political significance within English and Welsh Jacobitism than their Catholic peers.[19]

Instead, English and Welsh Jacobitism was dominated by its adherents in the Tory party. These were a mixed group. Some were crypto-Nonjurors, who convinced themselves that they should take the various oaths the better to work for the overthrow of the new order, and diligently endeavoured to achieve that end. Far outnumbering this group, however, were Tories who intermittently, in response to political developments they found alarming or personally grievous, moved into, and out of, sympathy with the Jacobite cause. The great majority of them were High Church Anglicans who were disturbed by the apparent rise of religious Dissent and the erosion of the social and political hegemony of the landowning élite since 1688. There was also a small group of disgruntled politicians associated with these Tory Jacobites who hoped to fulfil their political ambitions by taking a radical route back to the top, but they were usually an evanescent element with little practical impact on the Tory Jacobite group before 1715.[20] The impending, and then actual, death of Queen Anne and the collapse of the Tory hegemony of her last years that swiftly followed greatly boosted the number of Tories who found themselves in sympathy with the Jacobite cause, and, for a brief time, moved a significant tranche of the leaders of the party, such as Bolingbroke and Sir William Wyndham, to begin contemplating a Jacobite restoration.[21] The Whig purges swelled the ranks of these Tory Jacobites with professional soldiers, such as Ormond and Robert Echlin, who had been dismissed for their Toryism.[22] Taken all together this long-standing Jacobite element within the Tory party, boosted by those moving into alignment with it in 1714–15, looked more and more formidable, and it certainly impressed outside observers in the British Isles and overseas. Yet the Jacobite element was always a minority, and the number of English and Welsh Jacobite Tories who were willing to raise their tenants (in so far as that was even possible in England and Wales by the early eighteenth century), buckle on their swords and ride off to start what might well turn out to be another Great Civil War was probably even less. Yet the fact that there was certainly a barely concealed Jacobite element within the Tory party, and that a great many Tories were vocally expressing outrage at their treatment by the Hanoverian dynasty, created an impression that the whole party might be inclining towards the exiled Stuarts.[23] And because the allegiance of the English and Welsh Tory party as a whole would have been an enormous gain for James and his cause, those English and Welsh Tories who were truly Jacobites, and seemed to represent the shifting allegiance of the party, dominated the councils and decision-making of the Jacobite movement.[24] Image manifestly overmatched substance.

In Scotland, by contrast, the perception that the Scots Tories were sympathetic to the Jacobite cause was, largely speaking, absolutely correct. As in England and Wales, the Jacobite movement in Scotland was a composite of a number of different elements. There was a small Episcopalian Nonjuror group and an equally small Catholic minority. These were completely overshadowed, however, by the Scots Tories, who were routinely Jacobite.[25] Because of events in Scotland since 1688, especially the Union of 1707, they were also markedly more committed and determined than their English counterparts. Moreover, because of the very different dynamics of society in rural Scotland élite Scots Tories were not only willing to summon their tenants to war, but actually had the very real prospect that many of their tenants would heed them. Furthermore, while this was the case in the Lowlands, it was even more so in the Highlands.[26] Though the *fine* of a number of clans were split on the dynastic question, those leading elements that were pro-Jacobite could still mobilise proportionately large numbers of ordinary clansmen. The Highlands also contained a few clans who were overwhelmingly Catholic and could be relied on to bring out the great majority of their available manpower.[27] The upshot of this was that the Scots Jacobites were far more willing and able to rebel than their southern neighbours. They correspondingly carried some weight in the councils of the exiled dynasty.[28] Scotland alone, however, had not been able to withstand the might of the Anglo-Welsh state in arms since 1640 and was assumed to be incapable of doing so in 1715, not just by the Stuarts and their advisers but by the Scots Jacobites themselves.[29] Hence the English and Welsh dominance of the internal politics of the Jacobite court remained untouched by the implicit power of the Scots Jacobite movement.

The Irish Jacobite movement was in one sense the most powerful in the three nations, and in another the weakest of them all in 1715. Irish Jacobitism had two great advantages over the other two: it had an army in being overseas and very likely enjoyed the sympathy of the majority of the Irish population.[30] Its key problems were that the army overseas, while commanded by Jacobite sympathisers, was not under their control, and the widespread support it enjoyed in Ireland came overwhelmingly from a disarmed, largely plebeian, mass. There were still élite Catholic landowners in Ireland, but not very many, and they tended to disarmed, too, whenever there was a Jacobite scare.[31] The overwhelming majority of Jacobites in Ireland were therefore of very humble origins. Which is to say that any Jacobite revolt in Ireland, for all that it might very well have enjoyed great popular support, would have had uncertain leadership and been hard put to find arms. Any revolt by Irish Catholic Jacobites was also certain to antagonise and alarm their Protestant counterparts in mainland Britain. Neither the English and Welsh, nor the Scottish, Jacobites envisaged any substantive change in the power relationships between their polities and Ireland in the event of a successful Jacobite rebellion, and the spectacle of masses of plebeian Irish Catholics rising up against their mainly Protestant masters would have been certain to alienate any potential recruits beyond the immediate adherents of the Jacobite cause in England and Wales and Scotland.[32] Consequently the Stuart court, which well understood the religious animosities implicit in relationships between the three nations, shied away from exploiting the potential of its supporters in Ireland proper.[33] The army of Ireland overseas was another matter; they featured in all Stuart plans, but this still gave the Irish Jacobites no great sway in the councils of the exiled dynasty. In the final analysis, the Irish Jacobites had nowhere else to go than the Stuarts, and they could therefore be relied on to support any Jacobite attempt no matter how little their interests were consulted in the shaping of the Jacobite court's plans.

The Jacobite Mind in 1715

To understand the Jacobites', and particularly the Scottish Jacobites', decision to rebel we need to understand the parameters of the Jacobite mentality. Obviously there was a great deal of individual variation. Nonetheless, the general pattern is clear. Jacobitism was first and foremost a personal, political and religious commitment. An individual became a Jacobite, or if s/he were raised in a Jacobite family, remained a Jacobite, by choice.[34] Unless you were caught red-handed plotting, or fighting for, the overthrow of the new order it was not an irrevocable decision. Like any other political ideology, someone could embrace Jacobitism, then become disillusioned with it and move on to another political alignment and again perhaps move back into the Jacobite fold later in life.[35] By 1715 it was, too, not in any sense a 'natural' or 'default' option except among the Catholic minority in the British Isles, and had not been so for over a generation.

Jacobitism's marginal-cum-outlaw status stemmed directly from its successful characterisation as the illegitimate enemy of the status quo by the state and its agents in all three kingdoms. Early modern state churches always spent a great deal of time preaching and teaching the obligation to obey the state and its agents; one of their major functions as a social institution was to promote obedience to political and social authority in all its forms.[36] And since 1689 the state's authority in the British Isles depended on a general acceptance of the necessity of the Revolution of 1688 that had overthrown James II and VII, and the dynastic and politico-religious settlement that had accompanied the consolidation of the revolutionaries' seizure of power. The message endlessly rehearsed by the state and its protagonists was, therefore, that in 1688 William III and II and the revolutionaries had saved the British Isles from the popish menace which would certainly have extirpated Protestantism there and quite possibly beyond. On the verge of massacre akin to that believed to have taken place of the Irish Protestants in 1641, and persecution after the fashion of the reign of Bloody Mary, the three kingdoms had been saved by the blessed intervention of William III and II.[37] Henceforth, it was proclaimed, Church and state in the British Isles could only be safe if there was a Protestant on the throne and only Protestants sworn to uphold the revolution settlement in all public offices.[38]

There was a range of responses to this message. The Nonjuring and Catholic Jacobites rejected it entirely. The hardcore (crypto-Republican) Whigs who embraced Lockian contract theory celebrated the Revolution, but believed it did not go far enough. In between lay a complex range of shifting attitudes towards that pivotal event. For our purposes here the most important element on that spectrum was the Tories who were getting along, in terms of their consciences and principles, one way or another, with the aftermath of 1688. What was worrying about these Tories, as far as the protagonists of the new order were concerned, was the Jacobites hiding in their midst.

Theoretically Jacobitism posited a straightforward rejection of both the positions outlined above, in that it rejected the contention that the overthrow of James II and VII was necessary, just or divinely blessed. In fact, however, by 1715 only the Catholics and Nonjurors fully adhered to this uncompromising position.[39] The Jacobites who gravitated towards the movement out of the ranks of the post-1688 Tory party saw things differently. They were often ambivalent with respect to the Revolution itself, believing that James II and VII had made major errors of judgement that had provoked his overthrow, or even that just as revolution was justified in 1688, so it was now justified by the tyranny of the present government.[40] As Lord Pitsligo observed in the 1740s:

> To that surprising Revolution we owe the settlement of the German family; a measure as illegal and unwise (in the opinion of most people, natives and foreigners) as the former. There was also this remarkable difference; necessity was pleaded to justify the revolution. And to say the truth, some steps taken by King James (who acted from the sincerity of his heart) gave some grounds for popular apprehensions, but what had they to fear who made the last settlement?[41]

This tendency within Jacobitism, moreover, became more ubiquitous as time went on. Thus though the wellspring of Jacobitism was dynastic loyalty to the Stuarts, for many, if not most, Jacobites this had ceased to be the crucial motivation by 1715. Every Jacobite certainly believed that the Stuart dynasty should be restored to the thrones of the British Isles, but by then English, Irish and Scots Jacobites had different, and sometimes highly divergent, further reasons for wanting such a restoration. In each case the dynastic element was necessary, in that without a change of dynasty the changes desired by each nation's Jacobites could not come about, but in no case was the dynastic element (i.e. the restoration of the Stuarts) any longer sufficient to persuade thousands of men to throw up their livelihoods and pastimes and expose themselves to mortal danger.[42]

English Jacobitism by 1715 arose primarily from dissatisfaction with broad economic, social and political developments since 1688. Thomas Bruce, Earl of Ailesbury, though himself originally a hardcore dynastically inspired Jacobite, summed up the feelings of a great many when he reflected:

We landed men have smarted sorely for it since 1688, from the greatest landed man to the most small, at so much per pound on land when miserable misers and usurers, and those wealthy merchants that got honestly and before God (at least I ought to hope so) paid not one shilling towards carrying on our late long and cruel wars, and I wish to God that for the future a wise Parliament will take this into their serious consideration, as also as to what relates to the increasing of the poor.[43]

As far as English and Welsh Jacobites were concerned the wars flowing from the Revolution had impoverished the natural rulers of society and elevated bourgeois upstarts who were usurping the social and political authority of the landed élite. In addition, Protestant Anglo-Welsh Jacobites were virtually united in believing that the Church of England was in decline as a result of the revolution settlement (in large part because of Nonconformist efforts to undermine its authority), and, after the Hanoverian succession, that it was in danger of being dethroned as the dominant Church within the British Isles.[44] Thus Robert Patten recalled that he was drawn into Jacobitism by his gathering conviction 'of the church's being in danger', and William Paul's dying declaration challenged his readers:

as for your religion, is it not evident that the revolution, instead of keeping out popery, has let in atheism? Do not heresies abound every day? And are not the teachers of false doctrines patronized by the great men in the government? This shews the kindness and affection they have for the church.[45]

And, given the way their ideology and self-image centred on their role as defenders of the Church of England, it is not surprising that it was above all others the gathering belief that the Church was in danger that drew erstwhile Tories to Jacobitism. All of which said, it is clear that the English and Welsh

Jacobites were not unhappy with other consequences of the Revolution. Ireland's enhanced subjugation in the aftermath of the Williamite reconquest and Scotland's subordination by the operation of the Union found few critics among them.[46] As far as the English and Welsh Tory Jacobites were concerned the key to ensuring that things were right throughout the British Isles was the restoration of the Stuart dynasty followed by their reinstallation in power.[47] Nothing much else needed to change.

The Irish Jacobites, by contrast, wanted the most revolutionary changes of all. First and foremost they sought the restoration of Catholicism as the creed professed by the state Church in Ireland. This would necessarily have entailed the confiscation of most if not all of the existing church buildings and property in the possession of the Anglican Church of Ireland and its bestowal on Ireland's underground Catholic Church. In one blow, this would have overturned the basis of such religious reformation as had occurred in Ireland over the previous 150 years. The Irish Jacobites also sought the complete reversal of the land settlement in Ireland.[48] More than two generations of impoverished and dispossessed Catholic landowners had yearned for the full restoration of their property and the social authority that went with it; their restoration to their putative estates would have destroyed the economic basis of English control of Ireland. To round out this revolutionary agenda, the Irish Jacobites, finally, wanted to emancipate the Irish Parliament from Westminster's tutelage.[49] The Irish Parliament was constitutionally subject to oversight from the Privy Council in England and its legislation only had force in so far as English legislation did not specifically supersede it. The Irish Jacobites aimed at establishing the Irish Parliament as a fully sovereign body, hence an Irish Jacobite victory would have left the crown as the only formal, constitutional link between the two kingdoms. Needless to say, none of the above would have been acceptable to the great majority of Anglo-Welsh and Scottish Jacobites.

Scottish Jacobitism was, by 1715, second only in its radical import to its Irish counterpart. Scotland, like Ireland, had experienced a bitter civil war in the early 1690s, but unlike in Ireland it did not end decisively. The negotiated settlement that closed the Highland war allowed all those Jacobites willing to return quietly home and take an oath of allegiance to William III and II to do so, which the great majority – with the grudging permission of James II and VII – did.[50] The dynastic loyalists who were the core of the rising thus remained, for the most part, retired to the country, where they lurked in the background of Scottish politics. The numbers of Jacobites were also greatly swollen by the purge of the Kirk by the new order.[51] Consequently, as in Ireland, what the Scottish Jacobites wanted in a post-Restoration state involved radical change in the state institution that most nearly touched the lives of all Scots: the Kirk. A Jacobite victory would have led to the overturning of the government and doctrines of the Kirk for the fourth time in less than a century.

From a constitutional point of view, the Scots Jacobites' express aim of ending the Union of England and Scotland that became law in 1707 was just as radical.[52] This was not simply because the *de facto* domination of Scotland by Anglo-Welsh interests and mores would have come to an end, but because the Scottish Jacobites wanted more than a simple reversion to the status quo ante. What they envisaged was a wholesale transformation of the relationship between England and Scotland (including restrictions on the authority of the crown) which would have created a stronger, more fully sovereign Scottish Parliament.[53] It is not going too far to say that Scottish Jacobitism was, like Irish Jacobitism, a proto-nationalist movement.[54] As might easily be imagined, the independent polity it envisaged was not acceptable to the English and Welsh Jacobites.

Jacobitism in the British Isles was, then, a very complex phenomenon, involving national and confessional divisions in every one of the three kingdoms. The clashing aspirations of the Scots, English and Welsh, Irish, Anglican, Episcopalian, Nonjuror and Catholic strands that made up the Jacobite movement inevitably created chronic tension between them. As Ailesbury observed: 'It is wonderful, but true, that the English hate the Irish, and they are quits with them. And 'tis the same between the English and Scotch, as also between the Scotch and Irish.'[55] Hence a conviction that the time to strike a blow for the Stuarts had come was unlikely to be felt with equal force in all three nations at once. Particular political events resonated differently and distinctly with each of the national/confessional Jacobitisms, so it is not surprising to find them responding differently.

This brings us to the question of Scotland. Scotland was the epicentre of the 1715 rebellion, despite the fact that Jacobitism was intrinsically stronger in Ireland and richer in England and Wales. So what inspired the Scottish Jacobites, above all others, to take up arms in 1715?

* * *

Though there were religious sceptics, such as George Keith, Earl Marischal, and (in a later generation) David Wemyss, Lord Elcho, among the ranks of the Scottish Jacobites, they were certainly a tiny minority.[56] The mass of Scottish Jacobites were sincere, practising Episcopalians. Presbyterian Jacobites were so few that they do not merit separate consideration here.[57] And like the overwhelming majority of contemporary Christians throughout Europe the great majority of Jacobites of all stripes envisioned God as commonly, indeed constantly, intervening in human affairs. Nations and individuals all had their places in a divine plan, and the Episcopalian vision of the cosmos saw God's hand in what transpired at every level of the social and political order.[58] Humans nonetheless had free will, and it was believed that God could and would signal his approval or disapproval of their actions so as to give them fair warning to get in line with his plan. As a pamphleteer solemnly explained in 1710:

And if we consult history, we shall find, that there hath scarce been any notable apparation or prodigy in the heavens but it was attended with great changes here on earth. Neither is there any man, except he hath no religion, who is not affecte[d], with these strange appearances ... For God speaks to men not only by prophets, apostles, and teachers, but sometimes also by the elements, and extraordinary signs in the heavens, earth and sea to warn us of approaching judgments, thereby to warn us from evil practices, and reduce them to repentance and reformation ...[59]

On an individual level the trick was to surmise which way God meant you to respond to these signals, and Jacobite Episcopalians, like contemporary Christians of every other faith, scanned the news and their environment for signs of God's will on a regular basis. Since, of course, every Christian Scots Jacobite believed that his or her cause was God's cause this search for the appropriate signs was implicitly about timing.[60] There was no question in their minds that God favoured the Jacobite cause (hence the Jacobites' notorious over-optimism: 'les Jacobites toûjours determiner à croire ce qui leur fait plaisir', acidly commented the French ambassador in March 1715),[61] the only uncertainty was when he wanted the true believers to act.[62] Discerning that moment was the key to success.

Hence the importance which a great many Jacobites attached to visions, prophecies and prodigies. Writing to Middleton in 1705, an English Jacobite solemnly reported:

Wee talk of nothing but prodigies from all parts. Wee have had 4 cocks that run a liquor like blood for some hours, tho other cocks from the same pipe run clear. I have seen a letter which the party assured me was from as good a hand as any in Cheshire giving an account of a dog greyhound there that brought forth of his fundament a whelp which lived some time and sucked milk from a feather. The person saw it kept in spirit of wine and it was about the bigness of a mouse. Also that at Fradsham (as I remember) about the beginning of the month ships were seen sayling up the river, out of which an army landed, drew up in battle array with a man on a white horse at the head of them, that they fired – flashings being seen – but no noise heard, that this continued from 4 in the morning for about 2 hours till the sun dissipated the mist and clouds. It was a hard frost there, as the letter says. I saw the copy of another letter, which was affirmed to be from as sober a man as any in England, which mentioned these 2 and added a 3rd: that a mill of Mr Cholmeleys turned against the streame for above an hour and would have continued if the Miller had not taken much paines to make it go right. Here are also severall letters from the west that give an account of a thorn hedge that brought fo[rth] this year apples, peares, cheries, pease, beanes and stra[w]berryes, which people went far and neer to see. There are severall others here, and many from Scotland.[63]

And despite the possibly Jansenist-inspired scepticism which the exiled Stuarts themselves privately expressed about such stories, the increasing number reported to them by Scots and other correspondents and the appearance of cheap prints that conveyed the news to the wider Jacobite public hint at an increasing receptivity on the part of Scots Jacobite audiences.[64] The Catholic Bishop William Nicolson observed in 1706 that the fevered circulation of rumours and reported prodigies to be found in Scotland reminded him of the time just before Charles II's restoration:

We ar buzed with prophesies, dreams and visions in a transe, all of the King's returne. At least we had rumors of thes things, which is anofe to keep the people in motion, and some of them I beleeve well grounded. Mr Wilson, ane Episcopall minister, verie anticatholik, says he was two Sundays in the morneing last spring so transported that he was forced in a maner to write, and he was not sensible what he was doeing when he wrot, till afterwards he considered. And the writing was avowd his [and] made him and his freinds verie confident, as he owns still in print.[65]

When the refugee religious mystics known as the French Prophets visited Scotland and publicly proclaimed their ecstatic visions, it seems they particularly drew Jacobites to their witness.[66] Even those Scots Jacobites, like Dr George Garden, who doubted the heavenly origins of the messages conveyed by the French Prophets took them to be a sign of portentous change: 'Antichrist doth now reign, and hath at this present great dominion over the spirits of men, ensnaring them by false appearances of goodness and virtue, transforming himself into an angel of light that he may seduce the best meaning persons, and that the Devil can still speak of divine mysterys as well as when he was an Angel.'[67] If Antichrist was reigning, the end of days was nigh.

The tide of reported portents and visions was episodic and ebbed and flowed over the decade leading up to the '15, but it certainly seems to have become more intense in late 1714 and early 1715. Reports reaching the Jacobite court in autumn 1714 suggested that

> The late fire in London was very remarkable. It happened upon the day deputed for thanksgiving for George's accession to the crown. Thames street, where the chief merchants have their magazins, was burnt down, and the loss computed by some to a million and a half. Thus on his coronation day the scaffolds fall down, and killed many; and when he first landed, a boat was sunk, and all in it drowned. So that God's judgments seem to pursue him.[68]

By March 1715 London was abuzz with accounts of how an Irish prophet was predicting the fall of George I,[69] and the eclipse of the sun on 22 April was interpreted as a portent of momentous events to come.[70]

None of these accounts of portents and prodigies were out of the ordinary for early modern Britain. Publishers then and since have always profited from selling bizarre, extraordinary, or downright invented, stories to the general public. Their significance in the context of the '15 in general and Scotland in particular is that in the political circumstances of 1714–15, and in combination with a range of other, simultaneously operating stimuli examined below, they fostered an atmosphere of anticipation. As a Whig writer observed in 1715: 'In all civil wars . . . it is observable, that the generality of the people are fond of prophesies'.[71] The Scots Jacobites had come to expect great events to transpire, and by doing so they set themselves up for the thought to become mother to the deed.

Within the Jacobite milieu on both sides of the border, but especially in Scotland, the anticipation promoted by tales of prodigies and prophecies was mightily reinforced by the Jacobites' interactions with each other. Élite sociability in England was politically, and in Ireland confessionally, polarised, whereas in Scotland it was still governed more by conventional mores regarding kinship and good neighbourliness.[72] Yet it was in Scotland that the Jacobites' 'vanitie, insolence, arogance, and madness' became 'beyond all measure insupportable', by February 1715.[73] What seems to have happened is that hope of a Jacobite restoration and fear of the coming Hanoverian succession prompted the development of a mood of political hysteria among Jacobites all over mainland Britain, but particularly in Scotland, after 1708. This ebbed and flowed during the reign of Queen Anne and then reached a peak in the first half of 1715.

For the English and Welsh Jacobites this hysteria centred on their hope that Queen Anne would restore her half-brother to the throne on her death.[74] As Edward Gregg showed some time ago, such hopes were straightforward self-delusion, but they inspired such a turn towards Jacobitism as occurred in England before the queen died.[75] For a brief while after the Hanoverians peacefully succeeded to the throne the Anglo-Welsh Jacobites seem to have been chastened and dismayed, but the onset of the incendiary 'Church in Danger!' Tory election campaign for the first Parliament of George I's reign soon reignited their fervour.[76] By October 1714 the French ambassador, Charles François de la Bonde d'Iberville, marquis d'Iberville, noted that the number of Jacobites had greatly increased over the few he had observed at the end of the queen's reign, and that the new Jacobites were inspired by hostility to George I, whom they held personally responsible for their exclusion from power (and hence ability to protect the Church).[77] 'The High Church is above ten to one and it is incredible to you [sic] what their hatred and contempt of Hannover is, and what their veneration for James is. It is so now that the most Whiggish countys at the time of the revolution, are the most passionate and bold Jacobites now,' gleefully reported one Jacobite sympathiser at the end of the year.[78] This tide of pro-Jacobite feeling within the English and Welsh Tory party, furthermore, seems to have been deepened rather than checked by the Tories' catastrophic defeat in the 1715 general election. By the end of February the volume of sedition being spoken, preached and published around London convinced at least d'Iberville that England was on the verge of a civil war.[79] Indeed, approaches made to the Swedish ambassador by a group of leading Tories at the end of February 1715, forthrightly seeking Swedish military aid for a Tory rising, indicate a substantive basis to this belief.[80] Renewed, and more overtly Jacobite, rioting erupted again in late May around Restoration Day and in early June on the Old Pretender's birthday (10 June), and a wave of attacks on Dissenting chapels followed at the end of the month and went on into July.[81] The impeachment of the leading figures in Queen Anne's last ministry only fanned the flames, so that one Scots MP was soon writing home from London, 'I can assure you, the Tories here were never hyer in their looks or hopes, which they found upon a speedie invasion,'[82] while provincial Tories were longing to hear news of the Old Pretender's landing and they stayed up late at night to debate 'the common genius and inclination of the nation to another revolucion'.[83] The Anglo-Welsh Jacobites' zeal, however, appears to have begun to wane by the summer of 1715. The number and frequency of Tory riots fell off, and though this was in part owing to the draconian provisions of the new Riot Act, by late June d'Iberville found that at least some of the leading Tories had given over any thought of an uprising and were preparing to submit themselves and their party to the new order.[84] Nonetheless, until August other English and Welsh Tories apparently remained convinced that James was just about to land, and d'Iberville reported that only news of Louis XIV's terminal illness finally discouraged and disheartened them.[85]

By contrast, despite the greater propensity of Scotland's élite to socialise across party lines, the Jacobites' commitment to an armed confrontation there simply went from strength to strength. This may have been a function of the sheer numbers involved. For though there were a lot of increasingly alienated Tories in England and Wales, 'in England many were Tories who were not Jacobites, but in Scotland all the Tories were professed Jacobites . . .'[86] The practical repercussions of this were significant. Despite being the smaller party in a Scottish context (by contrast with England and Wales, where the Tory party probably enjoyed considerably more popular support than its Whig counterpart in 1715), the Scottish Tories were much more uniform in their Jacobite sympathies and their commitment to the cause.

Hence the steady rise in the emotional intensity of Scottish Jacobitism over the period 1708 to 1715. In large part this stemmed directly from the continued aggravation provided by the way the Union was developing with respect to Scotland and Scottish interests. 'The Union becomes dayly more insupportable and will at leng[th] entirely ensclave us,' bluntly asserted one Jacobite in 1709.[87] 'The more the English saw into our differences at home, the greater infractions they made of the Treatie of Union, and the less they saw any reason of keeping measures with us. . . . Almost every Parliament has produced new infractions . . .', bitterly recalled John, Master of Sinclair.[88] The queen's installation of a Tory ministry in 1710, because it was believed by many Scots Jacobites to presage James's restoration and consequently the end of the Union, was greeted by the Scottish Tories/Jacobites with great enthusiasm. The Reverend Robert Wodrow sourly observed, 'The Jacobits are mighty uppish, and plainly say that this 1710 is just another 1660; and they talk of nothing but resignation, restauration, and rescission, their three Rs; and they talk their king will be over, either by Act of Parliament or invasion, by A[u]gust nixt.'[89] Moreover, as the Tory majority at Westminster was persuaded by the Scots Episcopalians in their midst to take up legislation curtailing the power and authority of the Presbyterian Kirk, the conviction among Scottish Jacobites that their time was nigh steadily increased.[90] In 1712 there were major Jacobite demonstrations in Edinburgh and other towns on 10 June, the Old Pretender's birthday, in which, according to one witness,

> The streets wer crowded with gentlemen and Ladys going up and down with musick playing, 'When the King Enjoys his Own Again', but they made everyone they mett with drink, 'God bless and restore King James the eight[th]'. At Leith all the ships had out their flags except one, which being threatned with burning put out his likewayes, and upon the publick shoar ther was a great broad [banner] upon which the King's armes wer drawn with this subscription, 'God save the King, James the 8th. No abjuration. No Hanover.' This stood exposed at the end of the peer from one in the morning till four of the afternoon and then was taken down by the magistrats because none els durst. I know not what may have been done in other towns especially in the north, but I forgot to tell you that ther was upon the 10th at night a great bone fire within Edenburgh, and another upon the top of Arthur's seat . . .'[91]

The scale of the Jacobites' impertinence seems to have taken the authorities aback, but they were better prepared in 1713 and had troops standing by to intervene on the streets of Edinburgh if matters got out of hand again.[92] Unfortunately for their hopes of maintaining order, 10 June 1713 fell in the middle of the malt tax crisis and the prevailing mood was such that even a phlegmatic old soldier like Major-General Joseph Wightman felt moved to warn his superior, Argyll, 'how tumultous the people are in all respects, and I may venture to say ripe for an insurrection'.[93] The authorities decided that, in the circumstances, discretion would be the better part of valour and let the Jacobites celebrate their king's birthday and parade their hostility to the Union, but with the threat of immediate, drastic intervention by the troops if the Jacobites tried to burn the future George I in effigy. And the Jacobites duly refrained from provoking them on that score.[94] Such restraint was not, however, generally characteristic of Jacobite behaviour as the political crisis brought on by the queen's declining health deepened in the winter of 1713–14. Instead they zealously prepared and sent in loyal addresses that smacked of downright Jacobitism, more and more openly drank toasts to the Old Pretender at public gatherings and dabbled in some desultory military preparations.[95] All of this posed no effective challenge to the prevailing authorities or the planned accession of the house of Hanover, but did act as a powerful incentive for Scotland's Whigs to prepare for civil war.

For though the Jacobites' conduct in Scotland during the last years of Queen Anne was highly provocative, and well illustrates their rising hopes and aspirations, there was little focus or substance to it. Indeed, Jacobite agents found it very difficult to get even the most hardcore Scots Jacobites seriously to consider an uprising,[96] so confident were they that Queen Anne intended to restore her brother to the throne upon her death.[97] 'I've lost patience, yea and it has made me sick to find Mr Mark [the Jacobites] so pusillanimous and inactive,' inveighed one Jacobite agent in early 1714.[98] Ironically, however, the Scots Jacobites' posturing completely succeeded in convincing the Scottish Whigs that they posed a genuine threat to the Hanoverian succession, leading the Whigs to begin secret preparations for a seizure of power in Scotland in the name of George I in case the Jacobites' hopes materialised. This willingness to embrace civil war on the part of the Whigs arose directly from their apprehensions at the advance of the Episcopalian agenda at Westminster over the previous four years.[99] These fears took flight in the spring of 1712 with the passage of the Scottish Toleration Act, which officially broke the Kirk's monopoly on legal religious practice in Scotland, and associated legislation restoring kirk patronages to their owners. Implicit within the Toleration Act was also a new abjuration oath to be taken by all Protestant clergymen, of whatever Church, in Scotland. The oath was deliberately couched in language theologically unacceptable to many Presbyterians and provoked uproar and schism within the Kirk.[100] All of this further antagonised and alarmed Scotland's Whigs. By April 1712 devout Presbyterians like Sir John Clerk of Penicuik were listening to sermons on themes such as 'the axe is laid to the root of the tree, therefor every tree that bringeth not forth good fruit is hewn down and cast into the fire', and privately praying, 'O Lord prevent the evils thereof for thy sake and disappoint the fears of thy people who tremble for the [anger?] of God. O that I may be one of the mourners in Zion and may prefer the welfare of Zion to my chiefest joy.'[101] The opening of an Episcopal meeting-house in Glasgow and the first public appearance of Edinburgh's Episcopal clergy in surplices in October 1712 excited further anger, associated as it was with rumours that Presbyterians were about to be put out of their kirks and Episcopalians installed in their places, and a Jacobite agent warned that the Presbyterians were threatening 'to go to armes befor they quit their Kirks, so 'tis feared we may have a war of religion'.[102] Since there was certainly no intention on the part of the Oxford administration to overthrow the Presbyterian hegemony in the Kirk, such a dramatic over-reaction at first sight seems quite puzzling. Given, however, the increasing confidence with which the Jacobites were predicting their own imminent triumph and the rumours and prophecies circulating throughout Scotland, it is not surprising that Scotland's Whigs became apprehensive. Even a moderate Presbyterian like

Lieutenant-Colonel John Blackader felt moved to confide to his diary in February 1713,

> This town is full of stories and rumours; there is a busy lying people spreading scandal on all sides, to rankle and irritate men's spirits. I know, I among others am the butt of this malice and rage, – but who shall harm us if we be followers of that which is good? Lord, counsel and guide us to just and proper measures for the security of our holy religion, our liberties, and properties, all of which seem to be in great danger.[103]

The extent of the threat outlined in these rumours and reports also steadily grew to menacing proportions. Wodrow recorded that he heard a report that during the 1713 Parliamentary session the Scots Tory MPs were barely prevented from implementing 'a formed designe . . . of bringing in a clause in some act of Parliament, for oblidging all ministers in Scotland to renounce the Covenants'.[104] For our purposes the truth or falsehood of such reports is only marginally relevant; what they illustrate is the climate of fear building up among Scotland's Whigs. By January 1714 this had escalated to the point where rumours that the Catholic Irish had risen and were 'cutting all Protestants' throats' were circulating and some ministers were preaching 'that when magistrates are l[ax?] in putting down idolaters, the people, full of zeel for the Lord, should supply for the magistrats, etc.'[105] The government was by that stage alarmed enough for Mar, then Secretary of State with particular responsibility for Scotland, to admonish the Commissioners of the General Assembly of the Kirk:

> the behaviour of some of your brethren for some time past, in stirring up jealousies in the people's minds, as if their libertys and rights religious and civil were in danger under her Majestie's administration, and encourageing them to buy up arms, and put themselves in a posture of defence looks very odd from ministers of the gospel, who have had so great proofs of the Queen's favour, and whose duty it is to preach peace and obedience to her.[106]

Given Scotland's recent history of religious conflict and still very live, and very bitter, memories of the religious persecution the Presbyterians had suffered under Charles II it is hard to escape the conclusion that Scotland was facing civil war in the spring and summer of 1714 in much the same manner as it subsequently experienced it in the winter of 1715–16. The Scottish Whigs had armed themselves as best they could and they were probably as mentally prepared to fight to defend the Hanoverian succession and Presbyterian control of the Kirk as their Jacobite counterparts were to overthrow the succession and Kirk settlement a year later.[107] The Whig mob estimated at 5,000 people who confronted and forced out the troops stationed in Glasgow in April 1714 and the unusually destructive Presbyterian attacks on Episcopal meeting-houses that followed on the death of Queen Anne are a grim indication of the way religious tension was sliding towards civil conflict.[108] The upshot is that whichever party had prevailed in 1714, whether the Jacobites by some miraculous conversion of Queen Anne to their cause, or, as actually transpired, the Whigs by the succession of the house of Hanover, there was a strong likelihood of a civil war in Scotland.

Nevertheless, the Scottish Jacobites' decision to undertake a rebellion only finally crystallised in the year following the death of Queen Anne and the accession of the house of Hanover. It was at that point that their exclusion from power and the triumph of their political and religious enemies came home to roost. At the outset of the new reign they were distinctly dismayed by Queen Anne's refusal to restore the succession to James as she moved towards her death.[109] 'The Jacobits appear quiet and to lay asyde violent courses,' noted a Whig observer in September,[110] and John Haldane of Gleneagles cockily remarked in October, 'They doe not nou drink healths and talk of their King James.'[111] The Jacobites' acquiescence in the new order, however, was more apparent than real. Even before the end of August 1714 the more enthusiastic elements in the Scots Jacobite community were showing a 'certain joy and resolution', and as one correspondent writing to Deputy Lord Advocate Duncan Forbes of Culloden noted, despite showing some reserve, 'yet they are still positive, and persevere that he [James] will come, though the French should give him no assistance'.[112] The proclamation of George I in some of the more disaffected Scottish towns and cities, such as Inverness, Montrose, Elgin and Dundee, was also disapprovingly noted as 'uncivil and distracted'[113] by the *Edinburgh Gazette* and Mar, still in charge of Scotland's government at the time, was moved in mid-August sternly to demand that the magistrates of Aberdeen arrest and prosecute the Jacobite demonstrators who 'did, in the night time, and under the disguise of women's apparrell, proclaim the pretender'.[114] These incidents, rather than the despondency noted by Gleneagles, were to prove true auguries of what was to come.

Yet for a rebellion actually to begin the Scots Jacobites still had to move beyond a general faith in Jacobite righteousness and unfocused enthusiasm for the Stuart cause to a more hard-edged conviction that particular circumstances were right and the hour had at last arrived. This necessarily involved, too, an acceptance that the blood of their fellow countrymen would be spilled and lives taken, quite possibly, given Scotland's experience of internecine strife in the seventeenth century, on an epic scale.[115] This is not, and was not, an easy step, and it seems to have been taken only as a result of a process in which specific events struck a resonant chord with the internal dynamics of the Jacobite mentality.

First amongst these events was one the incoming dynasty was obliged by custom, law and the constitution to set in motion: the election of the first Parliament of the new reign. As we have already seen, the 1715 general election was fiercely contested, and well before it took place George I had indicated he would favour the Whigs.[116] They were delighted. Sir John Clerk happily confided to his spiritual journal, 'O blesd be the Lord for good news of our king's arrival, [and] his excellent declaration to his people, his removing the wicked and putting honest good men in their place'.[117] Likewise a Whig newsletter-writer in Edinburgh crowed: 'The Qween dead! Louis the Great declining! A consummat prince in the Brittish throne! And yet more likely to be swported by ane unanimous Whigg Parliament.'[118]

The Scots Tories naturally saw matters rather differently. Those who had hoped to work their passage into the new king's good graces were shocked and disillusioned by the speed with which the queen's old ministers were dismissed. As Harry Maule of Kellie sardonically observed,

They thought that there would be a mixture in the ministry, and the question would be among the courtiers as usual, who should have the ruling of the ro[a]st, but now when they see the Whigs onely are brought into favor, and every body els turned out that had the least affection for the queen, it inclines people mightily to stand to their principle who had litle thought that way.[119]

And by October 1714 they were 'dieply and sadly infected with the danger of the church and say plainly nothing can nou save it but a Torie Parliament'.[120] The feeling seems to have been general among the Scots Tories, and their yearning for a Tory Parliament very rapidly to have generated an absurd level of optimism about the outcome of the election. According to one reporter Colin Campbell of Glendaruel, a noted Tory/Jacobite, was, by December, assuring anyone who would listen 'that the House of Commons will be Torie by a great majority. And then he hopes this ministrie will turn out as fast as ever they turned in.'[121] By the end of 1714 party feeling had again risen so high that Blackader felt moved to deplore it in his diary: 'Every public meeting now becomes an occasion of snares and temptations, people are so divided in their opinions.'[122] The fall, when the election results came in, was that much more precipitous in that the Tories had hoped so much for a decisive result in their favour.[123] Indeed, they were initially so downcast by the outcome that Montrose and his friend and agent Mungo Graham of Gorthie were in turn hopeful that the Whig landslide would prove 'so disheartening a stroke to the enimys of the goverment that they'l give over their foolish projects'.[124] The subtext of concern in Montrose's and Gorthie's letters is nonetheless significant, for, by then, rumours and intelligence of 'foolish projects' in the Highlands and elsewhere in Scotland were turning from a trickle into a stream.[125]

The second strand in the confluence of events finally preparing the Scots Jacobites for war was the petitioning movement against the Union. 'There is a mighty fervowr about having the Union dissolvd,' observed a Whig newsletter-writer in January 1715. 'It is talked as fresh of now and with resentment as [if] it had comensed but last year and been browght about in King George's reign.'[126] As we have already seen, the campaign came to a head in February 1715 with the Faculty of Advocates' debate on whether or not to join the petitioning movement, and thereafter dissipated, at least from the point of view of being a threat to Whig solidarity in Scotland.[127] Yet such was the intensity of the anti-Union feeling aroused by the campaign that this disappointment, even when allied with their rout at the general election, failed to quell the Jacobites. Explaining his decision to rebel to his older brother, William Scott of Ancrum flatly stated that what inspired him to take up arms was his conviction

> that on of the greatest dutys incumbent on us here, as Cristians and Cuntrymen, was the serving our creator in the first place and in the nixt our cuntry and when either demanded noe respect whatsomever coud free us from engaging our lives for the support of either. The Union hes begune our nation's ruine and will, in all probability, in a short time compleat it. Upon this supposition, which I was convinced off, I must say houever had been king, when my nation's interest came to compeat with theirs I [w]ould [have] been their enemy because my principal obleiges me to prefere my cuntry's interest even befor my oun.[128]

The 'fervowr' aroused by the petitioning campaign correspondingly acted directly to inflame the Jacobites' hopes regardless of its outcome. Throughout Scotland it went hand in hand with a swelling tide of reports of Jacobite gatherings and arming, and Jacobites became more and more public in their conviction that the Old Pretender's arrival in Scotland was imminent.[129] 'Never was [there] more noise here of some attempt very soon to be made by the Pretender,' reported Montrose in February 1715.[130] Moreover, incidents like that near Falkirk in December 1714, when a group of drunken Jacobites leaving Sir Thomas Nicolson's house waylaid some passers-by and forced them to 'sitt down on their knees, praye for King James the eight and curse King George', are symptomatic of an illicit community that was beginning to abandon any attempt at concealing itself or its ambitions.[131] Such was the situation in Scotland when news began to arrive of gathering civil disorder in England.

This was the third strand in the confluence of events, the one that finally stoked the Scots Jacobites up to that pitch of excitement that made them willing to heed Mar's call to rebel. News of Tory rioting in England, associated at that point with George I's coronation, arrived with the weekly newsprints and in letters from Scots living south of the border in the autumn of 1714, and though there was some concern in Scottish Whig circles about the 'extraordinary ferment' in England, the Scots Jacobites, possibly because they generally 'looked with contempt upon the English', seem initially to have been less moved by that spate of civil disorder.[132] The Scottish Tory/Jacobites were also distracted by their own electioneering and the campaign against the Union. When the second wave of English Tory/Jacobite popular protest, this time targeting Dissenting meeting-houses, broke out in the spring and early summer of 1715, however, the Scots Jacobites were very interested indeed.[133] The Jacobite community had by then been abuzz for months with prophecies, rumours of arming and other preparations for rebellion and predictions of James's imminent arrival.[134] Hence they were much more receptive to news of civil disorder in England. Charles Cockburn, son of the Lord Justice Clerk, writing from Edinburgh in early June reported, 'Its impossible to conceive what a number of storyes we have set about here dayly from all which our Jacobites conclude that these High Church tumults will at last turn to an open declaration in favours of the Pretender or at least will soon occasion of necessity a change of this ministry.'[135] Brazenly public Jacobite demonstrations in Aberdeen and Inverness on the Old Pretender's birthday were also stoked by 'the account they have of the insolence of the High Church party in England'.[136] By the time Mar arrived in Scotland in August such reports had created a climate of expectation.[137] Sinclair recalled that when Mar assured the Scots Jacobites that the English were ready to rise he was easily believed, given 'that we had heard of nothing from thence but mobs and tumults'.[138] Hence the spectacle in September of the solidly Jacobite – but highly sceptical of Mar – James Maule, Earl of Panmure, who had initially rejected Mar's exhortations to rise with contempt, being moved to come out in rebellion simply by a report that James had landed in England.[139] The events of summer 1715 completed the priming of the Scots Jacobites for rebellion. They were implicitly prepared to believe Mar's promises of an Anglo-Welsh Jacobite uprising – if only the Scots would set the ball rolling.

For months, too, Jacobites had been talking to Jacobites about how the time and the stars were ripe for a rebellion in favour of the Stuarts, and, as is the way of these things, a rhetorical ratchet effect seems to have taken hold within the Jacobite community. At a secret meeting he attended to plan a rising in the central Lowlands Eglinton recalled, 'every one . . . was more forward than another'.[140] When Sinclair tried to persuade Major Henry Balfour of Dunbog and the north Fife Jacobites to postpone taking up arms until they had definite news of a rising or an invasion of England he found him so 'bloun up' 'that there was no speaking to him, and those young people in his neighbourhood, who used to spur him up, who all their lives were fools, were now turned mad'.[141] When Sinclair similarly continued to try and dissuade the west Fife Jacobites who were pledged to follow him from rising, they 'came at last to a peremptorie resolution', and sent a message telling him they were 'resolved to goe on' whether he led them or not.[142] Forced to choose, Sinclair explained some time later that 'after using all my endeavours to divert their madness, I out of friendship to them went with the torrent I could not stem, having often declared to them my readyness to joyn in any measures for the relieving of my country from the hardships it lay under from the Union .'[143] In the same vein, David Smythe of Methven, despite misgivings about the wisdom of the rising, felt he could not in conscience stay safe at home when all his friends were going out to rebel:

> The plain treuth was that there being ane apearance made in favours of what I had always professd to be my principalls, I thought I could not ward of the imputation of couhardice otherways than by embarking in it; just as a man that gets ane affront, be it never so slight it is be thought so in the eys of the world must either pass for a couheard all his life or else braick through the laws both sacred and civil, resolve to renounce his family and country and doubly risque his life to doe himselfe what the mistaken world calls justice.[144]

In effect, as one report of 'distributeing commissions, receiving of arms, and liverie cloths making for the regiments' built upon the next, any of which it was 'treason to doubt the truth of', none of the Jacobites wanted to appear behindhand and so, step by step, they talked themselves into rebellion.[145]

By the beginning of August 1715 it may fairly be said, then, that the Scottish Jacobites were set to rise almost whatever happened. A deep unreality had taken hold of the community. 'Those with whome I was concerned', recalled Sinclair, 'would hear reason no more.'[146] Mar's arrival and his manipulation of their conviction that the hour had arrived certainly played a pivotal role in sparking the rebellion (though he later claimed he 'could not allay the Scots heat').[147] Nevertheless, the degree to which the Jacobite leadership in Scotland had lost touch with reality was ultimately more important than anything one disgraced – and at the outset generally distrusted[148] – politician, however persuasive, could say or do. The Scots Jacobites, like most of the politically committed in any era, were subject to a certain intrinsic self-delusion stemming from their beliefs about themselves and the world around them. Thus, for instance, after 1707 many Scots Jacobites became unshakeably convinced that radical Presbyterians in the south-west of Scotland would join them in any uprising against the Union. There were absolutely no concrete grounds for such a belief (beyond the lying assurances of proven Whig double agents), and plenty of evidence that in a crisis radical Presbyterians in the region would rally to the house of Hanover, Union or no Union, yet many Jacobites continued implicitly to believe it for decades.[149] In the summer of 1715, however, the Scottish Jacobite élite almost as a whole seems to have lost its grip on reality. Nowhere is this more clearly illustrated than in their reaction to the foreclosure of the possibility of any substantive military support from France – something upon which they had always hitherto insisted as the *sine qua non* of their appearing in arms.[150]

In the months before the outbreak of the '15 a notable escalation in the scale of French involvement was projected in the rumours circulating through the Jacobite community about the imminent arrival of James and/or Berwick. The Scots Jacobites, one government informant reported in August 1714, believed that 'if the Pretender can but lett the French see that he has any thing like a party to back him either in England or Scotland worth the while . . . then the French king will assist him to the outmost of his power'.[151] By July 1715 the Lord Justice Clerk was receiving reports that 'in Angus and further north they talke confidently that the Duke of Berwick is to land in Brittain with 15 or 20,000 men and another army is to land in Ireland at the same time, and this is beleeved as the greatest certainty'.[152] In northern Scotland in early August it was reported that James was going to land there with one army while Berwick invaded western Scotland with another.[153] Hence when Mar told the Scots Jacobite leadership that Louis XIV was committed to sending 5,000 men with James and Ormond to invade England and 5,000 more with Berwick to Scotland, his audience was well prepared to believe him.[154]

This was despite the fact that the French king had publicly reaffirmed his commitment to stand by all the terms of the treaty of Utrecht, including his commitment to uphold the Protestant succession in Britain, in June 1715.[155] It was, of course, possible that Louis XIV was prevaricating (as, indeed, he was); and the Jacobites could be forgiven for not taking this French commitment to the status quo at face value. What they could not deny, however, was the old man's death. On 21 August 1715 Louis XIV died and Philippe de Bourbon, duc d'Orléans, became Regent for Louis XV, his great-grandson. Many senior Whigs at that point believed that the crisis was over and the English and Welsh Tories were certainly 'fort decourages', as soon as they heard news of his last illness.[156] The Scots Jacobites, however, on the whole saw things differently. Though some were 'apprehensive the pretender is stopt if [the] Duke [of] Orleans be Regent', many others were not.[157] When Sinclair told James Malcolm of Grange that the king's death was a blow to their plans, Grange simply denied there was any problem and declared he 'was very well pleasd to hear it, for a younge Prince, such as the Regent, would push our affair with more vigour then the old King, who was half doated; and my Lord [Mar] was positive, none in France was so well inclined to serve us as the Duke of Orleans, contrarie to all the false reports that were spread of him'.[158] Likewise, a Jacobite veteran, reflecting years later on his and his comrades' refusal to be deterred by this disaster, explained: 'they were in hopes that the Regent who succeeded in the Government of France would be no less a friend to the Chevalier, especially when he should be pushed on by his interest to doe everything that might favour the Roman Catholick religion'.[159]

To outside observers the slippage between vision and reality taking place in the Scots Jacobite community was all too apparent. 'The vanitie, insolence, arogance, and madness of the Jacobits is beyond all measure unsupportable,' complained a northern Scots Whig in February 1715. 'I bleeve they must be let blood.'[160] Charles Cockburn in July wonderingly likened them to 'mad desperate people in a frenzie' who had 'got up their spirits so far that they know not how to get themselves brought within bounds again'.[161] 'Mad and infatuat', ruefully agreed Solicitor-General Sir James Steuart of Goodtrees in September 1715.[162] Desperation, inspiration and zeal had indeed combined synergistically to turn the Scots Jacobite community into a powder keg in the summer of 1715. Very little is inevitable in history, but the Scots Jacobite rebellion of 1715 comes very close.

CHAPTER 4

'That Treason Thus Could Sell Us':
the Jacobite Conspiracy of 1715

Just as it is the business of the Opposition in Parliament to oppose, so it is the business of governments in exile to overthrow those who have supplanted them. The ultimate purpose of the alternative, Jacobite, government at Saint-Germain and Bar-le-Duc was the overthrow of the controllers of the new order at Whitehall. In a sense everything that transpired at the Stuart court, from the balls and theatrical performances, to the solemn religious services daily performed, to the exiled dynasty's patronage of the arts, turned on this single objective.[1] The only question was how it was to be realised.

In principle, there were three ways to achieve the overthrow of the post-Revolutionary order. The first was by a foreign invasion of the British Isles, with the Stuarts at its head, which would reconquer the three kingdoms by straightforwardly military means. The second was by a national revolution or revolutions which would sweep the controllers of the new order from power by dint of an overwhelmingly popular uprising, after the fashion of the Revolution of 1688 in England. The third, which was never considered at this time, was by assassination of the rival monarch and a sudden seizure of power. More realistically, given the enormity of the task and the vested interests opposed to them, the Stuarts always sought to put together a package that combined the first two options: an invasion by at least some regular military forces borrowed from a friendly great power, supported by as widespread an uprising as possible.[2] Almost every Jacobite plot hatched between 1689 and 1760 contained these basic elements; the difficulty lay in organising and managing the two so that the invasion struck at the point when the conspirators in the British Isles were prepared and ready to rise in support of it.[3]

What this meant in practice was that the Jacobite court, operating from its base on the continent and using secret agents and couriers, had to contact its adherents in the British Isles, persuade them to risk their lives and livelihoods to restore the Stuart dynasty, organise them into an underground army, supply this army with arms, ammunition and money and coordinate uprisings in multiple regions in a carefully orchestrated sequence. All this, moreover, had to be done in the teeth of British government resistance, in the form of infiltrators, spies, mass arrests and counter-propaganda, to say nothing of the inevitable human failings of individual Jacobites, some of whom were bound to get drunk and brag to the wrong people, sell out for love or money, become frightened and refuse to act, or just simply get distracted by life or making a living. In addition, the Jacobite court had at the same time to be negotiating – from a position of profound weakness – with the hard-nosed diplomatic representatives of the European great powers to try and secure the regular military support both the exiled Stuarts and their friends in the three kingdoms were agreed they desperately needed if they were to confront and defeat the British army. As will easily be appreciated, these tasks went beyond being simply difficult; taken in the round they look nigh impossible. But it had been done once before. In England in 1688 William of Orange and his allies organised regional revolts and paralysed royal government in coordination with a foreign invasion, and brought off a revolution.[4] All the Jacobites wanted to do was reproduce the same result.

The Origins of the '15

The Jacobite court was constantly working to this end throughout its early years in France, and on two occasions (1692 and 1695–96) brought its plotting and negotiations to the point where a French invasion was scheduled and a coordinated uprising in support of it prepared and ready to erupt. On both occasions the plot and the French invasion miscarried for reasons we need not explore here, but it is significant that both came close to realisation (though not necessarily success).[5] After the Peace of Ryswick in 1697, however, the somewhat demoralised Stuart court relaxed its efforts to overthrow the Williamite regime in the British Isles and there followed a five-year hiatus in serious Jacobite plotting.[6] This period ended with the outbreak of the War of the Spanish Succession in 1702, after which France, in increasing financial and military difficulties, began to look for a quick fix to its strategic problems by exercising the Jacobite option. This turn in French policy was also in part prompted by the Union crisis in Scotland, which, if properly exploited, seemed to offer a golden opportunity to disrupt the British war effort on the continent, and after some cautious investigation of the situation and the Scots Jacobites' willingness to rebel, the French government duly attempted to throw a small army with James at its head into Scotland in 1708, where it was supposed to be joined by an army of anti-Union rebels led by Atholl.[7] This was always a desperate venture, given that the English and Welsh Jacobites, who were generally very taken with Queen Anne, wanted no part of any uprising against her, and in any event it, too, miscarried. The exigencies of the war, which by 1709 had become a grim struggle for survival by France, subsequently precluded the investment of further military resources in a British venture, though this did not prevent the Jacobite court from doggedly trying to persuade Louis and his ministers to renew the attempt on Scotland.[8] Only after France emerged, battered but intact, from the war after the Peace of Utrecht in 1713 did any real interest in the Jacobite option begin to re-emerge, and then, as we have already noted, it was necessarily straitened by the determination of Louis XIV's government to maintain the peace.

If for no other than purely strategic reasons, Louis and his ministers could not fail to take an interest in the British succession crisis of 1713–14. France could not afford renewed war, but if, without a war, a pro-French monarch somehow succeeded the ailing queen then the balance of power in Europe would dramatically shift in France's favour. The Jacobite court soon picked up on this slight shift in the French government's attitude towards them, and alongside the frustrating and fruitless effort secretly to negotiate a second Stuart restoration with the Oxford ministry in the winter of 1713–14, James and his advisers began to explore the possibility of an uprising in the event that Anne died before she could restore her half-brother to his 'rightful' place as her heir.[9] The first concrete results of this revived French and Jacobite interest in a military solution came in November 1713 when the French government secretly committed itself to provide James with two ships to get him to the British Isles quickly in the event of Queen Anne's death.[10] In addition, Berwick was given permission to accompany James, and the French foreign minister Jean Baptiste Colbert de Croissy, marquis de Torcy, promised to allow a number of officers from the Irish brigade surreptitiously to join the expedition.[11] As regards overt supplies of troops, munitions and money, however, the French made it very clear that the Jacobites would have to fend for themselves and that James must travel through France to the waiting ships fast and incognito.[12]

The Jacobite court did not accept that this was all the support they could get from France and continued to try and persuade Louis and Torcy to provide all three, but in the interim James and Berwick began to explore the possibility of engineering an uprising in the British Isles based only on Jacobite resources.[13] This struck a particular chord with the Scots Jacobites. Quite apart from the intrinsically more activist mien of the Scots since before 1707, their anger and frustration at the Union had been rekindled with a

vengeance during the malt tax crisis of 1713. Some Scots Jacobites were there-
fore amenable to the idea of a rebellion. After consulting with a number of
pro-Jacobite clan chieftains in late 1713 a delegation composed of William
Mackintosh of Borlum and Charles Forbes of Brux secretly visited Saint-
Germain to consult with Berwick.[14] He in turn introduced them to Torcy, and
sent them back to Scotland with a message to be ready to rise in the event of
Anne's dying without restoring her brother.[15] In January 1714 Robert Dalzell,
Earl of Carnwath, visited Bar to pledge his support and to urge the Stuart
monarch to go to Scotland. James responded positively, flatly declaring, 'I
certainly will, if this Parliament of England don't give me encouragement and
hopes of a restoration.'[16] Yet despite James's apparent boldness, the Jacobite
court did little more to prepare for a rising. Although agents from Saint-
Germain sounded out prominent Jacobites in Scotland and England James
and Berwick made no attempt to smuggle arms or money into the British Isles
and no command structure or plan was developed.[17]

Those Scottish and English Jacobites who were inclined to support a rising
on Anne's death accordingly each made their own preparations and laid their
own plans. The result was a haphazard set of piecemeal responses.[18] In Fife,
for example, when Sinclair was asked by several of his Tory neighbours to
organise a troop of horse suitable for a rising, he found when he put his
potential recruits on the spot, 'most of them [were] surprised, and lookt on
those who advised armeing as rash people, who had a mind to ruine them'.[19]
Only with difficulty was he able to get them to agree to his purchase of
weapons and equipment, and he completely failed to persuade his fellow
Jacobites to hire demobilised veterans of the war as servants, 'in case they
might askt ten shillings more a year then the countrie servants'.[20] According to
James Keith, the future Marshal Keith, Ormond was asked by a group of
English Jacobites to lead a *coup d'état* immediately after Anne's death. He
agreed, but delayed while he first secured a port either for easy access for an
invasion force from the continent or for escape if the coup failed. That done,
he scheduled a muster by the rebels close to London, only to be informed by
his erstwhile co-conspirators the day before the rising was due to begin that
'most of those who were to have composed the body, wearied with the delays,
had gone to the country, and that they could not draw together above the fift
part of what they had first offered'.[21] Moreover, even by the time Anne died on
1 August James himself was clearly still uncertain what kind of a reception he
could expect from his adherents in the British Isles, and news that Atholl (who
was still believed to be pro-Jacobite) had gone south to take the oaths and that
John Campbell, Earl of Breadalbane (and a stalwart Jacobite), had concerted
a joint letter from the clan chieftains pledging their loyalty to the Hanoverian

dynasty seems to have completely disconcerted him. A message from Alexander Rose, the Episcopalian Bishop of Edinburgh and *de facto* leader of the Episcopal communion, on behalf of the Lowland Jacobites, 'not to stirr in this conjuncture on any account', finally left him at such a stand that he responded to the news of Anne's death by doing exactly what Louis XIV and Torcy had strictly enjoined him not to do: openly heading for Paris in the hope of personally soliciting the king for arms, men and money.[22] True to his word, Louis refused even to see the Stuart prince and ordered him back to Lorraine forthwith.[23] It was a humiliatingly public signal of the Jacobites' failure to prepare adequately for the inevitable climax of the succession crisis.

James was crestfallen at having to slink back to Lorraine, and rightly concerned that the débâcle would tarnish his reputation, but he seems to have soon recovered his drive.[24] He quickly drew up a trenchant declaration proclaiming his refusal to accept his exclusion from the throne and his intention to contest it at the first opportunity.[25] Allan Cameron, a younger son of the chief of clan Cameron, was also sent over at the end of the month to consult with the Scottish Jacobites and get a sense of how willing they might be to come out in a rising now the Guelph dynasty was on the throne.[26] His report does not survive, yet it seems to have been good enough to persuade James to dispatch a second wave of three or four emissaries detailed to survey the Jacobites' situation in various parts of the British Isles.[27] One of the most important of these was the Irish Brigade colonel Sir John Forrester, who was sent over in October. Forrester was particularly charged with distributing £4,000 amongst the Scottish Jacobites[28] to help them purchase arms and stores for the coming rising, encouraging them to 'keepp up their hearts', and passing on James's pledge

> that the vieu of no danger or evill whatsoever will bee capable to make me fayle in what I owe to my self and them, as well as to a nation so signally brave and loyall in all times and for the recovery of whose liberty, now groaning under the yoak of that shamefull Union (which shall bee broke at my landing) I will cheerfully expose my self to the greatest of hazards and doe every thing tending to the good and happiness of so valiant and faithfull a people.[29]

The Jacobite court also accumulated its own store of munitions and found a ship or two capable of carrying James and some Irish officers over to Scotland.[30] Forrester remained in Scotland, conferring with leading Jacobites, for nearly four months and only returned to make his report (which appears to have been very positive) in February 1715.[31] By then, however, news of the

English Tories' gathering alienation from the new dynasty had preceded him, and in mid-November Berwick, freshly back from recapturing Barcelona for the Spanish Bourbons, and James already felt they could promise the Scots Jacobites:

> That the King is firmly resolved to goe himself in person to them as soon as possibly he can, and to carry me [Berwick] along with him.
>
> That a little time must be allowed for getting together what is necessary, especially for raising of money and for taking measures with friends in England, without which little good is to be expected. The King is now actually about this. That for the better keeping the secret, the King's friends must not expect to know the precise time of his embarquing, but that he will give them sufficient warning that they may meet him, in the meane time they must keep up their harts, without giving jealousy to the governement, and they must give him regularly an account how matters stand.[32]

Persuading Torcy and Louis XIV to support a Jacobite rising now assumed critical importance.

The Jacobite Conspiracy of 1715

Again and again, when sounded on the subject of a rebellion the British Jacobites had stressed that James must come with a body of regular troops which would act as the hard nucleus around which Jacobite insurgents could coalesce.[33] Any body of regular troops would do, and much though the British Jacobites would have liked to have had good Protestant Swedes, they were quite prepared to take what they could get.[34] In practical terms, in 1715 that meant French troops; which, as we have seen, Louis XIV was dead set against providing for fear that it would embroil France in a renewed war against the Grand Alliance. By February, though, the possibility that another revolution might be in the offing in the British Isles seemed to be growing. D'Iberville secretly reported in January that, 'Il est impossible que l'animosité croissant chaque jour comme elle fait, et eclatant par des declarations vives de part et d'autre ne produire a la fin de grands troubles',[35] and a briefing prepared at the end of 1714 for the marquis d'Alegre forthrightly portrays a Britain seething with sedition and on the verge of civil war.[36] Torcy and Louis were nonetheless very cautious about responding to the news out of Britain, doubtless reasoning that if a revolution occurred France would benefit whether it aided the rebels or not.[37] What seems to have changed the king and his minister's

attitude was the Tories' approach to Gyllenborg. Though he remained sceptical about the significance of much that was going on in Britain, Torcy
admitted: 'il y a certainement beaucoup de hardiesse a ceux qui en ont parlé
de s'estre ouvert sur un pareil point a un ministre etranger. Quoyque l'affaire
puisse avoir de grandes suites.'[38] Torcy and his master accordingly began to
discuss matters such as arms and money at least with Berwick, who by this
time had become the principal liaison between the French government and
the Stuart government in exile.[39] And although Louis and Torcy were still 'not
for venturing anything to the prejudice of M. Porray [the peace], unless one
were very sure of the success',[40] it was clearly a breakthrough from the Jacobite
point of view. Louis also seems to have indicated that he wanted to see a definite plan rather than airy proposals, which quickly moved James and Berwick
to try and firm up the loose strands of the tentative plot into something more
solid they could offer the king.[41]

The Jacobite court had contacted various leading members of the Oxford
ministry in the course of its putative negotiations for a restoration during
the period 1710–14, most notably Oxford himself, Bolingbroke, the senior
Secretary of State, Mar and Ormond, the Captain-General of the army.[42] As
James began sounding out the British Jacobites on the subject of a rising in the
autumn of 1714 he accordingly attempted to resume contact with those same
Tory leaders, Oxford (whom nobody trusted by this stage) excepted.[43] Initially
there does not seem to have been much of a response. Only the Scots Jacobites
showed any enthusiasm for the project. James, however, was nothing if not
persevering, and as Tory disenchantment with the Hanoverians deepened, the
former ministers and a number of lesser lights, including Sir William
Wyndham, former Chancellor of the Exchequer (then a minor government
office), George Granville, Lord Lansdowne and former Treasurer of the Royal
Household, and Lieutenant-General Robert Echlin, began to respond to
Jacobite overtures.[44] None, of course, did so directly. All the negotiations were
carried on verbally via Jacobite agents such as Charles Kinnaird, John
Menzies, John Tunstal and Thomas Carte – men of no great status or significance whose accounts of what transpired in their meetings with the Tory leadership could be loftily, if not plausibly, denied in the event that they were
intercepted by the British government.[45] This was obviously an advantage to
the Tory leaders concerned, but it severely retarded the progress of the negotiations from James's point of view. Though they did their sincere best to relay
the responses of those they were meeting with accurately, Jacobite agents were
chosen for their loyalty, and were all too prone to lapse into enthusiasm and
inaccuracy. It is also probably the case that the leaders of the English Tories
were reluctant to commit themselves too far, too fast and used the indirect

system of communication via the Jacobite agents as a means of slowing the process.[46]

James and Berwick thus found it hard at first to pin the English and Welsh Tory/Jacobite leadership down on critical subjects like where and when James should make his appearance in England, who could be relied upon to turn out and what the English Jacobites needed in terms of arms and money. Most critically of all, the Tories were initially negative or evasive on the question of whether or not they would rise without the support of a French invasion force.[47] Even Ormond, the Tory leader in whom Berwick and James put most hope, indicated in early February 1715 that he expected 'M. Robinson [James] should carry with him to M. Elbeuf [Scotland] or M. Alençon [England] that able lawyer M. Alexandre [an army]'.[48] The presumably more dispassionate surveys of the Jacobites' general situation provided by Forrester and other agents dispatched on similar missions, which were apparently complete by the end of February, also indicated 'that nothing is yet in a reddiness, nor can be so soon'.[49]

Nothing daunted, James and Berwick kept up the pressure. Both were agreed in not obfuscating the virtual certainty that no French troops would be forthcoming – the critical lack as far as the Jacobites in Britain were concerned. 'Plain dealing is', James observed, 'now become a necessity', though neither man considered the want of regular military forces to be of sufficient weight to abort the projected rising.[50] Nor, it appears, did the Jacobites in Britain. Though they continued to harp on about the need for an invasion by regular troops, and how this would make any Jacobite rising a certain success, they did not break off negotiations when James and Berwick informed them that none would be forthcoming. It seems that they, too, were impressed by the political ferment and civil disorder sweeping England in the spring and summer of 1715. Bolingbroke's flight to France in advance of his impeachment by the new, Whig-dominated Parliament further boosted the likelihood that the plot would come to fruition. Bolingbroke was a quintessential man of business who well understood the Tory party and its leaders throughout the British Isles, warts and all, and when he quickly committed himself to James and took on the role of co-organiser of the plot in April 1715, the pace of preparations quickened.[51] Berwick had been accumulating ships, arms and money in France for several months, and James had secretly negotiated a substantial loan from the Duke of Lorraine;[52] they were both now inclined to set a date and launch the rising without further ado:

When Puisieux [Parliament] returns to the country, then will be the time for M. Raucourt [James] to visit Elbeuf [Scotland], and M. Orbec

[Ormond] must at the same time regulate his affairs so at Alençon [England] that the ablest lawyers may appear for M. Robinson [James]. Lett what hast be made, it will be July before this concert can be made, so no time is to be lost.[53]

Even a flat statement from Ormond and his co-conspirators, 'that without men, arms, money and ammunition they think the suit impracticable', was insufficient to deter James and Berwick, who pressed on with their preparations regardless.[54]

Bolingbroke was initially not averse to the Jacobites on the continent taking decisive action to carry forward the plot.[55] Only as he became aware of the lacunae in Berwick and James's plan, which at this time essentially consisted of the two of them throwing themselves into the midst of their friends either in England or in Scotland (the target varied according to the latest news out of the two kingdoms) with whatever resources they could scrape together, did he develop misgivings.[56] In part, this may have been due to personal alarm at the fact that James wanted Bolingbroke to accompany him in his dash to the British Isles (Bolingbroke was not especially physically brave, or ever a soldier), but he was also very appropriately concerned about the vagueness of the planning and, above all, about the leakage of information to the British authorities.[57] In particular he

found a general expectation gone abroad that your Majesty was to under-take somewhat immediately; and I was not a little concerned to hear, in two or three places, and among women over their tea, that arms were provided and ships got ready; but I confess I was struck with concern when I knew in such a manner as is to be depended upon, and as I beg your Majesty to depend upon, that the factor of Lawrence [George I, i.e. Stair, the British ambassador] in this country knew of the little armament and sent advices of it home.[58]

Just as importantly, for Bolingbroke, 'It is evident, that in Margaret's country [England] things are not ripe; that at least you cannot tell with certainty whether they are so or not; that the secret is divulged; that in the present method, the correspondence wants that preciseness and exactness which is indispensably necessary'.[59] Bolingbroke also evidently made these same arguments to Berwick and Torcy, who passed them on to Louis XIV who was correspondingly 'mightily in pain for fear of wrong measures taken, or of a miscarriage', when he heard that James had peremptorily set the date for his own sailing for 17 July and the date for the uprising for 30 July.[60] Berwick was duly swayed by the old king's distress and backed Bolingbroke's plea for a postponement. By the time James received these pleas he was already in Paris, having secretly departed Bar in disguise with only two servants on 10 July. Finally convinced of the need for a postponement by the united front presented by Bolingbroke, Berwick and the French, he reluctantly returned again to Bar.[61]

James's arrival in Paris, however, closely coincided with the arrival in France of the long-desired detailed response to the Jacobite court's plan for an insurrection from the leading Jacobite conspirators in London.[62] Dictated by Mar to Charles Kinnaird at the beginning of July, the memorandum was read over personally by Ormond and then presented by Ormond to Kinnaird as his 'instructions' in the presence of Mar and Lansdowne.[63] It provides a unique insight into the thinking of the leading Jacobites in the British Isles on the projected rising.

The conspirators stated from the outset that they were very reluctant even to consider a rebellion without a force of foreign regulars to back it: 'Their unanimous sense is, that there is no hope of succeeding in it without the assistance of a regular force, or without a general raising of the people in all parts of England, immediately upon the King's landing, and that the latter of these depends very much upon the former.'[64] This was despite the fact that 'the generality of the people are extremely averse from the Court and Ministry (whom they hate and despise) and well inclined to a restoration'. The problem was that the people would be afraid to show their sympathies without a proper army to protect them from the authorities in their localities. These local authorities themselves contained many who were ostensibly opposed to the ministry, but were no friends to the Jacobite cause, 'which is the case of many in the Tory party', and in an emergency they were liable, Whig and Tory alike, to cleave to the government, 'thinking themselves that way out of danger, whichever side prevail'.[65] As would, indeed, the bourgeoisie in general and the newly recruited soldiery. Hence if James came without a force of regular troops there would be no general uprising and he would have to pause near where he landed while he trained up and organised an army out of those Jacobite volunteers who could reach him (and, the conspirators warned, many even of the Jacobites would sit quiet at home in such circumstances). Opposed to him would be a force of at least 32,000 government troops: 8,000 each from England, Ireland, Hanover and the Netherlands, plus an indeterminate number of Whig volunteers. If, as seemed likely, James's attempt failed, the conspirators believed Britain was doomed to fall under a Whig military dictatorship.[66]

Having painted a very grim prospect in the event of James arriving without foreign troops to back him, the conspirators nonetheless went on to imply that a rising without foreign backing might still have a chance of success. James was directed to land in late September in Northumberland, preferably on Holy Island (Mar subsequently changed this to 'Alimont', by which he probably meant Alnwick or Alnmouth) if he came from the east, and in Lancashire if he came from the west.[67] In Northumberland he could expect to be joined by about 1,000 mounted gentry and many coal miners. From Holy Island (or Alnwick) James should be able easily to secure Newcastle and disrupt the east coast coal supply to London, which 'would either induce London to declare or at least distress the Government'.[68] A Jacobite army there would also be in a good position to seize Berwick and link up with a Scots Jacobite rising. Should James decide to head for Scotland he should land near Aberdeen, or Angus or the Mearns, 'these countries being well affected and near the Highlands'. Notice that James intended to land in Northumberland had to be given well in advance so that the Lancashire, Welsh, West Country and Irish Jacobites could plan simultaneous risings of their own in support.[69]

Since 'the whole country of England is ill provided with arms and particularly those parts of it which are best affected', James was to bring an artillery train and 10,000 stand of arms (i.e. muskets and their accoutrements) with him and distribute 10,000 more to designated counties in advance. Money was likewise to be got to county leaders in anticipation of the rising. Failing a proper force of regulars, James was, in addition, to bring with him 500 Irish Brigade officers, each accompanied by a servant, as a cadre for his rebel army. The conspirators estimated they could mobilise about 8,000 Highlanders who would not need the degree of training Lowland Scots troops would have to undergo if they were to be of any use, but warned that the Highlanders would have to be promptly paid from the outset, otherwise 'they will plunder the country, and by that means do more harm to the King's cause than they can do good'. Once James was landed, the conspirators stressed, he should order a *Te Deum* in the nearest Anglican church and regularly attend services there himself. Though the plan, such as it is, then tails off, reiterating that without foreign forces the difficulties were 'almost insuperable', that political events might swing public opinion still more in favour of the Jacobites (i.e. that it would all come right without anyone having to risk their lives) and so on, the conspirators had already made the critical concession as far as the Jacobite court was concerned: they had tacitly conceded that it might, just, be possible to overthrow the Whig regime without a regular military invasion force.[70] Everything else was negotiable.

Though it is possible that Ormond, Mar and Lansdowne thought they had underscored the low probability of success without a foreign invasion emphatically enough to deter James from deciding to go it alone, in all likelihood they knew this response was tantamount to a green light. Quite apart from the fact that they had admitted it might be possible to overthrow the Whig regime just using the Jacobite movement's intrinsic strength in the British Isles, they also exaggerated the military strength of the Whig regime in such a fashion as to be easily refuted. There was no way George I could or would strip Hanover of its defences by bringing over the Electoral army, the Irish army could not redeploy wholesale to mainland Britain for fear of Catholic rebellion there and, with the best will in the world, it was to take the Dutch nearly five months to get their troops into the British theatre of operations when the rebellion actually did break out. Moreover, when they signed off with the pledge: 'If the King shall judge the time to be now ripe for it, they are determined to do their utmost towards supporting it, and to take any part, without reserve, that he may think for his service', they made it virtually certain that James would go forward with the attempt.[71] James duly signalled his intention to do so on 17 July when he issued a warning order to the colonels of the Irish regiments in French and Spanish service to select suitable officers and men in anticipation of a Jacobite uprising and 'facilitate their escape and transportation' to Britain when the rising broke out.[72]

By this point, too, the French government had for some months quietly been shifting its position from sympathetic but inactive neutrality towards surreptitious aiding and abetting. Though Louis and Torcy remained adamant that there could be no question of overt French military support, and were balking at allowing Berwick to accompany James on the grounds that as a naturalised French subject and one of the most prominent generals in France Berwick's participation in a rising would glaringly expose French involvement, they had become more and more amenable to the proposal that they should covertly supply the Jacobites with arms and ammunition.[73] They were also prepared to facilitate James's transportation to the British Isles.[74] Because of France's parlous financial situation Louis insisted that he could not come up with substantial funding for the rebellion, but in response to an appeal by Ormond he wrote to ask his grandson, Philip V of Spain, to provide the money, which in due course Philip did, to the amount of £100,000.[75] The French diplomatic machine also began to facilitate the Jacobites' efforts to organise a rising. From March onwards specially sensitive correspondence between the chief conspirators in London and the Jacobite court began to move under French diplomatic covers, d'Iberville allowed his own dispatches to be a direct conduit between the conspirators and France, and Torcy did what he could to encourage Charles XII of Sweden to respond positively to the Jacobites' overtures.[76] The Jacobite court's progress in breaking down the French government's reserve was sufficiently encouraging for Bolingbroke to assure James in July, 'I have much greater hopes from Harry [Louis XIV] than you, Sir, seemed to entertain; and if you are well served, you will in my conscience meet with support.'[77]

Bolingbroke's optimism, furthermore, did seem to be borne out by the French response to Ormond when he arrived in Paris, having fled England just ahead of his arrest and impeachment. He was courteously welcomed by the French government and almost immediately gained access to Torcy. By the beginning of August Torcy, Ormond, Berwick and Bolingbroke were jointly drawing up final memoranda on the rising for the remaining conspirators in London.[78] Bolingbroke found Torcy's engagement at this point particularly encouraging because it 'seemed to be from a sense of their own interest, the only principle by which they are to be influenced'.[79] The document they were colluding to produce nonetheless made it bluntly clear that the French government had gone as far as it could go in terms of concessions to the Jacobites. Louis would add 10,000 stand of arms to the 10,000 he had already given and provide ships to get James and the weapons to the British Isles, but nothing further. 'No troops, no money, no officers, no appearance which may not be disavowed on the part of France.'[80] The French government would secretly intercede with Sweden and Spain for troops and money, but that was the limit of further French involvement. Though it was not explicitly stated, the memorandum also implied that Berwick was, like his fellow Jacobites in French service, forbidden to join the rising.[81] The memorandum, finally, asked for a clear and forthright answer, 'whether with this supply of arms only the King shall embark and where he shall land. Whether he shall wait the event of the negotiations on foot for other assistances. What he shall do in case after all endeavours these negotiations fail, and no further help can be procured.'[82] James was by this time on a hair trigger, ready to dash for the Channel at the slightest encouragement, as he told Berwick at the end of July:

I find Raucourt [James] very much sett on his journey, and he cannot heare with any patience of a long delay; he promised Sably [Bolingbroke] by Cameron that he woud have patience for a month counting thence, but after that, doth he not find things ready on this side, I feare I shall scarce be able to hinder him from passing the sea as he cann, and as he certainly will, for after all what a conjuncture is this, all the nation is in a flame, and his person single now, will do more good, than an army join'd to it some months hence, if dispositions change, and who cann inshure them in our country?[83]

Thus the whole project now hinged on Mar, Lansdowne and Wyndham's response.

The Jacobite court's plans, however, were already being overtaken by events. On 20 July the British Secretaries of State dispatched official letters warning of the impending Jacobite uprising to government officers and local authorities throughout the British Isles.[84] Parliament was addressed by the king and money for augmenting the army promptly voted. Recruits were soon being raised and the militia mustered. More immediately damaging, the Habeas Corpus Act was suspended and there was a government swoop on suspected Jacobites and mass arrests that soon cowed many of those still at liberty, at least in London.[85] 'It greives me to find that they have singled out just the persons we depended upon', wrote a worried Bolingbroke in early August.[86] Though some of the most prominent, including Mar, Lansdowne and Wyndham, as yet remained at large, they were quite rightly alarmed, and before Bolingbroke *et al.*'s memorandum could arrive in London Mar had departed for Scotland with Major-General George Hamilton to raise the Jacobite standard.[87] Just as ominously, on 2 August Berwick in a letter to James noted with concern, 'I like not M. Rethel's [Louis XIV's] state of health'.[88] On 4 August, as Bolingbroke and Berwick sat down to dinner with Torcy after agreeing on the final draft of the memorandum to be sent to the conspirators in London, news arrived that the king was seriously ill.[89] He was to linger until 21 August, but in the interim France's government was effectively paralysed as Louis's ministers concentrated on manoeuvring at court to ensure their political survival after the king's death.[90] The Jacobites, too, needed to find a way to secure their political future, and French support for the now imminent rising, and as soon as he heard of Louis's condition James directed that Ormond and Bolingbroke should immediately try to ingratiate themselves with Orléans, who had already been named as the future Regent of France for Louis's great-grandson and heir, Louis XV.[91]

Unfortunately for them, the Regent, then duc de Chartres, had years before clashed with James II and VII over a matter of court etiquette (a vital matter in Louis XIV's France) and still bore a grudge against the Jacobite court.[92] In addition, according to the terms of the Peace of Utrecht the Regent was to become the next king of France in the event of the sickly Louis XV dying before begetting an heir. But since Philip V of Spain had a better claim to the French throne (he was Louis XIV's grandson, whereas Orléans was Louis's nephew), and viewed the renunciation of his right to the succession he had been obliged

to make as part of the Utrecht agreement as illegitimate, it was clear that
Orléans's succession could transpire only if the Peace of Utrecht was backed,
if necessary with force, by the other signatories, foremost among which was
Great Britain. As was apparent to every statesman in Europe, Orléans there-
fore had considerable incentive to maintain the peace and good relations with
Britain.[93]

Few of the Jacobites in the British Isles were more than dimly aware that an
Orléans regency was liable to pose a major strategic problem.[94] Their energies
had for the previous eight months been concentrated on preparing for the
forthcoming rebellion. There was, however, a marked divergence between the
kind of preparations engaged in by Jacobites in England and those undertaken
by their counterparts in Scotland. The Irish Jacobites were supposed to be
organising a rising of their own, too, but though there were rumours and
alarms in Ireland there is no evidence that they ever got to the stage of war
planning or accumulating matériel of any kind.[95] In England, as we have
already seen, the spring and early summer were exciting times for the
Jacobites, as the country was swept by a wave of Tory/Jacobite-inspired civil
disorder. Even as late as the autumn, despite all the government had done in
the way of exemplary executions and draconian legislation, this disorder
could recrudesce and at times verged on downright insurrection, as is
apparent, for example, from an account of a confrontation between a mob in
Oxford and a king's messenger (these were government officers charged with
carrying important dispatches and seizing and guarding suspected persons)
in October 1715. Nathan Willcox, the messenger, having arrested the two
suspects he had been sent down to seize, found himself besieged in the Angel
Inn by a mob 'swearing they would murder the Messenger and rescue the
prisoners'. Willcox directed the Mayor to read the Riot Act to the crowd, 'but
that did not disperse them, but on the contrary they grew more outragious,
crying "damn the Mayor, don't mind him", and assaulted the house with
stones, etc'. Willcox then threatened to fire into their midst with his pistols
unless they dispersed, 'which they refused to do, and one of them crying out
"James the third, Ormond and Bullingbrook", the said Messenger fired his
pistolls, crying "God bless King George and damn the Pretender, Ormond and
Bullingbrook and all their adherents"'. This wounded several, and the Mayor
then persuaded the mob to withdraw, but only for a short time. At 1 a.m. a
crowd of hundreds marched on the inn, breaking the street lights on the way
to ensure they were covered by darkness. Willcox and three Whig volunteers
only finally routed them by launching a furious assault with pistols and
swords in which several more people were wounded.[96] Such Tory/Jacobite
mobs would doubtless have been very good recruiting grounds for a Jacobite

army, but little effort appears to have been made by élite English Jacobites to harness their enthusiasm to a Jacobite rebellion, or to lay in serious stocks of weapons with which to arm them.[97]

As will also be seen to be the case in Scotland, the quantity of warlike supplies accumulated and followers recruited in England was always going to depend on the personal initiative of individual members of the Jacobite élite, if for no other reason than that they were the only segment of the Jacobite community with the financial or social wherewithal to do either. The problem in England seems to have been that far fewer élite Jacobites were willing to court danger by undertaking such activities than in Scotland. Before Peregrine Osborne, the Duke of Leeds, fled to France he apparently accumulated horses, arms and ammunition at his Wimbledon home, and prepared commissions for officers in a Jacobite regiment.[98] Alun Prideaux in Cornwall 'armed his servants' in August.[99] 'Great quantities of warlike stores' are alleged to have been collected by one Hart, 'a merchant', in Bristol, and someone brought 'eleven chests of firearms, a hogshead full of basket-hilted swords, and another of cartouches, and three pieces of cannon' into Bath.[100] In so far as the evidence allows an assessment of the English Jacobites' efforts to prepare for a rising, however, these four examples seem to have been distinctly untypical. Even when the government swept up Sir Richard Vyvyan and the other ring-leaders of the planned West Country rising in September and October they found little in the way of warlike supplies, and absolutely no equivalent to, for example, the 4,000 pounds of Jacobite gunpowder seized by the Whig magis-trates of Aberdeen alone on the eve of the rising.[101] And certainly when the northern English Jacobite rebellion broke out in October observers were moved to comment on how ill-prepared most of the participants were, despite the fact that Jacobite agents – who included a number of Irish officers formerly in French service – sent out by the conspirators in London had been 'riding from place to place as travellers' throughout England, 'carrying intelli-gence, discoursing with persons and settling and appointing their business', since at least August.[102] The only exceptions were some small bodies of northern English Catholics, such as the retinue of James Radcliffe, Earl of Derwentwater, who were described as 'very well armed', and a group of 'well armed' plebeian Catholics who joined the rebels at Lancaster.[103] William Widdrington, Lord Widdrington, is also known to have cached nearly 600 military-quality swords in a tenant's house and Simon Scrope of Danby Hall surreptitiously accumulated arms and mounts for twenty men.[104] These cases reinforce Paul Monod's suggestion that an underground Catholic army had been organised in the north in the 1690s of which they were the heirs.[105] Nonetheless, despite ample warning, the majority of the English Jacobite gentry who could be persuaded to turn out at all (Scrope, for example, refused to rise) rode to war, 'not above 8 or 10 of a troop . . . better armed than with a whip and small sword, many of their horses . . . but indifferent, and their men raw and unactive'.[106] General Joseph Wightman was, it seems, only being accurate when he described the Northumbrian rebel horse as 'the worst that ever were seen'.[107] Crucially, moreover, it appears that no one amongst the erstwhile rebels had thought to amass any quantity of military-calibre muskets ('eleven chests of firearms' would not actually have gone very far) to arm the plebeian volunteers who tried to join the rebellion, most of whom as a consequence had to be turned away.[108]

Instead of preparing for a home-grown rising, in fact, the English Jacobites apparently dissipated their energies looking for some source of foreign troops who could do the fighting for them. Sweden was the ally they most ardently sought, and again and again the English Jacobites clutched at the slightest hope of Swedish troops backing up an invasion of England by James and Berwick.[109] As we have already seen, in February 1715 a syndicate of forty Tories/Jacobites was even prepared secretly to raise £200,000 – equivalent to over £23 million in 2004 – to bring this prospect closer to realisation, well illustrating how much they yearned for it.[110] Failing the Swedes, French or Spanish troops would do just as well, hence the repeated demands for a commitment from Louis XIV to provide an invasion force, despite the English Jacobites being told repeatedly that it was out of the question.[111] Ultimately they persuaded the Scots Jacobites to take up the role of liberators of England. As James Keith feelingly recalled: 'They pushed on the Scots (who wanted no spur), to the attempt, giving them all the fair promises imaginable of help howsoon they should take arms. And how well they performed it shall be afterwards discovered. They concerted with the Duke of Marr that he should immediatly go to Scotland, and there declare publickly for King James.'[112] Without doubt the English population was ill armed and unmilitary, and the bulk of the British army was stationed in England, but the Lowland Scots were little better in either respect, which makes the English Jacobites' risk-aversion all the more puzzling. The fact that for their own reasons the Scots Jacobites believed more passionately in their need for a Jacobite victory than their English counterparts may have made a difference; certainly the Scots seem to have been far less daunted than the English and Welsh by the government crackdown that began in late July (though it should also be noted that there were very few arrests in Scotland at that time as compared with England). D'Iberville had no doubts, reporting from London at the end of July that the government's repression 'a jetté le parti des Torris et des Jacobites dans un etônnement et une crainte'.[113] Bolingbroke reached the same conclusion, and foolishly let slip to the French government 'that the English Tories would do nothing. That they wanted zeal, spirit and every thing for so enterprising a work, so that if France could not do the whole work they were not to expect any thing from the English Tories.'[114] Ormond was equally bitterly disappointed in October when he turned up off the Cornish coast with what few arms and Irish officers he had been able to slip past the French authorities and the Royal Navy squadrons hovering off Saint-Malo, only to meet with no response when he fired his signal guns to alert the English Jacobites who were supposed to be waiting to join him.[115] Apparently, what the great majority of the English Jacobites desperately wanted was a convenient miracle – that some invincible outside force should come to their rescue – and *faute de mieux* they persuaded the Scots to try and provide it.

The Scots, by contrast, seem to have been far more diligent in preparing for their recourse to arms. Because they were, naturally enough, not keen to advertise their activities either before or after the rebellion the evidence for this is impressionistic. Nevertheless there is a clear contrast between England and Scotland in the number of accounts of ships landing arms, meetings to coordinate military planning and other activities related to getting a rebellion off the ground.[116] It is, of course, possible that this simply indicates that the English Jacobites were better at covering their tracks. The poor state of their forces when they did turn out, however, tells against this, and the balance of the evidence suggests the obvious conclusion: the Scots Jacobites were better armed and better organised because they had invested serious time and money preparing themselves to rebel.

Some Scottish Jacobites had, indeed, begun gathering military-standard equipment in the winter and spring of 1714.[117] The distribution of £4,000 by Sir John Forrester during his visit to Scotland seems, however, to have notably accelerated the pace of preparations and arms procurement. As early as mid-February 1715 a bemused Montrose observed to a friend:

We have a hundered particulars from different places, such as that arms have been lately carried into that countrie, that there are frequent meetings especiallie since Borlum of Mckintosh came last from France. That messages are carried thoru the disafected countrie, particularly by this man and Robert Roy, and in short are infinit number of particulars of this sort.[118]

Montrose still could not believe this presaged a rebellion ('I can not imagin what these people can propose to themselves if they should be so mad as to make any attempt, which I confess I can not belive they'l venture'), but over the next six months the evidence of Jacobite planning and preparations steadily accumulated beyond the point of reasonable doubt. Lord Justice Clerk Cockburn pointedly wrote to Atholl in March to warn him that his vassals in Glen Almond were being recruited by Rob Roy Macgregor, and that others who owed allegiance to the duke were independently trying to buy suspicious quantities of arms and ammunition in Edinburgh.[119] By the end of April Duncan Forbes of Culloden was observing a disturbing number of 'trysts and meetings' by local Highland Jacobites, and his brother John enjoined him from London to put his house in a defensible state.[120] As James's originally projected starting date for the rebellion, 30 July, approached, another £25,000 was distributed by Breadalbane, and the pace of Jacobite preparations stepped up still further.[121] Mungo Graham of Gorthie and an anonymous government informant in the Borders both noticed that local Jacobites were busy buying horses suitable for military service: 'Some privatt gentilmen of the neigbur-hood have not under five or six a peice, and I am certain some of them have not money of ther own unless they have a fond from abroad to support the charge they are att.'[122] Arms were reported landed at Aberdour for Patrick Lyon of Auchterhouse, and others elsewhere in Fife for James Drummond, the Marquess of Drummond, James Murray, Lord Nairn, and Lord James Murray of Dowally (Atholl's brother).[123] Around the same time half-pay officers and former soldiers were being surreptitiously recruited to provide some profes-sional expertise in the units being secretly enlisted by wealthy Jacobites in Midlothian and the Borders.[124]

By the beginning of August, the Scots Jacobites were, as a result of these preparations, as ready as they were ever going to be. All that remained was for James and Berwick to arrive in Scotland, and to evade arrest until that tran-spired important Highland and Lowland Jacobite leaders quietly left their regular residences and began moving, sometimes almost daily, from one safe house to another in the countryside.[125] The Highlands in particular seemed to be primed to explode and the sudden reticence of local Jacobites there, as compared with their usually brazen Jacobitism, worried the authorities in Edinburgh and London almost as much as their former effrontery had annoyed them. 'By all accounts I have ffrom the highlands', reported Sheriff-Depute James Graham to Montrose, 'ther is not the least stir, but all are ordered to be in readiness again [*sic*] a landing and not to make the least noyse till they hear from their masters and leaders. They are certainlie all ready and prepared with armes and ammunition. And the better they observe their orders by lying quiet they value themselves the more of it.'[126] The Scottish Jacobites' precautions proved effective. Few of their real leaders were caught by the government after the round-up of Jacobite suspects was extended to

Scotland in mid-August.[127] Instead, the government bag ultimately consisted of prominent, but for the most part harmless, Jacobites such as James Ogilvy, Lord Deskford, and Sir Patrick Murray of Ochtertyre.[128] Of those taken up in the first sweep, only George Lockhart of Carnwath was of any significance.[129] The Scots Jacobites were, then, apparently well situated to launch their uprising when Mar arrived back in Scotland.

Yet appearances, and especially the apprehensions of the government, may belie reality. When Sinclair first began to purchase military-grade weapons to distribute in a rising (as far as battlefield utility was concerned there was a considerable difference between a light fowling piece such as might be used for hunting and the heavy, robust smoothbore muskets used by the military), he was warned: 'That if any private methode were fallne on to provide armes', his gentry peers would 'think themselves affronted and take none of them when they came', and it was only with difficulty that he prevailed on his putative troopers to make a joint effort to provide themselves with arms.[130] The Jacobite movement in Scotland was, unsurprisingly given the dynamics of Scottish society, dominated by the landed élite. They considered themselves to be the natural officers and rightful leaders of their people. Thus if anyone other than they provided leadership or weapons for the tenants, servants or clients whom they expected to recruit into their units, it derogated their status, something they would automatically oppose. The upshot of this was that the arming and preparation of the Scottish Jacobites were done on an individual, piecemeal basis. So where a powerful Highland magnate, such as Alexander Gordon, Marquess of Huntly, or a wealthy Lowland nobleman, such as Panmure, actively prepared his people for the rising the results could be impressive: in both instances they were able to turn out a substantial, organised body of men reasonably well armed and well equipped.[131] By contrast, lesser figures, such as Linlithgow and William Livingstone, Viscount Kilsyth, who paid little attention to arming, organising and preparing their followers, drew few with them and those ill armed.[132] There was also the matter of financial resources.[133] Not all heritors or Highland chieftains could afford to strip their estates of hale young men (who also usually had to be paid, at least initially, out of the landowner's own pocket), and then feed and arm them appropriately. In the final event, because of the presence among the Scots Jacobites of large (*de facto*) feudal followings like those brought in by all the major clan chieftains and some of the Lowland nobility, the Scots rebels, taken as a whole, were intrinsically better prepared for a rebellion than the English Jacobites could ever be. Yet still the Scots Jacobites' level of military preparedness was more mixed than the government's fears would allow.

After Orléans's accession as Regent, moreover, the Jacobites were finally, it appeared, left with the stark alternative of either giving up on the whole enterprise, or essaying it with the resources they had to hand. The Regent's prompt response to Stair's demand for the arrest and unloading of the ships designated to carry the arms and ammunition supplied by Louis XIV greatly pleased the ministry in London, and struck directly at one of the Jacobites' key weaknesses.[134] If they could not get James and the few resources they had scraped together over to Britain there was clearly no hope at all of launching a successful rebellion there. For a month or so after the death of the king James and Bolingbroke were downcast if not downright despairing. 'The more I think, the more I hear, and the more I struggle forward in this business, the more impracticable it appears to me', wrote Bolingbroke in early September.[135] 'On the whole I must confess,' replied James, 'my affairs have a very melancholy prospect, every post almost brings some ill news or other.'[136] The Jacobite king refused to give up, however, and was in a manner vindicated by a distinct thawing in relations between the Jacobite court and the Regency at the end of September. In a conversation probably with Antoine Coiffier-Ruzé, marquis d'Effiat (a political ally of Orléans's), Bolingbroke was assured under conditions of strictest secrecy that, 'You may now expect . . . an absolute connivance, and even a concert in what manner Andrew's [James's] servants shall act that Harry [Orléans] may wink.'[137] The Regent nonetheless publicly continued to accede to Stair's demands that he block and suppress Jacobite attempts to use France as a springboard for rebellion in the British Isles, forbade Berwick to participate in the rebellion and even dispatched troops to Château Thierry ostensibly to prevent James passing through France on his way to the Channel coast.[138] Behind the scenes, though, Franco-Jacobite relations had improved to the point of real warmth by early October, when Ormond obtained a personal interview with Orléans, who 'made great professiones of his concerne and friendshipe for you [James]', and agreed to supply the Jacobites with arms and ammunition.[139]

The Regent was apparently moved to be more helpful, indeed to revive the policy of covert support adopted by Torcy and Louis XIV, by reports of Jacobite successes in Scotland.[140] Whether ruled by a regent or a king, the interests of France would clearly be served by a Jacobite victory and Orléans, like his predecessor, had doubtless by this time calculated that he could get away with covert support sufficient to win the Jacobites' gratitude without endangering the Peace of Utrecht. If the Jacobites won, France had aided them in their hour of need; if they lost, the peace settlement still stood, and could be improved to secure Orléans's own succession to the throne should the need arise. This two-faced approach to the warring parties in Britain prevailed for the remainder of the rising, to the growing annoyance and alarm of Stair and the British government.[141] Indeed, as the rebellion faded to its disastrous conclusion in early 1716, Stair became convinced that the Regent was planning to step up French support for the Jacobites to the extent of sponsoring a Franco-Swedish invasion:

It was very lucky that the rebellion ended at the time it did. If it had continued longer, I'm afraid France would very soon have taken another part in that matter than they had played hitherto. They were fitting out ships and they had troops actually marching towards Bayonne. The Duke of Ormonde was at Paris, publickly had a very great court and seemed very much elated at the time the King's [i.e. George I's] army was marching against Perth, and that in all appearance their game seemed desperate.[142]

In any event, Orléans's duplicity delivered exactly the results he had (presumably) calculated. When the rebellion was defeated he coolly switched over to ingratiating himself with the Whig regime, and within six months secured a military alliance with Britain, the Netherlands and, eventually, the Habsburgs, that proved more than sufficient to guarantee the peace settlement.[143]

Mar, meanwhile, had arrived in Scotland in mid-August to find the Scots Jacobites emotionally and psychologically committed to a rising and as well armed and well organised as their circumstances permitted. His strategic thinking at this point was never spelled out and is obscured in contemporary accounts of his conversations and debates with other Scots Jacobites by his immediate agenda: persuading them to come out in rebellion. But from his actions and retrospective judgements it seems that he (and presumably Lansdowne and Wyndham in England at the time he departed) envisaged a Scots rebellion drawing away government troops from putatively pro-Jacobite areas in England (and perhaps Ireland), thus enabling the English (and Irish) Jacobites to take the field. This in turn, it was hoped, would impress the French with the Jacobites' zeal and commitment and lead to full-scale French military intervention on their behalf and hence the rout of the Whig regime.[144] Mar's problem was that the Scots' intrinsic willingness to rise could not necessarily be counted on to overcome the caution inspired by their situation.[145] The final stage of the conspiracy, then, revolved around Mar and his close associates persuading the leaders of the Scots Jacobite community to overlook the implicit difficulties and drawbacks of a Scots-led British Jacobite rising. It was, in essence, a plot within the plot.

Mar left London on 9 August and arrived in Scotland on the 16th, in disguise, with Major-General Hamilton and £7,000 from the English

Jacobites.[146] David Colyear, Earl of Portmore, another professional soldier and Colonel of the élite 'Grey Dragoons' (the famous 'Scots Greys'), was supposed to have accompanied him too, but stayed in England, presumably to help with the abortive English rising.[147] Though he is open to a great deal of criticism at every stage of the rebellion, Mar did a very good job concealing his departure and his identity when he first reached Scotland. The ministry does not even appear to have been aware of his departure from London until 18 August and he deftly obscured what he was up to for over a week after notice arrived in Edinburgh.[148] Word of his arrival was quickly circulated through the Jacobite community, and it was not until then that some Jacobites became aware that he had been one of the lead conspirators in London, which well illustrates how disjointed the conspiracy was in Scotland even at this late stage.[149] From the outset Mar deliberately manipulated his fellow Jacobites by confidently assuring them of victory on whatever grounds he thought would get them to commit themselves. To some he maintained that the Jacobite army was going to be so huge and overwhelming that it could restore the Stuarts without need of foreign aid, and possibly even without a blow being struck.[150] Others were promised that Berwick and James were either on their way, or only waiting to hear that the Scots had risen, and that French troops, arms and munitions of all kinds would accompany them when they arrived in Scotland.[151] Even so, overcoming the Scottish Jacobites' disinclination to move first still took some time. In meetings at Aboyne at the end of July and Loch 'Spean' (possibly Loch Moy) in early August Highland and Lowland Jacobites had again agreed that there was to be 'no rising of men till once there be a landing'.[152] It was also generally expected, even by Mar, that Atholl would be the leader of the rebellion.[153] Yet Atholl, the Jacobites' putative commander in 1708, had firmly and publicly signalled his intention to remain loyal to George I at the beginning of August, which dismayed some of their number and left the question of who was to command ominously open to dispute.[154]

Since the question was obviously crucial to whether or not there would be a rebellion at all, Mar resolved it by assuming command himself.[155] Though at this time he certainly had no authority from James to do so, he plausibly presented himself as having a royal commission to act as the leader of the rising.[156] Under cover of his alleged authority from James, Mar then held a series of meetings with Highland and north-eastern Jacobites, culminating in a grand assembly of the Jacobites at Braemar on 26/27 August, under the guise of a *tinchal*, or Highland hunting, and followed it up with further, smaller meetings with other local Jacobite leaders.[157] At these meetings he continually reiterated the message he and his agents had been propounding since his arrival in Scotland, that James, Berwick, troops and munitions were either on their way or would be as soon as news of the rising was confirmed, that Orléans was backing the Jacobites, that the English were ready to rise and that the Hanoverian regime was already falling to pieces.[158] Given that the Scots Jacobites were primed to believe all of this, it is no great surprise that he successfully persuaded the majority of the élite Jacobites in the Highlands and north-east to agree to a rising beginning on or about 15 September.[159] Though there was still debate as to the wisdom of rebelling, and some instances of erstwhile Jacobites (such as John Farquharson of Invercauld and Sir Duncan Campbell of Loch Nell) getting cold feet as this date approached, it gave Mar an excellent opportunity to force the issue by an irretrievable action.[160] Mar accordingly began sending orders to muster and march to his putative subordinates and ostentatiously drew his own men together to proclaim James III and VIII at Kirkmichael on 6 September.[161] His fellow Jacobites, a great many of whom had by this point been summonsed to appear (and be incarcerated) at Edinburgh by the government, now had two choices: either rebel or turn themselves in.[162] And 'no bodie, in that great ferment of spirits, and great expectation, careing to give bad exemple by delivering up himself first, they were at last all caught in the same noose, their time being elapsed, and no place left to repent'.[163] All over Scotland armed men were on the move, and between 13 and 16 September the rebellion became general. The '15 had begun.[164]

* * *

The Jacobite conspiracy that underpinned the '15 was fairly typical of its ilk. The exigencies of negotiating a realistic and accepted plan, organising and arming an underground army and coordinating both of the foregoing with interested foreign powers while maintaining security and momentum all told against the conspiracy ever coming to fruition. In 1715 there was neither a realistic nor an agreed plan and an underground army was only partially organised (thanks to Scotland's special social dynamics more than anything else) and haphazardly armed north of the border and never really organised or armed at all in England or – as far as we can tell – in Ireland. Despite the Jacobite court's best efforts none of the European great powers was willing to intervene on its behalf, and the secret aid it had coaxed out of the French government was fatally delayed by the death of Louis XIV. Security was not maintained, and the British government successfully penetrated the Jacobites' secrets, though not all of them, in both the British Isles and France. Finally, the organisational and emotional momentum that was necessary to give a sense of purpose and direction to the plot was broken by disagreements among the

Jacobites themselves and the wave of arrests that followed the Whig ministry's crackdown at the end of July. The Jacobite conspiracy of 1715 was comprehensively defeated by both exigent circumstances and the Whig regime.

Common sense dictated that any question of a rebellion should have evaporated by the end of August at the latest. That it did not underscores what we already know about the inspirational power of the Jacobite cause, particularly in contemporary Scotland, and, too, Mar's clever, ruthless machinations. 'No man cane give judgement on the proceedings of [the] Earl of Mar. They looke the most rash, inconsiderate resolutions ever I heard of', observed Lord Justice Clerk Cockburn.[165] Yet this cannot be the whole story. To make a rebellion (i.e. the spontaneous generation of an alternative army and an alternative government) involving thousands of men, social authority/leadership and ideological inspiration, but also social mores, have to interact in a particular way. Some must, probably recklessly, act. Others must be moved to emulation, or required to follow by the structures of power, or a combination of both. Still others must be intimidated or flee. It is to the social dynamics of the outbreak of the rebellion, therefore, that we must now turn.

CHAPTER 5

'The English Steel We Could Disdain':
the Outbreak of the Rebellion

Around nine o'clock at night on 8 September 1715 Lord Justice Clerk Cockburn received an alarming message from his sister. Her husband, Dr William Arthur, had let slip that there was to be an attempt to seize Edinburgh castle by a *coup de main* that very night.[1] Wasting no time, Cockburn sent messengers running through the streets of Edinburgh to the magistrates and the Deputy Governor of the castle, Lieutenant-Colonel James Steuart, warning them of the impending attack. The magistrates promptly ordered an *ad hoc* patrol of Whig volunteers and city guards to sweep the area at the base of the castle walls.[2] Steuart, however, was difficult to reach and slow to react. By the time the message arrived the castle drawbridge was raised and the gates were all locked. As a consequence Cockburn's message did not reach him until after ten, and even then he 'made slight of it, whither out of knavrie or that he thowght it impracticable', and simply ordered the number of sentries increased and directed that they be put on alert.[3] The eighty or so plotters who were to storm the castle had, meanwhile, spent a happy evening toasting their presumptive success in various hostelries and private residences around Edinburgh.[4] From their various lodgings, taverns and private homes approx-imately forty of them assembled by the West Kirk, close to the south wall, at about nine, just as Cockburn was sounding the alarm. They were well armed, and their weapons had all been double-shotted so as to maximise the impact of their firing should they need to do so.[5] There they waited with increasing impatience for their 'ingeneer', Charles Forbes of Brux, who was supposed to be bringing specially lengthened rope ladders to supplement those Dr Arthur and his brother, Thomas, a former ensign in the Scots Guards and officer of the castle garrison, had brought with them, but which the conspirators feared were too short. Forbes, however, remained in a tavern drinking toasts to the success of the enterprise until after ten and did not rendezvous with his comrades before they were discovered.[6] About 11 p.m. one of the four castle sentries the plotters had suborned whispered down to them that they had better hurry for he was due to be replaced in an hour, and in desperation the plotters told him to lower the lead weight attached to a length of whipcord he had been supplied with in advance. He did so, and they quickly attached this to a grapnel tied to one of the rope ladders they had with them. The sentry hauled up the grapnel and wedged it to bear the weight of the ladder and the plotters, only to find, as the plotters had feared, that the rope ladder was 'above a fathome [six feet] too short'.[7] By this point, John Holland, another of the suborned sentries, who had been ordered to patrol along the walls down towards the sally port, was beginning to get nervous. When he saw his co-conspirator, James Thomson, on his stomach hauling up the grapnel he warned him to make haste. Thomson at this point decided the game was up, and called down to the Jacobites, 'God damn you all! You have ruined both yourselves and me! Here comes the round I have been telling you of this hour. I can serve you no longer', and threw down the grapnel. He and Holland then shouted, 'enemie!' and fired their muskets.[8] The Jacobites took the hint and promptly scrambled down the rocks to disperse into the city. All of them succeeded in doing so except Captain Allan Maclean, an old veteran of James II and VII's army, who fell and twisted his knee and was captured, and a couple of tardy Jacobites who came along late and were caught by the patrol sent round by the magistrates.[9]

Even though the attempt on the castle failed, it was so daring and so tellingly directed at the symbolic heart of government power in Scotland that it sent a *frisson* of fear through the Jacobites' enemies. Solicitor-General Steuart spoke for many relieved Whigs when he observed with fearful admiration, 'it was the best laid project ever I knew them engaged in and managed with the most secrecy considering how many must of necessity have been concerned in it'.[10] If they could come so near to success with one covert operation, and the government none the wiser until the very last moment, what else might the Jacobites have secretly planned? Fear that other Jacobite plots for sudden *coups de main* might be afoot ran through the ranks of the government's supporters, and the attempt was taken as evidence of a Jacobite master plan.[11]

But in fact it was not. It was a local initiative, put together on the fly by a couple of Jacobite activists and their friends through personal contacts with minimal involvement from the Jacobite élite beyond Midlothian.[12] Maclean, one of the few conspirators caught by the authorities, had been recruited for the assault only the very morning it was due to go off.[13] The rope ladders, as we have seen, were being adapted at the very last minute. The fact that the attack was about to take place was an open secret in the taverns frequented by the conspirators.[14] Only about half of the conspirators actually turned up at the West Kirk at the appointed time, and, crucially, Forbes of Brux was late. The only substantive outside help the Arthur brothers and their friends received was from Edward Drummond, Marquess of Drummond, who sent a small body of Highlanders, commanded by one Alexander Macgregor, to infiltrate the city and support their assault on the castle.[15] And, with consummate irony, an experiment carried out by General George Wade in 1727 indicates the whole operation was totally misdirected. Concerned about the castle's vulnerability to surprise attack, Wade selected four of his soldiers and had them try to get into the fortress. Without benefit of any equipment beyond their hands and feet and Wade's skilful military engineer's eye directing them, they slung their muskets on their backs, scrambled up the rocks at the spot their general had selected and were inside within five minutes.[16] Improvisation, enthusiastic amateurishness and spontaneity were the keynotes of the whole affair.

And that, in fact, makes the attempt on Edinburgh castle absolutely typical of the way in which the rebellion broke out across Scotland and northern England. There was supposed to be a grand plan, concerted by Mar with the rest of the Jacobite leadership, for everyone to rise on 15 September 1715.[17] In reality some, like Mar and the Arthur brothers, moved early, others late, the ultimate example of these being the gloriously tardy Caithness Jacobites, who did not make their move until the end of January 1716, when the rebellion was on the verge of disintegration.[18] The upshot of this is that the outbreak of the '15 should be thought of as a rolling process rather than a discrete event. And because each local uprising sprang from a local, community-derived chemistry, the way they unfolded offers us a direct insight into the sociology of the rebellion as a whole. This will be the subject of the next section.

Rebellions are, nonetheless, fundamentally military events. The whole point of the '15 was to create a rebel army to defeat and overthrow the government. To understand the course of the rebellion after its initial outbreak, then, we need first to look at the nature of the military machines opposed to each other in Scotland and northern England in the autumn and winter of 1715–16. The government, as much as the Jacobites, was engaged in hurriedly putting together a force capable of routing its opponents. Understanding their respective achievements, or lack of them, in this push to construct a viable army will open the way to a better appreciation of why the clash of arms outlined in the chapters that follow came out as it did. This will compose the second part of the chapter.

Sliding towards Civil War 1714–15

We have already seen that both sides, Tory/Jacobite and Whig, had been mentally and materially preparing themselves for a civil war in Scotland since 1708.[19] It was natural, given the nature of élite society in Scotland, for the growing political tension between the two periodically to express itself violently before ever the rising took place. This stemmed from the everyday rhythms and mores of élite society in Scotland. As part of the regular round of sociability Jacobites and Whigs were obliged to rub shoulders. Neighbourly hospitality, weddings, funerals, hunting parties – virtually all were bound to be cross-party affairs, given that Tory/Jacobite and Whig adherence cut across family lines at every level.[20] And sometimes in the heat of political passion, or inebriation, words would be exchanged, attitudes and even blows struck and violence follow.[21] *Prima facie*, this would appear to be direct evidence of the slide to war. There is, however, a methodological problem with taking such behaviour as part of a general drift towards civil strife: the Scots élite had been fighting and killing each other in duels and personal combats for hundreds of years and would continue to do so until the end of the eighteenth century.[22] It is thus very hard to be certain there was any political content to a particular act of interpersonal violence. To take only one example: Sir John Shaw was walking away from the law courts in Edinburgh in July 1715, having just lost an inheritance case before several Lords of Session who were subsequently to be dubbed the 'Bar Le Duck' (i.e. Jacobite) Lords for their decision. Shaw's opponent at law was John Houstoun of Houstoun, who was a notorious Jacobite and, in so far as there was any longer a head, the head of his name (in times past the tie to the head of the name in the Lowlands was almost equivalent to clan allegiance in the Highlands). So when Sir John Shaw encountered one James Houstoun on the street it did not take long for him to take umbrage at something Houstoun said or did. Sir John then 'struck with his kain when James was not lookeing that way, and imediatly drew and gave him two wounds before James could get his sword drawen', before fleeing.[23] The Lord Justice Clerk, James Houstoun's brother-in-law, was incensed, and claimed that Shaw simply lashed out at the first Houstoun he encountered, which is certainly possible.[24] On the other hand, the Lord Justice Clerk's fellow Whigs were much more sympathetic to Shaw. Lord Advocate Dalrymple regarded it as 'a rencounter', code for a 'legitimate' duel, and pointedly cited Shaw's services to the Whig cause as grounds for leniency:

Every body that knows Sir John's interest in the country must regrate that he is at this time disabled to doe the service to the government for which he is particularly fitted, for he armed 600 men and had them in readyness before the Queen's decease, for the common caus, and . . . the same hart and dependence on their master remaines and would be of more use than any one man of his country.[25]

Shaw's friends, and Houstoun's partial recovery from his wounds, seem to have enabled him to escape prosecution, and he subsequently fought bravely at Sherrifmuir alongside Islay.[26] As will easily be appreciated, it is hard to say what lay at the root of this incident. Was political tension involved, or was Shaw just a genteel thug?

There is a sense that civil order was eroding in Scotland during 1714 and 1715. In the spring of 1714, after a number of incidents in which Whigs wearing a particular party badge, a silver-trimmed hat, had been set upon by Edinburgh Jacobites, a group of élite Whigs were making their way back from dinner together when they encountered 'about a dozen of them in the habit of gentlemen, most of em with swords, others appeared to be writer lads. They begun with singing "the King shall Enjoy his own Again", then they cursed the Queen, Hanover, the Whigs and traced hats, and called "God blesse King James the 8th"'. The Whigs chose, initially, not to be provoked, but 'they began to throw stones at us, and [Lord]Forester, who was going to the bagnio in a chair, could not bear it, but got out of his chair, and lugged out his sword and made at these fellows who run all way. He cutt on or two of them so as to spoill their cloaths, and we, seing no resistance made, thought it best not to medle in it but allow him to beat the dozen of Jacobites by himself.' One of those wounded subsequently turned out to be a Tory justice of the peace.[27]

Over the year that followed there were more clashes of this kind, such as when some Crieff Jacobites took against an excise officer named Macallan who had boisterously celebrated George I's accession and 'brok in to the house where he was abed in the dead hour of night, and being twelve in number fell upon him and wounded him in the neck and breast. But their chief aim was to cut one of his ears out of his head, which they did and then went of.'[28] Equally nastily, one Geddes, a gentleman servant of James Carnegie, Earl of Southesk, who had a habit of forcing people at country festivities to toast James Stuart's health, 'dragged some people through a miln head for refusing it'.[29] When four or five Jacobites taunted a detachment of Whig volunteers in August 1715, a sentry opened fire on them, and the whole company then turned out and 'persued and fired' at the fleeing Jacobites, bringing down one of their number. Rather than being concerned to investigate the breakdown of civil order implicit in the affray, Lord Justice Clerk Cockburn instead exulted, 'so the first blood is drawn by those of our side'.[30] By summer 1715 the civic authorities in some cities, such as Aberdeen, were also clearly losing control of their communities. A visitor who was present on 10 June (James's birthday) in Aberdeen witnessed Jacobites openly drinking their king's health, lighting bonfires and discharging firearms in the streets. Even patrols by some of the troops garrisoned there did not dampen their enthusiasm. 'The hands of the magistrates', he opined, 'are much weakened by gentlemen of the shires residing in the place, who support and encourage the faction by talking openly in the coffee house, and other publick places, things reflecting on the Government both civil and ecclesiastick, and influencing the tradesmen to all the disorders they committ.'[31] The leaders of the rural social order, the heritors, were clearly setting themselves against the leaders of the urban social order, the municipal magistracy. By mid-June the magistrates of Aberdeen felt that only a continued military presence could prevent their being driven out by the students of the university, and when, despite their pleas, the troops were withdrawn, Jacobite mobs 'broke in to the warehouse and committed great disorders and threaten the magistrates' houses'.[32] The local Whigs retaliated in kind. When Alexander Gordon of Auchlyne junior heard a group of Jacobites was going to proclaim James VIII he and his servant attacked them and wounded nine of their number. Gordon proudly boasted, 'itt was the the first blood that was drawen, and the first advantage, that was obtained in Scotland in your Majesty's cause'.[33] Nor was the situation any better in parts of rural Scotland. Near Glasgow a gang of 30–40 Tory/Jacobite heritors were 'sculking from place to place neare the border, threatening and insulting the friends of the government upon all occasions', and George Keith, Earl Marischal, was repairing the fortifications of Dunnottar castle.[34]

Most ominously of all, the increasingly visible Jacobite preparations for a rising in the end provoked an equally bellicose reaction on the Whig side. The vehicle for this reaction was an association for 'the support and defence of his Majesty King George, our only rightful sovereign, and of the Protestant succession now happily established', which was formed in late July and publicly promulgated its agenda in early August.[35] To the modern eye the term 'association' smacks of nothing more sinister than community philanthropy or civic activism; indeed, the existence of a lively set of voluntary associations is generally regarded as betokening a healthy body politic.[36] In early eighteenth-century Scotland it had a quite different resonance. Associations of the kind formed in the summer of 1715 had antecedents stretching back to the civil strife of the late sixteenth century, were explicitly military in purpose and implicitly set themselves above the law.[37] The Associators of 1715 were armed zealots, primarily motivated by religion, and pledged to maintain the status quo by whatever means necessary. Their motivation stemmed in equal parts from fear of Jacobite invasion and fear for the Presbyterian religious order in Scotland. The Jacobite enemy, they asserted, threatened 'to involve these nations in blood and confusion, and wreath the yoke of popery and slavery about our necks', and the Associators pledged themselves

> to stand by and assist one another, to the utmost of our power . . . against all open and secret enemies, for the preservation and security of our holy religion, civil liberties, and most excellent constitution, both in church and state; and for that effect, we bind and oblige our selves, upon the first notice of the Pretender his landing in any part of Britain, or upon advice of any insurrection, or appearance of his friends and abettors at home in a hostile manner, for the support and assistance of the said Pretender, when he shall land, that upon such notice and advice, we shall assemble and meet together with our best arms and furniture, whether for foot or horse service, according to our stations and abilities at _____ and being there met, we oblige our selves, to the best of our power, to comply with, and obey such orders, as we shall receive from the government, for the supporting of his Majesty King George his person and government, and in defence of our sacred and civil liberties, in opposition to the Pretender and all his abettors.[38]

And the call was swiftly taken up all over southern Scotland.

Within two weeks companies and regiments of Association volunteers were being formed, and groups of vigilantes composed of Association members were being used by government officials to guard and patrol areas felt to be under threat from a Jacobite rising.[39] A further association, this time pledging to donate money to the cause, was also formed, and exhortations to stand up against 'an invasion of a Pretender to the crown, who has been educated in all the maxims of popish bigotry and French tyranny, and now comes against us with an army of Irish cut-throats, assisted (as we have no reason to doubt) by the grand enemy to the reformed interest in Europe, who hath embrued his hands so much in protestant blood [i.e. Louis XIV]', were being generally published and reinforced with enthusiasm from the pulpits of kirks across Scotland.[40] All the Associators asked of the authorities was arms, some officers to train them and orders; they would do the rest.[41] The government's officers in Scotland were understandably delighted with this outpouring of loyalism and almost unanimous in requesting the king's blessing and support for the Association movement.[42]

They were correspondingly very surprised when the ministry's response was distinctly cool. George I and his ministers expressed their appreciation of the Scots Whigs' zeal, but 'his Majesty hopes there will not be any occasion for their proceeding at this time any further in this matter'.[43] Just in case the government's officers did not take the hint, a second, private, letter clearly laid out the ministry's opposition to the whole project:

> After my Lord Tounshend and Mr Secretary Stanhope had signed the inclosed to your Lordship which was late yesternight, they directed me to acquaint you, that tho the not proceeding further at this time in the matter of the Association, is in a manner only insinuat, as what there seems no occasion for at this time, which they thought was sufficient in a letter which is to be communicated to so many, yet they are desirous your Lordship should know, that his Majestie's sentiments are that it should be lett fall altogether, of which your Lordship will make the proper use, as you may find occasion.[44]

The ministry, it appears, did not want any popular mass movement of Scots in arms, however loyal its intentions might be, as may also be implicit in the instructions issued to the newly appointed Lord-Lieutenants at the end of August (at a point when the ministry was beginning to relax, in the belief that the crisis was over): 'You are, at all times, to avoid the summoning, calling out, and assembling, disciplining or arming any of the Fensible men or heretors, concerning whom there can be any doubt as to their affection to our government.'[45] Given that anyone who had doubts about the Union was open to the imputation of 'disaffection', by 1715, this was tantamount to excluding a great many thoroughly non-Jacobite Scots from any military mobilisation in Scotland.[46] The Jacobites soon caught wind of what lay behind the official discountenancing of the Association and were 'so vilainous and impudent as to tell us that we are as little trusted as they are'.[47] Not surprisingly, Whitehall's response angered many Scots Whigs. President Dalrymple, for one, could not restrain himself from sarcastically observing, 'I rejoyce that our danger is so far over that ther is no need of extraordinary methods.'[48] The ministry, however, was unmoved, and in mid-August the Lord Justice Clerk was further instructed to 'take the most prudent and discreet method for preventing the country's proceeding any further in that matter of association and levying of troops', though the ministers did not want their intervention publicised and so the message was 'only in confidence to your Lordship'.[49]

The chilly official response from the king and Cabinet at Westminster does not diminish the significance of the short-lived Association movement for

Scotland. It was a token, and a powerful one, of how badly polarised Scottish society had become by the eve of the rising. Civil society was on the verge of eclipse.

The Rebellion Begins

Rebellions, like politics, are always local. In each case the élite Jacobites who were the initiators of the rebellion were responding to their local circumstances in a fashion that made sense for them and the onlookers they were trying to impress. It was, naturally enough, a highly symbolic moment and one they really wanted to get right, in the sense of conveying an appropriate feeling of solemn occasion while physically demonstrating the power of the new, Jacobite, order.

In the rural Highlands there was a matter-of-fact quality to the coming-out of the rebel *fine*. This clearly arose from the lingeringly bellicose nature of the clan system and the martial mien as yet maintained by the *fine* despite their growing role as the clan's land managers and principal businessmen.[50] Thus long before ever he committed himself openly to the uprising Huntly was purchasing and locating horses suitable for military use amongst his tenants, and had accumulated some 600, 'well equipt', by the beginning of August. He had, too, been 'using them to drum and to bide fire', i.e. inuring the horses to the din of the battlefield. So in September, when he finally decided he would come out in rebellion, Huntly's men were prepared and 'well appointed'.[51] He mustered them in systematic fashion, 'drawing out only the best and ablest of his men, to the number of eight out of every Paroch', first in a series of small rendezvous, then in one large one at Huntly castle. Each ploughland was also allotted a share of the burden of equipping Huntly's men with coats, plaids, trews and so on.[52] The Highland infantry were then sent off to Perth on 22 September and Huntly's Lowland levies on 4 October.[53] Throughout the whole process Huntly was utterly methodical about preparing for, and then marching to, war. He may not even have bothered publicly to proclaim James VIII before he got to Aberdeen on his own journey south. Ideology aside (and many of the common people in the region were undoubtedly Jacobite sympathisers, if for no other reason than that they were Catholic or Episcopalian),[54] it was legally and morally sufficient for most of his tenants that the Marquess was 'hosting and hunting'; their tacks laid down that they should attend him, and so they did.[55]

Elsewhere in the Highlands things did not always run quite so smoothly, but they were very much in the same pragmatic vein. Alexander Macdonald of Glengarry took his own time to mobilise his men and did not finally march off to join the rising until 24 September, when he defiantly paraded 500 of them past the isolated garrison of Fort William.[56] Before then he carefully eliminated the small detachment of government troops who had been placed in his house at Invergarry, capturing them all without bloodshed (this was probably coordinated with the seizure of Tioram castle and its garrison by Allan Macdonald, Captain of Clanranald, around the same time), and wrote a polite letter to Sir Robert Pollock, the commander at Fort William, disingenuously justifying his action on the grounds that he did it 'for the safety of the poor people who were threatned by the souldiers that they would fall upon them in absence if they should go from home and relieving my self of the many oppressions I suffered'. Glengarry then apologised for not being able immediately to parole his prisoners, made it clear that he had no complaints about Pollock's personal conduct towards him, promised that the Jacobite army would behave with restraint towards enemy property and genteelly stated that he hoped, 'since its not the quarrel of private gentlemen or noblemen', Pollock would deal civilly with Glengarry's wife and family while he was away.[57] The Camerons of Lochiel had even more of a problem with Fort William because of its proximity to the clan's heartland, and John Cameron, the *de facto* chieftain (Sir Ewen Cameron being in his dotage), found it very difficult to raise his men. At least four 'principal gentlemen of the Camerons' apparently refused to follow him, presumably because of the threat posed to their lands in Lochaber by Fort William, and in Morvern his men were 'threatned by Argyle's friends to be used with utmost rigour if they rise with their chief'.[58] In the end Cameron was obliged to supplement the numbers of *fine* (the traditional junior officers of the clans) willing to turn out by appointing common clansmen as officers, and was only finally able to follow his peers off to war on 24 October.[59] As with Huntly, proclamations of James VIII and other grand symbolic acts never seem to have featured prominently in anything done by these chieftains to raise their men; as was to be exactly the case among the Whig clans, all the organisation and inspiration was provided (or not) by the regular institutions of clan society.[60]

The rising in the Lowlands and northern England took rather different form. In both regions the internal, customary structure used to mobilise their men by the clan chieftains no longer existed and so power had to be seized, men of authority recruited or intimidated, and so on, by very different methods. The seizure of power in Dundee and Perth in September 1715 is representative of the way this worked.

The town council in Dundee had been badly split along party lines for some time. Several members of the council were open frequenters of the Episcopalian chapel and on 10 June 1714 at least two of their number,

Alexander Watson and Alexander Wilson, openly drank James's health by the market cross.[61] Another councilman, John Oliphant, was convicted in early July 1715 of 'bidding God damn King George's blood' in January, and, according to the local Whigs, disaffection remained rife on the council even when these three were removed.[62] The local Jacobite heritors were in contact with this Jacobite municipal élite and were duly covered by them when the government ordered watches posted and searches made for suspects amongst the rural élite. By 8 September it was being reported to the Lord Justice Clerk that the local Jacobites were about to seize the town, and though this prediction proved premature it may be an indication of a developing debate amongst the Jacobites as to when and how to act.[63] The looming crisis, however, panicked the leading pro-Whig elements and they desperately begged for government troops to be sent, 'or els we'll be forced to fly the town'.[64] A group of Angus heritors, led by William Graham of Duntrune, finally rode in to seize the town on 16 September. There they rendezvoused with a number of armed Jacobite sympathisers led by Baillie Rolstone, Oliphant and Watson, and together formally proclaimed James VIII at the market cross. Graham then produced a Jacobite patent ennobling him as Viscount Dundee (he was a collateral descendant of John Graham of Claverhouse, first Viscount Dundee and victor of the battle of Killiecrankie in 1689) and assumed authority over the local rebellion and town alike, dispatching parties to seize the magazine, the castle, the port and the castle of Brockly. An oath of allegiance to James was then administered to the municipal élite and those who would not take it were imprisoned. The Whig party at this point bolted, leaving behind their families, 'and what outrages may be committed on them we know not'; moreover, 'our shops since we came off are pillaged by his order'.[65] The next day, to drive home the point that the new order was now in charge, the market cross was solemnly covered with carpet, the church bells were rung, a formal loyal toast was drunk and James was publicly proclaimed king of Scots, in a form that may well have been standard wherever the Jacobites seized power in Lowland communities north of the Tay:

> Whereas the crown and royal dignities of this kingdome did by undoubted right of succession and inheritance devolve upon King James the eight our present gracious and dread soverain by the decease of the late King James the seventh, his father, of blessed memory. And whereas during the late usurpations this his Majestie's ancient kingdom was reduced to a very miserable and deplorable condition by many heavy and insupportable grievances and burdens, particularly by the late unhappy Union. Therefore

we his Majestie's most dutifull and loyall subjects, by his Majestie's special command, do publish and proclaim his Majestie King James the 8th our lawfull and undoubted soverain of these kingdoms, and exhort all his Majestie's faithfull subjects to concurr with us in vindicating his sacred Majestie's undoubted right and establishing our ancient happy constitution against popery, rebellion and all its other enemies and in dissolving and putting an end to that unhappy Union.[66]

In one fell swoop Dundee was captured, purged and secured.

Perth's experience was very similar, despite the complication added by Atholl having posted some 200 or so of his men in the town to defend it against precisely such a Jacobite *coup d'état*.[67] Perth was the gateway to the Highlands and naturally featured in the Jacobites' plans from the very inception. The first rendezvous of the forces generated in the various local risings was set by Mar at Tibbermore, a few miles west of the town, and Jacobite plans to march on through Perth to Stirling clearly show they assumed they would take it.[68] The Whig magistrates in control of Perth also assumed they were liable to attack in any Jacobite rising and had disarmed as many local Tories/Jacobites as they could and tried to repair the town's defences.[69] John Hay of Cromlix (the future Jacobite Earl of Inverness) nonetheless met with two Jacobites from Perth in August to coordinate its seizure, and on 17 September turned up on the other side of the Tay with about forty horse drawn mainly from Fife heritors who had taken up arms but not yet organised themselves into a body (or, apparently, decided what to do next) and so were 'skulking' in Perthshire.[70] The Perth Jacobites promptly seized a number of boats on the river and ferried Hay's force across before moving into the town with them to confront 120 of Atholl's Highlanders and 40 or so local Whigs who were drawn up, ready to fight, in the town centre. Atholl's Highlanders then asked the Provost of Perth if they should fire, but he appears to have been so daunted by the prospect of civil strife on the streets of his town that he replied, 'no blood, no blood', and a truce was agreed whereby the local Whigs surrendered their arms, and those of the Highlanders who did not want to remain were allowed to leave freely.[71] 'Immediately thereafter all the burgers who adherd to the magistrats were made prisoners till such time as they deliverd all their arms', and then released on parole.[72] Several prominent local Whigs promptly took the opportunity to flee the town. Hay and the Jacobites meanwhile seized all the available weapons and public moneys (aided by James Freebairn, the local Collector of the Excise) and then amidst pealing bells solemnly processed to the market cross, draped it with carpet and proclaimed James VIII king of Scotland. The whole Jacobite force 'then

made their hussas and cried "No Hannoverian!", "No Popery!", "No Union!",
before settling into residence.[73]

Implicit within these two cases are a number of key elements. In each a
well-known local Jacobite leader took decisive control. There was also planning and collusion between rural and urban Jacobites. Having secured the
town, principally by purging or intimidating the local Whigs, there was as
solemn a public confirmation of the new order as possible, with everything
done according to the customary forms associated with the accession of a
monarch, down even to the drinking of the loyal toast in ritual form by all
those assembled, 'otherwise the ceremonie was null and voide'.[74] As far as
possible the regular routine of government, from commercial regulation to
tax collection (though at pre-Union Scottish rates), was immediately
resumed.[75] At the same time, the normative values of eighteenth-century
Scottish society were clearly affirmed in the personal conduct of the Jacobite
conquerors. In Perth, a Whig correspondent admitted: 'they give no distur-
bance to the inhabitants but pays for what they get'.[76] Contemporary Scottish
cultural norms were also ostentatiously upheld, hence the paradox of a
Catholic monarch's proclamation being serenaded by his erstwhile Protestant
subjects with enthusiastic cries of 'No popery!' And crucially, there was no
serious military opposition, on the part of either local Whigs or regular
troops, to the seizure of power in Perth, Dundee or any of the other towns
captured by the Jacobites at this time.[77]

When all these factors did not fall into place quite so well matters could
easily hang fire or go awry. A fair few Jacobite heritors, like the Fife Horse who
helped Hay capture Perth, got out their weapons, mounted themselves and a
couple of servants and then wandered around for a while simply looking for
someone to join.[78] This of course made the seizure of power in selected towns
by more decisive Jacobite leaders all the more important, as they thereby
created Jacobite bases towards which these individuals could gravitate.
Indeed, Sinclair later observed of the capture of Perth that without it the
'whole designe must have proven abortive, for there was no other place where
an armie could [have] been formed'.[79] A major problem for the Jacobites who
came out for William Gordon, Viscount Kenmure, was that he failed to
capture Dumfries (largely because of the united hostility of the local community) or any other major town in the Borders to use as a base.[80] Kenmure's
force was consequently condemned to wander from one small burgh to the
next proclaiming James and essentially looking for something to do, and other
Jacobites like Sir Patrick Maxwell of Springkell, who had not joined Kenmure
at his first rendezvous, had considerable difficulty locating and joining him as
a result.[81] Probably the most dramatic instance of this problem and its

consequences may be seen in the attempted rising in Midlothian of George Seton, Earl of Winton. Winton had accumulated a large arsenal and conspicuously failed to appear when summonsed on 15 September despite living within an hour of Edinburgh. Then on 16 September he 'ordred his vassals and tennents to rendevouse . . . at Pinkie Park dyke, where he was to furnish them with arms and ammunition'.[82] He mustered 2–300 tenants, including his colliers, but then dithered, uncertain what to do next.[83] Winton was apparently acting alone, as the local Jacobites had agreed at a number of secret meetings – including one at least where he was personally present – not to rise unless Mar crossed the Forth or James landed in Scotland.[84] He was also unsure of the reception he would receive if he marched on the towns of Haddington or Dalkeith, and so when Argyll sent two troops of dragoons and a cannon to deal with him the next day his uprising collapsed and the dragoons 'found he had crossd in a boat to Fife that morning [18 September] with 12 men well armed'.[85]

Almost any level of military opposition could upset the process of rebellion. The northern English Jacobites, after an extended period of 'skulking', decided that 'since there was no safety any longer in shifting from place to place', they might as well openly rebel, and mustered sixty horse at Greenrig on 6 October.[86] They then rode into Warkworth where their putative leader, Thomas Forster, 'by the sound of trumpet, and all the formality that the circumstances and place would admit',[87] proclaimed James III in traditional style:

> Whereas by the laws and constitution of these realms our native born prince James the third immediatly upon his father's demise had the sole, unquestionable right to these his paternall hereditary dominions and our gratious sovereign now com[in]g to assert his own right and relieve his kingdoms from the tyrannical oppression, arbitrary power and forraign yoake under which they groan. Therefore, we noblemen, gentlemen and others, his Majesty's faithfull subjects being now met together in obedience to his royall commands and being fully resolved to spend our lives and fortunes in his Majesty's service for the promoting his happy restoration, the re-establishment of the constitution in church and state and the deliverance of our native country, do hereby unanimously and in concert with others, his dutyfull subjects in many different parts of these realms, with heart and voice proclaim, notifie and declare to all men that the most august and high born prince James the third, by the grace of God King of England, etc, Defender of the Faith, is the only rightfull and lawfull soveraign of these realms to whom alone we acknowledge our allegiance

and subjection to be due, inviting hereby all his Majesty's faithfull and loyall subjects of both nations to joyne with us in his service and promiseing to stand by them in the prosecuting of these glorious ends.[88]

However, Forster rather detracted from the impact of the ceremony on the onlookers by officiating 'in disguise'.[89] Casting around for their next move, Forster and Derwentwater turned towards Newcastle, where they apparently hoped there would be so many Jacobite sympathisers they would be able to take the city easily. This was not entirely beyond the bounds of possibility given that many expatriate Scots worked as keelmen there, and there were Jacobite sympathisers amongst them.[90] Forster and Derwentwater, however, seem to have coordinated no specific plans to this end with the city's Jacobites, and the Jacobites' alleged leader, Sir William Blackett, responded to the crisis by initially keeping himself 'out of the way', and subsequently turning himself in to the authorities.[91] Though they had by this time grown to a force of about 300 horse, of whom approximately a third were Scots from the Borders, they were completely disconcerted when the Whig magistrates barricaded the entrances to the city, summoned in the local militia and gentry volunteers and armed 700 loyalists to defend it, and so turned back to take Hexham, which was undefended.[92] Perfectly to underscore the point that any kind of vigorous resistance could overthrow the Jacobites' plans, such as they were, another small, but daring, group of Jacobites led by Lancelot Errington briefly seized Holy Island only to be promptly attacked and captured by a scratch force of militia and regulars out of Berwick.[93]

Hepburn of Keith's experience illustrates the same phenomenon north of the border. Hepburn was prepared and ready to rise in terms of weapons and horses, and clearly intended to rebel at the first opportunity, but was apparently waiting for others to come out so that he could join them. He thus found himelf besieged in his home by Dr Sinclair of Hermiston and a posse of Sinclair's and Thomas Hamilton, Earl of Haddington's servants and tenants, 'indifferently armed, three of them having only staves'.[94] Challenged by Hepburn to show his authority for arresting him, Sinclair produced his commission, upon which Hepburn declared, 'God damn him and the Lord Marquess [of Tweeddale, the Lord-Lieutenant], and bid him dight his breech with the commission', then attempted to fight his way out of the house. In the struggle that ensued one of Hepburn's sons was killed and Hepburn unhorsed and driven back into the building while the rest of the party (composed of Hepburn's other son, two of his brothers and two servants) cut their way through the besiegers. Hepburn subsequently escaped after the people of Keith attacked Sinclair's party 'with forks and flails', and then skulked in the nearby woods until Mackintosh of Borlum crossed the Forth and he could join him.[95] Even more ignominiously, Sir Thomas Bruce of Hope and Robert Balfour, Lord Balfour, took a small party of Fife Jacobites into Kinross to proclaim James VIII. The weather was, however, bad, so they retired to Bruce's home to socialise instead, only to be surprised there by John Leslie, Earl of Rothes, at the head of a troop of dragoons and a body of Fife Whig heritors on their way to retrieve some arms Rothes had stockpiled at his home at Leslie. The Jacobites ran for it, and Bruce was finally caught hiding in the gardens and carried back in triumph to Stirling by Rothes.[96]

It should be emphasised that the awe factor associated with any appearance of military expertise was not simply a Jacobite phenomenon. Apparently superior, or at least determined, Jacobite forces several times produced equal consternation amongst their Whig opponents. Just before the fall of Perth to the Jacobites Rothes tried to march the assembled *posse comitatus* of Fife to the aid of the Whig magistrates there. Few of the Fife heritors heeded his call to appear and only about 1,500 'mob', whom 'the ministers forced to goe', showed up at the muster.[97] The reluctant levies then convinced themselves that assembling on 'Cashmoor' was an ill omen, because of the terrible defeat suffered by the armies of the Covenant at Tibbermore at the hands of Montrose's Highlanders. They got progressively more jittery until they finally panicked at a (false) report that Jacobite Highlanders had taken Perth, threw away their arms and fled.[98] In like manner militia who believed they were about to fight Highlanders in Midlothian in October simply mutinied rather than march on to do battle.[99] And similarly, when Henry Lowther, Viscount Lonsdale, and William Nicolson, Bishop of Carlisle, led the Westmorland *posse comitatus*, numbering some 6–7,000 men, against the Jacobite army operating in northern England at Penrith they experienced an equally humiliating reverse. The Jacobites resolutely advanced towards them and the English levies threw down their weapons and fled.[100] Nor were Highlanders immune to being overawed in very similar fashion. When William Mackenzie, Earl of Seaforth, determinedly advanced on an army of Grants, Rosses, Munros, Gunns and others led by John Gordon, Earl of Sutherland, at the head of an army of 2–3,000 Mackenzies, Macdonalds, Mcleods, Mackinnons, Frasers and Chisholms, at the beginning of October, Sutherland's forces decided discretion was the better part of valour and promptly dispersed to their homes.[101] It is clear that on both sides the appearance, or reputation, of military expertise and a bold carriage were far more important in the first stages of a rising or a mustering of forces than any military reality.[102]

Creating an Army

Once the rebellion had begun and significant numbers of Jacobites and Whigs started drawing together with the intention of fighting each other the situation rapidly changed. Both sides had to try and create a serious military force as quickly as possible with whatever human and military resources they had to hand. Though the Whigs obviously held the advantage, controlling as they did the arsenals and stockpiles of other military stores held in fortresses like Edinburgh castle and Berwick, to say nothing of the hard core provided by the professional soldiers of the regular army, they, too, faced the same kinds of problems of organising and hurriedly training the militia, volunteers and levies mobilised for government service during the rebellion. The Jacobites also had the advantage of having strong support in the Highlands, where, as already noted, a more martial culture still prevailed. As Lord Advocate Dalrymple observed at the end of September:

> the people that have joined them [the regulars encamped at Stirling] from Glasgow and some other places are some of them very good and I hope for so far better [*sic*] then any as many of the highlanders, but their mob is better and more numerous than ours, and our volunteers are but of equal merite to theirs. The highlanders who are, as it were, born with arms in their hands have a kind of superiority or ascendant over men brought from keeping of catle or the plough to whom arms are more terrible till they are disciplined.[103]

Because of strategic decisions taken at Whitehall very early on in the rebellion with regard to the deployment of the professional forces of the crown throughout the three kingdoms, the recruiting and training of the rival armies in the actual theatres of conflict (Scotland and northern England) in essence became a race as to which army, Jacobite or Whig, could be brought to an adequate level of military competence first. Whichever of them got there first would have, at least briefly, a potentially decisive edge.

This brings us to a very salient question: how many Scotsmen and Englishmen appeared in arms for their respective monarch between September 1715 and March 1716? The evidence for this is for the most part impressionistic, so any numbers that may be suggested below must automatically be assumed to be approximate at best and informed guesswork at worst. Definitively the most accurate count of troops available stems from the regular returns of his troop strength compiled by Argyll's staff while his army was encamped at Stirling. These only related to the regulars under his command and they show a steady rise in the number of men available between September and the end of January 1716.[104] At the beginning of September no figures are available, but Sir Peter Fraser of Durres (a well-informed witness) specifically blamed the outbreak of the rebellion on the fact that there were only 600 regular troops stationed in Scotland.[105] This almost certainly does not take into account the garrisons of Fort William or Edinburgh castle, which probably added in the region of 400 more, to make a total of approximately 1,000 men.[106] This number, however, very rapidly expanded during the course of September as regiments were rushed north from England and shipped in from Ireland. By 1 October the field army of regulars at Stirling numbered 1,391 foot and 642 horse (2,033 total).[107] This increased somewhat by the end of the month, at which point Argyll had 1,511 foot and 679 horse, including Portmore's élite 'grey' dragoons. There was also a newly raised regiment of foot (Grant's) stationed in Edinburgh and a second élite dragoon regiment, Evans's 'black' dragoons, had arrived from Ireland and was on its way to Stirling, making a total of approximately 2,620 (1,813 foot and 807 horse) all found.[108] Further reinforcements then augmented Argyll's field army to roughly 3,700 (2,400 foot, 1,300 horse) by the time of the battle of Sherrifmuir on 13 November, though these numbers may include at least two squadrons (*c.* 330 men) of heritor Whig volunteer cavalry rather than regulars.[109] The substantial losses Argyll sustained at the battle took some time to replace and at the beginning of January 1716 his field army numbered just 3,358 (2,550 foot and 808 horse), plus two regiments of dragoons stationed in Glasgow (*c.* 300).[110] But later that month some 6,000 Dutch and Swiss infantry arrived, augmenting Argyll's total of regular troops to between 9,000 and 10,000.[111]

It is very hard to say how many men served in the government militia over the course of the rebellion. Though the Lord-Lieutenants mobilised the fencible men in virtually every county under government control, few of these militia regiments were kept together or under arms for any length of time. In part this was owing to misgivings about their political reliability, and in part to lack of military equipment.[112] Those kept in service were select units composed of men the Lord-Lieutenants regarded as politically trustworthy. Even so, Patrick Hume, Lord Polwarth, had to struggle to maintain just one regiment (about 300 men) until December.[113] There were probably in the region of about 2–3,000 of these militia in service at the height of the rebellion. More difficult still to assess are the numbers of the Whig volunteers of all ranks who turned out to fight for King George at various stages of the rebellion. Some of these were genuine volunteers, like the citizens of Edinburgh who defended the city against Mackintosh of Borlum in October, or the regiment of Glasgow volunteers who guarded the bridge at Stirling during the battle of Sherrifmuir and the heritor Whig volunteer cavalry who fought alongside Argyll's regulars.[114] At a guess, there may have been as many as 2,000 of these. Less clear cut, as to whether their service was voluntary or involuntary, is the participation of the clansmen mobilised by the Grants, Munros, Gunns, Rosses, Frasers and Campbells of Argyll, to say nothing of the few who adhered to Atholl. The strength of the government's forces in the north and west fluctuated dramatically during the course of the fighting, but there were roughly 3,000 in arms at the height of the conflict.[115] The very approximate total of Scots more or less willingly appearing in arms alongside the regulars, then, comes to about 8,000 men. The regulars, of course, also included Scots regiments, and both they and the other regular regiments vigorously recruited while they were waiting at Stirling (though some of their recruits were from the militia regiments already counted above), so there was also a strong Scots component among the regular forces of the crown.[116] This may be estimated at perhaps 1,000 men, making a maximum total of (very approximately) 9,000 Scots actively participating in the war on the government side.

On the Jacobite side the numbers involved are more difficult to assess. Once the rebellion was over those who had fought for King James were not keen to advertise the fact, and most of the records compiled by the Jacobite armies were destroyed either at the time of their surrender or after they dispersed. A handful of troop returns survive for the main Jacobite army at Perth, and there is a final count of the Jacobite army at Preston, in the sense that we know how many prisoners the government forces captured there (though not how many escaped); any broader estimate of the number of those involved in the central, western, northern and southern Jacobite campaigns must rely on anecdotal sources.[117]

That said, enough evidence survives to give a reasonable sense of the rise and fall of the Jacobite armies in terms of their relative strengths. The central Jacobite army, based in Perth, had reached a strength of 2,550 foot and 500 horse by the end of September.[118] As further local rebellions rolled on, more troops flowed in while others were detached for Mackintosh of Borlum's southern expedition, so that by mid-October the Jacobites' numbers there had risen only to 2,666 foot and 917 horse.[119] Thereafter the main Jacobite army grew significantly only by subsuming other Jacobite forces, notably the western Jacobite army that had hitherto been campaigning in Argyllshire and the northern Jacobite army that had been suppressing Whig resistance around Inverness. Approximately 2,500 foot joined the main army from the west and 2,000 foot and a few horse from the north.[120] In addition, about 200 foot from the southern army who were prevented from crossing the Forth straggled back to Perth, so the final tally on the eve of Sherrifmuir was in the region of 9,000 men (8,000 foot and 1,000 horse).[121] Government estimates also indicate that about 2,500 Jacobite foot were on detached duty elsewhere in Scotland at the time of the battle.[122] The army at Perth never recovered from its losses at Sherrifmuir and an account of the troops there, plus nearby detachments, that was probably compiled in early January 1716 comes to 4,105 foot and 269 horse.[123]

By early 1716 a northern army composed of Seaforth's and Huntly's men was back in existence, probably amounting to around 2,000 men, including an unknown number of horse.[124] The strength of the southern Jacobite army by all accounts fluctuated wildly. Before it crossed into England it may have numbered as many as 1,500 foot and 700 horse.[125] It then lost large numbers of men before it marched through Westmorland into Lancashire and on to Preston, by which time it was regaining strength. The government bag there was 688 English and 1,005 Scots, undifferentiated between horse and foot, but there were certainly more than that present on the day of the battle – as Patten delicately put it, 'a great many found means to escape'[126] (though probably many more English than Scots) – hence we may reasonably suppose that there were in the region of 1,000 English and 1,100 Scots in the southern army on 12/13 November. There were also local Jacobite units formed in Aberdeen and several Fife towns whose strength we have no means of assessing.

So the maximum Jacobite strength, on the eve of the battles of Sherrifmuir and Preston, was roughly 14,000 Scots and 1,000 English. At this point, however, we must take into consideration the impact of troop turnover on the respective sizes of the Jacobite and government armies. Armies are intrinsically dynamic institutions: soldiers are always dropping out through death, illness or desertion, while others are recruited or conscripted into their ranks as replacements or to expand the forces available. And since the number of combat casualties suffered by both armies in 1715 came in just two brief, though intense, moments during the campaign, and neither army was significantly affected by epidemic disease (usually the major cause of military mortality during this era), the main engines of turnover in the ranks of the government and rebel forces were recruitment/conscription and desertion.

Of all the government forces in Scotland only the regulars and the clans recruited very much. The militia and volunteers, once embodied, were not further augmented. The regulars had always to be recruiting in any event, but obviously made a particular effort during the autumn of 1715. The ministry in London authorised the addition of two extra companies (approximately 100 men) to each non-Irish regiment and offered lucrative bounties and unusually short terms of service to those who enlisted against the Jacobites;

there was apparently quite a good response from the Scots population south of the Tay.[127] This was sufficient to raise the average strength of Argyll's regular regiments from their peacetime level of about 200 to about 300. Unfortunately the government was then rather dilatory about paying the promised bounties and at the beginning of 1716 the Colonels of the regiments encamped at Stirling sent in a joint memorandum to Argyll, for transmission to the ministry, complaining that as a consequence, 'many of the men lately raised have deserted'.[128] Despite this problem late in the campaign, the general level of desertion among the regulars seems to have been low, the only instance of anything even mildly redolent of a mass event being the sixty or so brought over to the Jacobites by Arthur Elphinstone, Master of Balmerino, in January 1716.[129] By contrast, few details of the recruitment and desertion rates among the government militia and the Whig clan armies that served in Argyllshire and northern Scotland survive. Some militia units definitely contained men who regarded themselves as having been forced out, and so were prone to high rates of desertion, and others seem to have been very unenthusiastic, to the point where they took the first legal opportunity to disband themselves, despite pleas that they remain under arms.[130] We know that Argyll's Campbell clansmen generally obeyed his summons to defend Inverary and subsequently took against Islay (their commander) and deserted when he asked any more of them than home defence.[131] This army dissolved, moreover, when Islay dismissed them after the western Jacobite army withdrew. Colin Campbell of Fonab, on orders from Argyll, subsequently remobilised 300 of his Campbell clansmen to take part in Argyll's offensive against the Jacobite army in Perth in February 1716, but there is no indication whether they were the same men as had served before or fresh recruits.[132] Given that they were subsequently involved in a hard-marching, but bloodless, operation which was very lucrative from the point of view of the loot to be had, there does not appear to have been any significant amount of desertion from this body of clansmen.[133] The army of Whig clansmen first drawn together by Sutherland, on the other hand, was virtually entirely dispersed in early October after its near-encounter with the northern Jacobite army led by Seaforth.[134] It was then reconstituted by Sutherland with the help of Simon Fraser, Lord Lovat, at the beginning of November, but again whether these were the same men out in November as were out in October is impossible to say.[135] There was, furthermore, considerable turnover due to desertion in this reconstituted army owing to both the weather conditions, which were atrocious, and a basic disinclination to fight clan neighbours on the part of many ordinary clansmen.[136] In the round, however, it does seem reasonable to assume that many of the men in this second army had not served in the first mobilisation.

By contrast, the Jacobite army as a whole seems to have undergone considerable turnover, primarily due to desertion. This stemmed in large part from the way the Jacobite army was recruited. There were certainly a good many plebeian volunteers on the Jacobite side, and the southern Jacobite army, at least, was literally having to turn them away because they had no spare weapons with which to arm them.[137] Volunteer companies and troops of horse were also recruited in Jacobite towns like Elgin, Perth, Aberdeen, Arbroath and Brechin.[138] Plebeian Jacobites were also capable of voting with their feet when it came to demonstrating their political sympathies. When Atholl mustered his vassals, for example, he found they 'were mutinous', and 'treacherously running away and deserting from the place of randisvouz' to go and join Mar. He promptly tried to bully them into obedience by 'wounding' a couple of them, but instead, 'all of them . . . left him and joyned his son the Marques of Tullibarden except about 300 that were with the Duke in Blair castle'.[139] Yet without doubt the majority of Jacobite troops were brought out regardless of their political sympathies, in obedience to the orders of their landlords and clan chieftains. Even the Athollmen's apparent mass demonstration of pro-Jacobite sympathy is more ambiguous than appears at first sight. Who exactly deserted the duke on 16 September? Going by the post-rebellion count of Perthshire heritors who were out during the '15 (more than 130) his élite vassals turned against him wholesale, but what of the rank-and-file tenants?[140]

This brings us to the question of 'forcing'. After the rebellion was over almost every plebeian, and not a few élite, Jacobites claimed they were forced out against their will.[141] In some cases this was brazen effrontery, as when Coll Macdonald of Keppoch, chieftain of his clan and a notorious Jacobite and cattle thief, claimed to have been forced out by his putative superiors.[142] As everyone who had the misfortune to be one of his neighbours well knew, Macdonald of Keppoch always did precisely as he pleased. In other cases, there is probably a great deal more truth in the claim. Panmure's tenants were conscripted *en masse* into his regiment and ascribed their acquiescence to their 'being for the most part ignorant and inured to slavery', a claim which receives some validation from their subsequent resistance when Panmure tried to levy more men to replace those his regiment had lost at Sherrifmuir.[143] Mar himself applied the harshest coercion, as evidenced by the testimony of William Touch of Nether Kildrummy:

> they were forced and compelled to go out in the unhappy rebellion much against their inclination. And that they did to be free of the same flee from

their houses for severall dayes. And that by my Lord Marr's order, parties were sent, who did sett fire to their houses, and corn yards. And that after they had absconded for severall dayes, they were taken prisoners by the saids parties, and were sent prisoners to Braemar, where my Lord Marr then was.[144]

Drummond threatened his tenants with 'heading, hanging and burning our houses, destroying and takeing away our goods'.[145] Allan Macdonald, Captain of Clanranald, was, according to clan tradition, shot in the back by one of his own men at Sherrifmuir (symbolically, with a twisted silver sixpence), which betokens considerable resentment on the part of the ordinary clansmen at having been unwillingly dragged off to war.[146] Sir David Thriepland pressed his tenants 'to the rebelion mutch against there wills when a-couting the corns', and when one Patrick Duncan sought to resist, he 'was sor beat be Sir David for refoosing to obey him'.[147] The evidence for forcing having played a major role in the recruitment of the Jacobite army is overwhelming.[148]

It must be acknowledged, however, that the Jacobites' need to force people out may have arisen from something other than the basic unpopularity of their cause among the common people. In some areas where men had to be forced out the Jacobite cause was definitely unpopular, but in others it was not.[149] When he finally arrived in Scotland James was touched by the reception he received: 'the affection of the people', he told Bolingbroke, 'is beyond expression.'[150] Yet he was travelling through exactly the area where Panmure was at the same time having a good deal of trouble persuading more of his people to enlist in his regiment.[151] To take another example, in Strathdon, 'the rebellion was favoured by almost all the common people' in 1715.[152] Yet when their superiors tried to bring those common people out in rebellion, 'very few compeared, others told being the tyme of their harvest, the tennents could not come out'.[153] Therein lies part of the answer: the rebellion began literally in the middle of harvest time. In such circumstances, even the most enthusiastic of plebeian Jacobites (and Whigs) had pause for serious reflection before joining (or opposing) the rebellion.[154] Jacobite 'recruiters' also took by preference fit men of working age – men vital to the gathering of the harvest – leaving only women and children to get in the crops in some places.[155] The next Jacobite recruiting drive came in December and January – the depths of a winter so cold the Channel froze.[156] Hardly surprisingly, most ordinary Scotsmen were averse to leaving their homes at that time of year. Naturally enough, then, despite the popularity of the cause in large parts of northern Scotland the small producers of Scottish rural society resented additional trouble at those particular times of year and began to 'curse the Earle of Mar'.[157]

Resentment at being forced out had a natural corollary: those who had been pressed into service tended to find opportunities to slip away. Drummond's men, forced out at Comrie, some of them even while they were in church one Sunday, took the first opportunity to desert in droves when they were no longer under his eye. So did the men dragged away from the harvest by Sir David Thriepland, as doubtless did many others in the same situation.[158] The results could be dramatic: Mackintosh of Borlum lost at least 50 per cent of the force he brought over the Forth to desertion in the three weeks that followed his landing in Midlothian, and more just before he crossed into England.[159] Nor was it only the rank and file who absented themselves. The precipitous decline in the number of Jacobite cavalry, an arm composed disproportionately of heritors, well illustrates how widespread desertion had become amongst even élite Jacobites by early 1716.[160] For most of the rebellion, though, the desertion problem tended to be simply a low-level, steady drain that operated 'like a plague' on Jacobite resources of manpower.[161] Desertion was, though, not necessarily a final withdrawal from the Jacobites' ranks. An officer like Colonel Alexander Urquhart of Newhall could, and did, quietly abscond for a while, then drift back to the Jacobite army.[162] The same pattern appeared lower down the social scale. John Brodie, a slater, deserted after Sherrifmuir, but then rejoined three weeks later and stayed with the Jacobite army until it retreated to Dundee, when he deserted again.[163] A great many of the ordinary clansmen deserted after Sherrifmuir and some 'refuse[d] to come out again', even when threatened with 'the highest paines' by their superiors.[164] Others, however, were obliged/willing to take up arms and in all likelihood some of them were former deserters.[165] Indeed, upwards of 1,000 were already on their way back when Mar was compelled to begin his retreat north.

The upshot of this is that as we try finally to estimate how many men appeared in arms for King George and how many for King James we need to assume a turnover effect, particularly in the case of the Jacobite army. The maximum number of men in the vicinity of Perth at any one time may only have been in the region of 10,000, but many more were there, or elsewhere, in arms at some point during the rising. At a guess, the level of turnover in the Jacobite forces probably ran in the region of 50 per cent in Scotland and rather less in northern England (because the rising was very much briefer there). If this multiplier is roughly correct, it would suggest that something over 20,000 Scotsmen served, willingly or unwillingly, in the Jacobite armies in Scotland in 1715, and perhaps 1,200 Englishmen in northern England. Such numbers in Scotland are, interestingly, close to the maximum number (about 25,000) of men under arms for the Covenanters during the Great Civil War, and, since the population size of Scotland in the 1640s and 1710s was probably comparable and the Covenanters were unusually proficient at raising men, around 25,000 may represent the maximum number that any regime in this era could mobilise. The 20,000 men probably raised by the Jacobites in 1715 was certainly the largest number they ever mobilised in any of their risings in Scotland.[166] On the government side in Scotland, the clan followings were likely to have been the units that showed most turnover, which suggests, because they were a smaller proportion of the forces available, that a lower multiplier is appropriate for the government forces as a whole; say 15 per cent. This would put the size of the volunteer, militia and enlisted loyalist forces in Scotland at about 11,000 men. It is impossible to estimate how many volunteers and militia served on the government side in northern England because the evidence is so sparse and the geographic limits of an estimate would be so vague. Suffice it to say that they must have far outnumbered the native Jacobites who turned out to fight: the magistrates of Newcastle alone almost certainly mobilised more loyalist volunteers and militia than all the English Jacobites involved in the rising combined.[167]

Thus over 30,000 male Scots, or more than 12 per cent of the adult male population (in an early modern population approximately 25 per cent of the whole may be assumed to have been adult males), had direct experience of the rising through transient, or sustained, personal involvement. Of this 12 per cent, two-thirds (*c.* 8 per cent) served on the Jacobite side and one-third on the government side (*c.* 4 per cent). A handful may even have served on both sides.[168] To put these percentages in a modern perspective, if there was a Scots Nationalist Party rising in Scotland tomorrow that mobilised 8 per cent of the male population it would field an army in the region of 145,000 men (substantially larger than the modern British regular army). The sheer scale of the rising was impressive. If we add in the fact that the great majority of Jacobite troops, and a good many government troops, were recruited in Scotland north of the Tay, which at that time contained approximately half of the population, the proportion of adult males in that region who at some point experienced the war at first hand grows still larger (at a guess, something between 15 per cent and 20 per cent). Projecting the wider Scots experience, including women and children, is truly guesswork, but if we throw in women and children who probably saw their husbands, fathers, brothers and sons taken off to fight (some never to return), or witnessed the passage and/or casual depredations of the marching armies, the lives touched in Scotland by the rising may have been in the region of 50 per cent of the population. By dint of its limited geographic impact and the small numbers of native Jacobites involved the English experience of the rising (and its likely long-term impact) must have been proportionately far less than the Scots.

Training and Supply

Mobilising thousands of men was just the beginning of the process of creating an army. To be able to function as an effective military unit men must be armed and trained to fight. During the early modern era this was a function of the available pool of military experience: old soldiers both taught new recruits how to drill and fight and set them an example in actual combat.[169] In an emergency such as that prevailing in 1715 the pool of available trainers was thus generally set by the level of military experience in the population as a whole. Neither side had time or opportunity to import very much outside military talent; they had to go with what was locally available.

This gave the government forces a considerable advantage. The regular regiments opposing the rising, except for those newly raised in the summer of 1715, were largely composed of veterans of the War of the Spanish Succession. These veterans, who had been through the process of breaking down and building up incomers many times before, easily trained and socialised the new recruits brought into their midst. The results were very obvious in camp and on the battlefield: the old regular army regiments which had been properly maintained and disciplined by their colonels performed as well during the rising as they had done in Flanders and Spain during the war.[170] Those that had been neglected did not do as well, and it is easy to see why from Argyll's description of Echlin's regiment in 1715:

> The men, my Lord, are many of them old and little, the horses generally wrong turned and ill sized, the cloathing the very worst I ever saw – tho not old, the accoutrements both of men and horse unfit for service, and as I am informed have been worn these six years, the arms very bad, and the numbers incompleat. To the best of my memory not above twenty four men a troop the strongest, corporalls included.[171]

Nor were the newly raised regiments particularly impressive. Grant's foot, one observer noted, 'neither seem to have that assurance in themselves, nor are they able to beget that confidence in others, that regular troops easily obtain', and the new regiments thrown into the assault at Preston 'seemed unwilling to fight'.[172] The regulars' existence had, moreover, an odd down side, in that it made the militia and Whig volunteers more reluctant to risk themselves in combat; they preferred to leave it to the professionals. As Argyll bitterly observed in mid-October:

> our well affected people cannot be persuaded to defend themselves against the very smallest number of the rebells. Till they had arms and ammunition, from all corners of the country they assured me they would do wonders. Now they have them, whenever the smallest number of the rebells approaches they cry nothing can be done without regular troops, and wherever the rebells have sent any parties, they have not met with the least resistance.[173]

The old regulars were, nonetheless, an unmatchable advantage.[174] In addition to the embodied units of veterans, moreover, the government forces had access to a substantial number of 'half-pay' officers. These were former officers who were officially given a pension and semi-retired, in the sense that they had no regular duties, but who were recallable to the colours in time of need. Not all of them were of military value. Among their number there were always some who were superannuated, or so maimed they effectively could not serve, while others were virtual sinecurists with little or no real military experience. At this time, though, only three years after the end of a major war, most half-pay officers were still fit for service; all the government had to do was call them up. Which it did. All the new regular regiments, the militia and some of the volunteer units were quickly allotted a cadre of half-pay officers, who soon (for the most part) were busy training and drilling the men under their command and teaching the inexperienced officers elected or selected from their ranks how to do their jobs.[175] Many of the Whig clans were led by, or contained, half-pay officers of their own who could have trained them to fight in conventional military form, but in deference to the very different style of warfare prevailing in the Highlands left them to train and fight according to their own traditions.[176]

The Jacobites had a considerably greater problem with respect to knocking their recruits into shape. The great majority of officers, half-pay and otherwise, in Scotland and England, whether out of professionalism or political sympathy, cleaved to the government.[177] Though there were certainly more involved who managed to escape or conceal their identities, the government troops identified only five bona fide half-pay officers among the 1,693 rebels captured at Preston (four of whom they quickly court-martialled and shot).[178] Much to his consternation, Sinclair likewise found on his arrival in Perth shortly after its capture that only he and Urquhart of Newhall had any recent military experience.[179] There were a number of former soldiers on the Jacobite side, but they tended either to have done their time in the military a very long time previously – Kilsyth and Colonel John Balfour, for example, had been officers in the army of James II and VII (of the latter Sinclair scathingly observed, 'he could know little of a trade which he never saw much of, and which has been not a little improven since he served') – or, like Marischal and Hay of Cromlix, had only seen peacetime service ('all the service [Hay] had done was to have mounted the guard once or tuice at St James's') and barely knew their trade.[180] Though Sinclair subsequently moderated his exasperation with the grandfathers of the old Jacobite army, this nonetheless created a chronic tension within the Jacobites' ranks as recent veterans disputed planning, preparation and strategy with their apparently superannuated or inexperienced peers.[181] It was not meant to have been like that. The Jacobite rising was supposed to have been supported by a substantial cadre of expatriate Irish officers led by Berwick. Instead, the Jacobite army in Scotland effectively suffered from 'an intire want of officers', and had to make do with some who had last seen active service as much as fifty years previously and young men elected from the ranks of the rebels who had no military experience at all.[182] Yet, surprisingly given these shortcomings, most of the Jacobites' units managed to achieve a reasonable level of competence, and were for the most part as good in action as their equivalents on the government side (they never, of course, came up to the standard of the older regiments of regulars). Having encountered these Jacobite formations at Sherrifmuir, Argyll forthrightly admitted that he had not believed their numbers could be so large: 'nor did I think it possible that they could have been in the order and discipline that they are, or that they could have behaved themselves with half the resolution that they did'. In consequence the Jacobites could 'not only fight, but fight well'.[183] This achievement can only be ascribed to the relatively systematic schedule of drill and training inaugurated by Mar's close military advisers, General Hamilton and Lieutenant-Colonel William Clephane. Clephane in particular began forming the amorphous mobs turning up at Perth into regiments with officers and NCOs the day after he arrived, and instituted a training programme for the cavalry's horses, 'daily useing them to fire'.[184] By all accounts he achieved a great deal in terms of upgrading the Jacobite army, but ultimately Clephane's efforts were limited by political considerations.[185] Discipline, especially among the senior officers, was implicitly voluntary in all the Jacobite armies.[186] Thus while conscientious commanders like Panmure and Strathmore laid down a regular routine of training and exercise for their regiments, and enforced it by personal participation, more lackadaisical commanders, such as Drummond, did the bare minimum and got minimal results.[187] The Highland regiments also followed their own distinct routine of training according to the lights of their respective commanders.[188] The net effect was to create a very patchy competence in the Scottish Jacobite army. At its best it was at least the equivalent of the newly raised regiments of regulars; at its worst it remained a mob with firearms.[189] The best units were undoubtedly the Highland regiments, though this may be something of a misnomer, in that in 1715 the Jacobites apparently did the same as they did in 1745, which was to supplement the numbers in several Highland units with Lowlanders in Highland dress.[190] In any event, they provided the real punch of the Jacobite army.

The Jacobite army operating in northern England was beset with chronic problems, but it did at least have a few Irish and other officers who had seen foreign service (several of whom were also the principal agents of the conspiracy) to help it assume a more military mien.[191] These officers did what they could with the English recruits, and in particular instituted a system of double-officering. Patten, a profoundly unmilitary man, ascribed this as being done 'to oblige the several gentlemen that were among them'.[192] In fact it was a well-understood contemporary technique for bolstering green troops and accelerating the learning curve of potential officers, and was commonly used in other situations where such troops had to be deployed, for example in Sweden after 1709.[193] Despite their efforts, however, and principally because the southern army never had a secure base, there was not much opportunity to train the recruits they picked up in the Borders and northern England. In consequence throughout the southern Jacobite army's brief existence, 'the English were not altogether so well regulated, nor so well armed as the Scots', and the cutting edge of the southern Jacobite army remained its Scots troops, particularly the Highlanders.[194] Even among them, though, there was wide variation in quality. Because five of the six regiments of Scots infantry there wore Highland dress it has been assumed the men who composed them were Highlanders. In fact nearly half the Scottish infantry who crossed the Forth were Lowlanders (the regiments of Strathmore, Drummond and Nairn) who happened, in the case of the Drummond and Nairn regiments, by local custom to favour a mode of dress generally assumed only to have been worn by Highlanders.[195] And, of course, the plebeian recruits the army picked up in the Borders were very far from being clansmen. Polwarth contemptuously described Borlum's army as '4 or 500 fit for service, all the rest good for nothing', by the end of October.[196] In consequence, and especially after the mass desertions that took place from the army as it moved towards, and finally into, England, there were probably not many more than 300 or so Highlanders left in the southern Jacobite army by the time of Preston, and since they were the best troops the

Jacobites generally had, the southern army was qualitatively weaker than any of its peers.[197]

Arming the troops is obviously as vital a component of creating an army as raising and training recruits, and here, once again, the government held the advantage. In particular, 7,000 modern muskets were stored in Edinburgh castle in early August 1715, alongside an additional 4,000 in need of repair.[198] This was very fortunate as the potential recruiting base for loyalist forces was virtually unarmed. A very few members of the Whig élite, such as William Boyd, Earl of Kilmarnock, and Brigadier Alexander Grant of Grant, had retained some of the weapons they had stockpiled in 1714, or otherwise had access to a quantity of firearms.[199] Most, however, found their tenants and the militia regiments they were raising had next to no modern weapons. The fencible men of Midlothian, for example, mustered 7,000 strong at the end of August, but fewer than 100 possessed serviceable flintlocks and a similar number military-standard swords.[200] Polwarth flatly reported of the Berwickshire militia, 'I find there are no arms among them.'[201] Nor were the Whig clans necessarily better prepared. As already noted, the Grants do seem to have been well prepared for war (they were, indeed, 'the best armed by far in Scotland', according to one witness), but they were exceptional.[202] When Sutherland first gathered his forces to attack the Jacobites in the north he mustered 1,400 men, 'wherof about 400 wanted arms'.[203] Even when a Whig heritor was willing to buy military-grade firearms out of his own pocket, there was a problem. William Duff of Braco tried to do just that, only to find 'he cannot get them to purchase for money'.[204] The problem was resolved on the government side only by the careful distribution of what stocks of firearms existed in Edinburgh castle and elsewhere to selected militia and volunteer units.[205] Albeit that the mass of fencible men were not necessarily either politically reliable, or good military material, the government had little choice but to dismiss the great majority of them.

The only stockpiles of arms available to the Jacobites were those in private hands. As we have already seen, some Jacobite noblemen and heritors had diligently addressed this problem and were able to turn out well-armed forces of tenants and clansmen. Others were nowhere near as well prepared, and once they had mustered their men they faced a similar problem to Sutherland and Duff of Braco.[206] The 20,000 stand of arms promised first by Louis XIV and subsequently by Regent Orléans never made it out of France's ports. And in any event once the rebellion began the Royal Navy's patrols off the east coast of Scotland virtually closed off the possibility of importing any substantial quantity of weapons.[207] The population at large was unarmed, and do what they could in terms of combing local communities that fell under their control for any suitable weapons, the Jacobites could not requisition weapons where they did not exist. It is indicative of their desperation that almost the first thing any Jacobite force did when it swept into a given town or locality was to search for arms and confiscate them wherever it found them, even when the weapons concerned were of doubtful utility.[208] The upshot was that certain Jacobite units, such as Robert Stuart of Appin's, marched off to war 'but ill armd', and do what he could in the north, Seaforth's troops turned up for Sherrifmuir, 'the 3rd man of them not armed'.[209] Likewise the English recruited into the southern army were 'few or none well armed, all the greatest part altogether without armes; . . . their horses were light hunting horses, and hunting saddles and snaffles made up their accoutrements; . . . there was scarce a cutting suord amongst them all'.[210] Just as perniciously, because the population in general was unarmed the gunpowder necessary for the Jacobites to use the weapons they did have was in short supply. The nearly 4,000 pounds of powder the Jacobites had smuggled into Aberdeen by various means were seized on the eve of the rising, and when Sinclair arrived in Perth he found only 5–6 pounds there in total.[211] Rigorous searches for powder throughout northern Scotland and the fortuitous capture of a ship carrying three barrels of powder and 300 stand of arms north to Sutherland during a raid on Burntisland temporarily ameliorated the problem, but the battle of Sherrifmuir set the Jacobites back near where they had started.[212] General Hamilton, dispatched to France in December to beg urgently for immediate aid from the Regent, confided that there was less than 700 hundredweight accumulated at Perth, which was insufficient for even one day's fighting. The direness of this situation is well underscored by the Regent's response: he ordered 6,000 hundredweight sent forthwith and promised 50,000 to follow.[213]

The southern Jacobite army had a worse armaments and ammunition problem than its counterparts in Scotland, and was completely unable to remedy the situation from locally available resources.[214] It did, however, have a lucky break when it encountered, and routed, the *posse comitatus* of Cumberland and Westmorland. Though 'very few of them had any regular armes', the fact that the *posse* was large meant that when they fled, 'leaving most of their armes upon the said Fell', these amounted to a very useful windfall for the Jacobites.[215] There was a shortage of ammunition on the Jacobite side at the battle of Preston, but they were undoubtedly better off than they would have been a couple of weeks previously.[216]

If men, arms and ammunition are the necessary components of an army, they are by no means sufficient. To be effective troops must be regularly fed, and to be controllable they must be paid. Requisitioning food and raising money to supply their armies was, then, a critical element in sustaining the war effort on both sides. And here once again the government enjoyed a massive advantage. Not only could it draw on ample food supplies located safely away from the theatres of conflict, it had all the resources of one of the best revenue-raising administrations in contemporary Europe to supply it with money.[217]

Yet, for all that it was intrinsically so powerful, the British fiscal-military state's advantage did not immediately translate into tangible results for the government's forces in Scotland, primarily owing to the slowness with which the bureaucratic machine moved into action. In mid-August the Board of Ordnance rebuffed Townshend's request for £2,048 to repair the badly decayed defences of Fort William because 'there is no money allowed to this office for carrying on any works in North Brittain'.[218] In the same vein, only £3,000 of supplementary moneys had been sent to Scotland by the end of the month, as a consequence of which the Scottish administration had insufficient funds to recall half-pay officers resident in Scotland to the colours.[219] Even if these officers had been willing to take it on trust many were already in dire financial straits because of the accumulation of arrears of their pensions. The Irish army officers, for example, were twelve months in arrears.[220] When he arrived in Scotland Argyll faced further problems as a result of the Bank of Scotland being closed on 19 September, so that 'every body hoards up what specie they have in their hands'.[221] This left him unable to exchange the paper bills sent down by the Treasury and thus with insufficient hard currency to pay his troops and purchase supplies. In the end he had to dig into his own pocket to get things moving and for his pains still continued to encounter bureaucratic difficulties, verging on obstruction, at every level until the end of the year.[222] Argyll was so infuriated by this that he several times offered to resign and became positively paranoid with respect to the machinations of his political enemies in London, and Marlborough in particular, who he suspected were trying to starve him of resources so that he would fail against the Jacobites.[223]

Argyll was not alone in encountering such difficulties. Active Whig Lord-Lieutenants like Polwarth also had to extend their own credit to keep their militia embodied (the counties were only required to pay them for forty days) without any financial support from Westminster, and the government later privately indicated that it had no intention of reimbursing them.[224] In the same vein, Sutherland and Lovat had to borrow money in Inverness to keep their army together in December and the authorities in cities like Edinburgh and Glasgow were matter-of-factly stuck with the cost of maintaining Jacobite prisoners deposited in their gaols.[225] The situation only began to be remedied after the arrival of Marlborough's trusted lieutenant and henchman, William Cadogan, later Earl Cadogan, in December. Thereafter money, munitions and equipment all flowed north more smoothly and the all-important Dutch and Swiss auxiliary forces arrived in good shape, despite it being midwinter, and were regularly paid.[226] In northern England the regular military forces pursuing the Jacobites were closer to the administration in London and do not seem to have suffered from any shortages of either money or supplies.

The Whig clansmen who were mobilised in October and November–December, however, always lay outside the regular military bureaucratic structure and were not systematically recompensed. They accordingly paid themselves by looting friend and foe alike.[227] This only changed in the later stages of the campaign in 1716, when Cadogan mustered a force of 1,000 Monroes, Rosses and Frasers to supplement his regular troops during his operations in the western Highlands and Islands. These were regularly paid threepence a day – half the rate received by the regulars – and compensated for their low pay by being allowed 'all the plunder they can get'.[228]

As far as food was concerned, there generally does not seem to have been a problem for the government forces. Argyll's army was small enough to draw on Stirlingshire and the Lothians, two of contemporary Scotland's foremost agriculturally productive regions, without straining their resources.[229] Most of the food the government army needed seems to have been supplied on credit, but that was not at all exceptional. There were more problems in northern Scotland because Sutherland and Lovat were waging a campaign using clan troops with no administrative back-up in the depths of winter, so that on one occasion, 'the storme was so great and the weather so violent that it was impossible to hinder some desertion amongst our highlanders, whose stock lyes in cattle'.[230] Nonetheless, by reducing the size of their forces (except for the Frasers) they seem eventually to have secured sufficient food, at least in part through the plundering of local estates, both Jacobite and Whig.[231] The government's forces in northern England may have encountered some food shortages while they were on a forced march after the southern Jacobite army, but if so these were not serious and arose from the speed with which they were moving once they were away from major cities like Newcastle rather than any chronic problem of supply.[232]

Beyond their personal fortunes the Jacobites had no significant financial resources available to them at the outset of their rebellion(s) and were obliged to live hand to mouth. A regular part of the occupation of every town that fell to them, after the proclamation of James III and VIII and alongside the search for arms, was the collection of all the revenues in the hands of government officials.[233] Mar also initiated a forced loan and ordered the levying of an additional cess on all areas under rebel control (with known Whigs being subject to double assessment).[234] None of these measures yielded sufficient revenue to keep the Jacobite statelet afloat financially. As early as the beginning of October in Perth the rank-and-file troops were 'generally all complaining for want of money', and began 'to be very troublesome to all the country about'.[235] Mar tried to remedy the situation by instituting a regular system of pay, or at least the distribution of some cash, the accumulation of notional arrears and, where possible, payment in kind, but it was a stopgap system that was only partially successful.[236] Consequently Jacobite troops, and particularly the Highlanders, many of whom were a long way from home and thus had less compunction about plundering comparative strangers, 'begun to mutinie, for want of pay', and sometimes pillaged local communities in territory under their control.[237] When this did occur their depredations could be quite severe. One witness in Fife claimed that Macgregors under the command of Rob Roy and Gregor Macgregor took 'the cloaths of the people's very backs, plaids from women and seting men down and taking their shoes off their feet, and their cravats from their necks', even raiding Arngask one Sunday, where they 'came in to the Kirk befor the half got out, and took their cloaths off, and their bibles from them'.[238] Mar had instituted a controlled system of requisitioning, for which official IOUs were to be issued, but this applied only to the food and livestock being taken to supply the Jacobite armies.[239] Even then there was a fine line between 'requisitioning' and pillaging. One has to wonder if the thirty hogsheads of wine seized by John Gordon of Glenbuchat from the *Robert* of North Berwick at Burntisland at the end of October, or the wine Lieutenant David Ramsay seized from the cellars of David Carnegie, Earl of Northesk, were really vital to the survival of the Jacobite army.[240] Above and beyond such 'official' activity there was in any case a good deal of indiscriminate (in that it struck at both friend and foe) free enterprise looting.[241] Organised pillage was also the common mode of supply (and possibly payment) for Jacobite troops in the north and west.[242] The southern Jacobite army diligently collected the revenues as it meandered from town to town, and this plus the fact that it contained a disproportionate number of the economically better-off in its ranks enabled it to sustain itself and mostly pay its way as it marched towards Preston. It is notable that the Scots troops in the southern army, including the Highlanders, were not generally accused of having a proclivity to plunder (though they did take free quarter) while they were operating in England, very likely because they were being regularly paid.[243]

Food could have been a problem for the Jacobites at any other time of year than the autumn. The regular agricultural cycle in the early eighteenth century involved the planting and harvesting of two crops each growing season to provide for the winter. Rebelling in the autumn, then, virtually ensured that the Jacobites would have ample food supplies so long as there was a decent harvest. In 1715, there certainly was. 'Nothing favoured us so much', recalled Sinclair, 'as that year's plentiefull crop, for nobodie remembered they had ever seen such aboundance of corn in Scotland.'[244] The Jacobites were doubly fortunate in that they also held the Carse of Gowrie, which was the best grain-producing area in the whole of Scotland at the time, and this ensured that food supplies at Perth were initially good, though food did get scarcer as the winter came on.[245] It also enabled the Jacobite administration to boost the level of payment in kind to their troops. How extensive and relatively effective this was may perhaps be glimpsed in the tradition that when local people went up to Sherrifmuir to pick over anything the combatants had left behind after the battle they found many discarded Highland plaids (it was customary for Highlanders to take off their plaids and shoes before charging into action) with substantial packages of grain (but not money or stolen goods) secured in their folds.[246] The southern, northern and western Jacobite armies operated in the same relatively fortuitous circumstances, and there are no reports of Jacobite troops going hungry, other than by happenstance, in any of these theatres either.

* * *

The outbreak of the '15 was a strange, haphazard event. Clearly a great many Jacobites did not want to be the first ones to move, lest they rise alone and be left exposed, unsupported to the wrath of the government. Yet the decay of civil order in Scotland in 1714–15 insensibly threw up some very bold, or foolhardy, individuals who were willing to risk everything to strike a blow for their cause. They were truly the spark that set Scotland ablaze, and they did so in a fascinatingly choreographed fashion full of symbolic gestures that connected with the mores and traditions of their local communities as well as with their grievances and economic interests. Yet despite the best efforts of these brave few there was still a faltering and hesitant quality to many of the outbreaks of the rebellion and their counterparts, musters of Whig loyalists. Any kind of determined opposition by their opponents could disrupt the process and scatter the rebels or the assembled militia. In the opening stages of the rising appearances were everything.

Once they were out in rebellion, or assembled to oppose it, Jacobites and loyalists alike faced the formidable tasks of recruiting, training, arming, paying and feeding their respective armies. Given the size of the forces involved, relative in particular to the size of Scotland's population and economy (which effectively had to bear much the greater part of the burden), these were major hurdles. The government forces did quite well with respect to all of them, though not quite so well as might have been expected. There were lapses and failures on the government side that in many ways illustrate the limits of power in the early eighteenth century. Troops were not paid, weapons were not distributed in time and the training was clearly not always good. The British fiscal-military state was undoubtedly very strong, but it was not always able to apply that strength quickly, efficiently or effectively in emergencies. The fact that, given the vulnerability of the rebels in the opening stages of the rising, the state did not summarily put them to flight mutely underscores the point.

On the Jacobite side the results of their efforts were predictably patchy, but, significantly, quite effective given their circumstances. They managed, albeit not in northern England, to construct a passable, if green, army. It was not an army capable of defeating the veterans of the War of the Spanish Succession who made up the bulk of the old regular regiments, but, there again, neither was the thoroughly professional army of Louis XIV. The Highlanders, predictably, formed its cutting edge and there were problems associated with their culture and way of war. Nonetheless, the Jacobites recruited by force and otherwise were turned into soldiers. They were not always well armed (indeed, the Jacobites' military infrastructure was consistently fragile) nor regularly paid, but they were regularly fed, and though they had a tendency to plunder it never got totally out of hand.[247] The proof of the Jacobites' achievement is that despite all their problems, disappointments and military failures, and the menacing build-up of overwhelming government forces a scant few miles away from his base at Perth, Mar still had a viable, functioning army, if a reduced one, ready to take the field in January 1716.

CHAPTER 6

'Sae Famed in Martial Story': Military Operations, September 1715–April 1716, the Central Theatre

Taken in the round, everything the Jacobites and the government did, in terms of conspiracy, spying, preparation and making a rebellion actually happen or not happen on a particular day in a particular locality, was ultimately no more than the lead-in to the war that took place in Scotland and northern England for some seven months in 1715–16. As internecine wars go, it was not a bad one. Mutual hostility did not reach the levels of bitterness, or spark the incidence of atrocity, more generally associated with civil wars, though this may have been no more than a function of time. Rebellions are implicitly civil wars in the making; generally the longer they go on the more likely they are to degenerate into inchoate savagery. Thus because the '15 was relatively short the rules of contemporary civil society were never entirely forgotten. There were, admittedly, some very nasty moments, such as the murder of a number of prisoners of war by government troops on the battlefield at Sherrifmuir and after the surrender at Preston, and a number of rapes associated with the harrying of Munro lands by the Mackenzies and their allies in the north, but these were isolated incidents.[1] Plenty of property damage was committed on both sides, but the general population, friendly and unfriendly, was for the most part left physically unharmed and the contemporary laws of war were tacitly observed during both sides' military operations.[2] Baron of the Exchequer John Clerk tellingly assumed this would be the case when he told his father, Sir John Clerk of Penicuik, that his (Baron Clerk's) wife could remain at Penicuik even if Sir John had to flee before the rebels because 'she will be safe enough any where, as all other women will be'.[3]

Lest this give the impression that neither side, but particularly the rebels, was taking the war seriously, it should be borne in mind that internecine warfare of the kind they were engaged in is always a conversation in violence designed to bring over (by a combination of example, persuasion and intimidation) the mass of the population. And neither the Jacobites nor the Whigs wanted to make a desert and call it peace. Military operations were, therefore, trammelled by a moral framework set by as yet unbrutalised civilian sensibilities. Nor did either army reach the point, or see so good an opportunity to best its opponent, that it was willing to contemplate the alienation of the general population by its ruthless conduct of military operations. In sum, neither wanted a reputation for committing 'cruell barbaritys'.[4] An object lesson was the burning of the villages of Auchterarder, Blackford, Crieff, Dunning, Muthil and Dalreach in late January 1716, which was and is usually held to be a particularly vicious Jacobite atrocity.[5] Yet the Jacobites were hesitant about doing it and consequently ended up being both too ruthless, in that they themselves were clearly discomforted by what they had done and so tried to make belated attempts at restitution, and not ruthless enough, in that what they did was insufficient to achieve the effect they had hoped (forcing Argyll's army to desist from its advance on Perth by denying it shelter in dead of winter).[6] Military restraint, with regard to the impact of the war on the general population, was an implicit part of both sides' strategy.

Within those implicit constraints there was, nevertheless, a war to be won. The Jacobites' basic military strategy was intrinsically aggressive. As we have seen, they sought to set off as many local risings as possible, in the hope of overstretching the military resources available to the government. This would enable them to bring together a locally superior force to overwhelm the government troops opposed to them. If they could carry this off they would score a major coup in the battle for hearts and minds and, they hoped, provoke French intervention. Control of Scotland was obviously the key to this strategy. By defeating the government forces there and securing the country the Jacobites could give themselves a (more) secure military base and much improved diplomatic credibility; it was the vital stepping-stone to victory. The government's strategy, by contrast, was primarily defensive. Their objective was to prevent local uprisings occurring in the first place, limit their impact when they did occur and isolate areas that fell under Jacobite control. This would demonstrate that the Whig regime was still firmly in control, deter potential rebels and discourage foreign intervention. For this strategy control of England was the key. Holding on to as much of Scotland (and Ireland) as possible would be helpful in the long run, but keeping firm control of England was crucial. Hence military resources were initially allocated to Scotland only, as Townshend told Argyll, 'so far as was consistent with the care that lies on the government for the preservation of the whole'.[7] In practical terms this meant that government forces outside England were to be straitened for resources until all possibility of a general English rising had passed. Redeployment of the troops that had secured England would then enable the government to reconquer any territory it might lose in the interim. Bluntly put, within this strategy Scotland and the army in Scotland were strategically expendable.[8] All they could really be expected to do was limit the Jacobites' gains until the forces securing England could be redeployed.

These opposed strategies set the pattern for military operations during the '15. Because of the way the rebellion flared up and secured itself in different places at different times in response to local circumstances in Scotland and northern England, the war quickly resolved itself into a number of distinct theatres of operations. These episodically geared up and wound down in response to the strategic objectives outlined above, the progress of the war in that theatre and in response to events elsewhere. First and foremost the Jacobites needed to sweep Argyll's army aside to secure control of Scotland, and they were quite prepared to shut down their operations in northern and western Scotland in order to boost their strength in central Scotland so as to reach a decisive conclusion there. In the same vein, Mar threw Mackintosh of Borlum's little army into southern Scotland further to stretch available government resources. Nonetheless, from the point of view of effective analysis, the war resolves itself into four theatres: central (the most important), comprising eastern Perthshire, Clackmannan, Kinross, Stirlingshire and Fife; northern, comprising eastern Inverness-shire, Ross, Nairn and Elgin; western, comprising western Inverness-shire, western Perthshire, Argyllshire and the islands; and southern, comprising all operations south of the Forth into northern England. Each in turn will be analysed below.

Offstage, beyond these theatres, yet still vital to the outcome of events therein, were military operations designed to keep the Jacobites in England and Ireland down and restrict the flow of resources from the continent to areas under Jacobite control. Here the government had an asset the Jacobites had no possibility of matching: the Royal Navy. The navy had been gearing up for potentially offensive operations against Sweden in the Baltic from early in 1715, which required it to take on extra skilled workers and labourers in the naval dockyards, and thus when the Jacobite crisis broke it was not difficult to extend the recommissioning of mothballed warships to increase the number available for coastal patrols.[9] The first priority was to establish a strong presence off the French coast to watch for and intercept any attempt by James and Ormond to get to the British Isles, and by late July there were already six ships cruising the waters between Calais and Cherbourg.[10] In August this was upgraded to a full squadron of ten ships under Sir George Byng, Admiral of the White.[11] The risings in Scotland prompted further deployment of ships and by mid-September five ships were patrolling the waterways between the western isles and the mainland and four were making their way to the east coast.[12] The orders issued to Captain Charles Poole of HMS *Pearl* are probably typical:

> you are to use your utmost care and diligence to speak with and search all such ships or vessells as you may meet with, and have reason to suspect are going between France and Scotland. And if you shall find on board them any arms, ammunition, money, or persons whom you may have reason to apprehend are officers employed by the Pretender, or any other suspected persons, you are to take particular care that they be secured . . .[13]

Moreover, in the event of resistance by the ships he intercepted, Poole was 'to take, sink, or destroy them', and his orders pointedly made no mention of his needing to take account of the nationality of any ships he judged it necessary to attack.[14] By November there were some thirty Royal Navy warships hovering off the major ports of northern France or systematically patrolling the east and south coasts of England and eastern and western Scotland.[15]

This blockade was maintained until March 1716. It was certainly large and *prima facie* impressive, and definitely disrupted the Jacobite diaspora's efforts to get James, Ormond and their painfully accumulated supplies of munitions and money to the British Isles.[16] It was, however, of limited effectiveness.[17] The weather at that time of year was not conducive to maintaining a regular patrol schedule and there were so many ports under Jacobite control in Scotland that the navy could not hope to overawe them all, or even scout them regularly.[18] Mackintosh of Borlum successfully crossed the Forth despite the presence of several warships and he lost only about forty men to their attempts to intercept his flotilla of small boats and fishing smacks.[19] Once James got past the ships hovering off the French coast he had an uninterrupted voyage to Scotland, and he subsequently escaped from Scotland back to France without incident.[20] The main physical contribution of the navy to the suppression of the rebellion came in the form of the supplies it convoyed to Whig forces in northern Scotland and a few minor encounters and clashes with Jacobite authorities in various east coast ports.[21] The only major landing it supported came in December 1716, when navy warships guaranteed the uncontested reoccupation of Burntisland by a force of Edinburgh militia and Swiss auxiliary troops.[22] Overall, then, it seems fair to say that the main impact of the Royal Navy was psychological. Its visible presence added to the Scottish Jacobites' sense of isolation and beleaguerment.

Though they had an almost equally uneventful war, the government troops deployed in England and Ireland had far greater significance in terms of their impact on the outcome of the rebellion. Both the British and the Irish armies (the two military establishments were theoretically separated at this time) doubled in size between the end of July and the beginning of October. This put the British army at 28 battalions of foot and 50 squadrons of horse/dragoons and the Irish army at 22 battalions of foot and 14 squadrons of horse/dragoons.[23] In both kingdoms these substantial forces vigorously projected the government's authority by their physical presence in suspect communities. In a sense, the Irish army was the more successful, in that it effectively suppressed all but the most trivial Jacobite activity in 1715.[24] Since, however, the Irish end of the plot had apparently never got off the ground this is not a very remarkable achievement. The British army stationed in England and Wales, by contrast, did have to do some marching and fighting to secure the government's hold on power. In late September the successful arrest of what remained of the Jacobites' leadership in southern England, and particularly Wyndham and Lansdowne, demoralised their followers in the countryside (in so far as these would ever have been resolute enough to rise without outside support).[25] According to local tradition, around that time a number of putative rebels turned up at a horse-race near Bath supposedly ready to rise, milled around a little waiting for someone to step up and take command, then quietly dispersed.[26] Ormond certainly got no response to his signals when he sailed along the Devon coast trying to link up with his erstwhile supporters.[27] Yet in early October continued Jacobite activity was deemed sufficiently alarming to provoke further raids in attempts to arrest notorious local Jacobite leaders, such as 'Colonel Owen' in Oxford, and the installation of garrisons of government troops in strongly Tory/Jacobite cities like Oxford, Bristol and Bath.[28] This seems to have completely secured the government in southern England and Wales, so that at the end of the month Stanhope could confidently tell Stair, 'it will be impossible as our forces are now disposed for 500 men to gett together anywhere in England unless perhaps in the mountains of Wales, and even from thence they would be driven in a fortnight'.[29] The bulk of the forces in England and Wales were, though, concentrated in the south, the better to ensure control of that region and London in particular. This opened the way for the northern English rising at the beginning of October, which was then opposed by forces that had to march up from the south. This obviously took some little time, and that allowed the northern English rising to get off the ground, albeit in a minimal way. Once the northern rising was dealt with the bulk of the army in England and Wales again settled into the comfortable, if dull, watchfulness that was all that was required to keep the kingdom under control. And though it was increasingly obvious there was little likelihood of further trouble in England and Wales, the government took no chances. Few of these occupying troops were transferred to Scotland. Instead the bulk of the reinforcements received by Argyll in the later stages of the rebellion were Swiss and Dutch auxiliaries who arrived in England in December.[30]

Central Scotland, September 1715 to February 1716

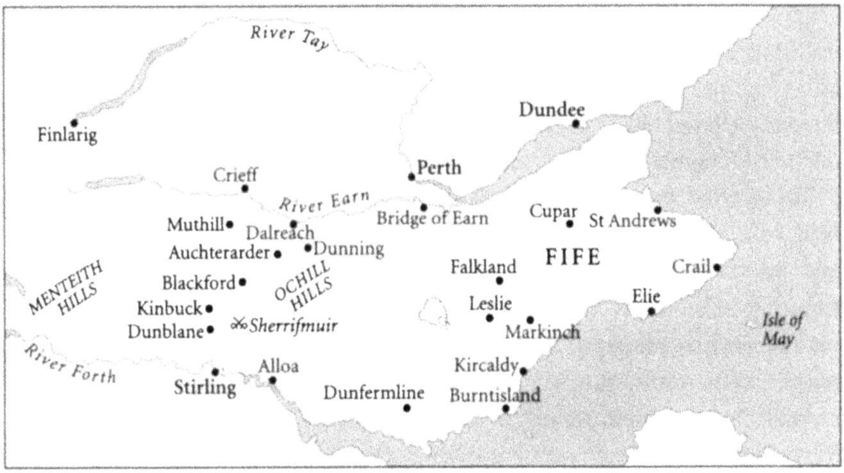

Map 2: Central Scottish theatre of operations.

The central theatre of operations was where the '15 would be won or lost, if for no other reason than that the main government army was encamped there at Stirling. If the Jacobites could defeat it and either take Stirling castle or otherwise bypass the bogs which trammelled the approaches to the town (the only easy route was via the bridge at Stirling, which was overlooked by the guns of the castle) to get into the Lowlands below the Forth, they would be well on the way to taking control of the whole of Scotland. For precisely that reason, plus the paucity of reliable troops he had under his command at that point, Argyll initially decided to go on the defensive and use his army as a blocking force, only risking a battle with the Jacobites if they tried to outflank him by passing the Forth to the west of him, in the Menteith Hills.[31] Mar likewise had an operational dilemma. If the pace of rebel success was allowed to falter, the rebel army was liable to become discouraged and waverers would be encouraged to stay neutral rather than join.[32] On the other hand, marching boldly south to attack Argyll with the raw troops he had gathered in and around Perth by the end of September was asking for a decisive defeat (which would have had even worse consequences for the progress of the rebellion). Mar's forces outnumbered Argyll's, but not enough to give the Jacobites a meaningful advantage, given that their troops were for the most part virtually untrained and that many were armed with improvised weapons. The best troops the Jacobites had were western clans (the Macdonalds of Clanranald, Glengarry and Sleat, the Macleans, the Stuarts of Appin and the Camerons) which were as yet mustering and had their own military objectives in view in the western theatre.[33] They were not likely to be free to join him for some time. Reinforcement from the north, particularly by Huntly and his vassals, was expected sooner, but its quality was for the most part liable to be as mixed as the troops Mar already had with him. Pausing at Perth to train and organise his army seemed the safest and most sensible option and Mar, probably on the advice of General Hamilton and Lieutenant-Colonel Clephane, took it.[34]

This locked the opposing armies into a well nigh static confrontation for nearly two months. In each camp, but much more so at Perth, frantic training and exercise regimes were implemented and military equipment was acquired, refurbished and repaired. Patrols and detachments were also sent out on various missions both for logistical reasons and to give the newly raised troops some experience in the field. It was, in contemporary military parlance, an extended period of *petite guerre* (i.e. a war of raids, patrols and skirmishes)[35] while each army readied itself for the real thing. And though it may seem that raids, patrols and skirmishes ought to be the regular fare of eighteenth-century warfare (as they are in modern war) they were, in fact, not within the usual experience of most professional officers, and still less of the amateurs. In European warfare at the time such duties were normally carried out by the cavalry, with the support of light infantry if any were available.[36] Hence, once again, Argyll's army had a considerable advantage over its opponent, including as it did a substantial number of regular cavalry, many of whom were War of the Spanish Succession veterans experienced in exactly the kind of operations that were about to become commonplace. Encounters between them and roving Jacobite forces correspondingly tended to be quite one-sided, as may be seen from the clash that occurred at Dunfermline on 24 October.

On 23 October Argyll received word from one of his outposts that a Jacobite force of approximately 80 horse and 300 Highlanders had marched past them heading for Fife, where they were going to levy contributions to supply the main Jacobite army at Perth.[37] He promptly detached a squadron of Portmore's 'grey' dragoons under Lieutenant-Colonel Charles Cathcart to intercept them. Cathcart caught up with the Jacobites at Dunfermline on 24 October. The Jacobites' security was very lax: James Malcolm of Grange, the Jacobite commander, was confident that he knew the area and its approaches so well that he posted only one sentry at the bridge into the Stirling end of the town and allowed his forces to divide when they took up quarters. The Highlanders, under Gordon of Glenbuchat, camped in a ruined abbey on the edge of the town while the horse took up residence without any order or forethought in taverns and private houses throughout it.[38] Cathcart scouted the Jacobite position overnight and then attacked at 5 a.m. from the opposite, eastern, side of Dunfermline with 120 mounted dragoons just after a detachment of 30 of his men who were dismounted commenced a noisy firefight with the Highlanders in the abbey. As Cathcart had planned, this brought the Jacobite cavalrymen scrambling out of their beds into the streets in confusion, trying to find their horses and get mounted. He then struck them with a charge, killing four and mortally wounding two more, before riding on through the town and rejoining his dismounted detachment with seventeen prisoners in tow.[39] Behind him, 'everie one run a different way', and, after trying and failing to draw the Highlanders out of the abbey by trailing his prisoners across their line of sight, Cathcart withdrew without interference to Stirling. His casualties amounted to one man and one horse wounded.[40]

Given the clear superiority they displayed in this encounter it might be assumed that Argyll would have sought every opportunity to use his cavalry to raid and ambush the Jacobites; in fact the skirmish at Dunfermline was the only occasion when he launched such a major raid before December. He thoroughly reconnoitred the whole area within a day's march of Stirling and personally familiarised himself with the landscape, but other than that attacks on the Jacobites were little more than vindictive sallies against Jacobite property unfortunate enough to be close by Stirling, such as that launched on 12 October which 'demolished the Laird of Keir's barn yeard'.[41] Argyll's reasoning was straightforward: in the event of a pitched battle, he told Townshend, 'whatever advantage we can hope for must be from the good behaviour of our cavallry'.[42] His regular cavalry were his trump card and he was correspondingly loath to risk them taking serious casualties in the course of the *petite guerre*.[43] Until the arrival of the Dutch and Swiss in December Argyll unleashed his cavalry for such operations only when they could be conducted close by Stirling, so that if they got into trouble they did not have far to retreat and he could quickly bring his infantry up to support them.[44] The net effect was to yield the initiative in the *petite guerre* to the Jacobites, so long as they gave Stirling a wide berth. Thus the Jacobites were allowed virtually free rein to exact contributions, recruit and otherwise do as they pleased in Fife until late December, which, aside from unhappy encounters like Dunfermline, in turn boosted both their confidence and the resources available to them until the end of the year.[45]

In the Highlanders, who were *ipso facto* light infantry, the Jacobites had a potential asset of their own in the *petite guerre*. Troops who operated in a similar fashion, such as the Croats and Pandours deployed by the Habsburgs, were highly effective in such warfare in the Balkans and later in central Europe.[46] Yet the Jacobites made limited use of their potential. This can only be ascribed to the limited vision of their senior officers. Mar is generally blamed for the military failures of the '15, but he was obviously no soldier, and never really pretended to be.[47] Despite Sinclair's claims that Mar arrogated the role of commander, and Hamilton's occasional peevishness about how he was being ignored, Mar in fact consistently took all his military decisions in consultation with both senior Jacobite leaders, such as the clan chieftains, Huntly, Sinclair and so on, and three close advisers who were professional military officers with considerable recent experience: Clephane (who had been a major in the British army), Hamilton (a major-general in the Dutch army) and Alexander Gordon of Auchintoul (who had been a major-general in the Russian army).[48] This is not to suggest that Mar's military decision-making was not profoundly influenced by political considerations, or that some very ill-judged moves were not thereby generated, but that in the round he was generally guided by this coterie of experienced officers. In turn, the problem with them was that they were blinkered by contemporary military orthodoxy. Clephane, a half-pay major, had defected to Mar when Argyll sent him up to Blair Atholl to assist Atholl in organising his men, and he was subsequently promoted to lieutenant-colonel and adjutant-general in the Jacobite army.[49] Sinclair grudgingly allowed 'the man is well enough', and that he knew 'the detaile of a regiment', which Clephane certainly put to good effect in organising and training the Jacobite army assembling at Perth.[50] The problem with Clephane was that beyond those essential, but mundane, tasks he was too junior an officer to swing much weight in Jacobite military councils. As Mar regretfully recalled, 'he did very good service, and it was a misfortoun to our affairs that some times for humouring of some for whom I was oblidged to have regard, I could not follow his advice, and particularly at Sherifmoor'.[51] Gordon of Auchintoul was a considerably more senior officer who was living in retirement in 1715. He, too, never seems to have been influential in Jacobite military decision-making, though in his case the reason is not clear. It may have been that he did not have the personality for it, or it is possible that the fact that he was recruited by Huntly (who did not get on well with Mar) and looked to the marquess as the head of his name limited his impact.[52] In any event, Gordon of Auchintoul did not play a leading role in setting the Jacobites' operational agenda. The man whose influence was decisive was General George Hamilton.

Hamilton is indelibly associated with the inconclusive battle at Sherrifmuir and the Jacobites' failure to make best use of their military assets, yet he was by no means incompetent.[53] Sinclair felt that in the court of general officers, which directed the Jacobites' military affairs, Hamilton did 'all that, in my weak judgement could be proposed in our circumstances'.[54] The problem, as James Keith discerned, was that:

> though an old officer, [he] was not in the least equal to the affair he was to undertake, for though he had served long and with very good reputation in the Dutch troops, yet being a man whom only experience, not natural genious, had made an officer, he did not know how to make use of his new troops, who are of a disposition as hot and quick as the Dutch are slow and flegmatick, and this certainly was the occasion of his misfortune at the affair of Dumblain [Sherrifmuir]. Besides, he having been always used to the regularty of the Dutch, thought all lost when he saw the first sign of confusion among the Highlanders.[55]

Without doubt Hamilton was a brave, solidly orthodox soldier.[56] Unfortunately for them, the Jacobites had more need of an unorthodox one. At Sherrifmuir Gordon of Glenbuchat is said to have lamented, 'Oh for an hour of Dundee! – for an hour's worth of the skill shown by Dundee at Killiecrankie in 1689.[57] Dundee, however, was another solidly conventional soldier who just happened to have one brilliant moment before getting himself killed.[58] It would have been more appropriate to wish for an hour of Alasdair Maccolla, the ferocious Macdonald warrior and master of Highland warfare who was primarily responsible for the victories usually credited to James Graham, Marquess of Montrose.[59]

Free rein in Fife, albeit at the cost of putting little or no *petite guerre* pressure on Argyll at Stirling, allowed the Jacobites to hone their troops and supplement their supplies and equipment. Sinclair successfully raided Burntisland on 2 October and carried off over 300 stand of arms and 300 pounds of gunpowder destined for Sutherland. A few days later he returned and provocatively proclaimed James VIII in a swathe of towns (St Andrews, Crail, Kilrenny, Anstruther, Pittenweem, Elie, Leven, Wemyss and Dysart), all the while collecting the cess and confiscating weapons wherever he found them.[60] These raids were followed by others led by Lord George Murray and Gordon of Glenbuchat.[61] Jacobite garrisons were also placed in Burntisland and Crail and the Fife ports became the regular conduit for communications between Mar and the southern Jacobite army.[62] And until the end of November Argyll's response was extremely limited. The only long-range raid he launched was the one carried out by Rothes in September that captured Sir Thomas Bruce.[63]

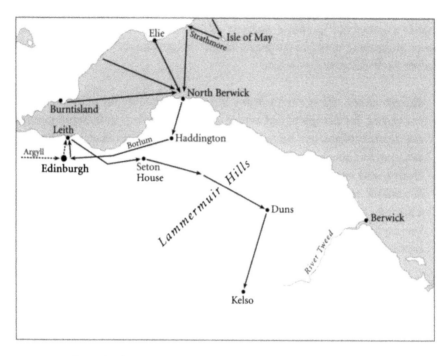

Map 3: Mackintosh of Borlum's crossing of the Forth and march south.

Argyll came in for a good deal of criticism for his inaction at the time and later, which he bitterly resented.[64] The extent of the problem that underlay his immobility is, however, well illustrated by the crisis that broke when Mackintosh of Borlum crossed the Forth in a daring night operation on 12/13 October. Originally this crossing was to have been commanded by Sinclair, but he had clashed with Mar too often, and demanded too great a share of the scant stockpile of munitions then available at Perth as a precondition for his undertaking it.[65] Mackintosh of Borlum accordingly replaced him, and was allotted six regiments of Jacobite infantry to carry it out. These were a very mixed group, consisting of three Highland units: the Mackintoshes, Mar's and Lord Charles Murray's, and three Lowland ones: Strathmore's, Thomas Drummond of Logiealmond's and Nairn's.[66] Mar and Sinclair had arranged for small boats to be accumulated at all the ports in southern Fife, and Borlum only had to coordinate their departure. He did not manage this terribly well, and some boats were delayed because the winds and tides in different ports did not mesh with the starting time he directed, but overall the crossing was a considerable success.[67] Argyll had warned the warships in the Forth to be on the alert for such a move by the Jacobites, and tried to get the navy to seize all suitable boats and impound them on the south side of the Forth.[68] The navy had reluctantly begun patrolling the Firth of Forth at the behest of Lord Advocate Dalrymple, but bluntly told him that given the number of boats in the Fife ports and the few warships available it was going to be difficult to stop the Jacobites reaching the south shore.[69] Nonetheless, though they only managed to intercept some 40 or so of the Jacobite troops, the warships forced 500 or more others, including Strathmore himself, either back into Fife or on to the Isle of May. These stragglers eventually escaped back to Fife, whence some deserted and others rejoined the army at Perth.[70] Something over 2,000 Jacobites set out and approximately 1,400 made it to the Midlothian shore, scattered in small groups between Dunbar and North Berwick. Within a day Mackintosh of Borlum nevertheless collected most of them together at Haddington and from there he advanced on Edinburgh, which was by then in a state of panic.[71]

Argyll was thus in a vice. If he did not reinforce Edinburgh it could fall to Borlum; if he did, he would leave his main army at Stirling dangerously weakened and vulnerable to attack by Mar and the rest of the Jacobite army in Perth.[72] On the 14th Argyll therefore left 1,500 men with General Thomas Whetham and force-marched 300 cavalry and 200 infantry, mounted on requisitioned horses, to Edinburgh. There he found that Borlum, apparently daunted by the determination of the Edinburgh magistrates to defend the city, had postponed attacking it and instead occupied Leith, where he was giving his men some much needed rest.[73] When Borlum heard that Argyll had arrived he promptly moved his army into the old Cromwellian citadel of Leith, which he barricaded and prepared to defend. Argyll meanwhile put together an impromptu force of militia and Whig volunteers to supplement his regulars and advanced on the citadel. On closer examination of the defences, however, he decided that throwing his regulars at the barricades erected by the Jacobites (the militia and volunteers apparently did not feature in his calculations here) was asking for a mauling. Argyll therefore decided to wait until he could bring up some artillery from the city or the warships hovering off the coast, and retired back to Edinburgh for the night.[74] Borlum promptly took the opportunity to slip away to the south towards Seton House, which was 'large and walled', leaving only a few stragglers behind in Leith who were the worse for wear after looting a shipload of brandy stored in the customs house. Argyll duly marched towards him next day with the same force as he had had at Leith plus some naval artillery. News then arrived from Whetham that Mar and the rest of the Jacobite army at Perth, some 3–4,000

strong, were advancing menacingly towards Stirling. Argyll dashed back to his
main army, reluctantly leaving behind a token force to bolster the timorous
defenders of Edinburgh.[75]

Argyll's determination, 'considering this small number of troops that I
have . . . to keep them together', was completely vindicated by Borlum's
crossing.[76] Had Argyll been waging a vigorous *petite guerre* many of his
troops, and especially his cavalry, would have been scattered in detachments
all over Stirlingshire and Fife and he would have had nothing with which to
counter Borlum's strike southward. Still, it was frustrating both for the army
and their general to watch the Jacobites 'doe what they please with all the
country that lyas on the north side of the Forth', while they awaited reinforcements, and Argyll complained increasingly bitterly about his lack of troops.[77]
Indeed, so vociferous did his complaints become by the end of October that
he earned a harsh rebuke from Westminster. Townshend and Stanhope flintily
informed him that the king, having reviewed Argyll's latest diatribe, had
'commanded' them 'to tell your Grace very plainly, that he was not a little
surprised at some expressions in them', and that: 'His Majesty hath had, and
has good reasons for all the resolutions he has taken, which a very little time
may possibly demonstrate. And however your Grace may please to treat his
ministers, certainly some respect is due to the resolutions of the King.'[78] Argyll
duly apologised, but continued to be frustrated by the slowness with which
his promised reinforcements trickled into Stirling.[79]

At source the problem was that Scotland and the Scottish army continued
to be viewed as expendable at Whitehall. Hence once they had dispatched
Carpenter's and Kerr's regiments northwards in late September, the ministers
in London were very reluctant to transfer any further troops from the army in
England, and only the strongest possible appeals from Argyll ('Sir, for my own
justification hereafter, I must end with insisting on a considerable reinforcement, for without it or a miracle, not only this country will be utterly
destroyed, but the rest of his Majestie's dominions put in the extreamest
danger')[80] and threats of resignation secured the grudging promise of three
further regiments of foot and one of dragoons from Ireland (of very mixed
quality)[81] in early October and an assurance that he could have the first
contingent of Dutch troops when they arrived.[82] Even then, as soon as problems arose with respect to operations against the southern Jacobite army, the
Dutch and Swiss auxiliaries were redirected to deal with that emergency.[83] Not
until the crisis in northern England was decisively resolved at Preston were
they finally ordered to march north and join Argyll.[84]

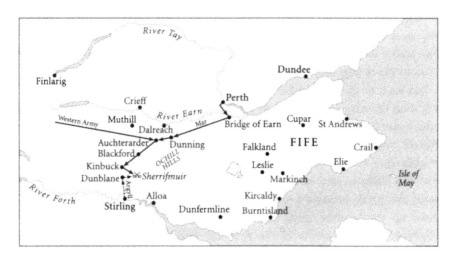

Map 4: The march to Sherrifmuir.

Mar, meanwhile, was reinforced by Huntly at the beginning of October and brought Seaforth and his army – which included a number of contingents from the smaller northern clans, and a large force of Macdonalds of Sleat – down in mid-October.[85] The virtual truce that ended hostilities in the west (see below, pp. 191–192) allowed the transfer east of Gordon of Auchintoul's forces there, which brought Mar's field army strength up to over 9,000, encamped at Perth and Auchterarder, by the beginning of November.[86] At that point Mar was in the best situation he could hope for. Though some elements of his army, such as the Mackenzies, were neither well motivated nor well armed, the bulk of his troops were now as well trained and as well equipped as they were ever going to be, he had the western clans (his best troops) to hand and he outnumbered Argyll by well over two to one. The rate of desertion from the central Jacobite army was, though, trending towards worrying levels, making it imperative that he use the army before it was further weakened.[87] Even so, Mar only cautiously advanced towards the Forth to the west of Stirling on 11 November with a view to outflanking his opponent. He had cause for trepidation. Argyll had not been wasting his time. After carefully scouting and reviewing the terrain between Stirling and Perth he had already decided if possible to fight the Jacobites on 'the rising grounds on the other side Dumblain, where we are sure of both provisions and forrage. When we are there where the ground is good, if the enemy should advance we can have no better ground to receive them in.'[88] Both armies were thus on a trajectory towards the open ground to the north-east of Dunblane: Sherrifmuir.

Argyll having been hitherto so cautious in committing his forces beyond the moss of Stirling, the vanguard of the Jacobite army was surprised on 12 November to hear from a sympathiser near Dunblane that he had advanced beyond the bridge and was deployed on the moor in battle order. Mar was at a loss what to do next, and allowed himself to be persuaded to encamp that night on the edge of the moor at Kinbuck.[89] The moor then froze overnight, which notably improved the ground for the cavalry (highly advantageous for Argyll), and the next morning was cold, creating a further problem in that the Highlanders were certain to throw off their plaids before going into action and this was likely to lead to their freezing on the field unless they fought, and won, the battle promptly. General Hamilton nonetheless took the time to draw up the Jacobite army in the customary two lines, with the western Highland clan regiments in the first line and the Lowland and northern Highland regiments in the second. The cavalry were divided into two sets of squadrons, four on the right of the first line, and three on the left of the second.[90]

The deployment of the main body of the army in this manner reflected a basic tactical problem facing the Jacobites: the Highlanders fought in very different fashion from the Lowland regiments. The Lowlanders by this point had acquired the rudiments of conventional infantry tactics, which consisted of forming the men into a firing line four or five men deep which was then marched forward to within musket shot (approximately 100 metres) of the enemy, whom they would then (hopefully) blast away with their disciplined volleys of musket fire.[91] This was the same tactical system as was used by the regular British army and, while effective when done well, was a hard fighting technique to manage because the key to success was keeping the firings regular and at least generally on target amidst the noise, smoke, screams and fear generated by a firefight. To do so required constant supervision and correction by NCOs and officers who knew what they were about.

The Highlanders fought in an entirely different fashion, making use of a motley variety of firearms, including not only regular muskets but also pistols, blunderbusses and dirks and, among the *fine* especially, the classic weapons of the contemporary Highlander: broadsword – basically a heavy, long-bladed one-handed sword – and targe, a light shield behind which an experienced Highland soldier might also carry a dirk or pistol.[92] Their classic battlefield tactics were observed by Sinclair in the ensuing battle. First they drew themselves up in a relatively deep mass, with the front two ranks composed of the *fine*. They then:

run towards the ennemie in a disorderlie manner, always firing some dropeing shots, which drew upon them a generall salvo from the ennemie, which begun at their left, opposite to us, and run to their right. No sooner that begun, the Highlandmen threw themselves flat on their bellies, and when it slackned, they started to their feet. Most threw away their fuzies [muskets], and, drawing their suords, pierced them everie where with ane incredible vigour and rapiditie, in four minutes time from their receaving the order to attack.[93]

This was a classic Highland charge of the kind that was to be highly effective in various encounters up to the mid-eighteenth century. Unfortunately it did not easily mesh with the tactics the Lowland regiments had been trained to use, and to compound the problem there was a basic language difficulty. The rank and file of the Highland units were for the most part monoglot Gaelic-speakers with very strong clan affiliation, but little respect for anyone outside it. This meant they could only be directed and controlled by their own officers (who were virtually all bilingual) and, in so far as they would heed orders from officers not of their clan, could not understand commands delivered in the Scots spoken by most of the senior Jacobite officers. Of these, only Gordon of Auchintoul, and possibly Drummond, could speak Gaelic.[94] In the confusion all contemporary battles invariably generated, this was a dangerous hostage to fortune.

Argyll, meantime, had camped overnight to the east of Dunblane near the village of Kippendavie, and in the morning also deployed his army in the customary two lines. He placed six regiments of foot in his first line with three squadrons of horse on each wing and a further squadron slightly set back behind those three, and in the second line two squadrons of horse in the centre and a regiment of foot on each wing. There was an additional nuance to this deployment in that Argyll placed both Portmore's grey dragoons and Evans's black dragoons on his right, thus ensuring consolidated striking power on that wing. His best infantry regiments were also on the right-hand side of the army.[95]

At this point both commanders had to decide whether they felt their circumstances favoured battle. Argyll had long since discussed this with his senior officers at Stirling and once he made sure exactly where the Jacobites were by personally scouting their position he proceeded forthwith into action, facing his lines to the right to turn them into columns and marching off to the north-east, further on to the moor, to prevent the Jacobites outflanking him.[96] By contrast, the Jacobites' senior officers now had to meet in their own impromptu council of war. So while their hungry men shivered for five hours

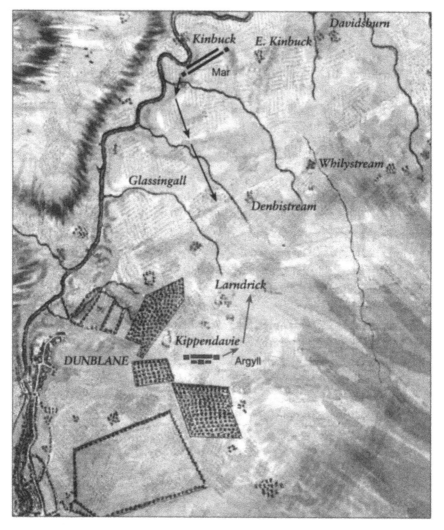

Map 5: Sherrifmuir, 13 November 1715: initial deployments.

in the November chill, their commanders debated whether to fight or fall back on Perth.[97] Mar finally assembled all the senior officers between the two lines and

> made us a very fine speech, where he laid out to us the injustice done our Royall familie, the miserie and slaverie of our countrie by being under a forreigne yoak, such as that of England occasioned by the Union, and since, to his certain knowledge, we had been longe languishing after ane opportunitie of retriveing our ancient libertie, he conjured us not to let such ane

occasion slip, which seemed to offer itself, as it were, by providence of Heaven, when, in all probabilitie, we could not meet with another so favourable, and concluded it was his opinion we should attack the enemie who were so near us, and inlarged on the whole in very stronge and moveing terms.[98]

Only Huntly raised any objection, and the council of war voted unanimously to endorse Mar's proposal to fight. This decision was certainly popular with the army. Though many of them were pressed men, the rank and file of the Jacobite army greeted the decision enthusiastically. As Sinclair recalled: 'we were no sooner got to our posts when a huzza begun, with tossing up of hats and bonnets, and run through our whole armie, on the hearing we had resolved to fight.'[99] Despite its unpromising origins and all its other difficulties morale was clearly not a problem for the Jacobite army on 13 November.

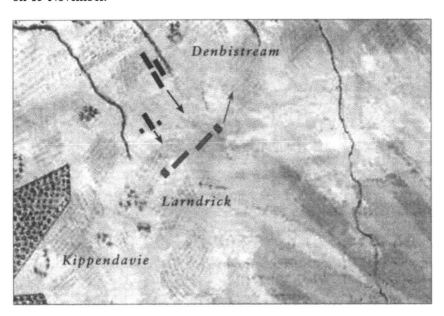

Map 6: Sherrifmuir: the armies closing.

Hamilton then reordered the army into four columns, each composed of half of the two lines, with four squadrons of horse at the front and three at the rear, and then marched these off in the general direction of Dunblane.[100] Unbeknown to either army they were now effectively marching on parallel tracks, but in opposite directions: Argyll northwards, Mar southwards. All that separated the two was a ridge of higher ground. What was about to transpire was that most intrinsically chaotic and scrambling of contemporary battles, the encounter battle (essentially one in which two armies collide with each other on the march). The actual fighting was precipitated by Mar when he observed a scouting party of Argyll's dragoons watching the Jacobite army from the high ground to the Jacobites' left and ordered the four squadrons of horse at the head of the Jacobite army and 700 Macdonalds commanded by Sir Donald Macdonald of Sleat to drive them off. When they got to the crest, however, Marischal, commanding the horse, and Sir Donald found themselves 'two musket shot' (approximately 200 metres) from Argyll's whole army, 'all marcheing in haste towards our left'.[101] Correctly discerning that Macdonald's infantry were now too close to the enemy to fall back safely, Marischal sent a galloper to Mar begging him to bring up the rest of the army as fast as possible. Mar did so, and in the process the Jacobite columns fell into total confusion. The lead column reinforced the Macdonalds, but columns two, three and four deployed higgledy-piggledy to the left of Marischal's horse, trapping his squadrons in the centre of the army when they needed to be on a wing to be in any way effective.[102] In the confusion the first and second lines also got mixed up, so that the Lowland foot ended up deploying in front of several Highland regiments and the cavalry at the rear of the Jacobite army were moved up to the right of the first column. To make matters worse, a half-unfrozen bog further disrupted the deployment of the Lowland foot.[103] Argyll, with his cavalry at the head of his own column, seems not to have been aware that the rear of his army was now in danger of attack by the Jacobites, and instead responded instinctively to the opportunity presented by the Jacobite infantry's confusion. He ordered Portmore's grey dragoons to outflank the Jacobites and then charged sword in hand at the head of Evans's black dragoons straight into the half-formed Jacobite lines, followed up by two of his eight regiments of foot. The Lowland regiments did their best to follow their recently learned drills and duly tried to fire and retire in an organised fashion, presumably so as to clear the way for the Highland infantry to move forward and attack. With the best will and the best troops in the world this would have been a difficult and dangerous manoeuvre in the face of charging cavalry, and the Lowland regiments were simply not up to it. Thus when Argyll's charge struck home they dissolved in panic, sweeping away the Highlanders massed behind them as they did so. So complete was the rout that Argyll assumed he had scored an equally complete victory and 'thought of nothing but pursuing them as long as we had day light'.[104]

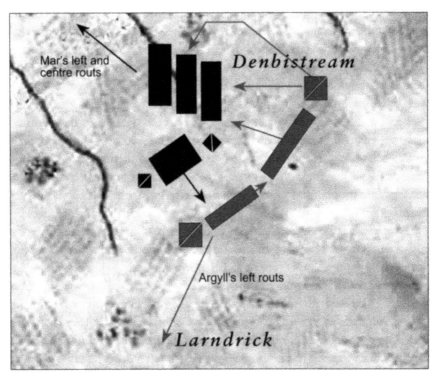

Map 7. Sherrifmuir: the battle proper.

Matters were not going so well, however, at the rear of his army. Though Marischal's four squadrons were trapped in the midst of the deploying infantry, Sinclair had deployed his three on the right of the Jacobite line in such a fashion as to deter Argyll's cavalry squadrons bringing up the rear of his army from doing to the right of the Jacobite army what Argyll was doing to the left.[105] Gordon of Auchintoul was also personally present on the crest and had been able to deploy the first column of the Jacobite army into battle order with much less confusion than elsewhere along the line. The troops under his command also consisted primarily of several regiments of Macdonalds (Sir Donald Macdonald's, Glencoe's, Glengarry's and Clanranald's), plus Sir John Maclean of Duart's regiment, the Breadalbane Campbells and Gordon of Glenbuchat's battalion of Huntly's men, who were among the best in the Jacobite army. Nonetheless he hesitated – perhaps another instance of an orthodox military commander nonplussed as to how best to use Highland troops – watching while the rear units of Argyll's army marched past, until an old officer of James II and VII's army remonstrated with him, 'with great oaths', to attack at once. Auchintoul looked for Mar to give him orders, but, finding his commander nowhere in sight, finally gave the order to attack.[106] The three infantry regiments at the rear of Argyll's column promptly turned towards the Jacobite charge and fired, killing amongst others Allan Macdonald, Captain (i.e. hereditary commander) of Clanranald, but were then struck by the Highland charge. This literally cut a great many of them to pieces and within minutes the survivors were fleeing for their lives. In the process they swept away all of Argyll's cavalry at the rear of the column, allowing virtually unhindered pursuit for some distance.[107] Marischal's cavalry squadrons, released from the centre by this success, tried charging three of Argyll's unbroken infantry regiments frontally but were mauled and correspondingly daunted by the volleys directed at them and so slid off to their right to join the pursuit of Argyll's broken foot with the Highlanders.[108]

In a manner quite characteristic of encounter battles, both armies were, by mid-afternoon, in complete chaos. Almost the only formed troops on the battlefield were Sinclair's three squadrons, incompletely held back from the pursuit by his threatening to kill any man who broke ranks.[109] On the Jacobite side, too, Mar had got involved in the pursuit of the routed government troops, Auchintoul appears to have got lost somewhere and Hamilton was caught up in the rout of the Jacobite left when he tried to take command there and rally the wavering Jacobites (one may legitimately speculate that his lack of Gaelic would have distinctly hindered his doing so).[110] Both the government and Jacobite routers were rallying by the time twilight drew on, but neither group was in a fit state to fight. General Whetham duly fell back on Stirling with what remained of the regiments on Argyll's left and individual Jacobite commanders like Cameron of Lochiel gathered what men they could and fell back towards Auchterarder.[111] On the battlefield itself Sinclair's squadrons became a nucleus around which returning pursuers rallied while he faced down Argyll's remaining cavalry. As a result, by late afternoon Mar, who had by this time reappeared, had perhaps 3,000 or so of his army regrouped and, at least theoretically, capable of further action. Argyll had, too, rallied his pursuing troops and had five regiments of foot and four squadrons of horse (probably something under 2,000 men) to fight with. The two tired and battered armies duly confronted each other for about thirty minutes, but Mar could not persuade the foot, 'who were extreamly fatigued, and had eat nothing in two days', to attack again and so the Jacobites simply watched as Argyll retired back towards Dunblane.[112] When he was safely gone Mar withdrew his own force into the night, back towards Ardoch. Next day both armies retreated to their respective bases, with each commander claiming a victory.[113]

In truth, if anyone won it was Argyll, who had at the very least fought almost two and a half times his own number to a standstill, yet he confronted no glad dawn the next day. The government's army had lost close to 40 per cent of its effectives, and though the scale of his losses diminished as stragglers returned to their units and the more lightly wounded returned to duty it was still a grave blow. Argyll estimated around 500 of his troops killed or taken prisoner. To that needs to be added the number of seriously wounded, which at this time would generally have been about equal in number, giving a net loss of approximately 1,000 men out of his total force of around 3,600, i.e. over a quarter of his army.[114] It was a grave blow, and small wonder that he warned the ministry soon after the battle that if the Jacobites advanced again he would have to fight or retreat, and 'in the first case I think both the country and this corps of troops will be lost, in the latter the country is lost, and which adds to our difficultys, our foot do not at all think they can beat more than their oun numbers'.[115] Indeed, further investigation into the collapse of the government army left led Argyll to the conclusion that 'you may depend upon it, if any action happens again they will throw down their arms, as many of them did that day, so that ... [Argyll] does not think he has above four battalions he can trust to'.[116] He duly held another council of war with his senior officers at which they agreed that if the Jacobites resumed their advance the army would abandon Stirling and retreat southwards.[117]

The Jacobites, however, were in no condition to advance anywhere, or fight anyone. Because of the phenomenal surge of desertion precipitated by the battle it is hard to be certain how many casualties the Jacobites suffered at Sherrifmuir. Mar claimed only sixty dead, but that was manifestly false. Government estimates suggest around 700 killed or captured, which sounds far more plausible, though Sinclair later observed, 'I have often wondered to see so few killed on all that ground over which he [Argyll] pursued with the dragoons'.[118] It seems, then, reasonable overall to assume the Jacobites probably suffered around 1,500 killed, seriously wounded and captured. Since this represented only about 17 per cent of their total forces they clearly came out ahead of their opponents and should have been able to pick themselves up and have another go without too much trouble. In addition, several Jacobite units, notably Rob Roy Macgregor's mixed regiment of Macgregors and Macphersons, Lord George Murray's regiment of Athollmen and John Steuart of Invernytie's regiment of Grandtully men (in the region of 1,000 men in total), were on their way to, but had not participated in, the battle and were still fresh and tolerably well equipped.[119] After 'the affair of Dumblain, in which neither side gained much honour', there was, though, no further will to fight on the Jacobite side.[120] In part this was because of the indecisive outcome of the battle and the far from negligible casualties the Jacobites had suffered. Far more important, however, was the massive surge in desertion that followed the battle. This stemmed from both Highland custom and the way the Jacobite army had been recruited. The tradition in the Highlands was for men who had done their duty and followed their chieftains to war to return home full of honour and booty after a battle. As far as many ordinary clansmen were concerned, they had fulfilled their obligation and they now took the opportunity to return home. Some Highlanders had, of course, also been forced out, as most probably had a great many of the Lowland troops, and in the chaotic aftermath of Sherrifmuir, removed as they were from the supervision of their officers and landlords, there was little or nothing to prevent them escaping home, which a great many now did. In the region of 7,500 Jacobites survived Sherrifmuir more or less unscathed; probably over half of these deserted in the days following the battle.[121] As previously noted, their desertion was not necessarily a final severing of their involvement with the uprising. Nonetheless, desertion on such a scale made further military action impracticable for some time to come.

In the interim, the Jacobites' strategic situation markedly worsened. In the south Forster's little army surrendered at Preston on 14 November, and in the north Inverness fell to the combined forces of Sutherland, Lovat and the Grants. There was still no word of where James was in his journey towards Scotland, and though the Orléans government was definitely warming to the idea of helping them the Jacobites in Scotland had no inkling that this was the case. In such circumstances it is not surprising that discussion of a negotiated end to the rebellion began to take off amongst the Jacobite leaders still at Perth. Individuals, such as Huntly, had mooted such an option even before Sherrifmuir; the debate now became general, and a faction among the Jacobites, whom for convenience I will label the 'peace' party (this included Huntly, Sinclair, Sir Robert Gordon of Gordonstoun and David Smythe of Methven), began lobbying for a formal approach to Argyll seeking terms.[122] Mar's response, though it appears two-faced, was actually quite intelligent. In Perth, as a precursor to any such formal negotiations about capitulation, he tried to persuade as many senior Jacobites as possible to sign an association committing themselves not to seek or accept separate terms.[123] At the same time he sought to establish a private line of communication with Argyll using Anne Stewart, Countess of Moray, Argyll's aunt, as an intermediary.[124] In the meantime both groups of Jacobites ill-temperedly agreed to request terms, using a government prisoner of war, Lieutenant-Colonel Albert Lawrence, as their representative to Argyll.[125]

Lawrence's arrival at Stirling at the end of November carrying the peace proposal was something of a bombshell. Argyll had spies at Perth and had got some inkling of what was afoot in advance of Lawrence's arrival, but even he was taken aback by the scope of what the Jacobites were offering. Lord Justice Clerk Cockburn's pungent response to the news – 'here is good news, peace' – well summarises the response of Scottish Whigs outwith Argyll's inner circle.[126] Lawrence brought, too, a separate, secret message from the peace party, offering 'that if they might seperately have his Majestie's mercy they would break of from the rest'.[127] Hardly surprisingly, Argyll wanted to capitalise on this golden opportunity: after all, the Jacobite army still outnumbered Argyll, had proved they could fight his regulars with at least some prospect of success, and he was privately very pessimistic about his army's condition and hence the likely outcome if it was forced to give battle again.[128] Though he returned a cautious response, telling Lawrence that he had no authority to negotiate and offer pardons, and that the Jacobites would have to wait for a response from the ministry, Argyll immediately pressed for plenipotentiary powers.[129] 'Your Lordship sees,' he forthrightly told Townshend, 'if I had power to save half a dozen of them I would tomorrow have broke this rebellion.'[130]

The response at Westminster, however, was not what the commander-in-chief in Scotland expected. The king and the Cabinet received the news very coolly indeed. Townshend made it clear in their reply that the government intended to have its full measure of retribution for the rebellion:

> Your Grace may be assured that his Majesty layes verry much to heart the sufferings of his faithful subjects by this unnatural rebellion and will most readily go into such just and honourable measures as may not only redress and recompense such as have been exposed to the fury and ravages of the rebels, but also such as may secure them from the like in the future.[131]

The king, he further informed Argyll, did not not think that 'in the present situation and circumstances of affairs, it is consistent with the honour of his government, or the future peace and quiet of his good subjects that the rebels should be admitted to any terms but those of surrendering their persons and entirely submitting to his Majesty's pleasure'.[132] Since the Jacobites who had surrendered at Preston had done so 'at pleasure', and were at that very time preparing to stand trial for treason (with all its grisly attendant penalties) where they were not already sentenced to death by firing squad (the case of the half-pay officers captured there), this was tantamount to blocking any negotiated settlement in Scotland. Argyll was clearly angered by this response. After icily thanking Townshend for explaining that his (Argyll's) orders did not give him the authority to negotiate, he sarcastically observed that the letters he had sent up in support of the rebels' requests for mercy stemmed from 'a thorough perswasion of its being for his Majestie's service, and for the good of my country, and it will be an infinite pleasure to me to find that I was entirely mistaken'.[133] He then bluntly warned that he now expected the war would be a long one, perhaps stretching into years.

It was to no avail. George I and his government had set their sights on total victory and swingeing postwar vengeance.[134] Argyll stubbornly continued to pick away at the subject until mid-January, and even thought he had found a chink in the ministry's refusal to compromise at the end of December when Townshend implied that he could assure rebels who brought over troops to the government side that they would receive clemency.[135] Unable to resist a swipe at a policy he manifestly considered wrongheaded and destructive, Argyll could not resist bitterly commenting that 'the rebellion had been over by this time', if he had had such authority in early December.[136] It was a mistake. The ministry was fed up with Argyll, his fulminations and his threats of resignation. Already in early January they had called his bluff and given him permission to return to London whenever he wanted.[137] They now firmly crushed his attempt to give himself some leeway with regard to negotiating with the Jacobites. The king, Townshend informed him, 'was surprized to find your Grace attribute the continuance of the rebellion to the orders his Majesty has thought fitt to send you'. Moreover, George I 'was from the beginning of the rebellion of an opinion that he could not either in honour or conscience go into any measures in relation to the rebells, but such as would effectually secure the future peace and quiet of his faithfull subjects'.[138] Nor could George I see any reason why Jacobite commanders like Sinclair, who had ravaged the estates of eminent, brave loyalists like Rothes, should receive any mercy even if they defected to the government. And finally, as far as the king was concerned,

> since they have put the nation to such vast expence and oblidged the king to call for the assistance of foreign troops, the greater the preparations are for the suppressing this rebellion, the less reason there is for listening to any offers of the rebells, but such as carry with them evident advantages to his Majesty's service, are absolutely consistent with the honour of his gouvernment and tending to the future quiet and security.[139]

All Argyll could do at that point was offer a grovelling apology for even raising the issue.[140] He did not, however, entirely give up. Though he was expressly forbidden to offer the rebels clemency he could and, as we shall see, did, do his best to subvert the government's efforts to impose a Carthaginian peace.

The government's frigid response to their overtures predictably delayed the disintegration of the main Jacobite army. If they were going to be treated harshly whether or not they fought on, they might as well continue the struggle in the hope that something would turn up. And, of course, they still hoped that James would arrive with French troops and stores aplenty.[141] James, for his part, had set out incognito, with just two servants, for the Channel ports on 17/28 October, dodging French officials and troops who might be forced to take cognisance of him, and doing his best to avoid detection by Stair's agents, a network of whom was keeping watch along the French coast. Stair was at the time, and has been subsequently, accused of directing these agents to assassinate James if they found him, but there is no concrete evidence that this was the case and the conduct of the ministry with respect to other would-be assassins does not suggest it would have favoured such a blatant violation of contemporary political mores.[142] Regardless, James's journey became a frustrating and increasingly desperate odyssey. He reached St Malo on the Channel coast on 28 October/8 November, but did not get a fair wind until 7/18 November. James then boarded a ship provided by the local Irish community, only to have to disembark when the wind turned contrary again. With no prospect of any break in the weather and uneasy at the lax security surrounding Ormond and his entourage, who were there too, James left them on 21 November/2 December and struck north for Dunkirk.[143] Finally, after nearly a week hiding in and around St Omer, the Irish diaspora (which had also been sheltering him) found him a ship and he sailed for Scotland on 16/27 December.[144] Though he had made secret arrangements with various Irish officers he encountered on his journey to follow him or accompany Ormond (which they later did their best to carry through), James arrived in Scotland at Peterhead on 22 December with only two attendants, a small war chest and no more arms or ammunition than would suffice for personal protection.[145] It was nothing like the reinforcement the Scottish Jacobites had been looking for.

The main Jacobite army's situation had to some extent bottomed out by mid-December. Many of the officers and chieftains of the western clan regiments had by then returned home to bring their clansmen and sub-tenants out again, and as far as we can tell their preparations to do so in the early spring were going reasonably well.[146] Huntly and Seaforth had returned to the north where they were remobilising their forces to defend their estates and the Jacobite position there, and while it is certainly the case that they were somewhat dispirited, their gathering forces did at least mean the Jacobites could hope at some point again to contest control of the region.[147] In any event, the harsh winter of 1715–16 precluded any realistic possibility of large-scale Jacobite military action. Indeed, the weather was so bad that it almost shut down the *petite guerre* that had hitherto been waged across Stirlingshire and Fife.[148] Even Argyll and his officers, with all the ferocious panoply of instruments of contemporary military discipline, from penal duties and fines to the lash, could not keep their men in camp at Stirling. Every evening crowds of rankers simply ignored their officers and took shelter in the town.[149]

Yet despite these climatic problems preparations were afoot on the government side for a winter campaign. Lieutenant-General William Cadogan arrived from London in early December with a definite remit: to wage a winter campaign that would drive the Jacobites back into the Highlands preparatory to a summer campaign that would corner and finally defeat them there.[150] Cadogan was an old soldier who had been Marlborough's right-hand man throughout the War of the Spanish Succession. Logistics and organisation were his particular specialities, though he was, too, an able officer in other circumstances.[151] Above all else, Cadogan was an absolutely loyal henchman of Marlborough's and a reliable agent of the ministry in London. From the beginning he reported back on Argyll's conduct in a damaging fashion and surreptitiously subverted his authority while maintaining outwardly good relations with him.[152] Crucially, because he was both energetic and Marlborough and the ministry's man he was able to get things moving in terms of securing the money, supplies and reinforcements necessary for a winter campaign. The captain-general and the king's ministers simply responded far better to his requests than ever they had done to Argyll's. Cadogan was also a very energetic officer, and it was characteristic of him that within a day of arriving at Stirling he was personally scouting the roads north to Perth and reviewing the battlefield at Sherrifmuir. Arrangements to transport a full siege artillery train and pontoon bridge system to Stirling were quickly made, and when the train was delayed by storms, Cadogan secured permission to strip Berwick and Edinburgh of the necessary heavy artillery instead.[153]

The whole conduct of operations by the government army was revitalised by Cadogan's presence. In mid-December Argyll used the threat of naval bombardment to force the Jacobite garrison out of Burntisland, and occupied the town with a battalion of Edinburgh militia.[154] This was only the precursor, however, to the dispatch of contingents of Dutch and Swiss troops to various outposts in Fife with a view to contesting control of the county with the Jacobites. The strategic intent was to 'protect the forrage for the use of the King's troops, there being a considerable quantity yet in that shire, nixt to hinder the enemie from getting coalls, they being straitened in firing'.[155]

Cadogan supplied Rothes with a force of 400 regulars, including 200 Dutch infantry, to set this in train in early January, but they were initially blocked by the Jacobites throwing a garrison of 300 into Falkland. This only briefly delayed the government foray, and by mid-January defensible houses were being held by government troops in the heart of Fife and even within eight miles of Perth.[156] The weather still hampered operations on both sides, but as far as was physically possible, the *petite guerre* was also back in full swing by that time, and clashes between government and Jacobite troops were again a regular occurrence. Though the Jacobites scored the most notable success in these encounters when Rob Roy Macgregor decoyed and then ambushed a party of militia and Swiss at Markinch, killing two and forcing the others to surrender, the net strategic effect was in the government's favour.[157] The Jacobites had accumulated more than sufficient food at Perth to see them through the winter, but by mid-January supplies of coal were so low that they began 'to burne their household furniture'.[158]

By then the accumulation of troops and supplies in and around Stirling was reaching the point where the winter campaign could commence. The key variable was now the weather. Snow and drifting had been almost continuous since 10 December, and when Argyll and Cadogan reconnoitred the roads north as far as Auchterarder on 23 January they found 'a vast depth of snow, in so much that we were obliged to march the whole way one horse after another, and for the most part up to the horse's bellies, which made Mr Cadogan and all of us of opinion that it was impossible to encamp'.[159] Quartermaster Charles Dubourgay, however, came up with a plan for coal wagons to accompany the army along with equipment to build temporary shelters, while Cadogan organised the impressment of local people along the roads to clear them of snow in advance of the army's march.[160] All was ready to go on 27 January, the official commencement of the march north (Cadogan was already probing ahead as far as Ardoch with the advance guard by that point). And as a result of these careful preparations, once launched the government army straitly marched from Stirling and Dunblane to Perth without being seriously inconvenienced by either the Jacobites or the weather. The only exception was the siege artillery train, which had to be sent back to Stirling after it had advanced only four miles in two days.[161]

The preparations for the march on Perth were so obvious that it was impossible to prevent the Jacobites learning of them. Given the weather, however, Mar and James could not believe that it would actually transpire, though they still took the precaution of ordering the burning of the six villages to make certain it would be impossible.[162] As Mar observed:

After all when they have no cover left them I see not how it is possible for them to march. We are like to be frose in the house and how they can endure the cold for one night in the fields I cannot conceive. And then the roads are so that but one can go abreast, as their party did yesterday, and ther is no going off the road for horse and scarce for foot without being lost in the snow.[163]

From the time he arrived in Perth James also sent out letters urgently requesting that the western clan chieftains Huntly and Seaforth bring up reinforcements forthwith, and the recruiting of new levies was ordered in friendly areas like Aberdeenshire and Angus.[164] As Argyll approached Perth, however, all this resolution rapidly faded and a few hours before the advance guard of the government army arrived there the Jacobites evacuated the town and retreated towards Dundee.[165]

Perth was certainly not the most defensible of Scottish towns. There was an old Cromwellian citadel just beyond the city, but it could have been no more than an outpost at best.[166] Sinclair, 'a French fellow, who had been a footman of Beaufort's, and had takne up the trade of being a danceing and fenceing master in the North', and subsequently Hamilton, had all tried to do something about preparing minimal fortifications, but the net result was far from impressive.[167] Baron John Clerk, who saw them in 1717, described them as consisting of 'several lines and redoubts for defending the avenues of the toun', plus a 'a small trench of about 8 feet wide with a parapit' around the rest of the town. Overall he considered them 'very poor defences'.[168] Sinclair agreed: Hamilton, he believed, 'had perfited [perfected] his lines by leaving out [the] high ground', as a consequence of which 'they had been so raked [by artillery] that a mouse could not [have] lived in his lines'.[169] Yet the Jacobites had a hugely important ally: one of the worst winters of the early eighteenth century. While it is true that Cadogan and Argyll had achieved the remarkable feat of getting the army from Stirling to Perth virtually intact, it is not clear they could have sustained it there if the Jacobites had had the resolution to stand even a brief siege. Each of the government soldiers was carrying five days' rations (plus a quota of official-issue brandy to ward off the cold) and a further eleven days' worth was transported in wagons with the army, so Argyll's food supply was more than adequate.[170] His siege artillery was, however, unable to get up to Perth and the light guns he had with him could not have wrought sufficient devastation on Perth's defences as to make a stormable breach.[171] Argyll could, of course, have launched an unprepared assault on the town, but even Perth's minimal defences would have made that an uncertain prospect, and Jacobite troops had shown at Preston how well even semi-amateurs like themselves could defend a town behind barricades. The key vulnerability of Argyll's army was that it could carry only a limited amount of coal to keep the men warm as they encamped in prefabricated shelters amidst the snowdrifts.[172] If the Jacobites had forced them to settle into a prolonged blockade of Perth they would have been in trouble. As one experienced soldier remarked before the march commenced: 'I'm apt to belive the cold will kill as many of our men as the enemy', and Argyll himself confided, 'if they take the measures which I would do were I in their place it will prove a difficult task'.[173] But if the Jacobites' mistake was in not allowing time for the weather to do their killing for them, their failure to do so points to a basic problem with the Jacobite army: by this time it and in particular its senior officers were badly demoralised.

James did his public duty when he arrived in Scotland, projecting himself as the returning king of popular mythology, graciously receiving delegations of Episcopalian clergymen with loyal declarations, holding court and touching for the King's Evil (a form of tuberculosis known as scrofula).[174] Privately, however, he was appalled at the state of affairs on the Jacobite side. 'To speak plain', he confided to Bolingbroke, the situation was 'none of the best'. Indeed, 'all was in confusion before my arrival; terms of accommodation pretty openly talked of, the Highlanders returned home, and but four thousand men left at Perth; and had I retarded some days longer, I might in all probability have had a message not to come at all.' The Jacobites' plan was to hold on until the spring, but if no reinforcements materialised at that point, 'it is impossible we can meet the advantages the enemies have over us in all particulars; it must make us unable to stand against them, and the greatest zeal and affection will cool at last, when all prospect of success is vanished'.[175] As we have already seen, large numbers of heritors had by this time deserted and what was left of the Jacobite leadership was increasingly quarrelsome. To compound the problem, Hamilton had been discredited by Sherrifmuir, Gordon of Auchintoul seems to have been unable to replace him and General Robert Echlin, newly arrived from France, had been sent north to assist Huntly, so the army even lacked central military direction.[176] James had some military experience, having several times accompanied the French army in Flanders during the War of the Spanish Succession, but he was no warrior prince, so this situation could not be remedied. All James could do was desperately to appeal to Orléans to send Berwick and some of the senior Irish officers to fill the void.[177]

This was the background to the collapse of the Jacobite army in the face of Argyll's advance north. Before leaving Perth they abandoned their baggage train and threw their artillery into the Tay, 'so that they took litle more with them then what they carryd on ther backs'.[178] They then retreated in two columns along separate roads towards Brechin, one via Coupar Angus, the other via Dundee, and there took the coast road towards Aberdeen, all the while losing men as desertion became rampant. Despite being joined by little parties of Irish officers belatedly arrived from France and detachments recalled from Fife, the army was disintegrating with literally every mile it marched away from Perth, and by the time it reached Montrose on 1 February it was probably down to less than 4,000 men.[179] This was despite the fact that the Jacobites were able to outmarch their opponents; as Argyll ruefully observed, 'they are in truth able to march three miles for our one'.[180] The Jacobite army, such as it was by this time, remained at Montrose until 5 February, but after two days of anguished consultation with Mar and his other senior officers, assessing what prospect there was of reconstituting the army in the north, on 4 February James called together a select group of those remaining and announced that he was going to leave that night on a French ship, the *Maria Theresa* of Saint-Malo, taking Mar and a handful of others with him.[181] His decision to do so was greeted with derision by the Whigs (and some Jacobites) at the time and distinctly angered the army, who, when they discovered he was gone, 'were in the greatest confusion imaginable, running from house to house seeking their king'.[182] But, in truth, given the way the Jacobite army was fast disintegrating he did not have much choice if he wanted to escape being captured, and his continued presence in Scotland was certainly making it more difficult for his followers to negotiate their submission. In what may be an indication that he saw the latter as the most urgent task ahead, James appointed Gordon of Auchintoul commander-in-chief in Scotland with full authority to negotiate surrender terms.[183]

Government forces took Montrose unopposed on 6 February, which effectively closed major military operations in the central theatre of the conflict. Detachments of Atholl's men subsequently chased off a couple of outlying Jacobite garrisons holding out near Blair Atholl without encountering serious resistance, and Argyll quartered detachments in Montrose, Dundee, Arbrothick and Brechin to disarm Angus and in Perth, Dunkeld and Coupar of Angus to disarm Perthshire, but these were just mopping-up operations.[184] By late February the commissioners of the customs in Scotland felt sufficiently confident of their officers' security once again to send them back into the region so that 'the revenue of excise will flourish as formerly'.[185] The looting of the area by government troops, of course, continued and was terminated only by the sudden transfer south of the bulk of Argyll's army (by that time commanded by Cadogan) in response to an alarmist report from Stair that a

Franco-Swedish invasion of southern England, with James in its baggage train, was imminent.[186]

The reimposition of the government's authority, though, should not be confused with the re-emergence of civil order. That took time to develop. New sets of Whig magistrates were installed in the burghs retaken by the government, but their authority was initially fragile and dependent as often as not on government troops stationed nearby.[187] The Kirk synods again began meeting and prosecuting Episcopalian interlopers and clergy who had accommodated the Jacobite order. Particularly notorious Episcopalian divines were also arrested and carted off to Edinburgh for trial.[188] Though the common people in Scotland were generally just disarmed (and doubtless robbed, if they had anything worth stealing) by the government troops, the back-country areas of Perthshire and Angus were full of fugitive heritors trying to wait out the government's interest in capturing them. The withdrawal of most of the government detachments holding down Angus, Perthshire and Stirlingshire southwards in March accordingly allowed a minor recrudescence of prewar civil disorder. At the end of May a number of Angus Whigs submitted a memorial complaining that they were being attacked, threatened and harassed by small groups of these fugitives, one of whom had been heard to declaim that 'he would think no more to shoot one of the Whigg party, if he could meet with him, than to shoot a mad dog upon the high road'.[189] Only with time, as habit and custom reinforced the exercise of Whig authority in the burghs, the élite reabsorbed its outlaw Jacobite members and government attempts at retribution faltered and failed (see below, pp. 236–48), did a truly civil order reassert itself.

CHAPTER 7

'Secure in Valour's Station': Military Operations, September 1715–April 1716, the Northern, Southern and Western Theatres

Notwithstanding the fact that the rebellion was won and lost in the central Scottish theatre of operations, the three peripheral theatres played a significant role in its course and development. The outcome in the southern Scottish/northern English theatre was potentially decisive for the whole, and victory in the western Scottish theatre of operations could have boosted the Jacobites to victory in Scotland at least. The northern Scottish theatre only episodically influenced events elsewhere. Regardless of their military importance, however, the ancillary theatres are worth closer examination because the course of military events there was an expression of their unique sociopolitical dynamics. The origins of defeat and victory obviously lay therein but, just as importantly, so did the seeds of the Jacobite movement's survival.

Southern Scotland and Northern England, October to November 1715

After the false start with Winton in mid-September the Jacobite conspirators in the southern Lowlands and Borders had remained quiet while the rest of the rebellion unfolded north of the Forth. That they were, however, merely biding their time is apparent from the clash between Hepburn of Keith and those trying to arrest him and a second, failed conspiracy to take Edinburgh by surprise at the end of September which was foiled by Islay.[1] Most of the region's leading Jacobites – noblemen such as David Murray, Viscount Stormont, Carnwath and William Gordon, Viscount Kenmure – had refused to answer their summonses to appear at Edinburgh to give sureties for their good behaviour and were skulking in remote areas, waiting to see what might turn up.[2] Their situation was transformed by the northern English rising on 6 October. As we have seen, this was something of a damp squib, but the first reports had Forster and Derwentwater mustering a great many more men than was actually the case and looking highly threatening.[3] The rebels' numbers, moreover, did markedly increase during their first uncertain probes southwards from Warkworth, in part as more northern English gentry horse joined them, and in part because the Scots Border Jacobites appear to have taken the English rising as their own signal to muster. Several bodies of Scots accordingly gathered and rode over the old frontier into Northumberland to join the coalescing southern Jacobite army.[4]

The Jacobites' key problem there was that their leaders really had no idea what to do after they failed to take Newcastle. Forster was the nominal commander, but only because he was the most prominent Protestant involved at that point. He had no military experience and an indecisive character. Derwentwater would have been an equally inexperienced, though more energetic, commander, but being a Catholic he could not be seen to command the army. The southern army consequently spent two weeks meandering from town to town and otherwise dawdling wherever it found relatively congenial lodgings, as it did at Hexham and Kelso.[5] By the end of this it probably still numbered less than 400 men. Meanwhile, the government was not wasting time. General George Carpenter was dispatched north within days with three regiments of dragoons and one regiment of foot (approximately 700 men), though the latter was so newly raised that it was still in civilian clothing.[6] Carpenter's orders were to track down the Jacobite army and destroy it, but before he could catch up with it Forster took his men north to join Kenmure's rebels at Rothbury on 19 October.[7]

Kenmure had raised his own standard at Moffat on 12 October and had quickly gathered in the region of 200 men. His plan was to seize Dumfries, in the heart of the most strongly Presbyterian country in Scotland.[8] Bad luck, however, prevented him intercepting the Lord-Lieutenant of Galloway, William Johnstone, Marquess of Annandale, who was travelling through Moffat on his way west and whose capture would have disrupted the efforts of local loyalists to resist the Jacobites. Annandale nonetheless had to take refuge in Lochwood House until he could be rescued and brought off to Dumfries in the middle of the night by a party of Whig gentry volunteers.[9] There he energetically barricaded the town and summoned in local Whigs of all stripes to aid in its defence. Though Kenmure's force 'were 200 horse, weell mounted and weell armed, wee much about the same numbers, but verie ill armed, and all foott, verie ill provided with ammunition', the prospect of having to drive out the defenders of Dumfries sword in hand daunted him and rather than attack the town he turned away south to join Forster.[10]

When their forces eventually united at Rothbury they were still probably no more than 600 horse, and over half of them Scots. Unfortunately for the southern army, moreover, the junction between Forster and Kenmure produced no fresh ideas as to what to do next. They were rescued from their indecision by the march southwards of the force Mackintosh of Borlum had led across the Forth, or rather, what was left of it. After prudently evacuating Leith citadel rather than face Argyll's imminent return with artillery, Borlum had withdrawn to Seton House, Winton's principal seat, on the way facing down at least one detachment of Whig volunteer horse that threatened his rearguard. There he forted up and prepared to defend the main building, which was 'a large old strong house with two courts well waled round', and thus capable of standing an assault, though not a siege.[11] Argyll, though forced to return to Stirling by Mar's feint southwards, left Wightman and 250 of his regulars, plus several units of militia and volunteers, to ensure the safety of Edinburgh and pursue the Jacobites, which Borlum seems to have considered too strong a force to attack.[12] Thus Borlum, too, was left uncertain what to do next. His original orders seem to have been to try and take Edinburgh or otherwise link up with Jacobite forces in southern Scotland, possibly with a view to moving west against Glasgow, but he was now in a very difficult situation.[13] His ammunition supply was so low that at the confrontation at Leith his men had had to hold their fire despite Argyll's troops lingering within musket-shot for some time, and his force was haemorrhaging men at a prodigious rate as desertion became rampant.[14] By 19 October Borlum was down to about 1,200 men. New orders from Mar, smuggled in via Port Seton, directing him 'to march toward England, to join the new-risen rebels in Northumberland', nonetheless set him marching south through Winton's estates and past Haddington ('the most disaffected place of the shire', according to Tweeddale), which brought in a number of local recruits.[15] Even so, when he got to Duns after a gruelling march across the Lammermuir Hills Borlum's men were 'exceedingly dispirited', and their numbers had only increased to about 1,400; the influx of new recruits was offset by the desertion of hundreds of those who had crossed the Forth.[16] After two days' rest there and some communication with Forster's forces near the border Borlum struck south to link up with them at Kelso on 22 October. Neither side was in the best of shape. The day prior to Forster and Borlum's arrival Sir William Bennet of Grubbet had tried to fortify Kelso with a view to defending it against the Jacobites, only to find his men slipping away rather than fight. He accordingly decamped before Forster entered the town.[17] Borlum, for his part, tried to enter the town in an impressive fashion, personally leading his men in with their bagpipes playing, 'but they made a very indifferent figure, for the rain and their long marches had extremely fatigued them'.[18]

The final coalescence of all the Jacobite forces in southern Scotland and northern England into one army also resurrected the question of what to do next. Borlum's new orders had only instructed him to link up with the northern English and southern Scottish rebels, and apparently did not direct him as to what he should do thereafter. A subsequent letter from Mar was no help at all, as he 'left it to themselves to do what was thought most expedient for the service'.[19] Hence the question became the subject of a running dispute for the next ten days within the leadership of the southern army. Essentially the issue pitted a section of the Scots leadership, led by Winton, against the English, led by Forster, Widdrington and Derwentwater. The great majority of the army was, of course, Scots, but most of the Scots leaders, such as Kenmure, Borlum and Nairn, apparently took a neutral position. Winton's contention was that the best course for the army, given the overall strategic situation, was to strike west towards Dumfries and Glasgow. Their capture would open the way for a march north to unite with the western Jacobite army which was, as far as they knew, busy besieging Inverary, and they could then outflank Stirling in a renewed march on Edinburgh. The English leaders countered by arguing that more campaigning in Scotland was not going to win the war, and that the best service they could do would be to spread the rebellion deep into England. They could point to the fact that there had been plenty of Tory/Jacobite rioting that summer and that, to their certain knowledge, many of their friends were disaffected and/or involved in Jacobite plotting.[20] A bona fide Jacobite army marching by their homes would be sure to embolden them to come out in rebellion.

With perfect hindsight it is easy to see that Winton's more conservative strategy would have made much more effective use of the southern army. In a purely strategic sense, however, the English leaders were right: in the long run the chances of the Scots Jacobites succeeding unsupported were very slim indeed. In any event, the English arguments prevailed. Borlum's observation, 'why the devil not go into England, where there is ... meat, men, and money?', is our best insight into why the majority of the Scots leaders finally agreed.[21] They did so, however, without asking the opinion of their junior officers and men, who overwhelmingly favoured Winton's strategy. The first time their senior officers tried to lead the army into England, on 29 October, the infantry *en masse* 'refused to goe, saying they would be all knockt on the head, at last drew up and threatened to fire on the horse, who were obliged to comply with the foot and they marcht last night to Hawick'.[22] For the next two days the army then paralleled the old frontier as the senior Scots officers tried to persuade their men to follow them south and their men insisted 'that they would fight if they would lead them on to the enemy, but they would not go to England'.[23] When this was finally essayed again, on 31 October, after 'making great promises, and giving money to the men', approximately 500 still refused to go and instead deserted in a body.[24]

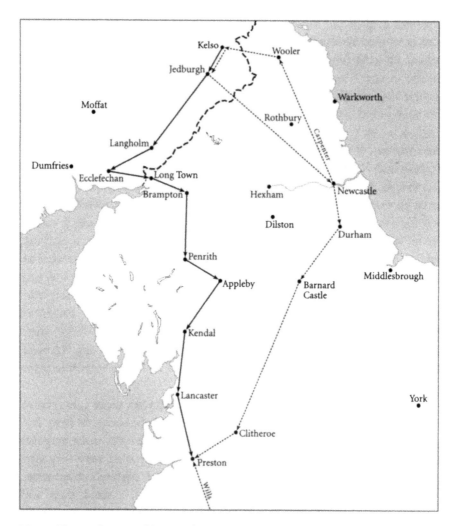

Map 8: The southern Jacobite army's march to Preston.

The army that marched into England on 1 November was, then, about 1,400 strong, roughly 50 per cent of it infantry. The only immediate gain from the move was that the rate of desertion among Borlum's foot seems to have fallen off to little or nothing thereafter, probably because those who were going to desert had already done so and because the ordinary Highlanders who remained were now truly moving through an alien land.[25] Desertion, however, continued amongst the horse, and probably for the same reasons as a 'Mr Aynsly' from Jedburgh and his friends departed: 'not liking the prospect of their affairs, nor their management'.[26] Morale was doubtless improved, too, by the regular payment of the infantry using the revenues collected in each town the army entered and by their first military success.[27] For though Carpenter had been force-marching after the southern army for nearly two weeks, and had exhausted his troops, the army's leaders had never been able to screw their courage up to the point of actually attacking him, despite the fact that Jacobite scouts had established 'that their horses were jaded', to say nothing of most of Carpenter's cavalry being newly raised and barely trained, and his infantry 'raw and undisciplined'.[28] Instead they had effectively avoided all combat. Fortunately for them, they now encountered troops even less prepared for it than they were: the *posse comitatus* of Cumberland and Westmorland assembled near Penrith. These, as noted above, simply refused to fight at all, instead throwing away their weapons and fleeing forthwith. It is possible there may even have been some Jacobite sympathisers amongst them, as, according to one Jacobite source, when the Jacobites released the prisoners they had taken in the encounter they, 'with joyful huzzas, cryed, "God save King James, and prosper his merciful army"'.[29] None, though, are noted as having volunteered to join their captors, and very few recruits indeed came in as the army continued its march south through Appleby and Kirby Lonsdale towards Lancaster.[30]

As with every other town they entered in northern England, the southern army's entry into Lancaster was unopposed, despite the efforts of local loyalists to throw something together at the last minute. The town did not have modern fortifications, but it was more defensible than Preston proved to be and there was clearly a body of opinion amongst the Jacobite officers that they should turn it into their base of operations.[31] Forster, officially commander of the army once it entered England, did not choose to do so, though he did rest the army there for a couple of days, during which time the first substantial numbers of recruits (200 or so, according to one estimate) began to come in. In principle these were very welcome, but in fact less so than they might otherwise have been because of their religion: 'they were most of them papists, which made the Scots gentlemen and the Highlanders mighty uneasy, very much suspecting the cause, for they expected all the High Church party to have joined them'.[32] Shortly before the southern army arrived in Lancaster it had also received word from the Manchester Jacobites that they were prepared and ready to rise as soon as the army reached them, which 'rouzed the spirits of the Highlanders, and animated them exceedingly', and, too, determined Forster to push on south.[33] The army duly marched via Garstang to Preston and proclaimed James III there on 10 November.[34]

Government forces were, however, closing in by this time. After giving his men some much needed rest, Carpenter had left his infantry at Newcastle and continued the pursuit with his three regiments of cavalry alone, 'with a designe to fall upon their rear'.[35] Meantime Major-General Charles Wills had occupied Manchester with eight regiments of horse and foot and was probing northward to locate the Jacobites with a view to attacking them. Two troops of Stanhope's horse were, in fact, reconnoitring Preston as the Jacobites arrived in the town and quickly carried the news back to him.[36] Wills, having left a regiment behind in Manchester to overawe the city, was by this time just a few miles away in Wigan with six regiments of dragoons and one of foot and there held a council of war with his senior officers at which they agreed they should attack the Jacobites in Preston as soon as possible. To boost his forces and provide labourers if he needed any siegeworks to be constructed he sent out an appeal to all the local loyalists to join him with as many men as they could, armed or unarmed, and sent a message to Carpenter asking him to come up with all speed.[37]

A substantial number of recruits had come in while the southern Jacobite army was at Preston, though again there was an 'abundance of Roman Catholics' amongst them.[38] The town was also generally friendly and the Jacobite officers spent most of their time there 'courting and feasting'.[39] Though he knew Wills was at Wigan and was warned the night before the battle that Wills intended to attack the next day, Forster nonetheless gave orders for the army to march on southward on 12 November, for some reason still confident that there were no government troops within forty miles of him.[40] He was thus greatly taken aback when he received news that Wills was advancing along the Wigan road towards Preston and clearly intended to attack the town. Rather than fight in the open Forster ordered all his outlying units, including a small unit of Highlanders holding a bridge over the River Ribble that Wills would have had to fight his way across, to withdraw into the town. Farquharson of Invercauld, who commanded there, only reluctantly did so, though, since the river was fordable elsewhere than at the bridge, he could at best have slowed Wills down, not stopped him. In Preston proper the other senior officers were meanwhile directing the barricading of the main roads into the town and their men were occupying defensible houses alongside them.[41]

Since the government forces had no artillery with them, Wills's only recourse, as he was determined to assault rather than blockade Preston, was to dismount most of his dragoons and use them in support of his solitary regiment of foot, who, in turn, were going to have to bear the brunt of the fighting. He apparently decided on this approach despite the fact that his troops were for the most part newly raised and barely trained.[42] And as any officer as experienced as Wills would have known that even poor-quality troops can put up stiff resistance in an urban environment, it seems reason-

1. Queen Anne.

2. John Campbell, Duke of Argyll.

3. Henry St John, Viscount Bolingbroke.

4. King George I.

5. King George II when Prince of Wales.

6. James Butler, Duke of Ormond.

7. James Stanhope.

8. James Francis Edward Stuart.

9. Charles Townshend, Viscount Townshend.

10. John Erskine, Earl of Mar.

able to surmise that he held the Jacobite army in such contempt that he did not think it could withstand any kind of determined attack. This hypothesis is supported by the careless manner with which he surrounded the town (leaving part of it unscreened) and directed his attacks. There was little attempt at coordination, and the Jacobites were thus allowed to move troops from one part of the town to another to meet particular crises and exploit opportunities.[43] Forster, for his part, seems to have been totally at a loss how to conduct the battle, and most of the vigorous defence the Jacobites offered stemmed from the personal initiative of lower-ranking officers.[44]

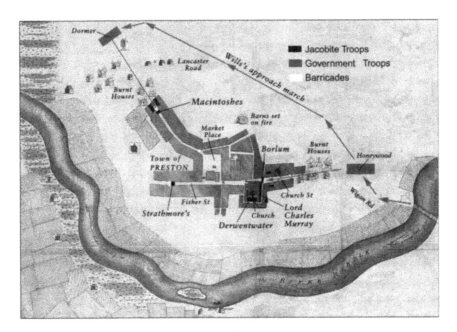

Map 9: The battle of Preston, 12/13 November 1715.

The first government attack, commanded by Brigadier Philip Honeywood, was launched against the barricade manned by Jacobite troops commanded personally by Borlum. There, Preston's regiment of foot and a composite unit of dismounted dragoons 'met with such a reception, and so terrible a fire was made upon them, as well from the barricado as from the houses on both sides, that they were obliged to retreat'.[45] This prompted some officers from Preston's (an old regular regiment now better known by its later designation: the Cameronians) to occupy the house of the Whig MP for Preston, Sir Henry Hoghton (which was large and overlooked all those around it), and the buildings opposite it in order to provide covering fire for a renewed assault. Lieutenant-Colonel George Baillie, Lord Forrester, then led the rest of the unit, plus the dismounted dragoons, via the side streets to get closer to the barricade defended by Lord Charles Murray and the remnants of the Atholl regiments. Once close enough, they 'came on very furiously', to fight the defenders hand to hand over the barricade. The struggle was a bloody, sustained one in which Lord Charles Murray personally killed several of the attackers, before reinforcements led by Derwentwater and Captain Philip Lockhart took the government troops in the flank and sent them reeling back in disorder. Preston's regiment was badly mauled in the course of these attacks, and Forrester himself was shot in the face, after which the regiment, which was the cutting edge of Honeywood's assault, lost its stomach for the fight and lapsed into desultory exchanges of fire with the Jacobite defenders from Hoghton's house for the rest of the day.[46]

The second attack, commanded by Brigadier James Dormer, was composed entirely of dismounted dragoons and directed at the barricade by the wind-mill defended by Colonel Lachlan Macintosh, the chieftain of the clan. He deployed about 300 men to defend it, the majority of them probably his own clansmen. There the government troops tried a straightforward advance on the barricade, but Macintosh's defenders 'made a dreadful fire upon the king's forces, killing many on the spot', which so unnerved the inexperienced soldiers engaged in the attack that they fell back and apparently could barely be persuaded to advance again.[47] Thereafter the fighting at this barricade died away to desultory exchanges of fire between the two sides. Elsewhere around the town the fighting never got beyond that stage. Nevertheless, in several places one or other side set fire to a number of houses either accidentally or deliberately and these burned on as darkness fell and the fighting finally petered out. The Jacobites then granted their opponents a ceasefire to retrieve their dead and wounded.[48] There seems to have been no question in the minds of either side that the Jacobites had had the better day. Wills later minimised his casualties in the official report, but the witnesses were all pretty much agreed that the government troops suffered badly, to the number of about 180 dead and seriously wounded and 50 or so taken prisoner. The Jacobites lost in the region of 35 on all counts.[49]

Even so, the southern Jacobite army was in a bad predicament. It had punished Wills for a premature and ill-considered series of attacks, and his infantry had been so badly mauled that they were unlikely to be up for another assault on the barricades. The Jacobites' problem was that they were now short of gunpowder and their barricades would not stand up to serious artillery bombardment, which meant they could not remain in Preston because it was merely a matter of time before the government forces brought some heavy guns up from elsewhere. On the other hand, any hope of coming out fighting was apparently foreclosed by the arrival of Carpenter and three more regiments of horse the next day (13 November). Carpenter superseded Wills and immediately instituted a proper blockade of the town.[50] Unless the Jacobites could break that blockade they faced mounting odds and certain defeat when heavy artillery arrived. In fact, however, their situation was not quite so desperate as it looked. Wills's troops were shaken, and the three regiments Carpenter had brought with him were all newly raised and barely trained horse – in other words little better than their Jacobite counterparts. Thus a sortie by the Jacobites offered them at least a fighting chance of both breaking out of what was fast becoming a trap and inflicting a comprehensive defeat on a major government army. That they did not take this option was a token not of how demoralised the army was (it was cock-a-hoop and keen to carry the battle to the enemy), but how traumatised their senior officers were by the fighting the previous day.[51]

Forster and Widdrington, in particular, seem to have been taken aback by the violence they had witnessed, and they correspondingly used the ceasefire which allowed the government forces to retrieve their dead and wounded secretly to send Colonel Henry Oxburgh to speak to Wills and ask for terms.[52] Contemporary customs of war usually allowed the successful defenders of a town the honours of war, according to which they would march out with 'drums beating, ball in mouth, match lighted at both ends, colours flying', plus all their personal baggage and full leave to carry on the war elsewhere, or else be made prisoners according to the rules laid down by existing 'cartels' between their respective governments.[53] These cartels, in turn, arranged for the prisoners' maintenance on parole and their eventual exchange or ransoming by their employers. Prisoners would certainly not be maltreated, though their personal possessions might be plundered. Forster, Widdrington and Oxburgh apparently believed they could obtain 'good terms', because Oxburgh was personally acquainted with several officers on the government side.[54] Wills, however, sensing weakness, demanded the Jacobites surrender at discretion, which is to say under the worst terms that could be allowed to besieged troops according to contemporary usage. If they surrendered at discretion the only thing their captors guaranteed them was that they would not immediately kill them.[55] In the meantime he demanded the Jacobites give hostages to ensure that they observed several secondary conditions he imposed on Oxburgh: that they cease to fortify the town and desist from attempts to escape from it.[56]

When Oxburgh returned with Wills's terms Forster and Widdrington wanted to accept them immediately, and only violence and threats of violence seem to have prevented their doing so. When the news broke more generally a furious row broke out among the Jacobite officers, 'and severall of the gentlemen reproached [Forster] to his face, and all he could answer was, that he was sensible of the incapacity he had for his office, cryed lyke a child, was sory for what he had done'.[57] Worse was to follow. According to John Patten, an Anglican minister who later turned king's evidence and wrote a memoir of the Preston campaign, fighting broke out amongst the Jacobites themselves, in which one man was killed and seven wounded for advocating acceptance of the surrender terms. Another Jacobite gentleman tried to shoot Forster, who was saved only when Patten knocked the pistol aside so the shot missed. When Colonel Cotton appeared under flag of truce next morning to demand the Jacobites' answer, and sent a drummer accompanying him to deliver an order to some government troops to cease fire while he talked with the Jacobites, the man was shot dead by some of the rebels, 'who were averse to all thoughts of surrender'.[58]

It was also clear to all present that 'the common men were one and all against capitulating, and were terribly enraged when they were told of it, declaring that they would die fighting, and that when they could defend their posts no longer, they would force their way out, and make a retreat'.[59] This encouraged a group of officers who included Winton, Nairn and Derwentwater to resolve to try and cut their way out. They asked Borlum for the support of the Scots infantry in doing this, which he at first promised, then failed to deliver.[60] It was a final token of what was by now the almost complete breakdown of command and control on the Jacobite side. The army had virtually collapsed and many Jacobites, including, one suspects, a lot of the local volunteers, simply discarded their weapons and slipped out of the town during the night. By morning on 14 November, the time Forster had agreed the surrender was to take place, there was practically no Jacobite army left. Lachlan Macintosh – who was one of the hostages sent over to the government lines as a token of the Jacobites' willingness to abide by Wills's subsidiary terms regarding fortification and escape – defiantly told him that morning, 'he could not answer that the Scotch would surrender in that manner, for that the Scots were people of desperate fortunes, and that he had been a soldier himself and knew what it was to be a prisoner at discretion'. Wills retorted by telling him to return to Preston and pledging, 'I will attack the town, and the consequence will be, I will not spare one man of you.'[61] When Macintosh got there he found that apart from Lockhart's troop of horse and Strathmore's regiment, who were still behaving as if they were military units, the rest of the army had degenerated into a demoralised mob incapable of resistance, and he had to return and humbly tell Wills that he and the rest of the Scots would accept the surrender terms along with the English.[62] In a final humiliation the government troops proceeded to enter the town even before the officially agreed time for the capitulation in order to begin plundering the prisoners and the townspeople willy-nilly (another of the contemporary customs of war was that when a town surrendered at discretion after initially offering resistance the ordinary soldiers had a right to sack it). It was a suitably sordid end to a thoroughly inglorious encounter.[63]

Northern Scotland, September 1715 to February 1716

The first public appearance of a body of men in arms to seize a town and proclaim James VIII – in many respects the irretrievable true beginning of the rising – actually took place in northern Scotland when Mackintosh of Borlum seized control of Inverness at the head of 2–300 men on 14 September.[64] His conduct there, and that of his men, very much fitted in with the general pattern already noted above. What was uncharacteristic of the fighting elsewhere, however, was the exceptional restraint exercised by both sides throughout the war in northern Scotland. Armies of several thousand Jacobites and Whigs at various times marched and counter-marched across each other's territory, offered battle, advanced and retreated and so on, and on the evidence seen by this author a total of two men were killed during the course of over five months of warfare.[65] Doubtless this low number is owing to partial survival of the sources, and there may well be evidence the author has missed, so that it is surely the case that more than two men died in the war in the north. But probably not a great many more. This means there was something crucially different about the war there that needs to be explained.

The key to the conduct of the war in the north is that it was very largely fought by Highland clansmen. Both sides put together composite armies consisting of men summoned and forced out by their landlords and chieftains. Thus the Whig army in the north consisted of a coalition of Rosses, Mackays, Forbes, Gunns, Frasers, Munroes, Grants, Raes and tenants of John Gordon/Sutherland, the Earl of Sutherland, while the Jacobites consisted of Gordons, Mackintoshes, Chisholms, Macdonalds, Macneills and Mackenzies.[66] This, in turn, meant that the war in the north was fought according to different rules from those in central and southern Scotland. This difference stemmed from the *fine*'s by this time primarily non-martial role in the economy and society.[67] In the course of their business dealings they naturally had a great deal to do with the *fine* of other clans, including those who were ancestral rivals and even enemies, and as was the way of these things in the early eighteenth century, marriage and kinship (to say nothing of friendship and good-neighbourliness) followed business as trade was to follow the flag in later centuries.

The overall effect was to establish a network of personal ties that criss-crossed political, religious and clan allegiances.[68] This was, of course, also the case with Lowland Jacobites, but in the Highlands these ties resonated more strongly and the consequences of breaking them were more grave. In partic-ular, though it had long since ceased to be a regular or recurrent feature of life in the Highlands, the concept of the blood feud, if not fully alive, at least retained some of its deterrent power.[69] In former times no one but a fool would deliberately provoke a blood feud without careful consultation with his kin and deep consideration of the consequences. And in 1715 the *fine* on both sides clearly wanted to avoid such consequences if at all possible.[70] Interestingly, it appears that the ordinary clansmen, too, were averse to getting into a real killing match with their counterparts on the other side. Thus when Simon Fraser, Lord Lovat, led a strong Whig force into Seaforth's lands in mid-December several hundred of Sutherland's men who were part of the army 'deserted upon hearing that they were to fight against the Mckenzies'.[71]

There is a kind of shadow-boxing quality to the war in the northern theatre which is best illustrated by an example of how it worked in practice.[72] In early November 1715 the Whig clans were on the march. Lovat had been given safe conduct north (he was an outlaw in Scotland for his abduction and rape of Amelia Murray, the dowager Lady Lovat in 1700) on the understanding that he would pluck the Frasers from the Jacobite camp and play a major role in a renewed Whig offensive.[73] His advent in early November certainly galvanised the pro-Whig elements in the region. Lovat, Deputy Lord Advocate Duncan Forbes of Culloden and Hugh Rose of Kilravock first called on the magistrates of Inverness to expel the Jacobite garrison, and when the magistrates disin-genuously claimed they could not do so, gathered a force of about 500 or so to attack the town.[74] The Jacobite Governor of Inverness, Sir Kenneth Mackenzie of Coull, promptly sent messages to Macdonald of Keppoch – who was plundering his way towards Perth in a leisurely fashion through lands belonging to the Grants – and the remaining Mackintoshes, asking for help. Keppoch turned towards Inverness and the Mackintoshes raised 500 men of their own in response.[75] Lovat, the master of this game, promptly advanced against Macdonald of Keppoch, who immediately retreated 'to the moun-taines', and then turned on the Mackintoshes, who 'make apology, swear they met to defend their land against Keppoch and that they will not assist the rebellion, upon which they promise to disperse'.[76] Lovat then crossed the water of Ness to blockade Inverness from the north while Forbes of Culloden and Rose of Kilravock blockaded it from the south.[77] At this point the besiegers were reinforced by 700 Grants, '[as] good men as we have in the north', who were apparently emboldened to re-emerge from their fastnesses by Lovat's successes and Keppoch's excesses.[78] These completed the blockade of Inverness to the south, and forced Mackenzie of Coull to retreat into Inverness's tollbooth. Rose of Kilravock also tried negotiating with Mackenzie of Coull, who was his son-in-law, but to no effect.[79] On 10 November a party of 100 of Culloden and Kilravock's men, led by Arthur Rose, Kilravock's brother, were seizing some boats on the Inverness shore when they opportunistically tried to force a sallyport into the tollbooth. In the ensuing fracas Arthur Rose, 'a bold resolute man, and long a slave in Turkie', was killed.[80] Immediately a proposal was made on the Whig side 'for burning the town at all ends'.[81] This was, however, averted by Mackenzie of Coull sending Rose of Kilravock his apologies (the deed was subsequently blamed on 'a ruffian' in the garrison),[82] requesting he and his men be allowed the honours of war. He then withdrew from the town by boat, abandoning his baggage to be plundered by the victorious Whigs the next day.[83]

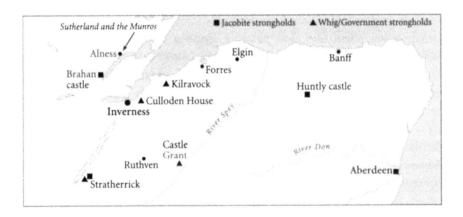

Map 10: The northern Scottish theatre of operations.

This was the way the fighting was carried on in the north from the very outset. Armies would be mustered and march against their foes. They would at some point confront each other, threatening battle, upon which the weaker army would retreat and the stronger pursue, though with little or no bloodshed. The winner would then plunder the loser's territory, make bloodcurdling threats of what he would do if there was any resistance and march home in triumph, upon which the clansmen involved in the expedition on both sides would disperse to their homes until next time.[84] In many ways it was a very civilised kind of war, at least in the sense that, by and large, it primarily targeted property rather than people. This was not at all to the taste of the more bellicose government officers. Lord Justice Clerk Cockburn, for example, was outraged that the Whig clans had allowed the Mackintoshes to capture Inverness unopposed: 'You will perhaps ask me what's become of the laird of Grant's hundereds? The Rosses, Munroes and Lord Stranaver's thousands? All I cane answer they are to the fore and have shed no blood; 'tis not fitt they should give occasion of feods with their neighbours.'[85] Regardless of the sentiments of outsiders, however, both sides in the north tacitly collaborated in maintaining this approach to the war clear through to the end of hostilities.

That said, there was plenty of military activity in northern Scotland, though it tended to come intermittently, with brief bursts of mustering and marching followed by long periods of virtual inactivity. The first blow was struck by the Mackintoshes at Inverness on 14 September, but they then marched home to prepare for the journey south to Perth. Inverness, which was the gateway to the north and the glittering prize in all that was to follow, might have been retaken by pro-government forces, but for the advent of Seaforth and several hundred Mackenzies a couple of days later. He not only occupied the town, but also placed a garrison of about 100 men there commanded by Mackenzie of Coull.[86] These moves gave the initiative to the Jacobites, and, the fact that Huntly, the greatest of the northern magnates, was still close by, mustering a large force of his tenants and clansmen near his eponymous castle, acted to give the Jacobites the decisive edge. The Whig clans prudently stayed at home defending their own territory while the Jacobites ranged around proclaiming James VIII (with as few as six men at Forres), levying the cess and mustering forces to send south. A few Whig heritors also negotiated local truces with powerful chieftains like Huntly that served to secure his lands from invasion for some time.[87] Only after Huntly marched away and Sutherland was landed in his own territory with 300 muskets and a commission as Lieutenant-General in early October did the war in the north revive.[88]

Sutherland was nothing if not energetic, and by 8 October had mustered some 1,800 of his own men plus contingents of Munroes and Raes near Alness, about 75 per cent of them armed. Seaforth had meantime drawn together a composite force of 4,000 Mackenzies, Macleods, Macdonalds, Mackinnons, Chisholms and Frasers and resolutely advanced towards Sutherland, offering battle. Sutherland consulted his allies, George Mackay, Lord Rae, and Captain Robert Monro of Foulis, and promptly decamped. In the course of the retreat one man was killed and a few were taken prisoner and the Whig army disintegrated. Sutherland's men held on to a couple of old fortified houses deep in his home territory, Sutherland himself fled on board a Royal Navy frigate in the Cromarty Firth and Rae and Monro of Foulis effectively went into hiding.[89] Seaforth allowed his men to plunder the Whigs' territory around Alness, then besieged Foulis, 'and vowed he would not leave it till he had Mr Monro dead or alive'.[90] From this position of strength he then negotiated a truce with the *fine* who remained, to the effect that they would not disturb the peace of the north on their own initiative, and took a number of hostages to ensure they observed the deal. News of the defeat also dismayed the Grants and Roses of Kilravock, who were marching north to join Sutherland at the time, and they immediately turned back. The Grants, at least, then subsequently negotiated a truce between themselves and the Mackenzies.[91] Seaforth duly returned in triumph to his own territory and only bestirred himself to recall his men and march south at the end of the month.

The rout at Alness damped the Whigs' enthusiasm until the beginning of November, when, as we have already seen, Lovat's arrival on the scene transformed the situation. Even so, the surge of Whig activity leading to the capture of Inverness ebbed fast thereafter. Sutherland was cautiously remustering his tenants preparatory to another strike at Inverness when he heard that Lovat and his allies had already retaken the town. He duly marched in two days later, after a brief pause to plunder Seaforth's lands around Brahan castle, and, along with Lovat and Captain Monro of Foulis, did what he could to ensure the Whigs could hold on to it after the troops under his command again dispersed. In the end, the best they could do was to install 400 Munroes as a garrison.[92] Matters then hung fire again until early December, when Sutherland marched into Elgin at the head of some 2,000 Whig clansmen before his army once more dispersed. By then Inverness was quite strongly held by the Whigs: 700 Grants had reinforced Captain Monro of Foulis and they had done their best to make the town more defensible.[93] Nor had the Jacobites been idle, and when Sutherland probed towards Huntly's territory with almost 1,500 men in mid-December, he was opposed by Gordon of Glenbuchat, sent north to bring back Huntly's men who had deserted after Sherrifmuir. Gordon, with a force of barely 200, proceeded to bluff the Whig army into retreating upon which the Whig army disintegrated as the rank and file dispersed to their homes with their plunder.[94] By the end of the month, too, Huntly and Seaforth were both back in the north and doing their best to cajole and force their men out again.[95] They had some success and when the next Whig surge of energy brought forth another army of about 1,500, this time commanded by Lovat, Huntly and Seaforth stood ready to defend their lands with 800 and more than 1,600 men respectively. Both men were also, however, by this time looking for an end-game to the rebellion that would allow them to escape with their lives and properties relatively intact, which put them firmly on the defensive with respect to the renewed Whig offensive.[96] This time it was directed at Seaforth, and after he had duly confronted the Whig army and brought it to a halt, Seaforth briskly turned to negotiation, initially using Sutherland of 'Rosecomon' and the dowager Countess of Seaforth (his mother) as intermediaries.[97] Lovat and his allies took the opportunity thoughtfully to inform Seaforth 'that he was playing the fool, and to their certain knowledge the Duke of Gordon [i.e. Huntly] was making up his peace with King George, when he encouraged him to hold out with a high hand. Which my Lord Seaforth then believed.'[98] This fairly quickly brought the talks to a conclusion, and the encounter might well have terminated to the satisfaction of both sides then and there, except that Sutherland suddenly rejoined them in an effort to get the military campaign moving again. The dreadful weather and the exhaustion of his troops' provisions (plus the fact that he was losing a great many to desertion) soon, however, forced him to agree to the terms Lovat had negotiated. The result was a truce between the Whigs and Seaforth pending the outcome of an application by him to George I for mercy, which Lovat pledged to support. Seaforth was also to release all the Munro hostages he had held since October.[99]

James's advent nonetheless bid fair to revitalise the Jacobite war effort in the north. Huntly's response to the news of his arrival – 'Now ther's no help for it, we must all ruine with him; would to God he had comed sooner' – was downbeat, but he repudiated neither the king nor the cause.[100] Huntly later claimed that he had detached himself from the Jacobites when he returned from Perth and did nothing further to aid the Jacobite cause. This was part of his political campaign to work his passage with the government once the rebellion was over and he had surrendered himself.[101] In fact, his conduct in December–January smacks of nothing so much as a man recharged. Huntly did his best to organise a viable force, and though he met with very limited success that has more to do with resistance to conscription on the part of his vassals and tenants and the scarcity of military-grade weapons and gunpowder amongst them after their losses at Sherrifmuir than with any lack of commitment on his part.[102] Glenbuchat warned him in mid-December:

I must tell you with great regret your own people have been very backward, notwithstanding the danger threatened you, and, if I had not got the few men together and made all possible haste I am afraid matters had been otherwise. This is the time you will know both men and friends, and, as I take the freedom to tell some, I hope in spite of all will say the contrary, the family of Huntly will be still, and that they will mind their friend[s] and punish their enemies.[103]

Huntly persevered regardless until early January, and even retook Elgin and Forres (albeit that there was neither a Whig garrison nor any resistance in either town) when, having learned of Seaforth's truce, he felt obliged to negotiate a similar deal of his own.[104] He appears, however, only to have done this with a view to regrouping his forces for a renewal of the war, and promised James that he would be back in the field by 22 January. Circumstances obliged him to extend the truce by a few days, but there seems little doubt that by the end of the month Huntly was gearing himself up for a full-scale attack on Inverness, with or without Seaforth, and he was certainly trying hard to persuade Lovat to defect to the Jacobites.[105]

The retreat from Perth necessarily changed everything. Huntly now faced the dreadful prospect of his lands and people becoming the venue for the Jacobites' last stand. This was, indeed, specifically recommended by Marischal just before James's flight from Montrose. Asked by Mar what he thought James should do, Marischal argued:

that though we were in a bad situation, he did not think the case so desperate as he represented. That the troops we had in the north would amount to about 7,000 foot and about 400 horse, which would make us very near equal to the enemy. That it was true we had little ammunition, but that we could get as much out of Aberdeen and the places where we passed as would serve to try the fate of a day, and that even if we lost it, we would be no worse than we would be in taking the present course. That as for the King's person, he did not apprehend it could be in danger, because by sending ships away to the west of Scotland, where there was so many harbors for them to lye in, he could make his escape from thence with less danger than even from the port they were at, the mouth of which was blocked up by two of the enemie's men of war. And that, to conclude all, he did not think it for the King's honour, nor for that of the nation to give up the game without putting it to a tryall.[106]

Sentiments with which Gordon of Glenbuchat manifestly agreed when he told Huntly: 'for God's sake let us do something worthy [of] memory, and, if we fall, let us die like men of honour and resolution. Our cause is good and just. By the Lord's assistance I shall have all your men I have concern with ready to march in haste and what more can be got together.'[107] Only when he heard that James and Mar had fled did Huntly abandon his efforts to remobilise his men. By the time the remnants of the main Jacobite army made it to Huntly castle, with Argyll in cautious pursuit, he had effectively ordered them all to stand down and put up no resistance to the government forces when they arrived, and himself gone into hiding. Gordon of Auchintoul, by then commander of the dispirited Jacobite army, had no choice but to continue on westward.[108] The formal war in the north was over.

This is not to say that military activity ceased. Before he relinquished command to Cadogan and went south to London Argyll set up a system of garrisons and large-scale patrols to disarm the common people and pursue the *fine*, and some prominent Jacobites, notably Gordon of Glenbuchat, ingratiated themselves with the authorities by helping at least the first part of the process along.[109] Looting by government forces also continued for another month or so, with even general officers like Wightman helping themselves on a grand scale to rebel property such as Seaforth's coach and horses and Fraser of Fraserdale's plate.[110] From hiding in Kintail, Seaforth also quietly ordered late arriving supplies and moneys from Europe to be secreted away pending a renewed uprising.[111] Resistance, however, subsided to virtually nothing, and might have ceased entirely had it not been for the government's insistence on punishing the Jacobite regional magnates. Huntly in due course surrendered himself and then sweated out the political process necessary to secure his pardon and release.[112] Seaforth was more nervous and less well connected and ended up going into exile. The result was that the Mackenzies continued to obstruct and resist government attempts to exert authority in the area, rising again in 1719 and ambushing small parties of government troops and officials into the 1720s, until Seaforth was finally permitted to return home at the end of the decade.[113] Social and civil order in the north of Scotland was still to a large extent dependent on magnate cooperation in the early eighteenth century, and it only fully returned when the government conceded that point.

Western Scotland, September 1715 to May 1716

The pattern in western Scotland was similar to that which prevailed in the north. There was remarkably little bloodshed, a good deal of plundering and a distinctly 'phoney war' quality to the conflict.[114] Until the final stages of the rebellion there was also not much in the way of a contest for control of the region, largely because of the overwhelming support for the Jacobites throughout most of the area. The government controlled a few fortified outposts, of which Fort William was the most strongly held, defensible and important, and Argyllshire, courtesy of Argyll as chief of clan Campbell, but for a long time they made little use of either to hamper the Jacobites' use of the area's resources (primarily its manpower).

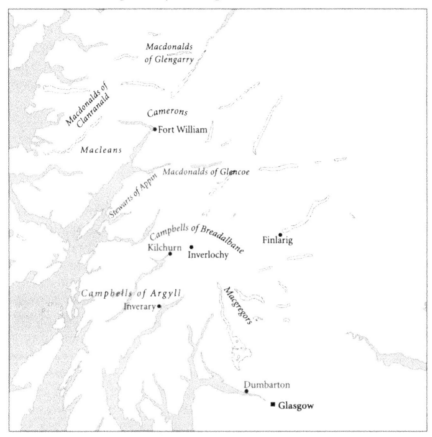

Map 11: The western Scottish theatre of operations.

Paradoxically, given that the region was so strongly Jacobite, the western clans, with the exception of the Macdonalds of Sleat, were relatively slow to gather their forces for the war. Sir Donald Macdonald ferried his men to the mainland in late September and led them off to help Seaforth in the north, where they took part in the advance that led to the rout at Alness, but it was mid-October before sufficient further forces were gathered in the west to allow offensive operations there.[115] This seems to have been due to the defection of Campbell of Lochnell and Campbell of Lawers, both of whom were regarded by their Jacobite peers as being key players. As we have already seen, they appear to have done so because they had no faith in an uprising that did not meet the criteria previously agreed among the Jacobite conspirators, but whatever their reasons their defection to the government side was a real blow to the Jacobite war effort in the region.[116] In particular, Campbell of Lochnell had been entrusted with command of Breadalbane's clansmen, who were thus left without their customary leaders and consequently made a poor showing throughout the rebellion.[117] Even so, by mid-October a Jacobite force commanded by Gordon of Auchintoul and composed of the Macgregors, the Macleans of Duart, the Macdonalds of Glengarry, Clanranald and Glencoe and the Stewarts of Appin had mustered, approximately 2,500 strong, at Strathfillan.[118]

From there they could easily strike two potential targets: Fort William or Inverary. Fort William was a relatively modern fortress, but it was in a poor state of repair and though it theoretically had a paper strength of over 600 in the garrison, the commander, Sir Robert Pollock of that ilk, found he had only 300 or so effectives. By the beginning of October all of his outposts except Castle Duart had fallen to the Jacobites and he was virtually blockaded within his fortress.[119] He did his best to shore up its crumbling defences with the peat he had stored for the winter, but it was an endless and dispiriting task: no sooner had he temporarily fixed one problem than another bastion collapsed. Throughout the uprising he remained in occasional contact by boat with the outside world, and exchanges of fire with Jacobite craft, indeed, were the highlight of what passed for military action by the garrison until January 1716.[120] For, although the presence of the fortress certainly inhibited nearby clans – notably the Camerons – from committing all the forces they could have done to the Jacobite war effort, the Jacobites decided in the end not to attack Fort William. Since their only means of assaulting it would have been with unsupported infantry (they apparently had no artillery in the west), this was probably a wise decision. The garrison of even a wreck of a fortress like Fort William would probably have inflicted heavy casualties on a storming party, and as Pollock had too few men to do much in the way of serious sorties he did not pose an inordinate threat to their base area.

Inverary was ultimately selected as the objective for more than the fact that it was the virtual capital of clan Campbell. Though there was certainly a tradition of rivalry and hostility between the Campbells and several of the clans making up the Jacobite army, such as the Macdonalds and Macleans, there were quite a number of Campbells fighting on the Jacobite side, and many of the clan chieftains, to say nothing of the other Jacobite *fine*, had either personal ties with Campbell *fine* loyal to the government or good, cordial relations with Argyll and Islay personally.[121] Indeed, some Jacobites, like Rob Roy Macgregor, had such close ties that it is debatable whether or not they were really fighting for the Jacobites at all, for all that they made an appearance or two in the Jacobite camp.[122] More important by far was the strategic significance of Inverary and Argyllshire generally. If the Jacobites could take Inverary and subdue the Campbells of Argyll they could with relative safety strike south towards Glasgow.[123] Only Dumbarton castle, with a far smaller garrison and in a much worse state of repair than Fort William, would stand in their way.[124] Moreover, the Jacobites knew that despite their mustering in large numbers, Glasgow's militia and volunteers were just as prone to panic when threatened by Highlanders as their Lowland counterparts elsewhere in Scotland. Rob Roy had raided the south shore of Loch Lomond in early October, looking for arms and, doubtless, other unconsidered trifles, and though he probably deployed fewer than 300 men (less than a fifth of the total forces in Glasgow) had paralysed the city and struck fear into its civic leaders.[125] Inverary was therefore the key to a potentially major breakthrough.

A counter-raid on the Macgregors' territory on the north shore of Loch Lomond by a small force of Whig militia and volunteers out of Dunbartonshire and Glasgow in mid-October further delayed the western army's march, so that it only finally reached Inverary on 20 October.[126] By then, however, the town was in a far more defensible state than it had been earlier in the rising. Islay had arrived to take command in early October with 1,000 military muskets and a good stock of ammunition.[127] Between then and the Jacobites' arrival at the end of the month he managed to mobilise some 1,500 Argyll Campbell clansmen, rapidly brought them into the town and put them to work pulling down outlying houses and building some basic defences. Islay tended to be rather brusque in doing all this, and anyway could barely conceal his contempt for the Highlands and Highlanders alike, which alienated a good number of the clansmen, but the net result was to create a real obstacle for the Jacobite army when it arrived.[128] Gordon of Auchintoul had the western army surround the town and ostentatiously prepare fascines and other impedimenta that an army about to storm a fortified position would need, probably in the hope of intimidating Islay, but it was a bluff.[129] One Jacobite probing attack, led by the ubiquitous Rob Roy, was met with such heavy fire that he was reported to have said, 'he would go half way to hell before he would go back again', and the rest of the Jacobite army apparently felt similarly disinclined to try storming Islay's position.[130] Lacking the artillery necessary to blow holes in Islay's defences, Auchintoul had little choice but to retreat.

As he did so he detached John Campbell of Glenlyon and 300 men to bring or force out some more of Breadalbane's men from Lorne, which Islay attempted to stop by dispatching Colin Campbell of Fonab to intercept him with 1,000 Argyll Campbells. Rather than fight, however, Fonab and Glenlyon agreed a truce whereby Campbell would not fight Campbell and the Lorne men could return home without interference or penalty. Islay was allegedly outraged when he heard of this, but was apparently unable to undo the pact, even after the Lorne men subsequently remustered and marched off to fight alongside the other western clans at Sherrifmuir.[131] It is not clear exactly what was agreed beyond the immediate truce between Glenlyon and Fonab, yet the relative inactivity of Argyll's Campbell clansmen in the west until the end of March 1716 is very suggestive. Islay was subsequently accused of having quietly negotiated an armistice in the west that preserved Argyllshire and the Jacobites' clan territories there pretty much inviolate throughout this period, and since Fonab clearly remained in favour with the Duke of Argyll it seems that whatever deal he made was not something the duke found offensive or wished to repudiate.[132] Suffice it to say that neither side went beyond the tacit rules that seem to have governed and restrained potential clan on clan conflicts elsewhere in Scotland during the rising, and until April they were not even plundering each other's territory very much either. It is especially notable, too, that the plundering, when it occurred, was peculiarly polite. When the western Jacobite army retreated from Argyllshire (where they did inflict extensive property damage in the vicinity of Inverary) they took some 100 horses belonging to local people with them. However, when the locals protested the Jacobites returned over sixty of them and promised, 'they would pay when they got money, or let Ilay pay them'.[133] This was not the kind of behaviour generally exhibited by clan troops in north or central Scotland and hints at exactly the kind of agreement Islay was later believed to have made.

The western Jacobite army's retreat and subsequent march eastward to Auchterarder to join the main Jacobite army's thrust southward that ended at Sherrifmuir signalled the almost complete termination of hostilities in the west until 1716. Islay had asked for and received the support of two Royal Navy ships with which he planned to raid and harass the island Jacobites' homes in the hope of forcing their return to defend them, but the season was late and the passages through the western islands too dangerous at that time of year for them to achieve very much.[134] John Macdougall of Dunollie's wife, Mary Macdonald of Sleat, tried to hang on to the weapons he had left behind in his house, and was bombarded by the Royal Navy for her pains, and Pollock's supply boats did exchange fire with local Jacobites a few times, but there is no mention of anybody being hurt in any of these incidents.[135] The only military moves of any significance were another Macgregor raid into Dunbartonshire, the occupation of Kilchurn and Finlarig and a cattle raid by Pollock out of Fort William. The Macgregor raid on Dunbartonshire was commanded by Rob Roy and Macgregor of Marchfield and took place in early December. The Macgregors took the local Whig volunteers and militia by surprise, audaciously seized the excise and proclaimed James VIII within twelve miles of Glasgow and then returned home, plundering Sir Humphrey Colquhoun of Luss's house *en route*.[136] Kilchurn and Finlarig were fortified houses belonging to Breadalbane, and they were taken by a force of 500 Campbell clansmen commanded by Campbell of Fonab at the end of December, in both cases, it seems, without violent opposition.[137] Fonab thereafter showed no inclination to advance further north, though it has to be said that the weather was dreadful at the time. Pollock's raid, also at the end of December, consisted of sending out 100 men to try and seize some Jacobite leaders he had heard were meeting in the vicinity to plan the return of the western clans' forces to Perth, or, failing that, to plunder their cattle and property. The sortie apparently took the Jacobites by surprise, and though the Jacobite leaders escaped, the raiding party was able to drive a fair number of cattle and seize various other items of plunder. Nonetheless local clansmen were soon gathering in force to oppose the raiders. It even looked as if there might be some real fighting when a Lieutenant Graham, commanding the raiding party, spurned an offer from the shadowing clansmen to let him pass safely if he would return the cattle and goods he had taken. His way was then blocked by a party of 200 clansmen who, when he advanced towards them, 'at first seemd to stand by throwing away their plaids and putting themselves in a condition to receive them'.[138] Graham's resolution apparently daunted the clansmen, however, and they finally drew off to a distance and contented themselves with sniping at the raiders as they hurried back to the fortress. A couple of soldiers were wounded.

Compared to the curious inactivity that had hitherto characterised the conduct of pro-government forces in the region these were major incidents. They were also a flash in the pan. Though Pollock made a good deal of noise about what he could do if he received more reinforcements he consistently proved reluctant to venture any action at all, even when such reinforcements arrived, and Campbell of Fonab and most of his men were withdrawn in January to act as light troops on the fringes of Argyll's advance on Perth and subsequent drive north.[139] The western clans, though, having received several urgent messages from Perth begging them to mobilise their forces and return to the main army as soon as possible, began to muster their men at Moy near Strath Dearn in late January. All the clans who had appeared in arms in the autumn came out again (including the Breadalbane Campbells) plus the Macleans of Lochbuie, who up to then had stayed quiet. Even so, at 1,500 men the force was about half the size of that the clans had first mustered the previous year, which may be taken as a token of the difficulty the chieftains were facing in getting their men out at that time of year and in the wake of Sherrifmuir. Some of the Cameron *fine*, such as Cameron of Glen Nevis, were also refusing to turn out at all and others insisted on staying at home to defend their lands from government raids. By then, too, the directions from Perth were for the western army to march first towards Inverness and there join Huntly, Seaforth and General Echlin in attacking the town.[140] The chieftains were consequently taken aback when they learned that the main army was in headlong retreat and James had fled to France. Uncertain what to do next, the chieftains dissolved the muster and the men made their own way home.[141]

The drive north in pursuit of the disintegrating main Jacobite army soon dissipated both the energy and the accumulated supplies that had sustained Argyll's army, so that as Argyll and Cadogan turned their efforts towards pursuing fugitive Jacobites, disarming the common people and reinstalling Whig loyalists in office throughout the north, they hoped that the western clans would simply accept their defeat and submit to the government without further ado.[142] This proved not to be the case. Probably in large part because the government was unwilling to offer any terms beyond surrender at discretion (and by February the risks of doing that were all too bloodily manifest on scaffolds in London and northern England), the western chieftains, notably Cameron of Lochiel and the Macdonalds of Sleat, Keppoch, Glengarry and Clanranald, began to contemplate further resistance. Most of the Lowland and Franco-Irish Jacobite fugitives who arrived in the west after the main army disbanded at Ruthven in Badenoch on 15 February were not interested in anything except escaping to France as soon as possible.[143] After a month or so of relative rest and quiet, however, Gordon of Auchintoul at least had somewhat recovered himself and Seaforth was also showing interest in the possibility of continued resistance. This was despite the fact that many of the chieftains involved had been making submissive overtures to local government commanders and prominent loyalists.[144] What seems to have persuaded the Jacobites to contemplate further resistance was the hope that if they hung together, and even fought back, they might yet be able to persuade the government to grant them an amnesty such as that obtained by the Jacobites in 1691. Rumours of imminent hostilities with France, and the arrival of several ships carrying arms, ammunition and money from the Jacobite diaspora may also have encouraged them to hold out.[145]

The western chieftains' prevarications, though, had not gone unnoticed, and in March Cadogan began preparing an invasion of the western Highlands with a view to enforcing their submission and surrender. The offensive was to be two-pronged, with Colonel Jasper Clayton striking west from Atholl via Inverlochy with 500 men plus assistance from Fort William and Cadogan advancing west down Loch Ness into Lochaber with 2,500 regulars and 1,000 Grants, Frasers and Munroes.[146] Cameron of Lochiel tried to persuade his fellow chieftains to act on their previous discussions and muster once more, and Gordon of Auchintoul indicated he would take command of an army if they could draw one together. In the event, however, the chieftains' resolution collapsed in the face of the onslaught and when the offensive began in early April one chieftain after another either submitted himself and/or instructed his clansmen not to resist disarmament.[147] Eventually only the Camerons were willing to stand out, and after an ambush Allan Cameron was trying to organise – of Cadogan himself – missed the target, even they gave up. The government army's offensive into the western Highlands became a progress as they received the peaceful submission of the *fine*, if not the chieftains, and the clans surrendered their weapons.[148] The last attempt at resistance – the Mackenzies aside – came in early May, when Brigadier Colin Campbell of Ormidale raised some men on Uist to resist Colonel Cholmley's force, landing to disarm the islanders. These 'made a show of resisting. But upon the approach of our Grenadiers to attack them, they immediately runn away', and Campbell of Ormidale was captured.[149] With that last little débâcle the military side of the '15 came to an end.

* * *

From a strictly military history perspective the '15 is not very interesting. There is very little evidence of strategic vision, operational initiative or tactical innovation on either side. The government's regular forces performed up to standard in most cases and the government militias and volunteers performed as poorly as could have been expected. The Jacobites certainly did better than their opponents thought they would, and might, in the right hands, even have developed into as formidable an army as they did in 1745–46, but Sherrifmuir took the heart out of the rebellion and marred their potential.[150] Mar and Forster were both unsuitable as military commanders and urgently needed good, firm professional advice. Neither got it. General Hamilton was a competent logistician rather than a field commander and had no understanding of how best to manage and use the main Jacobite army's prime military asset, the Highlanders. Forster was advised, in so far as he was advised, by Colonel

Henry Oxburgh, an old soldier with a good reputation who had apparently lost touch with his profession. By the time of the '15, 'he was better at his beads and prayers than at his business as a soldier, and we all thought him fitter for a priest than a field officer'.[151] Generalship on the Jacobite side correspondingly ranged from mediocre to poor.

By contrast, the command skills exhibited on the government side went from mediocre to good. The accolade for worst commander on the government side during the rebellion has undoubtedly to go to a professional army officer: Major-General Charles Wills. He was, though, very fortunate, in that if the Jacobites had responded as aggressively to his botched attacks at Preston as some of them were clamouring to do, he might have gained the special distinction of being the architect of a truly catastrophic defeat. Argyll was a difficult man to work with, but, there again, he was in a very difficult situation. He was, by and large, a soldier's general, in the sense that he essentially sought to keep his men well paid, well drilled, well fed and well armed and expected to lead them – from the front – to the enemy, slip the leash and have them do their job quickly and efficiently without much further input by him. This worked up to a point, but could have gone very badly awry at Sherrifmuir. Nonetheless, fighting nearly two and a half times his own number to a standstill in a sprawling encounter battle was no small credit to him and he did not deserve the obloquy he subsequently received for his conduct of the war in Scotland.[152] Cadogan's abilities as a general were like Argyll's in that on the battlefield they did not go much higher than a good competence, and given his contempt for the Highlanders on the Jacobite side ('for my part I think these formidable clans so despicable a rabble that the militia may be brought to beat them') it was probably a good job for him that he never had to fight a battle against them.[153] In the hundred or so years after Alasdair Maccolla first showed what could be done tactically with Highland troops they encountered a number of generals like Cadogan and they almost invariably defeated them. His genius was as a logistician, and there he was head and shoulders above any other military officer involved in combating the rebellion. Cadogan was certainly responsible for the smooth, relentless quality of the government advance against Perth and into the north, and was the architect of the easy and bloodless victory in the west. Nonetheless, it did not escape some observers that, 'the gordion knot was broken by another and the bunch of rods were scattered to his hand, which made it easy work to nip them asunder singly which yet united would require force'.[154]

Cadogan's success is also ironic, in that the winter and spring campaigns of 1716 are probably among the most needless a British army and its allies have ever waged. As Argyll immediately grasped when the Jacobites sent

Lieutenant-Colonel Lawrence to ask for terms on their behalf at the end of November 1715, the rebellion was already virtually dead by that point. If he had been allowed to offer free pardon, or at least much reduced punishment, to dissident Jacobites like Huntly and Sinclair in all likelihood the rebellion would have collapsed in short order. Scotland could have been at peace again before the end of 1715. The war only ground on because of Westminster's thirst for revenge. George I and the Whig ministry wanted to make frightening examples of the former rebels, the better to deter future uprisings. Yet that, too, may well have been redundant. As we will see below, Argyll, for all that he was a very Anglicised Scottish nobleman, understood his opponents and grasped the fact that the Jacobites' experience of rebellion and failure had been highly disillusioning. Their punishment did not need to be swingeing to drive the lesson home.

By far the most interesting insights the military events of the '15 offer us relate to the social pathology of contemporary Scotland and northern England, rather than to military affairs. One of these is the evidence for a deep cultural fear of venturing into England in arms on the part of the common people of Scotland. The southern Jacobite army's infantry corps came close to complete disintegration at the prospect: two mutinies and massive desertion straitly followed on their commanders' attempts to lead them over the border. Despite peace and increasing trading links for the previous half-century England and the English were clearly profoundly alien and dangerous in their view. Another is the hidden uprising within the '15. It is generally assumed that after 1569 Catholicism was no longer any kind of military threat in England. The small number of English Catholics, out of the population as a whole, would not seem to have posed much of a danger to the existing social and religious order. Yet in 1715 the only substantive reinforcements the southern Jacobite army received in England were Catholic; they turned out in hundreds whereas Protestant Jacobites turned out in dozens at best. The paranoid fears of anti-Catholic zealots, it seems, did have a basis in fact. There really was a secret Catholic army lurking in the remote fastnesses of northern England, waiting for the opportune moment to strike (though it should be noted that they were fighting to restore the Stuarts and true religious toleration rather than Catholicism as the national religion). But perhaps the most fascinating insight of all is the self-restraint exercised by both sides throughout the military conflict. A great many people were robbed by the brutal soldiery of whatever political complexion, but they were not usually physically harmed or murdered. War is always a grim business, yet in 1715 both Jacobites and Whigs, overall, tacitly did what they could to minimise its impact on the general population and each other. And none more so than the supposedly ferocious and bloodthirsty Highlanders. The degree to which all concerned sought to avoid bloodshed in Highlander on Highlander confrontations is quite remarkable, and is a clear token of the will to preserve civil relations throughout Scottish society even in the most extreme circumstances. This, as we shall see in the next two chapters, lay at the heart of what was to happen when the process of retribution which followed directly on from the end of military operations got under way in 1716.

CHAPTER 8

'Bought and Sold for English Gold': Prisoners, Fugitives and Exiles after the '15

The termination of military operations did not signal the end of the 1715 rebellion as far as a great many of the participants were concerned. Early modern European governments were great believers in deterrence, and consequently everyone knew there was bound to be retribution in store for the Jacobite communities directly involved in the rebellion. Of these, the Scots had most cause for apprehension simply because the rebellion had started and ended there and they had clearly posed the greatest threat to the Whig regime's hold on power. Any opportunity righteously to punish the English Catholic community – the ancestral enemy of all good Whigs – was also bound to be of great interest to any Whig-dominated government in the early eighteenth century. The only questions concerned who and how many were to be punished.

Legally, every single person who appeared in arms for the Jacobites, regardless of whether they were forced or not, and everyone who had actively supported the Jacobites' government of areas under their control, was liable to the most dreadful penalties: hanging, drawing and quartering for themselves personally, forfeiture of all their property and concomitant destitution for their families. The wholesale slaughter of tens of thousands of people and the immiseration of hundreds of thousands more, however, were never contemplated. One of the Whig party's most central beliefs about itself was that the Whigs had rebelled in 1688 to overthrow the kind of tyranny exemplified by James II and VII's treatment of the men who had followed James Scott, the Duke of Monmouth, into rebellion in 1685. They accordingly shied away from any notion that a Whig ministry might preside over the equivalent of the infamous Judge Sir George Jeffreys's 'Bloody Assize'.[1] From the outset of the rebellion the government at Westminster was, therefore, looking to impose exemplary punishment, but only on a small percentage of those involved.[2] This implicitly compromised the government's position and made that percentage subject to negotiation, an opening the Jacobites and their friends were to exploit to the hilt.

Such a negotiation, however, was a delicate matter and needed time to work out. It will be the subject of the next chapter. In the immediate aftermath of the rebellion the government had to deal with three groups of ex-rebels: the prisoners of war taken at Dunfermline, Sherrifmuir, Preston and other encounters, the fugitives who had dispersed to their homes when the Jacobite armies disintegrated, and the Jacobites who fled overseas. Each group posed a different set of problems for the government and had its own internal dynamic and repercussions for the Jacobite communities of Scotland and England, and each will be examined separately below.

The Prisoners of War

The government first confronted the problem of what to do with the prisoners of war in mid-September 1715. Before then a substantial number of suspected Jacobites had either been summoned to appear before the Court of Justiciary and then imprisoned or obliged to give bail, or had been summarily arrested on warrants sent down from London.[3] These men were, though, dealt with under peacetime (albeit emergency) law. Habeas Corpus, or, in the Scots case, the Act Anent Wrongeous Imprisonment, had been suspended by Act of Parliament in July, but those arrested or summoned were still entitled to appeal against their answering and/or incarceration by legal means. Consequently a fair number of those initially taken up had actually secured their release on bail by early September.[4] The attempt to capture Edinburgh castle changed everything. A number of participating Jacobites were arrested and they had clearly been part of a military operation (however amateurish). The obvious way of dealing with them, as criminals to be individually prosecuted before the regular courts, was the one initially favoured by Lord Justice Clerk Cockburn and his fellow officials, Lord Advocate Dalrymple and Solicitor-General Sir James Steuart of Goodtrees.[5] The regular legal process was, however, very soon complicated by the sheer extent of the rebellion in Scotland and the capture of government soldiers by the Jacobites. On the very first day of the rising in the north Borlum captured four regular army officers in Inverness. He quickly released them on parole, but it was obvious to all concerned that the prosecution of Jacobite soldiers under the criminal law could henceforth invite retaliation against government prisoners.[6] Indeed, as the rebellion went on the Jacobites specifically began to look to the capture of government troops as a means to ensure the safety of their own prisoners in government hands. Thus James urged Huntly to attack Inverness forthwith at the end of December 1715 precisely because 'the Earl of Sutherland's situation is such that he cannot escape being taken, with his troops in a manner at present surrounded by mine. Such a number of prisoners would not only be of consequence for my service, but a great security to our own prisoners in England, for whom I am in great concern'.[7]

This produced a distinct difference of opinion in the administration. Argyll clearly wished to treat the Jacobites as if they were regular opponents under contemporary European laws of war.[8] These generally entitled prisoners of war to civil treatment paid for by their own side through neutral channels, release on parole in the case of officers and periodic prisoner exchanges that would allow them honourably to rejoin their units. Such 'cartels' had applied in most of the British Isles during the Great Civil War and in Ireland at least during the Williamite conquest of the kingdom.[9] In addition, Lord Justice Clerk Cockburn, Argyll and Roxburgh joined in proposing that an amnesty with only a few exceptions be offered the rebels, because, as Cockburn glumly put it, 'the gangrine is spread so fare, no cure is to be left unessayed'.[10] While waiting to hear from London on the matter Argyll on his own initiative virtually allowed amnesty to a number of putative Jacobites, such as Campbell of Loch Nell and Campbell of Auchinbreck, and was clearly prepared to offer similar terms to a greater number.[11]

If the time they took to decide the matter is anything to go by, George I and his ministers were initially uncertain how to respond. They approved Argyll's dealings with Loch Nell and Auchinbreck, but gave no formal response to the proposal for a general indemnity until November, and returned no specific answer to Argyll's query as to what the officers paroled by Borlum ought to do.[12] Further clashes in the course of the *petite guerre*, and the taking of more prisoners on both sides, led to Mar pressing the question of a cartel in a formal approach to Argyll at the end of October. Under flag of truce he wrote to Argyll to complain: 'I am informed that the gentelmen who had the misfortoun to be taken at Dunfermling are very ill used at Stirling, that they are stript of their cloathes and ly on the bare boards in the comon guard room', and while he refused to believe that Argyll had ordered such treatment, he pointedly noted that the Jacobites were holding prisoners of war too, and that he personally had made sure they were 'well used'.[13] Argyll formally declined to respond, but sent unofficial reassurances that he would remedy the situation and seek leave to negotiate a cartel.[14] This, however, did not meet with the approval of the ministry. When urgently lobbied by Lord Justice Clerk Cockburn and others as to what to do with the hundreds of prisoners being picked up south of the Forth as Borlum's army haemorrhaged men on its march towards northern England, the government had responded that for the time being such prisoners were to be 'treated with all humanity'.[15] In early November, however, a meeting of the ministry decided to approve Argyll's refusal to respond officially to Mar's letter, 'His Majesty being determined to treat him and all with him as rebels'.[16]

As we have seen, this fateful decision was to lock the government into four more months of warfare; it also changed the official attitude towards the prisoners of war. Henceforth they were to be considered heinous criminals who would be subject to trial and execution. The government's legal officers in Scotland were accordingly directed to broaden their efforts to gather evidence sufficient to convict the prisoners – from just the leaders of the rebellion to the Jacobite officer corps as a whole – and to find means to distinguish between the common men who were truly forced out and those who had willingly followed their social superiors.[17] Government army officers and others held by the Jacobites were effectively abandoned to their fate. Argyll refused to accept this and eventually worked out an unofficial cartel with the Jacobites channelled through John Walkinshaw of Barrowfield, a Jacobite prisoner of war held at Stirling, to whom Argyll paid subsistence money for government troops held by the Jacobites without designating it as such, and who would then write to Mar notifying him of his receipt of the funds.[18] Argyll also continued, fruitlessly, to press for authority to exchange prisoners with the rebels.[19]

By the time Argyll launched his winter offensive towards Perth, then, the ministry had long since decided it was in principle going to treat all the rebels as criminals. Four of the five half-pay officers captured at Preston had already been court-martialled and shot (others escaped immediate execution by concealing their identities) and the ministry was preparing for exemplary trials and executions of the other Preston prisoners in Lancashire and London.[20] The potential scale of such an exercise in Scotland, however, quietly daunted the authorities. Lord Justice Clerk Cockburn and Lord Advocate Dalrymple had been urging the ministry to be very lenient indeed with the plebeian prisoners for months, claiming,

> These poor creatures are not engaged by any principle to rebell, but what they doe is the effect of the slavish obedience they pay to their masters.
>
> These numbers of deserters, too, show that a great many who compose the rebell's army have been forced into the service. We had these accounts from the north from the beginning and allmost every one of the prisoners that has been examined confirm it.[21]

Though it had instructed its legal officers to find a way to distinguish between unwilling rebel conscripts and true-blue plebeian Jacobites, the government did not object when Argyll, and subsequently Cadogan and his subordinates, adopted a policy of simply disarming captured rank-and-file rebels, sometimes having them formally swear allegiance to King George, and then releasing them without further penalty.[22] It was manifestly obvious that if the ministry wanted to prosecute former rebels in Scotland it would have a plethora of richer, more élite targets. In a belatedly vindictive gesture the ministry did, though, attempt to coerce the prisoners taken from among Borlum's deserters in October, still held in Edinburgh and Glasgow, into agreeing to their transportation to the colonies (under existing law criminals could not at this time be sentenced to transportation, only petition for it on conviction), as was being done with the Preston prisoners in England.[23] The law officers duly went through the motions of forcing the prisoners to comply, but the unanimity with which they refused to agree (only 28 out of 250 agreed to do so in Edinburgh, and none out of 353 in Glasgow), plus the prisoners' bold demand to be treated like the common prisoners elsewhere in Scotland, suggests they were in receipt of some good legal advice on the subject, and their refusal – reinforced by the pleas of the municipal authorities in both cities to be relieved of the burden of guarding and maintaining them – obliged the ministry to abandon this tactic.[24] The remaining plebeian prisoners held in Scotland were virtually all released in late June 1716.

A very different fate was planned for their élite counterparts. Though the king and his ministers had been grudgingly willing to acquiesce in a few individual cases of leniency, in terms of Argyll accepting particular Jacobites' surrender and releasing them on parole, the order to Cadogan in March that any further Jacobites surrendering themselves or captured were to be kept 'closs prisoners' marked a clear attempt to stem the drift towards milder measures.[25] About a hundred of the élite prisoners were eventually concentrated in Edinburgh at the end of March, and there they remained until August while the authorities gathered legal evidence of their treason, by which time the government was facing a legal crisis. The suspension of the Act Anent Wrongeous Imprisonment and Habeas Corpus was about to expire before any of the élite prisoners could be tried. Even if they were brought before the Scottish courts the legal officers were warning that there was a strong possibility that a jury of their peers would either acquit them or fail to reach a determination in many cases, as had happened in 1708.[26] Indeed, some of the legal officers, notably Lord Advocate Dalrymple and Deputy Lord Advocate Duncan Forbes, were trying hard to persuade the ministry to abandon any attempt to prosecute the great majority of the rebels lest it makes all those who had the misfortune to be seduced into the rebellion, with their children, relatives and such as depend upon them, forever desparate. And its hard to tell what occasions may offer for venting their rage. We see that want and hard circumstances lead men daily into follies, without any other temptation. But when those circumstances are brought on by adherence to any principle, or opinion, its certain the sufferers will not quit their attempts to better their condition, but with their lives. Second, as there are none of the rebels who have not friends among the king's faithful subjects, it is not easy to guess how far a severity of this kind, unnecessarily pushed, may alienate the affections even of those from the Government.[27]

It was, though, to no avail. At the end of the month the ministry directed that some eighty élite prisoners were to be moved to Carlisle to be dealt with by an English court.[28]

The reaction in Scotland to this decision was one of outrage. The social élite was virtually united in its hostility to any attempt to try Scotsmen for crimes committed in Scotland under English law before an English court. Subscriptions for the prisoners' defence were taken up from all sections of élite society, Whig and Tory, Presbyterian and Episcopalian, Highland and Lowland, and the legal profession united in its opposition to the whole project. Lord Advocate Dalrymple absented himself from Scotland with a politic illness, and Duncan Forbes refused to lead the prosecution even if it cost him his office.[29] When the trials came on before a commission of Oyer et Terminer in Carlisle the prisoners, now well provided with good legal counsel, contested every element of the case against each of them, bogging down the prosecution in detail and technicalities.[30] The government, at that point presided over by the Prince of Wales while his father was visiting Hanover, which had originally intended to secure just three or so executions and convict the rest of the prisoners in order to show them conspicuous official mercy, was deluged with petitions and intercessions from the prisoners and their friends, and in the end decided the game of picking victims was not worth the candle if the ministers were going to have to endure the relentless lobbying of their kith and kin. Less than a third of the prisoners lost their nerve, confessed and were convicted (and none of these were executed or transported); the remainder were released either straightaway or under the provisions of the amnesty that passed Parliament in 1717.[31] In the end only one man was convicted and executed in Scotland for his part in the rebellion: Sergeant William Ainslie, the NCO in the Edinburgh castle garrison suborned by Ensign Thomas Arthur as part of the Jacobite attempt to capture the fortress.

He was not even a Jacobite. In the course of his trial he revealed he had done it all for 100 guineas and the promise of promotion. He correspondingly went to his death with little or no sympathy expressed by his erstwhile political comrades; the Edinburgh mob watched him die unmoved and the élite Jacobites and their Whig kinsfolk made no effort to save him.[32]

This was in complete contrast to the way the retributive process played itself out in England and Wales. The government quickly separated over a hundred of the élite prisoners at Preston from the rest and moved them to London for some suitably grim show trials. To underscore the point they were paraded through the streets on their way to Newgate and the Tower so as to allow the government's plebeian supporters to celebrate its triumph in a kind of grand charivari.[33] The peers deposited in the Tower were then put on trial first, in February. As was their right, the court was the House of Lords solemnly assembled and the prosecution was conducted by the Lord Chancellor, William Cowper, Lord Cowper, himself. There was, of course, no possibility of acquittal, and six of the seven peers on trial (Carnwath, Derwentwater, Widdrington, Nairn, Nithsdale and Kenmure) duly did their best to save themselves by pleading guilty and throwing themselves on the mercy of the court.[34] Only Winton tried to use the process to escape punishment, and, indeed, delayed and obfuscated so well that by the time he was found guilty the ministry had decided that it wanted no further executions of noblemen and duly reprieved him.[35] Derwentwater and Kenmure were finally selected to die for their crimes because of their emblematic significance. Derwentwater was a wealthy and powerful English Catholic who also happened to be a direct (illegitimate) descendant of Charles II; Kenmure was a Nonjuring Scots Episcopalian. When they realised that further petitions and pleas would not save them, both men died boldly affirming the Jacobite cause. Derwentwater expressed his sorrow for having in any way acknowledged the authority of George I in the course of his attempts to escape the axe, and with regard to James proclaimed:

> . . . him I had an inclination to serve from my infancy, and was moved thereto by a natural love I had to his person, knowing him to be capable of making his people happy; and though he had been of a different religion from mine, I should have done for him all that lay in my power, as my ancestors have done for his predecessors, being thereto bound by the laws of God and man.[36]

Kenmure, more quietly, 'prayed for the Pretender, and repented of his having pleaded guilty, and died after a very courageous manner'.[37] The executions of these two were great public spectacles and seem to have swayed the mood of the London crowd. The handsome young Derwentwater in particular won their sympathy and the appearance soon after of the aurora borealis over central and northern England led to much superstitious speculation on whether these rare phenomena were indications of God's displeasure at his execution. Indeed, in northern England the aurora borealis became known for a century or so afterwards as 'Derwentwater's lights'.[38] Quite possibly in response to the tangible change in the public mood, the ministry proceeded to grant successive reprieves to the remaining peers (except for Nithsdale, who was smuggled out of the Tower disguised in women's clothing by his wife on the night before the executions, and Winton, who made an improvised saw from a watchspring and cut through the bars of his cell to escape), until their eventual release.[39]

The rest of the gentry and heritors dragged down to London to participate in the government's grim pageant of justice, except for the substantial number who escaped from Newgate (including Forster and Borlum) over the next couple of months, were then tried before the Court of Common Pleas and two ancillary courts specially established for the purpose. Predictably, the overwhelming majority were found guilty.[40] Again, most of them were reprieved, and only those judged especially heinous or exemplary offenders, such as John Hall, a Northumberland JP, the Reverend William Paul, a clergyman of the Church of England, Oxburgh, who at this point publicly revealed that he had been a crypto-Catholic for years, and Richard Gascoigne, another Catholic who had been one of the most energetic organisers of the English end of the conspiracy, were selected to die. All of them did so defiantly once they realised there was no hope of reprieve.[41]

These, however, were just the best known of the executions that followed the London trials. Special commissions of Oyer et Terminer were sent up to Liverpool and Preston to deal with the prisoners who remained there. These numbered almost 1,300, so there was no prospect of trying them all. Instead 34 men the government especially wanted to get were selected to stand trial and the rest of the prisoners' fates were decided by lottery: only one in twenty of these was to face a court. The exigencies of collecting sufficient evidence further winnowed the group selected by lot, so that in the end only a further 47 stood trial. The conviction of those who faced the judges was almost preordained (only seven were acquitted) and of the 34 particular enemies of the government 17 were actually executed, whereas 18 of the 47 losers in the lottery suffered the same fate. To maximise the deterrent effect on the local Jacobite community the government carefully organised and paid for executions at every major town and city visited by the rebels, all designed to bring home the dreadful consequences of rebellion. In all, counting three ex-officers convicted of plotting a rising in Oxford and three pro-Jacobite rioters executed in London, there seem to have been about 40 executions in England.[42]

This, of course, came nowhere near clearing the gaols of the remainder of the 1,500 or so prisoners left in government hands after Preston. Some resolved the problem themselves by dying in the foul and overcrowded prisons into which they were crammed, though not as many as might have been expected. This was probably owing to the efforts of sympathisers who brought them food and other creature comforts in gaol and, too, because they tended to be both young and relatively fit. A few dozen others escaped and then went into hiding or into exile.[43] What to do with the rest was a serious problem.

The local authorities were already complaining about the cost of main-taining the prisoners and the threat to public health posed by having them crowded together in insanitary conditions in their local gaols. They were also escaping in increasing numbers, which quickly moved the ministry towards disposing of them by transporting them to the colonies. This had first been proposed by some Glasgow merchants as a way of dealing with the prisoners in the city gaol, but would probably have been taken up as a solution in any event by the ministry.[44] There was plenty of precedent for transporting former rebels, and the exiling of the less serious categories of felon to the colonies was a well-established practice by the early eighteenth century. The only problem was that transportation was a for-profit business as far as the merchants involved were concerned (they only wanted fit men of working age whose indentures they could sell in the colonies) and the prisoners had to petition for transportation in order for it to be legal. The government therefore directed that pressure, in the form of threats of further trials and executions and more stringent confinement, be put on the prisoners to force them to agree to be sent to the colonies. This was not entirely successful, but did even-tually persuade the great majority of the remaining prisoners to agree, and in August 1716 the first of a number of ships carrying former rebels sailed for the colonies from Liverpool.[45]

Altogether 638 prisoners were transported (those remaining in the English gaols were eventually released), 495 to the North American colonies and 143 to the Caribbean. The king and his ministers originally expected that they would all be sold in the West Indies, where a seven-year indenture was always likely to prove a death sentence for transportees from the British Isles.[46] In fact, however, most were sold in their first port of call in the North American colonies, which were desperate for skilled, fit labour that did not come with a proven aptitude for common felony.[47] Quite a few wealthy prisoners also matter-of-factly bribed the ship captains either to let them off on the way to the Americas (a large group famously celebrated their release with a raucous party in Cork before disappearing), or to let them buy their own indentures when they arrived. The indentures of others were carefully bought up by sympathisers, family and friends and the Governor of South Carolina bought as many of the transportees as he could in order to arm them and send them to the frontier to fight the Yamassee Indians, with whom the colony was at war.[48] The great majority of the transportees seem to have quickly adapted to life in the colonies and quite a few made such a success of their new lives that they had little inclination to return home. The ministry was not best pleased at the outcome of its transportation effort, which hardly created much of a deterrent to future rebellion, but there was little it could do to make it more severe once the process had begun.

Because there were only 40 executions in connection with the rebellion and because the transportation of over 600 other prisoners of war to the colonies turned out not to be so harsh a punishment as the government intended does not mean, however, that their ordeals had no impact on the Jacobite communities in Scotland and England. Many families were devastated by the fate of their loved ones. Mary, Vicountess Kenmure, collapsed when it became clear that her husband really was about to die. Anna, Countess of Derwentwater, had a miscarriage when she heard the news that her husband had been executed. Baillie Nairn begged in tears for the life of his son.[49] Sympathisers and friends were likewise distressed by the prisoners' fates. David Lumsden of Cushny confessed, 'I am so afflicted with the fatal accounts of our unfortunate friends in England that I hardly know what hand to turn me to. The accounts are now confirmed every where, and such discouraging stories publicly talked that I have not patience to hear them, much less to write them.'[50] Henry Prescott, in Chester, found the sight of the prisoners 'melancholy and shocking', and was stunned when he heard the news of Derwentwater's execution.[51] The grim process of official retribution also promoted a generalised mood of despair within the two Jacobite communities. Wightman found his prisoners at Inverness 'damnably doune in the mouth upon hereing some of the Lords are capot at Tower Hill', and it is in all likelihood at this time that some prisoners and their families went beyond simply saving the lives of those in danger of execution or transportation and gave up on the Jacobite cause permanently.[52] As one former Jacobite put it years later, 'he was happily got out of the scrap and would not be tempted again to backslide, and as he belived the generality of his party was of the same opinion'.[53] The long-term consequences of this were profound and will be dealt with in the next chapter and the conclusion.

Fugitives and Exiles

When the rebellion collapsed in February 1716 the active participants who had thus far escaped being taken prisoner by the government had three choices. They could surrender themselves in the hope that submission would lead to more lenient treatment. They could go into hiding in the British Isles in the hope that the government would eventually lose interest in catching and punishing them. Or they could flee into exile overseas in the hope of waiting out the pursuit or returning in triumph as part of a Jacobite invasion force. Those who surrendered were generally treated in like fashion to the prisoners taken during the fighting and do not need to be separately dealt with here.[54] The experience of the internal and external fugitives was another matter entirely.

Much of what happened to the internal fugitives is shrouded in mystery. The essence of their strategy demanded that they actively avoid catching the attention of the local and national authorities, so they have left precious few records. There were, however, literally hundreds of heritors 'skulking' and 'lurking' in the aftermath of the rebellion (over 130 in Perthshire alone).[55] Colonel Cathcart explained the problem he was having catching them in early March:

I had intelligence at Stirling that severall of the Perthshyre rebelles were skulking in that country. Non of them venture upon being att their oun houses, but they shift about amongst their tenants, never twoe nights together in one place. This will render it difficult to catch any of them by sending out detachments of the regular troopes. They are too much on their guard.[56]

Moreover, as élite Whigs became more and more involved in efforts to save individual Jacobite prisoners and their estates (as we will see in the next chapter), they tended to become less and less interested in delating Jacobite fugitives. The authorities nonetheless remained interested in catching élite Jacobites to the end of 1716, but as time went on they focused on the more senior of the fugitives.[57] Small heritors who were on the run were simply not worth the effort of apprehending, and, for the most part, they began quietly to go home in late 1717 (despite the fact that as they were still legally fugitives from justice they were not covered by the Indemnity Act passed earlier that year), and even harass local Whigs who remained activist pursuers.[58]

Two counties where such painstaking study of local and family records has been done that we get a sense of the number of fugitives are Aberdeenshire and Banff, and there a considerable number of small heritors followed this course. Thus we know nothing of where Lumsden of Cushny was and how he survived after February 1716, but he was certainly back home by 1717. Lachlan Forbes of Bellabeg was noticed as lurking in 1716, yet he was openly back in residence by 1719. James Oliphant of Gask hid somewhere in Scotland, only to reappear quietly in 1718. After the death of his only son beside him at Sherrifmuir, Sir John Johnston of Caskieben never did return home; instead he simply took up residence in Edinburgh.[59] These cases can be multiplied by a great many more in Aberdeenshire and Banff who were known to be out in the '15, but of whose travails and eventual re-emergence from the shadows we know nothing at all.[60] Assuming, however, that the Jacobite community's experience in these two counties was fairly typical of that in Angus, Perthshire, Fife and Inverness-shire, it seems reasonable to suggest that a great many Jacobites quietly slipped home and effectively escaped official notice when the rebellion was over. This seems, too, to have been what happened in northern England with those gentry who escaped either from Preston or subsequently from one of the gaols in which the prisoners were held. Certainly former rebels were being sheltered by local sympathisers in northern England and slipping away to hide in other parts of the British Isles from November 1715 onwards.[61]

Those who fled overseas were in a very different position. Their experience was far more prolonged and traumatic. Though some sought to escape abroad immediately, most of those who eventually went into exile at first seem to have attempted to 'lurk' near their homes just like their comrades who remained in hiding in the British Isles.[62] 'Hundreds', Dr Patrick Abercromby informed Mar, 'were in Edinburgh, and in the Brae countries, resolved . . . to lurk as long as possible, till they see whether the rage of the Government will relent, and they be overlooked.'[63] Only when these hopes were dashed did they attempt to escape overseas. As Clephane feelingly recalled: 'it began to be so warm . . . that our friends advised me to take the first opportunity of getting off anywhere'.[64] In the late spring and summer of 1716 the western seaports of continental Europe, and those of France in particular, began to see ship after ship arriving carrying Jacobite, especially Scottish, refugees. The greatest influx came between May and July; thereafter the flow dwindled away to a trickle of holdouts and escapees from Britain's prisons.[65] Although it is impossible to know exactly how many left Scotland as a result of the rising, a list of court pensioners compiled in 1718 indicates it cannot have been fewer than 350 and other evidence suggests it was probably fewer than 2,000.[66]

Once they arrived on the continent, financial survival was their first priority. Most had gone to war with whatever ready money they had available. Many then spent weeks or even months in hiding in Scotland or England and this further depleted their financial resources. However sympathetic they may have been, the shipmasters who eventually smuggled many of the exiles out of the British Isles past Royal Navy patrols also needed to be paid and even then were often unable to take their passengers directly to ports in countries where they were likely to be allowed to stay. Hence despite their social status very few of the refugees brought any substantial quantity of cash with them, and the vicissitudes of the journey to a safe haven in France, Italy or the Netherlands often consumed most of what little they had on them when they departed for the continent.[67] The former Baillie of Dundee John Oliphant's case is typical of many. Writing to his former commander, Panmure, from Amsterdam he related that after the army dispersed:

> I went to Buchan; where I disguised my self with a countrie man's dress and goott a chapman's pacik. Where I traveled nyne or ten weiks; being drag-oned from place to place. And having att lastt mett with several gentlemen thatt werre in my conditione; wee by a little interest with the master whoo was then load bound for Bergen to vindicatt him att the Goverment's hands, came aboard him att sea with sword in hand; and iff the weind hade bein faeir wee desseigned him for Dunkirk. But bloweing southerlie weinds wee was putt to Bergen in Norrowa (where I remained a month) and sos I have come from that place here.[68]

Not surprisingly, Oliphant's financial resources had been exhausted and he begged Panmure for a loan.

As in the British Isles, élite society in Europe worked on the basis of personal connections, and the first recourse of refugees was to seek out their kinsmen and friends already living abroad. This was, however, an option for only a small minority of the new exiles. In the main, a mere handful of the noblemen and a few of the Catholics amongst them knew anyone at all on the continent. Thus when Dr Abercromby, a well-known patriotic author who was the brother of Lord Glasfoord and a pre-1715 convert to Catholicism, arrived in France he immediately applied for help to Berwick, trading on his acquaintanceship with Berwick's son, James Fitzjames, Lord Tynemouth.[69] Most of the refugees, however, had no other institutional source of charity available to them than the Jacobite court.

Consequently, as more and more refugee Jacobites made their way to France in the late spring and summer of 1716 James's court at Avignon and Queen Mary of Modena's at Saint-Germain found themselves overwhelmed with urgent requests for help. 'For God's sake what must be done with such people? . . . I have crowds of them about me several times a day,' despaired the Jacobite courts' Paris banker William Gordon.[70] Something clearly had to be done, for, as Mar succinctly put it: ''tis hard and neither for my Master's interest nor honour they should starve'.[71] Unfortunately for the refugees, the Jacobite courts had scant resources to meet their needs. They were still in receipt of the 50,000 *livres* a month pension paid by the French government to Queen Mary, of which 12,000 was passed on to James with the tacit connivance of the French authorities. This sum was supplemented by an annual pension from the Pope equivalent to 83,000 *livres* a year and sundry private gifts.[72] Merely maintaining the barest essentials of royal grandeur around Queen Mary and her son consumed the bulk of this money, so that there was little left over to alleviate the destitution confronting most of the Jacobite exiles.

James correspondingly dunned every sympathetic statesman he could to secure the extra funding that would allow the Jacobite courts to help them, deploying whatever arguments he thought might evoke a positive response. Thus he wrote to Orléans, invoking his honour and the national interest of France:

> j'ose me flatter que vous m'en donnerez des preuves en cette occasion, en m'accordant quelques secours d'argent pour subvenir a leurs necessites, et a cette effet votre propre gloire et l'interest de la France vous doivent estre de plus puissants motifs que tout ce que je pourois dire.[73]

Then in a letter to the Pope via Cardinal Albani he put his moral dilemma to the fore, lamenting that he was 'absolutely incapable out of the pension he gives me to support all these poor Scotsmen who arrive every day and to whom I cannot without cruelty refuse bread, after they have lost their all for my service'.[74] In another to Philip V of Spain and Queen Elizabeth Farnese, he appealed to 'la droiture et la bonté de leurs coeurs et leur generosité naturelle'.[75] In the meantime Mar plied the Jacobite courts' contacts in France, Sweden and Savoy with letters trying to persuade them to take on the refugees as officers in their armies.[76]

It was all to no avail. No extra funding was forthcoming and Mar failed to persuade any of the statesmen he wrote to to offer the new exiles honourable remunerative employment. The Jacobite courts were forced to deal with the problem out of their own resources. Queen Mary promptly instituted a programme of retrenchment with respect to the existing pensions paid out at Saint-Germain and Mar and the Treasurer of the Household at Avignon, Sir William Ellis, set about working out a graduated tariff that would provide all the needy exiles with at least a bare subsistence.[77] The resulting 'new list' of pensions was scaled according to need, service record and social and military rank and ran from tiny payments of 10 and 15 *livres* a month to the handful of former rankers in the Jacobite army who had fled to the continent, through the 30 *livres* paid to ex-lieutenants up to 150 for former brigadiers and clan chieftains, to culminate in the 200 *livres* paid to all exiled noblemen.[78] In contemporary terms it was a commendably fair and efficient distribution of meagre resources. It was also a considerable strain on the Jacobite courts' finances. Until the '15 James had carefully managed his finances so as to produce a small surplus on his annual expenditure for future use as a war chest.[79] Supporting the exiles eliminated the possibility of any further accumulation of funds. When all the expenses of the two Jacobite courts were met the net monthly surplus available to meet all other contingencies was a mere 2,247 *livres* – a sum bound to be consumed from month to month by incidental expenditure.[80]

The pension system was also less than impartially administered. It rapidly became a tool of faction within the exiled community as different parties vied for power at the exiled courts. These parties reflected the former organisation of the Jacobite army in Scotland. As was customary in regular military hierarchies, those who had served under a given military commander expected him to act as their patron thereafter, so former senior officers in the Jacobite army automatically found themselves at the centre of networks of exiled former officers who had served in their respective regiments. 'Having the honnouer to have ben ounder your Lordship's comand [and] being now safly arived heir,' wrote Lieutenant John Carnegy to Panmure, 'I pressume to thinck that I can adress my self to none that I can hop for mor proction [*sic*] then from your Lordship. My behavioor and sircomstances being knoun to you and att present is as a grat many more of our Country, of nott knowing hou to subsist, I beg your Lordship's advice and asistins . . .'[81] And, quite unexceptionally, the chief minister's kinsmen and friends tended to receive special favour. From the outset Mar, who was appointed Secretary of State when Bolingbroke was summarily dismissed in March, made sure his old (and new) network did not want and that they received special consideration whenever they ran into financial difficulties or when official posts became vacant at the Jacobite courts.[82] Thus while the Jacobite Secretary of State felt obliged regretfully to inform Archibald Seton of Touch that: '[King James] is in a very indifferent way just now, and cannot supply his friends as he wishes',[83] relations like Harry Maule of Kellie were assured that: 'though it be not much that [the king] . . . in his present unlucky situation has to bestow, when he has more occasion for it than ever he had, yet, if you want, he expects that you will freely let me know it, and he will do what he can to supply you'.[84] Mar's political connection was soon recognised as the best one with which to become engaged, and was correspondingly increasingly resented by rival connections centred on other Jacobite leaders such as Marischal.[85]

Despite the gathering political tension generated by the favouritism of those administering the pension scheme, it is worth reiterating that the system was generally well run and certainly saved many of the Jacobite refugees from immediately descending into abject poverty. The money was regularly paid every month through a set of regional agents such as Robert Gordon in Bordeaux, William Dundas in Rotterdam and Lancelot Ord in Saint-Omer.[86] Three hundred *livres* a year (i.e. a former lieutenant's pension for ten months) was sufficient to purchase 'lodgings and diet' and 'to be tolerably well used' in a small provincial French town.[87] Larger towns, such as Rotterdam, Brussels, Orléans and Bordeaux, were more expensive, and indeed beyond the means of most of the exiles. Paris was too expensive for any but the nobility.[88] Those who were on less than 30 *livres* a month seem generally to have been plebeian refugees, and it appears to have been assumed that they would soon be able to shift for themselves. They were certainly not generally felt to need sustained support. Thus after some Jacobite prisoners seized the ship in which they were being transported to the West Indies in 1716 and got safely to France one of their officers casually remarked: 'a great many of the common men will get service, and some are trades. The rest are content to go to Scotland again, and, I hope, will be sent in some Scots ships that are expected here daily'.[89]

Once they began receiving their pensions the exiles distributed themselves according to their means. Those who were receiving subventions from home or substantial sums from the Jacobite courts took up residence in the larger towns and cities or even Paris, those in more straitened circumstances in smaller and less expensive provincial towns. The pattern of settlement was also conditioned by the active intervention of officials at the Jacobite courts. Before the pension system was introduced one of their major objectives was to prevent the entire Jacobite exile community ending up at Avignon clamouring at James's door, and to this end Mar wrote politely discouraging letters to most of the exiles who contacted him preparatory to travelling to the Jacobite court there.[90] Instead, he recommended they call on Queen Mary at Saint-Germain while behind the scenes requesting that she 'speak them fair, and so prevent their coming so long a journey'.[91] Once at Saint-Germain they were 'advised . . . to go to the coast of Brittany and Normandy, where they may live very cheap',[92] and thus by the end of 1716 little groups of Jacobite exiles were duly to be found eking out their pensions in a wide range of French, Dutch and Flemish towns from Leyden to Marseilles. At the beginning of 1717, however, James's court at Avignon decided to relocate a select cadre of the pensioners with a view to creating a skeleton officer corps for any future rebel army close to a suitable seaport. The Highland chieftains and the pick of the professional military officers were ordered quietly to resettle in and about Toulouse and given supplementary moneys to enable them to do so.[93] The only other major movements among the refugees occurred in connection with personal financial crises, at which point many would go to Paris to beg for extra assistance from the court at Saint-Germain, and when James's court was obliged to move from Avignon into Italy, where it ultimately settled in Rome.[94]

The diplomatic machinations of the British government that brought about the eventual, reluctant departure of the Jacobite court from Avignon to Urbino in February 1717 also included a more general diplomatic effort to dissuade any of the continental great powers from either sheltering or employing the exiles.[95] This achieved a partial success because most European potentates were reluctant needlessly to antagonise the Whig rulers of the British Isles. The king of Piedmont-Sardinia, Victor Amadeus II, spoke for them all when he bluntly told a Jacobite emissary that his strategic situation meant that 'he could not disoblige England' by taking former Jacobite officers into his army.[96] Even so, Europe's princes do not seem to have been inclined specially to exert themselves to please the British government, and Jacobite refugees were tacitly allowed to settle in the territories of virtually every one of the European great powers. Even in the Dutch Republic a representative from a local group of exiles was told by the Rector of the University of Leyden and the chief magistrate of the town:

> that they would be very ready to do us all the service in their power . . . they acknowledged at the same time that they were overreached in the late treaty betwixt England and their State, by which among other things they are obliged to deliver up all persons attainted, on twenty days if insisted on by England, but they assured us, if such a demand was made about any of us, we should all have such advertisement before anything was done upon it that we might have time to be at Rome, if we pleased . . .[97]

Both there and in the Habsburg Netherlands the key issue for the local authorities seems to have been resentment at interference in their affairs from the political centre and a determination to uphold their autonomy and privileges rather than any love of the Jacobite cause *per se*, though some Jacobites hopefully interpreted as such the refusal of local magistrates to comply with orders to evict them.[98]

Even in France, which was also allied with Britain by the end of 1716, the authorities showed little enthusiasm for harassing refugee Jacobites. This is not to say that the government of Regent Orléans was above putting some crude pressure on them when it served its purposes. Thus in the autumn of 1716, on finding that James and his entourage were dragging their feet about moving on from Avignon (which was papal territory) as the Regent had been required to request they do by his new treaty obligations, he blandly allowed a hiatus to occur in the Jacobite courts' pension payments.[99] He also sent a clear warning that he could go further when challenged by a Jacobite sympathiser at the French court. Surely, claimed the questioner, he had no means to evict James from a state with which he was at peace? ' "Yes I have", said the Regent, "namely by means of starvation." '[100] James and Mar took heed and departed. Nonetheless, in general even Orléans was reluctant to move against Jacobite exiles on French territory. If forced to take official notice of them he and his ministers would oblige high-profile Jacobites to depart, and even on occasion issue an order to the Intendants (the principal state officials in the French provinces) instructing them to expel all Jacobite refugees from France.[101] But when a Jacobite emissary asked him what he meant by such a directive, he insouciantly responded that 'the order was a thing he was obliged to by the late treaty, which he was pressed to execute, but it was "un coup d'espé dans l'eau" ', and he advised the exile community to ignore it.[102]

So, with the wolf being held at bay by an official dole and the best efforts of the British government to harass them availing little, the new, primarily Scottish Jacobite diaspora had, at least temporarily, stabilised by the end of 1716. For the next year or so the most serious problems facing the refugees proved to be psychological rather than material. Key amongst them were loneliness and boredom.

The loneliness of the exiles stemmed in large part from their social isolation. Surprisingly few of them seem to have been able to speak even the most basic French, the common tongue of the social élite throughout Europe at the time and the most commonly spoken language in the regions where they were now domiciled. Even scions of the Scottish aristocracy such as Marischal, Lord George Murray and Arthur Elphinstone, the Master of Balmerino, arrived unable to speak it.[103] Many of the exiles correspondingly found themselves stuck in small European provincial towns unable to communicate with the rest of the population except through those of their number who could make themselves understood. They were in effect doubly confined. The only social intercourse they could have was with the handful of fellow English/Scots-speakers sharing their current abode.[104] And however much they liked their fellow Jacobites, an exclusive diet of their company was bound to pall over time. Moreover, the social isolation of many of the exiles was compounded by their penuriousness and their being domiciled in small provincial towns – in themselves a byword for stultifying tedium in the eighteenth century.

Indeed, boredom ultimately became the keynote of the Jacobites' experience of exile. A few, like Robert Leslie, took their enforced leisure in Europe as a golden opportunity for self-improvement. Writing to Mar in April 1716 he confided:

As to myself I propose to go to some place of retreat, I mean of leisure and opportunities of reading. If I know anything of my own mind, leisure is the greatest pleasure, and a desire for quiet the strongest appetite I have . . . I will, with the King's leave, pursue the scheme which brought me first into France, and amuse myself at Montpellier as well as I can with a few books and leisure enough to make use of them . . .[105]

In particular, Leslie planned to make a special study of Clarendon's *History of the Rebellion*. Likewise Harry Maule of Kellie was content to spend his involuntary stay in Europe studying antiquities and supervising the education of two of his sons at the university of Leyden and Alexander Forbes, Lord Pitsligo, was determined from the outset to study medicine either at Leyden under the internationally renowned Herman Boerhaave or else at Montpellier.[106] They were, however, exceptions. Most of the exiles seem to have simply vegetated wherever they happened to fetch up, though it is only fair to note that books and higher education were both expensive items and most of the exiles had scant resources to spare for them. The inevitable outcome, of course, of 'one day being as like the other as two eggs and these eaten without either pepper or salt', was a rising tide of fractiousness, quarrelling and petty jealousy within the exile community.[107]

Alastair and Henrietta Tayler observed over sixty years ago that 'every Jacobite distrusted his fellow', and Edward Gregg in 1987 described how a culture of political paranoia suffused Jacobite life at home and abroad.[108] If further evidence were needed to sustain their theses, a cursory examination of the Jacobite experience between 1716 and 1718 would provide it. By May 1716 there were already 'Marischal' and 'Mar' factions at Avignon, in Paris and wherever else a critical mass of Jacobites was to be found, and the disgraced Bolingbroke was constantly being accused of intrigues and treason.[109] Just as corrosive to the exiles' morale was their growing sense of uselessness. Some responded by desperately seeking honourable employment. Major David Nairne, for example, 'being perfectly weary of this way of living and very much ashamed of being a burden to his Majesty', begged Mar to help him obtain a commission anywhere at all.[110] Lieutenant John Hutcheson was implicitly willing to surrender his pretensions to gentility if James's court at Avignon could just loan him 1,000 *livres* to start a business.[111] Despite being an attaindered felon Major Nathaniel Forbes was so 'entirely wearied of this idle life' by September 1717 that he informed Mar he was going to slip away into Ireland and set up as a farmer.[112] The meagre employments the Jacobite courts could offer inevitably became the focus of intense competition. So much so that the stalwart Panmure exploded with rage when he heard that a younger man (James Murray of Stormont) had been appointed James's agent in Paris. Writing to Mar, he declared: 'This has been and is very bitter to me and adds a great deal to my sufferings for the King, which were otherwise very great. . . . the world will always conclude that he has most regard and esteem for those he trusts and employs in his service.'[113] An even more immediately damaging problem was the Jacobite refugees' gathering penchant for killing each other out of sheer ennui. As John Ogilvie acidly observed in 1718, 'our people cannot agree among themselves'.[114] Captain Charles Wogan, for example, fought a duel with Charles Forman Macmahon in 1718 for no better reason than that he thought Macmahon had squeezed his hand unduly hard when he shook it.[115] Macmahon survived that encounter only to die in a subsequent one with an unknown protagonist. In like fashion, Lachlan Maclean killed his friend and fellow lodger at Cahors, Robert Robertson (nephew of Alexander Robertson of Struan), one evening after being 'jostled' by him after a sudden quarrel earlier in the day.[116] In the same vein, Laurence Charteris in Rotterdam became convinced his fellow exiles were sending unfavourable reports about him to the Jacobite court at Rome and that these had resulted in his pension payments being suspended. He was so incensed by this that he vowed that if they continued (as he believed) to traduce him, 'I will pistol some of them by God'.[117]

Thus by the second half of 1717 a deepening mood of frustration and despair was evident among the exiles. This stemmed in part from external factors, principally the failure of successive Jacobite diplomatic efforts to persuade any of the great powers openly to espouse the Stuart cause. In equal part, however, it sprang from the by then all too familiar rubs and tensions implicit in living in a foreign land.

Because the overwhelming majority of those who turned out to fight for the Jacobite cause prided themselves on their patriotism,[118] they took considerable pleasure in things Scottish and English, from their country's history to its tastes and mores.[119] The corollary was that they did not fit easily into the rhythms and customs of everyday life in the backwoods of Europe.[120] Even the unfamiliar food made many of them seriously ill.[121] Homesickness was a chronic problem that steadily sapped the morale of the refugee community. Writing to a friend still in Scotland, Pitsligo wistfully observed: 'I hope we shall yet live together in a certain corner of a country which I protest has an abundance of charms to me. Your staying at home has been very lucky for you. If you ever come abroad you'll be content to be at home again . . .'[122] These were sentiments which most of the rest of the exiled community certainly shared.[123] In addition, the fundamentally Roman Catholic nature of most of the polities in which they resided dramatically compounded the problem of alienation for the Protestants (the great majority) among them.

As far as this author is aware, the only Protestant associated with Jacobitism who was ever proceeded against by the Inquisition in any Catholic country was an Italian servant of Mar's, one Laurence Bernardi, who had converted to Protestantism while he was a boy in Scotland. After James's court was obliged to relocate from Avignon to Urbino his parents learned of his apostasy and denounced him to the Inquisition. This eventually forced Bernardi to leave Mar's service and flee to Venice.[124] The case, however untypical, nonetheless nicely illustrates a very salient point. For despite the leverage his losses for his adherence to the Catholic Church gave James in his dealings with *dévot* Catholic potentates inside and outside the Vatican, there was nothing James could do to protect Bernardi. Indeed, he was specifically warned not even to try, lest it provoke further investigation of his court at Urbino. In essence this typifies the situation the vast majority of the exiles of 1716, most of whom were more or less devout Episcopalians, found themselves in. Religious services and other devotions were tolerated as long as the authorities did not have to take official notice of them. When they were obliged to do so, they were adamantly hostile. For example, in 1717 when it came to the attention of the Prior of Saint-Germain that an Anglican communion service was about to take place in one of the private apartments at the palace, he informed the authorities and they ordered it suppressed, much to the unhappiness of the participants.[125] In Avignon, Urbino and even Rome Protestant religious services took place regularly, but as Mar admitted, 'we must not make a noise about it'.[126] In any case, the fact that the authorities hard by the Jacobite courts could be persuaded to turn a blind eye to Protestant services was small comfort to the little groups of refugees parked in sundry French and Flemish and subsequently Italian and Spanish provincial towns. There were simply not enough exile Protestant clergymen to minister to them, so they were effectively abandoned to their own devices. Even had there been an adequate number of Protestant clergymen available, it is unlikely they would have been able to operate freely anywhere in Catholic Europe other than major, sophisticated (and effectively anonymous) metropolitan centres at this time. There was a good deal of old-fashioned bigotry against Protestants at the local level still, as may be seen from the exile community's continued need to inter deceased Protestants secretly in provincial towns lest Catholic mobs desecrate their graves.[127] Failure to do so could have distressing consequences. While on the road to Rome in 1716 a Scots Catholic priest, Alexander Paterson, encountered the bloated corpse of an unknown Protestant who had died in a nearby village and been buried at a crossroads in a grave so careless and shallow that wild dogs had dug it up and mauled it. 'I left him,' he recalled, 'thinking with my self that the Italians hade more faith than charity.'[128]

Protestant Jacobites were also subject to direct and indirect pressure to convert to Catholicism. James personally kept himself absolutely aloof from such proselytising, trenchantly observing in 1718: 'Je suis Roy mais, comme m'a dit le Pape luy meme, je ne suis pas Apotre, je ne suis pas obligé de convertir mes sujets que par l'exemple, ni de montrer une partialité apparente aux Catholiques, qui ne serviroit qu'a leur nuire effectivement dans la suitte.'[129] Other European Catholic princes were not always as enlightened. After eight years as an officer in the Spanish army James Keith bitterly recalled that when he petitioned for promotion:

> I received the answer I expected: that His Majesty assured me that howsoon he knew I was Roman Catholick, I should not only have what I asked, but that he would take care of my fortune. On the receipt of this letter, I went straight to Madrid, and desired His Majestie's recommendation to the Empresse of Russia, since I found my religion was an invincible obstacle to my continuing in his [service], which he immediately granted me . . .[130]

But such crude tactics were rare. For the most part the drift towards Catholicism among the Scottish refugees was a natural one, brought on by their daily exposure to Catholic ideas and values and their gradual acclimatisation to the mores and beliefs of the societies in which they were sojourning.[131] It was nonetheless a very sensitive issue. When a number of exiles living in Saint-Omer converted in 1718 there was a 'great outcry' among the Protestant Jacobites elsewhere and the regional administrator of the pension scheme, Lancelot Ord (a Northumberland Catholic), was accused of having pressured them into doing so with the help of the Jesuits of the city's English College.[132] He emphatically, and convincingly, denied it, as did the

Jesuit fathers and the officers of the Irish regiment stationed there (not one of whom, Brigadier Christopher Nugent sardonically observed, 'would give a bottle of wine to make 500 converts'), and the scandal eventually blew over.[133] The extreme response of the Protestant Jacobites to the report, however, well illustrates how vulnerable they felt on this score.

The Protestants were not the only members of the Jacobite diaspora in Europe to feel threatened by the situation they found themselves in after 1716. James's Secretaries of State from 1715 to 1718, Bolingbroke and Mar, and other eminent Protestant Jacobites, were not shy about telling him of his need visibly, even ostentatiously, to favour Protestants in appointments to court office and other posts and likewise to downplay his personal commitment to Catholicism.[134] This bid fair to upset the actual, as opposed to theoretical, status quo at the Jacobite court. For though, as we have already seen, the dynasty had long since committed itself to favouring Protestant claims to authority within the movement, the simple fact was that the vast majority of the Jacobites who went into exile in the 1690s were Irish and English Catholics or Catholics-in-waiting. Hence most of the offices at Saint-Germain, and later Bar-le-Duc, had come to be held by Catholics. These old servants were naturally put out when the reconstruction of the Jacobite court at Avignon gave pride of place to the new wave of Scottish Protestant exiles.[135] As long as Queen Mary lived, her court at Saint-Germain was a vital ancillary to that centred on her son, and her old Catholic servants continued to play a prominent role in Jacobite espionage, politics and diplomacy, which somewhat softened their resentment at their overall loss of influence. After her death the Catholic interest felt distinctly threatened. Father Archangel Graeme told Mar in August 1718 that among the Catholic Jacobites in Paris it was reported 'that not one Roman Catholic of the three nations was allowed to be with the King, and that nobody was to be seen at Court but Scots Protestants'.[136]

The resentment of many of the ageing veterans of the 1690s towards the upstarts straggling in from the British Isles demanding succour and honourable employment also expressed itself in a good deal of personal friction between the two groups. James's confidential secretary, David Nairne, confided to a friend in 1717 that as far as Mar was concerned: 'I never writt a scrape of a pen to him . . . tho I am not at all ignorant of his extraordinary favour, which shews you how ill a Courtier I am. I love old tryd friends, and cannot bring my self to admire some new great men so extraordinarly as I see a great many do.'[137] And even Queen Mary's court at Saint-Germain, which was for the most part generous and helpful to all Jacobites, found the new refugees' different perception of the Jacobite cause somewhat hard to take on occasion. Hence the injunction her Lord Almoner, Lewis Innes, passed on to his brother Thomas regarding Dr Abercromby (a well-known writer on Scottish history): 'You'll be civill to him, but keep only on fair generalls as to history matters.'[138] Conversely, the new arrivals disliked the older generation of exiles' assumption of an air of superiority. Mar was reported 'shy', 'dry' and 'reservd' to Nairne.[139] The Earl of Southesk made his feelings even plainer in 1717 when he told John Paterson:

> I was very glad to retire [from Urbino] to where I live at my ease [Rome], free from the chagrin of seeing myself looked down on by those who can pretend to no more than to be my equals, though they now give themselves their great Saint-Germain airs and esteem themselves the only sufferers for the King, while they have been growing rich by him these nine and twenty years, and are in better circumstances than they could ever hope for, had he been on his throne.[140]

The conflict was only finally resolved by the death of Queen Mary in May 1718, following which the old Catholic veterans were steadily eclipsed.

Capping all the other tensions and anxieties inherent in the Scottish exiles' situation was a deep concern for the families they had left behind them.[141] Few of the refugees had managed to dispose of their property before they departed in such a fashion as to make it secure against attempts to confiscate it by the authorities. Consequently their families were left exposed to the vindictiveness of the Whig regime and they themselves were denied subventions from home, though it was the former rather than the latter that most preyed on the exiles' minds.[142] Thus Harry Maule lurked in Scotland as long as he dared, desperately writing to old friends and acquaintances within the Whig regime in the hope he might 'get something done for my wife and children'.[143] Lieutenant-Colonel Nathaniel Forbes was likewise so haunted by the plight of his wife and eight children after he heard that 'my house is plundered and my substance destroyed by Cadogan's soldiers', that he planned to go back to Scotland to try and help them – despite the fact that he was a former officer in the British army and as such subject to immediate court-martial and execution if he was captured.[144] In the same vein, George Home of Whitefield was so worried about his son, who was ill, and the situation in which he had left his family that he actually did return surreptitiously to Britain.[145] Straightforward anxiety about those they had left behind was a constant condition for many in the refugee community.

Part of the unhappiness the exiles felt about the situation facing their spouses and families back in Scotland may well, however, have stemmed from another cause. For the journey into exile in many cases brought in its train an uncomfortable reversal of roles and a humiliating loss of power within their families. The Jacobite élite, once again in accord with the rest of patrician British society, assumed that a family should be dominated by its pater-familias. This was obviously impossible if said paterfamilias was forced to become a fugitive in Europe. In such circumstances authority necessarily devolved, in most cases, on the refugees' wives and to a lesser extent (where this was feasible) on their older children.

This was not a welcome development as far as most of the exiles' spouses were concerned. For many of them it meant that they were abruptly cata-pulted out of their accustomed sphere into a new, hostile public world of bailiffs, bankers, lawyers and politicians at a time when their distress left them ill-prepared to face such a challenge. The first reaction of many of the wives seems to have been shock and an inability to cope with the collapse of the emotional and social verities that had hitherto sustained their lives. Frances, Countess of Mar, who may always have been somewhat delicate mentally, went into 'a sad way for some time'.[146] Catherine Erskine confessed to her husband, Sir John Erskine of Alva, that initially she 'was not capable of haveing a right thought'.[147] Likewise Margaret, Countess of Panmure, fled back to Panmure House and immured herself there.[148] All three, however, and doubtless many more whose letters have not survived, were ultimately forced to deal with their situation. After a time Catherine Erskine found she 'could not live after that way', and though still going 'many days without speaking except when bussiness obligt me to it', she turned to the difficult task of securing permission for Sir John Erskine to return, which in the end she and his brother-in-law, Patrick Campbell of Monzies, managed so successfully that he was one of the first to be allowed home.[149] When she emerged from her depression, Margaret Panmure soon became adept at judicial and political manoeuvring and eventually retrieved a considerable part of the Panmure estate.[150] Frances Mar, recovered from her 'sadness' and a subsequent serious illness, developed a humorous resilience that sustained her through the struggle to secure her jointure and a nightmarish journey from London to Rome to see her husband in the late autumn of 1718.[151]

In the process of coping with the disaster that had befallen their families, a significant shift occurred in the relationship between the exiles and their wives. The exiles were obliged to become virtually helpless onlookers while their wives, and sometimes children, battled to hang on to at least a part of the family estates and intrigued to secure permission from the authorities for them to come home.[152] Because, by and large, the Whig regime ultimately allowed the wives' jointures to be exempted from the general confiscation of rebels' estates, the husbands often became their financial dependants too. The authority of the women expanded accordingly. Harry Maule was genuinely distressed to hear that his wife, Anna, was ill in 1718:

> My Dear Life . . . I am so uneasie till I hear hou you are and prays God to have a care of you and comfort you in your afflicted state and mine and to let me knou if ther be any thing I can doe for you that will in any measure make you easier than you are, for I judge the affliction you ar under is the cause of all trouble and indisposition, which I pray God to help . . .[153]

But in part too, his distress may have stemmed from the consequences of Anna's illness: the paralysis of the complex financial arrangements by which the resourceful Anna had contrived to maintain Maule and two of their sons at Leyden.[154] By November Harry was in serious difficulties:

> . . . I am like to be straitned because I can get no account of my affairs. I have no body to correspond with me or to let me knou what mony I have at home that I can call for, for I am needing mony and I have no vieu of what may com in to me and if your sickness continue and make you not able to act I knou not whome to employ but those that I am afraid will neglect it as they have done on other occasions.[155]

He who pays the piper calls the tune, and the views of the women the exiles had left behind began to carry greater weight in their deliberations on how to conduct themselves. When, for example, Catherine Erskine and Sir John Erskine's friends and kinsmen succeeded in negotiating the frankly corrupt deal with Townshend and other Whig ministers that allowed him to come home,[156] she applied the maximum emotional pressure on him to accept:

> I believe the first thoughts of this kind will be very disagreeable to you, but consider mee and your children and every particular circumstance and then I am sure you must be of my mind. This is the opinion of those freinds that did not condemn your goeing out and hass your interest as much at heart as there own . . .[157]

Despite his relatively favoured position in the Jacobite hierarchy as a kinsman of Mar's, Sir John duly submitted.[158] Likewise when Margaret Panmure, who otherwise had a highly affectionate relationship with her husband,[159] at last secured him the possibility of permission to return home on condition that he promise to live quietly thereafter, she forthrightly attacked his scruples on the subject:

. . . I cannot but say that I am both very much grieved and astonished to find you are so nicely scrupolous as to resolve that you will not so much as give security for your peaceable behaviour in time comming in case your attainder is taken off. I begg you may seriously consider this matter, after which I am perswaided you will think it is an incumbent duty on you to preserve your familly from utter ruine if so small an acknowledgement will do it. And on what pretext do you think your friends can pretend to solicit for you, if they and I may not give assurance of your living peacablie here-after? If you refuse this don't complean of the Government's being sever for in reason they cannot be blamed to abstract their favour from any that shall give so plaine an indication of their future designes when ever an oppertu-nity might offer . . . I cannot but expect that what I have writt will have weight with you, but if I am so unhappy as not to prevaill with you then I must still remain misserable . . .[160]

Cowed by this tirade, even the famously unbending Panmure, a Nonjuror since 1689, penned a draft submission to the Whig regime.[161] It is also prob-ably far from coincidental that despite his original determination to hold out, Harry Maule first asked for permission to return to Scotland in the wake of Anna Maule's debility and her wish, too, to have him come home, and that Frances Mar played a major role in the negotiations that led to Mar's attempt to get home by betraying the Jacobite cause in 1720–24.[162]

Ironically though, the final crisis that broke the initial resolve of many of the Jacobites to persevere in exile until a second restoration dawned stemmed not from their homesickness, frustration at their reduction to helpless depen-dants, chronic ennui or alienation from the milieu in which they were forced to live, though all of these predisposed them to give way.[163] Nor had their dete-riorating morale in the face of successive Jacobite diplomatic failures, or the pressure exerted by their wives and families back home acted as yet on their unhappiness to create more than a trickle of returnees (licit and illicit) before the summer of 1718. What finally opened the floodgates and persuaded the exiles in their hundreds to take advantage of the Indemnity Act if they could, but by all means to return home, was an entirely external event: the financial crisis created by the inability of the French government to meet its obligations in 1717–18.

As we saw earlier, France had emerged from the reign of Louis XIV heavily burdened with debt. For political reasons Regent Orléans could not immedi-ately take the drastic fiscal measures necessary to retrieve the situation. Correspondingly, the level of debt and the inability of the French government to fund its outgoings steadily worsened, eventually leading to the adoption of

John Law's bold, but ultimately disastrous, financial schemes (most infamously in the Mississippi Bubble).[164] In such circumstances subventions to clients like the exiled Stuarts inevitably assumed a low priority, which in practical terms meant they were paid intermittently or not at all. So by the end of 1717 the Jacobite courts were seriously in debt themselves. Queen Mary's Treasurer, William Dicconson, submitted a confidential account to James and his mother in October, which showed they were already owed nine months' arrears of pension. He had compensated for the shortfall by borrowing money from William Gordon, the Jacobites' banker in Paris, but there could be no more forthcoming from him until some of the arrears were met. The only solution Dicconson could see was a massive retrenchment in the pension system, for: 'all I can do, is to pay when I have wherewithal and to represent my inability when I have not'.[165] James balked at such a drastic proposal, but he could offer no solution other than the empty one of signing over his entire share of the 50,000 *livres* due to be paid monthly to Saint-Germain.[166] Queen Mary responded by breaking into one of her periods of contemplative seclusion at Chaillot in order personally to lobby the Regent, 'who gave her great hopes, or rather assurances of paying soon all he owes to her, and also some hopes of helping the King the beginning of the next year'.[167] The Jacobite diaspora in France also mobilised their friends at the French court to add their moiety of pressure on the administration.[168] They all failed. By March 1718 William Gordon was reporting to Mar's secretary, John Paterson, that 'the Queen's pension is so far behind that the necessaries of her family can't be paid', and the crisis was exacerbated in May by the sudden death of the queen.[169] According to the regular practice of the French government in such cases the (at this point notional) pension payments to Saint-Germain were suspended forthwith.[170] At the time he left Avignon James had been secretly promised that they would be surreptitiously continued after Queen Mary's demise, but he was entirely dependent on Orléans's goodwill for the implementation of this commitment. Since the Regent was at this time involved in a major political confrontation with the *parlement* of Paris he had little time to spare for Jacobite affairs and consequently James's urgent appeals were ignored and the financial crisis deepened.[171] By June Dicconson was reporting that the arrears had built up to eleven months, and by the end of the year only Berwick's personal intervention prevented the queen's old servants at Saint-Germain from becoming totally destitute.[172]

In some respects, they were the lucky ones. The old courtiers resident at Saint-Germain did at least have a roof over their heads and access to Parisian networks of credit that were relatively accustomed to intermissions in state doles. Out in the provinces, where the majority of the exiles were to be found, creditors were not so patient with strangers.[173] William Gordon and Dicconson found themselves besieged with letters from desperate refugees, with little more they could do than extend private loans to a handful of the most needy.[174] Apart from one payment in June, nothing further was forthcoming from the French government, and by the end of the year Gordon bluntly reported, 'most of them are starving'.[175] He was not exaggerating. Former regimental commanders like Panmure also found themselves being deluged with desperate pleas for help in the second half of 1718, reaching a crescendo in early 1719, and the plight of John Oliphant, as described in one of these letters, is typical of many:

> Having pleagd all my cloathes for to keap my creadit and most say from sterving, having not recivied my subsistance this eleven months, and I have contracted so much det with the man I loog [with] he threatens to put me in prison or fynd him security for what I ow him which is impossible for me to fynd having no acquaintance to mack my sircomstance knowen too. But I must beeg of your Lordship for God sack to be so good as speack ons more to Mr Gordon to advance me a 100 livers which he shall reten the first mony he receives for me, which if he does it not I most stervie heer.[176]

A few responded to the crisis by enlisting as common soldiers in the Irish Brigade.[177] Most, faced with the unenviable choice of going 'home and to be hanged or starve here or knock themselves on the head or beg their way to Urbino and throw themselves at the King's feet', chose to try their luck at home.[178]

Former Ensign James Douglas's motives and reasoning undoubtedly reflect those of many others: 'being unwilling to be any further troublesome to his Majesty or your Lordship and finding I can't stay abroad without it, I have some thoughts of returning home soon (since I expect at three years end, which is now approaching, to be safe) . . .'[179] And, indeed, Mar and James himself officially endorsed the departure of any who could safely do so as early as May 1717, on the grounds that: 'a man of honour and principle will be so wherever he is, nor will anything the Government can do make him alter or keep him from endeavouring to rescue his King and country when an opportunity offers, and one man at home in the interest is worth ten abroad'.[180] Panmure duly responded positively to Douglas's proposal that he return to Scotland: '[I] aprove of your resolution to returne home as soon as you can doe it with safety. I know nothing you can doe better in the present situation of affairs.'[181] Douglas duly departed, as did, doubtless, a legion of others whose passing over is occasionally to be found laconically noted, 'gon away', in

Dicconson's lists of pensioners.[182] By 1719–20 even some of the biggest fish, such as Gordon of Auchintoul, Pitsligo and James Stirling of Keir, were quietly slipping away home without the authorities officially taking notice.[183]

Love of place and love of family – two halves of a common élite patriotic ideal among the Jacobites[184] – were fundamental, intertwined features of the Jacobite psyche. This is strikingly illustrated by a reverie penned in the spring of 1716 by Margaret Panmure. Observing that though the weather in Angus was beautiful:

> I cannot say I am pleased with [it] since you are not here, but it is rather an aggravation to my sorrow and I do believe you would think this a pleasanter place then where you are as I am sure I should do should I ever see it. But since you think it fitt for me to be here I shall hold the grip as long as I can, however melancholy it may be. I confess I should much more rejoise at your comming here then at my goieng where you are. You will perhaps think this is a but a bad complement, but I must owne I never was so fond of this place as now when I am likely to be forced to leave it . . .[185]

The yearning for home this inspired was compounded by the alienation, frustration, boredom and poverty that for most Jacobites characterised their period of exile to make it a preternaturally difficult experience. The net effect was that their involuntary sojourn abroad more than anything else taught them how much they needed to be at home.

* * *

In many respects what happened after the rebellion disintegrated was as important a part of the Jacobite experience of 1715 as the actual rebellion itself, at least for the social élite who were the regime's preferred target for retribution. The executions, though few in number compared to the toll taken of defeated rebels in many previous uprisings, were a depressing vindication of the Whig triumph. The transportation of hundreds of Jacobite prisoners of war to the colonies, for all that it worked out fortuitously for quite a number of them, was a further psychological blow to the community they left behind.

The fugitives within the British Isles had to watch their families struggle to hang on to their estates while they lurked in disguise in the shadows, helpless to influence the course of events. A great many of the lesser heritors in Scotland, and doubtless some of the minor gentry fugitives in England and Wales, eventually slipped back into their old lives, but it is doubtful if they were ever quite so sure of their status and authority again. Sustaining loved ones who were on the run was expensive at home, and more than one family was beggared by it.[186] The financial costs and the emotional toll of maintaining the exiles overseas, however, was even greater. The Stuart court, it is fair to say, did all that it could to lighten the load on the exiles. It was, though, caught up in political and economic problems not of its own making and was thus unable to sustain them adequately. The exiles consequently had to add poverty and sometimes destitution to the emotional torment exile brought for them. The patriotism that inspired the Jacobites was a double-edged sword: by fixing their beliefs solidly in a community and a place it gave the cause resilience and the power to move men to take up arms; conversely, separation from that community and that place diminished them in every respect.

Yet in a larger sense the depressing postwar experience of the Jacobites had a potentially positive effect for society as a whole, particularly in Scotland. Will they nill they, the Jacobites and their families, whether prisoners, fugitives or exiles, needed help escaping retribution for what they had done. That help ultimately had to come from their erstwhile enemies, and, as we shall see in the next chapter, this created a reciprocal process that opened the way to the reintegration of the rebel community and more broadly to the regeneration of civil society.

CHAPTER 9

'Such a Parcel of Rogues in a Nation': Resistance and Social Reintegration after the '15

The Jacobite armies were very much products of contemporary social customs and mores. Great magnates, superiors, clan chieftains, heritors, landlords and masters mobilised their people to fight for the Stuart cause (albeit that many plebeian Jacobites were happy to follow them). And the basis of this Jacobite élite's social power was its property ownership. Correspondingly, the most effective way to strike at that social power was to use the rebellion as a justification for the expropriation of the property (and especially the landed property) that made the rebellion possible. This was recognised early. In October 1715 Islay recommended that when the rebellion was over the authorities break the power of the (rebel) clan chieftains: 'They are the only source of any real danger that can attend the disaffection of the enemies to the Protestant succession. Several thousands of men armed and used to arms, ready upon a few weeks' call, is what might disturb any goverment.'[1] For his part, Lord Advocate Dalrymple argued, 'the popish Lords and gentlemen who are engaged will afford the Government means to root out that seed of rebellion. Even tho any of them should be spared, their childeren should be bred protestants according to the constitution of the country.'[2] Lord Justice Clerk Cockburn went still further: he believed that it was necessary to bring low the enemies of the state, 'att one stroke', so as to secure 'our religion and libertys'.[3] When the rebellion was over the government's pursuit of the rebels accordingly did not stop at their persons. Those who were significant property owners now became the targets of a systematic attempt to wrest their estates from them.

The engine of their destruction was supposed to be the Commission for Forfeited Estates, established by Act of Parliament in the summer of 1716. Its remit was to make good on the theoretical forfeiture of the estates of every rebel landowner in northern England and Scotland, and specifically to seize the property of those individuals who had failed to heed the summonses to

Edinburgh issued in August 1715 or were named in the Act of Attainder passed later in the year.[4] By the time the Forfeited Estates Commission Bill passed, however, there were signs that its implementation was liable to meet with opposition. Already the Jacobites were being seen more as objects of contemptuous pity than as deadly enemies in need of extirpation. Polwarth had pungently characterised the Berwickshire Jacobites as 'our fools' as early as October 1715. By February they and their peers were being described as 'miserably misled', 'unluckily drawn in', 'willfull fools' and 'poor unthinking Gentlemen', whose revolt had 'evanish[ed] lyke smoak', by stalwart Whigs, and in April plebeian rioters in Edinburgh savagely attacked Dutch troops who made the mistake of drunkenly bragging about beheading Highlanders while moving wagonloads of what was presumed to be plunder through the city.[5]

It was, nonetheless, a serious threat to the Jacobite communities of northern England and Scotland. The Commission, which was effectively split into two separate bodies, one for England, Wales and Ireland and one for Scotland, employed a well-paid staff of surveyors, accountant-generals, clerks, messengers and criers with legal authority to seize property and search documents in the course of their investigations, and supplemented these with incentives and rewards to informers.[6] The Commission was also energised by men on the make like Denis Bond, John Birch, Patrick Haldane of Bearcrofts and Robert Monro of Foulis Jr, who went at their task with a will.[7] The upshot was that where the Commission was allowed to pursue its remit relatively unhindered it was capable of striking the Jacobites hard. This was manifestly demonstrated by its success in northern England. There its principal target was the Catholic community, and by a judicious mix of legal measures and the solicitation of information from disgruntled tenants, worried creditors, avaricious informers and greedy neighbours it was able to uncover not only the bulk of the landed property held by many wealthy landed Catholic families, but also the lands and other properties secretly dedicated to supporting the underground Catholic Church in northern England and its support network of colleges and religious houses on the continent.[8] Despite some egregious corruption (sufficient to result in the expulsion of Birch and Bond from the Commons in 1732) the damage done to the northern Catholic community was profound. The huge Derwentwater estate was exposed and confiscated wholesale and many other élite Catholic families were drastically reduced in terms of their property and influence. It was a blow from which their community was to take decades to recover.[9]

The Commission's encounter with Scotland, however, was very different. By the time the Commissioners got to work in the autumn of 1716 the Scots Jacobite community had already prepared its legal defences. From the very start the Commission thus faced not only the kind of physical obstruction and asset-stripping that it encountered in northern England, but also thickets of legal ploys designed to stop it in its tracks. Many estates, it seemed, owed vast sums to neighbours, friends and family. These creditors naturally used the customary recourse of creditors in Scotland to recover their money: they petitioned the courts to sequester the estate and appoint factors who would exploit it for their collective benefit and, of course, could legally defend their hold on the estate until all the alleged debts were paid off. Strangely enough, many of these factors were friends, kinsmen or former employees of the forfeited owners. Some were even their former comrades in arms in the Jacobite armies.[10] Surprisingly, other estates were apparently never the property of the men who had previously claimed to be their owners. Either legal ownership was vested in someone else entirely and the ostensible owner had only been a life tenant, or they were really the property of a feudal superior, who was of course entitled to repossess the forfeited property under the terms of the Clan Act of August 1715.[11] Where these legal ploys proved insufficient to stop the Commission's agents pursuing their investigations the friends, neighbours and kinsmen of the threatened families matter-of-factly used violence. In Cromarty, Seaforth's factor, Donald Murchison, kept a small force of armed clansmen under his hand with which he ambushed at least one posse of surveyors and their attendants who were becoming annoying, killing and wounding members of their party. On Sleat several members of an investigative team were waylaid and beaten by the locals.[12]

The government could, and did, belatedly support the Commission's staff with military force in the face of extreme violence, but the Commissioners had to deal with the Scottish courts on their own terms, and this was where they most signally failed.[13] The Court of Session regarded them as arrogant interlopers and quietly cooperated with the threatened families at every turn (always, of course, on solid legal grounds under Scottish law), so that by 1718 the Commission was at a standstill.[14] The Commissioners tried to use the legal stalemate to wait out their opponents, but that was never going to work as long as the Jacobites' friends and families remained physically resident on the estates. Law or no law, it would have been a bold tenant who chose to defy the demands of Panmure's, Clanranald's or Seaforth's factors (whether official or unofficial) for rent and services. They could expect next to no support from the local élite and redress against exaction and eviction was difficult and expensive to obtain from local courts. Even when the local heritor was unpopular with his people London was a long way away and the laird's powerful friends were very near; hardly surprisingly, few tenants chose to defy their landlords' customary – as opposed to legal – authority. In the end the

Commissioners were reduced to trying to circumvent the Court of Session's obstructiveness by expensively invoking the superior authority of Parliament. As part of a supplementary Act extending the Commission's authority in preparation for the sale of the forfeited estates in England, the Commissioners inserted several provisions empowering them to confiscate property without appeal to the Scottish courts and to ignore claims on the personal property of forfeited rebels. This immediately transformed the issue from a local, and Jacobite, one to a national cause, and anyway failed to stop the legal trench warfare. The Jacobite families and their allies simply filed new lawsuits challenging the Commission's jurisdiction over the properties they were seeking to confiscate.[15] Ultimately a special Court of Delegates had to be appointed to hear these cases. It ruled in favour of the Commission in most of them, only for a number of the defeated plaintiffs to appeal over its head to the House of Lords (the Jacobites' legal teams and their political supporters seem to have quietly dropped the national issue at that point). Only the expense of such an appeal deterred them all from trying this ploy. Those who did appeal nonetheless further tied the Commission up in court, at great expense to the government, until 1725, when it was finally able to try and sell some of the forfeited estates.[16] Even when the Commission did manage to bring confiscations to the point of sale, as began to happen after 1718 as particular families' legal defences failed, it also often failed to realise anything like their true value. Potential Scottish purchasers were reluctant to buy properties that were virtually certain to be subject to continuing litigation, to say nothing of earning them the antipathy of the friends and neighbours of the families concerned.[17]

The Commission seemed to have found a way out of this quagmire when it effectively entered into a partnership with the York Buildings Company, which looked to buy the estates, modernise their exploitation and disburse the profits among its shareholders. The properties, though, came with all the debts (real and fictitious) that the Commission had been unable to overturn in the courts so the company was unable ever to turn a profit on its Scottish holdings. It was soon reduced to conniving in the effective legal repossession of their estates by many of the forfeited families, ostensibly as leaseholders. Once they were legally back in residence, of course, the Jacobite families were virtually restored to their full status and authority, though henceforth burdened with a mountain of debt from the unending litigation and bribery implicit in their struggle to hang on to their property.[18] Viewed in the abstract, though the Commission undoubtedly failed in Scotland, it did harm the Jacobite community by imposing costs that were tantamount to a huge fine. The British taxpayer, however, barely benefited. Monro, Haldane ('the curse of Scotland', as he was soon known), Birch, Bond and their fellow

Commissioners all nicely feathered their nests, but after deducting the expenses it incurred paying for the Commission's legal defences and the generous salaries of the Commissioners and their staff all the Treasury got for ten years' work was a net profit of £1,107.[19]

The Reconstruction of Civil Society in England

Rebellions are incipient civil wars, and civil wars implicitly destroy civil society. The only question is how badly fractured a given society becomes as a result of internecine conflict. This in turn dictates how long it will take that society to reknit itself together in the aftermath, assuming that this is possible at all. Here we can again see a clear divergence between the northern English and Scottish experiences.

In northern England the rebellion was most visibly supported by the Catholic minority and in its aftermath became firmly associated with them. They were correspondingly by far the most harshly punished section of the Jacobite community. This does not mean they were entirely disconnected from their Protestant kinfolk and neighbours. Henry Prescott was appalled by the conduct of government troops in the region and particularly 'disturbed with accounts of the barbarous behavior of the soldiers in their plunder of the popish gentlemen's houses'.[20] Lady Mary Cowper, a hardcore Whig originally from northern England, would not go to see either the grand parade of Jacobite prisoners into London or attend the trial of the seven peers because 'I think it very wrong to make a parade upon so dismal an occasion as that of putting to death one's fellow creatures. Nor could I go to the trial to see them receive their sentences, having a relation among them, my Lord Widdrington.'[21] Nathaniel Ryder encountered some Whig friends who argued for mercy to the condemned peers, 'and hoped the government would pardon them all'.[22] The local community in which the rebels dwelt also did sometimes act to protect them. In Lancaster the locals passively obstructed investigators and process servers working for the Forfeited Estates Commission. Edward Shafto, who had turned king's evidence on his former comrades, was forced to leave his home because local people were ostracising his family. As Derwentwater's funeral cortège made its way home the roads were lined with local people and they took the appearance of the aurora borealis as a sign of divine disapproval of his execution.[23]

Nonetheless, the overall pattern in northern England was not one of local communities uniting to protect their members against the intrusive efforts of outsiders to harass and persecute them. Many of the plunderers of Catholic gentry homes and estates in Lancashire were locally recruited militia who well knew the people they were harming.[24] A mob of local people spontaneously arose in Liverpool and besieged the home of William Molyneux, Viscount Molyneux, in response to rumours that he and some friends were planning to join the rebellion.[25] Local Catholics executed in the aftermath of the rebellion do not appear to have been shown much sympathy by the crowds of onlookers who attended the spectacle.[26] The mainspring of this detachment and even active hostility is not hard to find: it lay in the recrudescence of anti-popish rhetoric and reportage that accompanied the onset of the rebellion.

Indeed, the Church of England's particular contribution to the government war effort was a blast of anti-popish rhetoric from churchmen all over the country.[27] With only one or two exceptions the bishops firmly and publicly aligned themselves with the government, declaring,

> We are not surprised that Papists should . . . endeavour to set a person upon the throne, who will establish their religion and ruin ours . . . but that professed members of the Church of England should joyn with them in this . . . is so vile and detestable a thing, as may justly make them odious both to God and man . . .[28]

Large numbers of their inferior clergy and sundry Whig hacks took the hint and sermon upon sermon was preached, and pamphlet after pamphlet published, warning of the dangers of popery. Therein the old standards of English and Welsh anti-popish rhetoric were deployed in full force. The public once again heard all about the fires of Smithfield, the sufferings of foreign Protestants, the deceitfulness and mendacity of all Catholics and the threat to English liberties posed by popish despotism.[29] And it appears to have worked. Reports of a secret Catholic plot to use the rebellion as a stalking horse for the extirpation of Protestantism were soon circulating (gravely endorsed by Joseph Addison in the *Freeholder*), and accounts of the discovery of two hundredweight of metal 'gags' developed by Catholics to torture Protestants in Preston were circulating in London in early 1716.[30] One of these 'frightful' devices was actually brought down from the north for the Princess of Wales, by a 'Mr Carter', and the alleged stockpiler, one 'Mr Shuttleworth', was reported as being 'famous for saying he hoped in a little time to see Preston streets running as fast with heretic blood as they do with water when it has rained twelve hours'.[31]

The net effect of all this was to attenuate the ties of kith and kin that had for a century buffered the impact of the state's hostility towards the Catholic minority in northern England. In any event such ties generally had less purchase in England and Wales than elsewhere in the British Isles, and as a consequence the northern English Catholics were hard hit by government attempts at retribution. Moreover, these did not end in 1716. The Registration Act, which sought to confiscate two-thirds of all Catholic property, soon followed, and when there was a renewed Jacobite scare, associated with the Atterbury plot in the early 1720s, the Whig regime levied a fine of £100,000 specifically aimed at the English and Welsh Catholics. Scarcely surprisingly, the northern English Catholic community was cowed by these repeated blows and had still not fully recovered its nerve thirty years later when another Jacobite army marched through the region.[32]

The Reconstruction of Civil Society in Scotland

The Scottish experience of the reconstruction of civil society had elements that were akin to what happened in northern England. The Kirk had been blasting away at the Episcopalians as *faux* Protestants and the whole rebellion as a popish plot from the very beginning.[33] Some members of the élite were also not averse to taking advantage of their neighbours' and kinsfolk's predicament, and some scores were certainly settled using it. Montrose doubtless enjoyed being able to buy up his old enemy Rob Roy Macgregor's estate, even though he was never able to make good on the purchase. More grimly, clan chieftains like Grant of Grant and Argyll made sure that clansmen who had defied their authority suffered for it, and Islay's inaction may have been indirectly responsible for the horrible fate of Archibald Burnet of Carlops.[34] Burnet had broken his word, personally given to Islay, that he would not join the rebellion, and it may not be coincidental that he was one of the few prisoners executed after the '15 who had to endure the full programme of hanging, drawing and quartering (as opposed to simply being hanged, like almost all the others). His screams could be heard miles away.[35]

Yet overall, the general pattern in Scotland was very different. The heritor class in Scotland was much more closely knit than its southern counterpart, as is easily seen from the way Whigs and Tories continued to interact socially despite their deeply felt political differences. In both town and country the heritors and their families were constantly visiting each other, dining together and exchanging gifts.[36] Indeed, judging by his diary, even a minor laird like George Home of Kimmerghame rarely went two days without calling on, or being visited by, his kinsfolk and neighbours, and senior officials like Robert Dundas of Arniston, later President of the Court of Session, were famously convivial.[37] Nor was this a peculiarly male activity. Women from élite families travelled and visited widely and consequently developed semi-independent networks of sociability of their own.[38]

What is striking about this, given the fractionated, partisan nature of the Scottish élite, is its eclecticism. Episcopalian/Tory and Presbyterian/Whig neighbours and kinsfolk commonly ignored their political and religious differences and regularly visited each other. They also honoured the traditions of both family and good neighbourship by scrupulous attendance at formal occasions such as weddings and funerals.[39] Those sources that record the participants' impressions of such visits suggest there was a certain tension in the proceedings when the visitors and the hosts were seriously at odds over religion and politics, but social custom demanded restraint on such occasions and all parties generally seem to have tried to avoid falling into open dispute.[40]

The natural consequence of such normative behaviour was that kinsfolk and neighbours of very different political and religious opinions could become socially close through the regular round of local élite fraternisation. Kinship networks were generally very broad – Edmund Burt observed in the 1720s that 'the better sort here are almost all of them related to one another in some degree, either by consanguinity, marriage, or clanship'[41] – and family ties traditionally carried greater weight than those of neighbourliness, but in terms of everyday social activity neighbours were probably more important than kin. Given their political and religious divisions it was also virtually certain that every heritor family would have members of the opposing party in its neighbourly and kinship networks.[42] Indeed, some large élite families, such as the ducal family of Hamilton, spanned the entire range of religion and contemporary politics within one generation.[43] Learning to live with the enemy was thus a normal part of élite life in early eighteenth-century Scotland.

It was also in the nature of Scottish élite society that such personal ties would become currency in the political arena. Because county electorates were so small, and largely composed of relatively well-to-do heritors, elections were really only susceptible to manipulation through personal connections rather than grand patronage and corruption.[44] Being returned to Westminster as a knight of the shire for a Scottish county therefore required a successful candidate to exploit his local and family networks to produce a coalition of friends, neighbours and kinsmen sufficient to vote him in. In most cases this was bound to include some who were ideologically adherents of the opposing party.[45] Beyond Parliamentary elections the corollary was that in emergencies such ties would be used by those in trouble to elicit the help of friends and relations in the opposing camp.

This is most clearly seen in the treatment of neighbours and friends of the opposite party in areas under the control of the Jacobite or British governments. In both cases the official position of the regime was discrimina-tory, in that the other side's partisans were subjected to special taxation, and particularly obnoxious individuals were either incarcerated or harassed. The Jacobites levied a double cess payment on all pro-Hanoverian families in Aberdeenshire and Banff in 1715, while their opponents arrested and impris-oned suspected Jacobites all over southern Scotland and hit Jacobite Nonjurors with swingeing financial penalties in the aftermath of the rising.[46]

This official harshness was, however, mitigated to a significant extent by the personal intervention of friends and neighbours who were partisans of the prevailing regime, who would appeal for special treatment of their particular friends on the other side. In December 1715 James Campbell of Ardkinglass, for example, appealed to Colonel Henry Hawley not to beggar the tenants of his neighbour, the Jacobite Viscount Kilsyth, by confiscating all their draught horses. At much the same time on the Jacobite side Malcolm of Grange was busy interceding for a neighbour who was a well-known partisan of the government and in imminent danger of having all her horses seized by a Jacobite foraging party and David Smythe of Methven was doing his best to protect his Whig neighbours and the Presbyterian ministers of Perthshire from harassment and impositions.[47] Captain Grant of Wester Elchies squared the conflicting demands of clan loyalty and good neighbourship by assuring Gordon of Glenbuchat that he and his men would not attack the estates of his neighbour Huntly unless their clan chief personally led them against him, and Lovat went one step further by vehemently denying he would ever contem-plate ravaging Huntly's lands.[48] For his part, Huntly persistently refused 'to attack my relations and friends'.[49] Sir Thomas Hope actually saved his diehard Whig neighbour Rothes's property 'from distruction', during Jacobite forays into Fife.[50] But although this process of mitigation was a two-way street, in that Jacobite friends would intercede on behalf of their Whig neighbours in areas under Jacobite control as much as vice versa, because the Whig regime had the last word in 1715–16 it is the softening of the Whig line by personal appeals that is most significant.

On one level such interventions by kinsmen, friends and neighbours helped restore local harmony and reconstitute fractured élite communities. Beyond this, they also facilitated the regeneration of civil society. It was always diffi-cult for the central authorities to control the localities without at least the tacit consent of the majority of the local élite in the early modern British Isles, and allowing loyalist intercessors to save their kith and kin made the job of re-establishing a regular administration in a given area much easier in the aftermath of the fighting. As Atholl somewhat peevishly observed while interceding on behalf of two Perthshire heritors who had been in rebellion:

I am perswaded both these gentlemen would be very serviceable to his Majesty and government in this shire, if their lives be spared, and that they may be depended upon hereafter. Wee will have much need of them, for there is above 130 heretors out of this shyre who have been concerned in the rebellion, of whom there is none yett surendered themselves except the Lord Rollo and [the] laird of Methvine.[51]

Likewise, allowing Gordon of Glenbuchat to work his passage by facilitating the surrender of arms and the return home of the ordinary clansmen considerably speeded up the pacification of the Highlands in 1716,[52] and the return of the Marquess of Seaforth ended a prolonged period of confrontation between the central authorities and his Mackenzie clansmen. 'We are daily threatened,' lamented two agents for the Commission for Forfeited Estates in 1721, by way of explaining their abject failure to collect any rents from Seaforth's tenants.[53] As the clan chieftain he was simply irreplaceable, and finally allowing him to return home de facto restored order in his clan's territory and meant that the government's writ henceforth had some possibility of running there.[54]

Elsewhere, negotiating the return of exiled and other élite Jacobites to their homes, families and social networks directly bolstered the Whig regime's authority. When Lockhart of Carnwath used his political clout in Midlothian to bargain for lenient treatment of a number of convicted Jacobites in the aftermath of the '15, the quid pro quo was that he would use his interest to support the Lord Advocate, Robert Dundas of Arniston, in his bid to represent the county at Westminster. The bargain was struck, the Jacobites secured a Lord Advocate who, 'thenceforwards acted a friendly part to them', thus saving several 'honest men' from being expropriated by the Commission for Forfeited Estates, and the government secured a lock on the most prestigious seat in Scotland.[55]

Personal deals between imprisoned and exiled Jacobites and their families and powerful individuals in the government also created obligations that such Jacobites were subsequently reluctant to dishonour by further activism. After Montrose personally interceded with George I to secure a free pardon for him, Smythe of Methven frankly, and as it turned out, sincerely, expressed himself as bound not to embarrass his benefactor even though his own principles had not changed:

Your grace's undertakeing for my peaceable behaviour to the king shall add a further ty upon me, for had I not found my self at freedom to practice according to my profession nothing could have tempted me to submitt; for as my fault proceeded from a principall, so does my submission, and I'll venture just as far in performing the on as I have done in my deffence of the other.[56]

After Alexander Murray of Stanhope was allowed to return to Scotland on the condition that he live quietly at home he apparently felt himself under no obligation to forsake either his friends or his principles, and cheerfully moved back into the Jacobite socio-cultural milieu. When, however, he was approached by a Jacobite agent to act as a liaison between the clans and the Lowland Jacobites he refused:

I like the king [James Stuart] and my countrey as well as ever I did, and I will draw my sword whenever there is to be a general effort for restoring the king and kingdom of Scotland, but in the interim my head and heart are set upon improving the Highlands estate I have purchased, and bringing the mines to perfection (which will be a service done my countrey) and I will think upon and undertake no other business of any kind. Besids, when I got my life, after the last affair, I enterd into engagements that will not allow me to be active in contriving or carrying on measures against the government, though when there's to be a push made, I will venture all with the first.[57]

From personal deals to save individual Jacobites flowed personal obligations to Whig benefactors which effectively acted to neutralise many of the Jacobites concerned as political actors. It was a classic, E. P. Thompsonesque, instance of how the amelioration of the 'awful majesty' of the law could act as social cement.[58]

Legal engagement with the Whig regime also had a marked impact on the ingrained Jacobitism of particular heritor families. This arose in the course of the Jacobites' generally successful defence of their estates, which was strongly buttressed by help from two sources. The most visible was provided by their Whiggish kinsfolk, friends and neighbours. This is not to deny the very real hostility the rebellion sometimes generated between kith and kin. In 1745 Lady Jane Nimmo feelingly recalled her previous encounter with the Jacobites when she observed: 'I believe neighbours about will be our greatest enemys, as it happened at the last rebellion'.[59] And in May 1716 Ogilvie of Coull, a solitary Whig in a strongly Jacobite area, was physically attacked by a gang of local Jacobites hiding thereabouts, who cursed him as a 'rascall, villain, rebell, betrayer of your neighbours'.[60] But in general old ties overcame new tensions once the rising was over. Thus it was Whig friends, neighbours and kin who undertook the legal defence of the alleged debts and leases that were obstructing the confiscation of Jacobite estates, and, furthermore, used their connections and acquaintances within the Whig regime to facilitate the fraud. By using such middlemen Margaret Panmure, for example, was able to weave such a fine net of interlocking debts and spoiling lawsuits by alleged creditors around the Panmure estates that the Forfeited Estates Commission was soon hopelessly entangled.[61] And in 1718 when they tried to sell off the one part of the estate that could be easily expropriated, Panmure's bank stocks, she simply let it be publicly known that she intended to repurchase them – leading to the larger moneyed interests withdrawing from the auction – and calmly instructed her agent, the supposed representative of Panmure's creditors, 'not to be out bid . . . for I shall still indeavour to keep in our own possession any thing that can be reckond heretage'.[62] Such aid and comfort created a reciprocal obligation on the rebels' families. They could not honourably continue to be active Jacobites because to do so risked embarrassing their friends and relations who had fronted for them in the courts and used their influence and connections to help them escape forfeiture. In effect, the families of the forfeited Jacobites incurred a dynastic debt of honour with each fictitious mortgage and lease they passed on to Whig friends and relations, and many paid it by withdrawing from active Jacobitism and cooperating with their Whig peers in the restoration and maintenance of government and social order throughout Scotland – quintessentially regenerating civil society.

The second, less obvious, source of help for Jacobite heritor families in their attempts to fend off government attempts to confiscate their property came from within the Whig regime itself. Despite the presence of some in the government who, like Lord Justice Clerk Cockburn, wanted a Carthaginian peace, there were many others who were quietly, but resolutely, opposed to dealing with their errant kith and kin in such a fashion.[63] Lord Advocate Dalrymple spoke for an influential and significant element within the civil administration that included Argyll (after he was replaced as commander-in-chief in Scotland),[64] Montrose and Stair[65] and, going by their conduct, many others who were less willing to act publicly or put their misgivings down on paper, when he expressed his unhappiness about mass reprisals. He prefaced his argument with good pragmatic reasons for showing mercy. In the first place, the Jacobites' families were certain to use the legal system to block any forfeitures, and overcoming their resistance would be difficult and expensive. In addition, there were political considerations that militated against swingeing punishment of the rebels, amongst which one of the most important was the possibility that:

three or four hundred noblemen and gentlemen of birth and interest in the countrie being chassed to the hills and islands and readie to escape to France or some other Catholike Countrie ... may afford such as are enemies to his Majestie and the reformed relegion ane oppertunitie to form bodies of British subjects as they have sometyme since done of Irish, which by reason of the great interest and influence which these people will have for many generations in the country where they were borne, will be recruited and keepd full.[66]

The upshot was that he urged that all the Jacobites, bar a handful of top leaders, should be granted amnesty and allowed to compound for their estates. Nor, when the administration at Westminster chose to ignore his advice, did Dalrymple shrink from outright sabotage of its attempts to prosecute former rebels and seize their property.[67]

Dalrymple's memo and his subsequent obstruction of government measures may, too, have stemmed in part from a degree of sympathy with *some* of the (non-dynastic) objectives of the rising on the part of Scotland's Whigs. Many of the grievances the Scots Jacobites had promised to redress were felt, too, by their Whig kinsmen and friends. The stalwartly Whiggish Stair, for example, argued in the aftermath of the '15 that the best way to prevent another Jacobite rising was not swingeing retribution but measures 'to make the Union not greivous to Scotland'.[68] This body of Whiggish opinion was further alienated by the harsh treatment the English courts were meting out to the Scots prisoners taken at Preston and the decision to move the trials of Jacobite prisoners captured in Scotland over the border to Carlisle.[69] The nationwide campaign to raise money to support the prisoners in Carlisle, which brought in contributions from Scots of all political persuasions, and the stubborn refusal to participate in the trials of some of the administration's senior legal officers, such as Forbes of Culloden, amply attests to the revulsion the Scottish élite felt at the government's conduct.[70] In addition, the treatment of the plebeian prisoners taken at Preston was distasteful to many Scots, who seem generally to have felt it was not appropriate to punish those who had simply followed their betters in turning out to fight for the Stuarts.[71] All of which must certainly have contributed to the willingness of many Scots Whigs to help their Jacobite kith and kin as they struggled to preserve their estates.

Another interaction with the authorities that also helped resuscitate a broad civil consensus was negotiations for permission to return to the British Isles for those who had fled into exile and pardons for those who had been condemned to death or transportation. The Indemnity Act of 1717 specifically excluded those who had fled the country to avoid prosecution for their participation in the uprising. Those Jacobites languishing on the continent who wished to return home were thus obliged to seek special exemptions from the strict terms of the Act.[72] The alternative was to risk sneaking home incognito and hope that the authorities would not bother to hunt them down. And while this was certainly a reasonable risk for the small fry of the exiled community, it was distinctly less so for more prominent Jacobites. James Stirling of Keir, who returned home with the 'conivance of the government', about 1718, and was 'so much favoured as to have the purchasing of his estate . . . for a very triffle', then 'lived retiredly at his countrie house' thereafter, was nonetheless arrested in 1727 as part of a government sweep following the interception of letters directed to Lockhart of Carnwath, by then James's premier agent in Scotland.[73] Stirling was completely inactive by that stage, and had absolutely nothing to do with Lockhart or the rest of the Jacobite under-ground, but he was one of the usual suspects, and so he and his family had to go through the whole expensive process of negotiating a pardon while he was incarcerated as a fugitive felon. Most of the leaders of the Jacobite community understandably wanted to avoid such problems if they returned home, and preferred to have their families bargain for a pardon while they were still safe (if bored and depressed) overseas.

Bargaining for a pardon or a remission of sentence was, of necessity, an intricate and sometimes corrupt business. The only sources for such exemp-tions from normal legal process were the ministers and senior administrators of the government at Westminster, well-connected Whig politicians and senior courtiers with access to the monarch. In those cases where the father had been resolutely loyal, but one or more of his sons was so ill-advised as to turn out for the Jacobites, reprieves and pardons in general seem to have come fairly easily, at least in high-profile cases. James Forbes, the son of William, Lord Forbes, obtained a free pardon specifically for this reason, as did James Fraser, a younger brother of Alexander Fraser, Lord Salton.[74] Atholl had more mixed success in persuading the authorities to forgive his errant offspring, possibly because three of his four sons and at least one of his brothers were on the rebel side in 1715, but he did obtain reprieves for Lord Charles Murray (despite the fact that he was a serving officer in the British army at the time he joined the rebels) and, eventually, one for Charles's more famous brother, Lord George Murray.[75]

When the family in question had no clear record of loyalism to boost its case for special treatment, however, some senior Whigs seem to have regarded their plight as nothing more than an excellent opportunity to make a little money. In Edinburgh, 'tho it be not posted in the Gazet, yet it's weel knouen where, hou, and with whom such bargains are to be meide', and middlemen representing well-connected courtiers negotiated prices with syndicates formed to raise money among the prisoners in the castle.[76] For his part, Huntly matter-of-factly paid £2,000 to secure leniency for his tenants and vassals.[77] Likewise Margaret Panmure had considerable trouble securing a grant of her jointure and in the end, as Panmure delicately put it, the grant 'cost her a great deal of money'.[78] In the same vein, Sir John Erskine of Alva had to surrender the secret of what was believed to be a fabulously lucrative silver mine on his lands to a consortium of Whig grandees that included Townshend before he was allowed to come home.[79] And though (for obvious reasons) little direct evidence of such corruption survives, there are sufficient references to it to indicate that graft may have been responsible for the return home of a fair number of lesser Jacobite prisoners.[80]

In many more cases, it would appear that the families of the prisoners and exiles were able to obtain permission for them to return home without any special connections or bribery beyond the usual round of élite present-giving. Solid Whigs such as Baron John Clerk, Stanhope, Cowper, Islay, Argyll, Montrose and Stair seem to have helped Jacobite prisoners and former rebels without asking for any kind of financial return.[81] Indeed Lord Advocate Dalrymple specifically refused to take any money when it was offered him by Alexander Hamilton, Margaret Panmure's agent in Edinburgh.[82] The usual pattern was for Jacobite families to use their friends, kith and kin to gain the attention of these senior Whigs, and for them then to use their influence at court and in government to intercede for the prisoners and the exiles. Thus when John Campbell's – Lord Glenorchy's – case for leniency appeared to be hanging fire William III and II's former mistress, Elizabeth Villiers, the Countess of Orkney, 'pressd Viscount Townshend so hard that for self defence he was oblidged to cause read your petition and certificates in the Comittee of Councel'.[83] Typically, the petitioners would claim extenuating circumstances of various kinds that their intercessors could use to argue for clemency. George Drummond, for example, pleaded that his stepson was 'not yett twentie years off age and was easilie seduced with the promise off a pair of collours to bear', and that the boy's mother had died of grief at hearing of his likely fate. Graham of Slipperfield asked that his stepson, Robert Smith, be pardoned because 'the lad was led away with bad company'. Alexander Murray, Lord Elibank, interceded for John Paterson of Prestonhall on the grounds that he was 'without a stain, if he had not ingaged in this unnatural rebellion, which indeed is to be imputed to prejudice of education, and his being too easily seduced by bad company'. Alexander Home, Earl of Home, begged for Montrose's intercession on behalf of his brother, James Home of

Eaton, on the grounds that 'he is young and unacquainted with the world. . . . and . . . has the honour to be your Grace's near relation'.[84]

Élite female networks overlapped with, but were often distinct from, their male counterparts. They were correspondingly activated in parallel with more generic family connections in order to save the former rebels. Although the chief recipient of petitions in Scotland, Argyll, lacked a wife connected to the great kin network of titled families, the wives of other Whig notables found themselves besieged by petitions from relatives or acted themselves to help Jacobite women and their families. The most common form of help was to influence a Whig husband to intercede for, or inquire into, the charges against an accused Jacobite, as when Margaret Hume of Wedderburn managed to get her aunt, Grizel Baillie, to persuade her husband, the powerful George Baillie of Jerviswood, to intercede for Hume's errant husband. In similar fashion, Grizel Cochrane added petitions to Christian, Duchess of Montrose, to her appeals to Montrose himself.[85]

Élite women from Whig families who helped their Jacobite peers seem to have been acting from a variety of motives. Some acted out of sympathy with other women left destitute by their husbands' roles in the rebellion, others out of a sense of family duty, and some, apparently, for the sheer thrill of aiding desperate rebels. Henrietta, Marchioness of Huntley and daughter of the Whig Earl of Peterborough, solicited friends of her father's in order to expedite the jointure case of Lady Jean Drummond, her sister-in-law, explaining that she both owed her deceased father-in-law for the kindness he had shown her as a young bride, and felt revulsion at the prospect of seeing a member of her family reduced to scraping and begging, regardless of politics. Mary, Lady Cowper, interceded on behalf of Carnwath, moved, apparently, by his youth and candour. Henrietta Paulet, Duchess of Bolton, attempted to intercede with George I on behalf of Anna Derwentwater after she 'came crying to her'. The Nithsdales benefited from the generosity of Christian Montrose, in whose London house Winifred Maxwell, Countess of Nithsdale, hid in the hours immediately after helping her husband escape from the Tower, and who went to court to discover what was being said about the escape. Christian Montrose, indeed, seemed to Winifred Nithsdale to be treating the whole business as a thrilling masquerade rather than a desperate bid to avert Nithsdale's imminent execution.[86]

Élite women, like their male relatives, also offered help in order to build up their own networks of social and political credit. One of the most striking examples of this is the way in which Sophia, Countess of Lippe-Buckenburg, one of George I's female Hanoverian courtiers, moved quickly to offer her help to Jacobite women in need of court connections. Margaret Nairn plied her with gifts to present a petition for leniency on behalf of Lord Nairn to the Princess of Wales, thus establishing Buckenburg as a woman of influence at court as well as someone owed considerable respect and favours by members of the British élite. Margaret Panmure, petitioning Atholl, was unctuously deferential to his second wife, Mary Ross, despite the fact that her pedigree was considerably less exalted than that of his first wife, Katherine Hamilton, Lady Panmure's sister, and Lady Panmure herself. Mary Atholl was thereby confirmed in her new status and her social ascendancy acknowledged. In a society in which one's power and rank were visibly denoted by the status of those who deferred to one, these represented significant gains on both Sophia Lippe-Buckenburg's and Mary Atholl's parts. Such manoeuvrings make it clear that in some cases the women were acting in a no less calculating a way than their menfolk.[87] Moreover, it appears that at least some of the Jacobite women, having engineered favours for their male kin, were even more acutely aware of the reciprocal obligations these entailed than their male counterparts, as may be seen from Margaret Panmure's stern injunction to her husband, 'I think it right both in the sight of God and man that whoever receives such a favor from any government, be their title what it will, are tied by both the rules of honour and gratitude never to disturb it again'.[88]

For when male Whig grandees responded to the Jacobites' appeals there was almost certainly an element of calculation in their behaviour, in that the returned exiles and released prisoners were virtually obliged to become the grateful clients of their benefactor once they were home. And when an early eighteenth-century magnate such as Huntly promised Montrose on behalf of himself and his following that: 'wee shall indevor to show your Grace wee ar men of honour and will ever show our great sence of your Grace's being pleased to patronis us in owr present unhappy sircomstances', none of their contemporaries would have been in any doubt that Montrose had substantively advanced his power and authority.[89] But there was also manifestly a good deal of humanity and compassion in the behaviour of some of the intercessors, notably Argyll, Islay and Montrose. Montrose, for example, overlooked both Smythe of Methven and Urquhart of Newhall's contumacy (both men were already clients of his before they joined the rebellion) and personally spoke to George I to save two men who freely admitted they could offer no excuse for their behaviour other than that by rebelling they were being true to principles they had held all their lives, and who had no substantial assets, either financial or political, with which to repay Montrose for his help.[90] In the same vein, Islay as Lord Justice General ordered the release of his old friend Lockhart of Carnwath from Edinburgh castle when he became seriously ill, thereby adding to the criticism he and his brother were already incurring for advocating leniency towards the defeated rebels, and drawing on himself the animus of James Carmichael, Earl of Hyndford, who specially wanted to see his estranged kinsman rot in prison.[91] Such behaviour on the part of Whig grandees undoubtedly softened the impact of the punitive legislation enacted to try and ensure there would be no further Jacobite rebellions – and was subject to considerable criticism by the more zealous or embittered Whigs as a consequence – but in the long term it may have been just as effective in undermining the Stuart cause in Scotland, the heartland of the rebellion.[92] For the matrix of obligation it established between the former rebels and their families and the Whig regime tended to be a lasting one, not just for the individuals concerned but for subsequent generations.

In this respect the enforced engagement between the Jacobite community in Scotland and its Whig counterpart in the aftermath of the rebellion of 1715 was of the first importance. It did not directly diminish the Jacobite community *per se*, because most of the returnees soon took up their old socio-cultural milieu again, and by the 1720s the clergy of the Episcopal Church had emerged from hiding and were once more teaching and preaching Jacobitism.[93] Its impact was more subtle. At the level of the family most of the Scottish Jacobite élite had always been willing to take advantage of suitably lucrative employment opportunities associated with the new British state, doubtless reasoning that investing a son or two in the army or the bureaucracy merely made good dynastic sense. Thus a number of the senior Jacobite military leaders in the rebellion, from Sinclair to Hamilton, had seen active service in the British army in the War of the Spanish Succession, and many of the lesser lights, from Thomas Bruce, the future Earl of Kincardine, to Harry Maule of Kellie, had served as minor functionaries in the state bureaucracy.[94] Their own employments were of course terminated by their conduct in 1715–16, but their family connections in both areas were greatly enhanced in importance. To take two cases in point, Sinclair's brother's – General James Sinclair's – loyal service to the Hanoverian state was in large part responsible for the fact that Sinclair was eventually allowed to return home, and John Maule of Inverkeillor's diligent performance of his duties as Islay's confidential secretary paved the way for the restoration of his family's estates and fortunes. In return, their families never embarrassed either man by further displays of active Jacobitism.[95] Rather the contrary: in the late 1730s on encountering the then zealously Jacobite David Wemyss, Lord Elcho, Sinclair earnestly advised him to take service with the Hanoverian state rather than continue in his adherence to the Stuarts.[96] In the same vein, though Harry Maule served throughout the 1720s as one of the 'trustees' overseeing Jacobite affairs in Scotland, in 1725 when he heard two of his fellow trustees begin serious discussion of a proposal for a new Jacobite rising,

> He turnd all into a jest, falling afterwards into a passion and swearing that it was madness to propose anything to be done for you [James], and that none but madmen would engage in such an affair. In short, he went on at such a rate, that after leaving him we concluded that tho he is content to be reckond a Jacobite in the present situation of affairs, he will not venture further or meddle if anything in earnest come in play, and would therefor have matters stand as they are.[97]

Huntly took this tendency a stage further when he deliberately turned the relationships he had established with members of the Hanoverian establishment such as Montrose and General George Carpenter in the process of saving himself and his followers in the aftermath of the '15 into a platform for his family's transformation from a bastion of Catholicism and Jacobitism in the Highlands to a Protestant pillar of the Hanoverian regime; a position cemented by his son Cosmo's marriage to Catherine Gordon, daughter of the Protestant Gordon Earl of Aberdeen.[98]

Indeed, so common was it for Argathelian nominees to state offices to have families that had a record of involvement with the Stuart cause, the Squadrone seem to have been genuinely offended. They certainly tried to use the pattern of appointments sponsored by the Campbell brothers to smear them with Jacobitism at Westminster.[99] Such allegations were manifestly ridiculous, though Argyll occasionally played along with Jacobite overtures when he wanted Tory political support.[100] Nevertheless, the number of Argathelian clients with close personal or familial Jacobite connections is striking, and there may be a case for arguing that Islay pursued a deliberate policy of allowing his patronage network to become a bridge into the new order for erstwhile Jacobites.[101]

* * *

Theoretically, there were two ways for the Whig regime to re-establish peace and civil society in northern England and Scotland in the aftermath of the rebellion. They could have pursued a policy of wholesale extirpation of the crucial noblemen, heritors and gentry, either by a massacre of the élite prisoners or by banishing them and their families from the British Isles, or they could have allowed them all to return home without further penalty. In truth, however, neither of these clear-cut options was politically or emotionally acceptable. Even those who argued for a harsh peace, like Lord Justice Clerk Cockburn, had 'good' Jacobites, and even those who wanted no more than mild retribution, like Lord Advocate Dalrymple, felt that 'the springs of this rebellion deserve no mercy'.[102] If we take these two solutions as the extreme ends of a possible range of government responses to the Jacobite threat reified in the rebellion, we get more of a sense of how the retributive phase of the phenomenon unfolded. In northern England, despite the manifestly less threatening quality of the rebellion (if the Scots had not reinforced the northern English rebels the rebellion there would have been a pathetically damp squib) the regime's vengeance was distinctly brutal. Thirty-three of forty of the executions related to the fighting there and all the prisoners transported to what the king and probably many of his ministers envisaged as an early death in the colonies had surrendered at Preston. The Commission for Forfeited Estates then went after the estates of the northern English rebels with great zeal and was considerably aided in its efforts to damage the Jacobite interest by local gentry and other, more humble, members of society, many of whom turned on their neighbours with no apparent qualms. In Scotland the case was very different, despite a great many more casualties and extensive economic damage to the estates and fortunes of the winners. Though there were individual exceptions, such as Monro of Foulis and Haldane of Bearcrofts, the nobility and the heritors as a class quickly rallied behind the threatened families, both to save the men facing death or transportation and to obstruct the seizure of their property. As Bruce Lenman perceptively observed some time ago, this was tantamount to a class decision, 'that there would be no social change in Scotland comparable to the process which created a new Whig ascendancy in the north of England'.[103]

Why did the majority of the Scottish Whig élite behave as they did in the face of this external threat to their kith and kin? There were many sound political reasons. When Robert Wemyss's estate was damaged by marauding Jacobites, and his wife so frightened by their threats that she fled their home, he complained directly to Harry Crawford of Crail, the chief Jacobite administrator in the area, demanding restitution and succinctly enjoining him: 'Doe as you wud be done to.'[104] It may be that many Scots Whigs were all too well aware of the abrupt reversals of fortune that had characterised Scottish politics over the previous century. Being kind to one's neighbours in their tribulations was credit in the social bank if the Jacobites one day triumphed. There was also the plain fact that the Jacobites were often former political allies at the local level and might easily become useful again. Thus in May 1716 Atholl instructed his son Lord James Murray of Garth particularly to look out for one former Perthshire rebel, 'since he was so freindly to you in your elections'.[105] Yet the political advantage individual Whigs gained by their benevolence is insufficient to explain the widespread nature of the phenomenon. Many élite Scottish Jacobites had little or nothing to offer in terms of political goods. What saved them was the close-knit integration of noble and heritor society, and beyond it, the deepening interconnection of the Anglo-Welsh and Scottish social élites. The Scots were effectively one large, fecund cousinage and those among them who had good connections outwith Scotland did not hesitate to use their influence to save their erring relatives. Alongside the Scots magnates like Montrose and Argyll who saved so many former Jacobites were English aristocrats like James Stanley, Earl of Derby, and women like Barbara Orkney, connected by blood or marriage to the Scottish élite (in both their cases to the great tribe of Hamiltons). Thus both their class unity and the extension of their class's social network beyond Scotland acted to rescue the Jacobites there from their predicament.

Conclusion

For the Whigs the '15 was, above all, 'the unnatural rebellion', and in an abstract sense they were correct to label it so. Rebellions in Europe in the early modern era had a particular political, social and economic physiognomy and the '15 accorded with few of them. It was essentially the rebellion that should never have happened. Any rational assessment of the odds against success, given their circumstances, should have persuaded the Jacobites at least to postpone or, more prudently, to call off the whole enterprise after the government crackdown in July 1715. Even if they were pig-headed enough to continue plotting after that, the death of Louis XIV should have signalled that the game was up. Instead, inspired by their conviction that God was telling them to seize the moment, and, 'growing sanguine upon difficulties', the Scots Jacobites rose.[1]

Though James and Berwick had been trying to organise an uprising for nearly a year, when it came the onset of the rebellion was a supremely local phenomenon, wholly dependent on the degree of commitment in the local population (especially the élite) and the extent of the preparation and planning undertaken by local Jacobite leaders. In many respects there was not a single Jacobite rebellion, but rather a very loosely coordinated set of rebellions. Where these went unopposed by government troops they mostly took off, at least in the sense that the rebels were able to muster and march without their little columns being broken up or their leaders arrested. The coalescence of many of these local rebellions then produced armies which could undertake simple military operations, like occupying undefended towns and levying contributions from the countryside. Moving up to more complex operations, such as fighting battles, was something they needed to work up to over the weeks that followed in the course of a *petite guerre* that ebbed and flowed across Stirlingshire and Fife. It is impossible to be sure how many men turned out to fight, and how willingly, for King James or King George, but it seems clear that in the region of 20,000 Scots and 1,000 English at some point adhered to the Stuarts and something like 11,000 Scots and a great many more English cleaved to the Guelphs (not counting the regular army). Many of these men on both sides were undoubtedly reluctant conscripts; others were ideologically inspired and, despite a massive amount of desertion, particularly from the Jacobite armies, they fought courageously in the main, central theatre of the conflict in Scotland. Elsewhere their record was more mixed. In southern Scotland and northern England the Jacobites were never able properly to settle down and train their army for any period of time, and the rank and file signalled their unhappiness at the shilly-shallying of their leaders, and their uncertain situation, by deserting in droves. This was fortunate for the government troops they encountered at Preston, because, given the hard fight the regulars got there from the nub of the army that might have been, the battle could well have turned into a real setback for the Whig regime. In northern and western Scotland an oddly civilised form of warfare, mainly comprised of feint and counter-feint, prevailed. This resulted in remarkably low casualties on all sides. Indeed, except for the military professionals, the level of casualties was generally low everywhere during the rising (with the exception of Sherrifmuir) – and therein lay the potential for the revival of civil society in Scotland when the fighting was over.

This is particularly important because though English and Irish Jacobites played a part in what transpired over the seven months of the rebellion it was the Scots who set the tone of the conflict and from its beginning to its end the rebellion was fundamentally a Scottish-driven event. The northern English rising, the only part of the great Anglo-Welsh Jacobite rebellion originally envisaged that actually materialised, was a feeble thing. Without massive Scots Jacobite intervention it would never have seriously troubled the Whig regime. As it was, only some of the hardest of hardcore English Jacobites, the northern Catholic community, showed themselves ready, willing and able to fight and in the end there were simply not enough of them to make up for the implicit baggage they carried with them. Their Scottish comrades in arms were uneasy at the disproportionately Catholic character of the English rebels; it is legitimate to speculate that the northern English Tories may have been still more disturbed. Contrary to the accusations levelled by Whig propaganda, the great majority of Jacobites in England and Scotland were devout Protestants who had no intention of restoring the Church of Rome, as the northern Catholic presence implicitly threatened.

So Scotland became the unplanned, unintended cockpit of the rebellion. In later years Mar confessed that recalling the way matters there went awry made 'the thinking of those things ever since disagreeable to me', and he was certainly, and in many ways justly, blamed for the disaster that subsequently unfolded.[2] Nonetheless he presided over a remarkable feat. The Scottish people were not, by the early eighteenth century, a specially martial race, and despite their reputation even most of the Highlanders were unused to arms. Yet in the space of two months the Jacobite government and military commanders at Perth managed to knock together a roughly competent military force. Because the Jacobite army failed to overwhelm Argyll at Sherrifmuir and disintegrated on the retreat north, this accomplishment has not received the respect it deserves, and both those military failures are more directly ascribable to failures of command than of the ordinary Jacobite fighting man. Yet in the round, it would probably have made no difference if matters had gone the other way on the frozen moor outside Dunblane on 13 November, or if Perth had stood a siege in January 1716 and the government forces besetting it had been defeated by General Winter. In all likelihood Jacobite Scotland alone would eventually have been reconquered by the Whig regime.

This was all too apparent to the better-informed leaders on both sides. Montrose percipiently observed to Stair in September 1715 that he was confident the Whigs would win the war,

> however I can not bring myself up to be so sanguin as some are here in imagining this affair will be over in ane instant. It will in my opinion still cost some time and a little trouble. In the conclusion Jacobitism must be ruind, but in the mean time our . . . country must suffer extreamly.[3]

He was proved correct on every score. Leaving aside the body count, Scotland's economy and infrastructure were badly damaged by the rebellion. Military operations are inherently destructive and the long-term consequences for the local people of, for instance, General Echlin cutting the bridges and 'spoiling' the fords around Perth, or Colonel Zoutland burning the laird of 'Garway Moor's' house and driving his tenants' cattle, can only be imagined.[4] In the natural course of things the opposing armies also casually requisitioned goods and services to the detriment of local communities. Coupar had the misfortune to be situated on a main overland route north and was consequently 'very much harassed by the frequent passing of the King's troups, by their taking free quarters and by furnishing baggage horses, for which rarely was there any hire payed'. Jedburgh was 'opresed and harassed by the army of the rebells who lived severall dayes amongst them at free quarters, as also Generall Carpenter's army who stayed some short time there att the same rate'. Selkirk was forced to pay Jacobite exactions and the shoemakers there 'obliged to furnish the whole highlanders with shoes for which they never gott one farthing'.[5] The straightforward plundering of towns and villages by Jacobite and government troops added greatly to the burden of the war. Charles Stewart, Earl of Moray, found his home, Castle Stuart, ruined by a government garrison, his rents lost and a shipment of bere he was contracted to deliver (one necessary for maintaining his credit in Edinburgh) seized without compensation by Whig forces. Sir William Gordon of Invergordon claimed he had sustained losses of £14,000. More reasonably, Atholl estimated that the looting of Tullibardine by Dutch troops cost him over £1,000.[6] The common people, however, probably suffered the most long-term damage to their lives and livelihoods. Northesk's tenants suffered £660 3s. 11d. worth of damage as a result of Jacobite depredations and £1,918 2s. 9d. as a consequence of government troops passing through. Huntly's tenants suffered at least as much.[7] Straightforwardly monetary claims, though, do not convey the disaster this could represent for ordinary people with little or no slack in their domestic economies, such as a former weaver Edmund Burt encountered in the 1720s. His home, loom and stock had been burned by Argyll's forces even though he was not out in the rebellion. Ruined by a war in which he had no part, the man was thereafter forced to scrape a living as a guide for visitors to the Highlands.[8]

Nor was the ministry at all prompt about paying its debts to its supporters in Scotland. The magistrates of Edinburgh and Glasgow had to plead with the ministers in London to obtain any recompense of their outlay in raising, arming and supplying the militia the government had directed them to call out. Lord Justice Clerk Cockburn ended up paying for the subsistence of the prisoners held in Edinburgh out of his own pocket.[9] When Atholl asked for some reimbursement of the expenses he incurred holding out behind Jacobite lines for four months the ministry nonchalantly tried to bargain him down. The duke was furious, telling Lord James Murray of Garth, 'this is treating my account like a taylior or appothecary's bill, which I did not expect after the services I have done the government'.[10] Atholl was being naïve; a king and a ministry that unceremoniously dismissed Argyll, their successful commander-in-chief, less than four months after his triumphant return was not likely to show much consideration for a lesser Scottish loyalist.[11] When the army was finished disarming the Jacobites they moved on to disarming their opponents. The Campbells, Grants and other Whig clans were comprehensively stripped of the weaponry the government had been so eager to put in their hands just a few months before.[12] Gratitude to its supporters in Scotland was not a high priority for the ministry in London.

There is no way of accurately gauging the net economic impact of the '15 on northern England and Scotland. It seems highly likely, however, that the long-term effects of the limited damage caused by the brief period of fighting in England were minimal (although Preston did suffer from the battle fought in its streets).[13] Scotland, by contrast, suffered considerably. The 'incidental' costs of the war, closely followed by the expenses of the struggle to rescue the Scottish prisoners, sustain and then recall the exiles and the long-drawn-out battle with the Commission for Forfeited Estates all amounted to a huge drain on Scotland's capital resources. We know it took until the mid-eighteenth century for Scotland to begin feeling widespread economic benefit from the Union; how much this tardiness was attributable to the '15 is difficult to say, but it probably had more than a little to do with it.

What of the wider costs and benefits of the rebellion? The Whig regime undoubtedly emerged from its travail stronger and more confident. The Jacobites had done their best to bring it down and had signally failed. The combined British and Irish armies henceforth never numbered fewer than 30,000 men, which easily secured the regime in power, and Whigs were soon entrenched in virtually every office of power and profit.[14] Famously, it was 'pudding time' for Whigs.[15] We now know the Hanoverian dynasty was never their prisoner, but the Guelphs were not fools and they now knew for certain who they could rely on in the British Isles. It is not at all surprising that they ultimately acquiesced in the forty years of Tory proscription that followed.[16] The dynasty also benefited from the respect it gained from other European monarchs as a consequence of defeating the Jacobites. The other great powers had watched the political disorders of spring and early summer 1715 with great interest. The British Isles had seemed to be on the verge of another of its periodic revolutionary upheavals and they were all looking to see where their advantage might lie in such an event. The government's victory effectively removed the question mark hanging over the dynasty and its future. In the aftermath they all briskly turned to dealing with the new regime as a regular rival and peer, as opposed to potential prey. Perhaps the most significant vote of confidence in the new Whig order came in early March 1716, when Orléans matter-of-factly dumped the Jacobites and began the process of *rapprochement* with the British government that was to culminate in the Anglo-French alliance of December 1716 – a diplomatic coup that shifted the balance of power in Europe in Britain's favour for the next fifteen years.[17]

The counterpart of Whig and Hanoverian triumph was, of course, Jacobite failure, and it was a failure that had very long-term repercussions. They had obviously been defeated, which is always disappointing. But this was no ordinary defeat. In the early summer of 1715 the Jacobites in general, and the Scots Jacobites in particular, had felt themselves to be on the cusp of great, divinely sanctioned events (which, of course, they believed would transpire in their favour). They seized the moment and it turned into a disaster. Their faith was strong enough to survive this: prophetic visions of imminent victory never ceased during the rebellion and were recrudescing in the Jacobite community by the summer of 1716.[18] And despite the wave of prosecution and persecution of the Episcopalians, Catholics and Anglican Nonjurors that followed the rebellion all three Churches valiantly continued to minister to their (somewhat shrunken) congregations.[19] The experience must, however, have been a sobering one. Apart from the piffling rebellion of 1719 – a rising marked by a distinct lack of enthusiasm on the part of its Scottish constituency – there was not to be another Jacobite rebellion for thirty years.[20] There were many reasons for this, a major one being the Whig regime's determined efforts to stay out of conflicts with other European great powers that might lead them to play the Jacobite card.[21] There were, though, quite sufficient reasons within the Scottish Jacobite community in and of itself.

One of the most important of these was the experience of the exiles, subsequently diffused through the Jacobite community as a whole after their return from the continent. Because of the peculiarly strong yearning for Scotland produced by the synergy between patriotism and love of place that was intrinsic to Scottish Jacobitism, they were bound to have a hard time in exile.[22] Their experience was further compounded by alienation, frustration, boredom and poverty to make it emotionally traumatic. The upshot was that they learned, in the keenest possible fashion, how closely their identity was tied to their homeland, and once they got back to Scotland, like Charles II, they were determined not to go on their travels again.

Prolonged contact with other Jacobites also proved profoundly disillusioning. There was an enduring tension between the ageing, overwhelmingly Catholic, veterans of the first wave of Jacobite emigration and the mainly Protestant newcomers of 1716–17. Beyond that, the circumstances in which the exiles were living made for an atmosphere of pettiness and backbiting that was capable of depressing even men as saintly as Pitsligo. 'Scotsmen,' he gently observed to Mar, 'when out of their own kingdom, are better in small companies than when many of them are together.'[23]

The sheer marginality of the Jacobite cause as far as the great powers of Europe were concerned was also inescapably brought home to the exiles during the years 1716–19. Though many of them were ready to blame Mar or Bolingbroke or unknown traitors for the failure to find a great power ally in contemporary Europe,[24] the financial crisis of 1718–19 demonstrated with brutal clarity how little the Jacobites mattered to any of them. They were not even worth feeding. Moreover, despite its best efforts, the Jacobite shadow-government had proved unable to relieve its destitute followers. Its impotence could not have been more cruelly laid bare.

Yet we know with hindsight that the '15 and '19 were not the last hurrah of the Stuart cause. Most importantly of all, defeat and exile manifestly did not destroy the Jacobite community in Scotland. In fact, paradoxically, the aid the exiles abroad and their families at home were obliged to offer each other may even have reinforced some of its social bonds. Though they returned from Europe chastened, sad and, doubtless in many cases, disillusioned, few overtly abandoned the Stuarts. There were not many *penitenti* like the famously embittered Sinclair.[25] Far more came back like Harry Maule, Thomas Bruce and Alexander Murray of Stanhope, still considering themselves Jacobites and thoroughly comfortable with that socio-cultural milieu.[26] The problem for the Stuarts was that these and many other veterans of 1715 who rose to dominate the internal politics of Jacobitism in Scotland from 1720 to 1740 were effectively burnt-out cases, ready to talk and theoretically to act, but *de facto* a permanent brake on Jacobite activity there. Like their English and Welsh counterparts, the leadership of the Scots Jacobites were now braver in the evening in convivial company than alone over breakfast in the cold light of morning. For a generation Jacobitism in Scotland was thus reduced to little more than the cultural window-dressing of a slowly dwindling minority community. Only with the passing of the old soldiers of 1715 and the rise of a new cohort of Jacobites steeped in tales of near-victory and frustrated glory, but with no memory of the travails of exile, could a significant Scottish Jacobite military threat to the British state re-emerge.

Equally important was the long-term impact of the Scottish Jacobites' engagement with the Whig regime in the aftermath of the rebellion. Collaboration was to some degree inescapable – even rigid Nonjurors like Pitsligo and Panmure had to pay their taxes – but the net effect on many, if not most, Jacobite families was catastrophic for the Jacobite cause. Defending their estates with the help of Whig kinsmen, friends and neighbours; activating their social network's connections within the upper ranks of the Whig regime; exploiting family scions' positions within the army and the administration to find friends willing to plead their cause at the political centre: all of these served to enmesh them in a network of obligations that it would have been dishonourable to ignore by undertaking further Jacobite activity; and the primary duty of the patriarchs of élite families was always to uphold their dynasties' status and honour.

Again, Jacobitism in Scotland was not, and could not be, killed as a result of such engagement. Not every Jacobite was successfully bought off by his Whig friends, and some who were did not stand by their obligations. John

Cameron of Lochiel, for example, refused the offer of an indemnity and (after some heart-searching) Lord George Murray rebelled again in 1745.[27] Moreover, the political, social, cultural and economic machinery for producing new Jacobites was still functioning efficiently. Quite apart from the Jacobite cause's continuing, broad ideological appeal in certain parts of the country, and the deep hold Jacobite culture continued to have on many élite families, Scotland's lingering post-Union economic depression and the accumulated (and accumulating) national grievances blamed on the English connection ensured that Jacobitism survived until the 1740s. What was critical to the future of Jacobitism in Scotland, however, was that the '15 created an opportunity to deracinate a large section of the Jacobite community by acts of clemency. The net effect was not visibly to destroy the Jacobite community, but to weaken it. Thus even though the '45 came in like a lion, full of charisma, drama and early successes, a significantly lower proportion of the potential pool of sympathisers felt able to take up arms once again.[28]

The strength of this tendency within the Jacobite community may be seen from the fact that while he was on the run after Culloden James Johnstone alone encountered at least three formerly active Jacobite heads of families who still wished for the restoration of the Stuarts (and did their best to help him and other Jacobite fugitives at considerable risk to themselves), but no longer felt able to act because of their ties to the Hanoverian regime. Grant of Rothiemurcus was representative of the three, and of many others like them:

> This worthy man, who was then about fifty years of age, and a delightful companion, took a strong liking for me, and frequently assured me of his friendship, as did also his eldest son, with whom I had been at school, but who was in the service of King George. The father was a partisan of the house of Stuart, but from prudential motives, did not openly declare himself; and both he and his vassals remained neutral during the whole of our expedition.[29]

Moreover, a further tranche of former Jacobites, whom Johnstone was fortunate not to encounter, converted to (as opposed to accepted) the new order, though some more sincerely than others. Charles Stewart of Ballechin, for example, hardly evinced any great enthusiasm for the Hanoverian regime when he admitted that he absented himself from home when the Jacobite army came through Atholl in September 1745, 'so as to be free of force and temptation'.[30] By contrast, Charles Erskine, Lord Tinwald of the Court of Session, scion of a Jacobite family thoroughly committed to the '15 and well known as a Jacobite at that time, who gave the exiled Stuart monarch's principal Scottish agent George Lockhart timely warning that he was in imminent danger of arrest for Jacobite conspiracy in 1727, in 1745 did his duty by his new masters so 'ably and zealously' that he earned the praise of no less a patron than Lord Chancellor Hardwicke.[31]

The normal dynamics of Scottish élite society made it not only possible, but completely reasonable, to cherish the Jacobite cause and take a pride in one's previous service to it, while simultaneously upholding the honour of the family through engagement with the Whig regime. Hence when individual Jacobites and their families were obliged to forswear further active support for the Stuarts in the aftermath of the '15, they were not breaching either the normative values of the heritor class or those of their own peculiar milieu. By remaining cultural Jacobites, but becoming day-to-day collaborators with the Whig regime, they squared the circle. And the cumulative impact of this process of enforced, yet honourable, accommodation was profound. When rebellion broke out again in 1745 the effective neutralisation of many Jacobites active in the '15 (and often, too, their heirs) denied the movement the public support from influential members of the élite it so badly needed. Without doubt a wide range of personal, political and economic factors played their part in many Jacobites' decision by 1745 to submit to, or even embrace, the Whig regime. Certainly one of the most important amongst them was the sense of obligation many Jacobites felt towards the friends, neighbours, kinsmen and patrons who had rescued them or their families thirty years previously.

As regards the Jacobite movement as a whole, the effective neutralisation of the Scots and Scotland for a generation shifted its focus elsewhere. In the aftermath of the rising it was all too clear that some other component of the Jacobite movement was going to have to take the lead for a while. Ireland was politically impossible, which only left England and Wales. For the next five years, therefore, James and his ministers concentrated on plotting an Anglo-Welsh uprising. These intrigues eventually came together in the Atterbury plot, which is now the subject of a major new study by Eveline Cruickshanks and Howard Erskine-Hill and does not need to be dealt with here.[32] Suffice it to say that the English and Welsh Jacobites once again proved unable to carry it through and Anglo-Welsh Jacobitism was once more thoroughly cowed by the Whig regime's retributive counter-measures. Thus in many respects the Atterbury plot was both a last echo of the '15 and yet implicitly pointed to the '45. When push came to shove the Stuarts could rely only on the Scots and the Irish, and since playing the Irish card was tantamount to political suicide in the rest of the British Isles, the dynasty's next attempt could only come when the Scots were ready to go again.

Notes

Preface

1. ©1998 by the North American Conference on British Studies. All rights reserved.

Introduction

1. *Secret Memoirs of Barleduc From the Death of Queen Anne to the Present Time* (1715), xxi; *All is Well: Or the Providence of God Praised, and the Government Justified in a Sermon Preached Upon Thursday June 7 1716. Being the Day of Thanksgiving for the Blessing of God Upon his Majesty's Counsels and Arms, in Suppressing the Late Unnatural Rebellion. By a Minister of the Church of England* (1716), p. 8; RH 2/4/306/91: Sir Robert Pollock to [Argyll?], Fort William, 28 Oct. 1715.
2. Mary E. Ingram, *A Jacobite Stronghold of the Church* (Edinburgh, 1907), p. 7; Wolfgang Michael, *England under George I. The Beginnings of the Hanoverian Dynasty* (Westport, repr. 1981), p. 132; Michael Lynch, *Scotland. A New History* (repr. 1994), p. 327.
3. For examples of scholarly presentations of the '45 that nonetheless bring out the excitement and drama associated with the rebellion remarkably well, see: F. J. McLynn, *The Jacobite Army in England, 1745* (Edinburgh, 1983); Jeremy Black, *Culloden and the '45* (2000); Christopher Duffy, *The '45. Bonnie Prince Charlie and the Untold Story of the Jacobite Rising* (2003).
4. George Rudé, *The Crowd in History 1730–1848* (2nd edn, 1981); Eric Hobsbawm, *Primitive Rebels. Studies in Archaic Forms of Social Movement in the 19th and 20th Centuries* (1963); Jeremy Black, *Eighteenth Century Europe 1700–1789* (1990), pp. 133–135.
5. Yves Bercé, *History of Peasant Revolts: the Social Origins of Rebellion in Early Modern France*, trans. Amanda Whitmore (Ithaca, NY, 1990); Roland Mousnier, *Peasant Uprisings in Seventeenth-century France, Russia, and China*, trans. Brian Pearce (New York, 1970); Robin Briggs, 'Popular Revolt in its Social Context', in *Communities of Belief: Cultural and Social Tensions in Early Modern France* (Oxford, 1989), pp. 106–177.
6. See for example: Keith Brown, *Bloodfeud in Scotland 1573–1625. Violence, Justice and Politics in an Early Modern Society* (Edinburgh, 1986), pp. 145, 148, 149; Conrad Russell, *The Fall of the British Monarchies 1637–1642* (Oxford, 1995), pp. 379–380; Peter Earle, *Monmouth's Rebels. The Road to Sedgemoor* (1977), p. 16.

7. Earle, *Monmouth's Rebels*, pp. 169–181; Paul Hopkins, *Glencoe and the End of the Highland War* (revised reprint, Edinburgh, 1998), pp. 99, 102–103; Margaret Sankey, *Jacobite Prisoners of the 1715 Rebellion: Preventing and Punishing Insurrection in Early Hanoverian Britain* (Aldershot, 2005), ix–x.
8. See for example: P. J. Marshall and Alaine Low (eds), *The Oxford History of the British Empire. Volume II. The Eighteenth Century* (Oxford, 1998), pp. 70, 106; Tony Claydon, *William III* (2002), pp. 92–93, 113, 135. A fuller review of this historiographic tendency can be found in: Daniel Szechi, *The Jacobites. Britain and Europe 1688–1788* (Manchester, 1994), pp. 1–7.
9. J. C. D. Clark, *Revolution and Rebellion. State and Society in England in the Seventeenth and Eighteenth Centuries* (1986), pp. 111–116; J. C. D. Clark, 'On Moving the Middle Ground: the Significance of Jacobitism in Historical Studies', in E. Cruickshanks and J. Black (eds), *The Jacobite Challenge* (Edinburgh, 1988), pp. 177–185.
10. Paul Langford, *A Polite and Commercial People. England 1727–1783* (Oxford, 1992), p. 200; Linda Colley, *In Defiance of Oligarchy. The Tory Party 1714–60* (1982), pp. 29, 31, 32, 33, 36.
11. Paul Kléber Monod, *Jacobitism and the English People, 1688–1788* (1989), pp. 346–349.
12. Thomas Kuhn, *The Structure of Scientific Revolutions* (3rd edn, 1996).
13. John Baynes, *The Jacobite Rising of 1715* (1970).
14. Cf. the chapters that follow with Baynes, *Jacobite Rising, passim*, and in particular, pp. xi-xv, and 83–161 with Chapters 1–3 and 6–7.
15. Alistair and Henrietta Tayler, *1715: the Story of the Rising* (1936).
16. Frances Dickinson, *The Reluctant Rebel: a Northumbrian Legacy of Jacobite Times* (Newcastle-upon-Tyne, 1996); William James Couper, *The Rebel Press at Perth in 1715* (1928); J . H. E. Bennett, 'Cheshire and The Fifteen', *Journal of the Chester Archaeological Society* (new series, xxi, 1915), 30–46; John Elliot Shearer, *The Battle of Dunblane Revised: Sherrifmuir, 1715* (Stirling, 1911); Albert Nicholson, 'Lancashire in the Rebellion of 1715', *Transactions of the Lancashire and Cheshire Antiquarian Society*, iii (1886), 66–88; *The History of the Earl of Derwentwater and the Rebellion of 1715* (Newcastle-upon-Tyne, 1868); William Sidney Gibson, *Dilston Hall, or, Memoirs of the Earl of Derwentwater, a Martyr in the Rebellion of 1715* (1850).
17. For examples of which, see: Daniel Defoe, *A Dialogue Between a Whig and a Jacobite, upon the Subject of the Late Rebellion; and the Execution of the Rebel-lords, &C. Occasion'd by the Phoenomenon in the Skie, March 6. 1715–16* (1716); John Withers, *The Perjury and Folly of the Late Rebellion Display'd: in a Sermon Preach'd at Exon, June the 7th, 1716. Being the Day Appointed for a Publick Thanksgiving, for the Success of His Majesties Forces Against the Rebels, at Preston, Dumblain, and Perth* (1716); Peter Rae, *History of the Late Rebellion* (1718).
18. Sir Charles Petrie, *The Jacobite Movement* (1932); Leo Gooch, *The Desperate Faction? The Jacobites of North-East England 1688–1745* (Hull, 1995); John L. Roberts, *The Jacobite Wars. Scotland and the Military Campaigns of 1715 and 1745* (Edinburgh, 2002).
19. Bruce Lenman, *The Jacobite Risings in Britain 1689–1746* (1980), pp. 107–154; Jonathan Oates, 'The Responses in North East England to the Jacobite Rebellions of 1715 and 1745' (University of Reading Ph.D. thesis, 2001).
20. T. F. Donald, 'Glasgow and the Jacobite Rebellion of 1715', *Scottish Historical Review*, xiii (1916), 127; A. and H. Tayler, *1715*, p. 95; Petrie, *Jacobite Movement*, pp. 130–131; Murray Pittock, *The Myth of the Jacobite Clans* (Edinburgh, 1997), pp. 50, 57.
21. Petrie, *Jacobite Movement*, pp. 128, 136; A. and H. Tayler, *1715*, p. 94; Roberts, *Jacobite Wars*, p. 47; David Laing and Thomas Macknight (eds), *Memoirs of the Insurrection in Scotland in 1715. By John, Master of Sinclair. With Notes by Sir Walter Scott, Bart* (Abbotsford Club, Edinburgh, 1858), pp. 16, 20, 36, 42, etc.

22. A. and H. Tayler, *1715*, p. 120; Sir Charles Petrie, *The Marshal Duke of Berwick. The Picture of an Age* (1953), p. 295; Baynes, *Jacobite Rising*, pp. 20, 166–167.

23. Joseph Addison, *The Free-Holder* (1716), no. 36, 23 Apr. 1716, pp. 209–214; Robert Chambers, *History of the Rebellions in Scotland under the Viscount of Dundee and the Earl of Mar in 1689 and 1715* (Edinburgh, 1829), pp. 159, 162; Andrew Balfour, *To Arms!* (Boston, Mass., 1898), pp. 384–385; Michael, *Beginnings of the Hanoverian Dynasty*, pp. 133–134.

24. Edward Corp with Edward Gregg, Howard Erskine-Hill and Geoffrey Scott, *A Court in Exile. The Stuarts in France, 1689–1718* (2004), pp. 210–214, 257–279.

25. Szechi, *Jacobites*, pp. 85–121.

26. Duffy, *'45*, pp. 615–620.

Chapter 1 'To Mark Where England's Province Stands': the Economy and Social Structure of the British Isles in 1715

1. William Ferguson, *Scotland's Relations with England: a Survey to 1707* (Edinburgh, 1977), pp. 235–237.

2. Linda Colley, *Britons. Forging the Nation 1707–1837* (1992), pp. 11–54.

3. Geoffrey Holmes and Daniel Szechi, *The Age of Oligarchy. Pre-industrial Britain 1722–1783* (1993), p. 133.

4. Geoffrey Holmes, *The Making of a Great Power. Late Stuart and Early Georgian England 1660–1722* (1993), pp. 61–68, 295–306, 447, 449; T. C. Smout, *A History of the Scottish People 1560–1830* (6th impression, 1985), p. 224; T. W. Moody, F. X. Martin and F. J. Byrne (eds), *A New History of Ireland III. Early Modern Ireland 1534–1691* (Oxford, 1976), pp. 184–186, 401–406.

5. Gordon Mingay, 'Agriculture and Rural Life', in H. T. Dickinson (ed.), *A Companion to Eighteenth-Century Britain* (Oxford, 2002), p. 141.

6. T. S. Ashton, *An Economic History of England: the 18th Century* (1955; reprint, 1964), pp. 31, 64–65, 66, 69–70, 140, 179–180; Charles Wilson, *England's Apprenticeship 1603–1763* (1975), p. 45; Douglas Hay and Nicholas Rogers, *Eighteenth Century English Society* (1997), p. 7.

7. Wilson, *England's Apprenticeship*, pp. 47, 51; Hay and Rogers, *English Society*, p. 7.

8. Holmes, *Making of a Great Power*, pp. 64–65, 67.

9. Ashton, *Economic History of England*, pp. 63–70; Wilson, *England's Apprenticeship*, pp. 280, 288–312; Joan Thirsk (ed.), *The Agrarian History of England and Wales. Volume V. 1640–1750* (2 vols, 1985), i. 366.

10. Holmes, *Making of a Great Power*, pp. 62–68; Wilson, *England's Apprenticeship*, pp. 160–184.

11. Wilson, *England's Apprenticeship*, pp. 141–159.

12. Maxine Berg, *The Age of Manufactures 1700–1820* (1985), pp. 98–99; Thirsk (ed.), *Agrarian History of England and Wales*, i. 358, 389; ii. 276.

13. Ashton, *Economic History of England*, pp. 43–44, 46, 47; Holmes and Szechi, *Age of Oligarchy*, p. 140; Thirsk (ed.), *Agrarian History of England and Wales*, ii. 73.

14. Ashton, *Economic History of England*, pp. 67–70.

15. Wilson, *England's Apprenticeship*, pp. 291, 294.

16. Holmes and Szechi, *Age of Oligarchy*, pp. 144–145.

17. Wilson, *England's Apprenticeship*, pp. 226–236, 294, 297.

18. Ibid., pp. 277, 290; Ashton, *Economic History of England*, p. 53.

19. Wilson, *England's Apprenticeship*, pp. 300–301.

20. Holmes, *Making of a Great Power*, p. 301; Wilson, *England's Apprenticeship*, p. 288.

21. Thirsk (ed.), *Agrarian History of England and Wales*, ii. 273, 274, 275–276.
22. Wilson, *England's Apprenticeship*, pp. 289, 294, 295–296, 299.
23. SP 35/3, f. 168: Commissioners of the Customs to the Barons of the Treasury, 5 July 1715.
24. Edward Hughes, *North Country Life in the Eighteenth Century. The North-East, 1700–1750* (reprint, 1969), pp. 3–5.
25. R. H. Campbell, *Scotland since 1707. The Rise of an Industrial Society* (revised 2nd edn, Edinburgh, 1992), p. 6.
26. Smout, *History of the Scottish People*, pp. 106–110.
27. Hopkins, *Glencoe*, pp. 180, 191, 267, 359; Smout, *History of the Scottish People*, pp. 224–225.
28. Christopher A. Whatley, *Scottish Society 1707–1830. Beyond Jacobitism, towards Industrialisation* (Manchester, 2000), pp. 31–41.
29. J. Prebble, *The Darien Disaster* (1968); Whatley, *Scottish Society*, p. 38.
30. William Ferguson, *Scotland. 1689 to the Present* (Edinburgh, reprint, 1994), p. 70; Whatley, *Scottish Society*, pp. 40–41.
31. I owe this caveat to a very interesting conversation about Scotland's 'black' economy with Professor Allan Macinnes, who will be developing this argument in his forthcoming book on the Union of 1707.
32. Ian D. Whyte, *Scotland before the Industrial Revolution. An Economic and Social History c. 1050–c.1750* (1995), pp. 284–285, 289, 297.
33. GD 220/5/382/12: Charles Cockburn of Ormiston to James Graham, Duke of Montrose, Edinburgh, 28 Dec. 1714. See also: GD 220/5/453/2: Lord Advocate Sir David Dalrymple of Newhailes to Montrose, Newhailes, 4 Jan. 1715.
34. GD 220/5/454/12: copy of Dysart magistrates' address vs Union, 22 Jan. 1715; Convention of Royal Burghs SL 30/233: petition by the burgh of Selkirk to the Royal Convention of Burghs, 9 July 1718; SL 30/233: petition by Jedburgh to the Royal Convention of Burghs, 1718. I am grateful to Professor Chris Whatley for pointing out these invaluable records to me.
35. Whyte, *Scotland before the Industrial Revolution*, pp. 299–300, 304, 305. For a different view with respect to Glasgow, see: Whatley, *Scottish Society*, p. 54.
36. Whyte, *Scotland before the Industrial Revolution*, pp. 297, 298, 302–303, 306; Whatley, *Scottish Society*, pp. 56–57.
37. Whyte, *Scotland before the Industrial Revolution*, pp. 285, 300.
38. Ibid., p. 297.
39. Whatley, *Scottish Society*, p. 60.
40. Robert Wodrow, *Analecta: Or Materials for a History of Remarkable Providences; Mostly Relating to Scotch Ministers and Christians* (4 vols, Maitland Club, Edinburgh, 1862), iii. 161–162: Aug. 1724.
41. Whyte, *Scotland before the Industrial Revolution*, p. 299.
42. SP 54/8/124: Earl of Sutherland to Secretary Stanhope [Aug./Sept. 1715]; Walter B. Blaikie (ed.), *Origins of the Forty-Five and Other Papers Relating to that Rising* (reprint, Edinburgh, 1975, of Edinburgh, 1916 edn), p. 122.
43. Robert Patten, *The History of the Rebellion in the Year 1715. With Original Papers, and the Characters of the Principal Gentlemen Concerned in it* (3rd edn, 1745), p. 37.
44. Whyte, *Scotland before the Industrial Revolution*, p. 259.
45. Allan I. Macinnes, *Clanship, Commerce and the House of Stuart, 1603–1788* (East Linton, 1996), pp. 143–150.
46. Whyte, *Scotland before the Industrial Revolution*, pp. 260, 261.
47. Macinnes, *Clanship, Commerce and the House of Stuart*, pp. 221–228.

48. Ferguson, *Scotland's Relations with England*, pp. 240–241; Whatley, *Scottish Society*, pp. 50–51.
49. RH 2/4/302/51: warrant appointing Commission of Police for Scotland [13 Dec. 1714].
50. GD 248/46/7/32: David Polson to Brigadier Alexander Grant of Grant, 'Kininyly', 1 Feb. 1715; RH 2/4/307/21b: 'Ane Account of the Earl of Sutherland's Proceedings From his Embarkation at Leith the 25th of September to the 2nd of November, 1715'.
51. Whatley, *Scottish Society*, p. 54.
52. Charles Carlton, *Going to the Wars. The Experience of the British Civil Wars, 1638–1651* (1992), p. 214.
53. Moody *et al.*, *Early Modern Ireland*, pp. 389–390, 390–396, 403–404.
54. Ibid., p. 407.
55. T. W. Moody and W. E. Vaughan (eds), *A New History of Ireland IV. Eighteenth-Century Ireland 1691–1800* (1986), pp. 132–133.
56. Ibid., pp. 133–135.
57. Ibid., p. 8; D. W. Hayton, *I. Introductory Survey*. Appendices, vol. 1 of Eveline Cruickshanks, Stuart Handley and D. W. Hayton, *The House of Commons 1690–1715* (5 vols, 2002), Appendices, 525–530.
58. Moody and Vaughan, *Eighteenth-Century Ireland*, pp. 142–144.
59. Ibid., pp. 159–185.
60. Ibid., pp. 647–649.
61. P. J. Corfield, 'Class by Name and Number in Eighteenth-century Britain', *History*, lxxii (1987), 38–61.
62. Holmes, *Making of a Great Power*, pp. 70–81, 410–411.
63. Hay and Rogers, *English Society*, pp. 22–24.
64. Faramerz Dabhoiwala, 'The Construction of Honour, Reputation and Status in Late Seventeenth- and Early Eighteenth-Century England', *Transactions of the Royal Historical Society* (6th ser., vi, 1996), pp. 201–213.
65. Peter Laslett, *The World We Have Lost – Further Explored* (3rd edn, 1983), pp. 22–52; E. P. Thompson, *Customs in Common* (New York, 1991), pp. 31–32, 63.
66. Thompson, *Customs in Common*, pp. 16–96.
67. Ibid., pp. 185–258.
68. Ibid., 234–235, 239.
69. Ibid., pp. 188–189.
70. Hay and Rogers, *English Society*, pp. 114–122; Thompson, *Customs in Common*, pp. 59–60.
71. P. Jenkins, *The Making of a Ruling Class: the Glamorgan Gentry 1640–1790* (1983), pp. 14–17.
72. Colley, *Britons*, pp. 12–14, 77.
73. Ibid., p. 82.
74. Holmes, *Making of a Great Power*, pp. 351–356.
75. Nicholas Rogers, *Whigs and Cities. Popular Politics in the Age of Walpole and Pitt* (Oxford, 1989), pp. 23, 271–274.
76. John Bossy, *The English Catholic Community 1570–1850* (1975), pp. 172–181.
77. Whyte, *Scotland before the Industrial Revolution*, p. 114.
78. Viz.: the clansmen's defiance of chieftains who went wholly against the political consensus within the clan, for examples of which see: A. and H. Tayler, *1715*, p. 47; Blaikie, *Origins of the Forty-Five*, p. 91.
79. Bruce Lenman, *The Jacobite Clans of the Great Glen 1650–1784* (1984), pp. 13–14; E. Burt, *Burt's Letters from the North of Scotland. With Facsimiles of the Original Engravings*, intro. by R. Jamieson, 2 vols (reprint, Edinburgh, 1974, of London, 1754 edn), i. 233; GD 220/5/631/10a–b: John Hope to Montrose, Inverness, 6 Apr. 1716, but

cf. John Campbell, Lord Glenorchy on the difficulty of preventing clansmen deserting: Philip C. Yorke (ed.), *The Life and Correspondence of Philip Yorke, Earl of Hardwicke, Lord High Chancellor of Great Britain* (3 vols, reprint, New York, 1977, of Cambridge, 1913 edn), i. 519: Glenorchy to Colonel Joseph Yorke, Taymouth, 10 Apr. 1746.

80. Robert Clyde, *From Rebel to Hero: the Image of the Highlander, 1745–1830* (East Linton, 1995), p. 7.
81. Eric Richards, *A History of the Highland Clearances: Agrarian Transformation and the Evictions 1746–1786* (London, 1982), pp. 60–64; Macinnes, *Clanship, Commerce and the House of Stuart*, pp. 1–24; *Burt's Letters*, i. 50.
82. Thompson, *Customs in Common*, pp. 16–259; Whyte, *Scotland before the Industrial Revolution*, pp. 151–152, 155–156, 161.
83. D. Szechi, *George Lockhart of Carnwath, 1689–1727. A Study in Jacobitism* (East Linton, 2002), p. 44.
84. Julia Buckroyd, *Church and State in Scotland 1660–1681* (Edinburgh, 1980), pp. 57–67, 117–131.
85. Julia Buckroyd, *The Life of James Sharp, Archbishop of St Andrews. A Political Biography* (Edinburgh, 1987), pp. 106–116.
86. Lenman, *Jacobite Risings*, p. 55.
87. Ibid., pp. 55–71.
88. Ferguson, *1689 to the Present*, pp. 104–106.
89. *Burt's Letters*, i. 224.
90. Blaikie, *Origins of the Forty-Five*, pp. 126–127.
91. RH 2/4/308/128: John Campbell, Provost of Edinburgh, to Townshend, Edinburgh, 14 Dec. 1715; Bruce Lenman, 'The Scottish Episcopal Clergy and the Ideology of Jacobitism', in Eveline Cruickshanks (ed.), *Ideology and Conspiracy. Aspects of Jacobitism, 1689–1759* (Edinburgh, 1982), pp. 36–48.
92. Ferguson, *1689 to the Present*, p. 103.
93. Macinnes, *Clanship, Commerce and the House of Stuart*, pp. 180–81, 247–249.
94. Pittock, *Myth of the Jacobite Clans*, p. 47.
95. RH 2/4/308/96b: Lord Advocate Dalrymple to Stanhope, Edinburgh, 29 Nov. 1715. And see, for example, GD 220/5/455/3 and 7: Lord Justice Clerk Cockburn of Ormiston to Montrose, Edinburgh, 18 June and 7 July 1715; GD 220/5/455/4: anonymous account of Jacobite disturbances in Aberdeen, Aberdeen, 13 June 1715; Blaikie, *Origins of the Forty-Five*, 'Memoirs of the Rebellion in Aberdeen and Banff', pp. 126–127.
96. RH 2/4/299/33, 34: Francis Philipson to [George Tilson], Edinburgh, 20 July and 7 Aug. 1708; Blaikie, *Origins of the Forty-Five*, pp. 156–157; T. N. Clarke, 'The Scottish Episcopalians 1688–1720' (Univ. of Edinburgh Ph.D. thesis, 1987), pp. 394–398; J. B. Craven, *History of the Episcopal Church in the Diocese of Moray* (1889), pp. 217–218, 234, 285; G. Hay, *History of Arbroath to the Present Time. With Notices of the Civil and Ecclesiastical Affairs of the Neighbouring District* (2nd edn, Arbroath, 1899), p. 183; Murray Pittock, *The Jacobites* (1998), pp. 48, 114.
97. Murray Pittock, *Inventing and Resisting Britain. Cultural Identities in Britain and Ireland, 1685–1789* (1997), p. 10; GD 45/14/220/21: Margaret Maule, Countess of Panmure, to James Maule, Earl of Panmure, Panmure, 13 Nov. 1716; GD 1/616/64: Lord Advocate Robert Dundas of Arniston's response to a complaint by the General Assembly of the Kirk, Edinburgh, 20 Sept. 1723; Chevalier [James] de Johnstone, *Memoirs of the Rebellion in 1745 and 1746* (1820), pp. 182–184; Blaikie, *Origins of the Forty-Five*, p. 149.
98. RH 2/4/306/103b: 'Admonition by the Synod of Glasgow and Air to all the Congregations Under Their Inspection', [Glasgow?, Oct.]1715; RH 2/4/307/5: 'A Seasonable Admonition by the Provincial Synod of Lothian and Tweeddale',

Edinburgh, 2 Nov. 1715. See also: RH 2/4/305/44: warning by Synod of Perth and Stirling, Stirling, 13 Oct. 1715; A. Whitford Anderson (ed.), *Papers of the Rev. John Anderson, Minister of Dumbarton, 1698–1718* (Dumbarton, 1914), p. 41: Anderson to Lieutenant Ross, Dumbarton, 19 Nov. 1715. It is interesting to note in this context that Lawrence Stone (*The Causes of the English Revolution 1529–1642* [1972], p. 140) takes the rise of 'Curse of Meroz' sermonising as a key emotional trigger in the outbreak of both the Great Civil War in England and Wales and the American Revolution.

99. Blaikie, *Origins of the Forty-Five*, pp. 126–127. See also: *Burt's Letters*, ii. 224–225; Patten, *History of the Rebellion*, p. 31.

100. Laing and Macknight (eds), *Memoirs of the Insurrection*, p. 100; Craven, *Episcopal Church in the Diocese of Moray*, pp. 234, 257; RH 2/4/305/27: Advyces from North Britain, [9?] Oct. 1715; RH 2/4/308/178: Anon. to ? [post-10 June 1716]; RH 2/4/310/168b: Glenorchy to Townshend [1716]; James Allardyce (ed.), *Historical Papers Relating to the Jacobite Period 1699–1750* (2 vols, New Spalding Club, Aberdeen, 1895, 1896), i. 62: records of Alford Presbytery, Alford Kirk, 24 Oct. 1715; ii. 591: extracts from King's College Records, Aberdeen, 1716; Patten, *History of the Rebellion*, p. 67; SP 54/9/7 and RH 2/4/307/32: proclamations by Mar, camp at Perth, 4 Oct. and 1 Nov. 1715.

101. Craven, *Episcopal Church in the Diocese of Moray*, pp. 302, 321; Hay, *History of Arbroath*, p. 182; Allardyce (ed.), *Historical Papers Relating to the Jacobite Period*, i. 33–35: minutes of the Synod of Moray, Forres, 24 Apr. 1716; Patten, *History of the Rebellion*, p. 30.

102. Lenman, *Jacobite Risings*, pp. 56–57, 60–64.

103. Pittock, *Myth of the Jacobite Clans*, pp. 50–51, 57, 78–83; Simon Macdonald Lockhart, *Seven Centuries. The History of the Lockharts of Lee and Carnwath* (Carnwath, 1976), pp. 223, 230–232; GD 18/2092/4: Sir John Clerk's spiritual journal for Apr. 1712–1715: 10, 11 and 13 Oct. 1715; Blaikie, *Origins of the Forty-Five*, p. 122.

104. Macinnes, *Clanship, Commerce and the House of Stuart*, pp. 248–249.

105. Moody and Vaughan (eds), *Eighteenth-Century Ireland*, pp. 34; Thomas Bartlett, 'An End to Moral Economy: the Irish Militia Disturbances of 1793', in C. H. E. Philpin (ed.), *Nationalism and Popular Protest in Ireland* (1987), pp. 192–193, 216–217.

106. Moody and Vaughan (eds), *Eighteenth-Century Ireland*, p. 37.

107. Ibid., pp. 16–21.

108. Ibid., pp. 34, 38–39.

109. Ibid., pp. 39–41, 110.

110. Ibid., p. 38.

111. Thompson, *Customs in Common*, pp. 42–49; Szechi, *Lockhart of Carnwath*, pp. 42–44; Moody and Vaughan (eds), *Eighteenth-Century Ireland*, pp. 54–56.

112. BL Add. MS 61636. Blenheim Papers Vol. DXXXVI, f. 191r: Edward Budgell to Joseph Addison, [Dublin], 28 July 1715. See also: BL, Stowe 228, f. 143r, 152v: Gustavus Hamilton to Robethon, Dublin, 8 and 20 Oct. 1715.

113. Moody and Vaughan (eds), *Eighteenth-Century Ireland*, p. 53.

114. Harman Murtagh, 'Irish Soldiers Abroad, *c.* 1600–1800', in Thomas Bartlett and Keith Jeffery (eds), *A Military History of Ireland* (1996), pp. 297–298.

115. Moody and Vaughan (eds), *Eighteenth-Century Ireland*, pp. 629–649.

116. Ibid., p. 638; Éamonn Ó Ciardha, *Ireland and the Jacobite Cause, 1685–1766. A Fatal Attachment* (Dublin, 2002), pp. 105–107.

117. Frank McLynn, *The Jacobites* (1985), p. 131.

118. Ó Ciardha, *Ireland and the Jacobite Cause*, pp. 121–122, 151–162.

119. Moody and Vaughan (eds), *Eighteenth-Century Ireland*, pp. 106–107; Ó Ciardha, *Ireland and the Jacobite Cause*, pp. 100–105.

120. Nicholas Rogers, 'Riot and Popular Jacobitism in Early Hanoverian England', in Cruickshanks (ed.), *Ideology and Conspiracy*, pp. 78–79.
121. AECP 268, ff. 22v–23r: Charles François de la Bonde d'Iberville, marquis d'Iberville, to Jean-Baptiste Colbert de Croissy, marquis de Torcy, London, 22 Apr./3 May 1715.

Chapter 2 'Fareweel e'en to the Scottish Name': the Politics and Geopolitics of the British Isles in 1715

1. John Cannon, *Aristocratic Century. The Peerage of Eighteenth-Century England* (1987), p. 125.
2. Ibid., pp. 93–123.
3. Holmes, *Making of a Great Power*, pp. 212–218, 220–226.
4. Ferguson, *1689 to the Present*, pp. 49–53.
5. *http://www.history.ac.uk/projects/elec/sem19.html*: Alex Murdoch, 'Management or Semi-Independence? The Government of Scotland 1707–1832' (Institute of Historical Research, archived electronic seminar paper, 1998).
6. Geoffrey Holmes, *British Politics in the Age of Anne* (revised edn, 1987), pp. 386, 398.
7. Whatley, *Scottish Society*, p. 56; RH 2/4/299/41: petition against the pressing of Scottish seamen from the Convention of Royal Burghs.
8. Geoffrey Holmes, 'The Hamilton Affair of 1711–12: a Crisis in Anglo-Scottish Relations', *English Historical Review*, lxxvii (1962), 257–282.
9. Ferguson, *1689 to the Present*, pp. 110–112.
10. Daniel Szechi, *Jacobitism and Tory Politics, 1710–14* (Edinburgh, 1984), pp. 122, 129–130.
11. Ferguson, *Scotland's Relations with England*, pp. 197–198, 234.
12. Holmes, *Making of a Great Power*, pp. 212–215, 339.
13. Ibid., pp. 334–335.
14. Jonathan Scott, *England's Troubles. Seventeenth-Century English Political Instability in European Context* (2000), pp. 454–473; Holmes, *Making of a Great Power*, pp. 245–246.
15. Holmes, *Making of a Great Power*, pp. 342–343; Scott, *England's Troubles*, p. 492; Holmes, *British Politics*, p. 56.
16. H. T. Dickinson, *Liberty and Property. Political Ideology in Eighteenth-Century Britain* (1977), pp. 79–90.
17. Holmes, *British Politics*, pp. 17, 62; J. P. Kenyon, *Revolution Principles. The Politics of Party 1689–1720* (1977), pp. 83–101.
18. *The Interest of England in Relation to Protestant Dissenters: in a Letter to the Right Reverend, the Bishop of* —— (1714), p. 21. This Whig charge did have some basis in fact, for an example of which see: Rogers, 'Riot and Popular Jacobitism', p. 73.
19. Hayton, *Introductory Survey*, i. 463; BL, Stowe 228, f. 135r: St Paul Bouquet(?) to Robethon, Windsor?, 2 Oct. 1715; AECP 271, f. 109r: d'Iberville to Nicolas de Blé, marquis d'Huxelles, London, 17/28 Nov. 1715; SP 54/8/74c: intelligence from Perth, Stirling, 18 Sept. 1715.
20. Dickinson, *Liberty and Property*, pp. 33–56.
21. Edward Gregg, *Queen Anne* (1980), pp. 298–320.
22. Ibid., pp. 334–342, 353–358. In fairness to Oxford, it should be noted that Britain's long-term strategic situation was dramatically compromised by the death of the Holy Roman Emperor Joseph I in 1711. His brother and successor, Charles VI, who had hitherto been Britain's candidate for the Spanish throne, thenceforward stood to resurrect the Habsburg empire of Charles V by reuniting the Holy Roman and Spanish empires in the event of an allied victory. From a British point of view this was every

bit as unwelcome as France and Spain united under a single dynasty, which was what the War of the Spanish Succession was originally designed to prevent.

23. Szechi, *Jacobitism and Tory Politics*, pp. 182–193.
24. Ragnhild Hatton, *George I. Elector and King* (1978), pp. 105–108; Szechi, *Jacobitism and Tory Politics*, pp. 167, 173–174.
25. J. Macpherson (ed.), *Original Papers; Containing the Secret History of Great Britain, from the Restoration to the Accession of the House of Hanover* (2 vols, 1775), ii. 499–500: Charles Spencer, Earl of Sunderland, to Hans von Bothmer, 1/12 Aug. 1713; ii. 515–517: John Churchill, Duke of Marlborough, to Jean de Robethon, Antwerp, 19/30 Nov. 1713; ii. 550–551: Ludwig Schütz to Bothmer and Robethon, London, 26 Jan./6 Feb. 1714.
26. Edward Gregg, 'Marlborough in Exile, 1712–14', *Historical Journal*, xv (1972), 593–618; K. A. Moody-Stuart, 'Lieutenant-Colonel James Steuart: a Jacobite Lieutenant-Governor of Edinburgh Castle', *Scottish Historical Review*, xxi (1923), 11–12.
27. Hayton, *Introductory Survey*, i. 474, 478; *The Management of the Four Last Years Vindicated* (1714), pp. 4–5.
28. Szechi, *Jacobitism and Tory Politics*, pp. 153–181.
29. Hatton, *George I*, pp. 123–127.
30. W. A. Speck, *Stability and Strife. England, 1714–1760* (Cambridge, Mass., 1977), pp. 174–175.
31. Michael, *Beginnings of the Hanoverian Dynasty*, p. 120; G. V. Bennett, *The Tory Crisis in Church and State, 1688–1730: the Career of Francis Atterbury, Bishop of Rochester* (1975), pp. 186–188.
32. Harold Williams (ed.), *Jonathan Swift. Journal to Stella* (2 vols, Oxford, 1948), i. 195.
33. John Addy and Peter McNiven (eds), *The Diary of Henry Prescott, LL.B., Deputy Registrar of Chester Diocese* (Record Society of Lancashire and Cheshire, 2 vols, 1992, 1994), ii. 407, 407–408, 408–409, 409, 411, 415, 417: 24, 26 and 28 Sept., 5, 8, 12 and 20 Oct., 12 and 16 Nov. and 3 Dec. 1714; Monod, *Jacobitism and the English People*, pp. 173–179.
34. Bennett, *Atterbury*, pp. 192–193.
35. Holmes, *Making of a Great Power*, pp. 329–332.
36. Monod, *Jacobitism and the English People*, p. 179.
37. Cited in Michael, *Beginnings of the Hanoverian Dynasty*, p. 114.
38. Romney Sedgwick (ed.), *The House of Commons 1715–1754* (2 vols, 1970), i. 19–20.
39. Michael, *Beginnings of the Hanoverian Dynasty*, pp. 119–121, 122–129.
40. Monod, *Jacobitism and the English People*, pp. 185–193; Rogers, 'Riot and Popular Jacobitism', pp. 73–74.
41. John Stevenson, *Popular Disturbances in England, 1700–1832* (2nd edn, 1992), pp. 6–7, 27–29.
42. Nicholas Rogers, 'Popular Protest in Early Hanoverian London', *Past and Present*, lxxix (1978), 78–80.
43. £12 in pre-Union Scots money (which continued to be used as a unit of account and even in regular commerce for some time after the Union) was equivalent to £1 sterling.
44. Hayton, *Introductory Survey*, i. 141–143.
45. Ibid., i. 161–167.
46. Ibid., i. 168–172, 176.
47. Ibid., i. 148, 151–153.
48. This was the case even in the midst of the rebellion, for an example of which see: SP 54/8/125: copy, Alexander Macdonald of Glengarry to Sir Robert Pollock of that Ilk (Governor of Fort William), 22 Sept. 1715.

49. Laing and Macknight (eds), *Memoirs of the Insurrection*, pp. 6, 16; Daniel Szechi, 'Scotland's Ruine'. *Lockhart of Carnwath's Memoirs of the Union* (Association for Scottish Literary Studies, Aberdeen, 1995), p. 85.
50. Frank McLynn, *Charles Edward Stuart. A Tragedy in Many Acts* (1988), p. 149.
51. Colin Kidd, 'Conditional Britons: the Scots Covenanting Tradition and the Eighteenth-century British State', *English Historical Review*, cxvii (2002), 1147–1176.
52. GD 220/5/440/2: John Hamilton, Earl of Rothes, to 'Count Tarriff', Leslie, 7 Dec. 1714; GD 220/5/1895/5: Charles Cockburn of Ormiston to Montrose, Edinburgh, 18 Dec. 1714.
53. P. W. J. Riley, *The Union of England and Scotland. A Study in Anglo-Scottish Politics in the Eighteenth Century* (Manchester, 1978), pp. 48–49, 332–334.
54. Szechi, *Lockhart of Carnwath*, pp. 54, 57; Riley, *Union of England and Scotland*, p. 334; Szechi, *Jacobitism and Tory Politics*, pp. 148–149.
55. GD 220/5/434/11: Lord Advocate Dalrymple to Montrose, Edinburgh, 18 Dec. 1714.
56. Though it pertains to English and Welsh politics, the best modern description of the structure of the Court party is to be found in Holmes, *British Politics*, pp. 345–404. It should be noted, however, that the Scottish Court party was until 1710–11 proportionately much larger and stronger than its Anglo-Welsh counterpart.
57. Riley, *Union of England and Scotland*, p. 332.
58. Ferguson, *Scotland's Relations with England*, pp. 224–231.
59. Hayton, *Introductory Survey*, i. 510, 517, 523.
60. Holmes, *British Politics*, pp. 242–245.
61. Hayton, *Introductory Survey*, i. 517–518, 521, 524.
62. Ibid., i. 509, 513, 517.
63. Ibid., i. 517–518, 521, 523–524.
64. Edward Gregg, 'The Jacobite Career of John, Earl of Mar', in E. Cruickshanks (ed.), *Ideology and Conspiracy. Aspects of Jacobitism, 1689–1759* (Edinburgh, 1982), pp. 179–181; Huntington Library, California, Loudoun Papers, LO 11429 (lspbox 23): James Erskine, Lord Grange of the Court of Session, to Hugh Campbell, Earl of Loudoun, Edinburgh, 10 Sept. 1715. I am indebted to Professor Allan Macinnes for letting me see his transcripts of the Loudoun correspondence. See also: RH 2/4/390/1/57–9: Mar to Grange, Whitehall, 7 Aug. 1714.
65. Gregg, 'Mar', p. 181.
66. Szechi, *Jacobitism and Tory Politics*, pp. 131–133; Riley, *Union of England and Scotland*, pp. 173, 265–266.
67. Atholl Papers, box 45, bundle 11/180: Mar to Atholl, Whitehall, 24 Aug. 1714; GD 150/2375/3: Mar to James Douglas, Earl of Morton, 28 Aug. 1714.
68. GD 124/15/1143/2: Harry Maule of Kellie to Lord Justice Clerk Erskine, 28 Sept. 1714.
69. GD 45/1/192/3: circular letter, autumn 1714.
70. GD 45/1/193: 'list of peers to be written to, and by whom', autumn 1714.
71. GD 45/1/192/3: circular letter, autumn 1714.
72. Clyve Jones, '"Venice Preserv'd; or a Plot Discovered": the Political and Social Context of the Peerage Bill of 1719', in Clyve Jones (ed.), *A Pillar of the Constitution: the House of Lords in British Politics, 1640–1784* (1989), pp. 84–87; Szechi, *Lockhart of Carnwath*, pp. 127–131.
73. GD 45/14/370/3: Eglinton to Harry Maule, 17 Nov. 1714.
74. Ibid.
75. GD 45/1/190: Addresses to George I, [15 Nov.] 1714.
76. RH 2/4/391/40: Montrose to the Lord Provost of Glasgow, Whitehall, 7 Jan. 1715. See also: RH 2/4/391/41–4: Montrose to Lord Advocate Dalrymple and Lord Justice Clerk Cockburn, Whitehall, 7 Jan. 1715.

77. A Nonjuror was someone who refused to *jure*, i.e. take oaths, imposed by the state. At this time all officials, pastors, military men and many others besides were required to take various oaths of loyalty to the crown and the established religious order. Nonjurors refused to do so for religious/ideological reasons.

78. GD 220/5/440/2: Rothes to 'Count Tarriff', Leslie, 7 Dec. 1714; GD 220/5/440/4: Rothes to Montrose, Edinburgh, 18 Dec. 1714; GD 220/5/351/15: Principal John Stirling of Glasgow University to Montrose, [Glasgow], 31 Dec. 1714.

79. GD 220/5/331/14: Lord Justice Clerk Cockburn to Montrose, Edinburgh, 16 Dec. 1714. See also: Loudoun Papers, LO 8687 (lspbox 33): Colin Lindsay, Earl of Balcarres, to Loudoun, 2 Jan. [1715].

80. GD 220/5/454/6: Lord Justice Clerk Cockburn to Montrose, Edinburgh, 11 Jan. 1715.

81. GD 220/5/468/3: Charles Cockburn to Montrose, Edinburgh, 22 Jan. 1715; GD 220/5/453/11: Lord Advocate Dalrymple to Montrose, Edinburgh, 22 Jan. 1715.

82. GD 158/1191/2: Charles Home, Earl of Home, to Patrick Hume, Earl of Marchmont, Hirsell, 7 May 1715; GD 158/1191/4: copy, Marchmont to Home, Redbreas, 8 May 1715; GD 158/1191/6: copy, order from Marchmont as Sheriff to James Winram, Sheriff-Clerk, 9 May 1715; RH 2/4/391/98–9: Montrose to Lord Justice Clerk Cockburn, Whitehall, 9 July 1715.

83. GD 220/5/1895/5, 11: Charles Cockburn to Montrose, Edinburgh, 18 and 21; GD 220/5/434/12: Lord Advocate Dalrymple to Montrose, Edinburgh, 23 Dec. 1714; GD 220/5/440/7a-b: Rothes to Cockburn, Leslie, 25 Dec. 1714; GD 220/5/440/10: [Allan Logan to Sir Peter Halkett, Dec.? 1714].

84. Wodrow Letters VIII, ep. 161: Flint to Wodrow, 21 Dec. 1714.

85. GD 45/14/337/1: Fletcher to Harry Maule of Kellie, London, 1 Feb. 1715.

86. SP 54/8/125: copy, Glengarry to Pollock, 22 Sept. 1715.

87. Moody and Vaughan (eds), *Eighteenth-Century Ireland*, pp. 108–109.

88. BL, Stowe 228, ff. 152v: Gustavus Hamilton to Robethon, 20 Oct. 1715.

89. Moody and Vaughan (eds), *Eighteenth-Century Ireland*, pp. 21, 74, 77.

90. Ibid., pp. 18, 19.

91. D. Szechi and D. Hayton, 'John Bull's Other Kingdoms: the Government of Scotland and Ireland', in C. Jones (ed.), *Britain in the First Age of Party, 1680–1745. Essays Presented to Geoffrey Holmes* (1987), pp. 268–269.

92. Ó Ciardha, *Ireland and the Jacobite Cause*, pp. 117, 167–179.

93. Moody and Vaughan (eds), *Eighteenth-Century Ireland*, pp. 105, 108–109; Ó Ciardha, *Ireland and the Jacobite Cause*, p. 123.

94. BL Add. MS 61636, f. 189: [Dublin], 9 July 1715.

95. Szechi and Hayton, 'John Bull's Other Kingdoms', pp. 271–272; Moody and Vaughan (eds), *Eighteenth-Century Ireland*, p. 109; BL, Stowe 228 (Hanover Papers), vii, ff. 152–153: Gustavus Hamilton to Robethon, 20 Oct. 1715.

96. Nathalie Genet-Rouffiac, 'Jacobites in Paris and Saint-Germain-en-Laye', in Eveline Cruickshanks and Edward Corp (eds), *The Stuart Court in Exile and the Jacobites* (1995), pp. 31–33.

97. Genet-Rouffiac, 'Jacobites in Paris and Saint-Germain-en-Laye', pp. 16–18.

98. Pierre Goubert, *Louis XIV and Twenty Million Frenchmen*, trans. Anne Carter (New York, 1970), pp. 280–282.

99. HMC, *Stuart*, i. 336: Berwick to James, Saint-Germain, 27 Nov. 1714.

100. Ó Ciardha, *Ireland and the Jacobite Cause*, pp. 114–115, 139–150, 157–163.

101. Genet-Rouffiac, 'Jacobites in Paris and Saint-Germain-en-Laye', pp. 16–17; John Davenport (ed.), *Memoirs of the Court of France, From the Year 1684 to the Year 1720 . . . From the Diary of the Marquis de Dangeau* (2 vols, 1825), i. 360: 17 Aug. 1698 and i. 418: 2 Apr. 1700.

102. HMC *Stuart*, i. 336, 337–338, 346–347: Berwick to James, Saint-Germain, 16/27 Nov., 26 Nov./7 Dec. and 28 Nov./9 Dec. 1714 and 25 Jan./5 Feb. 1715.
103. HMC *Stuart*, i. 346–7: Berwick to James, Saint-Germain, 25 Jan./5 Feb. 1715.
104. BL, Stowe 228, f. 184v: John Dalrymple, Earl of Stair, to Robethon, Paris, 19/30 Nov. 1715; HMC *Stuart*, i. 381: James to the commanding officers of the Irish regiments in France and Spain, Bar, 17/28 July 1715; i. 451: Bolingbroke to James, Paris, 22 Oct./2 Nov. 1715; ii. 96–7: Robert Flannagan to Mar, Rouen, 6/17 Apr. 1716; ii. 148: Owen O'Sheridan to Mar, Saint-Germain, 3/14 May 1716; ii. 170: Mar to Dillon, Avignon, 9/20 May 1716; ii. 283: Brigadier Gaydon to Mar, Caen, 5/16 July 1716.
105. Jeremy Black (ed.), *The Origins of War in Early Modern Europe* (Edinburgh, 1987), pp. 1–23.
106. Szechi, *Jacobites*, pp. 87–90.
107. Claude Nordmann, 'Louis XIV and the Jacobites', in Ragnhild Hatton (ed.), *Louis XIV and Europe* (1976), p. 83; François Bluche, *Louis XIV*, trans. Mark Greengrass (New York, 1990), p. 422.
108. Szechi, *Jacobites*, pp. 17–24.
109. Ibid., p. 54.
110. John J. Murray, *George I, the Baltic and the Whig Split of 1717* (1969), pp. 112–114, 146–147, 155–156.
111. John B. Wolf, *Louis XIV* (New York, 1968), p. 618; Goubert, *Louis XIV*, pp. 271–276, 280–282; BL, Stowe 228, ff. 70–71: Stair to Robethon, Paris, 26 July/6 Aug. 1715.
112. L. B. Smith, 'Spain and the Jacobites, 1715–16', in Cruickshanks, *Ideology and Conspiracy*, pp. 159–160; Simon Harcourt-Smith, *Alberoni, or, the Spanish Conspiracy* (1943), pp. 130–133.
113. G. S. Macquoid, *Jacobite Songs and Ballads* (1887), p. 110.
114. Szechi, *Jacobites*, pp. 104–105.
115. AECP 266, ff. 262r–267v: d'Iberville to Louis XIV, London, 17/28 Feb. 1715.
116. Paul S. Fritz, *The English Ministers and Jacobitism between the Rebellions of 1715 and 1745* (Toronto, 1975), pp. 8–19.
117. Ibid., p. 10.
118. David Bayne Horn, *Great Britain and Europe in the Eighteenth Century* (Oxford, 1967), pp. 115, 117.
119. Murray, *George I, the Baltic and the Whig Split*, pp. 117–160.
120. Geoffrey Holmes, *The Trial of Dr Sacheverell* (1973).
121. Cruickshanks *et al.* (eds), *House of Commons, 1690–1715*, iii. 20–22.

Chapter 3 'What Force or Guile Could not Subdue': the Jacobites in 1715

1. Baynes, *Jacobite Rising*, p. 36; Laing and Macknight (eds), *Memoirs of the Insurrection*, p. 36; SP 54/8/85: Solicitor-General Sir James Steuart of Goodtrees to [Under-Secretary Robert Pringle], Edinburgh, 23 Sept. 1715; GD 220/5/1919/2: Hope to Montrose, Kinross, 26 Feb. 1716.
2. GD 18/2099, p. 19: Baron John Clerk of Penicuik's notes for a book on the '15. I am indebted to Dr Martin Rackwitz for pointing out this manuscript to me. See also: SP 54/7/71b: Solicitor-General Steuart to [Under-Secretary Pringle], Edinburgh, 25 Aug. 1715; Thomas Constable (ed.), *A Fragment of a Memoir of Field-Marshall James Keith, Written by Himself. 1714–1734* (Spalding Club, Edinburgh, 1843), p. 13.

3. SP 54/8/34: intelligence from Dundee, Dundee, 9 Sept. 1715; SP 54/8/74c: intelligence from Perth, Stirling, 18 Sept. 1715; SP 54/9/3b: 'A Letter from a Gentleman in the Earl of Mar's Camp to his Friend in the West Country', 1 Oct. 1715.
4. J. S. Gibson, *Playing the Jacobite Card. The Franco-Jacobite Invasion of 1708* (Edinburgh, 1988), *passim*; RH 2/4/301/12: Major-General Joseph Wightman to [Argyll?], Edinburgh, 9 June 1713.
5. Monod, *Jacobitism and the English People*, pp. 179–193.
6. Gregg, 'Mar', pp. 179–181; Colley, *In Defiance of Oligarchy*, pp. 177–187.
7. GD 27/6/7/19: [Montrose to Colonel Cornelius Kennedy], Edinburgh, 1 Mar. 1715. See also: BL, Add. MS 37993, f. 3v: Patrick Hume, Lord Polwarth, to Lord Justice Clerk Cockburn, Redbreas, 17 Sept. 1715; BL, Stowe 228, f. 121r: Gustavus Hamilton to Robethon, Dublin, 24 Sept. 1715; William Fraser (ed.), *The Chiefs of Grant* (2 vols, Edinburgh, 1883), ii. 102: Daniel Mackenzie, minister of Aberlour to Brigadier Alexander Grant of Grant, Aberlour, 25 May 1716.
8. SP 54/7/95: President Dalrymple to Under-Secretary Pringle, 31 Aug. 1715.
9. Corp, *Court in Exile*, pp. 284–285, 290–291, 294–296.
10. Daniel Szechi, 'The Jacobite Revolution Settlement, 1689–1696', *English Historical Review*, cviii (1993), 610–628.
11. Edward Gregg, 'France, Rome and the Exiled Stuarts, 1689–1713', in Corp, *Court in Exile*, pp. 60–61.
12. Szechi, *Jacobitism and Tory Politics*, pp. 20–23.
13. Corp, *Court in Exile*, pp. 287, 289; *Memoirs of the Life of Simon Lord Lovat; Written by Himself, in the French Language* (1797), pp. 446–447.
14. Petrie, *Berwick*, pp. 291–292, 299–300, 301–303; AECP 263, ff. 76r–79r: [James to Torcy], Plombieres, 18/29 Sept. 1714 ns; BL, Add. MS 31259, f. 85r: David Nairne to Cardinal Filippo Antonio Gualterio, Protector of England, Bar, 22 Oct./2 Nov. 1714.
15. Petrie, *Berwick*, pp. 304–306; Corp, *Court in Exile*, pp. 294, 304.
16. Dickinson, *Bolingbroke* (1970), pp. 137–140.
17. Corp, *Court in Exile*, p. 295; AECP 263, ff. 89r–91r: Lewis Innes to [Torcy], Bar, 23 Sept./4 Oct. 1714 ns; Add. MS 31259, ff. 67–68: Nairne to Gualterio, Luneville, 17/28 Aug. 1714.
18. Corp, *Court in Exile*, pp. 76–157, 180–234.
19. Monod, *Jacobitism and the English People*, pp. 138–145.
20. Daniel Szechi, 'The Jacobite Movement', in Dickinson, *Companion to Eighteenth-Century Britain*, pp. 84–87.
21. Szechi, *Jacobitism and Tory Politics*, *passim*.
22. Cruickshanks *et al.* (eds), *House of Commons, 1690–1715*, iii. 954–955.
23. Colley, *In Defiance of Oligarchy*, pp. 53–60. Cf. Sedgwick (ed.), *The House of Commons, 1715–1754*, i. 62.
24. Szechi, 'Jacobite Revolution Settlement', pp. 620–628; Szechi, *Jacobitism and Tory Politics*, pp. 182–191.
25. *Burt's Letters*, i. 222, 223–224, 224–225; Hayton, *Introductory Survey*, i. 520–521.
26. See above, pp. 21–25.
27. Macinnes, *Clanship, Commerce and the House of Stuart*, pp. 248–249.
28. Gibson, *Playing the Scottish Card*, pp. 93–105.
29. BL, Add. MS 31259, ff. 100–101: Nairne to Gualterio, Bar, 3/14 Dec. 1714; Stuart Erskine (ed.), 'The Earl of Mar's Legacies to Scotland and to his son Lord Erskine 1722–1727', in *Wariston's Diary and Other Papers* (Scottish History Society, 1st ser. xxvi, 1896), p. 170.
30. See above, pp. 25–27.

31. Add. MS 61636. Blenheim Papers Vol. DXXXVI, f. 191v: Budgell to Addison, [Dublin], 28 July 1715.
32. Szechi, 'Jacobite Movement', pp. 89–91, 93.
33. Bodleian Library, Carte 256, p. 25: Middleton to the Earl of Mountcashell, Saint-Germain, 5/15 June 1693; Ó'Ciardha, *Ireland and the Jacobite Cause*, p. 137.
34. Szechi, *Lockhart of Carnwath*, pp. 40, 197–211; E. Charteris (ed.), *A Short Account of the Affairs of Scotland in the Years 1744, 1745, 1746. By David, Lord Elcho* (Edinburgh, 1907), pp. 1–46.
35. For examples of this see: J. C. D. Clark, *Samuel Johnson. Literature, Religion and English Cultural Politics from the Restoration to Romanticism* (Cambridge, 1994), p. 92, re: William Murray, Lord Mansfield; Lenman, *Jacobite Risings*, pp. 73–74, 145, 238, 275, re: Simon Fraser, Lord Lovat.
36. Black, *Eighteenth Century Europe*, pp. 173–174.
37. See for example: Benjamin Hoadly, *The Happiness of the Present Establishment and the Unhappiness of Absolute Monarchy* (1708), pp. 7–10, 15, 16; [Anon.], *A Letter to the Patriot, Relating to the Pretender, and the Growth of Popery in the City of York and Other Parts of Great Britain* (1714), pp. 1–8.
38. Dickinson, *Liberty and Property*, pp. 35–42, 70–79.
39. Bodleian Library, Carte 181, f. 629v: John, Jacobite Lord Caryll, to James Drummond, Earl of Perth, [Saint-Germain], 21/31 Oct. 1695; BL, Add. MS 31259, f. 73: Nairne to Gualterio, Plombieres, 8/19 Sept. 1714.
40. Szechi, *Jacobitism and Tory Politics*, pp. 42–44.
41. University of Aberdeen, MS 2740 (Pitsligo Papers)/18/1/14 (5).
42. Szechi, 'Jacobite Movement', pp. 84–93. And see, for example, Laing and Macknight (eds), *Memoirs of the Insurrection*, pp. 371–372; A. Aufrere (ed.), *The Lockhart Papers* (2 vols, 1817), i. 22–23, 24–25; GD 259/2/31: William Scott to [Patrick] Scott Jr of Ancrum, Marshalsea, 27 Dec. 1715; GD 241/380/22: public address of William, Marquess of Tullibardine, to the men of Atholl, Logiereat, 19 Nov. 1715.
43. W. E. Buckley (ed.), *Memoirs of Thomas, Earl of Ailesbury. Written by Himself* (2 vols, Edinburgh, Roxburghe Club, 1890), ii. 711.
44. Dickinson, *Liberty and Property*, pp. 50–56.
45. Patten, *History of the Rebellion*, A4r; *A Faithful Register of the Late Rebellion* (1718), pp. 323–324.
46. Bodleian Library, Carte 256, p. 25: Middleton to the Earl of Mountcashell, Saint-Germain, 5/15 June 1693; Aufrere (ed.), *Lockhart Papers*, i. 427.
47. RH 2/4/306/63b: proclamation of James III placed on Hexham market cross by Forster's rebels [19 Oct. 1715].
48. Ó Ciardha, *Ireland and the Jacobite Cause*, pp. 65–67.
49. Moody *et al.* (eds), *Early Modern Ireland*, p. 489.
50. Hopkins, *Glencoe*, pp. 120–286, 292–301, 310–317, 321–322.
51. Pittock, *Myth of the Jacobite Clans*, p. 47.
52. Patten, *History of the Rebellion*, p. 175.
53. W. D. Macray (ed.), *Correspondence of Colonel N. Hooke, Agent from the Court of France to the Scottish Jacobites in the Years 1703–1707* (2 vols, Roxburghe Club, Edinburgh, 1870), ii. 333–335; SP 54/9/3b: 'A Letter from a Gentleman in the Earl of Mar's Camp to his Friend in the West Country', 1 Oct. 1715.
54. Lenman, *Jacobite Risings*, p. 87; Murray Pittock, *Scottish Nationality* (2001), pp. 64–65; Szechi, *Lockhart of Carnwath*, pp. 208–211.
55. Buckley (ed.), *Memoirs of Thomas, Earl of Ailesbury*, i. 268. See also: i. 251, 253; John Buchanan-Brown (ed.), *The Remains of Thomas Hearne. Reliquiae Hearnianae* (reprint

of 1869 edn, Carbondale, 1966), p. 306: 15 Aug. 1726; 'The Earl of Mar's Legacies', pp. 164–165, 166, 187.

56. McLynn, *The Jacobites* , p. 152.

57. Ibid., pp. 64–65.

58. Diarmaid MacCulloch, *Reformation. Europe's House Divided 1490–1700* (Penguin edn, 2004), pp. 554–555; Bodleian Library, Carte 181, f. 626v: Caryll to Perth, [Saint-Germain] 1/12 Sept. 1695; G. D. Henderson (ed.), *Mystics of the North-East* (Third Spalding Club, Aberdeen, 1934), pp. 115–118: Dr James Keith to James Ogilvy, Lord Deskford, [London], 13 Dec. 1715

59. *The Age of Wonders* (1710), pp. 2–3.

60. Bodleian Library, Carte 181, f. 629v: Caryll to Perth, [Saint-Germain], 20/31 Oct. 1695; Henderson (ed.), *Mystics of the North-East*, pp. 74–75: Keith to Deskford, London, 10 Oct. 1713.

61. AECP 265, f. 97r: d'Iberville to Torcy, London, 15/26 Mar. 1715. See also: AECP 271, ff. 108v–109r: d'Iberville to d'Huxelles, London, 17/28 Nov. 1715; SP 54/8/110: Islay to Townshend, Edinburgh, 27 Sept. 1715; RH 2/4/307/80: Lord Advocate Dalrymple to Stanhope, Edinburgh, 25 Nov. 1715.

62. See, for example, SP 35/1, f. 24; AECP 266, ff. 110r: d'Iberville to Louis XIV, London, 21 Jan./1 Feb. 1715.

63. Westminster Diocesan Archives, London, Old Brotherhood MSS, III pt 3, ep. 260: Edward Hales to [Middleton?], 17 July 1705.

64. Martin Haile, *Queen Mary of Modena. Her Life and Letters* (1905), 444, 446; Scottish Catholic Archives, Edinburgh, Blairs Letters 2/124/11: James Carnegy to the Scots College, Paris, [Edinburgh] 19 Mar. 1706; Blairs Letters 2/192/9: Thomas Innes to Walter Stuart, [Paris], 5/16 July 1714.

65. Blairs Letters 2/134/3: Bishop William Nicolson to Thomas Innes, [Edinburgh?], 17 Aug. 1706.

66. H. Schwartz, *The French Prophets. The History of a Millenarian Group in Eighteenth-Century England* (1980), pp. 156–162; T. McCrie (ed.), *The Correspondence of the Rev. Robert Wodrow* (3 vols, Wodrow Society, Edinburgh, 1862), i. 169–170: Wodrow to Jas Webster, 20 Sept. 1710.

67. Henderson (ed.), *Mystics of the North-East*, p. 214.

68. Westminster Diocesan Archives, London, Ep. Var. V, ep. 85: John Ingleton to Laurence Mayes, Bar, 1/12 Feb. 1715. See also: AECP 266, ff. 198r: d'Iberville to Torcy, London, 3/14 Feb. 1715.

69. AECP 267, f. 69v: d'Iberville to Torcy, London, 3/14 Mar. 1715.

70. GD 18/2092/4: Sir John's journal for Apr. 1712–1715: 22 Apr. 1715; John Doran, *London in the Jacobite Times* (2 vols, 1877), i. 68; BL, Add. MS 29981, ff. 95–96: *Verses Fixt on King James the 2nd's Statue in Time of the Great Eclipse, April the 22nd 1715*; f. 97r: *On the Eclipse. Found in the King's Bench Walks in the Temple.*

71. Andrew Schethrum, *The Northumberland Prophecy: With an Introduction and a Postscript* (1715), p. 6.

72. W. A. Speck, 'Conflict in Society', in G. S. Holmes (ed.), *Britain after the Glorious Revolution, 1689–1714* (1969, repr. 1978), pp. 135–152; Paul Monod, 'The Politics of Matrimony: Jacobitism and Marriage in Eighteenth-Century England', in E. Cruickshanks and J. Black (eds), *The Jacobite Challenge* (Edinburgh, 1988), pp. 24–37; Moody and Vaughan (eds), *Eighteenth-Century Ireland*, pp. 37–39; Sankey and Szechi, 'Elite Culture', pp. 103–105.

73. [H. R. Duff (ed.)], *Culloden Papers: Comprising an Extensive and Interesting Correspondence From the Year 1625 to 1748* (1815), 37: 'J. B. Munro' of Foulis to John Forbes of Culloden, Foulis, 17 Feb. 1715.

74. Szechi, *Jacobitism and Tory Politics*, p. 41.
75. Edward Gregg, 'Was Queen Anne a Jacobite?', *History*, lvii (1972), 358–375.
76. AECP 265, f. 36v: d'Iberville to Torcy, London, 20/31 July 1714; Westminster Diocesan Archive, London, Ep. Var. V, ep. 79: Ingleton to Mayes, Bar, 27 Nov./7 Dec. 1714; Monod, *Jacobitism and the English People*, pp. 173–179.
77. AECP 265, ff. 51v: d'Iberville to Torcy, London, 20/31 Oct. 1714.
78. Westminster Diocesan Archives, London, Ep. Var. V, ep. 78: Edward Dicconson to Mayes [1714/15].
79. AECP 266, ff. 90v, 198r, 264v: d'Iberville to Torcy, London, 16/27 Jan. and 3/14 and 17/28 Feb. 1715; AECP 267, ff. 39rv: d'Iberville to Louis XIV, London, 25–27 Feb./8–10 Mar. 1715.
80. AECP 266, ff. 262rv: d'Iberville to Louis XIV, London, 17/28 Feb. 1715.
81. Monod, *Jacobitism and the English People*, pp. 179–192.
82. [Duff (ed.)], *Culloden Papers*, p. 38: John Forbes to Duncan Forbes, London, 30 Apr. 1715.
83. SP 35/3, f. 199v: 'Philopoliteius' to Townshend, Oxford, 26 July 1715; Addy and McNiven (eds), *Diary of Henry Prescott*, ii. 445: 3 June 1715.
84. Rogers, 'Riot and Popular Jacobitism', pp. 72, 80; AECP 269, f. 110v: d'Iberville to Louis XIV, London, 27–30 June/8–11 July 1715.
85. Duncan Warrand (ed.), *More Culloden Papers* (5 vols, Inverness, 1923), ii. 79: John Forbes to Jean Forbes, London, 30 July 1715; AECP 269, f. 324v: d'Iberville to Torcy, London, 12/23 Aug. 1715.
86. GD 18/6080, p. 183.
87. Blairs Letters 2/159/6: Carnegy to the Scots College, [Edinburgh?], 24 Nov. 1709.
88. Laing and Macknight (eds), *Memoirs of the Insurrection*, p. 3.
89. Wodrow, *Analecta*, i. 286: 1710.
90. Szechi, *Jacobitism and Tory Politics*, pp. 86–87, 110–113.
91. Blairs Letters 2/173/12: Carnegy to the Scots College, [Edinburgh?], 14 June 1712.
92. RH 2/4/300/73: Sir Robert Blackwood, Provost of Edinburgh, to William Legge, Earl of Dartmouth, Edinburgh, 12 June 1712.
93. RH 2/4/301/12: Wightman to [Argyll?], Edinburgh, 9 June 1713.
94. Wodrow, *Analecta*, ii. 221: 1713.
95. Cruickshanks *et al.*, *House of Commons, 1690–1715*, ii. 853, 877–878; Laing and Macknight (eds), *Memoirs of the Insurrection*, pp. 9–10.
96. Laing and Macknight (eds), *Memoirs of the Insurrection*, p. 9.
97. Erskine (ed.), 'The Earl of Mar's Legacies', p. 163.
98. Blairs Letters 2/188/3: Carnegy to the Scots College, [Edinburgh?], 19 Jan. 1714.
99. RH 2/4/299/53: proclamation of a fast by the General Assembly of the Kirk, Edinburgh, 6 May 1710; McCrie (ed.), *Correspondence of the Rev. Robert Wodrow*, i. 169–170: Wodrow to Webster, 20 Sept. 1710; Wodrow, *Analecta*, i. 286: 1710.
100. Szechi, *Jacobitism and Tory Politics*, pp. 110–112; RH 2/4/300/58: Addresses to Queen Anne from the Commission of the Kirk, Edinburgh, 5 and 27 Mar. 1712.
101. GD 18/2092/4: Sir John's journal for Apr. 1712–1715, 19 Apr. and 18 May 1712.
102. Blairs Letters 2/173/19: Carnegy to the Scots College, [Edinburgh?], 11 Oct. 1712.
103. *Blackader*, p. 445.
104. Wodrow, *Analecta*, ii. 225: 1713.
105. Blairs Letters 2/188/2: Carnegy to the Scots College, [Edinburgh?], 5 Jan. 1714.
106. RH 2/4/390/1/37: Mar to Messrs Wisheart, Carstairs and Mitchel, Whitehall, 27 Mar. 1714.

107. SP 54/7/31: Provost of Perth to [Under-Secretary Pringle], Perth, 10 Aug. 1715; SP 54/8/52: Lord Advocate Dalrymple to Stanhope, [Edinburgh] 12 Sept. 1715; GD 18/2092/5: Sir John Clerk of Penicuik's spiritual journal for 1716, 6 Mar. and 23 May 1716; Moody-Stuart, 'Lieutenant-Colonel James Steuart', pp. 11–12; GD 124/13/68/1, 4, 5: papers relating to arming in 1714; Laing and Macknight (eds), *Memoirs of the Insurrection*, p. 52.

108. Add. MS 33273, ff. 265–266: Wightman to Webb, 27 Apr. 1714; BL 2/188/2, 4, 5: Carnegy to the Scots College, [Edinburgh?], 5 Jan. and 9 and 11 Feb. 1714; Warrand (ed.), *More Culloden Papers*, ii. 37: Duncan Forbes to John Forbes, [Edinburgh], 28 Jan. 1714; AECP 265, ff. 32v–33r: d'Iberville to Torcy, London, 2/13 July 1714; AECP 263, f. 6v: 'A Londres', 23 Aug./3 Sept. 1714; RH 2/4/390/1/60–61: Mar to the Lords of Justiciary of Scotland, Whitehall, 16 Aug. 1714.

109. AECP 265, f. 36v: d'Iberville to Torcy, London, 20/31 July 1714.

110. NLS, Wodrow Papers, Quarto VIII, ep. 132: L. C. Erskine to Wodrow, Edinburgh, 25 Sept. 1714.

111. GD 220/357/3: John Haldane of Gleneagles to Montrose, Gleneagles, 28 Oct. 1714.

112. [Duff (ed.)], *Culloden Papers*, 29–30: Anon. to Duncan Forbes, Culloden, 28 Aug. 1714.

113. *Edinburgh Gazette*, no. 50: 7–9 Sept. 1714.

114. Allardyce (ed.), *Historical Papers Relating to the Jacobite Period*, i. 28: Mar to the magistrates of Aberdeen, Whitehall, 21 Aug. 1714.

115. Cf. Carlton, *Going to the Wars*, pp. 211–212, 340.

116. Michael, *Beginnings of the Hanoverian Dynasty*, pp. 89–103. Cf. Hatton, *George I*, pp. 126–127.

117. GD 18/2092/4: Sir John's journal for Apr. 1712–1715: 29 Sept. 1714.

118. Steuart *Newsletters*, p. 12 [Edinburgh, autumn 1714].

119. GD 124/15/1143/2: Harry Maule to the Lord Justice Clerk, 28 Sept. 1714.

120. GD 220/357/3: John Haldane of Gleneagles to Montrose, Gleneagles, 28 Oct. 1714.

121. [Duff (ed.)], *Culloden Papers*, 34: John Forbes to Duncan Forbes, Culloden, 18 Dec. 1714.

122. *Blackader*, p. 453: 29 Dec. [1714].

123. Warrand (ed.), *More Culloden Papers*, ii. 50: John Forbes to Duncan Forbes, Culloden, 26 Nov. 1714.

124. GD 27/6/7/21: [Montrose and Graham of Gorthie to Cornelius Kennedy], Edinburgh, 3 Mar. 1715.

125. [Duff (ed.)], *Culloden Papers*, 33–4: John Forbes to Duncan Forbes, Culloden, 18 Dec. 1714; Warrand (ed.), *More Culloden Papers*, ii. 57–58: John Forbes to Duncan Forbes, Culloden, 14 Jan. 1715; GD 220/5/454/11: Lord Justice Clerk Cockburn to Montrose, Edinburgh, 29 Jan. 1715; J. Murray Graham, *The Annals and Correspondence of the Viscount and the First and Second Earls of Stair* (2 vols, Edinburgh, 1875), i. 275: Montrose to Stair, Feb. 1715.

126. Steuart *Newsletters*, p. 13: Edinburgh, 26 Jan. 1715.

127. See pp. 42–43.

128. GD 259/2/31: William Scott to [Patrick] Scott of Ancrum, Marshalsea, 27 Dec. 1715.

129. GD 18/3152/21: Baron John Clerk to Sir John Clerk of Penicuik, Edinburgh, 7 Aug. 1714; GD 27/6/10: Anon. to Lord Advocate Thomas Kennedy of Dalquharran, 'Coll', 28 Aug. 1714; Wodrow, *Analecta*, ii. 296: 1714; RH 2/4/390/1/73: Mar to Lieutenant-General James Maitland, Whitehall, 9 Sept. 1714; Warrand (ed.), *More Culloden Papers*, ii. 44–45: R. Gordon to John Forbes, Edinburgh, 16 Sept. 1714; and ii. 57: John Forbes to Duncan Forbes, Culloden, 14 Jan. 1715; [Duff (ed.)], *Culloden Papers*, 34: John Forbes to Duncan Forbes, Culloden, 18 Dec. 1714.

130. Graham, *Annals and Correspondence of . . . of Stair*, i. 275: Montrose to Stair, Feb. 1715.
131. GD 220/5/331/14: Lord Justice Clerk Cockburn to Montrose, Edinburgh, 16 Dec. 1714.
132. Warrand (ed.), *More Culloden Papers*, ii. 46: Duncan Forbes to John Forbes, Edinburgh, 16 Nov. 1714; GD 18/2099: Baron John Clerk's account of a journey to Perth, researching 1715, 1717, p. 20.
133. See pp. 35–36, 41–43, 71–73.
134. GD 18/3152/21: Baron John Clerk to Sir John Clerk, Edinburgh, 7 Aug. 1714; Wodrow, *Analecta*, ii. 296: 1714; RH 2/4/390/1/73: Mar to Lieutenant-General Maitland, Whitehall, 9 Sept. 1714; Warrand (ed.), *More Culloden Papers*, ii. 57: John Forbes to Duncan Forbes, Culloden, 14 Jan. 1715; GD 220/5/454/11: Lord Justice Clerk Cockburn to Montrose, Edinburgh, 29 Jan. 1715; Graham, *Annals and Correspondence of . . . Stair*, i. 275: Montrose to Stair, Feb. 1715; GD 27/6/7/13, 17: [Montrose to Cornelius Kennedy], Durham and Edinburgh, 4 and 19 Feb. 1715; [Duff (ed.)], *Culloden Papers*, 37: 'J. B. Munro' of Foulis to John Forbes of Culloden, Foulis, 17 Feb. 1715; Add. MS 38507, ff. 129–130: Montrose to Townshend, Edinburgh, 3 Mar. 1715.
135. GD 220/5/468/17: Charles Cockburn to Montrose, Edinburgh, 6 June 1715.
136. GD 220/5/455/4: anonymous account of 10 June, Aberdeen, 13 June 1715; Warrand (ed.), *More Culloden Papers*, ii. 77–78: Robert Baillie to John Forbes, Inverness, 22 July 1715.
137. SP 54/7/22: ['Mr Orr'] to ?, Inverness, 6 Aug. 1715; SP 54/7/35b: Sir Peter Fraser to Lord Justice Clerk Cockburn, Durres, 8 Aug. 1715.
138. Laing and Macknight (eds), *Memoirs of the Insurrection*, p. 20.
139. Ibid., p. 36; SP 54/7/79b: Lord Justice Clerk Cockburn to [Stanhope], Edinburgh, 26 Aug. 1715; SP 54/7/85a: Alexander Wedderburn and Charles Hamilton to the Commissioners of the Excise, Dundee, 27 Aug. 1715; SP 54/8/64: Solicitor-General Steuart to [Stanhope], Edinburgh, 15 Sept. 1715.
140. Wodrow, *Analecta*, ii. 359: 6 Feb. 1722.
141. Laing and Macknight (eds), *Memoirs of the Insurrection*, p. 23. See also: GD 220/5/645: Colonel Charles Cathcart to Montrose, Aberdeen, 14 Feb. 1716; GD 220/5/654: Alexander Rose, Bishop of Edinburgh, to Montrose, Edinburgh, 23 Feb. 1716; GD 220/5/655: Lord Charles Ker to Montrose, Edinburgh, 23 Feb. 1716.
142. Laing and Macknight (eds), *Memoirs of the Insurrection*, p. 43.
143. BL, Add. MS 61632, f. 141r: John, Master of Sinclair, to Sunderland, [Liège or Aix la Chapelle, post-1715].
144. GD 220/5/642/1: David Smythe of Methven to Montrose, Aberdeen, 12 Feb. 1716. See also: GD 220/5/662: Colonel Alexander Urquhart of Newhall to Montrose, [Feb. 1716].
145. SP 54/7/35b: Sir Peter Fraser to Lord Justice Clerk Cockburn, Durres, 8 Aug. 1715; Laing and Macknight (eds), *Memoirs of the Insurrection*, p. 38.
146. Laing and Macknight (eds), *Memoirs of the Insurrection*, p. 41.
147. Ibid., p. 17.
148. Ibid., pp. 16, 18, 25, 34, 41; Constable (ed.), *Fragment of a Memoir*, p. 11.
149. Macray (ed.), *Correspondence of Colonel N. Hooke*, ii. 310, 311: information from the Duchess of Gordon, 23 May/3 June 1707; Aufrere (ed.), *Lockhart Papers*, i. 197–198, 224–226; Blairs Letters 2/192/9: Thomas Innes to Walter Stuart, [Paris], 5/16 July 1714; AECP 270, f. 220v: d'Iberville to Huxelles, London, 9/20 Oct. 1715. I am pleased to find myself in agreement here with Dr Jeffrey Stephen, who was so kind as to allow me to see the relevant chapter of his Ph.D. thesis ('Scottish Presbyterians and

Anglo-Scottish Union, 1707', Aberdeen, 2004, pp. 281–329), which it is to be hoped will soon be in print.

150. Szechi, *Jacobites*, p. 57; AECP 268, f. 329v: d'Iberville to [Torcy], London, 8/19 June 1715.

151. GD 27/6/10: Anon. to Lord Advocate Kennedy, 'Coll:', 28 Aug. 1714.

152. GD 220/5/455/26: Lord Justice Cockburn to Montrose, Edinburgh, 19 July 1715.

153. SP 54/7/20: George Monro to ?, 5 Aug. 1715.

154. Laing and Macknight (eds), *Memoirs of the Insurrection*, p. 20.

155. AECP 268, f. 329v: d'Iberville to [Torcy], London, 8/19 June 1715.

156. SP 54/7/94a: Lord Justice Clerk Cockburn to Townshend, Edinburgh, 30 Aug. 1715; SP 54/8/2a: Lord Justice Clerk Cockburn to [Stanhope], Edinburgh, 1 Sept. 1715; BL, Stowe 228, f. 123r: Charles Dubourgay to Robethon, Stirling, 24 Sept. 1715; AECP 269, f. 324v: d'Iberville to Torcy, London, 12/23 Aug. 1715; SP 35/4, f. 48: Charles Paulet, Duke of Bolton, to Townshend, Dorset, Aug. 1715.

157. SP 54/7/73: Lord Justice Clerk Cockburn to [Under-Secretary Pringle], Edinburgh, 25 Aug. 1715.

158. Laing and Macknight (eds), *Memoirs of the Insurrection*, p. 25. Not all Scots Jacobites were so sanguine: Major-General George Hamilton, like the Master of Sinclair, advocated abandoning the rebellion at this point (ibid., p. 32).

159. GD 18/2099: Baron John Clerk's account of a journey to Perth, researching 1715, 1717, p. 20.

160. [Duff (ed.)], *Culloden Papers*, 37: 'J. B. Munro' of Foulis to John Forbes of Culloden, Foulis, 17 Feb. 1715.

161. GD 220/5/468/19: Charles Cockburn to Montrose, Edinburgh, 9 July 1715.

162. SP 54/8/64: to [Stanhope], Edinburgh, 15 Sept. 1715. See also: SP 54/8/29b: Lord Justice Clerk Cockburn to Under-Secretary Pringle, Edinburgh, 8 Sept. 1715.; SP 78/160, f. 136v: Stanhope to Stair, Whitehall, 31 Oct. 1715.

Chapter 4 'That Treason Thus Could Sell Us': the Jacobite Conspiracy of 1715

1. Corp, *Court in Exile*, pp. 76–256, *passim*.

2. Szechi, *Jacobites*, pp. 53–57.

3. Ibid., pp. 83–87.

4. J. R. Jones, *The Revolution of 1688 in England* (1972), pp. 288–310.

5. Szechi, *Jacobites*, pp. 55–56.

6. George Hilton Jones, *The Mainstream of Jacobitism* (Cambridge, Mass., 1954), pp. 51–60.

7. Gibson, *Playing the Scottish Card*, pp. 14–19, 93–131.

8. Szechi, *Jacobitism and Tory Politics*, pp. 18–19; Bodleian, Carte 180, f. 227: response to a new Scots project (proposed answer), Apr. 1709; Macray (ed.), *Hooke*, ii. 539–558.

9. Szechi, *Jacobitism and Tory Politics*, pp. 182–191.

10. HMC *Stuart*, i. 282–283: Berwick to James, 10/21 Nov. 1713; AECP 250, ff. 86–87: Torcy to James, 10/21 Nov 1713.

11. HMC *Stuart*, i. 284–285: Berwick to James, 1/12 Dec. 1713; i. 305–306: Berwick to James, 21 Feb./4 Mar. 1714.

12. AECP 262, ff. 344–346: Torcy to James, 1/12 Aug. 1714. That the French were serious about trying to make this potential Jacobite sortie viable may be seen from: SP 35/2, f. 97: petition for mercy by Captain Alexander Dalzeel [undated].

13. Szechi, *Jacobitism and Tory Politics*, p. 19.

14. William Mackay, 'The Camerons in the Rising of 1715: a Vindication by Their Leader, John Cameron, Younger of Lochiel', *Transactions of the Gaelic Society of Inverness* (1909), p. 9; Laing and Macknight (eds), *Memoirs of the Insurrection*, p. 91.
15. HMC *Stuart*, i. 284: Berwick to James, 29 Nov./10 Dec. 1713; i. 287–288: Berwick to James, 13/24 Dec. 1713.
16. *Diary of Mary Countess Cowper, Lady of the Bedchamber to the Princess of Wales 1714–1720* (1864), p. 83.
17. HMC *Stuart*, i. 310, 310–311, 311–312: Berwick to James, 16/27, 17/28 Mar. and 21 Mar./1 Apr. 1714.
18. RH 2/4/390/28: petition by Alexander Macdonald of 'Bracklet' in Glencoe to Mar [1714]; Blairs Letters 2/188/3: Carnegy to the Scots College, [Edinburgh?], 19 Jan. 1714; Laing and Macknight (eds), *Memoirs of the Insurrection*, pp. 70–71.
19. Laing and Macknight (eds), *Memoirs of the Insurrection*, pp. 11–12. Mar responded in similar vein when sounded out about a rebellion after the death of Queen Anne by some Stirlingshire Jacobites: ibid., pp. 70–71.
20. Ibid., p. 12.
21. Constable (ed.), *Fragment of a Memoir*, pp. 5–6.
22. BL, Add. MS 38851, f. 62r: Sir John Fisher's [Forrester's] instructions, 20 Oct. 1714.
23. SP 78/159, ff. 79v–80v: Matthew Prior to Bolingbroke, Paris, 12/23 Aug. 1714.
24. BL, Add. MS 31259, ff. 67r–v: Nairne to Gualterio, Luneville, 17/28 Aug. 1714.
25. SP 35/1, f. 100: Plombieres, 18/29 Aug. 1714.
26. GD 27/6/14: Hugh Rose of Kilravock to John Forbes of Culloden, 27 Aug. [1714]; Mackay, 'Camerons in the Rising of 1715', p. 9.
27. HMC *Stuart*, i. 349: Berwick to James, Saint-Germain, 11/22 Feb. 1715.
28. Bodleian, MS Carte 211, f. 320: 'disbursement of 4,000ll sterling carryd to Scotland'; Add. MS 31259, f. 100v: Nairne to Gualterio, Bar, 3/14 Dec. 1714; GD 220/5/454/36: Lord Justice Clerk Cockburn to Montrose, Edinburgh, 6 May 1715.
29. BL, Add. MS 38851, f. 62v: Sir John Fisher's [Forrester's] instructions, 20 Oct. 1714.
30. BL, Add. MS 31259, f. 81v: Nairne to Gualterio, Bar, 8/19 Oct. 1714; Add. MS 38851, f. 62v: Sir John Fisher's [Forrester's] instructions, 20 Oct. 1714.
31. HMC *Stuart*, i. 349: Berwick to James, Saint-Germain, 11/22 Feb. 1715.
32. HMC *Stuart*, i. 336–337: Berwick to James, 17/28 Nov. 1714.
33. See for example: Macray (ed.), *Hooke*, ii. 34–35: 'Mr Fleming's English memoire, which he gave to the queen in the beginning of February 1706'; ii. 541: 'Reponses aux questions proposées touchant l'Ecosse', 14/25 Jan. 1710;
34. AECP 263, f. 412v: d'Iberville to [Torcy], London, 12/23 Dec. 1714; AECP 266, f. 36r: d'Iberville to Louis XIV, London, 3/14 Jan. 1715.
35. AECP 266, f. 90v: d'Iberville to Torcy, London, 16/27 Jan. 1715.
36. AECP 264, ff. 288r–309v: [Jérome Phélypeaux, comte de Pontchartrain?] to Torcy, [Paris?, late] 1714.
37. AECP 267, f. 75v: Torcy to d'Iberville, Versailles, 28 Feb./11 Mar. 1715.
38. AECP 266, f. 274: Torcy to d'Iberville, Versailles, 22 Feb./5 Mar. 1715.
39. HMC *Stuart*, i. 347, 348: Berwick to James, Saint-Germain, 1/12 and 6/17 Feb. 1715. An undated memorandum from the Jacobite court may also date from this period: AECP 263, ff. 440–441 [James to Torcy].
40. HMC *Stuart*, i. 349: Berwick to James, Saint-Germain, 11/22 Feb. 1715.
41. HMC *Stuart*, i. 349, 350, 353: Berwick to James, Saint-Germain, 11/22 Feb., 21 Feb./4 Mar. and 4/15 Mar. 1715; i. 352–353: James to Ormond, [Bar], 2/13 Mar. 1715; i. 361: James to Berwick, Bar, 13/24 Apr. 1715.
42. Szechi, *Jacobitism and Tory Politics*, pp. 39–40, 182–191.

43. HMC *Stuart*, i. 357: Berwick to James, Saint-Germain, 3/14 Apr. 1715.; BL, Add. MS 61636, f. 175v: Anon. to Dean Jonathan Swift, London, 3 May 1715.
44. Cruickshanks *et al.*, *House of Commons 1690–1715*, iii. 954–955; iv. 79–83; v. 941–943; HMC *Stuart*, i. 391: Bolingbroke to Torcy, 3/14 Aug. 1715.
45. HMC *Stuart*, i. 341–342: Berwick to Tunstal, [Dec. 1714]; i. 345: Berwick to James, Saint-Germain, 11/22 Jan. 1715; i. 357: James to Berwick, [Bar], 5/16 Apr. 1715.
46. HMC *Stuart*, i. 518–520: memo by James for Queen Mary and Berwick, [Bar?], 7/18 May 1715.
47. HMC *Stuart*, i. 339–340, 378: Berwick to James, Saint-Germain and Marly, 17/28 Dec. 1714 and 14/25 July 1715; i. 405: Bolingbroke to James, Paris, 12/23–15/26 Aug. 1715.
48. HMC *Stuart*, i. 348: Berwick to James, Saint-Germain, 6/17 Feb. 1715.
49. HMC *Stuart*, i. 349: Berwick to James, Saint-Germain, 12/23 Feb. 1715.
50. HMC *Stuart*, i. 357: James to Berwick, [Bar], 5/16 Apr. 1715. See also: i. 360: Berwick to James, Saint-Germain, 15/26 Apr. 1715.
51. Cruickshanks *et al.*, *House of Commons 1690–1715*, v. 339–358; HMC *Stuart*, i. 362: Berwick to James, Saint-Germain, 20 Apr./1 May 1715.
52. HMC *Stuart*, i. 348, 355: Berwick to James, Saint-Germain, 6/17 Feb. and 13/24 Mar. 1715; Bodleian, MS Carte 211, f. 325: 'An account of the Duke of Lorrain's Gold', Mar. 1716.
53. HMC *Stuart*, i. 360: Berwick to James, Saint-Germain, 15/26 Apr. 1715.
54. HMC *Stuart*, i. 518: memo by James for Queen Mary and Berwick, [Bar?], 7/18 May 1715; i. 365: Berwick to James, Fitzjames, 10/21 May 1715.
55. HMC *Stuart*, i. 362: Berwick to James, Saint-Germain, 20 Apr./1 May 1715.
56. HMC *Stuart*, i. 365, 367: Berwick to James, Fitzjames, 10/21 May and 3/14 June 1715.
57. HMC *Stuart*, i. 375: James to Bolingbroke, Bar, Friday night [19 July 1715]; Dickinson, *Bolingbroke*, p. 10.
58. Lord Mahon, *History of England from the Peace of Utrecht to the Peace of Aix-La-Chapelle* (3 vols, 2nd edn, 1839), i., appendix, p. x: Bolingbroke to James, Paris, 12/23 July 1715.
59. Mahon, *History*, i., appendix, p. xi: Bolingbroke to James, Paris, 12/23 July 1715.
60. HMC *Stuart*, i. 378: Berwick to James, Marly, 14/25 July 1715. See also: i. 375–376: Berwick to James, Fitzjames, 8/19 July 1715.
61. Corp, *Court in Exile*, p. 295.
62. HMC *Stuart*, i. 352: James to Ormond, 2/13 Mar. 1715.
63. HMC *Stuart*, i. 525: memo from Mar to James [5/16 July 1715].
64. HMC *Stuart*, i. 520: memo from Mar to James [5/16 July 1715].
65. Ibid.
66. HMC *Stuart*, i. 521: memo from Mar to James [5/16 July 1715].
67. Ibid.; i. 525: Mar to Kinnaird, Whitehall, 6/17 July 1715.
68. It is worth noting that this was precisely the strategy successfully used by the Scots Covenanters against Charles I in 1640.
69. HMC *Stuart*, i. 522: memo from Mar to James [5/16 July 1715].
70. HMC *Stuart*, i. 523–524: memo from Mar to James [5/16 July 1715].
71. HMC *Stuart*, i. 525: memo from Mar to James [5/16 July 1715].
72. HMC *Stuart*, i. 381: James to the colonels or commanding officers of the Irish regiments in France and Spain, Bar, 17/28 July 1715.
73. HMC *Stuart*, i. 348, 359, 368, 371: Berwick to James, Saint-Germain, Fitzjames and Marly, 6/17 Feb., 13/24 Apr., 7/18 June, 22 June/2 July 1715.
74. HMC *Stuart*, i. 379: James to Bolingbroke, Bar, 15/26 July 1715; i. 381: Berwick to James, Fitzjames, 22 July/2 Aug. 1715.

75. SP 78/160, f. 142: Thomas Crawford (Stair's secretary) to Under-Secretary Pringle, Paris, 16/27 Nov. 1715; Smith, 'Spain and the Jacobites', pp. 161–162.
76. AECP 267, ff. 174v, 325r: Torcy to d'Iberville, Versailles, 23 Mar./3 Apr. and 20 Apr./1 May 1715; f. 234v: d'Iberville to Torcy, London, 29–30 Mar./9–10 Apr. 1715; Fritz, *English Ministers and Jacobitism*, pp. 9–10.
77. Mahon, *History*, i., appendix, p. xii: Bolingbroke to James, Paris, 12/23 July 1715.
78. HMC *Stuart*, i. 389: Berwick to James, Paris, 2/13 Aug. 1715.
79. HMC *Stuart*, i. 389: Bolingbroke to James, Paris, 4/15 Aug. 1715.
80. HMC *Stuart*, i. 529: memorandum for the Jacobite conspirators, [Paris] 2/13 Aug. 1715.
81. HMC *Stuart*, i. 376: Berwick to James, Fitzjames, 8/19 July 1715; i. 376–377: James to Berwick, Bar, 12/23 [endorsed, 27] July 1715.
82. HMC *Stuart*, i. 529: memorandum for the Jacobite conspirators, [Paris] 2/13 Aug. 1715.
83. HMC *Stuart*, i. 384–385: James to Berwick, Bar, 26 July/6 Aug. 1715.
84. RH 2/4/391/101–102, 103–104, 104–105, 106: Montrose to the Baillies of Edinburgh, the Provost of Glasgow, the Governor of Dumbarton castle, the Governor of Blackness castle and the commander of Fort William, Whitehall, 20 July 1715; SP 35/3, f. 180: Townshend to the Lord Mayor of London, Whitehall, 22 July 1715.
85. AECP 269, ff. 218v, 224r: d'Iberville to Torcy, London, 25–26 July/5–6 Aug. 1715.
86. HMC *Stuart*, i. 391: to James, Paris, 4/15 Aug. 1715.
87. Gregg, 'Mar', p. 182.
88. HMC *Stuart*, i. 389: Paris, 2/13 Aug. 1715.
89. HMC *Stuart*, i. 389–390: Bolingbroke to James, Paris, 4/15 Aug. 1715.
90. HMC *Stuart*, i. 395: Bolingbroke to James, Paris, 8/19 Aug. 1715; i. 400: James to Bolingbroke, [Bar?], 12/23 Aug. 1715.
91. HMC *Stuart*, i. 402–403, 408–409: Bolingbroke to James, Paris, 12/23–15/26 and 19/30 Aug. 1715.
92. Corp, *Court in Exile*, p. 172.
93. Jeremy Black, *Natural and Necessary Enemies. Anglo-French Relations in the Eighteenth Century* (1986), p. 8.
94. Laing and Macknight (eds), *Memoirs of the Insurrection*, p. 25.
95. HMC *Stuart*, i. 352–353: James to Ormond, 2/13 Mar. 1715; i. 522: memo from Mar to James, [5/16 July 1715]; i. 441: Bolingbroke to James, Paris, 9/20 Oct. 1715; i. 457: James to Lewis Innes, Saint-Malo, 31Oct./11 Nov. 1715; SP 54/8/28: copies of intercepted letters from Mar, [*c.* 21 Oct. 1715]; BL, Stowe 228, ff. 152v, 164r–v: Gustavus Hamilton to Robethon, Dublin, 20 and 25 Oct. 1715; SP 78/160, f. 136: Stanhope to Stair, Whitehall, 31 Oct. 1715; Stowe 228, f. 209r: Stair to Robethon, Paris, 10/21 Jan. 1716; RH 2/4/393/98: Townshend to Argyll, Whitehall, 4 [Feb.] 1716.
96. SP 35/2, f. 40: Willcox to Townshend, [Oct.] 1715.
97. SP 35/4, f. 31: Thomas Mason to Townshend(?), Wellingborough, 24 Aug. 1715; SP 35/3, ff. 199–200: 'Philopoliteius' to Townshend, Oxford, 26 July 1715; Bank of England CCXLII, Morice MSS: Walter Moyle to Humphrey Morice, 26 Sept. 1715 – I am indebted to Dr Eveline Cruickshanks for her kindness in drawing my attention to, and supplying me with a copy of, this letter. The élite English Jacobites' failure to exploit their plebeian supporters' potential was very obvious to the Scots Borderers who fought alongside them: RH 2/4/305/107: account of Kenmure's rising all the way to Preston.
98. BL, Add. MS 38507, f. 144: information re Leeds's household, 2 Aug. 1715.
99. BL, Add. MS 38507, f. 150: Charles Trelawney to Jonathan Trelawney, Bishop of Winchester, 18 Aug. 1715.

100. Patten, *History of the Rebellion*, pp. 219–220.
101. Michael, *Beginnings of the Hanoverian Dynasty*, pp. 164–165; Morice MSS: Walter Moyle to Humphrey Morice, 26 Sept. 1715; BL, Stowe 228, f. 146r: Charles Bodville Robartes, Earl of Radnor, to Robethon, Lanhydrock, 13 Oct. 1715; SP 54/8/37c: Lord Justice Clerk Cockburn to Townshend, Edinburgh, 10 Sept. 1715.
102. Patten, *History of the Rebellion*, pp. 16, 17; GD 220/5/1902/3: [James Carmichael, Earl of Hyndford, to Montrose], Bath, 5 Oct. 1715; BL, Add. MS 38851, f. 75v; Sir William Fraser (ed.), *The Annandale Family Book of the Johnstones, Earls and Marquises of Annandale* (2 vols, Edinburgh, 1894), ii. 257: Brigadier-General Thomas Stanwix to William Johnston, Marquess of Annandale, Carlisle, 21.00, 14 Oct. 1715.
103. Patten, *History of the Rebellion*, p. 19; RH 2/4/305/107: account of Kenmure's rising all the way to Preston.
104. Gooch, *Desperate Faction?*, pp. 42, 60.
105. Monod, *Jacobitism and the English People*, pp. 309–316, 318–326.
106. RH 2/4/305/107: account of Kenmure's rising all the way to Preston; SP 35/2, f. 29: petition of John Hall to Townshend, 1715.
107. RH 2/4/306/83: Wightman to [General George Carpenter?], Edinburgh, 24 Oct. 1715.
108. Patten, *History of the Rebellion*, pp. 21, 22.
109. AECP 266, f. 36r: d'Iberville to Louis XIV, London, 3/14 Jan. 1715; AECP 268, f. 376: d'Iberville to Louis XIV, London, 16/27 June 1715.
110. AECP 266, f. 262r: d'Iberville to Louis XIV, London, 17/28 Feb. 1715.
111. HMC *Stuart*, i. 395: Bolingbroke to James, Paris, 8/19 Aug. 1715. This continued even after the rebellion in Scotland had begun: Mahon, *History*, i., appendix, pp. xxxii: Bolingbroke to James, Paris, 14/25 Sept. 1715.
112. Constable (ed.), *Fragment of a Memoir*, p. 9.
113. AECP 265, ff. 161r: to Torcy, 30 July/10 Aug. 1715. See also: AECP 269, ff. 110v, 218v: d'Iberville to Louis XIV, London, 27–30 June/8–11 July and 26 July/6 Aug. 1715; ff. 224r, 268v: d'Iberville to Torcy, London, 25–26 July/5–6 Aug. and 1/12 Aug. 1715.
114. BL, Add. MS 38851, ff. 97r: official explanation of Bolingbroke's dismissal by James, [Mar.?] 1716. Patten vehemently agreed: *History of the Rebellion*, p. 78.
115. HMC *Stuart*, i. 532–533: minutes of James–Bolingbroke meeting, 3/14 Oct. 1715; Jones, *Mainstream of Jacobitism*, pp. 111–112.
116. Steuart *Newsletters*, p. 30: [Edinburgh], 28 Aug. 1715; GD 220/5/454/48: Lord Justice Clerk Cockburn to Montrose, Edinburgh, 4 June 1715; GD 220/5/455/27: 'Killraick and Foulks etc' to Lord Justice Clerk Cockburn, [Inverness?], 14 July 1715; GD 220/5/455/33, 34, 36: Lord Justice Clerk Cockburn to Montrose, Edinburgh, 23, 24 and 26 July 1715; Aufrere (ed.), *Lockhart Papers*, i. 487, 491–493; SP 54/7/34a: James Spence to Solicitor-General Steuart, Edinburgh, 9 Aug. 1715; SP 54/8/37c: Lord Justice Clerk Cockburn to Townshend, Edinburgh, 10 Sept. 1715; SP 54/8/71: Hugh Dalrymple to [Argyll], [North Berwick?], 16 Sept. 1715; *Memoirs of the Life of Simon Lord Lovat*, pp. 410–411.
117. RH 2/4/390/28: petition by Alexander MacDonald of Bracklet in Glencoe to Mar [1714]; Laing and Macknight (eds), *Memoirs of the Insurrection*, p. 12.
118. GD 27/6/7/17: [Montrose to Cornelius Kennedy], Edinburgh, 19 Feb. 1715.
119. Atholl Papers, box 45, bundle 12/15: Lord Justice Clerk Cockburn to Atholl, Edinburgh, 23 Mar. 1715.
120. [Duff (ed.)], *Culloden Papers*, p. 38: John Forbes to Duncan Forbes, London, 30 Apr. 1715.
121. SP 54/7/23: Pollock to Montrose, Fort William, 6 Aug. 1715; SP 54/7/79b: Lord Justice Clerk Cockburn to [Stanhope], Edinburgh, 26 Aug. 1715.

122. GD 220/5/455/21: 'D.B.' to Lord Justice Clerk Cockburn, Dirleton?, 10? July 1715; GD 220/5/815/2: Graham of Gorthie to Montrose, Edinburgh, 7 July 1715; J. Maidment (ed.), *The Argyle Papers* (Edinburgh, 1834), p. 134: 'Memorial for his Grace the Duke of Argyle'.
123. GD 220/5/455/26: Lord Justice Clerk Cockburn to Montrose, Edinburgh, 19 July 1715; GD 220/5/1912/5: [Lawrence Drummond? to Montrose], Edinburgh, 24 July 1715; SP 54/7/21: anon. report, 5 Aug. 1715.
124. GD 220/5/455/21: 'D.B.' to Lord Justice Clerk Cockburn, Dirleton?, 10? July 1715; Aufrere (ed.), *Lockhart Papers*, i. 489–490, 495.
125. GD 220/5/455/44a: Lord Justice Clerk Cockburn to Montrose, Edinburgh, 30 July 1715; Mackay, 'The Camerons in the Rising of 1715', p. 10; SP 54/7/22: ['Mr Orr'] to ?, Inverness, 6 Aug. 1715; SP 54/7/24: [Lord Justice Clerk Cockburn] to Montrose, 6 Aug. 1715.
126. SP 54/7/19: Buchanan, 4 Aug. 1715.
127. RH 2/4/391/121–122: Townshend to General Thomas Whetham, Whitehall, 12 Aug. 1715 (list of those to be arrested: Earls of Nithsdale, Linlithgow, Home, Wigton, Traquair and Carnwath; Viscounts Stormont, Kenmure, Kilsyth and Kingston; Lord Rollo; George Lockhart of Carnwath and George Home of Whitefield); RH 2/4/391/127–129: Townshend to Whetham, Whitehall, 18 Aug. 1715 (this added the Earl of Kinnoull, Lord Deskford, Sir Hugh Paterson of Bannockburn, Graham 'of Bucklivie', Sir John Maclean and Colin Campbell of Glendaruel).
128. SP 54/8/1: Deskford to Townshend, Edinburgh, 1 Sept. 1715; SP 54/8/77: Lord Justice Clerk Cockburn to [Under-Secretary Pringle], Edinburgh, 20 Sept. 1715.
129. Szechi, *Lockhart of Carnwath*, pp. 118–120; SP 54/7/89: Whetham to Townshend, Edinburgh, 28 Aug. 1715.
130. Laing and Macknight (eds), *Memoirs of the Insurrection*, pp. 11, 12.
131. SP 54/8/30: intelligence from northern Scotland, 8 Sept. 1715; GD 45/1/201: Panmure regiment official return, c. Oct. 1715.
132. Laing and Macknight (eds), *Memoirs of the Insurrection*, p. 33.
133. See for example: Aufrere (ed.), *Lockhart Papers*, i. 484, 488, 491.
134. SP 78/160, ff. 103–104: Stair to Stanhope, Paris, 3/14 Sept. 1715; BL, Stowe 228, f. 105: Stair to Robethon, Paris, 10/21 Sept 1715; RH 2/4/391/163: Townshend and Stanhope to Argyll, Whitehall, 15 Sept. 1715; SP 78/160, f. 119: Stanhope to Stair, Whitehall, 5 Oct. 1715.
135. Mahon, *History*, i., appendix, p. xxviii: Bolingbroke to James, Paris, 10/21 Sept. 1715.
136. HMC *Stuart*, i. 425: James to Bolingbroke, [Bar], 12/23 Sept. 1715.
137. HMC *Stuart*, i. 431: Bolingbroke to James, Paris, 26 Sept./7 Oct. 1715. See also: i. 431: Berwick to James, Saint-Germain, 26 Sept./7 Oct. 1715.
138. Mahon, *History*, i., appendix, p. xl: Bolingbroke to James, Paris, 28 Oct./8 Nov. 1715; A. de Boislisle (ed.), *Mémoires de Saint-Simon* (41 vols, Paris, 1879–1928), xxix. 273–274; Petrie, *Berwick*, pp. 304–306.
139. HMC *Stuart*, i. 442: Ormond to James, 10/21 Oct. 1715.
140. Mahon, *History*, i., appendix, p. xxxi: Bolingbroke to James, Paris, 14/25 Sept. 1715; BL, Stowe 228, f. 110r: Stair to Robethon, Paris, 15/26 Sept. 1715.
141. HMC *Stuart*, i. 435, 454: Bolingbroke to James, Paris, 7/18 Oct. and 28 Oct./8 Nov. 1715; GD 220/5/1908/5: [Stair] to Montrose, Paris, 28 Nov. 1715; BL, Stowe 228, ff. 216r: Stair to Robethon, Paris, 17/28 Jan. 1716; GD 220/5/1926/4: Crawford to Montrose, Paris, 17/28 Jan. 1716.
142. GD 220/5/624/2: [Stair to Montrose], Paris, 18/29 Feb. 1716. See also: RH 2/4/393/115: Stair to Stanhope (extract), [Paris], 24 Feb./7 Mar. 1716.
143. Michael, *Beginnings of the Hanoverian Dynasty*, pp. 311–319.

144. Erskine (ed.), 'Earl of Mar's Legacies', p. 170. See also: Constable (ed.), *Fragment of a Memoir*, pp. 9–11, which basically supports Mar's assertion that this was the plan, but claims that he was originally intending still to lie low and wait for James's arrival, and was forced to rebel prematurely because of the wave of arrests of suspected Jacobites by the government; Laing and Macknight (eds), *Memoirs of the Insurrection*, p. 27.

145. SP 54/7/11: James Graham, Sheriff-Depute of Dumbartonshire, to Montrose, [Dumbarton], 2 Aug. 1715; Aufrere (ed.), *Lockhart Papers*, i. 488.

146. SP 54/7/56b: confidential memo from Lord Justice Clerk Cockburn to [Townshend], Edinburgh, 19 Aug. 1715; SP 54/7/71a: [James Spence] to Solicitor-General Steuart, Edinburgh, 25 August 1715; Constable (ed.), *Fragment of a Memoir*, p. 9.

147. Constable (ed.), *Fragment of a Memoir*, p. 9; HMC *Stuart*, i. 408: James to Bolingbroke, [Bar], 28 Aug. 1715.

148. RH 2/4/391/127: Townshend to General Thomas Whetham, Whitehall, 18 Aug. 1715; SP 54/7/62: Mar to James Erskine, Lord Grange of the Court of Session (his brother), Braemar, 20 Aug. 1715; GD 220/5/815/20: Graham of Gorthie to Montrose, Edinburgh, 27 Aug. 1715; SP 54/7/87: Solicitor-General Steuart to Under-Secretary Pringle, Edinburgh, 28 Aug. 1715.

149. Laing and Macknight (eds), *Memoirs of the Insurrection*, p. 16; Aufrere (ed.), *Lockhart Papers*, i. 485.

150. SP 54/7/91: Provost Robert Stewart of Aberdeen to Lord Justice Clerk Cockburn, Aberdeen, 29 Aug. 1715; SP 54/8/30: intelligence from northern Scotland, 8 Sept. 1715.

151. Laing and Macknight (eds), *Memoirs of the Insurrection*, pp. 16–18, 20.

152. SP 54/7/22: ['Mr Orr'] to ?, Inverness, 6 Aug. 1715. See also: SP 54/8/8a: Solicitor-General Steuart to [Under-Secretary Pringle], Edinburgh, 1 Sept. 1715; SP 54/8/18: summary of intelligence [from James Spence], Edinburgh, 3 Sept. 1715.

153. HMC *Stuart*, i. 525: Mar to Kinnaird, Whitehall, 6/17 July 1715; Atholl Papers, box 45, bundle 12/57: John Douglas to Atholl, Edinburgh, 25 July 1715; HMC *Stuart*, i. 415: James Murray of Stormont to James, 23 Aug./3 Sept. 1715; Laing and Macknight (eds), *Memoirs of the Insurrection*, pp. 20, 28, 35.

154. Atholl Papers, box 45, bundle 12/63: Townshend to Atholl, Whitehall, 11 Aug. 1715; AECP 269, f. 325r: d'Iberville to Torcy, London, 12/23 Aug. 1715; SP 54/7/67: summary of intelligence reports, [Edinburgh?], 23 Aug. 1715.

155. Huntly, for example, refused, 'to raise any of his men under any subject's command' (SP 54/8/13: intelligence from Aberdeen, Aberdeen, 2 Sept. 1715).

156. SP 54/8/124: Sutherland to Stanhope, [Aug./Sept. 1715]; Laing and Macknight (eds), *Memoirs of the Insurrection*, pp. 24–25; SP 54/8/38: Brigadier Grant to Whetham, Castle Grant, 9 Sept. 1715; HMC *Stuart*, i. 415–416: James to Mar, Bar, 27 Aug./7 Sept. 1715.

157. SP 54/7/67: summary of intelligence reports, [Edinburgh?], 23 Aug. 1715; SP 54/7/71a: [Spence] to Solicitor-General Steuart, Edinburgh, 25 Aug. 1715; SP 54/7/96: intelligence on Jacobite movements, [end of Aug. 1715]; SP 54/7/91: Provost Stewart of Aberdeen to Lord Justice Clerk Cockburn, Aberdeen, 29 Aug. 1715.

158. Laing and Macknight (eds), *Memoirs of the Insurrection*, pp. 20–21; HMC *Stuart*, i. 422, 424: Mar to Macdonald of Glengarry, Invercauld, 11/22 Sept. 1715.

159. SP 54/8/44: W. Gordon to [Under-Secretary Pringle], Fort William, 11 Sept. 1715.

160. Mackay, 'Camerons in the Rising of 1715', pp. 12–13; Laing and Macknight (eds), *Memoirs of the Insurrection*, p. 22; SP 54/8/17: extract of Colonel William Grant's letter to Whetham, 3 Sept. 1715; SP 54/8/30: intelligence from northern Scotland, 8 Sept. 1715; Laing and Macknight (eds), *Memoirs of the Insurrection*, pp. 32, 37.

161. SP 54/8/30: intelligence from northern Scotland, 8 Sept. 1715; HMC *Stuart*, i. 417, 419: Mar to John Gordon of [Glenbuchat], Aboyne and Invercauld, 1/12, 5/16 and 8/19 Sept. 1715; i. 422: Mar to Macdonald of Glengarry, 11/22 Sept. 1715; Henry Paton (ed.), *The Mackintosh Muniments, 1442–1820. Preserved in the Charter-Room at Moy Hall, Inverness-shire* (Edinburgh, 1903), p. 156: no. 702. Order by Mar, Aboyn, 1 Sept. 1715.

162. BL, Add. MS 38091, f. 50r: newsletter on the progress of the rebellion, 10 Sept. 1715.

163. Laing and Macknight (eds), *Memoirs of the Insurrection*, p. 37.

164. SP 54/8/57: Alexander Stuart of 'Barkie' to Townshend, Inverness, 14 Sept. 1715; SP 54/8/62: Pollock to Townshend, Fort William, 14 Sept. 1715.

165. SP 54/8/29b: Lord Justice Clerk Cockburn to Under-Secretary Pringle, Edinburgh, 8 Sept. 1715.

Chapter 5 'The English Steel We Could Disdain': the Outbreak of the Rebellion

1. SP 54/8/37c: Lord Justice Clerk Cockburn to Townshend, Edinburgh, 10 Sept. 1715; BL, Add. MS 38091, f. 51v: newsletter on the progress of the rebellion, Aug.–Sept. 1715.

2. SP 54/8/37c: Lord Justice Clerk Cockburn to Townshend, Edinburgh, 10 Sept. 1715; NLS Wodrow Papers, Quarto X, ep. 10: ? to Wodrow, Glasgow, 9 Sept. 1715.

3. SP 54/8/37b: Charles Cockburn to [Under-Secretary Pringle], Edinburgh, 10 Sept. 1715.; Steuart *Newsletters*, p. 33: [Edinburgh, after 9 Sept. 1715].

4. Laing and Macknight (eds), *Memoirs of the Insurrection*, p. 31; SP 54/8/36: declarations taken by the Lord Provost and Baillies of Edinburgh, 9 Sept. 1715.

5. SP 54/8/36: declarations taken by the Lord Provost and Baillies of Edinburgh, 9 Sept. 1715; NLS Wodrow Papers, Quarto X, ep. 11: ? to Wodrow, [Edinburgh?], 10 Sept. 1715.

6. SP 54/8/33: Dubourgay to [Stanhope?], Edinburgh, 9 Sept. 1715; Laing and Macknight (eds), *Memoirs of the Insurrection*, p. 30.

7. Wodrow Papers, Quarto X, ep. 11: ? to Wodrow, [Edinburgh?], 10 Sept. 1715; Laing and Macknight (eds), *Memoirs of the Insurrection*, pp. 30–31.

8. SP 54/8/35: affidavit by John Holland, Edinburgh castle, 9 Sept. 1715; Laing and Macknight (eds), *Memoirs of the Insurrection*, p. 31.

9. Wodrow Papers, Quarto X, ep. 11: ? to Wodrow, [Edinburgh?], 10 Sept. 1715.

10. SP 54/8/39: Solicitor-General Steuart to [Under-Secretary Pringle], Edinburgh, 10 Sept. 1715. See also: Wodrow Papers, Quarto X, ep. 11: ? to Wodrow, [Edinburgh?], 10 Sept. 1715; SP 54/8/120a: Islay to Townshend, Edinburgh, 29 Sept. 1715; BL, Stowe 228, f. 121r: Gustavus Hamilton to Robethon, Dublin, 24 Sept. 1715.

11. BL, Add. MS 38091, ff. 51v–52r: newsletter on progress of the rebellion, Aug.–Sept. 1715; RH 2/4/391/204–7: Townshend to Lord Justice Clerk Cockburn, Whitehall, 15 Sept. 1715; SP 54/8/84: [Charles Cockburn] to [Under-Secretary Pringle], Edinburgh, 22 Sept. 1715.

12. Laing and Macknight (eds), *Memoirs of the Insurrection*, p. 29; BL, Add. MS 37993, f. 42v: Polwarth to Townshend, Redbreas, 27 Dec. 1715; GD 18/2099: Baron John Clerk's account of a journey to Perth, researching 1715, 1717: pp. 30–31; Moody-Stuart, 'Lieutenant-Colonel James Steuart', pp. 24–25.

13. SP 54/8/36: declarations taken by the Lord Provost and the Baillies of Edinburgh, 9 Sept. 1715.

14. Laing and Macknight (eds), *Memoirs of the Insurrection*, p. 31; GD 18/2099: Baron John Clerk's account of a journey to Perth, researching 1715, 1717: pp. 30–31.

15. SP 54/8/36: declarations taken by the Lord Provost and the Baillies of Edinburgh, 9 Sept. 1715; Laing and Macknight (eds), *Memoirs of the Insurrection*, p. 29.
16. RH 2/4/325/25a: Wade to Islay, Edinburgh, 16 July 1727. My thanks are due to Professor Roger Emerson for drawing my attention to this letter.
17. See above, pp. 99–100.
18. SP 54/8/109: copy, Lord Strathnaver to Captain James Stuart of the galley *Royal Ann* in Cromarty roads, Dunrotin, 27 Sept. 1715; SP 54/9/2b: C. McNachton to John McNachton, Finlarig, 28 Sept. 1715; RH 2/4/305/31: Captain Stuart (of the galley *Royal Ann*) to the Admiralty, at sea off Ardhead, 1 Oct. 1715; RH 2/4/309/116: list of Caithness and Orkney heritors who proclaimed James VIII, 26 Jan. 1716; Laing and Macknight (eds), *Memoirs of the Insurrection*, pp. 335, 342, 353.
19. See above, Chapters 2 and 3.
20. Sankey and Szechi, 'Elite Culture and the Decline of Scottish Jacobitism', pp. 103–105.
21. See, for example: GD 345/540/47: William Forbes to ?, 'Farnbeg', 5 June 1715.
22. See, for example: V. G. Kiernan, *The Duel in European History. Honour and the Reign of Aristocracy* (Oxford, 1989), pp. 92–115; Brown, *Bloodfeud in Scotland, passim*; GD 220/5/221/1: John Walkinshaw of Barrowfield to Montrose, Edinburgh, 24 Dec. 1709; Henry Rutherfurd, '"The Bloody Well": a Fatal Encounter between the Lairds of Fairnington and Muirhouselaw, 1716', *Transactions of the Hawick Archaeological Society*, liv (1922), 18–20; SP 35/62/109: depositions taken by the JPs at Jedburgh, 12 Aug. 1726.
23. GD 220/5/455/26: Lord Justice Clerk Cockburn to Montrose, Edinburgh, 19 July 1715; Cruickshanks *et al.*, *House of Commons 1690–1715*, iv. 398–400.
24. GD 220/5/455/31 and GD 220/5/1917/2: Lord Justice Clerk Cockburn to Montrose, Edinburgh, 21 July 1715 and 28 Jan. 1716.
25. SP 54/8/52: Lord Advocate Dalrymple to Stanhope, 12 Sept. 1715.
26. RH 2/4/307/51: Argyll to Townshend, Stirling, 15 Nov. 1715; GD 220/5/1917/2: Lord Justice Clerk Cockburn to Montrose, Edinburgh, 28 Jan. 1716.
27. GD 220/5/1929/8: ? to Montrose, Edinburgh, [Spring 1714].
28. GD 220/5/453/5: Lord Advocate Dalrymple to Montrose, Edinburgh, 11 Jan. 1715. See also: RH 2/4/310/202: Lord Justice Clerk Cockburn to [Stanhope], Edinburgh, 29 Mar. 1716.
29. SP 54/7/40b: [James Spence] to Solicitor-General Steuart, Edinburgh, 13 Aug. 1715. See also: GD 220/5/331/14: Lord Justice Clerk Cockburn to Montrose, Edinburgh, 16 Dec. 1714.
30. SP 54/7/12: Lord Justice Clerk Cockburn to Montrose, Edinburgh, 3 Aug. 1715.
31. GD 220/5/455/4: account of 10 June in Aberdeen, Aberdeen, 13 June 1715.
32. GD 220/5/455/5, 7: Lord Justice Clerk Cockburn to Montrose, Edinburgh, 21 June and 7 July 1715.
33. Allardyce (ed.), *Historical Papers Relating to the Jacobite Period*, i. 59: petition by Gordon, [1715].
34. SP 54/7/34a: James Spence to Solicitor-General Steuart, Edinburgh, 9 Aug. 1715; SP 54/7/41a: Lord Justice Clerk Cockburn to [Under-Secretary Pringle], Edinburgh, 13 Aug. 1715. NB: in contemporary parlance 'insulting' in this kind of context usually meant someone was committing violence, though short of bloodshed.
35. SP 54/7/7: Pledge of Association, Edinburgh, 1 Aug. 1715.
36. Robert D. Putnam, *Bowling Alone. The Collapse and Revival of American Community* (New York, 2000).
37. Jenny Wormald, *Court, Kirk and Community. Scotland 1470–1625* (Edinburgh, 1981; repr. 1991), pp. 114, 115–116.

38. SP 54/7/7: Pledge of Association, Edinburgh, 1 Aug. 1715. See also: SP 54/7/14: President Dalrymple to Montrose, Edinburgh, 3 Aug. 1715.

39. SP 54/7/12: Lord Justice Clerk Cockburn to Montrose, Edinburgh, 3 Aug. 1715; SP 54/7/19: Sheriff-Depute James Graham to Montrose, Buchanan, 4 Aug. 1715; SP 54/7/26: Provost and Baillies of Glasgow to George I, Glasgow, 8 Aug. 1715; GD 18/2092/4: Sir John Clerk's journal for Apr. 1712–1715: 9 Aug. 1715.

40. SP 54/7/14: President Dalrymple to Montrose, Edinburgh, 3 Aug. 1715; SP 54/7/37, printed proclamation of day of fasting, humiliation and prayer, Edinburgh, 11 Aug. 1715.

41. SP 54/7/13: Principal John Stirling to Montrose, Glasgow, 3 Aug. 1715; SP 54/7/34a: James Spence to Solicitor-General Steuart, Edinburgh, 9 Aug. 1715; SP 54/7/31: Provost of Perth to [Under-Secretary Pringle], Perth, 10 Aug. 1715.

42. SP 54/7/14: President Dalrymple to Montrose, Edinburgh, 3 Aug. 1715; SP 54/7/24: [Lord Justice Clerk Cockburn] to Montrose, 6 Aug. 1715; SP 54/7/33: Solicitor-General Steuart to [Under-Secretary Pringle], Edinburgh, 11 Aug. 1715; SP 54/7/48: John Hamilton, Earl of Ruglen, to [Under-Secretary Pringle], Barnton, 16 Aug. 1715.

43. RH 2/4/391/115: Stanhope and Townshend to President Dalrymple, Whitehall, 8 Aug. 1715.

44. SP 54/7/29:[Under-Secretary Pringle] to President Dalrymple, Whitehall, 9 Aug. 1715.

45. SP 54/7/98: instructions for Scottish Lord-Lieutenants, Whitehall, 25 Aug. 1715.

46. SP 54/7/45: Solicitor-General Steuart to [Under-Secretary Pringle], Edinburgh, 16 Aug. 1715.

47. Ibid.

48. SP 54/7/42: President Dalrymple to [Under-Secretary Pringle], Edinburgh, 13 Aug. 1715. See also: SP 54/7/45: Solicitor-General Steuart to [Under-Secretary Pringle], Edinburgh, 16 Aug. 1715; SP 54/7/63c: Lord Justice Clerk Cockburn to Townshend, Edinburgh, 23 Aug. 1715.

49. RH 2/4/391/132, 135: Townshend to Lord Justice Clerk Cockburn, Whitehall, 18 Aug. 1715.

50. Macinnes, *Clanship, Commerce and the House of Stuart*, pp. 169–173.

51. SP 54/7/40b: [James Spence] to Solicitor-General Steuart, Edinburgh, 13 Aug. 1715.

52. SP 54/8/30: intelligence from the north, 8 Sept. 1715; SP 54/8/41: Atholl to [Stanhope?], Blair Atholl, 10 Sept. 1715; SP 54/8/43: intelligence from the north, [Perth], 10 Sept. 1715; SP 54/8/45: intelligence from the north, Perth, 11 Sept. 1715; GD 44/51/167/4: list of matériel and men provided by the tenants of Ruthven, Gairtly, Cawnie, Dunbennam, Kinoir, Raws and Rhynie [1715–16].

53. SP 54/8/88: James Cockburn to Under-Secretary Pringle, Stirling, 23 Sept. 1715; RH 2/4/309/78c: Huntly to the Laird of Mayen, Gordon castle, 30 Sept. 1715.

54. Macinnes, *Clanship, Commerce and the House of Stuart*, p. 248.

55. SP 35/2, f. 35: tack of Gibstown to John Hamilton by Huntly, 8 Aug. 1715.

56. SP 54/8/94: Pollock to Townshend, Fort William, 24 Sept. 1715.

57. SP 54/8/125: Glengarry to Pollock, 22 Sept. 1715.

58. RH 2/4/310/174: Sir Robert Pollock to Townshend, Fort William, 10 Mar. 1716; A. Whitford Anderson (ed.), *Papers of of the Rev. John Anderson, Minister of Dumbarton 1698–1718* (Dumbarton 1914), p. 36: Tobias Martine to Anderson, Inverary, 28 Oct. 1715; [Anon.], *The Loch Lomond Expedition, with Some Short Reflections on the Perth Manifesto* (Glasgow, 1715), pp. 26–27: Gregor Macgregor to [Lieutenant-General Thomas Gordon of Auchintoul?], Achnacarry, 14 Oct. 1715; Mackay, 'Camerons in the Rising of 1715', pp. 12–13.

59. RH 2/4/311/21: Sir William Gordon to Townshend, Fort William, May 1716.

60. SP 54/8/15: Captain Robert Monro to [Stanhope?], Fowly in Ross, 2 Sept. 1715.

61. GD 220/5/357/4: John Haldane of Gleneagles to Montrose, Gleneagles, 1 Nov. 1714; GD 220/5/453/13a: Lord Advocate Dalrymple to Montrose, Edinburgh, 27 Jan. 1715.
62. GD 220/5/455/13: Lord Justice Clerk Cockburn to Montrose, Edinburgh, 5 July 1715; GD 220/5/455/23: sentence of the Court of Justiciary on the Dundee magistrates, Edinburgh, 11 July 1715; SP 54/7/28: extract of letter from James Yeoman, Baillie of Dundee, to Lord Advocate Dalrymple, Dundee, 8 Aug. 1715.
63. SP 54/7/87a: Lord Justice Clerk Cockburn to [Under-Secretary Pringle?], Edinburgh, 28 Aug. 1715; SP 54/8/29a: Lord Justice Clerk Cockburn to Townshend, Edinburgh, 8 Sept. 1715.
64. SP 54/8/34: intelligence from Dundee, Dundee, 9 Sept. 1715.
65. SP 54/8/70: James Yeaman and Thomas Wardroper to Lord Justice Clerk Cockburn, Woodhaven, 16 Sept. 1715.
66. SP 54/8/129: short proclamation of James VIII [1715]; SP 54/8/77: Lord Justice Clerk Cockburn to [Under-Secretary Pringle], Edinburgh, 20 Sept. 1715.
67. Laing and Macknight (eds), *Memoirs of the Insurrection*, p. 38.
68. SP 54/7/78: Whetham to Townshend, Edinburgh, 26 Aug. 1715; SP 54/8/27: intelligence from Aberdeen, 7 Sept. 1715; SP 54/8/30: intelligence from the north, 8 Sept. 1715.
69. SP 54/7/31: Provost of Perth to [Under-Secretary Pringle], Perth, 10 Aug. 1715.
70. SP 54/7/71a: [James Spence] to Solicitor-General Steuart, Edinburgh, 25 Aug. 1715; Laing and Macknight (eds), *Memoirs of the Insurrection*, p. 39; SP 54/8/74c: intelligence from Perth, Stirling, 18 Sept. 1715.
71. Atholl Papers, box 45, bundle 12/175/4: Atholl to George I, 1716; SP 54/8/74a: Argyll to Stanhope, camp at Stirling, 18 Sept. 1715; SP 54/8/74c: intelligence from Perth, Stirling, 18 Sept. 1715.
72. SP 54/8/74c: intelligence from Perth, Stirling, 18 Sept. 1715.
73. Ibid.
74. Laing and Macknight (eds), *Memoirs of the Insurrection*, p. 113.
75. SP 54/8/57: Alexander Stuart Barkie to Townshend, Inverness, 14 Sept. 1715; SP 54/8/77: Lord Justice Clerk Cockburn to [Under-Secretary Pringle], Edinburgh, 20 Sept. 1715; SP 54/8/75: licence by Marischal and consuls and senators of Peterhead for Alexander Smith to trade with Bergen in non-matériel goods, 16 Sept. 1715; RH 2/4/307/12: Captain Robert Monro to Townshend, Inverbreaky, 3 Nov. 1715; Warrand (ed.), *More Culloden Papers*, ii. 84–85: Harry Maule of Kellie to Henry Crawfurd of Crail, Perth, 21 Nov. 1715; Constable (ed.), *Fragment of a Memoir*, p. 12.
76. SP 54/8/74c: intelligence from Perth, Stirling, 18 Sept. 1715.
77. SP 54/8/77: Lord Justice Clerk Cockburn to [Under-Secretary Pringle], Edinburgh, 20 Sept. 1715; RH 2/4/305/31: Captain James Stuart (*Royal Ann Galley*) to the Admiralty, at sea off Ardhead, 1 Oct. 1715; RH 2/4/306/56a: Lord Justice Clerk Cockburn to Townshend, Edinburgh, 19 Oct. 1715.
78. Laing and Macknight (eds), *Memoirs of the Insurrection*, pp. 33–34, 39; SP 54/7/54a: Lord Justice Clerk Cockburn to [Townshend], Edinburgh, 19 Aug. 1715; BL, Add. MS 37993, f. 28v: Polwarth to George Baillie of Jerviswood, Redbreas, 13 Nov. 1715; f. 30r: Polwarth to Sir William Bennet of Grubbet, Redbreas, 14 Nov. 1715; GD 220/5/655: Lord Charles Ker to Montrose, Edinburgh, 23 Feb. 1716.
79. Laing and Macknight (eds), *Memoirs of the Insurrection*, p. 40.
80. Fraser (ed.), *Annandale*, ii. 255–256: Annandale to Stanwix, Dumfries,14 Oct. 1715.
81. Fraser (ed.), *Annandale*, ii. 264: Maxwell to Kenmure, 31 Oct. 1715.
82. SP 54/8/64: Solicitor-General Steuart to [Stanhope], Edinburgh, 15 Sept. 1715; SP 54/8/71: Hugh Dalrymple to [Argyll], [North Berwick?], 16 Sept. 1715.
83. GD 18/2092/4: Sir John Clerk's journal for Apr. 1712–1715, 18 and 20 Sept. 1715.

84. Aufrere (ed.), *Lockhart Papers*, i. 488, 492.
85. SP 54/8/73: Argyll to Townshend, Edinburgh, 17 Sept. 1715; SP 54/8/72a: Lord Justice Clerk Cockburn to Townshend, Edinburgh, 17 Sept. 1715; GD 18/2092/4: Sir John Clerk's journal for Apr. 1712–1715, 20 Sept. 1715.
86. Patten, *History of the Rebellion*, p. 19.
87. Ibid., p. 20.
88. RH 2/4/306/63b: proclamation fixed to Hexham market cross by Forster's rebels, [19 Oct. 1715].
89. Patten, *History of the Rebellion*, p. 20.
90. Ibid., p. 29.
91. Ibid., p. 23; Sedgwick, *House of Commons 1715–1754*, i. 464–465.
92. SP 54/8/119: Lord Justice Clerk Cockburn to Under-Secretary Pringle, Edinburgh, 29 Sept. 1715; Patten, *History of the Rebellion*, pp. 20–21, 22, 24–25.
93. Patten, *History of the Rebellion*, p. 21.
94. RH 2/4/305/28: 'A Full and True Account of the Action at Keith Upon the Eight Day of October 1715', Edinburgh, 1715.
95. Ibid.; RH 2/4/305/36b: account of the affair at Keith, 12 Oct. 1715; Wodrow Papers, Quarto X, ep. 45: J. Erskine to Wodrow, Edinburgh, 8 Oct. 1715.
96. GD 220/5/458/43/a–c: Rothes to John Leslie, Lord Leslie, Stirling, 29 Sept. 1715 (my thanks are due to Dr Tristram Clarke of the NAS for drawing my attention to this letter); Laing and Macknight (eds), *Memoirs of the Insurrection*, p. 52.
97. SP 54/8/58: Rothes to Townshend, Edinburgh, 14 Sept. 1715; SP 54/8/67: Charles Cockburn to [Under-Secretary Pringle], Edinburgh, 15 Sept. 1715; Laing and Macknight (eds), *Memoirs of the Insurrection*, p. 38.
98. Laing and Macknight (eds), *Memoirs of the Insurrection*, p. 39.
99. BL, Add. MS 37993, f. 11v: Polwarth to Andrew Hume, Lord Kimmerghame, Edinburgh, 20 Oct. 1715; RH 2/4/306/89: Charles Hay, Marquess of Tweeddale to Under-Secretary Pringle, Edinburgh, 27 Oct. 1715.
100. RH 2/4/305/107: account of Kenmure's rising all the way to Preston.
101. RH 2/4/305/27: 'advyces from North Britain', [9?] Oct. 1715; RH 2/4/305/46: intelligence from the north, Inverness, 14 Oct. 1715; RH 2/4/307/21b: 'Ane Account of the Earl of Sutherland's Proceedings From his Embarkation at Leith the 25th of September to the 2nd of November, 1715'.
102. Laing and Macknight (eds), *Memoirs of the Insurrection*, p. 40; RH 2/4/306/73: Lord Advocate Dalrymple to Stanhope, Edinburgh, 22 Oct. 1715.
103. SP 54/8/117: to [Under-Secretary Pringle], Edinburgh, 29 Sept. 1715. Argyll agreed: SP 54/9/24: Argyll to Townshend, camp at Stirling, 7 Oct. 1715.
104. SP 54/9/2e: weekly return of dragoons and foot, camp at Stirling, 1 Oct. 1715; RH 2/4/306/92: weekly return of dragoons and foot, [camp at Stirling], 29 Oct. 1715; RH 2/4/309/2b: weekly return of dragoons and foot, [camp at Stirling], 2 Jan. 1716.
105. BL, Stowe 228, f. 140v: to Robethon, Edinburgh, 5 Oct. 1715; SP 54/8/7: Whetham to Stanhope, Stirling, 1 Sept. 1715.
106. Chris Tabraham and Doreen Grove, *Fortress Scotland and the Jacobites* (repr. 1997), p. 53.
107. SP 54/9/2e: weekly return of dragoons and foot, camp at Stirling, 1 Oct. 1715.
108. RH 2/4/306/92: weekly return of dragoons and foot, [camp at Stirling], 29 Oct. 1715; RH 2/4/391/198: Townshend to Argyll, Whitehall, 4 Oct. 1715.
109. RH 2/4/307/48: Argyll to Townshend, Stirling, 14 Nov. 1715. This number is a projection based on the average of 302 men listed per regiment of foot and 168 per regiment of horse found in the weekly return above (29 Oct. 1715).

110. *Blackader*, p. 470: 19 Nov. 1715; RH 2/4/309/2b: weekly return of horse and foot, [camp at Stirling], 2 Jan. 1716.
111. RH 2/4/309/2a: James Cockburn to Under-Secretary Pringle, Stirling, 2 Jan. 1716; RH 2/4/309/19: Argyll to Townshend, Stirling, 10 Jan. 1716; RH 2/4/309/32: order of battle, [Jan. 1716].
112. SP 54/7/98: instructions for the Whig Lord-Lieutenants, Whitehall, 25 Aug. 1715; Add. MS 37993, ff. 2v–3r: Polwarth to Argyll, Redbreas, 15 Sept. 1715; f. 5r: Polwarth to the Deputy-Lieutenants of Berwickshire, Lauder, 21 Sept. 1715.
113. BL, Add. MS 37993, ff. 3r–v: Polwarth to Argyll, Redbreas, 17 Sept. 1715; ff. 5r, 5v: Polwarth to the Deputy-Lieutenants of Berwickshire, Lauder, 21 Sept. 1715; ff. 7v–8r: to Sir Alexander Cockburn of Langton, Sir Robert Sinclair of Longformacus, Sir John Pringle of Stitchel, Sir Alexander Don of Newton, Sir Joseph Stewart of Allinbank, Sir John Swinton of that ilk, and James Car of Cavers, Lauder, 24 Sept. 1715; f. 14r: Polwarth to Argyll, Edinburgh, 28 Oct. 1715; RH 2/4/307/42[b]: Polwarth to 'dear Cusen', Redbraes, 13 Nov. 1715; BL, Add. MS 37993, f. 30v: Polwarth to William Hay of Drummelzier, Redbreas, 16 Nov. 1715.
114. RH 2/4/305/53: Argyll to Townshend, camp at Stirling, 18 Oct. 1715; *Blackader*, p. 468: 13 Nov. 1715; RH 2/4/307/51: Argyll to Townshend, Stirling, 15 Nov. 1715.
115. RH 2/4/307/21b: 'Ane Account of the Earl of Sutherland's Proceedings From his Embarkation at Leith the 25th of September to the 2nd of November, 1715'; RH 2/4/307/83b: Anon. to Sir James Stewart, Inverness, 18 Nov. 1715.
116. RH 2/4/306/90: proclamation by Argyll, camp at Stirling, 27 Oct. 1715; BL, Add. MS 37993, f. 10r–v: Polwarth to George Drummond, Commissioner of the Excise, Leith, 13 Oct. 1715; RH 2/4/308/101: Argyll to Townshend, [Stirling], 1 Dec. 1715.
117. SP 54/9/2d: spy report from Perth, Stirling, 1 Oct. 1715 (it should be noted that the meat of this report is based on the Jacobite Adjutant-General Lieutenant-Colonel William Clephane's review of 29 September, but the numbers are suspiciously neat, which suggests they have been rounded off); GD 124/10/496: 'List of the armie at the camp of Perth', Perth, 13 Oct. 1715; Atholl Papers, box 45, bundle 12/97: muster of Jacobite army Dec. 1715/Jan. 1716, compiled by Brigade Major Alexander Maitland; Monod, *Jacobitism and the English People*, p. 321; Patten, *History of the Rebellion*, p. 123. NB: I am in agreement with Paul Monod's estimate of the English component of the southern Jacobite army by the time of the battle of Preston, but differ in my estimate of the number of Scots.
118. SP 54/9/2d: spy report from Perth, Stirling, 1 Oct. 1715.
119. GD 124/10/496: 'List of the armie at the camp of Perth', Perth, 13 Oct. 1715.
120. RH 2/4/306/80: Islay to Townshend, Inverary, 23 Oct. 1715; RH 2/4/307/1: Atholl to Argyll, Blair castle, 1 Nov. 1715; RH 2/4/307/8: Argyll to Townshend, camp at Stirling, 3 Nov. 1715.
121. RH 2/4/306/65: Mar to 'Mr Forrester' [i.e. Forster], camp before Perth, 21 Oct. 1715.
122. RH 2/4/307/62: James Cockburn to Under-Secretary Pringle, Stirling, 18 Nov. 1715.
123. Atholl Papers, box 45, bundle 12/97: muster of the Jacobite army Dec. 1715/Jan. 1716.
124. Laing and Macknight (eds), *Memoirs of the Insurrection*, pp. 345–346, 350.
125. RH 2/4/306/63a: General George Carpenter to Stanhope, Newcastle upon Tyne, 21 Oct. 1715; RH 2/4/306/71: Dalrymple to Stanhope, Edinburgh, 22 Oct. 1715.
126. Patten, *History of the Rebellion*, p. 123.
127. RH 2/4/306/90: proclamation by Argyll, camp at Stirling, 27 Oct. 1715; RH 2/4/307/19: minute, of Cabinet meeting?, Whitehall, 5 Nov. 1715; RH 2/4/307/20: James Cockburn to Under-Secretary Pringle, camp at Stirling, 4 Nov. 1715.
128. RH 2/4/309/7b: memo from the Colonels of the Foot regiments to Argyll, [Stirling], Jan. 1716.

129. GD 220/5/623/3: Hyndford to Montrose, Edinburgh, 21 Jan. 1716; Steuart *Newsletters*, p. 120: [Edinburgh], 3 Feb. 1716; E. Maxtone Graham, *The Oliphants of Gask. Records of a Jacobite Family* (1910), p. 120: Scone, 30 Jan. 1716.

130. Huntington Library, California, Loudoun Papers, LO 12290 (lspbox 38): John Montgomerie *et al.* of the Carrick militia troop to Loudoun (petition), Ayr, 4 Apr. 1716; Loudoun Papers, LO 11359 (lspbox 21): Colonel William Dalrymple of Glenmure to Loudoun, Glasgow, 21 Nov. 1715; BL, Add. MS 37993, f. 14r: Polwarth to Argyll, Edinburgh, 28 Oct. 1715.

131. RH 2/4/306/80: Islay to Townshend, Inverary, 23 Oct. 1715; RH 2/4/307/8: Argyll to Townshend, camp at Stirling, 3 Nov. 1715; Anderson (ed.), *Papers of the Rev. John Anderson*, pp. 37, 38: Martine to Anderson, Inverary, 4 and 17 Nov. 1715.

132. RH 2/4/309/81: Argyll to Townshend, Erroll, 2 Feb. 1716.

133. GD 220/1926/10: ? to Montrose, Dundee, 4 Feb. 1716; GD 220/5/631/3a–b: John Hope to Montrose, Montrose, 6 Feb. 1716.

134. RH 2/4/305/46: intelligence from the north, Inverness, 14 Oct. 1715.

135. RH 2/4/307/83b: Anon. to Sir James Stewart, Inverness, 18 Nov. 1715.

136. A. Fergusson (ed.), *Major Fraser's Manuscript* (2 vols, Edinburgh, 1889), ii. 83; RH 2/4/309/1: Sutherland to Townshend, Inverness, 1 Jan. 1716.

137. Constable (ed.), *Fragment of a Memoir*, pp. 12–13; Blaikie (ed.), *Origins of the '45*, p. 122; Patten, *History of the Rebellion*, p. 29.

138. RH 2/4/308/178: Anon. to ?, [post-10 June 1716]; Hay, *History of Arbroath*, p. 178; GD 241/380/23: statement by John Brodie, Perth, 21 Feb. 1716; Henderson (ed.), *Mystics of the North-East*, p. 50.

139. SP 54/8/85: Solicitor-General Steuart to [Under-Secretary Pringle], Edinburgh, 23 Sept. 1715; Atholl Papers, box 45, bundle 12/74: Atholl to Sutherland, Blair Atholl, 9 Oct. 1715; Atholl Papers, box 45, bundle 12/175/5: Atholl to George I, 1716. According to a friend (admittedly one indulging in special pleading), Coll Macdonald of Keppoch faced a similar threat on the part of his clansmen if he refused to lead them out in the Jacobite cause (RH 2/4/311/55b: 'Kyllihuntly' to General Joseph Sabine [1716]).

140. Atholl Papers, box 45, bundle 12/137: Atholl to Lord James Murray of Garth, Huntingtower, 1 May 1716.

141. See, for example: SP 35/2, f. 29: petition of John Hall of Otterburn to Townshend, 1715; GD 220/5/664/2: William Stirling of Northside to John Napier of Kilcroich, 1 Feb. 1716; RH 2/4/310/165: John Farquharson of Invercauld to [Under-Secretary Pringle?], Marshalsea prison, 1 Mar. 1716. NB: public 'forcing' was also sometimes done collusively by fellow Jacobites who were going along with a sympathiser's prudential caution, for an example of which see: Laing and Macknight (eds), *Memoirs of the Insurrection*, p. 115.

142. RH 2/4/310/154b: Macdonald of Keppoch to Pollock, [Keppoch] 25 Feb. 1716; Laing and Macknight (eds), *Memoirs of the Insurrection*, pp. 266–267.

143. Hay, *History of Arbroath*, p. 180; GD 45/14/280: James Irving to Margaret Maule, Countess of Panmure, Aberdeen, 24 Jan. 1716.

144. Allardyce (ed.), *Historical Papers Relating to the Jacobite Period*, i. 55–56: Justice of the Peace court records, Kirktoune of Alford, 15 Mar. 1716. This is not the sole instance of such harsh coercion: SP 54/8/84: [Charles Cockburn] to [Under-Secretary Pringle], Edinburgh, 22 Sept. 1715.

145. RH 2/4/310/168c: petition of Patrick Drummond, Duncan Ferguson, Patrick Ferguson, John King, John Kenock Snr and Jr, John McInroy, John Ferguson, Patrick Dow, Murdoch King, Dougall Thomson, William Carmichael, William Kenock,

McInnes, all of Comrie, to Lord Justice Clerk Cockburn, Edinburgh and Stirling castles [1716].

146. Alexander Carmichael, 'Some Unrecorded Incidents of the Jacobite Risings', *Celtic Review*, vi (1897), pp. 281–283. I owe thanks to Professor Allan Macinnes for his illuminating explanation of this folk tradition.

147. RH 2/4/310/156c: Brigadier George Preston to Townshend, Edinburgh castle, 25 Feb. 1716.

148. RH 2/4/307/20: James Cockburn to Under-Secretary Pringle, camp at Stirling, 4 Nov. 1715.

149. Laing and Macknight (eds), *Memoirs of the Insurrection*, p. 111; Graham (ed.), *Annals and Correspondence of . . . Stair*, i. 281: Montrose to Stair, 3 Oct. 1715.

150. Mahon, *History*, i., appendix, pp. xlii: Kinnaird, 2 Jan. 1716; GD 220/5/621: Lady Lauderdale to Montrose, Edinburgh, 14 Jan. 1716; Steuart *Newsletters*, p. 89: [Edinburgh, 22 Jan. 1716]. NB: not everyone was quite so charmed with James when they encountered him, for an example of which see Fraser (ed.), *Chiefs of Grant*, ii. 97: Anon. to ?, Aberdeen, 11 Jan. 1716.

151. GD 45/14/280: James Irving to Margaret Panmure, Aberdeen, 24 Jan. 1716.

152. Blaikie (ed.), *Origins of the Forty-Five*, p. 122. See also: BL, Stowe 228, ff. 130–131: Sir Peter Fraser to Robethon, Edinburgh, 24 Sept. 1715; Charles S. Terry, 'Allan Cameron's Narrative, February–April 1716', *Scottish Historical Review*, v (1908), p. 146; Constable (ed.), *Fragment of a Memoir*, p. 12.

153. SP 54/8/13: intelligence from Aberdeen, Aberdeen, 2 Sept. 1715.

154. SP 54/8/106: James Cockburn to Under-Secretary Pringle, camp at Stirling, 26 Sept. 1715; SP 54/8/86: Polwarth to [Under-Secretary Pringle], Lauder, 23 Sept. 1715; GD 220/5/458/43/a–c: Rothes to John, Lord Leslie. Stirling, 29 Sept 1715.

155. SP 54/8/127: examination of the postmaster of Inverness, Edinburgh, 28 Sept. 1715; GD 44/17/11/47: claim by James Anderson, tenant in 'Garberane' [post-1716].

156. SP 78/160, f. 191: Thomas Crawford to Under-Secretary Pringle, Paris, 7/18 Jan. 1716.

157. SP 54/8/13: intelligence from Aberdeen, Aberdeen, 2 Sept. 1715.

158. RH 2/4/310/168a: Lord Justice Clerk to Under-Secretary Pringle, Edinburgh, 3 Mar. 1716; RH 2/4/310/168c: Petition of Patrick Drummond, Duncan Ferguson, Patrick Ferguson, John King, John Kenock Snr and Jr, John McInroy, John Ferguson, Patrick Dow, Murdoch King, Dougall Thomson, William Carmichael, William Kenock, McInnes, all of Comrie, to the Lord Justice Clerk, Edinburgh and Stirling castles, [1716]; RH 2/4/310/156b: John Knox, surgeon to the garrison, to Townshend, Edinburgh castle, 25 Feb. 1716.

159. Alistair and Henrietta Tayler, 'Lord Forfar and the '15', *Journal of the Society for Army Historical Research*, xv (1936), 139: Archibald Douglas, Earl of Forfar, to Cornelius Kennedy, camp at Stirling, 4 Nov. 1715; RH 2/4/307/32: James Cockburn to Under-Secretary Pringle, camp at Stirling, 8 Nov. 1715; Patten, *History of the Rebellion*, pp. 38–39.

160. Blair Atholl castle, Atholl Papers, box 45, bundle 12/97: muster of Jacobite army Dec. 1715/Jan. 1716; Laing and Macknight (eds), *Memoirs of the Insurrection*, pp. 261, 321; RH 2/4/308/107, 130, 139: Argyll to Townshend, Stirling, 4, 15 and 20 Dec. 1715.

161. Laing and Macknight (eds), *Memoirs of the Insurrection*, p. 164.

162. GD 220/5/662: Urquhart to Montrose, [Feb. 1716]; *A Letter From an Officer in the King's Army After it had Marched Northward From Aberdeen, to his Friend at London. February 1715/16* (London?, 1716), p. 10; Patten, *History of the Rebellion*, pp. 57, 68.

163. GD 241/380/23: statement by John Brodie, Perth, 21 Feb. 1716.

164. RH 2/4/308/96b: Lord Advocate Dalrymple to Stanhope, Edinburgh, 29 Nov. 1715.

165. GD 44/17/11/67: claim by George Davidson, tenant in Rhynie [post-1716]; -/129:

claim of James Brown, tenant in Raws of Huntly [post-1716]; RH 2/4/308/123 and RH 2/4/309/9, 34: Pollock to Townshend, Fort William, 11 Dec. 1715 and 4 and 14 Jan. 1716.

166. Edward M. Furgol, *A Regimental History of the Covenanting Armies 1639–1651* (Edinburgh, 1990), pp. 5–6; Pittock, *Myth of the Jacobite Clans*, pp. 57–58, 59. I owe this insight to Professor Murray Pittock of Manchester University.

167. Patten, *History of the Rebellion*, pp. 24–25.

168. Laing and Macknight (eds), *Memoirs of the Insurrection*, p. 259; Dumfries House, Bute Papers A546/344: James Stewart, Earl of Bute, to (Murdoch?) Maclean of Lochbowie, Inverary, 12 Nov. 1715 (I am grateful to Professor Allan Macinnes for allowing me to use his transcripts of the Bute Papers).

169. David Chandler, *The Art of Warfare in the Age of Marlborough* (1976), pp. 47–49, 102–108.

170. RH 2/4/307/39, 54: Argyll to Townshend, Stirling, 10 and 16 Nov. 1715; RH 2/4/307/55: James Cockburn to Under-Secretary Pringle, Stirling, 16 Nov. 1716; Steuart *Newsletters*, pp. 64–65: St Ringan's, 9 Nov. 1715.

171. BL, Add. MS. 61136, f. 195: Argyll to Marlborough, 1716 [rect. early 1715]. See also: RH 2/4/307/18: Argyll to Townshend, camp at Stirling, 4 Nov. 1715; RH 2/4/307/55: James Cockburn to Under-Secretary Pringle, Stirling, 16 Nov. 1716.

172. RH 2/4/306/73: Lord Advocate Dalrymple to Stanhope, Edinburgh, 22 Oct. 1715; Patten, *History of the Rebellion*, p. 86; GD 220/5/631/1: John Hope to Montrose, Stirling, 28 Jan. 1716.

173. RH 2/4/305/53: Argyll to Townshend, camp at Stirling, 18 Oct. 1715. See also: RH 2/4/306/73: Lord Advocate Dalrymple to Stanhope, Edinburgh, 22 Oct. 1715.

174. NB: the fear inspired among the Jacobites by Portmore's 'grey' dragoons, for which see Laing and Macknight (eds), *Memoirs of the Insurrection*, p. 85; GD 220/5/1913/12: [?] to Montrose, Stirling, 5 Oct. 1715.

175. BL, Add. MS 37993, f. 3r: Polwarth to Argyll, Redbreas, 15 Sept. 1715; SP 54/9/6a: Argyll to Stanhope, camp at Stirling, 4 Oct. 1715; RH 2/4/306/55: Argyll to Stanhope, camp at Stirling, 19 Oct. 1715; *Blackader*, p. 463: 23 Sept. 1715.

176. RH 2/4/307/66: Sutherland to Stanhope, Inverness, 19 Nov. 1715.

177. SP 54/9/18a: Charles Cockburn to Under-Secretary Pringle, Edinburgh, 7 Oct. 1715.

178. BL, Add. MS 61315. Vol. CCXV, f. 231: Wills to Marlborough, Preston, 27 Nov. 1715; Atholl Papers, box 45, bundle 12/91: John Douglas to Atholl, Edinburgh, 12 Dec. 1715. Lord Charles Murray was reprieved.

179. Laing and Macknight (eds), *Memoirs of the Insurrection*, p. 43.

180. Ibid., pp. 45, 46, 180.

181. Ibid., pp. 45–49, 137, 217.

182. Ibid., p. 78; RH 2/4/305/34: orders of the day for the Jacobite army, 18 Sept.–11 Oct. 1715.

183. RH 2/4/307/64: Argyll to Townshend, Stirling, 19 Nov. 1715. See also: RH 2/4/307/48: Argyll to Townshend, Stirling, 14 Nov. 1715.

184. SP 54/8/127: examination of the postmaster of Inverness, Edinburgh, 28 Sept. 1715; SP 54/9/2d: spy report from Perth, Stirling, 1 Oct. 1715; RH 2/4/305/34: orders of the day for the Jacobite army, 18 Sept.–11 Oct. 1715.

185. GD 18/2099: Baron John Clerk's account of a journey to Perth, researching 1715, 1717: [p. 35]; RH 2/4/307/64: Argyll to Townshend, Stirling, 19 Nov. 1715.

186. Laing and Macknight (eds), *Memoirs of the Insurrection*, pp. 112–113.

187. Ibid., pp. 52, 73, 133–134, 136, 138.

188. GD 18/2099: Baron John Clerk's account of a journey to Perth, researching 1715, 1717: p. 17.

189. RH 2/4/307/54: Argyll to Townshend, Stirling, 16 Nov. 1715.
190. SP 54/9/2d: spy report from Perth, Stirling, 1 Oct. 1715; SP 54/9/18c: intelligence from Perth, [Edinburgh], 6 Oct. 1715; Pittock, *Myth of the Jacobite Clans*, p. 51.
191. Patten, *History of the Rebellion*, pp. 16, 110–119 *passim*.
192. Ibid., p. 51.
193. HMC *Stuart*, v. 179: Lieutenant-Colonel John Steuart to Mar, Leyden, 25 Oct./5 Nov. 1717.
194. Patten, *History of the Rebellion*, p. 47.
195. Ibid., pp. 120–122; SP 54/9/2d: spy report from Perth, Stirling, 1 Oct. 1715; Laing and Macknight (eds), *Memoirs of the Insurrection*, pp. 40, 54.
196. BL, Add. MS 37993, f. 14v: Polwarth to Carpenter, Edinburgh, 28 Oct. 1715.
197. RH 2/4/307/26a: Lord Justice Clerk Cockburn to Under-Secretary Pringle, Edinburgh, 6 Nov. 1715; GD 220/5/1909/7: John Stirling to Montrose, Glasgow, 9 Nov. 1715.
198. SP 54/7/24: [Lord Justice Clerk Cockburn] to Montrose, 6 Aug. 1715.
199. SP 54/7/39: Earl of Kilmarnock to Montrose, 12 Aug. 1715; RH 2/4/308/133: Argyll to Townshend, Stirling, 17 Dec. 1715.
200. SP 54/7/80: Solicitor-General Steuart to Townshend, Edinburgh, 26 Aug. 1715.
201. BL, Add. MS 37993, f. 2v: Polwarth to Argyll, Redbreas, 15 Sept. 1715. Even the Glasgow volunteers were very poorly armed: SP 54/8/74a: Argyll to Stanhope, camp at Stirling, 18 Sept. 1715.
202. Fraser (ed.), *Chiefs of Grant*, ii. 100: Huntly to Brigadier Grant, Inverness, 10 Mar. 1716.
203. RH 2/4/305/27: 'Advyces from North Britain', [9?] Oct. 1715.
204. SP 54/7/41[b]: memo by Duff [Aug. 1715]. See also: RH 2/4/305/38: Lord Advocate Dalrymple to Stanhope, Edinburgh, 12 Oct. 1715.
205. BL, Add. MS 37993, f. 4v: Polwarth to Argyll, Redbreas, 20 Sept. 1715; SP 54/9/24: Argyll to Townshend, camp at Stirling, 7 Oct. 1715; RH 2/4/305/47: John Sibbit, Mayor of Berwick, to Stanhope, 14 Oct. 1715.
206. Laing and Macknight (eds), *Memoirs of the Insurrection*, pp. 45, 48, 143.
207. PRO, ADM 8/14: 1 Oct., 1 Nov. and 1 Dec. 1715 and 1 Jan. 1716.
208. SP 54/9/26b: intelligence from the north, Inverness, 30 Sept. 1715; SP 54/9/2c: John Anderson and Robert? Colquhoun to the Provost of Glasgow, Dunbarton, 30 Sept. 1715; SP 54/9/18c: intelligence from Perth, [Edinburgh], 6 Oct. 1715; Patten, *History of the Rebellion*, p. 38; Laing and Macknight (eds), *Memoirs of the Insurrection*, pp. 45, 81.
209. RH 2/4/305/30: Pollock to Lord Justice Clerk Cockburn?, Fort William, 9 Oct. 1715; RH 2/4/307/26a: Lord Justice Clerk Cockburn to Under-Secretary Pringle, Edinburgh, 6 Nov. 1715.
210. Laing and Macknight (eds), *Memoirs of the Insurrection*, p. 191; Atholl Papers, box 45, bundle 12/77: account of the southern army to Preston.
211. Allardyce (ed.), *Historical Papers Relating to the Jacobite Period*, i. 40–1: Aberdeen Burgh records, 15 Sept. 1715; Laing and Macknight (eds), *Memoirs of the Insurrection*, p. 40.
212. SP 54/9/6d: George Thomson, Baillie of Burntisland, to Lord Justice Clerk Cockburn, Burntisland, 3 Oct. 1715; Constable (ed.), *Fragment of a Memoir*, pp. 24, 26, 27.
213. HMC *Stuart*, i. 502–503, 503–504: Hamilton to James, Paris, 2/13 Feb. 1716; Constable (ed.), *Fragment of a Memoir*, p. 26.
214. 'Lord Forfar and the '15', p. 137: Archibald Douglas, Earl of Forfar to Cornelius Kennedy, camp at Stirling, 31 Oct. 1715.

215. Samuel Hibbert Ware (ed.), *Lancashire During the Rebellion of 1715* (Chetham Society, 1st ser. v., 1845), p. 73; Patten, *History of the Rebellion,* p. 65.
216. Patten, *History of the Rebellion,* pp. 85–87, 92; Atholl Papers, box 45, bundle 12/77: account of the Jacobite southern army to Preston.
217. John Brewer, *The Sinews of Power. War, Money and the English State, 1688–1783* (New York, 1988), *passim.* Cf. Jeremy Black, *Britain as a Military Power, 1688–1815* (1999), pp. 267–293.
218. SP 54/7/60a: Board of Ordnance to Townshend, [London] 20 Aug. 1715.
219. SP 54/7/87: Solicitor-General Steuart to [Under-Secretary Pringle?], Edinburgh, 28 Aug. 1715.
220. RH 2/4/390/2/40–42: Lieutenant-General James Maitland to Mar, Fort William, 24 July 1714; SP 54/7/87: Solicitor-General Steuart to [Under-Secretary Pringle?], Edinburgh, 28 Aug. 1715; SP 54/8/79: James Cockburn to Under-Secretary Pringle, Stirling, 21 Sept. 1715.
221. SP 54/8/77: Lord Justice Clerk Cockburn to [Under-Secretary Pringle,], Edinburgh, 20 Sept. 1715; SP 54/9/24: Argyll to Townshend, camp at Stirling, 7 Oct. 1715; RH 2/4/306/55: Argyll to Stanhope, camp at Stirling, 19 Oct. 1715.
222. SP 54/8/121: Islay to Townshend, Edinburgh, 30 Sept. 1715; SP 54/9/21: Islay to Townshend, Inverary, 7 Oct. 1715; RH 2/4/306/55: Argyll to Stanhope, camp at Stirling, 19 Oct. 1715; RH 2/4/306/85: James Cockburn to Under-Secretary Pringle, camp at Stirling, 25 Oct. 1715; RH 2/4/306/70: Lord Justice Clerk Cockburn to Under-Secretary Pringle, Edinburgh, 22 Oct. 1715.
223. RH 2/4/306/101b: Argyll to Stanhope, camp at Stirling, 31 Oct. 1715; RH 2/4/307/18, 70, 82: Argyll to Townshend, Stirling, 4, 20 and 25 Nov. 1715.
224. RH 2/4/307/42[a]: Polwarth to [Townshend?], Redbraes, 13 Nov. 1715; BL, Add. MS 37993, f. 35r: Polwarth to Townshend, Redbreas, 28 Nov. 1715 (see also: ff. 35v, 37r, 37v–38r, 39v); RH 2/4/391/238–239: Townshend to Argyll, Whitehall, 4 Nov. 1715.
225. RH 2/4/307/83b: Anon. to Sir James Stewart, Inverness, 18 Nov. 1715; RH 2/4/310/229: magistrates of Glasgow, Glasgow, 13 Apr. 1716; RH 2/4/310/240: [Lord Justice Cockburn to Under-Secretary Pringle] Edinburgh, 27 Apr. 1716.
226. RH 2/4/308/179[a]: Cadogan to Stanhope, Edinburgh, 19 Dec. 1715; RH 2/4/309/47, 120: Argyll to Townshend, Stirling and Aberdeen, 21 Jan. and 15 Feb. 1716; RH 2/4/309/55: Cadogan to Stanhope, Stirling, 25 Jan. 1716.
227. SP 54/9/21: Islay to Townshend, Inverary, 7 Oct. 1715; Fergusson (ed.), *Fraser's Manuscript,* ii. 79; HMC *Stuart,* i. 476–477: [Glenbuchat] to [Mar?], Fochabers, 14/25 Dec. 1715; Fraser (ed.), *Chiefs of Grant,* ii. 95: Brigadier Alexander Grant to Captain George Grant, Stirling, 22 Dec. 1715.
228. GD 220/5/631/10a–b: John Hope to Montrose, Inverness, 6 Apr. 1716.
229. RH 2/4/307/18: Argyll to Townshend, camp at Stirling, 4 Nov. 1715.
230. RH 2/4/309/1: Sutherland to Townshend, Inverness, 1 Jan. 1716.
231. RH 2/4/308/133: Argyll to Townshend, Stirling, 17 Dec. 1715; HMC *Stuart,* i. 477, 479: [Glenbuchat] to [Mar?], Fochabers, 14/25 Dec. 1715; RH 2/4/309/1: Sutherland to Townshend, Inverness, 1 Jan. 1716.
232. RH 2/4/305/107: account of Kenmure's rising all the way to Preston; RH 2/4/306/98: Lord Justice Clerk Cockburn to Townshend, Edinburgh, 30 Oct. 1715; Patten, *History of the Rebellion,* p. 89.
233. SP 54/8/57: Barkie to Townshend, Inverness, 14 Sept. 1715; SP 54/8/69: Pollock to Townshend, Fort William, 16 Sept. 1715; Patten, *History of the Rebellion,* pp. 37–38.
234. RH 2/4/305/43: Mar to John Horn of Westhall, camp at Perth, 13 Oct. 1715; SP 54/9/4: Mar to Lady Rathton and Baillie David Maxwell of Dundee, camp at Perth, 3 Oct. 1715.; Alistair and Henrietta Tayler (eds), *The Jacobite Cess Roll for the County of*

Aberdeen in 1715 (Third Spalding Club, Aberdeen, 1932), *passim*; RH 2/4/306/105: formal summons to heritors and other landowners in Fife to pay levy by Mar [Oct. 1715]; GD 45/1/198: order from Mar for the payment of a levy by shire of Forfar, Perth, 4 Oct. 1715; RH 2/4/306/73: Lord Advocate Dalrymple to Stanhope, Edinburgh, 22 Oct. 1715.

235. SP 54/9/18c: intelligence from Perth, [Edinburgh], 6 Oct. 1715.

236. SP 54/9/2d: spy report from Perth, Stirling, 1 Oct. 1715; Laing and Macknight (eds), *Memoirs of the Insurrection*, pp. 72, 190, 276; RH 2/4/307/74: Argyll to Townshend, Stirling, 21 Nov. 1715; HMC *Stuart*, i. 472: accounts of moneys paid to sundry Jacobite units, Oct. and Nov. 1715.

237. Laing and Macknight (eds), *Memoirs of the Insurrection*, pp. 72, 101, 192; SP 54/9/9: Lord Advocate Dalrymple to [Under-Secretary Pringle?], Edinburgh, 4 Oct. 1715; RH 2/4/305/27: 'Advyces from North Britain', [9?] Oct. 1715; RH 2/4/306/59: Sibbit to Stanhope, Berwick, 20 Oct. 1715.

238. *Loch Lomond Expedition*, pp. 40, 41: J. Row to [Wodrow?], Leslie, 28 Mar. 1716. Asked why they were so 'rude', a Macgregor officer answered: 'I see many good shoes here, and my men are going barefoot.'

239. RH 2/4/307/78: proclamation by Mar, camp at Perth, 24 Nov. 1715; *Loch Lomond Expedition*, p. 42: J. Row to [Wodrow?], Leslie, 28 Mar. 1716; Patten, *History of the Rebellion*, p. 74.

240. HMC *Stuart*, i. 457, 458: Mar to [Glenbuchat], camp at Perth, 31 Oct./11 Nov. and 1/12 Nov. 1715; Hay, *History of Arbroath*, p. 178.

241. Laing and Macknight (eds), *Memoirs of the Insurrection*, pp. 101, 267; RH 2/4/309/18: James Cockburn to Under-Secretary Pringle, Stirling, 7 Jan. 1716; Warrand (ed.), *More Culloden Papers*, ii. 86–87: Robert Wemyss to Crawford of Crail, Grange, 17 Jan. 1716; HMC *Stuart*, i. 508: John Gordon, Earl of Aboyne, to Lieutenant-General Gordon, Aberdeen, 7/18 Feb. 1716; GD 220/5/612/5: Northesk to Montrose, 25 Feb. 1716.

242. GD 46/6/98: Seaforth to Ranald McDonald, Inverness, 20 Oct. 1715; Anderson (ed.), *Papers of the Rev. John Anderson*, p. 34: Martine to Anderson, Inverary, 28 Oct. 1715; Warrand (ed.), *More Culloden Papers*, ii. 88: John Pattullo to Crawford of Crail, Balhoussie, 30 Jan. 1716; Fergusson (ed.), *Fraser's Manuscript*, ii. 70; GD 220/5/611/3: Colin Graham of Drenny to James Graham, 'Inarbreases', 30 Jan. 1716.

243. RH 2/4/305/107: account of Kenmure's rising all the way to Preston; J. D. Marshall (ed.), *The Autobiography of William Stout of Lancaster, 1665–1752* (Chetham Historical Society, 1967), p. 173; Patten, *History of the Rebellion*, pp. 58, 67; GD 18/2092/4: Sir John Clerk's journal for Apr. 1712–1715: 14 Oct. 1715; Ware (ed.), *Lancashire During the Rebellion of 1715*, pp. 78, 82, 97.

244. Laing and Macknight (eds), *Memoirs of the Insurrection*, p. 84.

245. RH 2/4/306/95: Lord Advocate Dalrymple to Stanhope, Edinburgh, 29 Oct. 1715; Laing and Macknight (eds), *Memoirs of the Insurrection*, pp. 93, 249, 266.

246. [Anon.], *The Battle of Sherrifmuir* (Stirling, 1898), p. 45.

247. *Loch Lomond Expedition*, pp. 34–39: [G. Archer?] to Alexander Archer, L[eslie], 13 and 20 Jan. and 9 Feb.1716; pp. 39–50: J. Row to [Wodrow?], Leslie, 28 Mar. 1716.

Chapter 6 'Sae Famed in Martial Story':
Military Operations, September 1715–April 1716,
the Central Theatre

1. Laing and Macknight (eds), *Memoirs of the Insurrection*, p. 219; RH 2/4/307/12: Captain Robert Monro to Townshend, Inverbreaky, 3 Nov. 1715; RH 2/4/305/107: account of Kenmure's rising all the way to Preston.
2. RH 2/4/306/70: Lord Justice Cockburn to Under-Secretary Pringle, Edinburgh, 22 Oct. 1715; RH 2/4/306/89: Tweeddale to [Under-Secretary Pringle], Edinburgh, 27 Oct. 1715; RH 2/4/306/101a: Mar to Argyll, camp at Perth, 30 Oct. 1715.
3. GD 18/3152/9: to Sir John Clerk, [Edinburgh, *c.* 18?] Oct. 1715; RH 2/4/306/89: Tweeddale to [Under-Secretary Pringle], Edinburgh, 27 Oct. 1715; Ware (ed.), *Lancashire During the Rebellion of 1715*, p. 77; Steuart *Newsletters*, p. 110: [Edinburgh], 27 Jan. 1716.
4. RH 2/4/309/68: Argyll to Townshend, Dunblane, 29 Jan. 1716; RH 2/4/306/62: Dalrymple to Stanhope, Edinburgh, 20 Oct. 1715; GD 18/3152/8: Baron John Clerk to Sir John Clerk, Edinburgh, [*c.* 24 Oct? 1715]; RH 2/4/309/108: Captain Robert Monro of Foulis to Stanhope, Inverness, 13 Feb. 1716; Ware (ed.), *Lancashire During the Rebellion of 1715*, pp. 77, 82, 96–97, 107.
5. *Miscellany of the Maitland Club* III (Edinburgh, 1843), pp. 441–474: 'Accounts of the Burning of the Villages of Auchterarder, Muthill, Crieff, Blackford, Dalreoch and Dunning, about the beginning of the year 1716'; Patten, *History of the Rebellion*, p. 183; A. and H. Tayler, *1715*, p. 137; Baynes, *Jacobite Rising*, p. 168.
6. HMC *Stuart*, i. 497: Mar to General Gordon, Scone, 26 Jan./6 Feb. 1716; Chambers, *History of the Rebellions in Scotland*, pp. 312–314: James to Argyll, Montrose, 4 Feb. 1716; *Loch Lomond Expedition*, appendix, pp. 44–46 footnote.
7. RH 2/4/391/188–99: Townshend to Argyll, Whitehall, 4 Oct. 1715. See also: RH 2/4/391/171–172: Townshend to Argyll, Whitehall, 24 Sept. 1715; RH 2/4/391/182: Stanhope to Argyll, Whitehall, 26 Sept. 1715.
8. This was not something Argyll was at all happy about: BL, Add. MS. 61136, f. 170r: Argyll to Marlborough, camp at Stirling, 7 Oct. 1715.
9. ADM 8/14: 1 May and 1 June 1715; Murray, *George I, the Baltic and the Whig Split*, pp. 112–113, 161–165.
10. ADM 8/14: 1 July 1715.
11. ADM 8/14: 1 Aug. 1715.
12. ADM 8/14: 1 Sept. 1715.
13. N. Hill, 'A Side Light on the 1715', *Scottish Historical Review*, xvii (1920), 225–226.
14. Ibid., p. 226.
15. ADM 8/14: 1 Nov. 1715.
16. Mahon, *History*, i., appendix, p. xxii: Bolingbroke to James, [Paris?] 9/20 Sept. 1715; HMC *Stuart*, i. 454: Bolingbroke to James, Paris, 28 Oct./8 Nov. 1715; HMC *Stuart*, i. 471: James to Bolingbroke, [Saint-Malo?], 20 Nov./1 Dec. 1715.
17. SP 54/8/104: Islay to Townshend, camp at Stirling, 30 Sept. 1715; RH 2/4/308/119: Argyll to Townshend, Stirling, 10 Dec. 1715; GD 220/5/610/2: Lord Justice Clerk Cockburn to Montrose, Edinburgh, 7 Jan. 1716.
18. SP 54/8/111: Argyll to Townshend, camp at Stirling, 28 Sept. 1715; Hill, 'Side Light on the 1715', p. 230; RH 2/4/306/51e: Captain James Stuart of *Royal Ann Galley* to Secretary of the Navy Josias Burchett, off Inchkeith Island, 11 Oct. 1715.
19. RH 2/4/305/53: Argyll to Townshend, camp at Stirling, 18 Oct. 1715.
20. Martin Haile, *James Francis Edward. The Old Chevalier* (1907), pp. 206–207, 215.

21. SP 54/8/51: Sutherland to Townshend, aboard HMS *Queenborough* at the Nore, 12 Sept. 1715; RH 2/4/305/31: Captain Stuart (*Royal Ann Galley*) to the Admiralty, at sea off Ardhead, 1 Oct. 1715; RH 2/4/305/27: 'advyces from North Britain', [9?] Oct. 1715; Henrietta Tayler (ed.), *The Seven Sons of the Provost. A Family Chronicle of the Eighteenth Century Compiled from Original Letters 1692–1761* (1949), p. 66: William Kennedy to Thomas Kennedy, [camp at Stirling], 12 Oct. 1715.
22. RH 2/4/308/139: Argyll to Townshend, Stirling, 20 Dec. 1715; Steuart *Newsletters*, p. 83: [Edinburgh?], 28 Dec. 1715.
23. SP 54/8/105: Argyll to Townshend, camp at Stirling, 26 Sept. 1715; BL, Add. MS 61640. Vol. DXL, ff. 25–26: return of the army in Ireland, Aug. 1714; BL, Add. MS 61640. Vol. DXL, f. 193: present state of the establishment in Ireland [*c.* June 1715].
24. Ó Ciardha, *Ireland and the Jacobite Cause*, pp. 135–136; BL, Stowe 228, ff. 164, 197r: Gustavus Hamilton to Robethon, Dublin, 25 Oct. 1715.
25. See above, pp. 65–66, 92–94.
26. Monod, *Jacobitism and the English People*, p. 317.
27. Haile, *James Francis Edward*, pp. 189, 195; HMC *Stuart*, i. 456: James to Lewis Innes, Saint-Malo, 31 Oct./11 Nov. 1715.
28. SP 54/9/1: instructions for General George Wade, St James, 1 Oct. 1715; GD 220/5/1902/2: [Hyndford to Montrose], Bath, 3 Oct. 1715; C. E. Doble (ed.), *Remarks and Collections of Thomas Hearne* (6 vols, 1885), v. 125, 149: 9 Oct. and 30 Nov. 1715; Patten, *History of the Rebellion*, pp. 219–220.
29. SP 78/160, f. 136: Whitehall, 31 Oct. 1715.
30. RH 2/4/309/32: Argyll's order of battle, [Jan. 1716].
31. SP 54/8/74a: Argyll to Stanhope, camp at Stirling, 18 Sept. 1715; SP 54/8/111 and 54/9/24: Argyll to Townshend, camp at Stirling, 28 Sept. and 7 Oct. 1715; Laing and Macknight (eds), *Memoirs of the Insurrection*, p. 94.
32. RH 2/4/307/18: Argyll to Townshend, camp at Stirling, 4 Nov. 1715.
33. RH 2/4/306/99: [Charles Cockburn to Under-Secretary Pringle], Edinburgh, 30 Oct. 1715; Constable (ed.), *Fragment of a Memoir*, p. 13.
34. SP 54/8/127: examination of the postmaster of Inverness, Edinburgh, 28 Sept. 1715; Laing and Macknight (eds), *Memoirs of the Insurrection*, pp. 29, 83.
35. *Petite guerre* can also be translated as 'guerrilla' warfare, but the modern image and connotations of this term markedly differ from the actual practice and understanding of guerrilla warfare in the early eighteenth century. Hence I have deliberately used the French, rather than the now far more common Spanish term, to describe the low-intensity warfare being waged at this time.
36. Chandler, *Art of Warfare*, pp. 27, 68–72.
37. HMC *Stuart*, i. 450: Mar to Gordon of [Glenbuchat], camp at Perth, 21 Oct./1 Nov. 1715; Laing and Macknight (eds), *Memoirs of the Insurrection*, pp. 166, 168.
38. Laing and Macknight (eds), *Memoirs of the Insurrection*, p. 168; W. L. Burn, 'Charles Cathcart and the Affair at Dunfermline', *Journal of the Society for Army Historical Research*, xvi (1937), p. 56.
39. Burn, 'Affair at Dunfermline', pp. 56–57.
40. Laing and Macknight (eds), *Memoirs of the Insurrection*, p. 169; Burn, 'Affair at Dunfermline', p. 57.
41. SP 54/8/80a: Argyll to Stanhope, camp at Stirling, 21 Sept. 1715; Tayler (ed.), *Seven Sons of the Provost*, pp. 65, 67: William Kennedy to Thomas Kennedy, [camp at Stirling] 1 and 12 Oct. 1715; A. and H. Tayler, 'Lord Forfar and the '15', p. 132: Archibald Douglas, Earl of Forfar, to Cornelius Kennedy, camp nr Stirling, 10 Oct. 1715; RH 2/4/306/101a: Mar to Argyll, camp at Perth, 30 Oct. 1715.
42. SP 54/8/111: camp at Stirling, 28 Sept. 1715.

43. RH 2/4/307/18: Argyll to Townshend, camp at Stirling, 4 Nov. 1715.
44. Tayler (ed.), *Seven Sons of the Provost*, pp. 65, 66: William Kennedy to Thomas Kennedy, [camp at] Stirling, 8 and 12 Oct. 1715.
45. SP 54/9/6a: Argyll to Stanhope, camp at Stirling, 4 Oct. 1715; Tayler (ed.), *Seven Sons of the Provost*, p. 65: William Kennedy to Thomas Kennedy, [camp at] Stirling, 8 Oct. 1715; HMC *Stuart*, i. 456: Mar to [Glenbuchat], camp at Perth, 30 Oct./10 Nov. 1715; Steuart *Newsletters*, p. 83: [Edinburgh?], 28 Dec. 1715.
46. Chandler, *Art of Warfare*, pp. 72–73.
47. A. and H. Tayler, *1715*, p. 193; Gregg, 'Mar', p. 182; Mahon, *History*, i., appendix, pp. xliii: James to Bolingbroke, Kinnaird, 2 Jan. 1716.
48. Laing and Macknight (eds), *Memoirs of the Insurrection*, pp. 22, 55, 83, 96, 131, 166, 196–197, 213, 246; A. and H. Tayler, *1715*, p. 231.
49. SP 54/8/89: Argyll to Townshend, camp at Stirling, 24 Sept. 1715; Laing and Macknight (eds), *Memoirs of the Insurrection*, p. 83; Warrand (ed.), *More Culloden Papers*, ii. 87–88: Adjutant-General Clephane to [Henry Crawfurd], court at Scone, 21 Jan. 1716.
50. Laing and Macknight (eds), *Memoirs of the Insurrection*, p. 83.
51. Erskine (ed.), 'The Earl of Mar's Legacies', p. 174.
52. A. and H. Tayler, *1715*, p. 232; Laing and Macknight (eds), *Memoirs of the Insurrection*, pp. 158, 159.
53. Mahon, *History*, i., appendix, p. xli: James to Bolingbroke, Kinnaird, 2 Jan. 1716; HMC *Stuart*, i. 486: Mar to Bolingbroke, Kinnaird, 3/14 Jan. 1716.
54. Laing and Macknight (eds), *Memoirs of the Insurrection*, p. 246.
55. Constable (ed.), *Fragment of a Memoir*, p. 10.
56. Laing and Macknight (eds), *Memoirs of the Insurrection*, p. 336.
57. A. and H. Tayler, *1715*, p. 238; Laing and Macknight (eds), *Memoirs of the Insurrection*, p. 223 note 1; Andrew M. Scott, *Bonnie Dundee. John Graham of Claverhouse* (Edinburgh, 2000), pp. 207–223.
58. Lenman, *Jacobite Risings*, p. 31.
59. David Stevenson, *Alasdair MacColla and the Highland Problem in the 17th Century* (Edinburgh, 1980), pp. 82–84, 127–128, 133–134.
60. SP 54/9/6d: George Thomson, Baillie of Burntisland, to Lord Justice Clerk Cockburn, Burntisland, 3 Oct. 1715; GD 220/5/1913/12: [?] to Montrose, Stirling, 5 Oct. 1715; Laing and Macknight (eds), *Memoirs of the Insurrection*, pp. 95–100, 107–122.
61. HMC *Stuart*, i. 450: Mar to [Glenbuchat], camp at Perth, 21 Oct./1 Nov. 1715; i. 453: James Malcolm of Grange to [Glenbuchat], Falkland, 27 Oct./7 Nov. 1715; RH 2/4/306/56a: Lord Justice Clerk Cockburn to Townshend, Edinburgh, 19 Oct. 1715.
62. HMC *Stuart*, i. 456: Mar to [Glenbuchat], camp at Perth, 30 Oct./10 Nov. 1715; GD 124/10/497: 'copie of the instructions to Mrs Miller to be communicated to the King's friends besouth Forth', Perth, 23 and 24 Oct. 1715; RH 2/4/393/51–52: Townshend to Polwarth, Whitehall, 22 Dec. 1715; Fergusson (ed.), *Fraser's Manuscript*, ii. 50–51.
63. A. and H. Tayler (eds), 'Lord Forfar and the '15', p. 132: Forfar to Cornelius Kennedy, camp nr Stirling, 10 Oct. 1715; Laing and Macknight (eds), *Memoirs of the Insurrection*, pp. 52–53.
64. RH 2/4/307/39 and 2/4/309/47, 67: Argyll to Townshend, camp at Stirling, 10 Nov. 1715 and 21 and 28 Jan. 1716.
65. Laing and Macknight (eds), *Memoirs of the Insurrection*, pp. 54–56.
66. Patten, *History of the Rebellion*, pp. 120–122.
67. Tayler (ed.), *Seven Sons of the Provost*, p. 66: William Kennedy to Thomas Kennedy, [camp at Stirling], 12 Oct. 1715; Laing and Macknight (eds), *Memoirs of the Insurrection*, pp. 115, 118, 124, 127–128.

68. SP 54/9/6a, 24: Argyll to Stanhope, camp at Stirling, 4 and 7 Oct. 1715; Hill, 'Side Light on the 1715', p. 229: Stirling, 8 Oct. 1715.
69. SP 54/9/10: Lords Commissioners of the Admiralty to Stanhope, London, 5 Oct. 1715; RH 2/4/305/51d: Captain Poole to Josiah Burchett, Leith Roads, 10 Oct. 1715; RH 2/4/306/51e: Captain Stuart of *Royal Ann Galley* to Josias Burchett, off Inchkeith Island, 11 Oct. 1715.
70. Steuart *Newsletters*, p. 38: Edinburgh, 15/20 Oct. 1715; RH 2/4/305/49: Postmaster Anderson of Edinburgh to John Lloyd, Edinburgh, 16 Oct. 1715; RH 2/4/306/65: Mar to 'Mr Forrester' [i.e. Forster], camp before Perth, 21 Oct. 1715.
71. RH 2/4/305/39: Lord Advocate Dalrymple to Stanhope, [Edinburgh], 13 Oct. 1715; RH 2/4/305/47: John Sibbit, Mayor of Berwick, to Stanhope, [Berwick], 14 Oct. 1715; RH 2/4/305/53: Argyll to Townshend, camp at Stirling, 18 Oct. 1715; RH 2/4/306/56a: Lord Justice Clerk Cockburn to Townshend, Edinburgh, 19 Oct. 1715.
72. RH 2/4/305/53: Argyll to Townshend, camp at Stirling, 18 Oct. 1715; RH 2/4/306/83: Wightman to [General George Carpenter?], Edinburgh, 24 Oct. 1715.
73. RH 2/4/305/53: Argyll to Townshend, camp at Stirling, 18 Oct. 1715; GD 220/5/455/55: Lord Justice Clerk Cockburn to Montrose, Edinburgh, 19 Oct. 1715; Steuart *Newsletters*, p. 39: Edinburgh, 15–20 Oct. 1715.
74. Steuart *Newsletters*, pp. 44–45: Edinburgh, 16 Oct. 1715; BL, Add. MS 37993, f. 12r : Polwarth to Lord of Session Kimmerghame, Edinburgh, 20 Oct. 1715; A. and H. Tayler, 'Lord Forfar and the '15', p. 137: Forfar to Cornelius Kennedy, camp at Stirling, 31 Oct. 1715.
75. RH 2/4/305/49: Postmaster Anderson of Edinburgh to John Lloyd, Edinburgh, 16 Oct. 1715; RH 2/4/305/53: Argyll to Townshend, camp at Stirling, 18 Oct. 1715; Tayler (ed.), *Seven Sons of the Provost*, p. 67: William Kennedy to Thomas Kennedy, Edinburgh, 25 Oct. 1715.
76. RH 2/4/305/53 and RH 2/4/307/18: Argyll to Townshend, camp at Stirling, 18 Oct. and 4 Nov. 1715.
77. A. and H. Tayler, 'Lord Forfar and the '15', p. 132: Forfar to Cornelius Kennedy, camp nr Stirling, 10 Oct. 1715; SP 54/8/68: Argyll to Townshend, Edinburgh, 15 Sept. 1715; SP 54/8/80a: Argyll to Stanhope, camp at Stirling, 21 Sept. 1715; BL, Add. MS. 61136, f. 170r: Argyll to Marlborough, camp at Stirling, 7 Oct. 1715; RH 2/4/307/18: Argyll to Townshend, camp at Stirling, 4 Nov. 1715.
78. RH 2/4/391/227–229: Whitehall, 2 Nov. 1715.
79. RH 2/4/307/30, 54: Argyll to Townshend, camp at Stirling, 8 and 16 Nov. 1715.
80. SP 54/8/80a: Argyll to Stanhope, camp at Stirling, 21 Sept. 1715.
81. RH 2/4/307/18, 39: Argyll to Townshend, camp at Stirling, 4 and 10 Nov. 1715.
82. SP 54/8/89: Argyll and Townshend, camp at Stirling, 24 Sept. 1715; RH 2/4/391/149: Townshend to Lord Justice Clerk Cockburn, Whitehall, 3 Sept. 1715; RH 2/4/391/162: Townshend and Stanhope to Argyll, Whitehall, 15 Sept. 1715; RH 2/4/391/195: Townshend to Argyll, Whitehall, 4 Oct. 1715; RH 2/4/391/212: Stanhope to Argyll, Cockpit, 11 Oct. 1715; RH 2/4/391/232: Townshend to Lord Justice Clerk Cockburn, Whitehall, 4 Nov. 1715.
83. RH 2/4/391/250: Townshend to Argyll, Whitehall, 8 Nov. 1715.
84. RH 2/4/393/3, 15: Townshend to Argyll, Whitehall, 15 and 26 Nov. 1715; RH 2/4/393/6–7: Stanhope to Argyll, Whitehall, 22 Nov. 1715.
85. RH 2/4/305/49: Postmaster Anderson of Edinburgh to John Lloyd, Edinburgh, 16 Oct. 1715; Laing and Macknight (eds), *Memoirs of the Insurrection*, p. 144.
86. RH 2/4/306/101b: Argyll to Stanhope, camp at Stirling, 31 Oct. 1715; A. and H. Tayler, 'Lord Forfar and the '15', pp. 139–40: Forfar to Cornelius Kennedy, camp at Stirling, 4 Nov. 1715.

87. Laing and Macknight (eds), *Memoirs of the Insurrection*, pp. 144, 158, 164, 189.
88. RH 2/4/307/18, 39: Argyll to Townshend, camp at Stirling, 4 and 10 Nov. 1715.
89. Constable (ed.), *Fragment of a Memoir*, p. 16; Laing and Macknight (eds), *Memoirs of the Insurrection*, pp. 204, 207–208; Mackay, 'Camerons in the Rising of 1715', p. 14.
90. RH 2/4/307/48: Argyll to Townshend, Stirling, 14 Nov. 1715; Constable (ed.), *Fragment of a Memoir*, p. 17; Laing and Macknight (eds), *Memoirs of the Insurrection*, pp. 209, 214.
91. Chandler, *Art of Warfare*, pp. 102–104, 117–121.
92. Atholl Papers, box 45, bundle 12/117: weapons turned in to Atholl, 12–22 Mar. 1716; Nicholas Maclean-Bristol (ed.), *Inhabitants of the Inner Isles, Morvern and Arnamurchan 1716* (Scottish Record Society, xxi, Edinburgh, 1998), p. 173: list of arms handed in at Duart, Apr. 1716.
93. Laing and Macknight (eds), *Memoirs of the Insurrection*, p. 217; Stevenson, *Alasdair MacColla*, pp. 82–84.
94. Laing and Macknight (eds), *Memoirs of the Insurrection*, pp. 78, 101, 102–103, 171.
95. RH 2/4/307/48, 54: Argyll to Townshend, Stirling, 14 and 16 Nov. 1715; Patten, *History of the Rebellion*, p. 152.
96. SP 54/9/24: Argyll to Townshend, camp at Stirling, 7 Oct. 1715; RH 2/4/307/48: Argyll to Townshend, Stirling, 14 Nov. 1715.
97. Laing and Macknight (eds), *Memoirs of the Insurrection*, pp. 209, 212; Mackay, 'Camerons in the Rising of 1715', p. 14; Constable (ed.), *Fragment of a Memoir*, p. 17.
98. Laing and Macknight (eds), *Memoirs of the Insurrection*, p. 212.
99. Ibid., pp. 213–214; Mackay, 'Camerons in the Rising of 1715', p. 14.
100. Laing and Macknight (eds), *Memoirs of the Insurrection*, p. 214.
101. Constable (ed.), *Fragment of a Memoir*, pp. 17–18; Laing and Macknight (eds), *Memoirs of the Insurrection*, p. 216; Mackay, 'Camerons in the Rising of 1715', p. 14.
102. Constable (ed.), *Fragment of a Memoir*, pp. 17–18; Laing and Macknight (eds), *Memoirs of the Insurrection*, pp. 214–216; Henrietta Tayler, *The Jacobite Court at Rome in 1719. From Original Documents at Fettercairn House and at Windsor Castle* (Scottish History Society, 3rd ser. xxxi, Edinburgh, 1938), p. 87.
103. Mackay, 'Camerons in the Rising of 1715', pp. 14–15; RH 2/4/307/48: Argyll to Townshend, Stirling, 14 Nov. 1715; Laing and Macknight (eds), *Memoirs of the Insurrection*, pp. 215–216, 225.
104. RH 2/4/307/48: Argyll to Townshend, Stirling, 14 Nov. 1715; Tayler (ed.), *Seven Sons of the Provost*, p. 70: William Kennedy to Thomas Kennedy, [Stirling?] 15 Nov. 1715; Patten, *History of the Rebellion*, p. 159; Steuart *Newsletters*, p. 70: Stirling, 16 Nov. 1715.
105. Laing and Macknight (eds), *Memoirs of the Insurrection*, pp. 219–220.
106. Ibid., pp. 216–217; Patten, *History of the Rebellion*, pp. 159, 167; Dumfries House, Bute Papers, A546/394: Campbell of Fonab to Bute, Glenfalloch, 17 Nov. 1715.
107. RH 2/4/307/48: Argyll to Townshend, Stirling, 14 Nov. 1715; RH 2/4/308/95: Lord Torpichen's account of Sherrifmuir, Nov. 1715; Constable (ed.), *Fragment of a Memoir*, pp. 18–19; Laing and Macknight (eds), *Memoirs of the Insurrection*, pp. 217–218; Steuart *Newsletters*, p. 71: Stirling, 16 Nov. 1715; *Blackader Diary*, p. 469.
108. Laing and Macknight (eds), *Memoirs of the Insurrection*, pp. 218, 226; Tayler (ed.), *Seven Sons of the Provost*, p. 71: William Kennedy to Thomas Kennedy, [Edinburgh?], 15 Nov. 1715.
109. Laing and Macknight (eds), *Memoirs of the Insurrection*, p. 219.
110. Ibid., p. 225; Mackay, 'Camerons in the Rising of 1715', p. 15.

111. Mackay, 'Camerons in the Rising of 1715', pp. 15–16; RH 2/4/308/95: Lord Torpichen's account of Sherrifmuir, Nov. 1715; Laing and Macknight (eds), *Memoirs of the Insurrection*, p. 236.
112. Laing and Macknight (eds), *Memoirs of the Insurrection*, pp. 219–222; Patten, *History of the Rebellion*, p. 160; Constable (ed.), *Fragment of a Memoir*, p. 19.
113. RH 2/4/307/48, 51: Argyll to Townshend, Stirling, 14 and 15 Nov. 1715; Steuart *Newsletters*, pp. 75, 77: [Stirling], 19 and 22 Nov. 1715; Laing and Macknight (eds), *Memoirs of the Insurrection*, p. 224; RH 2/4/307/45: Mar to Colonel Balfour, Governor of Perth, [Ardoch?], 13 Nov. 1715.
114. RH 2/4/307/51: Argyll to Townshend, Stirling, 15 Nov. 1715.
115. RH 2/4/307/64: Argyll to Townshend, Stirling, 19 Nov. 1715.
116. RH 2/4/307/55: James Cockburn to Under-Secretary Pringle, Stirling, 16 Nov. 1716; RH 2/4/307/74 and RH 2/4/308/115: Argyll to Townshend, Stirling, 21 Nov. and 6 Dec. 1715.
117. RH 2/4/307/70: Argyll to Townshend, [Stirling], 20 Nov. 1715.
118. RH 2/4/307/45: Mar to Colonel Balfour, Governor of Perth, [Ardoch?], 13 Nov. 1715; RH 2/4/307/48: Argyll to Townshend, Stirling, 14 Nov. 1715; Tayler (ed.), *Seven Sons of the Provost*, p. 71: William Kennedy to Thomas Kennedy, [Edinburgh?], 15 Nov. 1715; Laing and Macknight (eds), *Memoirs of the Insurrection*, p. 225.
119. Laing and Macknight (eds), *Memoirs of the Insurrection*, pp. 221, 233; RH 2/4/307/62: James Cockburn to Under-Secretary Pringle, Stirling, 18 Nov. 1715.
120. GD 18/2099: Baron John Clerk's account of a journey to Perth, researching 1715, 1717: p. 35; Constable (ed.), *Fragment of a Memoir*, p. 20.
121. Constable (ed.), *Fragment of a Memoir*, p. 22; Laing and Macknight (eds), *Memoirs of the Insurrection*, pp. 240, 244; Atholl Papers, box 45, bundle 12/97: muster of Jacobite army Dec. 1715/Jan. 1716.
122. Constable (ed.), *Fragment of a Memoir*, p. 23; Mackay, 'Camerons in the Rising of 1715', p. 16; Laing and Macknight (eds), *Memoirs of the Insurrection*, pp. 210, 212–213, 272–273, 279.
123. Laing and Macknight (eds), *Memoirs of the Insurrection*, pp. 274–275, 278–279, 283–284, 293–294; RH 2/4/308/107: Argyll to Townshend, Stirling, 4 Dec. 1715.
124. Laing and Macknight (eds), *Memoirs of the Insurrection*, pp. 302–303; RH 2/4/308/96d: Argyll to Townshend, 30 Nov. 1715; Steuart *Newsletters*, p. 121: [Edinburgh, beginning of Feb. 1716].
125. Laing and Macknight (eds), *Memoirs of the Insurrection*, pp. 297–299.
126. RH 2/4/307/84 and RH 2/4/308/86: Argyll to Townshend, Stirling, 26 and 27 Nov. 1715; GD 220/5/455/56: Lord Justice Clerk Cockburn to Montrose, Edinburgh, 29 Nov. 1715.
127. RH 2/4/308/86: Argyll to Townshend, Stirling, 27 Nov. 1715.
128. GD 220/5/453/16: Lord Advocate Dalrymple to Montrose, [Edinburgh?], 5 Dec. 1715.
129. Laing and Macknight (eds), *Memoirs of the Insurrection*, pp. 299, 301; RH 2/4/308/96d, 101, 107: Argyll to Townshend, 30 Nov. and 1 and 4 Dec. 1715.
130. RH 2/4/308/86, 101: Stirling, 27 Nov. and 1 Dec. 1715.
131. RH 2/4/393/28: to Argyll, Whitehall, 6 Dec. 1715.
132. RH 2/4/393/29: to Argyll, Whitehall, 6 Dec. 1715.
133. RH 2/4/308/130: Argyll to Townshend, Stirling, 15 Dec. 1715.
134. RH 2/4/307/19: minute, of a Cabinet meeting?, Whitehall, 5 Nov. 1715; RH 2/4/391/248 and RH 2/4/393/28, 58–59: Townshend to Argyll, Whitehall, 8 Nov. and 6 and 27 Dec. 1715; RH 2/4/393/40–42: Stanhope to Lord Advocate Dalrymple, Whitehall, 22 Dec. 1715.

135. RH 2/4/308/133, 139, 150: Argyll to Townshend, Stirling, 17, 20 and 24 Dec. 1715; RH 2/4/393/59: Townshend to Argyll, Whitehall, 27 Dec. 1715.

136. RH 2/4/309/7a: Argyll to Townshend, Stirling, 3 Jan. 1716.

137. RH 2/4/393/63: Townshend to Argyll, Whitehall, 3 Jan. 1716.

138. RH 2/4/393/73: Townshend to Argyll, Whitehall, 10 Jan. 1716.

139. RH 2/4/393/76–77: Townshend to Argyll, Whitehall, 10 Jan. 1716.

140. RH 2/4/309/41: Argyll to Townshend, Stirling, 19 Jan. 1716.

141. Laing and Macknight (eds), *Memoirs of the Insurrection*, pp. 307–309, 313, 316; GD 18/2099: Baron John Clerk's account of a journey to Perth, researching 1715, 1717, pp. 36–37.

142. W. Seton, 'The Itinerary of King James III, October to December, 1715', *Scottish Historical Review*, xxi (1924), 251; SP 78/160, ff. 163–164: Mr Douglas to Stanhope, Paris, 3/14 Dec. 1715; GD 220/5/1926/4: Thomas Crawford to Montrose, Paris, 17/28 Jan. 1716; Corp, *Court in Exile*, p. 297; SP 35/18/27: Paul Müller to [Stanhope?], [London], 28 Sept. 1719.

143. Seton, 'Itinerary of King James III', p. 252; HMC *Stuart*, i. 461, 463–464: James to Bolingbroke, [Saint-Malo], 13/24 Nov. 1715.

144. Seton, 'Itinerary of King James III', pp. 259–265.

145. Ibid., pp. 258, 265; HMC *Stuart*, i. 451: Bolingbroke to James, Paris, 22 Oct./2 Nov. 1715; RH 2/4/310/181b: list of Irish officers noted as aboard Captain Battelet's ship out of Calais; RH 2/4/310/243c: deposition by James Livingstone, 28 Apr. 1716; RH 2/4/309/71, 74: Daniel Moore to the Admiralty, Calais, 18/29 and 19/30 Jan. 1716.

146. Mackay, 'Camerons in the Rising of 1715', p. 16; GD 220/5/615/1, 2a: Pollock to Montrose, Fort William, 4 and 12 Jan. 1716.

147. RH 2/4/308/96b: Lord Advocate Dalrymple to Stanhope, Edinburgh, 29 Nov. 1715; RH 2/4/308/162: Wightman to Stanhope, Stirling, 29 Dec. 1715; Laing and Macknight (eds), *Memoirs of the Insurrection*, pp. 330–331.

148. Steuart *Newsletters*, p. 83: [Edinburgh?], 28 Dec. 1715; Laing and Macknight (eds), *Memoirs of the Insurrection*, p. 331.

149. Tayler (ed.), *Seven Sons of the Provost*, pp. 65, 80: William Kennedy to Thomas Kennedy, camp at Stirling, 1 Oct. 1715 and 10 Jan. 1716; Constable (ed.), *Fragment of a Memoir*, p. 25; HMC *Stuart*, i. 491: Mar to Huntly, Scone, 18/29 Jan. 1716; GD 18/2092/5: Sir John Clerk's journal for 1716: 20 Jan. 1716; RH 2/4/307/18: Argyll to Townshend, camp at Stirling, 4 Nov. 1715.

150. RH 2/4/308/127: James Cockburn to Under-Secretary Pringle, Stirling, 13 Dec. 1715; RH 2/4/308/179[a]: Cadogan to Stanhope, Edinburgh, 19 Dec. 1715.

151. David Chandler, *Marlborough as Military Commander* (2nd edn, 1979), pp. 67, 78, 132–133, 176, 182, 214, 218.

152. RH 2/4/308/179[b]: Cadogan to Townshend, Edinburgh, 19 Dec. 1715; Tayler (ed.), *Seven Sons of the Provost*, p. 78: William Kennedy to Thomas Kennedy, Touch, 7 Jan. 1716.

153. RH 2/4/308/127: James Cockburn to Under-Secretary Pringle, Stirling, 13 Dec. 1715; RH 2/4/309/5, 24: Cadogan to Stanhope, Stirling and Edinburgh, 3 and 10 Jan. 1716; RH 2/4/393/70: Stanhope to Cadogan, Whitehall, 8 Jan. 1716.

154. RH 2/4/308/139: Argyll to Townshend, Stirling, 20 Dec. 1715; Steuart *Newsletters*, p. 83: [Edinburgh?], 28 Dec. 1715.

155. GD 220/5/610/2: Lord Justice Clerk Cockburn to Montrose, Edinburgh, 7 Jan. 1716.

156. Steuart *Newsletters*, p. 84: [Edinburgh?], 28 Dec. 1715; RH 2/4/308/168: Rothes to Stanhope?, Stirling, 30 Dec. 1715; GD 220/5/610/2: Lord Justice Clerk Cockburn to Montrose, Edinburgh, 7 Jan. 1716; RH 2/4/309/39: Cadogan to Stanhope, Edinburgh,

18 Jan. 1716; Tayler (ed.), *Seven Sons of the Provost*, p. 76: William Kennedy to Thomas Kennedy, [camp at Stirling, rect. Jan. 1716].

157. Steuart *Newsletters*, pp. 84, 97–98: [Edinburgh?], 28 Dec. 1715 and 25 Jan. 1716; *Loch Lomond Expedition*, 34–37: [G. Archer?] to Alexander Archer, L[eslie], 13–20 Jan. 1716.

158. Tayler (ed.), *Seven Sons of the Provost*, p. 76: William Kennedy to Thomas Kennedy, [camp at Stirling, rect. Jan. 1716]; Steuart *Newsletters*, p. 117: Edinburgh, 2 Feb. 1716; Laing and Macknight (eds), *Memoirs of the Insurrection*, p. 331.

159. RH 2/4/309/57: Argyll to Townshend, Stirling, 25 Jan. 1716; GD 18/2092/5: Sir John's journal for 1716: 20 Jan. 1716.

160. Steuart *Newsletters*, p. 112: Edinburgh, 28 Jan. 1716; RH 2/4/309/57, 68: Argyll to Townshend, Stirling, 25 and 29 Jan. 1716; RH 2/4/309/55: Cadogan to Stanhope, Stirling, 25 Jan. 1716.

161. RH 2/4/309/66: James Cockburn to Under-Secretary Pringle, 28 Jan. 1716; Steuart *Newsletters*, p. 105: Edinburgh, 26 Jan. 1716; RH 2/4/309/68, 81: Argyll to Townshend, Dunblane and Errol, 29 Jan. and 2 Feb. 1716.

162. Warrand (ed.), *More Culloden Papers*, ii. 87–88: Clephane to [Henry Crawfurd], court at Scone, 21 Jan. 1716; HMC *Stuart*, i. 495: James to James Graham Jr of Braco, Scone, 22 Jan./2 Feb. 1716.

163. GD 124/10/498: draft letter by Mar, Scone, 24 Jan. 1716.

164. GD 220/5/615/3: Sir Robert Pollock to Montrose, Fort William, 14 Jan. 1716; Laing and Macknight (eds), *Memoirs of the Insurrection*, pp. 346–347; Fraser (ed.), *Chiefs of Grant*, ii. 97: intelligence report, Aberdeen, 11 Jan. 1716; Allardyce (ed.), *Historical Papers Relating to the Jacobite Period*, i. 50: Aberdeen Burgh records, 21 Jan. 1716.

165. RH 2/4/309/78a: Argyll to Townshend, camp at Tullibardine, 31 Jan. 1716.

166. Tabraham and Grove, *Fortress Scotland*, p. 17 and colour plate 4.

167. Laing and Macknight (eds), *Memoirs of the Insurrection*, pp. 50, 197–198, 199.

168. GD 18/2099: Clerk's account of a journey to Perth, 1717: pp. 16–17.

169. Laing and Macknight (eds), *Memoirs of the Insurrection*, p. 199.

170. Steuart *Newsletters*, pp. 106, 112: Edinburgh, 26 and 28 Jan. 1716.

171. RH 2/4/309/68, 81: Argyll to Townshend, Dunblane and Errol, 29 Jan. and 2 Feb. 1716.

172. Steuart *Newsletters*, pp. 112: Edinburgh, 28 Jan. 1716.

173. Tayler (ed.), *Seven Sons of the Provost*, p. 81: William Kennedy to Thomas Kennedy, Touch, 24 Jan. 1716; RH 2/4/309/19: Argyll to Townshend, Stirling, 10 Jan. 1716.

174. Mahon, *History*, i., appendix, p. xlv: James to Bolingbroke, Kinnaird, 2 Jan. 1716; GD 124/10/498: Address by the Episcopalian clergy of Aberdeen diocese and James's reply, 29 Dec. 1715; Buchanan-Brown (ed.), *Remains of Thomas Hearne*, 182: 2 Dec. 1716.

175. Mahon, *History*, i., appendix, pp. xlii: Kinnaird, 2 Jan. 1716.

176. HMC *Stuart*, i. 486: Mar to Bolingbroke, Kinnaird, 3/14 Jan. 1716; RH 2/4/309/18: James Cockburn to Under-Secretary Pringle, Stirling, 7 Jan. 1716; GD 220/5/631/1: John Hope to Montrose, Stirling, 28 Jan. 1716.

177. Corp, *Court in Exile*, pp. 65, 132, 278–279; Mahon, *History*, i., appendix, p. xliii: James to Bolingbroke, Kinnaird, 2 Jan. 1716; HMC *Stuart*, i. 504–505: James to Orléans, Montrose, 3/14 Feb. 1716.

178. Steuart *Newsletters*, p. 119: [Edinburgh] 3 Feb. 1716; GD 220/5/631/2: John Hope to Montrose, Dundee, 3 Feb. 1716.

179. HMC *Stuart*, i. 495: Mar to Commanding Officer at Dunkeld, Scone, 23 Jan./3 Feb. 1716; i. 500: Mar to Gordon of Auchintoul, Scone, Sunday night [29 Jan./9 Feb. 1716]; Steuart *Newsletters*, p. 117: Edinburgh, 2 Feb. 1716; RH 2/4/309/81: Argyll to

Townshend, Erroll, 2 Feb. 1716; GD 220/5/1927/3: ? to Montrose, Montrose, 6 Feb. 1716; Constable (ed.), *Fragment of a Memoir*, p. 26.
180. RH 2/4/309/81: Argyll to Townshend, Erroll, 2 Feb. 1716. See also: GD 220/5/631/2: John Hope to Montrose, Dundee, 3 Feb. 1716.
181. Constable (ed.), *Fragment of a Memoir*, pp. 26–29; Laing and Macknight (eds), *Memoirs of the Insurrection*, pp. 358–359; GD 220/5/1927/3: ? to Montrose, Montrose, 6 Feb. 1716.
182. GD 220/5/631/3a–b: John Hope to Montrose, Montrose, 6 Feb. 1716; RH 2/4/309/95: Lord Justice Clerk Cockburn to Under-Secretary Pringle, Edinburgh, 8 Feb. 1716; Steuart *Newsletters*, p. 140: Edinburgh, 11 Mar. 1716.
183. Patten, *History of the Rebellion*, pp. 205–207; Constable (ed.), *Fragment of a Memoir*, p. 27; HMC *Stuart*, i. 505: James to Gordon of Auchintoul, Montrose, 4/15 Feb. 1716.
184. Atholl Papers, box 45, bundle 12/100, 101: Captain James Menzies to Atholl, Comrie and Wemys, 5 and 6 Feb. 1716; 12/102: account of Atholl's actions 8–11 Feb. 1716; RH 2/4/309/126: Argyll to Townshend, Aberdeen, 17 Feb. 1716.
185. RH 2/4/310/142: Francis Philipson to Under-Secretary Pringle, Edinburgh, 21 Feb. 1716.
186. GD 220/5/635: [David Grahame of Orchill to Montrose], Perth, 2 Feb. 1716; GD 220/1926/10: ? to Montrose, Dundee, 4 Feb. 1716; RH 2/4/393/108–109: Townshend to Argyll, Whitehall, 17 Feb. 1716; RH 2/4/393/115: extract from Stair letter to Stanhope, [Paris], 24 Feb./7 Mar. 1716; RH 2/4/393/112–114: Townshend to Cadogan, Whitehall, 3 Mar. 1716.
187. RH 2/4/309/89: Argyll to Townshend, Dundee, 4 Feb. 1716; RH 2/4/309/113 and RH 2/4/310/156a: Lord Justice Clerk Cockburn to Townshend, Edinburgh, 14 and 27 Feb. 1716.
188. Allardyce (ed.), *Historical Papers Relating to the Jacobite Period*, i. 33–35, 37–38: Minutes of Synod of Moray, Forres and Elgin, 24 Apr. and 30 Oct. 1716; i. 64–66, 66–68: records of Alford Presbytery, Kirk of Clate and Alford Kirk, 14 Mar. and 2 May 1716; i. 124–128: John Alexander of Kildrummy to his wife, Edinburgh, 14 Apr. 1716.
189. RH 2/4/311/20: memorial on the state of Angus and the Mearns, Brechin, 31 May 1716.

Chapter 7 'Secure in Valour's Station': Military Operations, September 1715–April 1716, the Northern, Southern and Western Theatres

1. SP 54/8/115: Lord Justice Clerk Cockburn to Under-Secretary Pringle, Edinburgh, 28 Sept. 1715; SP 54/8/120a, 121: Islay to Townshend, Edinburgh, 29 and 30 Sept. 1715
2. GD 220/5/455/44a: Lord Justice Clerk Cockburn to Montrose, Edinburgh, 30 July 1715; SP 54/8/85: Solicitor-General Steuart to [Under-Secretary Pringle], Edinburgh, 23 Sept. 1715.
3. RH 2/4/391/213: Townshend to Lord Justice Clerk Cockburn, Whitehall, 11 Oct. 1715.
4. Patten, *History of the Rebellion*, pp. 19–22; *A Letter About the Occurrences in the Way to, and at Preston. By a Gentleman who was an Eye-witness to the Said Transactions* [Edinburgh? 1717?], p. 1; Add. MS 37993, f. 9v: Polwarth to the Deputy-Lieutenants of Berwickshire, Stirling, 8 Oct. 1715.
5. Patten, *History of the Rebellion*, pp. 22, 23, 25, 28, 30, 37, 83, 97; RH 2/4/306/63a: George Carpenter to Stanhope, Newcastle, 21 Oct. 1715; GD 1/811/9a, 9b: sundry receipts given by Mackintosh of Borlum at Kelso, 24 and 28 Oct. 1715.

6. RH 2/4/306/63a: Carpenter to Stanhope, Newcastle, 21 Oct. 1715; Tayler (ed.), *Seven Sons of the Provost*, p. 67: William to Thomas, Edinburgh, 25 Oct. 1715; RH 2/4/391/216–17: Townshend to Lord Justice Clerk Cockburn, Whitehall, 27 Oct. 1715.

7. Patten, *History of the Rebellion*, p. 28; *Letter About the Occurrences*, p. 2.

8. RH 2/4/305/29: Lord Justice Clerk Cockburn to Under-Secretary Pringle, Edinburgh, 8 Oct. 1715; RH 2/4/305/107: account of Kenmure's rising all the way to Preston; Fraser (ed.), *Annandale*, ii. 254–255: Robert Corbett, Provost of Dumfries, to Annandale, Dumfries, 12 Oct. 1715.

9. Fergusson (ed.), *Fraser's Manuscript*, ii. 33–35; RH 2/4/306/56b: Corbet to Lord Justice Clerk Cockburn, Dumfries, 14 Oct. 1715.

10. RH 2/4/307/15: Annandale to Townshend, [Edinburgh], 3 Nov. 1715. See also: RH 2/4/306/56b: Corbet to Lord Justice Clerk Cockburn, Dumfries, 14 Oct. 1715.

11. RH 2/4/305/53: Argyll to Townshend, camp at Stirling, 18 Oct. 1715; RH 2/4/305/47: John Sibbit, Mayor of Berwick, to Stanhope, 14 Oct. 1715; Steuart *Newsletters*, p. 46: Edinburgh, 16 Oct. 1715; GD 18/3152/12: Baron John Clerk to Sir John Clerk, 16 Oct. 1715; RH 2/4/305/49: Postmaster Anderson of Edinburgh to John Lloyd, Edinburgh, 16 Oct. 1715.

12. GD 18/3152/9: Baron John Clerk to Sir John Clerk, [Edinburgh, c. 18?] Oct. 1715; RH 2/4/306/61: Postmaster Anderson to ?, Edinburgh, 20 Oct. 1715; BL, Add. MS 37993, f. 12v: Polwarth to Andrew Hume, Lord Kimmerghame, Edinburgh, 20 Oct. 1715.

13. Cf. RH 2/4/306/65: Mar to 'Mr Forrester' [i.e. Forster], camp before Perth, 21 Oct. 1715; Laing and Macknight (eds), *Memoirs of the Insurrection*, pp. 54–56; Steuart *Newsletters*, p. 44: Edinburgh, 15–20 Oct. 1715.

14. A. and H. Tayler, 'Lord Forfar and the '15', pp. 135–136: Forfar to Cornelius Kennedy, camp at Stirling, 19 Oct. 1715; Steuart *Newsletters*, p. 46: Edinburgh, 16 Oct. 1715; GD 18/2092/4: Sir John Clerk's journal for Apr. 1712–1715: 21 Oct. 1715.

15. Patten, *History of the Rebellion*, p. 13; RH 2/4/306/89: Tweeddale to [Under-Secretary Pringle], Edinburgh, 27 Oct. 1715; RH 2/4/305/47: Sibbit to Stanhope, 14 Oct. 1715; GD 18/3152/9: Baron John Clerk Clerk to Sir John Clerk, [Edinburgh, c. 18?] Oct. 1715.

16. RH 2/4/306/76: Patrick Hume, Earl of Marchmont, to Townshend, Berwick, 22 Oct. 1715; RH 2/4/306/68: Sibbit to Stanhope, Berwick, 21 Oct. 1715; GD 18/3152/11: Baron John Clerk to Sir John Clerk, Edinburgh, 22 Oct. 1715; RH 2/4/306/71: Lord Advocate Dalrymple to Stanhope, Edinburgh, 22 Oct. 1715.

17. Patten, *History of the Rebellion*, pp. 14, 38; Fraser (ed.), *Annandale*, ii. 266: Sir William Johnstone of Westerhall to Annandale, [Dumfries?], 4 Nov. 1715; *Letter About the Occurrences*, pp. 2–3.

18. Patten, *History of the Rebellion*, p. 30.

19. GD 124/10/497: 'copie of the instructions to Mrs Miller to be communicated to the King's friends besouth Forth', Perth, 23 and 24 Oct. 1715.

20. Patten, *History of the Rebellion*, pp. 39–40, 51, 56; RH 2/4/305/107: account of Kenmure's rising all the way to Preston; Atholl Papers, box 45, bundle 12/77: account of the Jacobite southern army to Preston; *Letter About the Occurrences*, p. 4.

21. *Letter About the Occurrences*, p. 4.

22. RH 2/4/306/98: Lord Justice Clerk Cockburn to Townshend, Edinburgh, 30 Oct. 1715; Patten, *History of the Rebellion*, pp. 53–54; Tayler (ed.), *Seven Sons of the Provost*, p. 68: William Kennedy to Thomas Kennedy, Edinburgh, 1 Nov. 1715.

23. Patten, *History of the Rebellion*, p. 53.

24. Ibid., p. 56; RH 2/4/307/14b: Corbett to Lord Justice Clerk Cockburn, Dumfries, 1 Nov. 1715; RH 2/4/307/13: Annandale to Under-Secretary Pringle, Edinburgh, 3 Nov. 1715;

Fraser (ed.), *Annandale*, ii. 266: Johnstone of Westerhall to Annandale, [Dumfries?], 4 Nov. 1715.

25. *Letter About the Occurrences*, p. 4.
26. Patten, *History of the Rebellion*, p. 68. See also: RH 2/4/307/26a: Lord Justice Clerk Cockburn to Under-Secretary Pringle, Edinburgh, 6 Nov. 1715; RH 2/4/307/33: Provost of Edinburgh to [Under-Secretary Pringle], Edinburgh, 8 Nov. 1715; BL, Add. MS 37993, f. 29v–30r: Polwarth to Bennet of Grubbet, Redbreas, 14 Nov. 1715; *Letter About the Occurrences*, p. 5.
27. Patten, *History of the Rebellion*, p. 58; Ware (ed.), *Lancashire During the Rebellion of 1715*, pp. 84, 91, 99.
28. *Letter About the Occurrences*, p. 3; Patten, *History of the Rebellion*, pp. 51, 77; Atholl Papers, box 45, bundle 12/77: account of Jacobite southern army to Preston.
29. *Letter About the Occurrences*, pp. 4–5. See also: Patten, *History of the Rebellion*, p. 65.
30. Patten, *History of the Rebellion*, pp. 67, 70; Atholl Papers, box 45, bundle 12/77: account of Jacobite southern army to Preston; Ware (ed.), *Lancashire During the Rebellion of 1715*, pp. 77, 80, 84.
31. Patten, *History of the Rebellion*, pp. 71–73, 78; Ware (ed.), *Lancashire During the Rebellion of 1715*, pp. 85, 87.
32. Patten, *History of the Rebellion*, p. 78. See also: Atholl Papers, box 45, bundle 12/77: account of Jacobite southern army to Preston; Ware (ed.), *Lancashire During the Rebellion of 1715*, pp. 89–97, 100.
33. Patten, *History of the Rebellion*, pp. 71, 79–80; RH 2/4/393/1: Townshend to Argyll, Whitehall, 15 Nov. 1715; Atholl Papers, box 45, bundle 12/77: account of Jacobite southern army to Preston.
34. Patten, *History of the Rebellion*, p. 80.
35. Tayler (ed.), *Seven Sons of the Provost*, pp. 69–70: William Kennedy to Thomas Kennedy, Edinburgh, 8 Nov. 1715; RH 2/4/306/98: Lord Justice Clerk Cockburn to Townshend, Edinburgh, 30 Oct. 1715; Fraser (ed.), *Annandale*, ii. 269: Johnstone of Westerhall to Annandale, [Dumfries?], 4 Nov. 1715; RH 2/4/391/250: Townshend to Argyll, Whitehall, 8 Nov. 1715.
36. RH 2/4/393/1: Townshend to Argyll, Whitehall, 15 Nov. 1715; Patten, *History of the Rebellion*, p. 79; Tayler (ed.), *Seven Sons of the Provost*, p. 70: William Kennedy to Thomas Kennedy, Edinburgh, 8 Nov. 1715.
37. BL, Add. MS 37993, f. 30r: Polwarth to Bennet of Grubbet, Redbreas, 14 Nov. 1715; Ware (ed.), *Lancashire During the Rebellion of 1715*, p. 117.
38. Ware (ed.), *Lancashire During the Rebellion of 1715*, p. 100.
39. Ibid., p. 107.
40. *Letter About the Occurrences*, p. 5; Patten, *History of the Rebellion*, p. 80.
41. Patten, *History of the Rebellion*, pp. 81–83, 104; RH 2/4/305/107: account of Kenmure's rising all the way to Preston; *Letter About the Occurrences*, p. 6; Atholl Papers, box 45, bundle 12/77: account of Jacobite southern army to Preston; Baynes, *Jacobite Rising*, p. 115.
42. Atholl Papers, box 45, bundle 12/77: account of Jacobite southern army to Preston; RH 2/4/305/107: account of Kenmure's rising all the way to Preston; Patten, *History of the Rebellion*, p. 85; RH 2/4/393/1: Townshend to Argyll, Whitehall, 15 Nov. 1715.
43. Patten, *History of the Rebellion*, pp. 86, 91; *Letter About the Occurrences*, pp. 6–7; RH 2/4/305/107: account of Kenmure's rising all the way to Preston.
44. *Letter About the Occurrences*, p. 7; Atholl Papers, box 45, bundle 12/77: account of Jacobite southern army to Preston.
45. Patten, *History of the Rebellion*, pp. 83, 90; Ware (ed.), *Lancashire During the Rebellion of 1715*, p. 125.

46. Patten, *History of the Rebellion*, pp. 85, 86; Atholl Papers, box 45, bundle 12/77: account of Jacobite southern army to Preston; *Letter About the Occurrences*, pp. 6–7; RH 2/4/305/107: account of Kenmure's rising all the way to Preston; *Blackader*, p. 473: 24 Nov. 1715. Though Patten has Lord Charles Murray's barricade attacked by different troops, the other sources differ substantially from his account.

47. Patten, *History of the Rebellion*, p. 88; Ware (ed.), *Lancashire During the Rebellion of 1715*, p. 132.

48. Patten, *History of the Rebellion*, p. 87; Ware (ed.), *Lancashire During the Rebellion of 1715*, p. 133; RH 2/4/305/107: account of Kenmure's rising all the way to Preston.

49. RH 2/4/305/107: account of Kenmure's rising all the way to Preston; *Letter About the Occurrences*, p. 7; Atholl Papers, box 45, bundle 12/77: account of Jacobite southern army to Preston; Patten, *History of the Rebellion*, p. 95.

50. Patten, *History of the Rebellion*, pp. 90–92; *Letter About the Occurrences*, p. 7.

51. Atholl Papers, box 45, bundle 12/77: account of Jacobite southern army to Preston; RH 2/4/305/107: account of Kenmure's rising all the way to Preston; Patten, *History of the Rebellion*, p. 92; Buchanan-Brown (ed.), *Remains of Thomas Hearne*, p. 240: 4 Oct. 1721.

52. Patten, *History of the Rebellion*, p. 92.

53. Browning (ed.), *English Historical Documents*, vii., no. 293: Treaty of Limerick, 1691.

54. Patten, *History of the Rebellion*, p. 92.

55. Ibid., pp. 94–96.

56. Ibid., p. 95.

57. Atholl Papers, box 45, bundle 12/77: account of the Jacobite southern army to Preston; RH 2/4/305/107: account of Kenmure's rising all the way to Preston.

58. Patten, *History of the Rebellion*, pp. 93, 96–97.

59. Ibid., pp. 92, 96.

60. *Letter About the Occurrences*, pp. 7–8; RH 2/4/305/107: account of Kenmure's rising all the way to Preston; Atholl Papers, box 45, bundle 12/77: account of Jacobite southern army to Preston.

61. Patten, *History of the Rebellion*, p. 95.

62. Ibid., p. 96; Atholl Papers, box 45, bundle 12/77: account of Jacobite southern army to Preston; *Letter About the Occurrences*, p. 8; RH 2/4/305/107: account of Kenmure's rising all the way to Preston.

63. Patten, *History of the Rebellion*, p. 100; Atholl Papers, box 45, bundle 12/77: account of Jacobite southern army to Preston; RH 2/4/305/107: account of Kenmure's rising all the way to Preston; Ware (ed.), *Lancashire During the Rebellion of 1715*, p. 111.

64. SP 54/8/57: Alexander Stuart Barkie to Townshend, Inverness, 14 Sept. 1715.

65. RH 2/4/305/46: intelligence from northern Scotland, Inverness, 14 Oct. 1715; Fergusson (ed.), *Fraser's Manuscript*, ii. 77.

66. RH 2/4/305/27: 'Advyces from North Britain', [9?] Oct. 1715; RH 2/4/305/46: intelligence from northern Scotland, Inverness, 14 Oct. 1715; Warrand (ed.), *More Culloden Papers*, ii. 96; RH 2/4/309/126: Argyll to Townshend, Aberdeen, 17 Feb. 1716; Fergusson (ed.), *Fraser's Manuscript*, ii. 83; Laing and Macknight (eds), *Memoirs of the Insurrection*, p. 341.

67. Macinnes, *Clanship, Commerce and the House of Stuart*, pp. 30–52, 142–148.

68. See, for example: RH 2/4/305/46: intelligence from northern Scotland, Inverness, 14 Oct. 1715; RH 2/4/307/1: Atholl to Argyll, Blair castle, 1 Nov. 1715; RH 2/4/391/129: Townshend to Whetham, Whitehall, 18 Aug. 1715; HMC *Stuart*, i. 492: Lovat to [Glenbuchat], Inverness, 20/31 Jan. 1716.

69. Macinnes, *Clanship, Commerce and the House of Stuart*, pp. 37–46; Brown, *Bloodfeud in Scotland*, p. 33.

70. SP 54/8/77: Lord Justice Clerk Cockburn to [Under-Secretary Pringle], Edinburgh, 20 Sept. 1715; GD 44/40/6/1/39: George Grant of Grant to Huntly, Castle Grant, 23 Jan. 1716.
71. Fergusson (ed.), *Fraser's Manuscript*, ii. 83. This phenomenon was first noticed by Rosalind Mitchison in 1970: Mitchison, 'The Government and the Highlands, 1707–1745', in N. T. Phillipson and Rosalind Mitchison (eds), *Scotland in the Age of Improvement. Essays in Scottish History in the Eighteenth Century* (Edinburgh, repr. 1996), pp. 27–28.
72. This was sometimes the case, too, in the Lowlands, for an example of which, see: GD 18/3152/9: Baron John Clerk to Sir John Clerk, [Edinburgh, *c.* 18?] Oct. 1715, in which Baron John recommends the defenders of Sir John's home should only fire blanks if the house is attacked.
73. Lenman, *Jacobite Clans*, pp. 63–71; Fergusson (ed.), *Fraser's Manuscript*, ii. 44–45.
74. RH 2/4/307/83b: Anon. to Sir James Stewart, Inverness, 18 Nov. 1715; [Duff (ed.)], *Culloden Papers*, 39–40: Provost and Council of Inverness to Hugh Rose, John Forbes and Duncan Forbes, Inverness, 7 Nov. 1715.
75. RH 2/4/307/83b: Anon. to Sir James Stewart, Inverness, 18 Nov. 1715; Fergusson (ed.), *Fraser's Manuscript*, ii. 70.
76. RH 2/4/307/83b: Anon. to Sir James Stewart, Inverness, 18 Nov. 1715.
77. Fergusson (ed.), *Fraser's Manuscript*, ii. 72, 74–76; RH 2/4/307/83b: Anon. to Sir James Stewart, Inverness, 18 Nov. 1715.
78. RH 2/4/307/83b: Anon. to Sir James Stewart, Inverness, 18 Nov. 1715.
79. Ibid.; Fergusson (ed.), *Fraser's Manuscript*, ii. 76.
80. Fergusson (ed.), *Fraser's Manuscript*, ii. 77.
81. RH 2/4/307/83b: Anon. to Sir James Stewart, Inverness, 18 Nov. 1715.
82. Fergusson (ed.), *Fraser's Manuscript*, ii. 77.
83. Ibid., 77–78.
84. RH 2/4/307/21b: 'Ane Account of the Earl of Sutherland's Proceedings From his Embarkation at Leith the 25th of September to the 2nd of November, 1715'; RH 2/4/305/27: 'Advyces from North Britain', [9?] Oct. 1715; RH 2/4/309/1: Sutherland to Townshend, Inverness, 1 Jan. 1716.
85. SP 54/8/77: Lord Justice Clerk Cockburn to [Under-Secretary Pringle], Edinburgh, 20 Sept. 1715.
86. SP 54/8/69: Pollock to Townshend, Fort William, 16 Sept. 1715; SP 54/8/109: Lord Strathnaver to Captain James Stuart, of *Royal Ann Galley* in Cromarty roads, Dunrotin, 27 Sept. 1715.
87. SP 54/8/77: Lord Justice Clerk Cockburn to [Under-Secretary Pringle], Edinburgh, 20 Sept. 1715; SP 54/8/127: examination of the postmaster of Inverness, Edinburgh, 28 Sept. 1715; HMC *Stuart*, i. 478–479: [Glenbuchat to] Huntly, np, 14/25 Dec. 1715.
88. RH 2/4/307/21b: 'Ane Account of the Earl of Sutherland's Proceedings From his Embarkation at Leith the 25th of September to the 2nd of November, 1715'.
89. RH 2/4/305/27: 'Advyces from North Britain', [9?] Oct. 1715; RH 2/4/305/46: intelligence from northern Scotland, Inverness, 14 Oct. 1715.
90. RH 2/4/305/27: 'Advyces from North Britain', [9?] Oct. 1715; BL, Stowe 228, ff. 173–174: Sutherland to George I, [mid-Oct. 1715?].
91. SP 54/8/109: Strathnaver to Captain James Stuart, of *Royal Ann Galley* in Cromarty roads, Dunrotin, 27 Sept. 1715; RH 2/4/305/46: intelligence from northern Scotland, Inverness, 14 Oct. 1715; RH 2/4/307/21b: 'Ane Account of the Earl of Sutherland's Proceedings From his Embarkation at Leith the 25th of September to the 2nd of November, 1715'; GD 220/5/615/5: terms agreed between Seaforth and Lovat, Brewlie and Brahan, 28–30 Dec. 1715; RH 2/4/307/4: petition by Monro of Foulis, Sutherland,

Ross, Strathnaver, etc, to Townshend, Inverbreakie, 2 Nov. 1715; Baynes, *Jacobite Rising*, pp. 158–159.

92. RH 2/4/307/21b: 'Ane Account of the Earl of Sutherland's Proceedings From his Embarkation at Leith the 25th of September to the 2nd of November, 1715'; RH 2/4/307/83b: Anon. to Sir James Stewart, Inverness, 18 Nov. 1715; Fergusson (ed.), *Fraser's Manuscript*, ii. 79; RH 2/4/308/105: Captain Monro of Foulis to Townshend, Inverness, 2 Dec. 1715.

93. GD 248/46/7/43: anon informant to [Brigadier Grant?], Aberdeen, 12 Dec. 1715; RH 2/4/308/133: Argyll to Townshend, Stirling, 17 Dec. 1715.

94. HMC *Stuart*, i. 470: Mar to [Glenbuchat], camp at Perth, 18/29 Nov. 1715; i. 470: Mar to Collectors and Receivers of Cess and Excise in Aberdeenshire and Banff, camp at Perth, 18/29 Nov. 1715.

95. HMC *Stuart*, i. 476–478: [Glenbuchat] to [Mar?], Fochabers, 14/25 Dec. 1715; HMC *Stuart*, i. 478–479: [Glenbuchat to] Huntly, 14/25 Dec. 1715; Fergusson (ed.), *Fraser's Manuscript*, ii. 82.

96. Fergusson (ed.), *Fraser's Manuscript*, ii. 82–83; RH 2/4/309/1: Sutherland to Townshend, Inverness, 1 Jan. 1716; Laing and Macknight (eds), *Memoirs of the Insurrection*, pp. 345–346.

97. HMC *Stuart*, i. 483: resolutions of Whig Council of War, Inverness, 26 Dec.–6 Jan. 1715/16; Fergusson (ed.), *Fraser's Manuscript*, ii. 84; RH 2/4/309/1: Sutherland to Townshend, Inverness, 1 Jan. 1716.

98. Fergusson (ed.), *Fraser's Manuscript*, ii. 84.

99. RH 2/4/308/167: Seaforth to Lovat, Brahan, 30 Dec. 1715; RH 2/4/309/30c: Sutherland to [Brigadier Grant?], Inverness, 30 Dec. 1716; RH 2/4/309/1: Sutherland to Townshend, Inverness, 1 Jan. 1716.

100. Laing and Macknight (eds), *Memoirs of the Insurrection*, p. 333.

101. RH 2/4/309/106: Argyll to Townshend, Aberdeen, 12 Feb. 1716; RH 2/4/309/111a: Sutherland to Stanhope, Inverness, 13 Feb. 1716; HMC *Stuart*, i. 511: Huntly to Lovat, 14/25 Feb. 1716.

102. HMC *Stuart*, i. 478: [Glenbuchat to] Huntly, 14/25 Dec. 1715; Laing and Macknight (eds), *Memoirs of the Insurrection*, p. 330; HMC *Stuart*, i. 483: Huntly to [James Gordon of] Kerremenoch, Gordon castle, 27 Dec./7 Jan. 1715/16; RH 2/4/309/9: Pollock to Townshend, Fort William, 4 Jan. 1716.

103. HMC *Stuart*, i. 478: [Glenbuchat to Huntly], 14/25 Dec. 1715.

104. Fraser (ed.), *Chiefs of Grant*, ii. 97: Anon. to ?, Aberdeen, 11 Jan. 1716; HMC *Stuart*, i. 486: Huntly to Seaforth, Gordon castle, 9/20 Jan. 1716; Laing and Macknight (eds), *Memoirs of the Insurrection*, pp. 340–341.

105. Laing and Macknight (eds), *Memoirs of the Insurrection*, pp. 331, 341, 349, 350–351; HMC *Stuart*, i. 489: James to Huntly, Scone, 17/28 and 18/29 Jan. 1716; RH 2/4/309/73b: Lovat to Pollock, Inverness, 19 Jan. 1716; HMC *Stuart*, i. 500–501: Huntly to Lovat, Gordon castle, 2/13 Feb. 1716.

106. Constable (ed.), *Fragment of a Memoir*, p. 28.

107. HMC *Stuart*, i. 507: [Glenbuchat] to Huntly, Inverbucket, 4/15 Feb. 1716.

108. Laing and Macknight (eds), *Memoirs of the Insurrection*, pp. 361, 363; HMC *Stuart*, i. 508: Huntly to [Glenbuchat], Gordon castle, 5/16 and 7/18 Feb. 1716; i. 510: Huntly to Lovat, 11/22 Feb. 1716.

109. RH 2/4/309/111a: Sutherland to Stanhope, Inverness, 13 Feb. 1716; RH 2/4/309/126: Argyll to Townshend, Aberdeen, 17 Feb. 1716; Fraser (ed.), *Chiefs of Grant*, ii. 99: Wightman to Brigadier Grant, Inverness, 10 Mar. 1716; [Duff (ed.)], *Culloden Papers*, p. 43: Robert Baillie to John Forbes, Inverness, 23 Mar. 1716.

110. [Duff (ed.)], *Culloden Papers*, pp. 44, 47: Robert Baillie to John Forbes, Inverness, 30 Mar. and 6 Apr. 1716; p. 46: John Hossack to Duncan Forbes, Inverness, 6 Apr. 1716.
111. Terry, 'Allan Cameron's Narrative', p.138; HMC *Stuart*, i. 510: Seaforth to Brigadier Rattray, Brahan, 10/21 Feb. 1716; RH 2/4/309/111a: Sutherland to Stanhope, Inverness, 13 Feb. 1716; Tayler (ed.), *Seven Sons of the Provost*, p. 82: William Kennedy to Thomas Kennedy, [Elgin], 28 Feb. 1716.
112. See below, pp. 203–204, 244, 246, 248.
113. Lenman, *Jacobite Risings*, pp. 178, 193, 204.
114. GD 112/39/272/24: ? to Alex. Campbell of Barcaldine, Inverary?, 2 Oct. 1715; GD 112/39/273/6: John Campbell to John Campbell, Lord Glenorchy, 'Inish'?, 2 May 1716.
115. SP 54/8/69, 94, 116 and RH 2/4/305/50: Pollock to Townshend, Fort William, 16, 24 and 28 Sept. and 16 Oct. 1715; SP 54/9/14: Charles Cockburn to Under-Secretary Pringle, Edinburgh, 5 Oct. 1715; SP 54/9/21: Islay to Townshend, Inverary, 7 Oct. 1715; RH 2/4/305/30: Pollock to Lord Justice Clerk Cockburn?, Fort William, 9 Oct. 1715.
116. SP 54/8/80b: Anon. to Argyll, 21 Sept. 1715; SP 54/9/24: Argyll to Townshend, camp at Stirling, 7 Oct. 1715; RH 2/4/306/80: Islay to Townshend, Inverary, 23 Oct. 1715.
117. SP 54/8/80b: Anon. to Argyll, 21 Sept. 1715; GD 112/39/272/26: Breadalbane to Alexander Campbell of Barcaldine, Kilchurn?, 28 Oct. 1715.
118. RH 2/4/306/80: Islay to Townshend, Inverary, 23 Oct. 1715.
119. SP 54/8/94, 116 and RH 2/4/305/30: Pollock to Townshend, Fort William, 24 and 28 Sept. and 9 Oct. 1715; GD 174/1217/1: John Hardie to Maclean of Lochbuie, Duart castle, 1 Oct. 1715.
120. SP 54/8/116 and RH 2/4/307/77 and RH 2/4/308/92: Pollock to Townshend, Fort William, 28 Sept. and 23 and 28 Nov. 1715; RH 2/4/307/23, 27, 52: Pollock to Argyll, Fort William, 5, 7 and 15 Nov. 1715.
121. Macinnes, *Clanship, Commerce and the House of Stuart*, pp. 248–249; SP 54/8/106: James Cockburn to Under-Secretary Pringle, camp at Stirling, 26 Sept. 1715; Warrand (ed.), *More Culloden Papers*, ii. 102–103: Robert Baillie to Duncan Forbes, [Inverness, 14] Apr. 1716.
122. SP 54/8/113: James Cockburn to Under-Secretary Pringle, camp at Stirling, 28 Sept. 1715; SP 54/8/116: Pollock to Townshend, Fort William, 28 Sept. 1715; SP 54/9/2c: John Anderson and Robert? Colquhoun to Peter Murdoch, Provost of Glasgow, Dumbarton, 30 Sept. 1715; Nigel Tranter, *Rob Roy Macgregor* (Glasgow, 1995), p. 181.
123. Glasgow was the western Jacobites' ultimate objective (SP 54/8/46: Pollock to Townshend, Fort William, 11 Sept. 1715), and its fall something Argyll greatly feared: SP 54/8/111: Argyll to Townshend, camp at Stirling, 28 Sept. 1715.
124. SP 54/7/90: William Cunningham, Earl of Glencairn, to Townshend, Dumbarton castle, 29 Aug. 1715.
125. SP 54/9/2c: John Anderson and Robert? Colquhoun to Provost Murdoch of Glasgow, Dumbarton, 30 Sept. 1715; SP 54/9/2a: Argyll to Stanhope, camp at Stirling, 1 Oct. 1715.
126. *Loch Lomond Expedition, passim*.
127. SP 54/8/74a: Argyll to Stanhope, camp at Stirling, 18 Sept. 1715; SP 54/8/98: Sutherland to Townshend, Leith, 25 Sept. 1715; SP 54/8/121: Islay to Townshend, Edinburgh, 30 Sept. 1715; SP 54/9/15: Islay to [Under-Secretary Pringle?], 'Kilmund', in Argyll, 5 Oct. 1715.
128. SP 54/9/21: Islay to Townshend, Inverary, 7 Oct. 1715; RH 2/4/306/74: Islay to John Campbell, Provost of Edinburgh, Inverary, 22 Oct. 1715; Dumfries House, Bute Papers A546/400: Islay to Bute, Inverary, 9 Oct. 1715; *Papers of of the Rev. John Anderson*, p. 38: Tobias Martine to Anderson, Inverary, 17 Nov. 1715.

129. RH 2/4/306/74: Islay to John Campbell, Provost of Edinburgh, Inverary, 22 Oct. 1715.
130. RH 2/4/306/80: Islay to Townshend, Inverary, 23 Oct. 1715; Anderson (ed.), *Papers of the Rev. John Anderson*, p. 35: Martine to Anderson, Inverary, 28 Oct. 1715.
131. Anderson (ed.), *Papers of of the Rev. John Anderson*, pp. 35, 36–37: Martine to Anderson, Inverary, 28 Oct. and 4 and 17 Nov. 1715; RH 2/4/307/18: Argyll to Townshend, camp at Stirling, 4 Nov. 1715.
132. BL, Stowe 228, f. 159v: Dubourgay to Robethon, Stirling, 25 Oct. 1715; Steuart *Newsletters*, pp. 101–102, 121: Edinburgh, 25 Jan. [and beginning of Feb.] 1716.
133. Anderson (ed.), *Papers of of the Rev. John Anderson*, p. 35: Martine to Anderson, Inverary, 28 Oct. 1715.
134. SP 54/8/78: Islay to Townshend, Edinburgh, 20 Sept. 1715; RH 2/4/391/180: Commissioners of the Admiralty to Captain Stuart of HMS *Alborough*, [London], 26 Sept. 1715; SP 54/8/111: Argyll to Townshend, camp at Stirling, 28 Sept. 1715; SP 54/9/15: Islay to [Under-Secretary Pringle?], 'Kilmund', in Argyll, 5 Oct. 1715.
135. Anderson (ed.), *Papers of of the Rev. John Anderson*, p. 38: Martine to Anderson, Inverary, 17 Nov. 1715; RH 2/4/308/92: Pollock to Townshend, Fort William, 28 Nov. 1715.
136. *Loch Lomond Expedition*, pp. 31–32.
137. RH 2/4/308/165: Argyll to Townshend, Stirling, 29 Dec. 1715; RH 2/4/309/69: James Cockburn to Under-Secretary Pringle, Dunblane, 29 Jan. 1716.
138. RH 2/4/308/172: Pollock to Townshend, Fort William, 31 Dec. 1715; Mackay, 'Camerons in the Rising of 1715', p. 17.
139. GD 220/5/615/7: Pollock to Montrose, Fort William, 30 Jan. 1716; RH 2/4/309/79: James Cockburn to Under-Secretary Pringle, Perth, 1 Feb. 1716; RH 2/4/393/99–100: Townshend to Pollock, Whitehall, 6 Feb. 1716; RH 2/4/310/132, 154a: Pollock to Townshend, Fort William, 19 Feb. and 1 Mar. 1716.
140. Mackay, 'Camerons in the Rising of 1715', pp. 16–17; GD 220/5/615/1, 3: Pollock to Montrose, Fort William, 4 and 14 Jan. 1716; RH 2/4/309/34, 45, 73a: Pollock to Townshend, Fort William, 14, 16 and 30 Jan. 1716.
141. GD 220/5/615/8, 10: Pollock to Montrose, Fort William, 6 and 16 Feb. 1716; RH 2/4/310/132: Pollock to Townshend, Fort William, 19 Feb. 1716; Mackay, 'Camerons in the Rising of 1715', p. 17.
142. RH 2/4/309/126 and RH 2/4/310/144a: Argyll to Townshend, Aberdeen, 17 and 23 Feb. 1716; GD 248/46/7/33: Cadogan to Brigadier Grant, Elsick, 4 Mar. 1716.
143. RH 2/4/393/110: Townshend to Argyll, Whitehall, 21 Feb. 1716; RH 2/4/393/136–137: Stanhope to Pollock, Whitehall, 21 Mar. 1716; RH 2/4/310/132: Pollock to Townshend, Fort William, 19 Feb. 1716; Terry, 'Allan Cameron's Narrative', p. 140; Constable (ed.), *Fragment of a Memoir*, p. 31.
144. See, for example: Atholl Papers, box 45, bundle 12/107: Lord Justice Clerk Cockburn to Atholl, Edinburgh, 25 Feb. 1716; RH 2/4/310/154a: Pollock to Townshend, Fort William, 1 Mar. 1716.
145. Terry, 'Allan Cameron's Narrative', p. 141; RH 2/4/310/173: Wightman to Under-Secretary Pringle, Inverness, 10 Mar. 1716; GD 220/5/615/17: Pollock to Montrose, Fort William, 18 Mar. 1716; GD 220/5/631/8, 10a–b: Hope to Montrose, Perth and Inverness, 23 Mar. and 6 Apr. 1716.
146. GD 220/5/631/8: Hope to Montrose, Perth, 23 Mar. 1716; GD 220/5/615/18: Pollock to Montrose, Fort William, 30 Mar. 1716; RH 2/4/310/204: Atholl to Townshend, Blair castle, 31 Mar. 1716; RH 2/4/310/215: Cadogan to Townshend, Inverness, 6 Apr. 1716.
147. Mackay, 'Camerons in the Rising of 1715', pp. 17–20; RH 2/4/310/215: Cadogan to Townshend, Inverness, 6 Apr. 1716; RH 2/4/310/219: Wightman to Stanhope, 7 Apr. 1716; GD 220/5/631/12: Hope to Montrose, Inverness, 10 Apr. 1716.

148. Terry, 'Allan Cameron's Narrative', pp. 142–150; GD 220/5/631/9: Hope to Montrose, Blair Atholl, 1 Apr. 1716; [Duff (ed.)], *Culloden Papers*, 47: Robert Baillie to Duncan Forbes, Inverness, 6 Apr. 1716; RH 2/4/310/215: Cadogan to Townshend, Inverness, 6 Apr. 1716; RH 2/4/310/221: Cadogan to Stanhope, Inverness, 10 Apr. 1716.
149. RH 2/4/311/3a: Cadogan to Stanhope, Perth, 4 May 1716.
150. RH 2/4/308/96c: Andrew Hume, Lord Kimmerghame, to Under-Secretary Pringle, Edinburgh, 29 Nov. 1715; Constable (ed.), *Fragment of a Memoir*, p. 24; GD 18/2099: Baron John Clerk's account of a journey to Perth, researching 1715, pp. 35–36.
151. Patten, *History of the Rebellion*, p. 97.
152. RH 2/4/309/77: Cadogan to Townshend, camp at Tullibardine, 31 Jan. 1716; Steuart *Newsletters*, pp. 122–124: [Edinburgh, beginning of Feb. 1716]; RH 2/4/393/100: Stanhope to Cadogan, Whitehall, 10 Feb. 1716.
153. RH 2/4/308/179[b]: Cadogan to Townshend, Edinburgh, 19 Dec. 1715.
154. Warrand (ed.), *More Culloden Papers*, ii. 103: Robert Baillie to Duncan Forbes, [Inverness, 14] Apr. 1716.

Chapter 8 'Bought and Sold for English Gold': Prisoners, Fugitives and Exiles after the '15

1. Sankey, *Jacobite Prisoners*, xi–xii. What follows below is profoundly indebted to Dr Sankey's work and broadly follows her interpretation.
2. SP 54/8/39: Solicitor-General Steuart to [Under-Secretary Pringle?], Edinburgh, 10 Sept. 1715; SP 54/8/78: Islay to Townshend, Edinburgh, 20 Sept. 1715; RH 2/4/306/62: Lord Advocate Dalrymple to Stanhope, Edinburgh, 20 Oct. 1715.
3. RH 2/4/391/121–122: Townshend to Whetham, Whitehall, 12 Aug. 1715; SP 54/8/85: Solicitor General Steuart to [Under-Secretary Pringle], Edinburgh, 23 Sept. 1715.
4. SP 54/8/7: Whetham to Stanhope, Stirling, 1 Sept. 1715; SP 54/8/16: Kinnoull to Townshend, Edinburgh castle, 3 Sept. 1715; SP 54/8/23: Lord Justice Clerk Cockburn to Townshend, Edinburgh, 6 Sept. 1715.
5. SP 54/8/35: affidavit by John Holland, Edinburgh castle, 9 Sept. 1715; SP 54/8/36: declarations taken by Lord Provost and Baillies of Edinburgh, 9 Sept. 1715; SP 54/8/37a: affidavit by James Thomson, Edinburgh castle, 10 Sept. 1715; SP 54/8/53a: Lord Justice Clerk Cockburn to Townshend, Edinburgh, 12 Sept. 1715.
6. SP 54/8/57: Stuart Barkie to Townshend, Inverness, 14 Sept. 1715; SP 54/8/125: Macdonald of Glengarry to Pollock, 22 Sept. 1715.
7. HMC *Stuart*, i. 484: James to Huntly, Fetteresso, 28 Dec./8 Jan. 1715/16. See also: *Loch Lomond Expedition*, p. 32: 9 Dec. 1715.
8. SP 54/8/106: James Cockburn to Under-Secretary Pringle, camp at Stirling, 26 Sept. 1715; RH 2/4/306/101b: Argyll to Stanhope, camp at Stirling, 31 Oct. 1715; RH 2/4/307/81: James Cockburn to Under-Secretary Pringle, Stirling, 25 Nov. 1715.
9. Sankey, *Jacobite Prisoners*, x; John Childs, *The British Army of William III, 1689–1702* (Manchester, 1987), p. 242; RH 2/4/307/81: James Cockburn to Under-Secretary Pringle, Stirling, 25 Nov. 1715.
10. SP 54/8/99: Lord Justice Clerk Cockburn to Townshend, Edinburgh, 25 Sept. 1715. See also: Stowe 228, f. 123v: Dubourgay to Robethon, Stirling, 24 Sept. 1715.
11. SP 54/8/106: James Cockburn to Under-Secretary Pringle, camp at Stirling, 26 Sept. 1715; SP 54/9/24: Argyll to Townshend, camp at Stirling, 7 Oct. 1715.
12. RH 2/4/391/212–214: Townshend to Lord Justice Clerk Cockburn, Whitehall, 11 Oct. 1715; RH 2/4/391/224: Stanhope to Lord Justice Clerk Cockburn, Whitehall, 2 Nov. 1715; RH 2/4/307/65: James Cockburn to Under-Secretary Pringle, 19 Nov. 1715.

13. RH 2/4/306/101a: Mar to Argyll, camp at Perth, 30 Oct. 1715.
14. Sankey, *Jacobite Prisoners*, pp. 104–105; RH 2/4/306/101b: Argyll to Stanhope, camp at Stirling, 31 Oct. 1715.
15. RH 2/4/306/70: Lord Justice Clerk Cockburn to Under-Secretary Pringle, Edinburgh, 22 Oct. 1715; RH 2/4/306/73: Lord Advocate Dalrymple to Stanhope, Edinburgh, 22 Oct. 1715; RH 2/4/391/224: Stanhope to Lord Justice Clerk Cockburn, Whitehall, 2 Nov. 1715.
16. RH 2/4/307/19: minute, of Cabinet meeting?, Whitehall, 5 Nov. 1715; RH 2/4/391/248: Townshend to Argyll, Whitehall, 8 Nov. 1715.
17. RH 2/4/391/167, 230: Stanhope to Lord Justice Clerk Cockburn, Whitehall, 20 Sept. and 2 Nov. 1715; RH 2/4/391/241–242: Townshend to Lord Justice Clerk Cockburn, Whitehall, 8 Nov. 1715
18. RH 2/4/309/31: Argyll to Townshend, Stirling, 14 Jan. 1716.
19. RH 2/4/307/65, 71: James Cockburn to Under-Secretary Pringle, 19 and 20 Nov. 1715; RH 2/4/308/150: Argyll to Townshend, Stirling, 24 Dec. 1715.
20. Sankey, *Jacobite Prisoners*, pp. 42, 44, 45–46.
21. RH 2/4/306/71: Lord Advocate Dalrymple to Stanhope, Edinburgh, 22 Oct. 1715. See also: RH 2/4/307/14a: Lord Justice Clerk Cockburn to Townshend, Edinburgh, 3 Nov. 1715.
22. RH 2/4/310/173: Joseph Wightman to Under-Secretary Pringle, Inverness, 10 Mar. 1716; Atholl Papers, box 45, bundle 12/115; [Duff (ed.)], *Culloden Papers*, 43: Robert Baillie to John Forbes, Inverness, 23 Mar. 1716.
23. RH 2/4/393/131–132: Stanhope to Cadogan, St James's, 14 Mar. 1716; RH 2/4/393/132–134: Stanhope to Lord Justice Clerk Cockburn, Whitehall, 14 Mar. 1716.
24. RH 2/4/310/194: Lord Justice Clerk Cockburn to [Stanhope], Edinburgh, 23 Mar. 1716; RH 2/4/393/162, 163: Stanhope to the Provosts of Glasgow and Edinburgh, Whitehall, 15 May 1716; RH 2/4/311/16, 35: magistrates of Glasgow to Stanhope, Glasgow, 23 May and 20 June 1716; RH 2/4/311/40: 25 June 1716.
25. RH 2/4/393/49–50: Townshend to Argyll, Whitehall, 23 Dec. 1715; RH 2/4/308/170a: Lord Justice Clerk Cockburn to Under-Secretary Pringle, Edinburgh, 31 Dec. 1715; RH 2/4/309/89: Argyll to Townshend, Dundee, 4 Feb. 1716; RH 2/4/393/114: Townshend to Cadogan, Whitehall, 3 Mar. 1716.
26. Fraser (ed.), *Chiefs of Grant*, ii. 99: Wightman to Grant, Inverness, 10 Mar. 1716; Gibson, *Playing the Jacobite Card*, pp. 144–145; Sankey, *Jacobite Prisoners*, pp. 118–119.
27. [Duff (ed.)], *Culloden Papers*, 62: [Duncan Forbes] to Robert Walpole, c. Aug. 1716. See also: GD 220/5/631/6: memo by Lord Advocate Dalrymple, Feb.? 1716.
28. Sankey, *Jacobite Prisoners*, p. 120.
29. Ibid., pp. 119–120, 122–124.
30. Ibid., pp. 124–125.
31. Ibid., pp. 122, 125–126, 128–129.
32. Ibid., pp. 12–14.
33. Ibid., pp. 22–25.
34. Ibid., pp. 26–27.
35. Ibid., pp. 27–28, 36–37.
36. T. B. Howell (ed.), *A Complete Collection of State Trials* (33 vols, 1816–26), xv. 802.
37. Ibid., xv. 806.
38. Sankey, *Jacobite Prisoners*, pp. 32–33, 34–35; Howell (ed.), *State Trials*, xv. 803–805.
39. Sankey, *Jacobite Prisoners*, pp. 33, 34, 36, 37–38.
40. Ibid., pp. 81, 83.
41. Ibid., pp. 83–84, 86–88; Add. MS 38851, ff. 75–77: extract from the trial of Gascoigne, 1716; *Faithful Register*, pp. 288–289, 295–330.

42. Sankey, *Jacobite Prisoners*, pp. 46–47, 47–48, 48–49, 50–51, 56.
43. Ibid., pp. 48–49, 53–55, 88–91.
44. Ibid., p. 59; RH 2/4/307/32: James Cockburn to Under-Secretary Pringle, camp at Stirling, 8 Nov. 1715.
45. Sankey, *Jacobite Prisoners*, pp. 55, 60–63.
46. Ibid., pp. 55, 63, 71–72.
47. Ibid., pp. 65, 67.
48. Ibid., pp. 63–64, 65, 66–67, 70.
49. Atholl Papers, box 45, bundle 12/110: Lady Nairn to her daughter [not clear which one], the Tower, 25 Feb. 1716; RH 2/4/307/75: Lord Advocate Dalrymple to Stanhope, Edinburgh, 22 Nov. 1715. See also: GD 220/5/646/2: John Maxwell, Lord Pollock of the Court of Session, to Montrose, Pollock, 19 Mar. 1716.
50. HMC *Stuart*, i. 474: to Gordon of [Glenbuchat], Cushnay, 6/17 Dec. 1715.
51. Addy and McNiven (eds), *Diary of Henry Prescott*, ii. 476, 495: 27 Nov. 1715 and 27 Feb. 1716. See also: *Diary of Mary Countess Cowper*, p. 78.
52. A. and H. Tayler (eds), *Jacobite Cess Roll*, pp. 59–60 (John Farquharson of Invercauld); Henderson (ed.), *Mystics of the North-East*, pp. 42–43; GD 220/5/635: [David Grahame of Orchill to Montrose], Perth, 2 Feb. 1716.
53. GD 18/2099: Baron John Clerk's account of a journey to Perth, researching 1715, 1717, p. 39.
54. RH 2/4/393/110: Townshend to Argyll, Whitehall, 21 Feb. 1716; RH 2/4/310/163: Brigadier Preston to Argyll, Edinburgh castle, 1 Mar. 1716; RH 2/4/393/114: Townshend to Cadogan, Whitehall, 3 Mar. 1716.
55. HMC *Stuart*, ii. 71: Dr Patrick Abercromby to Mar, Saint-Germain, 27 Mar./7 Apr. 1716; Atholl Papers, box 45, bundle 12/137: Atholl to Lord James Murray of Garth, Huntingtower, 1 May 1716; Steuart *Newsletters*, p. 147: Edinburgh, 11 Mar. 1716.
56. RH 2/4/310/169: Cathcart to Argyll, Edinburgh, 3 Mar. 1716. See also: RH 2/4/310/144a: Argyll to Townshend, Aberdeen, 23 Feb. 1716.
57. RH 2/4/311/76: minutes of committee of Cabinet meeting, Whitehall, 18 July 1716; Add. MS. 61632, ff. 155–157: Roxburgh to Sunderland, Edinburgh, 8 Sept. 1716.
58. RH 2/4/311/20: memorial on the state of Angus and the Mearns, Brechin, 31 May 1716; RH 2/4/311/55a: General Sabine to Townshend, Perth, 6 July 1716; Allardyce (ed.), *Historical Papers Relating to the Jacobite Period*, i. 61: petition by Alexander Gordon of Auchlyne Jr.
59. A. and H. Tayler (eds), *Jacobite Cess Roll*, pp. 98–99, 112, 138; Graham, *Oliphants of Gask*, p. 123.
60. See for example: A. and H. Tayler (eds), *Jacobite Cess Roll*, pp. 37 (George Forbes of Skellater), 46 (Patrick and Alexander Duguid of Auchinove), 56 (Lewis Farquharson of Auchindryne), 61 (James Farquharson of Balmurrell); 78 (Alexander Leith of Threefield and New Rain).
61. Addy and McNiven (eds), *Diary of Henry Prescott*, ii. 475: 23 Nov. 1715; Patten, *History of the Rebellion*, p. 75; GD 158/1200: John Brown to Marchmont, Coldstream, 16 Feb. 1716.
62. HMC *Stuart*, ii. 31–32: William Pigault to Mar, Calais, 9/20 Mar. 1716.
63. HMC *Stuart*, ii. 71: Saint-Germain, 27 Mar./7 Apr. 1716.
64. HMC *Stuart*, ii. 175: Clephane to Mar, Amsterdam, 10/21 May 1716.
65. HMC *Stuart*, v. 180, 188.
66. Stuart Papers 40/149: list of pensioners [1718]. C. Nordmann, 'Les Jacobites écossais en France au XVIIIᵉ siècle', in M. S. Plaisant (ed.), *Regards sur l'Écosse au XVIIIᵉ siècle* (Lille, 1977), p. 84, puts the number of Scots in the French army after 1715 at 5,000 in addition to others who found alternative employment in France. The French army was

large and it is conceivable that there were 5,000 expatriate Scots in it, but I differ with Professor Nordmann over their origins. The government of Regent Orléans refused to employ the refugees of 1716 except as ordinary enlisted men, and, as well, punished Irish officers who had gone to Scotland to participate in the rising (GD 45/14/219/3/2: Panmure to John Oliphant, Avignon, 21 Sept./2 Oct. 1716; HMC *Stuart*, ii. 283: Mr Gaydon to Mar, Caen, 5/16 July 1716). It would seem likely, therefore, that Scots serving in the French army in the years immediately following 1715 were recruited before then, or were the children of the Jacobite exiles of the 1690s, rather than men taken in from among the new *émigrés*.

67. See, for example, HMC *Stuart*, ii. 55–56: Hay to Mar, Dunkirk, 23 Mar./3 Apr. 1716; ii. 104–105: Lieutenant-Colonel Nathaniel Forbes to Mar, Paris, 11/22 Apr. 1716.

68. GD 45/14/219/1/1: 2 June 1716.

69. Blairs Letters 2/200/2: Abercromby to Thomas Innes, Avignon, 6/17 Sept. 1716.

70. HMC *Stuart*, ii. 295–296: to John Paterson, Paris, 9/20 July 1716.

71. HMC *Stuart*, ii. 118–119: Mar to Lieutenant-General Arthur Dillon, Avignon, 15/26 Apr. 1716.

72. HMC *Stuart*, v. xx–xxi. The Jacobite court also received two gifts, amounting to 65,230 *livres*, from the Spanish government in 1716: Stuart Papers 44/82: 'An account of what mony was advanced by foreign princes or lent by particular persons for the King's use . . .' [Saint-Germain], 18/29 Aug. 1719. Cf. L. B. Smith, *Spain and Britain 1715–1719. The Jacobite Issue* (1987), p. 90.

73. HMC *Stuart*, ii. 5: to Orléans, 23 Feb./6 Mar. 1716.

74. HMC *Stuart*, ii. 188: [Avignon], 15/26 May 1716.

75. HMC *Stuart*, ii. 398: Avignon, 20/31 Aug. 1716.

76. HMC *Stuart*, ii. 118–119: Mar to Dillon, Avignon, 15/26 Apr. 1716; ii. 266–267: [G. Bagnall to James], [Turin?], [8?] July 1716.

77. HMC *Stuart*, vii. 573: Lady Anne Lytcott to James, Paris, 15/26 Nov. 1718; ii. 174–175: William Gordon to Mar, Paris, 10/21 May 1716; ii. 336–337, 470: Dicconson to John Paterson, [Saint-Germain], 30 July/10 Aug. and 14/25 Sept. 1716; ii. 376: Mar to Sir Hugh Paterson of Bannockburn, [Avignon], 15/26 Aug. 1716; ii. 414: Dicconson to Mar, Saint-Germain, 29 Aug./9 Sept. 1716.

78. Stuart Papers 40/149: [1718].

79. HMC *Stuart*, iv. 278: Mar to Harry Maule, 15/26 May 1717.

80. HMC *Stuart*, v. 593–595: account by Dicconson, [Saint-Germain], 25 Sept./6 Oct. 1717.

81. GD 45/14/219/5/1: Lille, 17/28 Oct. 1716.

82. Dickinson, *Bolingbroke*, pp. 140–142.

83. HMC *Stuart*, ii. 94–95: Avignon, 6/17 Apr. 1716.

84. HMC *Stuart*, ii. 216–218: [Avignon], 30 May/10 June 1716.

85. HMC *Stuart*, ii. 211–213: Mar to Lewis Innes, [Avignon], 29 May/9 June 1716; ii. 216–217: Mar to Maule, 30 May/10 June 1716.

86. HMC *Stuart*, v. 425–428: account by Dicconson, [Saint-Germain], 20/31 Jan. 1718.

87. HMC *Stuart*, ii. 405: Captain Robert Erskine to John Paterson, Avalon, 23 Aug./3 Sept. 1716.

88. HMC *Stuart*, ii. 182: Captain Robert Kay to John Paterson, Paris, 15/26 May 1716.

89. HMC *Stuart*, iii. 305: Andrew Ramsay to John Walkinshaw of Barrowfield, Bordeaux, 29 Nov./10 Dec. 1716.

90. HMC *Stuart*, ii. 163, 164: Mar to Southesk, Avignon, 8/19 May 1716.

91. HMC *Stuart*, ii. 165: Mar to Lewis Innes, Avignon, 8/19 May 1716.

92. HMC *Stuart*, iii. 83: Lewis Innes to Mar, [Saint-Germain], 4/15 Oct. 1716.

93. HMC *Stuart*, iii. 503–504: Mar to Dicconson, Avignon, 22 Jan./2 Feb. 1717; Stuart Papers 17/55: 'List of Those that are to Stay in France, or Flanders'.

94. HMC *Stuart*, iii. 459: Dr Abercromby to Mar, Paris, 7/18 Jan. 1717; Stuart Papers 17/55: 'List of his Majestie's Subjects that are to goe to Italy'.
95. Michael, *Beginnings of the Hanoverian Dynasty*, p. 13; HMC *Stuart*, ii. 55: Hay to Mar, Dunkirk, 23 Mar./3 Apr. 1716; iv. 334–335: Thomas Bruce to Mar, Brussels, 29 May/9 June 1717.
96. HMC *Stuart*, ii. 266–267: [G. Bagnall to James], [Turin?], [8?] July 1716.
97. HMC *Stuart*, ii. 191: Sir Hugh Paterson of Bannockburn to Mar, Leyden, 17/28 May 1716.
98. HMC *Stuart*, ii. 246–247: John Walkinshaw [of Scottstown] to Mar, Brussels, 20 June/1 July 1716; iv. 341–342: Bruce to Mar, Brussels, 31 May/11 June 1717.
99. Michael, *Beginnings of the Hanoverian Dynasty*, p. 323.
100. HMC *Stuart*, ii. 220: [marquis de Magny] to [Queen Mary?], 3/14 June 1716.
101. HMC *Stuart*, vii. 22–23: Marquess of Tullibardine to Mar, 28 June/9 July 1718; vii. 61: William Gordon to John Paterson, Paris, 8/19 July 1718; vii. 195: Dillon to Mar, [Paris], 12/23 Aug. 1718.
102. HMC *Stuart*, vi. 539–541: Fanny Oglethorpe to Mar, [Paris?], 6/17 June 1718; vii. 128: Dillon to Mar, Paris, 28 July/8 Aug. 1718.
103. HMC *Stuart*, ii. 63–64: Sir John Erskine of Alva to Mar, Beaune, 26 Mar./6 Apr. 1716; ii. 148: Thomas Forster to Mar, Paris, 2/13 May 1716; ii. 277–278: Clephane to Mar, Avignon, 2/13 July 1716; ii. 333–334: James Edgar to Paterson, 27 July/7 Aug. 1716; iii. 162: Lord George Murray to Mar, Turin, 20/31 Oct. 1716; iii. 164: Elphinstone to Paterson, Blois, 21 Oct./1 Nov. 1716; v. 68: Mar to James, Liège, 11/22 Sept. 1717.
104. Despite the presence of many Highlanders among them (and the fact that many of the soldiers of the Irish Brigades spoke the language – W. D. Griffin, 'The Irish on the Continent in the Eighteenth Century', *Studies in Eighteenth Century Culture*, v (1976), p. 461), there appear to have been no exclusively Gaelic-speaking communities of Scots exiles.
105. HMC *Stuart*, ii. 102–103: Leslie to Mar, 10/21 Apr. 1716.
106. GD 45/14/376: Maule to Anna Maule, Leyden, 11/22 Nov. 1718; A. and H. Tayler, *1715*, p. 274; HMC *Stuart*, iii. 428–429: Pitsligo to Mar, Leyden, 31 Dec. 1716/11 Jan. 1717.
107. HMC *Stuart*, v. 487: Mar to Panmure, Urbino, 6/17 Feb. 1718.
108. A. and H. Tayler, *1715*, p. 295; Edward Gregg, 'Politics of Paranoia', in Cruickshanks and Black (eds), *The Jacobite Challenge*, pp. 42–56.
109. HMC *Stuart*, ii. 164–167 and 211–213: Mar to Lewis Innes, Avignon, 8/19 May and 29 May/9 June 1716; ii. 216–218: Mar to Maule, [Avignon], 30 May/10 June 1716; ii. 260–261: Lewis Innes to Mar, [Saint-Germain], 26 June/7 July 1716.
110. HMC *Stuart*, v. 48: Nairne to Mar, Xaintes, 6/17 Sept. 1717.
111. GD 45/14/219/6: Hutcheson to Panmure, Bordeaux, 22 Nov./3 Dec. 1716.
112. HMC *Stuart*, v. 58: Forbes to Mar, Rotterdam, 7/18 Sept. 1717.
113. HMC *Stuart*, vi. 416: Panmure to Mar, Paris, 28 Apr./9 May 1718.
114. HMC *Stuart*, vii. 173: Ogilvie to Mar, Dunkirk, 7/18 Aug. 1718. It is interesting to observe that the first wave of Jacobite *émigrés*, in the 1690s, also had a distinct propensity towards violence in their relationships with each other and the native population: Genet-Rouffiac, 'Jacobites in Paris and Saint-Germain-en-Laye', pp. 35–37.
115. HMC *Stuart*, vii. 73: Mar to Ormonde, 11/22 July [1718]; vii. 173–174: Ogilvie to Mar, Dunkirk, 7/18 Aug. 1718.
116. HMC *Stuart*, vii. 106–107: Sir John Forrester to Mar, Cahors, 23 July/3 Aug. 1718; vii. 206: Colin Campbell of Glendarule to Mar, Orléans, 16/27 Aug. 1716. See also Stuart Papers 60/73A: Lord George Murray to James, Paris, 11/22 June 1722.
117. HMC *Stuart*, vii. 274–275: to Mar, 1/12 Sept. 1718.

118. See for example, Laing and Macknight (eds), *Memoirs of the Insurrection*, pp. 1–2; HMC *Stuart*, ii. 107–114: Ronald Macdonald of Clanranald to Mar, Ormaclett (south Uist), 11/22 Apr. 1716; v. 21: Maule to Mar, Leyden, 27 Aug./7 Sept. 1717.

119. For examples of which see: HMC *Stuart*, iii. 305: Andrew Ramsay to Walkinshaw, Bordeaux, 29 Nov./10 Dec. 1716; Szechi (ed.), 'Scotland's Ruine', pp. 239–244; Patrick Abercromby, *The Martial Achievements of the Scottish Nation* (2 vols, Edinburgh, 1711/15), i. preface (last paragraph), 622–623; ii. iv, 305–306, 318, 487, 543; Buchanan-Brown (ed.), *Remains of Thomas Hearne, passim*.

120. For an amusing example of which see HMC *Stuart*, iv. 191–192: Clanranald to Mar, Toulouse, 4/15 Apr. 1717.

121. Tayler (ed.), *Jacobite Court at Rome*, p. 138 note 1.

122. A. and H. Tayler, *1715*, p. 278: Pitsligo to George Cumine of Pitullie, [1718?].

123. HMC *Stuart*, ii. 191: Sir Hugh Paterson to Mar, Leyden, 17/28 May 1716; G. E. Cokayne, *The Complete Peerage of England, Scotland, Ireland, Great Britain and the United Kingdom* (13 vols, 1910–40), iv. 497 note c.

124. HMC *Stuart*, vii. 143–144: Mar to Thomas West, [Urbino?], 1/12 Aug. 1718.

125. HMC *Stuart*, iv. 466–468: Dicconson to Queen Mary, [Saint-Germain], 15/26 July 1717.

126. HMC *Stuart*, ii. 216–218: Mar to Maule, [Avignon], 30 May/10 June 1716.

127. HMC *Stuart*, vii. 106–107: Sir John Forrester to Mar, Cahors, 23 July/3 Aug. 1718. Cf. iii. 92: Dr Roger Kenyon to Mar, Rome, 6/17 Oct. 1716.

128. Blairs Letters 2/210/16: Paterson to William Stuart, Leghorn, 9/20 June 1716.

129. HMC *Stuart*, v. 515: to Fr Gaillard (Queen Mary's confessor), Fano, 17/28 Feb. 1718.

130. Constable (ed.), *Fragment of a Memoir*, pp. 75–76.

131. For an example of which, see: Tayler (ed.), *Jacobite Court at Rome*, pp. 232–233: James Murray of Stormont to James Edgar, [Autun], 12/23 Sept. 1751.

132. HMC *Stuart*, vi. 314–315: Robert Freebairn to Hay, Calais, 4/15 Apr. 1718.

133. HMC *Stuart*, vii. 20–21: Lancelot Ord to Dicconson, [Saint-Omer?], 27 June/8 July 1718; vii. 24: statement by Lancelot Ord, John Wood, James Kay, John English, John Coughlan, Henry Anderson and George Dallas, Saint-Omer, 28 June/9 July 1718; vii. 33–34: Richard Plowden (Provincial of the English Jesuits) to Mar, Saint-Omer, 2/13 July 1718; vii. 89: Nugent to Mar, Saint-Germain, 15/26 July 1718.

134. Dickinson, *Bolingbroke*, pp. 139–140; HMC *Stuart*, iv. 349–355: Mar to James, [Urbino?], 3/14 June 1717; iv. 370: Ormond to James, 9/20 June 1717; Tayler (ed.), *Jacobite Court at Rome*, pp. 143–146: Mar to James, 24 Jan./4 Feb. and 25 Jan./5 Feb. 1719.

135. A. and H. Tayler, *1715*, pp. 330–336.

136. HMC *Stuart*, vii. 178–179: Fr Archangel Graeme to Mar, Calais, 8/19 Aug. 1718.

137. Blairs Letters 2/217/2: Nairne to [Thomas Innes?], [Rome?], 26 Oct./6 Nov. 1717.

138. Blairs Letters 2/208/15: [Saint-Germain], 14/25 Dec. 1716.

139. Blairs Letters 2/210/7: Nairne to Thomas Innes, [Avignon], 26 Aug./6 Sept. 1716.

140. HMC *Stuart*, v. 205: Rome, 2/13 Nov. 1717.

141. Though this was not universal, for which see: HMC *Stuart*, ii. 138: Captain Simon Fraser to Paterson, Sens, 26 Apr./7 May 1716.

142. See, for example, Stuart Papers 41/32: Panmure to Mar, Paris, 29 Dec. 1718/9 Jan. 1719.

143. HMC *Stuart*, ii. 261: Maule to Mar, Leyden, 26 June/7 July 1716.

144. HMC *Stuart*, ii. 104–105: Forbes to Mar, Paris, 11/22 Apr. 1716; ii. 190: Forbes to John Paterson, Paris, 17/28 May 1716.

145. HMC *Stuart*, vii. 279–281: Home to Mar, London, 2 Sept. 1718.

146. HMC *Stuart*, ii. 85–86: Mar to Hay, Avignon, 2/13 Apr. 1716; Gregg, 'Mar', pp. 193–194.

147. GD 1/44/7: Catherine Erskine to Sir John Erskine, 4 May 1716.
148. GD 45/14/220/3: Margaret Panmure to Panmure, Panmure, 12 Mar. 1716.
149. GD 1/44/7: Catherine Erskine to Sir John Erskine, 4 May 1716; HMC *Stuart*, ii. xxvi–xxvii; iii. 44: Sir John Erskine to Mar, 27 Sept./8 Oct. 1716.
150. GD 45/14/220/38/1–62: Margaret Panmure to Panmure, London and Panmure, 23 July 1717–19 June 1718.
151. HMC *Stuart*, vii. 319–320, 351–352, 442–443 and 482–483: Frances, Countess of Mar, to Mar, Boulogne, [12/23] Sept., 22 Aug./2 Oct., 15/26 Oct. and 21 Oct./1 Nov. 1718.
152. HMC *Stuart*, ii. 129: Sir Hugh Paterson of Bannockburn to Mar, Leyden, 18/29 Apr. 1716; v. 20–21: Maule to Mar, Leyden, 27 Aug./7 Sept. 1717; vii. 156–157: Panmure to Mar, Paris, 4/15 [Aug.] 1718; Stuart Papers 50/9: Panmure to James, Paris, 31 Oct./11 Nov. 1720.
153. GD 45/14/376: Maule to Anna Maule, Leyden, 25 Feb./8 Mar. 1718.
154. GD 45/14/376: Maule to Anna Maule, Leyden, 5/16 Aug. and 6/17 Sept. 1718.
155. GD 45/14/376: Maule to Anna Maule, Leyden, 11/22 Nov. 1718.
156. HMC *Stuart*, iii. 44: Sir John Erskine to Mar, 27 Sept./8 Oct. 1716; Sankey, *Jacobite Prisoners*, pp. 110–111.
157. GD 1/44/7: Catherine Erskine to Sir John Erskine, 3/14 May 1716.
158. As is tacitly demonstrated by the general assumption that he was a man of influence, for which see HMC *Stuart*, ii. 322: Mary Drummond, Duchess of Perth, to Erskine, [Saint-Germain?], 23 July/3 Aug. 1716.
159. GD 45/14/220/1, 2, 5, 31: Margaret Panmure to Panmure, Panmure, 22 Feb. and 9 and 29 Mar. 1716 and 22 Apr. 1717.
160. GD 45/14/220/73: Margaret Panmure to Panmure, 18 Dec. 1718.
161. This is on the back of Margaret Panmure's letter cited above. Panmure was, however, clearly ashamed of having given in and denied he would ever accept such conditions in a letter to Mar (though at the same time this may possibly have been a hint that if the Jacobite monarch gave him permission to do so he could accept the British government's terms): Stuart Papers 41/32: Paris, 29 Dec. 1718/9 Jan. 1719.
162. GD 45/14/377: copies of letters from Maule to Roxburgh and Montrose, [Leyden], 6/17 Jan. 1719; Gregg, 'Mar', pp. 180, 185, 186, 192.
163. HMC *Stuart*, ii. 113: Clanranald to Mar, Ormaclett (south Uist), 11/22 Apr. 1716; ii. 138–139: Fraser to John Paterson, Sens, 26 Apr./7 May 1716; ii. 157–158: Alexander Gordon to John Paterson, Paris, 5/16 May 1716.
164. J. H. Shennan, *Philippe, Duke of Orléans. Regent of France 1715–1723* (1979), pp. 97–125.
165. HMC *Stuart*, v. 593–595: account by Dicconson, [Saint-Germain], 25 Sept./6 Oct. 1717.
166. HMC *Stuart*, v. 600–601: memo on his financial situation by James, [Urbino?], Oct. 1717.
167. HMC *Stuart*, v. 132–133: Queen Mary to Mar, Chaillot, 11/12 Oct. 1717.
168. HMC *Stuart*, v. 404: Cardinal de Noailles to James, Conflans, 13/24 Jan. 1718; vi. 75: William Gordon to Paterson, Paris, 18 Feb./1 Mar. 1718.
169. HMC *Stuart*, vi. 75: Gordon to Paterson, Paris, 18 Feb./1 Mar. 1718.
170. HMC *Stuart*, vii. 271: Dicconson to James, 1/12 Sept. 1718.
171. Shennan, *Duke of Orléans*, pp. 80–87; HMC *Stuart*, vi. 488–489: James to Orléans, [Urbino], 17/28 May 1718.
172. HMC *Stuart*, vi. 526–527: William Gordon to Mar, Paris, 3/14 June 1718; vii. 622: James to Dicconson, Rome, 1/12 Dec. 1718.
173. HMC *Stuart*, vii. 497–498: William Gordon to Mar, Paris, 25 Oct./5 Nov. 1718.

174. HMC *Stuart*, vi. 216: William Gordon to Mar, Paris, 18/29 Mar. 1718; vii. 8–9: Dicconson to Mar, [Saint-Germain], 23 June/4 July 1718. See also: Stuart Papers 42/10: Robert Gordon to Mar, Bordeaux, 27 Jan./7 Feb. 1719; 43/114A: account by William Dundas, Rotterdam, 31 May/11 June 1719.

175. HMC *Stuart*, vii. 587: Gordon to John Paterson, Paris, 18/29 Nov. 1718; Stuart Papers 42/10: Robert Gordon to Mar, Bordeaux, 27 Jan./7 Feb. 1719.

176. GD 45/14/219/20/1: Carnegy to Panmure, Lille, 3/14 May 1719.

177. HMC *Stuart*, vii. 2–3: George Maxwell to Mar, Cahors, 20 June/1 July 1718; vii. 314–315: [Lancelot Ord] to Mar, Saint-Omer, 11/22 Sept. 1718; Stuart Papers 40/151.

178. HMC *Stuart*, vi. 395: Captain John Ogilvie to Mar, Dunkirk, 21 Apr./2 May 1718.

179. GD 45/14/219/15/1: Douglas to Panmure, Leyden, 18/29 Nov. 1718.

180. HMC *Stuart*, iv. 277–278: Mar to Maule, 15/26 May 1717.

181. GD45/14/219/15/2: Panmure to Douglas, Paris, 29 Nov./10 Dec. 1718.

182. SP 40/151, [Dicconson, end of 1718].

183. A. and H. Tayler, *1715*, pp. 233–234, 282; Szechi (ed.), *Lockhart Letters*, p. 323: Lockhart to James, [Aix-la-Chapelle?], 26 Sept./7 Oct. 1727.

184. For examples of which see: Aufrere (ed.), *Lockhart Papers*, i. 250–253; ii. 427–429; A. and H. Tayler, *1715*, p. 186; Ó Ciardha, *Ireland and the Jacobite Cause*, pp. 151–163, Buckley (ed.), *Memoirs of Thomas, Earl of Ailesbury*, i. 236, 304, ii. 518.

185. GD 45/14/220/7: Margaret Panmure to Panmure, Panmure, 7 May 1716. See also: Tayler (ed.), *Jacobite Court at Rome*, p. 36.

186. A. and H. Tayler (eds), *Jacobite Cess Roll*, pp. 55–56 (James Mackenzie of Dalmore Jr), 185 (Thomas Forbes of Tolquhon).

Chapter 9 'Such a Parcel of Rogues in a Nation': Resistance and Social Reintegration after the '15

1. SP 54/9/21: Islay to Townshend, Inverary, 7 Oct. 1715.

2. RH 2/4/306/62: Lord Advocate Dalrymple to Stanhope, Edinburgh, 20 Oct. 1715.

3. GD 220/5/455/57: Lord Justice Clerk Cockburn to Montrose, Edinburgh, 29 Dec. 1715.

4. A. and H. Tayler, *1715*, pp. 317–323.

5. BL, Add. MS 37993, f. 15v: Polwarth to George Baillie of Jerviswood, Edinburgh, 29 Oct. 1715; GD 220/5/635: [Grahame of Orchill to Montrose], Perth, 2 Feb. 1716; GD 220/5/645: Cathcart to Montrose, Aberdeen, 14 Feb. 1716; RH 2/4/309/121: Lord Justice Clerk to Under-Secretary Pringle, Edinburgh, 16 Feb. 1716; Atholl Papers, box 45, bundle 12/112: Grizel Lyon, Lady Airlie, to Atholl, Corlachie, 27 Feb. 1716; RH 2/4/310/217: Lord Justice Clerk Cockburn to Under-Secretary Pringle, Ormiston, 7 Apr. 1716.

6. Sankey, *Jacobite Prisoners*, pp. 133, 134.

7. Sedgwick, *House of Commons 1715–1754*, i. 462, 470–471; ii. 95–96, 282; RH 2/4/310/158, 213: Munro to Townshend, Inverness and Ruthven, 28 Feb. and 4 Apr. 1716.

8. Sankey, *Jacobite Prisoners*, pp. 134–136.

9. Ibid., pp. 136–138.

10. Ibid., pp. 138–139.

11. Ibid., pp. 138, 143–144.

12. Ibid., p. 141.

13. Ibid., p. 141.

14. Ibid., pp. 139–140, 143.

15. Ibid., pp. 143–144.

16. Ibid., pp. 144–146.
17. Ibid., p. 146.
18. Ibid., pp. 147–149.
19. J. R. N. Macphail, *Highland Papers. Volume II* (Scottish History Society, 2nd ser., Edinburgh, 1916), pp. 290–291.
20. Addy and McNiven (eds), *Diary of Henry Prescott*, ii. 475: 20 Nov. 1715. See also: ii. 474, 476: 17, 18 and 25 Nov. 1715.
21. *Diary of Mary Countess Cowper*, p. 72. Despite her deep-dyed Whiggery she was also delighted by Nithsdale's escape (p. 87).
22. William Matthews (ed.), *The Diary of Dudley Ryder 1715–1716* (1939), p. 182: 14 Feb. 1716.
23. Sankey, *Jacobite Prisoners*, pp. 35, 82, 136; *Diary of Mary Countess Cowper*, pp. 91–92.
24. Nicholson, 'Lancashire in the Rebellion of 1715', p. 84; J. J. Bagley (ed.), *The Great Diurnal of Nicholas Blundell of Little Crosby, Lancashire* (The Record Society of Lancashire and Cheshire, 2 vols, 1970[?]), ii. 144, 148, 151, 152: 18 Aug., 2 Oct. and 13 and 16–21 Nov. 1715.
25. Matthews (ed.), *Diary of Dudley Ryder*, p. 175: 30 Jan. 1716.
26. Sankey, *Jacobite Prisoners*, p. 51; *Faithful Register*, p. 331.
27. Susannah Abbott, 'Clerical Responses to the Jacobite Rebellion in 1715', *Historical Research* lxxvi (2003), 332–346.
28. 'A Declaration of the Arch-bishop of Canterbury, and the Bishops in and near London, Testifying Their Abhorrence of the Present Rebellion; with an Exhortation to the Clergy and People under Their Care, to Be Zealous in the Discharge of Their Duties to His Majesty King George', 3 Nov. 1715, cited in Michael, *Beginnings of the Hanoverian Dynasty*, p. 205.
29. See for example: Charles Lambe, *The Popish Plot a Fair Caution to Protestants not to Engage in a Popish Rebellion. A Sermon Preached on Sunday November the 6th, 1715. At St Katherine Cree-Church and All-Hallows Barkin [sic]* (1715), pp. 3–4, 12–13, 17, 20–21; White Kennett, *The Witchcraft of the Present Rebellion. A Sermon Preached in the Parish Church of St Mary Aldermary, in the City of London, on Sunday the 25th of September, 1715. The Time of Publick Ordination* (1715), pp. 9, 16–18, 20–22; *Rebellion Display'd: or, Our Present Distractions set Forth in Their True Light* (1715), pp. 4, 5, 8, 9, 14–15; *A King and no King: Or, the Best Argument for a Just Title. Being the Present Case of Great Britain Briefly Considered in a Seasonable Address to the People* (1716), pp. 245, 246, 247–248, 252; Edmund Gibson, *The Deliverances and Murmerings of the Israelites, and These Nations Compar'd* (1716), pp. 16, 22.
30. Addison, *Free-Holder*, no. 12, 30 Jan. 1716, p. 74; Matthews (ed.), *Diary of Dudley Ryder*, pp. 176, 181–183: 30 Jan. and 14 Feb. 1716.
31. *Diary of Mary Countess Cowper*, pp. 84–85; *Faithful Register*, p. 28.
32. Monod, *Jacobitism and the English People*, pp. 327–330; Fritz, *English Ministers and Jacobitism*, p. 105.
33. RH 2/4/305/44: warning by Synod of Perth and Stirling, Stirling, 13 Oct. 1715; RH 2/4/306/103b: 'Admonition by the Synod of Glasgow and Air to all the Congregations Under Their Inspection', [Glasgow?, Oct.]1715; RH 2/4/307/5: 'A Seasonable Admonition by the Provincial Synod of Lothian and Tweeddale', Edinburgh, 2 Nov. 1715.
34. Sankey, *Jacobite Prisoners*, p. 147; Fraser (ed.), *Chiefs of Grant*, ii. 95–96: Brigadier Grant to Captain George Grant, Stirling, 22 Dec. 1715; RH 2/4/309/38: Lord Justice Clerk Cockburn to Under-Secretary Pringle, Edinburgh, 18 Jan. 1716.
35. Steuart *Newsletters*, pp. 48–49: [Edinburgh, latter half of Nov. 1715]; GD 220/5/610/5: [Walter Stirling to ?], *c.* 17 Mar. 1716.

36. Henry Grey Graham, *The Social Life of Scotland in the Eighteenth Century* (New York, reprint, 1971 of London 2nd edn, 1901), pp. 12–13; GD 18/2092/2: Sir John Clerk's spiritual journal for 1699–1709, 17 Mar. 1701; D. Szechi (ed.), *The Letters of George Lockhart of Carnwath 1698–1732* (Scottish History Society, 5th ser., ii, Edinburgh, 1989), pp. 52–53; Wodrow, *Analecta*, i, 345. This subject has recently been explored in an English context, from which it is clear that many of the mores of Scottish sociability were common to England too: Susan E. Whyman, *Sociability and Power in late-Stuart England: the Cultural Worlds of the Verneys, 1660–1720* (Oxford , 1999).

37. Helen and Keith Kelsall (eds), *An Album of Scottish Families 1694–96. Being the First Instalment of George Home's Diary, Supplemented by Much Further Research into the Edinburgh and Border Families Forming his Extensive Social Network* (Aberdeen, 1990), p. 15 and *passim*; George W. T. Omond (ed.), *The Arniston Memoirs: Three Centuries of a Scottish House, 1571–1838* (Edinburgh, 1887), p. 59.

38. GD 18/5246/1/46: James Stewart, Earl of Galloway, to Sir John Clerk, Glasertoun, 30 Mar. 1713; GD 27/6/16: Thomas Kennedy to Grizel Kennedy, London, 5 May 1716; GD 18/5271/4: Elizabeth, dowager Countess of Stair, to Sir John Clerk, 3 September 1715; Johnstone, *Memoirs of the Rebellion*, pp. 239–243, 296.

39. *Burt's Letters*, i. 230, 234.

40. GD 18/2092/2: Sir John Clerk's spiritual journal for 1699–1709, 12 Feb. and 26 Sept. 1702 and 1 and 9 Feb. 1708.

41. *Burt's Letters*, i. 233.

42. Lenman, *Jacobite Clans*, p. 187; John B. Stewart, *Opinion and Reform in Hume's Political Philosophy* (Princeton, 1992), p. 9; Wodrow, *Analecta*, ii. 307: Nov. 1715; GD 220/5/623/4: Hyndford to Montrose, Edinburgh, 5 Mar. 1716; Moody-Stuart, 'Lieutenant-Colonel James Steuart', p. 22.

43. Sir James Balfour Paul, *The Scots Peerage: Founded on Wood's Edition of Sir Robert Douglas's Peerage of Scotland. Containing an Historical and Genealogical Account of the Nobility of That Kingdom* (9 vols, Edinburgh, 1904), *passim*.

44. Ronald M. Sunter, *Patronage and Politics in Scotland, 1707–1832* (Edinburgh, 1986), pp. 2–8.

45. Ibid., pp. 48–60; GD 18/2092/3: Sir John's journal for 1710–Apr. 1712, 26 Aug. and 8 Nov. 1710; Szechi (ed.), *Letters of George Lockhart*, pp. 69–70.

46. A. and H. Tayler (eds), *Jacobite Cess Roll*; Holmes and Szechi, *Age of Oligarchy*, p. 90; Szechi (ed.), *Letters of George Lockhart*, p. 200.

47. GD 220/5/1913/7: Hawley to Campbell of Ardkinglass, Falkirk, 2 Dec. 1715; HMC *Stuart*, i. 458: Malcolm to Gordon of Glenbuchat, Kirkcaldy, 31 Oct. 1715; GD 220/5/642/9: 10 ministers of the Kirk in Perthshire to Lord Justice Clerk Cockburn, Perth, 3 Aug. 1716.

48. HMC *Stuart*, i. 478: [Gordon of Glenbuchat to Huntley, 14/25 Dec. 1715]; i. 492: Lovat to Glenbuchat, Inverness, 20 Jan. 1716.

49. HMC *Stuart*, i. 501–502: Huntly to ?, Gordon castle, 2 Feb. 1716.

50. GD 220/5/631/7: John Hope to Montrose, Edinburgh, 17 Mar. 1716.

51. Atholl Papers, box 45, bundle 12/137: Atholl to Lord James Murray of Garth, Huntingtower, 1 May 1716.

52. Baynes, *Jacobite Rising*, p. 202; A. and H. Tayler, *1715*, pp. 239–240; GD 220/5/631/11: John Hope to Montrose, Inverness, 7 Apr. 1716.

53. NLS, E609/22/5 (Commission for Forfeited Estates Papers): William and Robert Ross to the Commissioners, 13 Jan. 1721.

54. Macinnes, *Clanship, Commerce and the House of Stuart*, pp. 196–197; *Burt's Letters*, ii. 178–180.

55. Szechi (ed.), *Letters of George Lockhart*, p. 179.

56. GD 220/5/721/2: Smythe of Methven to Montrose, Edinburgh castle, 15 Feb. 1717.
57. Szechi (ed.), *Letters of George Lockhart*, p. 293.
58. Douglas Hay, 'Property, Authority and the Criminal Law', in Douglas Hay, Peter Linebaugh, John G. Rule, Edward Thompson and Cal Winslow, *Albion's Fatal Tree: Crime and Society in Eighteenth-Century England* (London, reprint, 1988, of London 1975 edn), pp. 40–56.
59. G. F. C. Hepburne Scott (ed.), 'Marchmont Correspondence Relating to the '45', in *Miscellany of the Scottish History Society* (Scottish History Society, 3rd ser., v, Edinburgh, 1933), p. 323: Lady Jane Nimmo to Marchmont, Redbraes, 30 Sept. 1745. See also: GD 45/14/220/21: Margaret Panmure to Panmure, Panmure, 13 Nov. 1716; GD 220/5/611/3: Colin Graham of Drenny to James Graham, 'Inarbreases', 30 Jan. 1716; Laing and Macknight (eds), *Memoirs of the Insurrection*, p. 100.
60. RH 2/4/311/20: memorial on the state of Angus and the Mearns, Brechin, 31 May 1716.
61. GD 45/14/220/10–18, 21, 28: Margaret Panmure to Panmure, Panmure and Edinburgh, 1716.
62. GD 45/14/220/67: Margaret Panmure to Panmure, Panmure, 25 Aug. 1718.
63. GD 220/5/455/56, 57: Lord Justice Clerk Cockburn to Montrose, Edinburgh, 29 Nov. and 29 Dec. 1715. See also, GD 220/5/631/4a–b: John Hope to Montrose, Aberdeen, 8/10 Feb. 1716 and GD 220/5/615/17: Sir Robert Pollock to Montrose, Fort William, 18 Mar. 1716.
64. Aufrere (ed.), *Lockhart Papers*, ii. 5; A. and H. Tayler (eds), *Jacobite Cess Roll*, p. 98.
65. GD 220/5/624/1: [Stair to Montrose], Paris, 17/28 Jan. 1716. See also [Duff (ed.)], *Culloden Papers*, p. 61: Duncan Forbes of Culloden to Sir Robert Walpole, Aug. 1716.
66. GD 220/5/631/6: memo by Sir David Dalrymple, Feb.? 1716.
67. Omond (ed.), *Arniston Memoirs*, p. 60; Lenman, *Jacobite Risings*, p. 163; George W. T. Omond, *The Lord Advocates of Scotland*, 2 vols (Edinburgh, 1883), i. 306; Sir David Dalrymple, *The Laws and Judicatures of Scotland* (London, 1718), pp. 9, 14.
68. GD 220/5/624/2: [Stair to Montrose], Paris, 18/29 Feb. 1716. See also: GD 220/5/624/3: [Stair to Montrose], Paris, 10/21 Apr. 1716; Huntington Library, California, Loudoun Papers, LO 7670 (lspbox 20): Stair to Loudoun, Paris, 15/26 May 1716.
69. Lenman, *Jacobite Risings*, p. 159; A. and H. Tayler, *1715*, pp. 174–176; Tayler (ed.), *Seven Sons of the Provost*, p. 84: William Kennedy to Thomas Kennedy, Edinburgh, 25 Aug. 1716.
70. [Duff (ed.)], *Culloden Papers*, p. 58: Duncan Forbes to Islay, Edinburgh, 7 July 1716; p. 68: circular letter signed by William Drummond of the Bank of Scotland, Edinburgh, 6 Nov. 1716.
71. Baynes, *Jacobite Rising*, p. 202; Atholl Papers, box 45 bundle 12/117: numbers of former Perthshire rebels who took the oaths, 12–22 Mar. 1716; GD 220/5/631/6: memo by Sir David Dalrymple (copy), Feb.? 1716; GD 220/5/610/5: [Walter Stirling to ?], *c.* 17 Mar. 1716.
72. HMC *Stuart*, v. 600–601.
73. Szechi (ed.), *Letters of George Lockhart*, p. 323.
74. A. and H. Tayler (eds), *Jacobite Cess Roll*, pp. 114, 153.
75. GD 220/5/634/4: Grizell Cochrane to Montrose, Levenside, 23 Feb. 1716; Katherine Tomasson and Francis Buist, *Battles of the '45* (reprint, 1978), p. 32.
76. GD 220/5/642/23, 24: Smythe of Methven to Montrose, Edinburgh castle, 16 and 27 Nov. 1716.
77. GD 220/5/642/23: Smythe of Methven to Montrose, Edinburgh castle, 16 Nov. 1716.

78. GD 45/14/220/10–17: Margaret Panmure to Panmure, Edinburgh, June–Sept. 1716; HMC *Stuart*, vii. 669: Panmure to Mar, Paris, 15/26 Dec. 1718.
79. HMC *Stuart*, iii. 44: Sir John Erskine to Mar, 27 Sept./8 Oct. 1716; vii. 668–670: Panmure to Mar, Paris, 15/26 Dec. 1718.
80. A. and H. Tayler (eds), *Jacobite Cess Roll*, pp. 56, 58, 63; Aufrere (ed.), *Lockhart Papers*, i. 496; National Library of Scotland, Abbotsford 902/60. Even the more important prisoners were sometimes obliged to oil the wheels of the state bureaucracy to ensure that their remissions passed through it in a timely manner, for an example of which see: GD 112/39/273/34: Patrick Campbell of Monzies, Lord Monzies of the Court of Session, to Glenorchy, London, 29 Sept. 1716.
81. GD 18/5245/5: petition by Laurence Charteris to Sunderland (care of Baron John Clerk), the Hague, 23 Aug./3 Sept. 1720; GD 220/5/619/1: Nairne to Montrose, Tower of London, 11 Jan. 1716; GD 220/5/611/4: James Graham, Judge Admiral, to Montrose, Edinburgh, 28 Feb. 1716; GD 112/39/273/37: Campbell of Monzies to Glenorchy, London, 25 Oct. 1716; GD 220/5/623/3: Hyndford to Montrose, Edinburgh, 21 Jan. 1716; HMC *Stuart*, vi. 498: Panmure to Mar, Paris, 20/31 May 1718; *Diary of Mary Countess Cowper*, pp. 72, 81, 88.
82. E650/63/21: Alexander Hamilton's expenses charged to Margaret Panmure, 1716.
83. GD 112/39/273/10: Campbell of Monzies to Glenorchy, London, 31 May 1716.
84. GD 220/5/616: Drummond to Montrose, Callander, 7 Jan. 1716; GD 220/5/611/2: James Graham to Montrose, Edinburgh, 23 Feb. 1716; GD 220/5/636/2: Elibank to Montrose, Balincrieffe, 26 Mar. 1716; GD 220/5/641: Home to Montrose, Edinburgh castle, 11 Feb. 1716.
85. GD 267/19/15: Grizel Baillie to Margaret, Lady Wedderburn, 7 Feb. 1717; GD 220/5/540/3: Grizel Cochrane to Montrose, Levenside, 23 Dec. 1715.
86. GD 160/217/4: Henrietta Gordon to ?, 25 Mar. 1717; Henrietta Tayler, *Lady Nithsdale and Her Family* (London, 1939), pp. 46–58, 61; *Diary of Mary Countess Cowper*, pp. 80–81.
87. GD 38/2/2/48: Sophia Lippe-Buckenburg to Margaret Nairn, St James, 22 Mar. 1716; GD 45/14/270/12 Margaret Panmure to Mary, Duchess of Atholl, 1716.
88. GD 45/14/220/73: Margaret Panmure to Panmure, London, 18 Dec. 1718. See also: GD 1/44/7/6 Sophia Erskine to Sir John Erskine of Alva, 4 May, 1716.
89. GD 220/5/672/1: Huntly to Montrose, Edinburgh castle, 7 Apr. 1716. See also: GD 220/5/658/1: John Murray, Earl of Dunmore, to Montrose [London, 21 Feb. 1716]; GD 220/5/637/2: Kinnoull to Montrose, 'Inderaske', 10 Mar. 1716; GD 220/5/646/3: John Maxwell, Lord Pollock of the Court of Session, to Montrose, Pollock, 23 Apr. 1716.
90. GD 220/5/721/1: Montrose to Smythe of Methven, London, 5 Feb. 1717; GD 220/5/642/1: Smythe of Methven to Montrose, Aberdeen, 12 Feb. 1716; GD 220/5/662: Urquhart of Newhall to Montrose, [Feb. 1716]; Sedgwick, *House of Commons 1715–1754*, ii. 490.
91. GD 220/5/453/16: Dalrymple to Montrose, [Edinburgh?], 5 Dec. 1715; GD 220/5/455/57: Lord Justice Clerk Cockburn to Montrose, Edinburgh, 29 Dec. 1715; GD 220/5/623/3: Hyndford to Montrose, Edinburgh, 21 Jan. 1716.
92. Omond (ed.), *Arniston Memoirs*, 102; Wodrow, *Analecta*, iii. 145; Scott (ed.), 'Marchmont Correspondence', pp. 317–18: George Carre to Marchmont, Nisbet, 10 Sept. 1745.
93. Szechi (ed.), *Letters of George Lockhart*, pp. 309–310, 344; *Burt's Letters*, i. 223–225; Clarke, 'Scottish Episcopalians', pp. 411–412.
94. Lenman, *Jacobite Risings*, p. 167; Baynes, *Jacobite Rising*, p. 27, 142; Szechi, *Jacobitism and Tory Politics*, pp. 204–205; A. and H. Tayler, *1715*, p. 273.

95. Lenman, *Jacobite Risings*, p. 167; John Stuart Shaw, *The Management of Scottish Society 1707–1764. Power, Nobles, Lawyers, Edinburgh Agents and English Influences* (Edinburgh, 1983), p. 70; Szechi (ed.), *Letters of George Lockhart*, pp. 254–255. General Sinclair was also helpful in getting permission to return home for other exiled Jacobites: Tayler (ed.), *Seven Sons of the Provost*, pp. 122, 130.

96. Charteris (ed.), *Short Account*, p. 37.

97. Szechi (ed.), *Letters of George Lockhart*, p. 255.

98. A. and H. Tayler, *1715*, pp. 199–218, 252; A. and H. Tayler (eds), *Jacobite Cess Roll*, pp. 31, 196–197; Jeremy Black, *The Grand Tour in the Eighteenth Century* (Stroud, 1997), p. 171; Yorke (ed.), *Hardwicke*, i. 512: Joseph Yorke to Hardwicke, Aberdeen, 9 Mar. 1746. Huntly was graciously wining and dining government officers within little more than a month of the rebellion's disintegration: Tayler (ed.), *Seven Sons of the Provost*, 83: William Kennedy to Thomas Kennedy, Edinburgh, 24 Mar. 1716.

99. Scott (ed.), 'Marchmont Correspondence', pp. 331–332: Lady Jane Nimmo to Marchmont, Redbraes, 27 Oct. 1745; pp. 334–335: James Nimmo to Marchmont, 21 Dec. 1745; Omond (ed.), *Arniston Memoirs*, pp. 101, 102.

100. Aufrere (ed.), *Lockhart Papers*, i. 395–399; Szechi (ed.), *Letters of George Lockhart*, pp. 132–133; Ferguson, *1689 to the Present*, pp. 137–138.

101. Aufrere (ed.), *Lockhart Papers*, i. 395–399; Shaw, *Management of Scottish Society*, p. 70; Macinnes, *Clanship, Commerce and the House of Stuart*, p. 197. I am grateful to Professor David Hayton of Queen's University, Belfast, for a thought-provoking conversation with him in London in 1997 regarding his work on Scottish Parliamentary politics, and to Senator John Stewart for letting me see an early draft of several chapters of his book and for the stimulating discussion of Islay's clientage network I had with him in Edinburgh, also in 1997.

102. SP 54/8/77: Lord Justice Clerk Cockburn to [Under-Secretary Pringle], Edinburgh, 20 Sept. 1715; RH 2/4/306/62: Lord Advocate Dalrymple to Stanhope, Edinburgh, 20 Oct. 1715.

103. Lenman, *Jacobite Risings*, p. 178.

104. Warrand (ed.), *More Culloden Papers*, ii. 86–87: Wemyss to Crawfurd, Grange, 17 Jan. 1716.

105. Atholl Papers, box 45, bundle 12/147: Atholl to Garth, Dunkeld, 30 May 1716.

Conclusion

1. SP 54/8/110: Islay to Townshend, Edinburgh, 27 Sept. 1715.

2. Erskine (ed.), 'Earl of Mar's Legacies', p. 158; Laing and Macknight (eds), *Memoirs of the Insurrection, passim.*

3. GD 220/5/1908/1: Montrose to Stair, London, 26 Sept. 1715.

4. RH 2/4/309/18: James Cockburn to Under-Secretary Pringle, Stirling, 7 Jan. 1716; GD 220/5/631/10a–b: John Hope to Montrose, Inverness, 6 Apr. 1716.

5. SL 30/232: petition of William Rigg, Commissioner for Coupar, to the Royal Convention of Burghs, 1717; SL 30/233: petition of Jedburgh to the Royal Convention of Burghs, 1718; SL 30/233: petition of Selkirk to the Royal Convention of Burghs, 9 July 1718.

6. Fraser (ed.), *Chiefs of Grant*, ii. 97–98: [Moray] to Brigadier Grant, Dunibrisle, 19 Jan. 1716; Warrand (ed.), *More Culloden Papers*, ii. 111: John Forbes to Duncan Forbes, London, 12 Apr. 1716; Atholl Papers, box 45, bundle 12/147: Atholl to Lord James Murray of Garth, Dunkeld, 30 May 1716.

7. Hay, *History of Arbroath*, p. 178; GD 44/17/11/115–116, 120–121, 126, 134, 178, 192, 203, 209, 229.
8. *Burt's Letters*, i. 210–211.
9. RH 2/4/310/203, 228: John Campbell, Provost of Edinburgh, to Stanhope, Edinburgh, 31 Mar. and 17 Apr. 1716; Donald, 'Glasgow and the Jacobite Rebellion of 1715', p. 131; RH 2/4/311/29: Lord Justice Clerk Cockburn to Under-Secretary Pringle, Edinburgh, 9 June 1716.
10. Atholl Papers, box 45, bundle 12/157: Atholl to Lord James Murray of Garth, Huntingtower, 23 June 1716.
11. Warrand (ed.), *More Culloden Papers*, ii. 124–125: John Forbes to Duncan Forbes, London, 29 June 1716.
12. Ibid., 117: John Forbes to Duncan Forbes, [London] 15 May 1716; BL, Add. MS 38851, ff. 102–103: inventory of weapons received at Inverary; ibid., ii. 156–160, 160–161: lists of weapons handed in at Inverness, prior to 1 Nov. 1716.
13. Sankey, *Jacobite Prisoners*, p. 135.
14. Correlli Barnett, *Britain and Her Army 1509–1970* (New York, 1970), p. 165; Alan Guy, 'The Irish Military Establishment, 1660–1776', in Thomas Bartlett and Keith Jeffery (eds), *A Military History of Ireland* (Cambridge, 1996), p. 216; Holmes, *Making of a Great Power*, pp. 322, 394–395.
15. The phrase comes from 'The Vicar of Bray':

> When George in pudding time came o'er,
> And moderate men looked big, sir,
> My principles I chang'd once more,
> And so became a Whig, sir:
> And thus preferment I procur'd,
> From our faith's great defender,
> And almost every day abjur'd
> The Pope, and the Pretender.
> And this is law, I will maintain
> Unto my dying day, sir,
> That whatsoer king shall reign,
> I will be Vicar of Bray, sir!

16. Colley, *In Defiance of Oligarchy*, pp. 188–235.
17. SP 78/160, ff. 216–218: Orléans to Stair, [Paris], 2/13 Mar. 1716; Michael, *Beginnings of the Hanoverian Dynasty*, pp. 311–326; Black, *Natural and Necessary Enemies*, pp. 6–20.
18. BL 2/211/6: Perth to ?, 9 Feb. 1716; BL 2/202/5: Carnegy to the Scots College, [Edinburgh?], 21 Aug. 1716.
19. RH 2/4/308/128: John Campbell, Provost of Edinburgh, to Townshend, Edinburgh, 14 Dec. 1715; RH 2/4/311/15: Lords of Justiciary to Stanhope, Edinburgh, 21 May 1716; E. M. Graham, 'Margaret Nairne: a Bundle of Jacobite Letters', *Scottish Historical Review*, iv (1907) 17: Amelia Lovat to Margaret Nairne, Edinburgh, 3 July 1716; Allardyce (ed.), *Historical Papers Relating to the Jacobite Period*, i. 124–128: John Alexander of Kildrummy to his wife, Edinburgh, 14 Apr. 1716; Monod, *Jacobitism and the English People*, pp. 272–307.
20. Constable (ed.), *Fragment of a Memoir*, pp. 51–52.
21. Paul Langford, *Modern British Foreign Policy. The Eighteenth Century 1688–1815* (1976), pp. 78–103; Black, *Natural and Necessary Enemies*, pp. 15–16.

22. GD 45/14/220/7: Margaret Panmure to Panmure, Panmure, 7 May 1716; Tayler (ed.), *Jacobite Court at Rome*, p. 36.
23. HMC *Stuart*, vi. 180: Leyden, 23 Mar. 1718 ns.
24. HMC *Stuart*, vi. 527: William Gordon to Mar, Paris, 3/14 June 1718.
25. Laing and Macknight (eds), *Memoirs of the Insurrection, passim.*
26. Szechi (ed.), *Letters of George Lockhart*, pp. 251–252, 290: Lockhart to James, [Dryden?], 18 Dec. 1725 and 29 July 1726.
27. John Sibbald Gibson, *Lochiel of the '45: The Jacobite Chief and the Prince* (Edinburgh, repr. 1995), pp. 24–25, 26.
28. A. and H. Tayler (eds), *Jacobite Cess Roll*, pp. 196–197, 221–222; Leah Leneman, *Living in Atholl: A Social History of the Estates 1685–1785* (Edinburgh, 1986), pp. 232–233.
29. Johnstone, *Memoirs of the Rebellion*, p.162. See also pp. 197, 225.
30. Leneman, *Living in Atholl*, pp. 232–233.
31. Omond (ed.), *Arniston Memoirs*, p. 102; Szechi (ed.), *Letters of George Lockhart*, p. 308; Yorke (ed.), *Hardwicke*, i. 459; 551–552: Hardwicke to Thomas Pelham-Holles, Duke of Newcastle, London, 21 Oct. 1748.
32. Eveline Cruickshanks and Howard Erskine-Hill, *The Atterbury Plot* (2004). See also: Bennett, *Tory Crisis in Church and State*, pp. 223–257; Fritz, *English Ministers and Jacobitism*, pp. 67–136.

Bibliography

1. Archives

University of Aberdeen, Special Collections
  MS 2740 (Pitsligo Papers)
  Macbean Collection
Archives des Affaires Étrangères, Quai d'Orsai, Paris
  AECP (Affaires Étrangères, Correspondance Politique (Angleterre)), 230–262
Auburn University
  SP 35 (*The Complete State Papers Domestic. Series Two, 1714–1782* [Hassocks, Sussex, microform]).
  AECP (Quai d'Orsai, Paris, Archives des Affaires Étrangères, Correspondance Politique (Angleterre) [microform]), 263–271
Bank of England
  CCXLII, Morice MSS
Blair Atholl castle, Perthshire
  Atholl Papers, boxes 45 and 45a
Bodleian Library, Oxford
  Carte 180, 181, 211, 256 (Carte Papers)
British Library
  Add. MS 31259 (Gualterio Correspondence)
  Add. MS 33273 (Watkins Correspondence)
  Add. MS 37993 (Polwarth Letter Book)
  Add. MS 38091 (newsletters)
  Add. MS 38507 (Townshend Papers)
  Add. MS 38851 (Hodgkin Papers)
  Add. MS 61136, 61155, 61315, 61632, 61636, 61640 (Blenheim Papers)
  Stowe 228 (Hanover Papers)
Dumfries House
  Bute Papers (Macinnes transcripts)[1]
Edinburgh City Archives
  SL 30 (Convention of Royal Burghs Records)

---

1. I am very grateful to Professor Allan Macinnes of Aberdeen University for letting me use his transcripts of this collection and of the Loudoun Papers at the Huntington Library in California.

Huntington Library, California
  Loudoun Papers (Macinnes transcripts)
National Archives of Scotland
  GD 1 (Miscellaneous Jacobitism)
  GD 18 (Clerk of Penicuik Papers)
  GD 27 (Kennedy of Dalquharran Papers)
  GD 38 (Stewart of Dalguise Papers)
  GD 44 (Gordon Castle Muniments)
  GD 45 (Dalhousie Papers)
  GD 112 (Breadalbane Papers)
  GD 124 (Mar and Kellie Papers)
  GD 158 (Hume of Marchmont Muniments)
  GD 160 (Drummond Papers)
  GD 174 (Maclean of Lochbuie Muniments)
  GD 220 (Montrose Papers)
  GD 241 (Thomson and Baxter W.S. Papers)
  GD 248 (Seafield Muniments)
  GD 259 (Scott of Ancrum Papers)
  GD 267 (Home of Wedderburn)
  GD 345 (Grant of Monymusk)
  RH 2/4/- (State Papers, Scotland, photocopied volumes)
National Library of Scotland
  Wodrow Papers, Quarto VIII, X
  Abbotsford Papers
Public Record Office, Kew
  ADM 8 (Admiralty papers)
  SP 54 (State Papers Domestic)
  SP 78 (State Papers Foreign)
Scottish Catholic Archives, Edinburgh
  Blairs Letters
Westminster Diocesan Archives, London
  Ep. Var.
  Old Brotherhood MSS

2. Printed Primary Sources

Patrick Abercromby, *The Martial Achievements of the Scottish Nation* (2 vols, Edinburgh, 1711/15)

Joseph Addison, *The Age of Wonders* (1710)

Joseph Addison, *The Free-Holder* (1716)

John Addy and Peter McNiven (eds), *The Diary of Henry Prescott, LL.B., Deputy Registrar of Chester Diocese* (Record Society of Lancashire and Cheshire, 2 vols, 1992, 1994)

James Allardyce (ed.), *Historical Papers Relating to the Jacobite Period 1699–1750* (2 vols, New Spalding Club, Aberdeen, 1895, 1896)

All is Well: Or the Providence of God Praised, and the Government Justified in a Sermon Preached Upon Thursday June 7 1716. Being the Day of Thanksgiving for the Blessing of God Upon his Majesty's Counsels and Arms, in Suppressing the Late Unnatural Rebellion. By a Minister of the Church of England (1716)

A. Whitford Anderson (ed.), *Papers of the Rev. John Anderson, Minister of Dumbarton, 1698–1718* (Dumbarton, 1914)

A. Aufrere (ed.), *The Lockhart Papers* (2 vols, 1817)

J. J. Bagley (ed.), *The Great Diurnal of Nicholas Blundell of Little Crosby, Lancashire* (The Record Society of Lancashire and Cheshire, 2 vols, 1970[?])

Walter B. Blaikie (ed.), *Origins of the Forty-Five and Other Papers Relating to that Rising* (reprint, Edinburgh, 1975, of Edinburgh, 1916 edn)

A. de Boislisle (ed.), *Mémoires de Saint-Simon* (41 vols, Paris, 1879–1928)

Andrew Browning (ed.), *English Historical Documents, vii: 1660–1714* (1953)

John Buchanan-Brown (ed.), *The Remains of Thomas Hearne. Reliquiae Hearnianae* (repr. of 1869 edn, Carbondale, 1966)

W. E. Buckley (ed.), *Memoirs of Thomas, Earl of Ailesbury. Written by Himself* (2 vols, Edinburgh, Roxburghe Club, 1890)

E. Burt, *Burt's Letters From the North of Scotland. With Facsimiles of the Original Engravings,* intro. by R. Jamieson, 2 vols (reprint, Edinburgh, 1974 of London, 1754 edn)

E. Charteris (ed.), *A Short Account of the Affairs of Scotland in the Years 1744, 1745, 1746. By David, Lord Elcho* (Edinburgh, 1907)

Thomas Constable (ed.), *A Fragment of a Memoir of Field-Marshall James Keith, Written by Himself. 1714–1734* (Spalding Club, Edinburgh, 1843)

J. B. Craven, *History of the Episcopal Church in the Diocese of Moray* (1889)

A. Crichton [ed.], *The Life and Diary of Lieutenant Colonel John Blackader of the Cameronian Regiment, and Deputy Governor of Stirling Castle* (1824)

Sir David Dalrymple, *The Laws and Judicatures of Scotland* (London, 1718)

John Davenport (ed.), *Memoirs of the Court of France, From the Year 1684 to the Year 1720 . . . From the Diary of the Marquis de Dangeau* (2 vols, 1825)

Daniel Defoe, *A Dialogue Between a Whig and a Jacobite, upon the Subject of the Late Rebellion; and the Execution of the Rebel-lords, &C. Occasion'd by the Phoenomenon in the Skie, March 6. 1715–16* (1716)

Diary of Mary Countess Cowper, Lady of the Bedchamber to the Princess of Wales 1714–1720 (1864)

C. E. Doble (ed.), *Remarks and Collections of Thomas Hearne* (6 vols, 1885)

[H. R. Duff, (ed.)] *Culloden Papers: Comprising an Extensive and Interesting Correspondence From the Year 1625 to 1748* (1815)

Stuart Erskine (ed.), 'The Earl of Mar's Legacies to Scotland and to his son Lord Erskine 1722–1727', in *Wariston's Diary and Other Papers* (Scottish History Society, 1st ser. xxvi.,1896)

A Faithful Register of the Late Rebellion (1718)

A. Fergusson (ed.), *Major Fraser's Manuscript* (2 vols, Edinburgh, 1889)

William Fraser (ed.), *The Chiefs of Grant* (2 vols, Edinburgh, 1883)

Sir William Fraser (ed.), *The Annandale Family Book of the Johnstones, Earls and Marquises of Annandale* (2 vols, Edinburgh, 1894)

Edmund Gibson, *The Deliverances and Murmerings of the Israelites, and These Nations Compar'd* (1716)

E. M. Graham, 'Margaret Nairne: a Bundle of Jacobite Letters', *Scottish Historical Review*, iv (1907) 11–23

E. Maxtone Graham, *The Oliphants of Gask. Records of a Jacobite Family* (1910)

J. Murray Graham, *The Annals and Correspondence of the Viscount and the First and Second Earls of Stair* (2 vols, Edinburgh, 1875)

Martin Haile, *Queen Mary of Modena. Her Life and Letters* (1905)

G. Hay, *History of Arbroath to the Present Time. With Notices of the Civil and Ecclesiastical Affairs of the Neighbouring District* (2nd edn, Arbroath, 1899)

G. D. Henderson (ed.), *Mystics of the North-East* (Third Spalding Club, Aberdeen, 1934)

HMC, *Calendar of the Stuart Papers Belonging to His Majesty the King Preserved at Windsor Castle* (8 vols, 1902–20)

Benjamin Hoadly, *The Happiness of the Present Establishment and the Unhappiness of Absolute Monarchy* (1708)

T. B. Howell (ed.), *A Complete Collection of State Trials* (33 vols, 1816–26)

The Interest of England in Relation to Protestant Dissenters: in a Letter to the Right Reverend, the Bishop of ——— (1714)

Chevalier [James] de Johnstone, *Memoirs of the Rebellion in 1745 and 1746* (1820)

Helen and Keith Kelsall (eds), *An Album of Scottish Families 1694–96. Being the First Instalment of George Home's Diary, Supplemented by Much Further Research into the Edinburgh and Border Families Forming his Extensive Social Network* (Aberdeen, 1990)

White Kennett, *The Witchcraft of the Present Rebellion. A Sermon Preached in the Parish Church of St Mary Aldermary, in the City of London, on Sunday the 25th of September, 1715. The Time of Publick Ordination* (1715)

A King and no King: Or, the Best Argument for a Just Title. Being the Present Case of Great Britain Briefly Considered in a Seasonable Address to the People (1716)

David Laing and Thomas Macknight (eds), *Memoirs of the Insurrection in Scotland in 1715. By John, Master of Sinclair. With Notes by Sir Walter Scott, Bart* (Abbotsford Club, Edinburgh, 1858)

Charles Lambe, *The Popish Plot a Fair Caution to Protestants not to Engage in a Popish Rebellion. A Sermon Preached on Sunday November the 6th, 1715. At St Katherine Cree-Church and All-Hallows Barkin* [*sic*] (1715)

A Letter About the Occurrences in the Way to, and at Preston. By a Gentleman who was an Eye-witness to the Said Transactions [Edinburgh? 1717?]

A Letter From an Officer in the King's Army After it had Marched Northward From Aberdeen, to his Friend at London. February 1715/16 (London? 1716)

A Letter to the Patriot, Relating to the Pretender, and the Growth of Popery in the City of York and Other Parts of Great Britain (1714)

The Loch Lomond Expedition, with Some Short Reflections on the Perth Manifesto (Glasgow, 1715)

William Mackay, 'The Camerons in the Rising of 1715: a Vindication by Their Leader, John Cameron, Younger of Lochiel', *Transactions of the Gaelic Society of Inverness* (1909), pp. 1–21

Nicholas Maclean-Bristol (ed.), *Inhabitants of the Inner Isles, Morvern and Arnamurchan 1716* (Scottish Record Society, xxi, Edinburgh, 1998)

J. R. N. Macphail, *Highland Papers. Volume II* (Scottish History Society, 2nd ser., Edinburgh, 1916)

J. Macpherson (ed.), *Original Papers; Containing the Secret History of Great Britain, from the Restoration to the Accession of the House of Hanover* (2 vols, 1775)

G. S. Macquoid, *Jacobite Songs and Ballads* (1887)

W. D. Macray (ed.), *Correspondence of Colonel N. Hooke, Agent from the Court of France to the Scottish Jacobites in the Years 1703–1707* (2 vols, Roxburghe Club, Edinburgh, 1870)

T. McCrie (ed.), *The Correspondence of the Rev. Robert Wodrow* (3 vols, Wodrow Society, Edinburgh, 1862)

Lord Mahon, *History of England from the Peace of Utrecht to the Peace of Aix-La-Chapelle* (3 vols, 2nd edn, 1839)

J. Maidment (ed.), *The Argyle Papers* (Edinburgh, 1834)

The Management of the Four Last Years Vindicated (1714)

J. D. Marshall (ed.), *The Autobiography of William Stout of Lancaster, 1665–1752* (Chetham Historical Society, 1967)

William Matthews (ed.), *The Diary of Dudley Ryder 1715–1716* (1939)

Memoirs of the Life of Simon Lord Lovat; Written by Himself, in the French Language (1797)

Miscellany of the Maitland Club III (Edinburgh, 1843)

George W. T. Omond (ed.), *The Arniston Memoirs: Three Centuries of a Scottish House, 1571–1838* (Edinburgh, 1887)

Henry Paton (ed.), *The Mackintosh Muniments, 1442–1820. Preserved in the Charter-Room at Moy Hall, Inverness-shire* (Edinburgh, 1903)

Robert Patten, *The History of the Rebellion in the Year 1715. With Original Papers, and the Characters of the Principal Gentlemen Concerned in it* (3rd edn, 1745)

Peter Rae, *History of the Late Rebellion* (1718)

Rebellion Display'd: or, Our Present Distractions set Forth in Their True Light (1715)

Andrew Schethrum, *The Northumberland Prophecy: With an Introduction and a Postscript* (1715)

G. F. C. Hepburne Scott (ed.), 'Marchmont Correspondence Relating to the '45', in *Miscellany of the Scottish History Society* (Scottish History Society, 3rd ser., v, Edinburgh, 1933)

Secret Memoirs of Barleduc From the Death of Queen Anne to the Present Time (1715)

W. Seton, 'The Itinerary of King James III, October to December, 1715', *Scottish Historical Review*, xxi (1924), 249–266

A. Francis Steuart (ed.), *News Letters of 1715–16* (1910)

Daniel Szechi (ed.), *The Letters of George Lockhart of Carnwath 1698–1732* (Scottish History Society, 5th ser., ii, Edinburgh, 1989)

Daniel Szechi, *'Scotland's Ruine'. Lockhart of Carnwath's Memoirs of the Union* (Association for Scottish Literary Studies, Aberdeen, 1995)

Alistair and Henrietta Tayler (eds), *The Jacobite Cess Roll for the County of Aberdeen in 1715* (Third Spalding Club, Aberdeen, 1932)

Alistair and Henrietta Tayler, 'Lord Forfar and the '15', *Journal of the Society for Army Historical Research*, xv (1936), 126–143

Henrietta Tayler, *The Jacobite Court at Rome in 1719. From Original Documents at Fettercairn House and at Windsor Castle* (Scottish History Society, 3rd ser., xxxi, Edinburgh, 1938)

Henrietta Tayler (ed.), *The Seven Sons of the Provost. A Family Chronicle of the Eighteenth Century Compiled from Original Letters 1692–1761* (1949)

Charles S. Terry, 'Allan Cameron's Narrative, February–April 1716', *Scottish Historical Review*, v (1908), 137–150

Samuel Hibbert Ware (ed.), *Lancashire During the Rebellion of 1715* (Chetham Society, 1st ser., v., 1845)

Duncan Warrand (ed.), *More Culloden Papers* (5 vols, Inverness, 1923)

Harold Williams (ed.), *Jonathan Swift. Journal to Stella* (2 vols, Oxford, 1948)

John Withers, *The Perjury and Folly of the Late Rebellion Display'd: in a Sermon Preach'd at Exon, June the 7th, 1716. Being the Day Appointed for a Publick Thanksgiving, for the Success of His Majesties Forces Against the Rebels, at Preston, Dumblain, and Perth* (1716)

Robert Wodrow, *Analecta: Or, Materials for a History of Remarkable Providences; Mostly Relating to Scotch Ministers and Christians* (4 vols, Maitland Club, Edinburgh, 1862)

Philip C. Yorke (ed.), *The Life and Correspondence of Philip Yorke, Earl of Hardwicke, Lord High Chancellor of Great Britain*, (3 vols, reprint, New York, 1977 of Cambridge, 1913 edn)

3. Secondary Works

Susannah Abbott, 'Clerical Responses to the Jacobite Rebellion in 1715', *Historical Research*, lxxvi (2003), 332–346

[Anon.] *The Battle of Sherrifmuir* (Stirling, 1898)

T. S. Ashton, *An Economic History of England: the 18th Century* (1955; reprint, 1964)

Correlli Barnett, *Britain and Her Army 1509–1970* (New York, 1970)

Thomas Bartlett, 'An End to Moral Economy: the Irish Militia Disturbances of 1793', in C. H. E. Philpin (ed.), *Nationalism and Popular Protest in Ireland* (1987)

John Baynes, *The Jacobite Rising of 1715* (1970)

G. V. Bennett, *The Tory Crisis in Church and State, 1688–1730: the Career of Francis Atterbury, Bishop of Rochester* (1975)

J . H. E. Bennett, 'Cheshire and The Fifteen', *Journal of the Chester Archaeological Society* (new ser., xxi, 1915), pp. 30–46

Yves Bercé, *History of Peasant Revolts: the Social Origins of Rebellion in Early Modern France*, trans. Amanda Whitmore (Ithaca, NY, 1990)

Maxine Berg, *The Age of Manufactures 1700–1820* (1985)

Jeremy Black, *Natural and Necessary Enemies. Anglo-French Relations in the Eighteenth Century* (1986)

Jeremy Black (ed.), *The Origins of War in Early Modern Europe* (Edinburgh, 1987), pp. 1–23

Jeremy Black, *Eighteenth Century Europe 1700–1789* (1990)

Jeremy Black, *The Grand Tour in the Eighteenth Century* (Stroud, 1997)

Jeremy Black, *Britain as a Military Power, 1688–1815* (1999)

Jeremy Black, *Culloden and the '45* (2000)

François Bluche, *Louis XIV*, trans. Mark Greengrass (New York, 1990)

John Bossy, *The English Catholic Community 1570–1850* (1975)

John Brewer, *The Sinews of Power. War, Money and the English State, 1688–1783* (New York, 1988)

Robin Briggs, *Communities of Belief: Cultural and Social Tensions in Early Modern France* (Oxford, 1989)

Keith M. Brown, *Bloodfeud in Scotland 1573–1625. Violence, Justice and Politics in an Early Modern Society* (Edinburgh, 1986)

Julia Buckroyd, *Church and State in Scotland 1660–1681* (Edinburgh, 1980)

Julia Buckroyd, *The Life of James Sharp, Archbishop of St Andrews. A Political Biography* (Edinburgh, 1987)

W. L. Burn, 'Charles Cathcart and the Affair at Dunfermline', *Journal of the Society for Army Historical Research*, xvi (1937), 55–58

R. H. Campbell, *Scotland since 1707. The Rise of an Industrial Society* (revised 2nd edn, Edinburgh, 1992)

John Cannon, *Aristocratic Century. The Peerage of Eighteenth-Century England* (1987)

Charles Carlton, *Going to the Wars. The Experience of the British Civil Wars, 1638–1651* (1992)

Alexander Carmichael, 'Some Unrecorded Incidents of the Jacobite Risings', *Celtic Review*, vi (18?), pp. 281–283

Robert Chambers, *History of the Rebellions in Scotland under the Viscount of Dundee and the Earl of Mar in 1689 and 1715* (Edinburgh, 1829)

David Chandler, *The Art of Warfare in the Age of Marlborough* (1976)

David Chandler, *Marlborough as Military Commander* (2nd edn, 1979)

John Childs, *The British Army of William III, 1689–1702* (Manchester, 1987)

J. C. D. Clark, *Revolution and Rebellion. State and Society in England in the Seventeenth and Eighteenth Centuries* (1986)

J. C. D. Clark, 'On Moving the Middle Ground: the Significance of Jacobitism in Historical Studies', in Cruickshanks and Black, *Jacobite Challenge*, pp. 177–185

J. C. D. Clark, *Samuel Johnson. Literature, Religion and English Cultural Politics from the Restoration to Romanticism* (Cambridge, 1994)

Tony Claydon, *William III* (2002)

Robert Clyde, *From Rebel to Hero: the Image of the Highlander, 1745–1830* (East Linton, 1995)

G. E. Cokayne, *The Complete Peerage of England, Scotland, Ireland, Great Britain and the United Kingdom* (13 vols, 1910–40)

Linda Colley, *In Defiance of Oligarchy. The Tory Party 1714–60* (1982)

Linda Colley, *Britons. Forging the Nation 1707–1837* (1992)

P. J. Corfield, 'Class by Name and Number in Eighteenth-century Britain', *History*, lxxii (1987), pp. 38–61

Edward Corp with Edward Gregg, Howard Erskine-Hill and Geoffrey Scott, *A Court in Exile. The Stuarts in France, 1689–1718* (2004)

William James Couper, *The Rebel Press at Perth in 1715* (1928)

Eveline Cruickshanks (ed.), *Ideology and Conspiracy. Aspects of Jacobitism, 1689–1759* (Edinburgh, 1982)

E. Cruickshanks and J. Black (eds), *The Jacobite Challenge* (Edinburgh, 1988)

Eveline Cruickshanks and Howard Erskine-Hill, *The Atterbury Plot* (2004)

Eveline Cruickshanks, Stuart Handley and D. W. Hayton, *The House of Commons 1690–1715* (5 vols, 2002)

Faramerz Dabhoiwala, 'The Construction of Honour, Reputation and Status in Late Seventeenth- and Early Eighteenth-Century England', *Transactions of the Royal Historical Society* (6th ser., vi, 1996), pp. 201–213

Frances Dickinson, *The Reluctant Rebel: a Northumbrian Legacy of Jacobite Times* (Newcastle-upon-Tyne, 1996)

H. T. Dickinson, *Bolingbroke* (1970)

H. T. Dickinson, *Liberty and Property. Political Ideology in Eighteenth-Century Britain* (1977)

H. T. Dickinson (ed.), *A Companion to Eighteenth-Century Britain* (Oxford, 2002)

T. F. Donald, 'Glasgow and the Jacobite Rebellion of 1715', *Scottish Historical Review*, xiii (1916), 126–132

John Doran, *London in the Jacobite Times* (2 vols, 1877)

Christopher Duffy, *The '45. Bonnie Prince Charlie and the Untold Story of the Jacobite Rising* (2003)

Peter Earle, *Monmouth's Rebels. The Road to Sedgemoor* (1977)

William Ferguson, *Scotland's Relations with England: a Survey to 1707* (Edinburgh, 1977)

William Ferguson, *Scotland. 1689 to the Present* (Edinburgh, reprint 1994)

Paul S. Fritz, *The English Ministers and Jacobitism between the Rebellions of 1715 and 1745* (Toronto, 1975)

Edward M. Furgol, *A Regimental History of the Covenanting Armies 1639–1651* (Edinburgh, 1990)

Nathalie Genet-Rouffiac, 'Jacobites in Paris and Saint-Germain-en-Laye', in Eveline Cruickshanks and Edward Corp (eds), *The Stuart Court in Exile and the Jacobites* (1995), pp. 15–38

John Sibbald Gibson, *Playing the Scottish Card. The Franco-Jacobite Invasion of 1708* (Edinburgh, 1988)

John Sibbald Gibson, *Lochiel of the '45: The Jacobite Chief and the Prince* (Edinburgh, reprint 1995)

William Sidney Gibson, *Dilston Hall, or, Memoirs of the Earl of Derwentwater, a Martyr in the Rebellion of 1715* (1850)

Leo Gooch, *The Desperate Faction? The Jacobites of North-East England 1688–1745* (Hull, 1995)

Pierre Goubert, *Louis XIV and Twenty Million Frenchmen*, trans. Anne Carter (New York, 1970)

Henry Grey Graham, *The Social Life of Scotland in the Eighteenth Century* (New York, reprint, 1971 of London 2nd edn, 1901)

Edward Gregg, 'Marlborough in Exile, 1712–14', *Historical Journal*, xv (1972), 593–618

Edward Gregg, 'Was Queen Anne a Jacobite?', *History*, lvii (1972), 358–375

Edward Gregg, *Queen Anne* (1980)

Edward Gregg, 'The Jacobite Career of John, Earl of Mar', in E. Cruickshanks (ed.), *Ideology and Conspiracy. Aspects of Jacobitism, 1689–1759* (Edinburgh, 1982), pp. 179–200

Edward Gregg, 'The Politics of Paranoia', in Cruickshanks and Black (eds), *The Jacobite Challenge*, pp. 42–56

Edward Gregg, 'France, Rome and the Exiled Stuarts, 1689–1713', in Corp, *Court in Exile*, pp. 11–75

W. D. Griffin, 'The Irish on the Continent in the Eighteenth Century', *Studies in Eighteenth-Century Culture*, v (1976), pp. 453–473

Alan Guy, 'The Irish Military Establishment, 1660–1776', in Thomas Bartlett and Keith Jeffery (eds), *A Military History of Ireland* (Cambridge, 1996), pp. 211–230

Martin Haile, *James Francis Edward. The Old Chevalier* (1907)

Simon Harcourt-Smith, *Alberoni, or, the Spanish Conspiracy* (1943)

Ragnhild Hatton, *George I. Elector and King* (1978)

Douglas Hay, 'Property, Authority and the Criminal Law', in Douglas Hay, Peter Linebaugh, John G. Rule, Edward Thompson and Cal Winslow, *Albion's Fatal Tree: Crime and Society in Eighteenth-Century England* (reprint 1988 of London 1975 edn)

Douglas Hay and Nicholas Rogers, *Eighteenth Century English Society* (1997)

N. Hill, 'A Side Light on the 1715', *Scottish Historical Review*, xvii (1920), 225–233

The History of the Earl of Derwentwater and the Rebellion of 1715 (Newcastle-upon-Tyne, 1868)

Eric Hobsbawm, *Primitive Rebels. Studies in Archaic Forms of Social Movement in the 19th and 20th Centuries* (1963)

Geoffrey Holmes, 'The Hamilton Affair of 1711–12: a Crisis in Anglo-Scottish Relations', *English Historical Review*, lxxvii (1962), 257–282

Geoffrey Holmes (ed.) *Britain after the Glorious Revolution, 1689–1714* (1969; repr. 1978)

Geoffrey Holmes, *The Trial of Dr Sacheverell* (1973)

Geoffrey Holmes, *British Politics in the Age of Anne* (revised edn, 1987)

Geoffrey Holmes, *The Making of a Great Power. Late Stuart and Early Georgian England 1660–1722* (1993)

Geoffrey Holmes and Daniel Szechi, *The Age of Oligarchy. Pre-industrial Britain 1722–1783* (1993)

Paul Hopkins, *Glencoe and the End of the Highland War* (Edinburgh, 1986; revised reprint 1998)

David Bayne Horn, *Great Britain and Europe in the Eighteenth Century* (Oxford, 1967)

Edward Hughes, *North Country Life in the Eighteenth Century. The North-East, 1700–1750* (reprint, 1969)

Mary E. Ingram, *A Jacobite Stronghold of the Church* (Edinburgh, 1907)

P. Jenkins, *The Making of a Ruling Class: the Glamorgan Gentry 1640–1790* (1983)

Clyve Jones, '"Venice Preserv'd; or a Plot Discovered": the Political and Social Context of the Peerage Bill of 1719', in Clyve Jones (ed.), *A Pillar of the Constitution: the House of Lords in British Politics, 1640–1784* (1989), pp. 79–112

George Hilton Jones, *The Mainstream of Jacobitism* (Cambridge, Mass., 1954)

J. R. Jones, *The Revolution of 1688 in England* (1972)

J. P. Kenyon, *Revolution Principles. The Politics of Party 1689–1720* (1977)

Colin Kidd, 'Conditional Britons: the Scots Covenanting Tradition and the Eighteenth-century British State', *English Historical Review*, cxvii (2002), 1147–1176

V. G. Kiernan, *The Duel in European History. Honour and the Reign of Aristocracy* (Oxford, 1989)

Thomas Kuhn, *The Structure of Scientific Revolutions* (3rd edn, 1996)

Paul Langford, *Modern British Foreign Policy. The Eighteenth Century 1688–1815* (1976)

Paul Langford, *A Polite and Commercial People. England 1727–1783* (Oxford, 1992)

Peter Laslett, *The World We Have Lost – Further Explored* (3rd edn, 1983)

Leah Leneman, *Living in Atholl: a Social History of the Estates 1685–1785* (Edinburgh, 1986)

Bruce Lenman, *The Jacobite Risings in Britain 1689–1746* (1980)

Bruce Lenman, *The Jacobite Clans of the Great Glen 1650–1784* (1984)

Simon Macdonald Lockhart, *Seven Centuries. The History of the Lockharts of Lee and Carnwath* (Carnwath, 1976)

Michael Lynch, *Scotland. A New History* (1991; revised reprint 1994)

Diarmaid MacCulloch, *Reformation. Europe's House Divided 1490–1700* (Penguin edn, 2004)

Allan I. Macinnes, *Clanship, Commerce and the House of Stuart, 1603–1788* (East Linton, 1996)

Frank McLynn, *The Jacobite Army in England, 1745* (Edinburgh, 1983)

Frank McLynn, *The Jacobites* (1985)

Frank McLynn, *Charles Edward Stuart. A Tragedy in Many Acts* (1988)

P. J. Marshall and Alaine Low (eds), *The Oxford History of the British Empire. Volume II. The Eighteenth Century* (Oxford, 1998)

Wolfgang Michael, *England under George I. The Beginnings of the Hanoverian Dynasty* (1936; Westport, repr. 1981)

Rosalind Mitchison, 'The Government and the Highlands, 1707–1745', in N. T. Phillipson and Rosalind Mitchison (eds), *Scotland in the Age of Improvement. Essays in Scottish History in the Eighteenth Century* (Edinburgh, 1970; paperback 1996), pp. 24–46.

Paul Kléber Monod, 'The Politics of Matrimony: Jacobitism and Marriage in Eighteenth-Century England', in Cruickshanks and Black (eds), *Jacobite Challenge*, pp. 24–41

Paul Kléber Monod, *Jacobitism and the English People, 1688–1788* (1989)

T. W. Moody and W. E. Vaughan (eds), *A New History of Ireland IV. Eighteenth-Century Ireland 1691–1800* (1986)

T. W. Moody, F. X. Martin and F. J. Byrne (eds), *A New History of Ireland III. Early Modern Ireland 1534–1691* (Oxford, 1976)

A. Moody-Stuart, 'Lieutenant-Colonel James Steuart: a Jacobite Lieutenant-Governor of Edinburgh Castle', *Scottish Historical Review*, xxi (1923), 1–25

Roland Mousnier, *Peasant Uprisings in Seventeenth-century France, Russia, and China*, trans. Brian Pearce (New York, 1970)

John J. Murray, *George I, the Baltic and the Whig Split of 1717* (1969)

Harman Murtagh, 'Irish Soldiers Abroad, c. 1600–1800', in Thomas Bartlett and Keith Jeffery (eds), *A Military History of Ireland* (1996)

Albert Nicholson, 'Lancashire in the Rebellion of 1715', *Transactions of the Lancashire and Cheshire Antiquarian Society*, iii (1886), 66–88

Claude Nordmann, 'Louis XIV and the Jacobites', in Ragnhild Hatton (ed.), *Louis XIV and Europe* (1976), pp. 82–114

Claude Nordmann, 'Les Jacobites écossais en France au XVIIIe siècle', in M. S. Plaisant (ed.), *Regards sur l'Écosse au XVIIIe siècle* (Lille, 1977)

Éamonn Ó Ciardha, *Ireland and the Jacobite Cause, 1685–1766. A Fatal Attachment* (Dublin, 2002)

George W. T. Omond, *The Lord Advocates of Scotland,* (2 vols, Edinburgh, 1883)

Sir James Balfour Paul, *The Scots Peerage: Founded on Wood's Edition of Sir Robert Douglas's Peerage of Scotland. Containing an Historical and Genealogical Account of the Nobility of That Kingdom* (9 vols, Edinburgh, 1904)

Sir Charles Petrie, *The Jacobite Movement* (1932)

Sir Charles Petrie, *The Marshal Duke of Berwick. The Picture of an Age* (1953)

Murray Pittock, *Inventing and Resisting Britain. Cultural Identities in Britain and Ireland, 1685–1789* (1997)

Murray Pittock, *The Myth of the Jacobite Clans* (Edinburgh, 1997)

Murray Pittock, *The Jacobites* (1998)

Murray Pittock, *Scottish Nationality* (2001)

J. Prebble, *The Darien Disaster* (1968)

Robert D. Putnam, *Bowling Alone. The Collapse and Revival of American Community* (New York, 2000)

Eric Richards, *A History of the Highland Clearances: Agrarian Transformation and the Evictions 1746–1786* (London, 1982)

P. W. J. Riley, *The Union of England and Scotland. A Study in Anglo-Scottish Politics in the Eighteenth Century* (Manchester, 1978)

John L. Roberts, *The Jacobite Wars. Scotland and the Military Campaigns of 1715 and 1745* (Edinburgh, 2002)

Nicholas Rogers, 'Popular Protest in Early Hanoverian London', *Past and Present*, lxxix (1978), 70–100

Nicholas Rogers, 'Riot and Popular Jacobitism in Early Hanoverian England', in Cruickshanks, *Ideology and Conspiracy*, pp. 70–88

Nicholas Rogers, *Whigs and Cities. Popular Politics in the Age of Walpole and Pitt* (Oxford, 1989)

Nicholas Rogers, *Crowds, Culture, and Politics in Georgian Britain* (Oxford, 1998)

George Rudé, *The Crowd in History 1730–1848* (2nd edn, 1981)

Conrad Russell, *The Fall of the British Monarchies 1637–1642* (Oxford, 1995)

Henry Rutherfurd, '"The Bloody Well"': a Fatal Encounter between the Lairds of Fairnington and Muirhouselaw, 1716', *Transactions of the Hawick Archaeological Society*, liv (1922), 18–20

Margaret Sankey, *Jacobite Prisoners of the 1715 Rebellion: Preventing and Punishing Insurrection in Early Hanoverian Britain* (Aldershot, 2005)

Margaret Sankey and Daniel Szechi, 'Elite Culture and the Decline of Scottish Jacobitism 1716–1745', *Past and Present*, clxxiii (2001), 90–128

Hillel Schwartz, *The French Prophets. The History of a Millenarian Group in Eighteenth-Century England* (1980)

Andrew M. Scott, *Bonnie Dundee – John Graham of Cleverhouse* (Edinburgh, 2000)

Jonathan Scott, *England's Troubles. Seventeenth-Century English Political Instability in European Context* (2000)

Romney Sedgwick (ed.), *The House of Commons 1715–1754* (2 vols, 1970)

John Stuart Shaw, *The Management of Scottish Society 1707–1764. Power, Nobles, Lawyers, Edinburgh Agents and English Influences* (Edinburgh, 1983)

John Elliot Shearer, *The Battle of Dunblane Revised: Sherrifmuir, 1715* (Stirling, 1911)

J. H. Shennan, *Philippe, Duke of Orléans. Regent of France 1715–1723* (1979)

L. B. Smith, 'Spain and the Jacobites, 1715–16', in Cruickshanks, *Ideology and Conspiracy*, pp. 159–178

L. B. Smith, *Spain and Britain 1715–1719. The Jacobite Issue* (1987)

T. C. Smout, *A History of the Scottish People 1560–1830* (6th impression, 1985)

W. A. Speck, 'Conflict in Society', in Holmes, *Britain after the Glorious Revolution*, pp. 135–152

W. A. Speck, *Tory and Whig. The Struggle in the Constituencies 1701–1715* (1970)

W. A. Speck, *Stability and Strife. England, 1714–1760* (Cambridge, Mass., 1977)

David Stevenson, *Alasdair MacColla and the Highland Problem in the 17th Century* (Edinburgh, 1980)

John Stevenson, *Popular Disturbances in England, 1700–1832* (2nd edn, 1992)

John B. Stewart, *Opinion and Reform in Hume's Political Philosophy* (Princeton, 1992)

Lawrence Stone, *The Causes of the English Revolution 1529–1642* (1972; reprint 1973)

Ronald M. Sunter, *Patronage and Politics in Scotland, 1707–1832* (Edinburgh, 1986)

Daniel Szechi, *Jacobitism and Tory Politics, 1710–14* (Edinburgh, 1984)

Daniel Szechi, 'The Jacobite Revolution Settlement, 1689–1696', *English Historical Review*, cviii (1993), 610–628

Daniel Szechi, *The Jacobites. Britain and Europe 1688–1788* (Manchester, 1994)

D. Szechi, *George Lockhart of Carnwath, 1689–1727. A Study in Jacobitism* (East Linton, 2002)

Daniel Szechi, 'The Jacobite Movement', in Dickinson, *Companion to Eighteenth-Century Britain*, pp. 84–93

D. Szechi and D. Hayton, 'John Bull's Other Kingdoms: the Government of Scotland and Ireland', in C. Jones (ed.), *Britain in the First Age of Party, 1680–1745. Essays Presented to Geoffrey Holmes* (1987), pp. 241–280

Chris Tabraham and Doreen Grove, *Fortress Scotland and the Jacobites* (1995, reprint 1997)

Alistair and Henrietta Tayler, *1715: the Story of the Rising* (London, 1936)

Henrietta Tayler, *Lady Nithsdale and Her Family* (London, 1939)

Joan Thirsk (ed.), *The Agrarian History of England and Wales. Volume V. 1640–1750* (2 vols, 1985)

E. P. Thompson, *Customs in Common* (New York, 1991)

Katherine Tomasson and Francis Buist, *Battles of the '45* (reprint 1978)

Nigel Tranter, *Rob Roy Macgregor* (Glasgow, 1995)

Christopher A. Whatley, *Scottish Society 1707–1830. Beyond Jacobitism, Towards Industrialisation* (Manchester, 2000)

Susan E. Whyman, *Sociability and Power in late-Stuart England: the Cultural Worlds of the Verneys, 1660–1720* (Oxford, 1999)

Ian D. Whyte, *Scotland before the Industrial Revolution. An Economic and Social History c. 1050–c.1750* (1995)

Charles Wilson, *England's Apprenticeship 1603–1763* (1975)

John B. Wolf, *Louis XIV* (New York , 1968)

Jenny Wormald, *Court, Kirk and Community. Scotland 1470–1625* (Edinburgh, 1981; reprint 1991)

4. Unpublished Theses, Papers and Dissertations

T. N. Clarke, 'The Scottish Episcopalians 1688–1720' (University of Edinburgh Ph.D. thesis, 1987)

http://www.history.ac.uk/projects/elec/sem19.html: Alex Murdoch, 'Management or Semi-Independence? The Government of Scotland 1707–1832' (Institute of Historical Research, archived electronic seminar paper, 1998)

Jonathan Oates, 'The Responses in North East England to the Jacobite Rebellions of 1715 and 1745' (University of Reading Ph.D. thesis, 2001)

Margaret Sankey, 'Jacobite Prisoners of the 1715 Rebellion' (Auburn University Ph.D. dissertation, 2002)

Jeffrey Stephen, 'Scottish Presbyterians and Anglo-Scottish Union, 1707' (University of Aberdeen Ph.D. thesis, 2004)

Index

Milton Keynes UK
Ingram Content Group UK Ltd.
UKHW022228280723
425983UK00001B/12/J

9 780300 111002